Harnessing Happiness and Wisdom for Organizational Well-Being

Minh Tung Tran
FPT University, Vietnam

IGI Global
Scientific Publishing
Publishing Tomorrow's Research Today

Published in the United States of America by
IGI Global Scientific Publishing
701 East Chocolate Avenue
Hershey, PA, 17033, USA
Tel: 717-533-8845
Fax: 717-533-8661
Website: https://www.igi-global.com E-mail: cust@igi-global.com

Library of Congress Cataloging-in-Publication Data

Names: Tran, Minh Tung, 1981- editor.
Title: Harnessing happiness and wisdom for organizational well-being / edited by Minh Tung Tran.
Description: Hershey, PA : IGI Global Scientific Publishing, [2025] | Includes bibliographical references and index. | Summary: "This book goes beyond traditional happiness programs, proposing a framework that integrates the pursuit of happiness with the cultivation of wisdom. It argues that by harnessing both happiness and wisdom, organizations can create a more positive, resilient, and ultimately successful work environment"-- Provided by publisher.
Identifiers: LCCN 2024051498 (print) | LCCN 2024051499 (ebook) | ISBN 9798369384572 (hardcover) | ISBN 9798369384589 (paperback) | ISBN 9798369384596 (ebook)
Subjects: LCSH: Psychology, Industrial. | Organizational behavior. | Quality of work life. | Happiness.
Classification: LCC HF5548.8 .H37 2025 (print) | LCC HF5548.8 (ebook) | DDC 158.7--dc23/eng/20241219
LC record available at https://lccn.loc.gov/2024051498
LC ebook record available at https://lccn.loc.gov/2024051499

British Cataloguing in Publication Data
A Cataloguing in Publication record for this book is available from the British Library.

Table of Contents

Detailed Table of Contents

This chapter investigates the critical role of emotional intelligence (EI) in nursing education as a tool for cultivating organizational well-being, happiness, and wisdom within healthcare settings. As healthcare environments become increasingly complex, emotionally intelligent nurses are better equipped to manage interpersonal dynamics, lead effectively, and foster positive work environments. The chapter provides a theoretical overview of EI and its application in organisational well-being, focusing on the intersection between nursing education and emotional intelligence development. Strategies for embedding EI into the curriculum, fostering emotional resilience, and promoting a culture of empathy, wisdom, and happiness within healthcare organizations are examined. By integrating EI into the core of nursing education, we can better prepare nurses to contribute not only to patient care but also to the broader organisational ethos, promoting a work environment where both emotional and psychological well-being are prioritised.

This chapter aims to study the impact of internal branding (IB) on employee engagement (EE) and organizational citizenship behaviour (OCB). This study indicated understanding the meditational effect of EE between IB and OCB in the manufacturing industries of India country. The study analyzed the relationship from the data collected from Indian countries like Karnataka, Delhi NCR, and Odisha. The study used reliability, validity, confirmatory factor analysis, and structural equation modelling to test the hypothesis in AMOS version 20. The study shows that IB has a substantial positive impact on EE and OCB. EE has a strong mediation effect between IB and OCB. However, EE could not predict the dimensions of altruism and sportsmanship in OCB. Additionally, there is no significant relationship between IB and OCB in EE. The IB on EE and OCB has been lightly studied previously, and neither has been analyzed to understand its impact on OCB and EE.

This chapter delves into the importance of purpose and meaning in employee engagement and its impact on corporate success. In today's changing workplace, employees want more than simply a salary; they want meaningful employment that reflects their values. It looks into tactics for cultivating a purpose-driven culture, such as leadership influence, job creation, and the establishment of a supportive work environment. The chapter also looks at how well-being programs, continual development, and engagement assessment can help to maintain a vibrant workplace. This chapter equips business executives, HR experts, and personal development enthusiasts with the skills they need to improve employee well-being, increase engagement, and create a more meaningful and productive work environment.

This chapter provides a comprehensive guide for organizations to create and maintain a positive work environment, emphasizing employee well-being. It explores strategies to enhance physical, mental, and emotional health, including fostering a positive work culture, implementing health and safety programs, and promoting work-life balance. The chapter highlights leadership's role, continuous improvement, and strong workplace relationships. By adopting these strategies, organizations can boost productivity, job satisfaction, and overall success. The chapter covers understanding well-being, creating a positive work culture, physical and mental health initiatives, building strong relationships, and continuous improvement and feedback. It concludes by emphasizing the continuous effort required from both leaders and employees to build a foundation of well-being, leading to greater productivity, job satisfaction, and overall success.

Creating a happy and productive workplace requires more than meeting deadlines or offering competitive salaries. It's about cultivating an environment where employees feel valued, supported, and motivated to grow. Flexibility is key and remote options or adaptable hours help employees balance their personal lives without stress. Promoting diversity and inclusion through open conversations and training ensures every employee feels welcomed. Regular check-ins between managers and teams foster communication and personal development. Prioritizing physical and mental well-being with wellness programs or mental health resources shows employees their well-being matters. Recognition of accomplishments, whether through bonuses or simple acknowledgments, reinforces a positive culture. Team building across departments fosters a sense of community. Leaders should model respect and positivity, engaging in open dialogue with employees to ensure continuous improvement. These strategies create a workplace where employees thrive, and success becomes a shared journey.

Organizations are rapidly adjusting their strategies, operations, and employee value propositions in response to the disruptive era and evolving employee expectations. They acknowledge the necessity of crisis-specific strategies and flexible resource allocation to navigate varied challenges and opportunities effectively. This underscores the critical need to establish a resilient environment that encourages agile decision-making and improved time management. Organizations are dedicated to cultivating self-reliant work teams, culturally astute leadership, and adaptable leaders capable of fostering a skilled workforce. This chapter offers readers a comprehensive insight into organizational strategies for building resilience, enabling workers to adapt better manage resources and conflicts and build employee connectedness throughout the organization. Resilient organizations must prioritize cultivating adaptable leadership capable of facilitating behavioural adjustments and fostering the necessary changes in mindset to maintain resilience in the face of change.

This chapter explores the essential role of character education in universities, emphasizing its capacity to foster organizational well-being through the development of practical wisdom and virtues. Drawing upon Ken Wilber's integral theory and neo-Aristotelian perspectives, the chapter examines how intellectual, civic, moral, and performance virtues can be systematically integrated into higher-education curricula. The significance of practical wisdom, particularly as articulated through the three-dimensional wisdom model, is highlighted in promoting psychosocial growth and well-being among students, thereby reducing self-centeredness and enhancing ethical decision-making. Furthermore, the chapter investigates how character education equips students to navigate the complexities of modern life, contributing to a more just and compassionate society. By integrating these theoretical frameworks with practical applications, the chapter presents a comprehensive approach to character education that is both philosophically rigorous and practically effective.

The science of happiness at work explores the multifaceted dimensions of employee well-being and its impact on organizational success. This field integrates insights from psychology, business, and neuroscience to understand how positive emotions, engagement, relationships, meaning, and accomplishment (PERMA) contribute to a thriving workplace. Research indicates that happier employees are more productive, creative, and committed, leading to enhanced teamwork and reduced health issues. This study reviews various theoretical frameworks, including the job demand-resources model, social exchange theory, and broaden-and-build theory, to provide a comprehensive understanding of workplace happiness. Practical strategies for fostering a positive work environment, such as gratitude practices, mindfulness, and socially intelligent leadership, are discussed. The findings underscore the importance of prioritizing happiness as a core organizational goal to boost engagement, productivity, and overall employee satisfaction.

This chapter highlights the crucial role of wisdom in improving well-being and happiness within organizations. In high-pressure work environments, employee well-being is essential for success. Wisdom—comprising creativity, curiosity, judgment, love of learning, and perspective, as identified by Peterson and Seligman—is key for navigating complex settings and promoting continuous improvement. The chapter focuses on nurturing these strengths to enhance workforce engagement, satisfaction, and productivity. It explores how cultivating wisdom at various organizational levels boosts happiness and accountability. A conceptual model is proposed to show how wisdom supports organizational happiness and outlines strategies for developing these strengths among employees. By integrating wisdom into organizational practices, leaders can create thriving environments that achieve sustainable success and improved employee engagement, with practical strategies provided for actionable steps.

Happiness in the form of pleasant moods and emotions, well-being, and positive attitudes has been attracting increasing attention throughout psychology research. This chapter introduces the happy wisdom framework, an integrative approach designed to nurture joyful insights and address the multifaceted challenges of modern workplaces. By combining the principles of wisdom and happiness, the authors propose a comprehensive strategy for enhancing individual well-being, team dynamics, and organizational culture. The framework builds on established conceptualizations of wisdom and happiness, drawing from extensive theoretical and empirical research. It identifies key workplace issues at different levels, including individual stress and lack of meaning, team incivility and abusive supervision, and organizational deficits in ethical, social, and environmental responsibility. The chapter concludes by presenting practical insights and recommendations for integrating the happy wisdom framework into workplace practices that benefit employees and organizations alike.

Mindfulness techniques have been proposed to address teacher burnout and enhance well-being in the academic environment. However, limited research has hindered understanding of their impact on teachers' well-being and professional growth. This project explores the effects of mindfulness interventions on teacher well-being, aiming to improve teaching and research skills. Using a qualitative approach, the study involved focus groups, narrative, and content analysis with 60 lecturers and academic staff from a mindfulness program between Swinburne University and FPT Education in Vietnam. The findings suggest mindfulness helps teachers maintain a positive mindset, reduce stress, and improve emotional resilience and professional performance. This research extends beyond individual teachers, influencing the broader educational environment and policy development, while contributing to the understanding of mindfulness in higher education.

Happiness, a universally valued and significant positive emotional state, is essential for a meaningful and fulfilling existence in the workplace across cultures. The present chapter explores the interconnected effect of mindfulness, organizational identification, work-life balance, and family support on employee happiness at the workplace. The study surveyed 385 married working women in the Indian banking and IT industry, and the data was analyzed using PLS SEM 4. Further, the bootstrapping method was also employed to assess the significance of the relationships between variables. The study revealed that all the examined factors have a positive and significant impact on the happiness of the Indian female workforce. The findings provide useful insights for organizations and policymakers to create inclusive and enlightened workplace cultures that prioritize the welfare of the female workforce, thereby enhancing their happiness, involvement, and proficiency. The chapter also discusses the theoretical implications as well as the limitations and potential avenues for future research.

The main aim of this study is to investigate the relationship of personality traits and wellbeing and impact of personality on mental health. Wellbeing of the people is also one of the goals for attaining sustainability. Due to increased globalisation, the competition level has been increased. Due to which in some organisation the employees are treated as a machine This study is descriptive in nature with qualitative data. The secondary data will be collected from research papers, articles, book chapters, and official websites to evaluate the relationship between personality traits and wellbeing and its impact. Research has shown that positive extraverted people tend to be happier than negative introverted people who are more likely to fret. The clinical disorder paradigm has generally been the center of personality evaluation. Positive emotionality, conscientiousness, and behavioural control are the psychological traits that have been discovered to be associated with mental wellness.

In today's fast-paced and increasingly complex work environment, organizations are under immense pressure to ensure not just productivity but also the overall well-being of their employees. Through the exploration of real-world success stories, this chapter will illustrate the innovative strategies adopted by organizations to create environments where employees flourish. Additionally, "Happiness Wisdom Framework," a practical guide that organizations can adopt to cultivate a culture of well-being, is proposed. Methodology relies on secondary sources and focussed group discussions conducted among Generation Z participants to provide a comprehensive analysis of employee well-being practices and the formulation of the Happiness Wisdom Framework. This chapter will be helpful for HR and organizational leaders looking to implement effective well-being strategies and benefit researchers and consultants interested in understanding how to create sustainable, positive workplace cultures through the adoption of innovative frameworks like the Happiness Wisdom Framework.

Preface

In a world where the workplace often feels fast-paced, demanding, and stressful, the importance of fostering happiness, wisdom, and well-being within organizations has never been clearer. *Harnessing Happiness and Wisdom for Organizational Well-Being* is an essential resource for those seeking to explore how positive psychology, emotional intelligence, and practical wisdom can be effectively cultivated to promote a thriving and sustainable organizational culture.

As the workplace landscape evolves, it is evident that success cannot solely be defined by profits or performance metrics. Instead, it is increasingly tied to the well-being of employees, the fostering of meaningful connections, and the ability to create environments that inspire both personal and professional growth. This book sets out to highlight the profound role that happiness and wisdom can play in transforming organizational life, unlocking creativity, improving productivity, and fostering resilience.

Edited by Minh Tung Tran and published by IGI Global, this book brings together a diverse range of thought-provoking chapters that cover every aspect of happiness and wisdom within the modern workplace. With contributions from leading experts in the field, the chapters offer valuable insights into the science of happiness, organizational well-being, the role of wisdom in leadership, and practical frameworks for integrating these principles into the fabric of any organization.

The book is organized into four key parts:

- **Part 1: Foundations of Organizational Well-Being and Happiness** explores the importance of building a foundation rooted in happiness, engagement, and purpose. It provides the necessary context for why organizations should prioritize the well-being of their employees and how this can lead to improved outcomes for both individuals and the organization as a whole.
- **Part 2: Science and Application of Happiness and Wisdom** delves into the deeper, more philosophical aspects of organizational life, examining how organizations can cultivate wisdom that goes beyond short-term thinking

and profit-driven goals. It looks at how long-term thinking, ethical decision-making, and balancing profit with purpose can lead to a more sustainable and meaningful approach to business.

- **Part 3: Leadership and Mindfulness in Organizational Well-Being** offers a step-by-step guide to implementing a "Happy Wisdom" culture, including how to assess progress, overcome obstacles, and build a lasting culture of well-being and wisdom. This practical section is grounded in real-world case studies that demonstrate the power of these concepts in action.
- **Part 4: Sustainability, Personality, and Success Stories** reflects on the lasting impact of happy wisdom on organizations, offering a vision for the future and outlining potential directions for research and practice.

This book also includes additional topics such as mindfulness, the role of technology in shaping well-being, the importance of diversity and inclusion, and the unique challenges faced by multinational organizations. These diverse perspectives ensure that readers will walk away with a comprehensive understanding of how to cultivate happiness and wisdom in their organizations.

Whether you are a leader, HR professional, or researcher, *Harnessing Happiness and Wisdom for Organizational Well-Being* offers a wealth of knowledge, practical tools, and inspiration to guide your journey toward creating a more engaged, wise, and happy workplace.

We invite you to explore the chapters, engage with the ideas presented, and join us in the quest to foster happiness and wisdom in organizations for a more prosperous and fulfilling future for all.

Minh Tung Tran
FPT University, Vietnam

Acknowledgment

The journey of bringing *Harnessing Happiness and Wisdom for Organizational Well-Being* to fruition has been both inspiring and rewarding. This book would not have been possible without the support, collaboration, and contributions of many Reviewers of this book, to whom I am deeply grateful.

First and foremost, I would like to express my sincere gratitude to the authors and contributors who have shared their expertise, time, and thoughtful insights. Your work has elevated this book, and each chapter provides a unique perspective on the crucial role of happiness and wisdom in the workplace. Without your dedication and commitment, this project would not have been as impactful and comprehensive. Thank you for your collaboration and for making this book a truly valuable resource.

I would also like to extend my appreciation to the editorial team and the publisher, IGI Global. Your professionalism, encouragement, and meticulous attention to detail have been instrumental in bringing this book to life. Your support throughout the entire process has been unwavering, and I am incredibly grateful for your guidance every step of the way.

A special thanks goes to my colleagues, mentors, and friends who have been constant sources of inspiration and guidance. Your unwavering belief in the potential of organizations to foster well-being and wisdom has shaped my own understanding of these concepts, and for that, I am eternally thankful.

I am particularly grateful to my family for their love, patience, and understanding. Their encouragement provided me with the strength and motivation to push through challenging moments during this project. You have always been my foundation, and your support is deeply appreciated.

Lastly, to all those who are working tirelessly to build organizations that prioritize human well-being, kindness, and wisdom—this book is dedicated to you. Your efforts are shaping a better, more compassionate future for workplaces everywhere, and I hope this book serves as a resource to aid you in your journey.

Thank you to everyone who has contributed, supported, or believed in this project. Your involvement has made this book a reality, and I am truly grateful for each and every one of you.

Introduction

In today's rapidly changing world, organizations are no longer solely focused on profits and operational efficiency. Instead, the emphasis has shifted towards creating environments that nurture the well-being of employees, foster personal growth, and contribute to a sustainable future. *Harnessing Happiness and Wisdom for Organizational Well-Being* is a timely and vital contribution to this evolving narrative, offering a comprehensive exploration of how happiness and wisdom can transform not only individual lives but also entire organizations.

As someone who has spent a significant portion of my career working with organizations across various sectors, it is clear that the link between employee well-being and organizational success is undeniable. Happy employees are not only more engaged, productive, and creative, but they also tend to be more loyal and motivated. Yet, creating a work culture that prioritizes happiness is not a simple or automatic process. It requires intentionality, thoughtful leadership, and the integration of emotional intelligence and wisdom into the very fabric of the organization.

This book, edited by Minh Tung Tran, goes beyond surface-level concepts and dives deep into the complex relationship between happiness, wisdom, and organizational well-being. It brings together research, theory, and practical insights from some of the foremost thought leaders in the field, offering a rich and diverse set of perspectives. The chapters tackle the multifaceted nature of organizational life—from building a foundation of well-being and cultivating organizational wisdom to implementing the "Happy Wisdom Framework" in practice.

What stands out in this collection is its holistic approach to organizational health. It goes beyond the traditional focus on profits and goals, incorporating the broader elements of purpose, ethics, and long-term vision. The integration of mindfulness, diversity and inclusion, and positive psychology into this framework presents a nuanced approach that is highly relevant for today's workplace.

As a reader, you will find a wealth of practical tools and strategies for creating workplaces that not only excel in performance but also in employee happiness and well-being. From the importance of fostering a positive organizational culture to the practical steps for implementing a wisdom-driven framework, this book provides a roadmap for those looking to make meaningful change.

What is particularly inspiring about this work is the collective effort to redefine success in organizational contexts. The idea of "Happy Wisdom" challenges us to rethink traditional business models and strive for a more compassionate, ethical, and sustainable approach to leadership and organizational growth. It is a call to action for all of us—leaders, managers, employees, and scholars alike—to embrace the values of happiness and wisdom in our daily work and interactions.

This book is not just for those in leadership positions but for anyone committed to creating work environments that prioritize the well-being of employees. Whether you are looking to initiate small changes in your team or embark on a large-scale transformation, this work will serve as a guiding light, offering inspiration, practical tools, and a deeper understanding of how to harness the power of happiness and wisdom for organizational success.

As you journey through the chapters, I encourage you to reflect on how these principles can be applied to your own organization and your personal approach to work. The ideas presented here are not just theories—they are transformative tools that can help shape the future of work and create environments where people can truly thrive.

May this book inspire you to take action and join the movement towards a more joyful, wise, and sustainable way of working.

Chapter 1

Cultivating Emotional Intelligence for Organizational Well-Being:

Fostering Happiness and Wisdom in Nursing Education

Tiago Manuel Horta Reis da Silva
https://orcid.org/0000-0001-5220-1718
King's College London, UK

ABSTRACT

This chapter investigates the critical role of emotional intelligence (EI) in nursing education as a tool for cultivating organizational well-being, happiness, and wisdom within healthcare settings. As healthcare environments become increasingly complex, emotionally intelligent nurses are better equipped to manage interpersonal dynamics, lead effectively, and foster positive work environments. The chapter provides a theoretical overview of EI and its application in organisational well-being, focusing on the intersection between nursing education and emotional intelligence development. Strategies for embedding EI into the curriculum, fostering emotional resilience, and promoting a culture of empathy, wisdom, and happiness within healthcare organizations are examined. By integrating EI into the core of nursing education, we can better prepare nurses to contribute not only to patient care but also to the broader organisational ethos, promoting a work environment where both emotional and psychological well-being are prioritised.

DOI: 10.4018/979-8-3693-8457-2.ch001

1. INTRODUCTION

The chapter begins by exploring the rising importance of emotional intelligence within healthcare organisations. Emotional Intelligence (EI) has emerged as a foundational element for fostering well-being, happiness, and wisdom within organizations, particularly in professions like nursing, where emotional labour is intrinsic to daily responsibilities. This section sets the stage for understanding how EI can be cultivated through nursing education, linking it to broader concepts of organizational well-being.

In recent years, the significance of emotional intelligence (EI) in nursing education has gained considerable attention, reflecting a paradigm shift in how healthcare professionals are trained to interact with patients and colleagues. Emotional intelligence, defined as the ability to perceive, understand, manage, and utilise emotions effectively in oneself and others, is increasingly recognised as a critical competency for nurses (da Silva, 2022; Reis da Silva, 2024a). This chapter, entitled "Cultivating Emotional Intelligence for Organisational Well-Being: Fostering Happiness and Wisdom in Nursing Education," aims to explore the intricate relationships between emotional intelligence, happiness, wisdom, and organizational well-being within the context of nursing education.

1.1 Background and Rationale

The background of this chapter is rooted in the understanding that nursing is not merely a technical profession but also a deeply emotional one. Nurses frequently encounter high.stress situations that require them to manage their emotions while providing compassionate care to patients (Reis da Silva, 2024b; 2024c; 2024d). Research indicates that higher levels of emotional intelligence among nurses correlate with improved communication skills, enhanced job satisfaction, and better patient outcomes (Mariati et al., 2022; da Silva, 2022; Farhana, 2023; Reis da Silva, 2024d). Furthermore, the integration of emotional intelligence training into nursing curricula has been advocated to prepare future nurses for the emotional demands of their profession (Reis da Silva, 2024e; Reis da Silva, 2024f).

The rationale for focusing on emotional intelligence in nursing education stems from the recognition that emotional competencies can significantly influence the overall well-being of healthcare organizations. A workforce equipped with high emotional intelligence is better positioned to foster positive relationships, manage conflicts, and enhance teamwork, all of which contribute to a healthier organisational culture (Li et al., 2021; Xu, 2023; da Silva, 2024). Moreover, the interplay between emotional intelligence and happiness is particularly relevant, as studies have shown that nurses who possess strong emotional intelligence tend to report higher levels of job satisfaction and overall happiness (Varughese & Rema, 2021; Baghdadi, 2023).

1.2 Purpose of the Chapter

The purpose of this chapter is to elucidate the role of emotional intelligence in cultivating happiness and wisdom among nursing students, ultimately contributing to organizational well-being. By examining the existing literature, this chapter will highlight the importance of emotional intelligence as a foundational element in nursing education, emphasising its potential to enhance both individual and collective outcomes within healthcare settings.

1.3 Overview of Key Concepts: EI, Happiness, Wisdom, and Organizational Well-Being in Nursing Education

Key concepts that will be explored in this chapter include emotional intelligence, happiness, wisdom, and organisational well-being. Emotional intelligence encompasses a range of skills, including self-awareness, self-regulation, empathy, and social skills, all of which are essential for effective nursing practice (da Silva, 2024; da Silva, 2024b; Reis da Silva, 2024d). Happiness, in the context of nursing, refers to the subjective well-being and job satisfaction experienced by nurses, which can be significantly influenced by their emotional competencies (Varughese & Rema, 2021; Farhana, 2023; Xu, 2023). Wisdom, often characterised by sound judgment and the ability to apply knowledge in practical situations, is crucial for nurses as they navigate complex clinical environments (Jung & Kang, 2020). Finally, organisational well-being pertains to the overall health of the workplace, including factors such as employee engagement, morale, and the quality of interpersonal relationships within the healthcare team (Li et al., 2022).

2. THEORETICAL FOUNDATIONS OF EMOTIONAL INTELLIGENCE

This section offers a deep dive into the theoretical underpinnings of EI. The definition of EI varies across disciplines, but core concepts include self-awareness, self-regulation, motivation, empathy, and social skills. Goleman's model of EI, as well as Salovey and Mayer's ability-based model, will be explored to frame the discussion in the context of healthcare and organizational well-being. A brief historical overview of how EI has evolved in organizational psychology and healthcare leadership will be presented.

2.1 Definitions and Conceptual Frameworks of Emotional Intelligence

Emotional Intelligence (EI) is increasingly recognised as a critical competency in various fields, particularly in healthcare and organisational psychology. At its core, EI encompasses the ability to recognise, understand, and manage one's own emotions, as well as the emotions of others. Salovey and Mayer, who are credited with coining the term, define emotional intelligence as a set of four interrelated abilities: perceiving emotions, using emotions to facilitate thought, understanding emotions, and managing emotions in oneself and others (Salovey et al., 2009; da Silva, 2022). This framework highlights the multifaceted nature of EI, emphasising that it is not merely about emotional awareness but also involves the application of emotional knowledge to enhance cognitive processes and interpersonal interactions.

In the context of nursing education, EI is particularly pertinent. notes that EI is pivotal in the development of healthcare professionals, as it fosters empathy and effective communication, which are essential for patient care (Shrestha & Mandal, 2021). The integration of EI into nursing curricula can enhance students' abilities to navigate the emotional demands of their profession, ultimately leading to improved patient outcomes and job satisfaction (Shrestha & Mandal, 2021). Furthermore, the conceptualisation of EI as a blend of cognitive, affective, and behavioural components underscores its relevance in teaching and learning environments, where emotional management plays a crucial role in educational success (Koshechko, 2019).

2.2 Historical Evolution of EI in Healthcare and Organizational Psychology

The historical evolution of emotional intelligence can be traced back to the early 1990s when psychologists began to explore the role of emotions in cognitive processes. Daniel Goleman's influential book, "Emotional Intelligence," published in 1995, popularised the concept and linked it to success in various domains, including leadership and organisational effectiveness (Farmer et al., 2020). Goleman's model emphasised the importance of EI in fostering effective leadership, particularly in high-stress environments such as healthcare, where emotional labour is prevalent (figure 1 and table 1).

Figure 1. Emotional intelligence and high-performing leaders

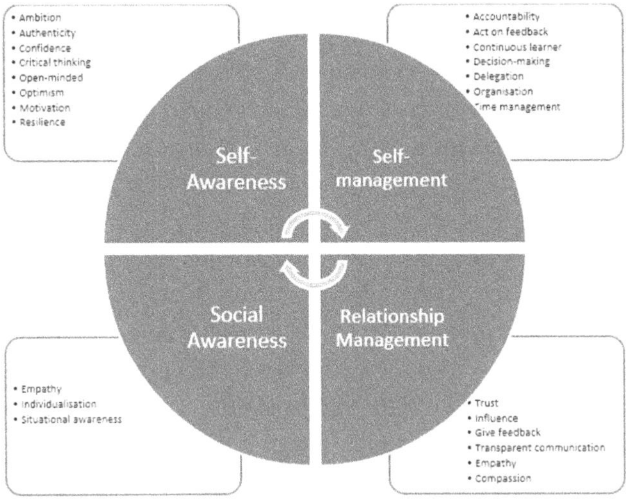

Table 1. Concepts in Emotional Intelligence

Self.awareness	Self.management
Accurately recognising and understanding your own emotions, thoughts, perceptions, strengths, limitations and identity	Using your self.awareness to positively manage your actions and behaviours
Social Awareness	**Relationship Management**
Accurately recognising and understanding the emotions, thoughts, perceptions, strengths, limitations and identities of others	Using your self.awareness, self.management and social awareness to build and maintain healthy connections

In healthcare, the recognition of EI's significance has grown alongside the increasing complexity of patient care. As healthcare professionals face emotionally charged situations, the ability to manage emotions becomes essential for maintaining professional relationships and ensuring patient satisfaction (Koutsioumpa, 2023). Studies have shown that healthcare leaders with high EI are better equipped to inspire and motivate their teams, leading to improved organizational performance and employee engagement (Gupta, 2023). This historical perspective highlights the transition from viewing intelligence primarily through a cognitive lens to embracing a more holistic understanding that includes emotional competencies.

2.3 Relevance of EI in Leadership and Nursing Education

The relevance of emotional intelligence in leadership, particularly within healthcare settings, cannot be overstated. Effective leaders are often characterised by their ability to connect with their teams, understand their emotional needs, and foster a supportive work environment. Research indicates that leaders who exhibit high levels of EI are more adept at conflict resolution, team building, and enhancing employee morale (Hammett et al., 2018; Reis da Silva, 2024d; Reis da Silva, 2024e). In nursing education, cultivating EI among future leaders is crucial for preparing them to navigate the complexities of modern healthcare systems, where emotional resilience and interpersonal skills are paramount (Carragher & Gormley, 2016). Moreover, the integration of EI into nursing curricula has been shown to enhance students' clinical performance and retention rates (Carragher & Gormley, 2016). By equipping nursing students with the tools to understand and manage their emotions, educators can foster a generation of healthcare professionals who are not only technically proficient but also emotionally intelligent. This dual focus on cognitive and emotional skills is essential for delivering compassionate care and improving patient outcomes (Carragher & Gormley, 2016; Hammett et al., 2018). As the healthcare landscape continues to evolve, the emphasis on emotional intelligence in both leadership and education will play a pivotal role in shaping the future of nursing practice (figure 2).

Figure 2. 10 Traits of a High Emotional Intelligence Quotient Leader

3. THE ROLE OF EI IN FOSTERING ORGANISATIONAL WELL-BEING

Here, the discussion shifts to EI's relevance in creating positive workplace environments in healthcare settings. Research evidence will be examined to demonstrate how emotionally intelligent nurses contribute to job satisfaction, reduce turnover, and improve patient outcomes. The section will argue that a focus on EI can lead to sustainable happiness and wisdom within organisations, promoting emotional and psychological well-being at all levels of healthcare operations.

3.1 EI and Its Impact on Healthcare Organisational Culture

Emotional Intelligence (EI) plays a pivotal role in shaping the organisational culture within healthcare settings. A culture that values EI fosters an environment where employees feel understood and supported, which is crucial in high-stress professions like nursing. Research indicates that organisations with high EI are characterised by improved communication, collaboration, and conflict resolution among staff members (Dâmbean & Gabor, 2021). This positive organisational culture not only enhances employee morale but also contributes to a more cohesive team dynamic, ultimately leading to better patient care outcomes (Lee & Wong, 2017). Moreover, EI facilitates the development of empathy and compassion among healthcare professionals, which are essential traits in patient-centred care. When healthcare workers possess high emotional intelligence, they are better equipped to manage their own emotions and respond effectively to the emotional needs of patients and colleagues (Farhana, 2023). This ability to navigate emotional landscapes contributes to a supportive work environment where staff members feel valued and engaged, thereby enhancing overall organizational well-being (Li et al., 2021).

3.2 How EI Contributes to Happiness and Wisdom in the Workplace

The relationship between emotional intelligence, happiness, and wisdom in the workplace is well-documented. High levels of EI are associated with increased job satisfaction and overall happiness among employees (Jufrizen, et al. 2023). When individuals can effectively manage their emotions and understand the emotions of others, they are more likely to experience positive interactions, leading to a greater sense of fulfilment and well-being at work (Kwabena et al., 2022). This emotional competence allows employees to navigate workplace challenges with resilience and adaptability, fostering a culture of wisdom where informed decision-making and ethical considerations are prioritised (Kwabena et al., 2022). Furthermore, organisations that prioritise EI training and development create an environment conducive to personal and professional growth. Employees who engage in EI training often report enhanced self-awareness, improved interpersonal relationships, and greater emotional regulation, all of which contribute to a more harmonious workplace (Kwabena et al., 2022). This cultivation of emotional intelligence not only promotes individual happiness but also encourages a collective wisdom that benefits the organisation as a whole, as employees become more adept at collaborating and problem-solving (Kwabena et al., 2022).

3.3 Evidence of EI's Influence on Staff Retention, Job Satisfaction, and Patient Outcomes

The influence of emotional intelligence on staff retention, job satisfaction, and patient outcomes is supported by a growing body of evidence. Studies have shown that healthcare professionals with high EI are more likely to remain in their positions, as they experience greater job satisfaction and lower levels of burnout (Shepherd, 2021). For instance, a study among nurses revealed that those with higher emotional intelligence reported significantly higher job satisfaction and were less likely to consider leaving their jobs (Doğru, 2022). This correlation underscores the importance of EI in fostering a stable workforce, which is essential for maintaining continuity of care in healthcare settings. Additionally, emotional intelligence has been linked to improved patient outcomes. Healthcare providers who exhibit high levels of EI are better able to establish rapport with patients, leading to enhanced patient satisfaction and compliance with treatment plans (Aznan et al., 2019). The ability to empathise with patients and effectively communicate their needs not only improves the patient experience but also contributes to better health outcomes (Kiziloğlu & Şahin, 2022). This relationship between EI and patient care highlights the critical role that emotional intelligence plays in the overall effectiveness of healthcare delivery systems.

4. EMBEDDING EMOTIONAL INTELLIGENCE IN NURSING EDUCATION

This section offers practical strategies for embedding EI into nursing curricula. Approaches such as experiential learning, simulation-based education, and reflective practice will be examined. The value of mentorship in developing emotional intelligence among student nurses will also be discussed, alongside case studies that demonstrate successful integration of EI in nursing education programs. This part will emphasize the importance of EI in preparing nurses for the emotional demands of their profession.

4.1 Curriculum Development strategies for Teaching Emotional Intelligence

The integration of Emotional Intelligence (EI) into nursing education is essential for preparing future nurses to navigate the complex emotional landscapes of healthcare environments. Curriculum development strategies aimed at embedding EI can include the incorporation of specific learning outcomes related to emotional competencies, such as self-awareness, empathy, and emotional regulation (Fitzpatrick et al., 2023; Cowley et al, 2023; Reis da Silva and Mitchell, 2024a). For instance, Lu and Shorey (2021) emphasise the need for formal EI education and training activities within undergraduate nursing curricula, suggesting that these competencies can significantly enhance nursing practice and patient care. Moreover, the curriculum can be designed to include both theoretical and practical components, ensuring that students not only understand the concepts of EI but also apply them in real-world scenarios. This can be achieved through the development of case studies, role-playing exercises, and simulations that allow students to practice emotional skills in a controlled environment (Reis da Silva and Mitchell, 2024a). Additionally, interdisciplinary collaboration and the use of service users can be encouraged, where nursing students engage with peers from other healthcare disciplines or use service users to foster a holistic understanding of emotional dynamics and enhance empathy in patient care (Jung & Kang, 2020; Reis da Silva and Mitchell, 2024b).

4.2 Pedagogical Approaches: Experiential Learning, Reflective Practice, and Mentorship

To effectively teach EI in nursing education, various pedagogical approaches can be employed. Experiential learning, which emphasises learning through experience, is particularly effective in developing emotional competencies. This approach allows nursing students to engage in hands-on activities that challenge them to apply their emotional intelligence in real-life situations, thereby reinforcing their learning (Li et al., 2022). Reflective practice is another critical pedagogical strategy that can enhance EI among nursing students. By encouraging students to reflect on their emotional responses to various clinical scenarios, educators can help them develop greater self-awareness and emotional regulation skills. This reflective process can be facilitated through journaling, group discussions, and guided debriefing sessions after clinical placements (Baghdadi, 2023).

Mentorship also plays a vital role in fostering EI in nursing education. Experienced nurses can serve as mentors, providing guidance and support to students as they navigate the emotional challenges of clinical practice. This mentorship relationship can help students develop their emotional competencies through observation, feedback, and shared experiences (Prihandhani & Hakim, 2022).

4.3 Case studies of Successful EI Integration in Nursing Programs

Several nursing programs have successfully integrated EI into their curricula, demonstrating the positive impact of such initiatives on student outcomes. For example, a study conducted by highlighted the effectiveness of an emotional intelligence training program in improving interpersonal relationships among nursing staff at a general hospital (Huang et al., 2019). The program not only enhanced the emotional competencies of the nurses but also led to improved patient care and satisfaction. Another notable case study involved a nursing program that implemented a comprehensive EI curriculum, which included workshops, simulations, and reflective practice sessions. The results indicated significant improvements in students' emotional intelligence scores, as well as enhanced clinical performance and communication skills (Huang et al., 2019). These findings underscore the importance of embedding EI in nursing education to prepare students for the emotional demands of their profession.

5. EMOTIONAL RESILIENCE AND COPING MECHANISMS

Building emotional resilience is essential for nurses working in high-stress environments. This section discusses the significance of emotional resilience and offers methods to build it through emotional intelligence training. Techniques such as mindfulness, empathy-building exercises, and self-regulation strategies will be explored. The role of EI in helping nurses cope with stress and prevent burnout will be emphasised.

5.1 Importance of Emotional Resilience in Nursing

Emotional resilience is a critical attribute for nurses, enabling them to cope effectively with the emotional demands of their profession (Figure 3 and table 2). The nature of nursing involves frequent exposure to high-stress situations, including patient suffering, loss, and the pressures of healthcare environments (Reis da Silva, 2024g; Reis da Silva, 2024h; Reis da Silva, 2024i; Reis da Silva, 2024j; Reis da Silva, 2024k). Resilience allows nurses to maintain their mental health and well-being while providing compassionate care to patients. Research indicates that resilient nurses are better equipped to handle stress, recover from setbacks, and sustain their commitment to patient care (Foster et al., 2018). The ability to bounce back from adversity not only enhances personal well-being but also contributes to improved patient outcomes, as resilient nurses are more likely to engage positively with their patients and colleagues (Yang et al., 2023). Moreover, emotional resilience is linked to job satisfaction and retention rates among nursing staff. Nurses who demonstrate resilience are less likely to experience burnout and emotional exhaustion, which are prevalent in the profession (Foster et al., 2018) (figure 3 and table 2). This connection underscores the importance of fostering resilience through targeted educational and training programs within nursing curricula. By equipping nursing students with the tools to develop resilience, educational institutions can help prepare them for the emotional challenges they will face in their careers (Yang et al., 2023).

Figure 3. Six Domains of Resilience

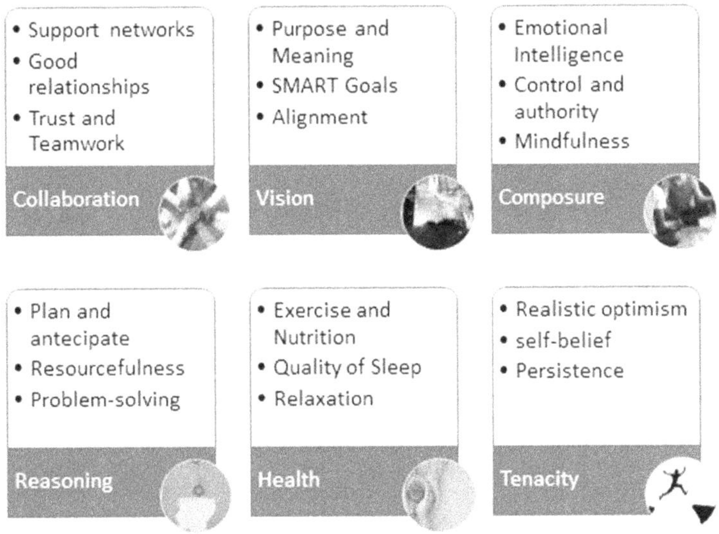

5.2 Techniques for building Resilience Through Emotional Intelligence

Building emotional resilience in nursing can be effectively achieved through the development of emotional intelligence (EI). Techniques that enhance EI, such as self-awareness, emotional regulation, and empathy, are essential for fostering resilience (da Silva, 2022; da Silva, 2024). Self-awareness allows nurses to recognise their emotional triggers and responses, enabling them to manage their emotions more effectively (da Silva, 2022). Emotional regulation skills help nurses maintain composure in stressful situations, allowing them to respond thoughtfully rather than react impulsively (Wang, 2023) (table 2). Training programs that focus on enhancing emotional intelligence can include workshops, role-playing scenarios, and reflective practice exercises. These activities encourage nurses to practice self-regulation and develop coping strategies that can be employed in real-world situations (Cabrera. Aguilar, 2023). For instance, mindfulness practices can be integrated into training to help nurses cultivate a greater awareness of their emotional states and develop techniques for managing stress (Wang, 2023).

Furthermore, fostering a supportive workplace culture that encourages open communication and emotional expression can significantly enhance resilience. When nurses feel supported by their colleagues and supervisors, they are more likely to engage in positive coping strategies and seek help when needed (Liu, 2023). This collaborative environment not only strengthens individual resilience but also promotes a culture of well-being within healthcare organisations.

Table 2. Methods for increasing resilience

	Goggins 40% rule	Cognitive reframing	Premeditation Malorum
	The mind will be the first thing to give up, embrace the uncomfortable and keep going	Your outlook shapes your experiences, explore and change your pessimistic thoughts	The stoic rule encourages you to prepare for the worst case scenario by visualisation
Action	When your mind is telling you to stop, you have only reached 40% of your limit, keep going.	Identify negative thoughts as they occur. Evaluate their accuracy and counter them with evidence.based, realistic positive statements	Visualise and explore the worst case scenario to reduce any anxiety and stress around this outcome

continued on following page

Table 2. Continued

	McGonigal's Challenge Response	Stockdale Paradox	The 5 x 5 Rule
	Transform stress into a powerful ally	Face the brutal truth, yet never lose faith	Do not sweat the small stuff, think long term
Action	When faced with stress, consciously choose to see it as a challenge to overcome rather than a threat to avoid	Acknowledge the severity of your situation without sugarcoating it but maintaining faith in your eventual success and take active steps towards the solution.	If it will not matter in five years, do not spend more than five minutes being upset by it.

Source: Liu et al., 2023; Min, 2024

5.3 Role of Mindfulness, Empathy, and Self-Regulation

Mindfulness, empathy, and self-regulation are three interrelated components that play a vital role in enhancing emotional resilience among nurses. Mindfulness practices, such as meditation, visualisation, and deep breathing exercises, help nurses develop present moment awareness and reduce stress levels. Research has shown that mindfulness can improve emotional regulation and increase resilience by enabling individuals to respond to stressors with greater clarity and composure (Wang, 2024).

Empathy, the ability to understand and share the feelings of others, is another crucial element of emotional resilience. Empathetic nurses are better able to connect with their patients, which can lead to improved patient satisfaction and outcomes (Min, 2024). Moreover, empathy fosters a sense of community and support among nursing staff, further enhancing resilience within the workplace (Mariati et al., 2022). Self-regulation, the ability to manage one's emotions and behaviours in response to stress, is essential for maintaining resilience in nursing practice. Nurses who can effectively regulate their emotions are less likely to experience burnout and are better equipped to handle the emotional demands of their roles (Min, 2024; da Silva, 2024). Training programs that focus on developing self-regulation skills can include techniques such as cognitive restructuring, which helps nurses reframe negative thoughts and adopt a more positive outlook (Elam & Taku, 2022).

6. PROMOTING A CULTURE OF EMPATHY, WISDOM, AND HAPPINESS

This section addresses the broader organizational culture and how EI can foster empathy and wisdom within nursing teams. It explores the connections between EI, empathy, and ethical decision-making, showing how these elements contribute to organizational happiness. Practical strategies for creating an emotionally intelligent workplace culture, including training programs, leadership models, and peer support systems, will be highlighted.

6.1 Strategies for Nurturing Empathy Within Nursing Teams

Nurturing empathy within nursing teams is essential for fostering a supportive and compassionate healthcare environment. One effective strategy is to implement training programs focused on emotional intelligence (EI), which can enhance nurses' ability to understand and respond to the emotions of their colleagues and patients. Research has shown that teams with high emotional intelligence exhibit improved communication, collaboration, and conflict resolution skills, all of which are critical for nurturing empathy (Lee & Wong, 2017). Additionally, creating opportunities for team-building activities can strengthen interpersonal relationships among nursing staff. These activities can include workshops, retreats, or collaborative projects that encourage open dialogue and shared experiences. Such initiatives not only promote empathy but also enhance team cohesion and trust (Lee & Wong, 2017). Furthermore, incorporating reflective practices into the nursing curriculum can help students and staff develop greater self-awareness and empathy (da Silva, 2022). By encouraging nurses to reflect on their interactions with patients and colleagues, they can better understand the emotional dynamics at play and respond more compassionately (Lee & Wong, 2017).

Mentorship programs can also play a significant role in fostering empathy within nursing teams. Experienced nurses can serve as mentors, providing guidance and support to newer staff members. This relationship can help cultivate a culture of empathy, as mentors model empathetic behaviours and encourage mentees to prioritise emotional connections with patients and colleagues (Lee & Wong, 2017). Overall, a multifaceted approach that includes training, team-building, reflective practices, and mentorship can effectively nurture empathy within nursing teams.

6.1.1 Importance to Develop Empathy at Work

The development of empathy within the workplace is crucial for fostering a positive organisational culture and enhancing overall employee well-being. One of the primary benefits of empathy is its ability to improve communication among team members. When employees practice empathy, they create an environment of open and honest dialogue, which significantly reduces misunderstandings and conflicts (Ahsan, 2023). This open communication is essential in high.stress environments, such as healthcare, where clear and effective communication can directly impact patient outcomes.

Empathy also enhances collaboration within teams. By understanding and sharing the feelings of their colleagues, employees can build stronger relationships, leading to improved teamwork and cooperation (Hajibabaee et al., 2018). This collaborative spirit is vital for achieving organisational goals, as it encourages individuals to work together towards common objectives rather than in silos. Moreover, fostering an empathetic workplace can lead to increased employee satisfaction. When employees feel valued and understood, their morale and job satisfaction improve, which can result in higher levels of engagement and productivity (Prado et al., 2022). This sense of belonging and appreciation is particularly important in retaining talent, as employees are less likely to leave organizations where they feel supported and recognised.

Empathy in leadership is also linked to promoting innovation. Leaders who demonstrate empathy are more open to new ideas and feedback from their teams, creating a culture that encourages creativity and innovation (Munira et al., 2022). This openness not only enhances problem.solving capabilities but also empowers employees to contribute their unique perspectives and solutions. Additionally, a culture of empathy can significantly reduce turnover rates. When employees feel heard and supported, they are less likely to seek employment elsewhere. This stability is beneficial for organisations, as it reduces the costs associated with recruiting and training new staff (Munira et al., 2022). Furthermore, empathetic leaders build trust and loyalty among their teams, which are essential qualities for effective leadership. Trust fosters a safe environment where employees feel comfortable expressing their thoughts and concerns, leading to a more cohesive and resilient team (Munira et al., 2022). Finally, empathy contributes to resilience within teams. By understanding and supporting each other through challenges and setbacks, employees can navigate difficulties more effectively, fostering a culture of resilience that benefits the entire organization (Sadeghi et al., 2018).

6.1.2 How to Increase Empathy at Work

Increasing empathy in the workplace requires intentional strategies and practices. One effective approach is active listening, where individuals give their full attention to the speaker, show genuine interest, and respond thoughtfully to their concerns. This practice not only demonstrates respect but also encourages open dialogue (Ahsan, 2023). Another strategy is to practice empathy daily by making a conscious effort to understand others' feelings and perspectives in every interaction. This can be achieved by asking open.ended questions and engaging in meaningful conversations that allow for deeper understanding (Hajibabaee et al., 2018).

Creating an environment that encourages open communication is also vital. Employees should feel safe to express their thoughts and emotions without fear of judgment or retribution. This can be facilitated through regular team meetings, feedback sessions, and informal gatherings that promote relationship.building (Safiullah et al., 2023). Showing genuine concern for colleagues' well-being, both personally and professionally, is another important aspect of fostering empathy. Leaders and team members should actively demonstrate care and support, which can be as simple as checking in on a colleague's workload or offering assistance during challenging times (Safiullah et al., 2023).

Working on emotional intelligence is crucial for enhancing empathy. Employees should develop the ability to recognize and manage their own emotions as well as the emotions of others. Training programs focused on emotional intelligence can provide valuable skills for improving interpersonal relationships (Kiishi, 2024). Providing constructive feedback in a considerate manner is also essential. Feedback should be framed in a way that helps others grow without being hurtful, promoting a culture of learning and development (Pan et al., 2020). Creating a supportive culture where team members encourage one another and share their challenges openly can significantly enhance empathy within the workplace. This culture of support fosters a sense of community and belonging (Pečiuliauskienė, 2021). Finally, leaders should lead by example, modelling empathetic behaviour in their interactions. By demonstrating empathy in their leadership style, they set a standard for the team and encourage others to follow suit (Mercader.Rubio, 2023).

6.2 How EI Fosters Wisdom in Decision-Making and Leadership

Emotional intelligence is a critical factor in fostering wisdom in decision-making and leadership within nursing and healthcare settings. Leaders with high EI are better equipped to navigate complex emotional landscapes, allowing them to make informed decisions that consider both the emotional and practical implications of their choices. Research indicates that emotionally intelligent leaders are more adept at recognizing and managing their own emotions, as well as understanding the emotions of their team members, which enhances their decision-making capabilities (Jeong et al., 2022). Moreover, EI contributes to wisdom by promoting a collaborative decision-making process. Leaders who exhibit high emotional intelligence are more likely to encourage input from their team members, fostering an inclusive environment where diverse perspectives are valued. This collaborative approach not only leads to more comprehensive decision-making but also enhances team morale and engagement (Davaei & Gunkel, 2023). Additionally, emotionally intelligent leaders are better at managing conflicts and navigating difficult conversations, which are essential skills for effective leadership in healthcare settings (Davaei & Gunkel, 2023).

The integration of EI into leadership development programs can further enhance the wisdom of nursing leaders. By focusing on emotional competencies such as empathy, self.regulation, and social awareness, these programs can prepare leaders to make decisions that prioritize the well-being of their teams and patients (Rožman et al., 2022). Ultimately, the cultivation of emotional intelligence within leadership can lead to more effective decision-making and a more positive organizational culture.

6.3 Impact of Emotionally Intelligent Teams on Organisational Happiness and Well-being

The presence of emotionally intelligent teams has a profound impact on organisational happiness and well-being. Research has shown that teams with high emotional intelligence are more cohesive, innovative, and effective in their collaborative efforts (Fang et al., 2022). This enhanced teamwork contributes to a positive work environment, where employees feel valued and supported, leading to increased job satisfaction and overall happiness (Peláez.Fernández et al., 2021). Emotionally intelligent teams are also better equipped to handle stress and adversity, which is particularly important in high-pressure healthcare settings. By fostering a culture of emotional awareness and support, these teams can mitigate the negative effects of stress and burnout, promoting a healthier work-life balance for their members (Algarni & Alemeri, 2023). Furthermore, the positive emotional climate created by emotionally intelligent teams can lead to improved patient outcomes, as satisfied and engaged staff are more likely to provide high-quality care (Peláez.Fernández et al., 2021).

7. LEADERSHIP AND EMOTIONAL INTELLIGENCE IN NURSING

Nurse leaders play a pivotal role in promoting emotional intelligence within healthcare organizations. This section examines how nurse leaders can use EI to enhance teamwork, manage conflicts, and empower staff. Leadership theories related to emotional intelligence will be analysed, and case studies demonstrating successful EI leadership in healthcare will be provided.

7.1 The Role of Nurse Leaders in Promoting Driven Organisational Well-Being

Nurse leaders play a pivotal role in fostering an emotionally intelligent (EI) organisational culture that enhances overall well-being within healthcare settings. By prioritising emotional intelligence, nurse leaders can create an environment that promotes open communication, collaboration, and trust among staff members. Research indicates that nurse leaders who exhibit high levels of EI are more effective in managing their teams, as they can recognise and respond to the emotional needs of their colleagues (Wang, 2024). This emotional awareness enables leaders to address conflicts proactively, ensuring that misunderstandings are minimised and that a supportive atmosphere is cultivated. Moreover, nurse leaders can model empathetic behaviour, which encourages staff to adopt similar practices in their interactions with patients and each other. By demonstrating empathy, leaders can build strong relationships with their teams, fostering a sense of belonging and commitment (Moloney et al., 2020). This supportive culture not only enhances job satisfaction but also contributes to lower turnover rates, as employees are more likely to remain in an organization where they feel valued and understood (Moloney et al., 2020).

Additionally, nurse leaders can implement training programs focused on developing emotional intelligence among their staff. Such initiatives can enhance communication skills, promote resilience, and empower nurses to take ownership of their emotional well-being (Cheng et al., 2020). By investing in the emotional intelligence of their teams, nurse leaders can create a more engaged and motivated workforce, ultimately leading to improved patient care and organizational performance (Mulyatsih, 2023).

7.2 EI as a Tool for Conflict Resolution, Collaboration, and Staff Empowerment

Emotional intelligence serves as a powerful tool for conflict resolution, collaboration, and staff empowerment within nursing teams. In high-stress environments, conflicts are inevitable; however, leaders with high EI can navigate these challenges effectively. By recognising the emotional undercurrents of conflicts, they can facilitate constructive conversations that address the root causes of disagreements (Pedroso et al., 2020). This approach not only resolves conflicts but also strengthens relationships among team members, fostering a culture of collaboration. Collaboration is further enhanced when team members feel empowered to express their emotions and perspectives. Nurse leaders who promote emotional intelligence encourage open dialogue, allowing staff to share their thoughts and feelings without fear of judgment (Prado-Gascó et al., 2019). This inclusive environment fosters teamwork, as employees are more likely to collaborate effectively when they feel heard and respected. Research has shown that emotionally intelligent teams are more innovative and productive, as they leverage diverse perspectives to solve problems and improve patient care (Wang, 2023).

Moreover, emotional intelligence empowers nurses to manage their own emotions and stress levels, leading to greater job satisfaction and resilience. When nurses feel supported by their leaders and colleagues, they are more likely to engage in self-care practices and seek help when needed (Atthayasai, 2023). This empowerment not only enhances individual well-being but also contributes to a healthier organizational culture, where employees are motivated to perform at their best.

7.3 Leadership Case studies Illustrating EI in Action

Several case studies illustrate the successful application of emotional intelligence in nursing leadership. For instance, a study conducted by highlighted how nurse leaders who embraced transformational leadership styles and demonstrated empathy were able to create a supportive work environment during public health emergencies (Wang, 2024). These leaders effectively communicated with their teams, addressing concerns and fostering a sense of unity, which ultimately improved staff morale and patient care outcomes.

Another case study by examined how healthcare organisations that prioritised emotional intelligence in their leadership practices experienced significant improvements in employee well-being and job satisfaction (Moloney et al., 2020). By implementing training programs focused on developing EI skills, these organizations empowered their nursing staff to engage in compassionate care, resulting in enhanced patient experiences and reduced burnout among nurses.

Furthermore, a qualitative study by explored the impact of head nurses' empathy on their teams' performance and well-being (Cheng et al., 2020). The findings revealed that head nurses who actively practiced empathy not only improved their relationships with staff but also fostered a culture of support and collaboration. This environment allowed nurses to thrive, ultimately leading to better patient care and organizational success.

8. CHALLENGES AND BARRIERS TO IMPLEMENTING EI IN NURSING EDUCATION

Despite its benefits, there are challenges in integrating EI into nursing education. Institutional inertia, resistance to change, and cultural barriers within healthcare organizations can impede the implementation of EI-focused curricula. This section discusses these challenges and offers strategies to overcome them, focusing on the importance of institutional support, faculty development, and leadership buy.in.

8.1 Institutional and Cultural Barriers

Implementing emotional intelligence (EI) in nursing education faces several institutional and cultural barriers. One significant barrier is the existing educational framework, which often prioritises technical skills and clinical competencies over emotional and interpersonal skills (Mudzi & Bruce, 2023). Many nursing programs are still rooted in traditional pedagogical approaches that do not adequately address the emotional aspects of patient care. This lack of emphasis on EI can lead to a workforce that is technically proficient but lacks the emotional skills necessary for effective patient interactions and teamwork (Reis da Silva and Mitchell, 2024a; Reis da Silva and Mitchell, 2024b). Cultural barriers also play a critical role in the resistance to integrating EI into nursing curricula. In many healthcare settings, there is a prevailing culture that undervalues emotional competencies, viewing them as secondary to clinical skills (Lateef & Mhlongo, 2019). This cultural mindset can hinder the acceptance of EI training and development initiatives, as both faculty and students may perceive them as unnecessary or irrelevant to their professional practice. Additionally, the hierarchical nature of healthcare organizations can stifle open discussions about emotions and interpersonal relationships, further entrenching these cultural barriers.

8.2 Resistance to Change and Strategies for Overcoming It

Resistance to change is a common challenge when attempting to implement EI in nursing education. This resistance can stem from various sources, including faculty reluctance to adopt new teaching methods, student apprehension about engaging in emotional discussions, and institutional inertia (Çulha et al., 2017). To overcome this resistance, it is essential to foster a culture of openness and support within nursing programs. Educators can begin by providing evidence of the benefits of EI, such as improved patient outcomes and enhanced team collaboration, to encourage buy.in from both faculty and students (Blaauw et al., 2014). One effective strategy for overcoming resistance is to involve stakeholders in the development and implementation of EI initiatives. Engaging faculty, students, and healthcare professionals in the design of EI training programs can help ensure that these initiatives are relevant and tailored to the specific needs of the nursing community (Nye et al., 2022). Additionally, providing ongoing professional development opportunities for faculty can equip them with the skills and knowledge necessary to effectively teach EI concepts (Nye et al., 2022). Another strategy is to incorporate EI training into existing curricula gradually. By integrating EI concepts into courses that already focus on communication, leadership, and teamwork, educators can demonstrate the relevance of emotional intelligence without overwhelming students or faculty with entirely new content (Mediarti et al., 2018). This gradual approach can help ease the transition and reduce resistance to change.

8.3 Addressing EI Gaps in Traditional Nursing Curricula

Traditional nursing curricula often lack a comprehensive focus on emotional intelligence, which can create significant gaps in students' preparedness for the emotional demands of nursing practice. To address these gaps, nursing programs must revise their curricula to include explicit training in emotional intelligence skills, such as empathy, self-awareness, and emotional regulation (da Silva, 2022; Reis da Silva, 2024a). This can be achieved by integrating EI concepts into core nursing courses, clinical practice, and simulation experiences. Furthermore, nursing educators should prioritise experiential learning opportunities that allow students to practice and develop their emotional intelligence skills in real-world settings. For example, incorporating role-playing scenarios, reflective journaling, and peer feedback can help students gain insights into their emotional responses and improve their interpersonal skills (Shibata et al., 2020). Additionally, partnerships with healthcare organisations can provide nursing students with exposure to emotionally intelligent practices in clinical settings. By observing and participating in environments that prioritise emotional intelligence, students can better understand its importance and applicability in their future careers (Iheduru-Anderson & Waite, 2022).

9. FUTURE DIRECTIONS: ENHANCING EI FOR SUSTAINABLE ORGANIZATIONAL WELL-BEING

The future of EI in nursing education and organisational well-being is promising, with new innovations emerging. This section explores the potential of digital tools, AI, and e-learning platforms in teaching emotional intelligence. Research gaps will be identified, and future research directions will be proposed, with an emphasis on interdisciplinary approaches to studying EI in healthcare.

9.1 Innovations in Teaching EI Within Nursing Education

To enhance emotional intelligence in nursing education, innovative teaching methods must be employed. One promising approach is the use of simulation-based learning, which allows students to engage in realistic clinical scenarios that require the application of emotional intelligence skills (Aronsson et al., 2020). These simulations can provide valuable opportunities for students to practice empathy, communication, and conflict resolution in a safe and controlled environment. Another innovative strategy is the incorporation of interprofessional education (IPE) into nursing curricula. By collaborating with students from other healthcare disciplines, nursing students can develop a broader understanding of emotional intelligence in the context of team-based care (Park & Park, 2022). This exposure can enhance their ability to communicate effectively and work collaboratively with diverse healthcare teams, ultimately improving patient outcomes.

9.2 Leveraging Technology and Digital Tools for EI Training

The integration of technology and digital tools into nursing education can also enhance the teaching of emotional intelligence. Online training modules, virtual reality simulations, and mobile applications can provide nursing students with interactive and engaging ways to develop their emotional intelligence skills. For instance, virtual reality simulations can immerse students in challenging clinical scenarios that require them to navigate complex emotional dynamics, allowing for experiential learning without the risks associated with real-life patient interactions. Additionally, digital platforms can facilitate peer-to-peer learning and support, enabling nursing students to share experiences and strategies for developing emotional intelligence. Online forums and social media groups can serve as valuable resources for students to connect with their peers and mentors, fostering a sense of community and shared learning.

9.3 Research Gaps and Future Opportunities for Exploring EI in Healthcare Settings

Despite the growing recognition of the importance of emotional intelligence in nursing education, there remain significant research gaps in this area. Future studies should focus on the long-term impact of EI training on nursing practice, patient outcomes, and organisational well-being (Wałaszek et al., 2021). Additionally, more research is needed to explore the specific emotional intelligence competencies that are most relevant to different nursing specialties and practice settings (Wałaszek et al., 2021). Furthermore, there is an opportunity to investigate the role of emotional intelligence in addressing healthcare disparities and promoting health equity. Understanding how EI can be leveraged to improve communication and relationships with diverse patient populations can enhance the quality of care provided by nurses.

10. CONCLUSION

This chapter provided a comprehensive overview of how cultivating emotional intelligence can lead to enhanced happiness and wisdom among nursing students, thereby promoting organisational well-being. By integrating these concepts into nursing education, we can better prepare future nurses to meet the emotional and psychological demands of their profession, ultimately leading to improved patient care and a healthier work environment. The theoretical foundations of emotional intelligence encompass a rich tapestry of definitions, historical developments, and practical applications in healthcare and organisational psychology. As the importance of EI continues to gain recognition, particularly in nursing education, it is imperative to further explore its implications for leadership and patient care. By fostering emotional intelligence, healthcare professionals can enhance their ability to connect with patients and colleagues, ultimately leading to improved organisational well-being and patient satisfaction.

Emotional intelligence is a vital component in fostering organisational well-being within healthcare settings. Its impact on organisational culture, employee happiness, and patient outcomes underscores the necessity for healthcare organizations to prioritise EI in their training and development programs. By cultivating emotional intelligence among staff, healthcare organisations can enhance job satisfaction, improve staff retention, and ultimately provide better care for patients. Embedding emotional intelligence in nursing education requires a multifaceted approach that includes curriculum development strategies, diverse pedagogical methods, and successful case studies. By prioritising EI in nursing programs, educators can equip future nurses with the emotional competencies necessary for effective patient care and professional success. Emotional resilience is a vital component of nursing practice, enabling nurses to cope with the emotional challenges of their profession. By fostering emotional intelligence through targeted training and support, healthcare organizations can enhance the resilience of their nursing staff. Techniques such as mindfulness, empathy, and self-regulation are essential for building resilience, ultimately leading to improved job satisfaction, reduced burnout, and better patient care. Promoting a culture of empathy, wisdom, and happiness within nursing teams requires a multifaceted approach that emphasises emotional intelligence. By nurturing empathy through training, team-building, and mentorship, fostering wisdom in decision-making and leadership, and recognizing the impact of emotionally intelligent teams on organizational well-being, healthcare organizations can create a supportive and thriving work environment.

The role of nurse leaders in promoting emotional intelligence is essential for fostering organisational well-being. By leveraging EI as a tool for conflict resolution, collaboration, and staff empowerment, nurse leaders can create a positive work environment that enhances job satisfaction and patient care. The case studies presented demonstrate the tangible benefits of emotional intelligence in nursing leadership, underscoring its importance in today's healthcare landscape.

Addressing the challenges and barriers to implementing emotional intelligence in nursing education is essential for fostering a workforce that is equipped to navigate the emotional complexities of healthcare. By embracing innovative teaching methods, leveraging technology, and conducting further research, nursing programs can enhance emotional intelligence training and contribute to sustainable organizational well-being.

REFERENCES

Ahsan, M. (2023). The role of emotional intelligence in effective corporate social responsibility leadership. *International Journal of Organizational Analysis*, 31(8), 75.91. DOI: 10.1108/ijoa.02.2023.3615

Algarni, M., & Alemeri, M. (2023). The role of employee engagement, job satisfaction and organizational commitment on happiness at work at a Saudi organization. *International Journal of Business and Management*, 18(2), 27. DOI: 10.5539/ijbm.v18n2p27

Aronsson, J., Clarke, D., Grose, J., & Richardson, J. (2020). Student nurses exposed to sustainability education can challenge practice: a cohort study. *Nursing and Health Sciences*, 22(3), 803.811. DOI: 10.1111/nhs.12734

Atthayasai, J. (2023). Surgical nurses' perceptions of strategies to enhance pain management proficiency: a qualitative study. *Nursing Reports*, 13(2), 923.933. DOI: 10.3390/nursrep13020081

Aznan, E., Kassim, A., Othman, N., Yusof, M., & Amir, N. (2019). The relationship between job satisfaction and social skill. *Jurnal Intelek*, 14(2), 251.256. DOI: 10.24191/ji.v14i2.258

Baghdadi, N., Sankarapandian, C., Arulappan, J., Taani, M. H., Snethen, J., & Andargeery, S. Y. (2023). The association between nursing students' happiness, emotional intelligence, and perceived caring behavior in Riyadh city, Saudi Arabia. *Health Care*, 12(1), 67. DOI: 10.3390/healthcare12010067 PMID: 38200973

Blaauw, D., Ditlopo, P., & Rispel, L. (2014). Nursing education reform in South Africa – lessons from a policy analysis study. *Global Health Action*, 7(1), 26401. Advance online publication. DOI: 10.3402/gha.v7.26401 PMID: 25537941

Cabrera.Aguilar, E., Zevallos-Francia, M., Morales-García, M., Ramírez-Coronel, A. A., Morales-García, S. B., Sairitupa-Sanchez, L. Z., & Morales-García, W. C. (2023). Resilience and stress as predictors of work engagement: The mediating role of self.efficacy in nurses. *Frontiers in Psychiatry*, 14, 1202048. Advance online publication. DOI: 10.3389/fpsyt.2023.1202048 PMID: 37649562

Carragher, J. & Gormley, K. (2016). Leadership and emotional intelligence in nursing and midwifery education and practice: a discussion paper. *Journal of Advanced Nursing*, 73(1), 85.96. DOI: 10.1111/jan.13141

Cheng, L., Yang, J., Li, M., & Wang, W. (2020). Mediating effect of coping style between empathy and burnout among Chinese nurses working in medical and surgical wards. *Nursing Open*, 7(6), 1936.1944. DOI: 10.1002/nop2.584

Cowley, S. A., Tzouvara, V., & Horta Reis da Silva, T. (2023). Public Health: healthy ageing and well-being. In *Redfern's Nursing Older People*. Fifth edition. Elsevier.

Çulha, Y., Turan, N., & Kaya, H. (2017). Entrepreneurship in nursing education. *Pressacademia*, 4(1), 50.53. DOI: 10.17261/Pressacademia.2017.516

da Silva, T. H. R. (2022). Emotional awareness and emotional intelligence. *British Journal of Community Nursing*, 27(12), 573–574. DOI: 10.12968/bjcn.2022.27.12.573 PMID: 36519463

Dâmbean, C. & Gabor, M. (2021). Implications of emotional intelligence in human resource management. *Economics*, 9(2), 73.90. DOI: 10.2478/eoik.2021.0016

Davaei, M. & Gunkel, M. (2023). The role of intelligences in teams: a systematic literature review. *Review of Managerial Science*, 18(1), 259.297. DOI: 10.1007/s11846.023.00672.7

Doğru, Ç. (2022). A meta.analysis of the relationships between emotional intelligence and employee outcomes. *Frontiers in Psychology*, 13, 611348. Advance online publication. DOI: 10.3389/fpsyg.2022.611348 PMID: 35548499

Elam, T., & Taku, K. (2022). Differences between posttraumatic growth and resiliency: Their distinctive relationships with empathy and emotion recognition ability. *Frontiers in Psychology*, 13, 825161. Advance online publication. DOI: 10.3389/fpsyg.2022.825161 PMID: 35418895

Fang, Y., Mirza, F., Chaudhary, N., Arshad, R., & Wu, Y. (2022). Impact of perceived skillset and organizational traits on digital wellbeing of teachers: Mediating role of resilience. *Frontiers in Psychology*, 13, 923386. Advance online publication. DOI: 10.3389/fpsyg.2022.923386 PMID: 35719496

Farhana, A. (2023). Effect of emotional intelligence on job satisfaction among nurses: descriptive study. *PJMHS*, 17(6), 127.129. DOI: 10.53350/pjmhs2023176127

Farmer, J., Mistry, M., & Jainer, A. (2020). Emotional intelligence for healthcare. *Sushruta Journal of Health Policy & Opinions,* 13(1), 26.27. DOI: 10.38192/13.1.8

Fitzpatrick, J. M., Bianchi, L. A., Hayes, N., Da Silva, T., & Harris, R. (2023). Professional development and career planning for nurses working in care homes for older people: A scoping review. *International Journal of Older People Nursing*, 18(1), e12519. DOI: 10.1111/opn.12519 PMID: 36441621

Foster, K., Cuzzillo, C., & Furness, T. (2018). Strengthening mental health nurses' resilience through a workplace resilience programme: a qualitative inquiry. *Journal of Psychiatric and Mental Health Nursing*, 25(5.6), 338.348. DOI: 10.1111/jpm.12467

Gupta, R. (2023). Emotional intelligence for health professionals. *Journal of Internal Medicine and Health Affairs*, 2(3). Advance online publication. DOI: 10.58489/2836-2411/024

Hajibabaee, F., Farahani, M., Ameri, Z., Salehi, T., & Hosseini, F. (2018). The relationship between empathy and emotional intelligence among Iranian nursing students. *International Journal of Medical Education*, 9, 239.243. DOI: 10.5116/ijme.5b83.e2a5

Hammett, R. D., Arenas, F., & Scherer, J. (2018). Facilitating full.range leadership with emotional intelligence in the USAF Squadron Officer College. *The International Journal of Transformative Emotional Intelligence*, 5.

Huang, H., Liu, L., Yang, S., Cui, X., Zhang, J., & Wu, H. (2019). Effects of job conditions, occupational stress, and emotional intelligence on chronic fatigue among Chinese nurses: a cross.sectional study;. *Psychology Research and Behavior Management*, 12, 351.360. DOI: 10.2147/PRBM.S207283

Iheduru.Anderson, K., & Waite, R. (2022). Illuminating antiracist pedagogy in nursing education. *Nursing Inquiry*, 29(4), e12494. Advance online publication. DOI: 10.1111/nin.12494 PMID: 35543498

Jeong, J., Kang, S., & Choi, S. (2022). A multilevel study of the relationship between csr promotion climate and happiness at work via organizational identification: Moderation effect of leader–followers value congruence. *International Journal of Environmental Research and Public Health*, 19(11), 6637. DOI: 10.3390/ijerph19116637 PMID: 35682221

Jufrizen, J., Khair, H., & Loviky, F. B. (2023). Work Engagement and Emotional Intelligence on Personnel Performance: The Mediating Role of Job Satisfaction. *International Journal of Business Economics (IJBE), 5*(1), 77.91. DOI: 10.30596/ijbe.v5i1.16499

Jung, H., & Kang, S. (2020). Collective efficacy and communication ability according to emotional intelligence in nursing students. *Indian Journal of Public Health Research & Development*. Advance online publication. DOI: 10.37506/ijphrd.v11i12.13232

Kiishi, V. (2024). The role of emotional intelligence in effective leadership and its impact on team performance: a study of the university of Ibadan, Nigeria. *International Journal of Business and Management Review*, 12(2), 75.138. DOI: 10.37745/ijbmr.2013/vol12n275138

Kiziloğlu, E., & Şahin, M. (2022). *The mediating role of burnout in the effect of emotional intelligence on job satisfaction: an application on coachs*. Equinox Journal of Economics Business and Political Studies. DOI: 10.48064/equinox.1060496

Koutsioumpa, E. (2023). Development of emotional intelligence and leadership aspects applied in health professionals. a scoping review. *Technium Biochemmed*, 6, 22.36. DOI: 10.47577/biochemmed.v6i.9533

Kwabena, F., Asare, K., & Ackah, R. (2022). Does emotional intelligence influence an employee's job satisfaction? an empirical assessment. *Asian Journal of Social Sciences and Management Studies,* 9(4), 75.84. DOI: 10.20448/ajssms.v9i4.4349

Lateef, A., & Mhlongo, E. (2019). Factors influencing nursing education and teaching methods in nursing institutions: A case study of southwest Nigeria. *Global Journal of Health Science*, 11(13), 13. DOI: 10.5539/gjhs.v11n13p13

Lee, C. & Wong, C. (2017). The effect of team emotional intelligence on team process and effectiveness. *Journal of Management & Organization*, 25(6), 844.859. DOI: 10.1017/jmo.2017.43

Li, M., Qin, G., & Li, Y. (2022). Mediating effects of emotional intelligence on the relationship between empathy and humanistic care ability in nursing students: A cross.sectional descriptive study. *Medicine*, 101(46), e31673. DOI: 10.1097/MD.0000000000031673 PMID: 36401377

Li, X., Fang, X., Wang, L., Geng, X., & Chang, H. (2021). Relationship between emotional intelligence and job well-being in Chinese registered nurses: mediating effect of communication satisfaction. *Nursing Open*, 8(4), 1778.1787. DOI: 10.1002/nop2.820

Liu, H., Zhang, L., Yan, J., Huang, H., Yi, Q., & Peng, L. (2023). The relationship between social support, empathy, self.efficacy, and humanistic practice ability among clinical nurses in China: A structural equation model. *Journal of Nursing Management*, 2023(1), 9. DOI: 10.1155/2023/1378278

Mariati, L., Jakri, Y., & Djerubu, D. (2022). The effect of emotional intelligence on nurse's communication skill. *Jurnal Ners Dan Kebidanan (Journal of Ners and Midwifery),* 9(2), 218.226. DOI: 10.26699/jnk.v9i2.art.p218.226

Mediarti, D., Rehana, R., & Abunyamin, A. (2018). Nurses education and motivation towards nursing documentation. *Jurnal Ners*, 13(1), 31.35. DOI: 10.20473/jn.v13i1.3478

Mercader.Rubio, I., Ángel, N. G., Teixeira, A., & Brito-Costa, S. (2023). Relationships between informal sports leadership and emotional intelligence: A cross. sectional study. *Sustainability (Basel)*, 15(19), 14571. DOI: 10.3390/su151914571

Min, H., Park, S.-H., Lee, S.-H., Lee, B.-H., Kang, M., Kwon, M. J., Chang, M. J., Negi, L. T., Samphel, T., & Won, S. (2024). Building resilience and social–emotional competencies in elementary school students through a short.term intervention program based on the see learning curriculum. *Behavioral Sciences (Basel, Switzerland)*, 14(6), 458. DOI: 10.3390/bs14060458 PMID: 38920790

Moloney, W., Fieldes, J., & Jacobs, S. (2020). An integrative review of how healthcare organizations can support hospital nurses to thrive at work. *International Journal of Environmental Research and Public Health*, 17(23), 8757. DOI: 10.3390/ijerph17238757 PMID: 33255725

Mudzi, P., & Bruce, J. (2023). How ready are nursing colleges to be integrated into higher education? a scoping review of influential factors. *Journal of Nursing Education and Practice*, 13(11), 1. DOI: 10.5430/jnep.v13n11p1

Mulyatsih, M., Nursalam, , Sriyono, , Duwiyani, N. N., & Siregar, S. (2023). Nurses' perception of caring.based nursing care for stroke patients with thrombolysis and influencing factors. *Journal of Law and Sustainable Development*, 11(11), e1268. DOI: 10.55908/sdgs.v11i11.1268

Munira, K., Rahman, D., & Akhter, S. (2022). Impact of emotional intelligence on sustainable leadership. *Business Perspective Review*, 4(2), 1.15. DOI: 10.38157/bpr.v4i2.446

Nye, C., Tengelin, E., & Somayaji, D. (2022). Developing a theory of norm.criticism in nursing education. *Advances in Nursing Science*, 46(2), E66.E79. DOI: 10.1097/ANS.0000000000000440

Pan, T., Trakulmututa, J., & Youravong, N. (2020). Self.perception of leadership style of dentists: heads of dental departments in community hospitals, southern Thailand. *International Dental Journal*, 70(3), 193.200. DOI: 10.1111/idj.12544

Park, J. & Park, J. (2022). Identifying the knowledge structure and trends of nursing informatics. *Cin Computers Informatics Nursing*, 41(1), 8.17. DOI: 10.1097/CIN.0000000000000919

Pečiuliauskienė, P. (2021). Emotional intelligence and transformational leadership of gymnasium teachers'. *Society Integration Education Proceedings of the International Scientific Conference*, 2, 457.467. DOI: 10.17770/sie2021vol2.6194

Pedroso, T., Pedrão, L., & Perroca, M. (2020). Approaches to workload in psychiatric and mental health nursing. *Revista Brasileira De Enfermagem*, 73(suppl 1). DOI: 10.1590/0034.7167.2019.0620

Peláez.Fernández, M., Mérida.López, S., Sánchez-Álvarez, N., & Extremera, N. (2021). Managing teachers' job attitudes: The potential benefits of being a happy and emotional intelligent teacher. *Frontiers in Psychology*, 12, 661151. Advance online publication. DOI: 10.3389/fpsyg.2021.661151 PMID: 34017291

Prado, J., Zárate-Torres, R., Tafur-Mendoza, A., Prada-Ospina, R., & Sarmiento, C. (2022). Impact of leadership practices on manager's pathways to goal attainment: the mediating effect of emotional intelligence. *International Journal of Organizational Analysis*, 31(7), 2889.2902. DOI: 10.1108/ijoa.01.2022.3110

Prado.Gascó, V., Giménez.Espert, M., & Valero-Moreno, S. (2019). The influence of nurse education and training on communication, emotional intelligence, and empathy. *Revista Da Escola De Enfermagem Da USP*, 53. DOI: 10.1590/s1980.220x2018015903465

Prihandhani, I., & Hakim, N. (2022). Training course on emotional intelligence effect of nurses' interpersonal relationship style on Tabanan general hospital. *International Journal of Research in Medical Sciences*, 10(9), 1878. DOI: 10.18203/2320-6012.ijrms20222262

Reis, , & da Silva, T. H. (2024a). Gender Equity In Healthcare: Integrating Emotional Intelligence To Achieve The United Nations Sustainable Development Goals. *J Comm Med and Pub Health Rep*, 5(12). Advance online publication. DOI: 10.38207/JCMPHR/2024/JUL051202106

Reis da Silva, T. (2024a). The Evolution of Nursing for Older Adult: A Historical Perspective. *Associative J Health Sci*. 3(3). AJHS. 000561. 2024. https://crimsonpublishers.com/ajhs/pdf/AJHS.000561.pdf

Reis da Silva, T. (2024j). Can supplementing vitamin B12 improve mental health outcomes?: A literature review. *British Journal of Community Nursing*, 29(3), 137–146. DOI: 10.12968/bjcn.2024.29.3.137 PMID: 38421889

Reis da Silva, T. H. (2024c). Oncology and Cancer Medicine: Understanding the complexities in Older Patients. *Biomedical Journal of Scientific & Technical Research*, 55(3), 2024. DOI: 10.26717/BJSTR.2024.55.008720

Reis da Silva, T. H. (2024e). Navigating Healthcare Complexity: Integrating Business Fundamentals into Nursing Leadership. In Sedky, A. (Ed.), *Resiliency Strategies for Long.Term Business Success. Pp. 145.168.* IGI Global. DOI: 10.4018/979-8-3693-9168-6.ch006

Reis da Silva, T. H. (2024f). Integrating business essentials into Gerontological Nursing: Enhancing Care for Older Adults in Diverse Settings. In Sedky, A. (Ed.), *Resiliency Strategies for Long.Term Business Success. Pp. 283.316.* IGI Global. DOI: 10.4018/979-8-3693-9168-6.ch011

Reis da Silva, T. H. (2024g). Oncology and Cancer Medicine: Understanding the complexities in Older Patients. *Biomedical Journal of Scientific & Technical Research*, 55(3), 2024. DOI: 10.26717/BJSTR.2024.55.008720

Reis da Silva, T. H. (2024i). Loneliness in older adults. *British Journal of Community Nursing*, 29(2), 60–66. DOI: 10.12968/bjcn.2024.29.2.60 PMID: 38300245

Reis da Silva, T.H. (2024k) Pharmacokinetics in older people: an overview of prescribing practice. *Journal of Prescribing Practice.* 6(9). 374.381. DOI: 10.12968/jprp.2024.6.9.374

Reis da Silva, T. H., & Mitchell, A. (2024a). Integrating Digital Transformation in Nursing Education: Best Practices and Challenges in Curriculum Development. In Lytras, M., Serban, A. C., Alkhaldi, A., Malik, S., & Aldosemani, T. (Eds.), *Digital Transformation in Higher Education, Part B Cases, Examples and Good Practices.* Emerald Publishing Limited.

Reis Da Silva, T. H., & Mitchell, A. (2024b). Simulation in nursing: The importance of involving service users. *British Journal of Nursing (Mark Allen Publishing)*, 33(5), 262–265. DOI: 10.12968/bjon.2024.33.5.262 PMID: 38446515

Reis da Silva Tiago. (2024d) The Value of Emotional Intelligence in Midwifery: Enhancing Care and Outcomes for Mothers and Infants through Sustainable Development Goals and Leadership. *Journal of Womens Healthcare & Midwifery Research.* https://www.onlinescientificresearch.com/articles/the.value.of.emotional.intelligence.in.midwifery.enhancing.care.and.outcomes.for.mothers.and.infants.through.sustainable.developme.pdf

Rožman, M., Oreški, D., & Tominc, P. (2022). Integrating artificial intelligence into a talent management model to increase the work engagement and performance of enterprises. *Frontiers in Psychology*, 13, 1014434. Advance online publication. DOI: 10.3389/fpsyg.2022.1014434 PMID: 36506984

Sadeghi, T., Kiani, M., Saeidi, M., Moghaddam, H., Ghodsi, M., & Hoseini, R. (2018). The relationship between emotional intelligence with administrators' performance at Mashhad university of medical sciences. *Electronic Physician*, 10(3), 6487.6493. DOI: 10.19082/6487

Salovey, P., Mayer, J., Caruso, D., & Yoo, S. (2009). The positive psychology of emotional intelligence., 236.248. DOI: 10.1093/oxfordhb/9780195187243.013.0022

Shepherd, T. (2021). The influence and interplay of emotional intelligence and leadership type on early childhood educators' organizational commitment. *International Journal of Business and Management Research,* 9(2), 168.177. DOI: 10.37391/IJBMR.090207

Shibata, K., Naruse, K., & Boonyanurak, P. (2020). Does the mutual recognition agreement on nursing services accelerate nurse migration in member countries of the association of southeast Asian nations?. *Nursing Open*, 7(4), 1187.1196. DOI: 10.1002/nop2.504

Shrestha, M. and Mandal, P. (2021). Emotional intelligence among nursing students of a government campus in eastern Nepal. *Journal of Kathmandu Medical College*, 10(1), 39.42. DOI: 10.3126/jkmc.v10i1.38970

Varughese, J. and Rema, M. (2021). Perceived stress, emotional intelligence and self.efficacy among nursing students during the covid.19 pandemic. *International Journal of Research and Studies Publishing*, 11(4), 201.207. DOI: 10.29322/IJSRP.11.04.2021.p11225

Wałaszek, M., Jaślan, D., Kołpa, M., Wójowska.Mach, J., Gniadek, A., & Różańska, A. (2021). Nurses' views on and compliance with the guidelines of hand hygiene, including nail hygiene in a multi.profile hospital in lesser Poland province – the evidence for need of continuous education and training. *Pielegniarstwo Xxi Wieku / Nursing in the 21st Century*, 20(3), 180.189. DOI: 10.2478/pielxxiw.2021.0029

Wang, L. (2023). The beneficial effect of empathy on work related quality of life among oncology nurse: mediating role of resilience. DOI: 10.21203/rs.3.rs.3327160/v1

Wang, X. (2024). Nurses' personality traits and perceived work environments during public health emergencies: implications for nursing workforce planning. *Risk Management and Healthcare Policy*, 17, 1199.1209. DOI: 10.2147/RMHP.S458235

Xu, J., Zhang, L., Ji, Q., Ji, P., Chen, Y., Song, M., & Guo, L. (2023). Nursing students' emotional empathy, emotional intelligence and higher education.related stress: A cross.sectional study. *BMC Nursing*, 22(1), 437. Advance online publication. DOI: 10.1186/s12912-023-01607-z PMID: 37981672

Yang, R., Gao, Y., & Ji, Z. (2023). The relationship between self.regulated learning, mindful agency, and psychological resilience in Chinese master of nursing specialists: A cross.sectional study. *Frontiers in Psychology*, 14, 1066806. Advance online publication. DOI: 10.3389/fpsyg.2023.1066806 PMID: 37008842

Chapter 2

An Empirical Study in Between Internal Branding and Organizational Citizenship Behavior: Mediation Effect of Employee Engagement

Smruti Rekha Sahoo
https://orcid.org/0009-0002-2328-1944
GIET University, Gunupur, India

Saumendra Das
https://orcid.org/0000-0003-4956-4352
GIET University, Gunupur, India

Sadananda Sahoo
https://orcid.org/0000-0001-9222-1684
GIET University, Gunupur, India

Neyyila Saibabu
https://orcid.org/0000-0001-6054-2053
Aditya Institute of Technology and Management, India

ABSTRACT

This chapter aims to study the impact of internal branding (IB) on employee engagement (EE) and organizational citizenship behaviour (OCB). This study indicated

DOI: 10.4018/979-8-3693-8457-2.ch002

understanding the meditational effect of EE between IB and OCB in the manufacturing industries of India country. The study analyzed the relationship from the data collected from Indian countries like Karnataka, Delhi NCR, and Odisha. The study used reliability, validity, confirmatory factor analysis, and structural equation modelling to test the hypothesis in AMOS version 20. The study shows that IB has a substantial positive impact on EE and OCB. EE has a strong mediation effect between IB and OCB. However, EE could not predict the dimensions of altruism and sportsmanship in OCB. Additionally, there is no significant relationship between IB and OCB in EE. The IB on EE and OCB has been lightly studied previously, and neither has been analyzed to understand its impact on OCB and EE.

1. INTRODUCTION

In India, manufacturing firms have emerged as a fast-growing sector due to their population. India has invested huge capital in initiatives like 'Make in India' with the aim of making the South Asian country into a worldwide manufacturing hub. During the financial year 2022, the annual growth rate of manufacturing firms was 11.4% (Manya Rathore, 2023). In addition, during that fiscal year, the new investment and ordering activity also had a great pick-up, with a 210% increase compared to the previous fiscal year 2020–21 (Goldman Sachs, 2022).

It was found that from the Economic Survey 2021–22, there is an overall positive expansion in totalling of the manufacturing sector. Entire employee engagement in this sector has improved from 57 million in the year 2017-18 to 62.4 million in 2019-20 (PBNS, 2022).

Several initiatives, like the PLI scheme, the MITRA scheme, Operation Green scheme, etc., have been taken by the government of India to endorse a vigorous atmosphere in the growth of manufacturing sector in India (Central Statistics Office, FICCI and Economic Survey of India).

> *"The manufacturing sector has been expanding, and this positive trend has to be maintained if India is to achieve its goal of being self-sufficient" (Rajiev Luthra, 2022).*

The manufacturing industry in India is regarded as a rising sector and has the potential to improve the economic development of the country. To extend this diversity, it is only possible through changes in internal branding of company. Internal branding is deliberate, advancing the branding within the organization to influence the brand image by adjusting the organization's values with the member of staff's values. In manufacturing companies, employees may not have any direct communication with customers. Here, the internal branding strategy helps to ensure all associates, apart from their jobs, know the firm's mission and values and are attached to the company's objectives. And this attachment creates a positive and cohesive culture, which is directly linked with employee satisfaction, engagement, and citizenship behavior. Internal branding also helps improve communication and partnership with the company, especially in industries where it highly needs collaboration. There is a great deal of internal branding to make it easier and better to work together to acquire and retain the best talent in the company. It also helps to foster a set of values and a common understanding of the company's aims among the employees. Investment in internal branding concepts in organizations is helpful to improve the satisfaction and pride of employees, enhance the reputation of the company, and increase employee engagement (Chris Jarratt, Guest Columnist, 2023).

In this contemporary market, to survive for a long time, every organization must establish a powerful brand and encourage performance (Lee et al., 2008). Branding is a concept that is considered for improving organizational performance. Consequently, organizations should focus on how to promote brand-supportive behaviour, which helps them to create an optimistic organizational climate as well as develop understanding capacity of employees towards product potentials (Matanda and Ndubisi, 2013).

Internal Branding

Internal branding concepts are illustrated in several papers of works. From existing works, internal branding borrowed by the concept of internal marketing (Garas et al., 2018; Punjaisri et al., 2009a; Saleem & Iglesias, 2016).

Internal branding is the adverse version of internal marketing, which attains mainly the improvement and promotion of the brand. It is a technically structured method that helps to motivate and carry employees' satisfaction toward brand activities. It also helps them to communicate a complete message of the brand promise to customers (M. J. Matanda and N. O. Ndubisi, 2013). Employees are internal customers, and without their support, the brand message can weaken the brand's reputation. The purpose of internal branding is to civilize the common understanding of features, objectives, and positioning of the brand promise, give harmony between the values of employees, and also design the commitment of an employee (M. J. Matanda and N. O. Ndubisi, 2013).

Internal branding is a key factor in establishing a product launching which allows an employee to express a product potential for carrying out product creating events (Kaur et al., 2020). Theory of internal branding primarily focuses on internal employees because external customer loyalty happens due to the internal customer relationship through brand orientation (Eid et al., 2019).

Branding is a multi-faceted concept, but as it is treated with employees of an organization, this can be counted as internal branding (Hasni et al., 2018). Internal branding is recognized by establishing strong values for the firm. Internal branding considers as the brand values are communicated to internal member of staffs by the brand to their external clients, society, or customers (Punjaisri and Wilson, 2017).

Many researchers have cultivated their study of internal marketing for 45 years. Their major study has focused on how to initiate and the consequences of the implementation of internal marketing concepts (Rafiq& Ahmed, 1993).

Organizational Citizenship Behavior

OCB is defined as "individual behavior that is discretionary, not directly or explicitly recognized by the formal reward system, and in the aggregate promotes the efficient and effective functioning of the organization". A high level of motivation generates citizenship behavior towards organizations. Through citizenship behavior, the behavior indicates employees, high level of job satisfaction and more dedication to the organization and also to society (Dennis W. Organ 2006). OCB plays a supporting role in the effective function of organizations (Robbins and Judge, 2012). Organizational citizenship behaviors define the behaviors that ease the performance of duties within an organization (Podsakoff et al., 2016). OCB may inspire employees by encouraging more gratifying relationships with co-workers (Parke et al., 2021). Recently, a study found that those employees are highly engaged with tasks, which implies that he or she has a strong sense of direction towards his work (Liu et al., 2022).

Employee Engagement

Employee engagement is the jargon between academicians and business practitioners around the globe. Even though this concept has gained high acknowledgment but still it lacks something in its definition in academic ground (Saks, 2006). Employees those who having attachment with the company's values and objectives, they are more likely motivated, satisfied and engaged at the work place.

In the days of professional practice the concept in its initial phase of development was referred to as work engagement and was defined as a state of mind that functions as an instrument explaining how motivations lead to employees' positive outcomes (Stoeber and Damian, 2016).

Employee engagement is defined as "an individual's sense of purpose and focused energy, evident to others in the display of personal initiative, adaptability, effort, and persistence directed toward organizational goals" (Macey et al. 2009, p. 7).

The most widely cited meaning of employee engagement is as "a positive, fulfilling, work- related state of mind that is characterized by vigor, dedication, and absorption" (W. B. Schaufeli et al. 2002, p. 74).

When employees are properly engaged themselves with job, then the results become positive while employees show their productivity and creativity then it is valuable, for individuals and organizations (Smruti and Sasmita, 2019). High levels of employee engagement are socially responsible, especially they act as good motivator for others and positive benefactors to an organization (Jagannathan Anitha, 2014). High involvement of employee in work engagement increases positive outcomes like financial revenues, turnover, increased job performance, improved client and customer satisfaction and better relationships between superiors and subordinates (Bakker et al., 2012 & Kataria et al., 2013).

Most of the past literatures are done on the relationships among IB, EE and OCB; but very few researches are on the relationship among each of the fundamental dimensions of IB and citizenship behaviors. Most of the research is found to be silent on this point. The present study is an attempt to find out several factors influencing engagement and citizenship behavior, with respect to the dimensions of IB like, communication, training and development, motivation, empowerment and HR involvement in Indian manufacturing sector. The major issues in this study to deal with the internal branding, EE and OCB by using several dimensions of research construct. Different research questions are therefore arising in the Manufacturing sector mentioned as below:

> RQ1: Are all the dimensions like communication, training, motivation, HR involvement and empowerment of internal branding important in exhibiting citizenship behavior and engagement?
>
> RQ2: What is the key role of employee engagement in establishing the relation between internal branding and organizational citizenship behavior in Indian manufacturing sector?

The study has been used structural equation model (SEM) to ensure the empirical validity. The study uses SEM to reveal the fundamental relationships and formulation of hypotheses and theoretical frameworks. The present study scrutinizes the role of IB, OCB and EE. In addition to that it examines the mediating role of EE in between IB and OCB.

The remaining part of the article is ordered as follows: After the introduction, the literature review is presented in Section 2. The theoretical framework and hypotheses are developed in Section 3. The research methodology is provided in Section 4. The results of the present research are provided in Section 5. The discussion is provided in Section 6, which is followed by managerial implications in Section 7, and the paper concludes with a conclusion, limitations, and future research direction in Section 8.2. Literature Review:

2. INTERNAL BRANDING AND ORGANIZATIONAL CITIZENSHIP BEHAVIOR

Internal branding is the action to encourage a product within organization for improving requisite behaviours. Every company must encourage its internal customers to hold brand skills through proper training and communication programs given by management to improve the necessary behaviours. Consequently, employees exhibit positive behaviours during working hours. It has been found that internal branding reconstructs defiance and behaviors of employees (Garas et al., 2018; Ngo et al., 2019).

In recent decades, research has attempted to examine the relationship among internal branding and organizational citizenship behavior (Dewan et al., 2022). It shows that internal branding and organizational citizenship behavior is positively related with each other. Recently, one study reveals regarding internal branding influences the OCB in case of bank employees (Gupta et al., 2021). In addition, it has been seen that the organizational citizenship behavior levels of the college faculties are developed by internal branding, which is possible because of their connection to organizational brand values (Srivastava et al., 2019).

There is a positive leverage of internal branding on job satisfaction, brand commitment, and brand citizenship behavior among Pharma employees. As well, this study has found that the positive impact of internal branding on employees' job satisfaction, brand commitment, and brand citizenship behavior can raise organizational performance (Nagaraju Kolla, 2019).

Similarly, it has been seen that internal branding has a positive relationship with organizational citizenship behavior in case of teaching staff (Tanisa et al., 2020).

Likewise, it is examined that relationship between internal marketing and internal customer citizenship behavior at universities with the mediating role of employees perceived value and satisfaction. The result reveals that internal marketing has a significant effect on customer citizenship behavior. As well as employee's perceived value and satisfaction has positive mediation effect in between IM and customer citizenship behavior (Mohsen Akbari et al. 2019).

Internal branding has a positive association with organizational citizenship behavior, and there was no mediation effect of person-organization fit in between the two constructs. (Gaye Özçelik, Mine Afacan Fındıklı, 2014).

On the other hand, internal brand management has significant effect on brand citizenship behavior in terms of brand commitment and job satisfaction among bank employees (Arezoo Gkenaatgar and Seyyed Mehdi Jalali, 2016).

All the components of internal marketing, such as organizational vision and mission, performance evaluation, training, psychological costs, reward, communication, and participation, have a significant impact on OCB (Sanjar Salajeghe et al., 2015; Smruti and Sasmita, 2019).

Most of the past surveys have focused on the relationships among internal branding and citizenship behavior in the service industry rather than the manufacturing sector. Some of the fundamental dimensions of internal branding are silent in past literature. The current study also attempts to locate several factors of IB influencing citizenship behavior, like communication, training and development, motivation, empowerment, and HR involvement.

2.1 Internal Branding and Employee Engagement

Several previous studies have investigated internal branding in various sectors, exploring its correlation with organizational citizenship behavior, employee engagement, brand commitment, organizational commitment, job satisfaction, and person-organization fit. One study, using the social exchange theory (SET) concept, found a significant and positive association between internal branding and the engagement level of medical staff. (Asha Binu Raj, Vol. 11 No. 3 (2020): Indian Journal of Public Health Research & Development).

Internal branding created a strong correlation with employee engagement and job satisfaction. And affective commitment has a mediating effect in between internal branding and employee engagement, rather than job satisfaction and resulting in a significant positive relationship (Prabhjot Kaur, Keshav Malhotra, and Sanjeev K. Sharma in 2020).

A recent study has confirmed that internal branding can boost employee engagement level and job satisfaction, leading to improved employee performance. The study has found that the association in between internal branding and employee performance with a mediation effect of employee engagement and job satisfaction (Latifah & Muafi, 2021).

A study conducted on front-line employees in the hotel industry, South Korean (Lee et al., 2014) found that internal branding increases employee engagement with their job. Another study showed that effective HR policies, such as training programs and reward systems, positively impact service employees' engagement levels (Gupta and Sharma, 2018).

Research has shown that internal branding has a notable impact on employee engagement, job satisfaction, and loyalty. In a study conducted on this topic, it was found that internal branding affects employee engagement both with their job and the organization as a whole. The study also found that employee engagement has a significant mediation effect on the relationship between internal branding and job satisfaction. (Yong-Ki Lee et al., 2014)

Past surveys have mainly examined the equation between internal branding and employee engagement in the service industry, neglecting to explore this relationship in the manufacturing sector. Additionally, certain fundamental aspects of internal branding have not been fully examined in past literature, and there has been limited research on the interplay between internal branding, organizational citizenship behavior, and employee engagement. While the concept of internal branding is widely recognized in the service sector, this study focuses on examining the relationship between these three variables in the manufacturing industry. Furthermore, the investigation seeks to identify various dimensions that impact engagement and citizenship behavior, specifically related to dimensions of internal branding such as communication, training and development, motivation, empowerment, and HR involvement.

2.2 Employee Engagement and Organizational Citizenship Behavior

Past literature focuses the essential role of work engagement, nurturing both attitudinal and behavioral consequences (Alfes et al., 2013; Rich et al., 2010; Schaufeli & Bakker, 2004). Employee engagement derives from two concepts of academic recognition that is commitment and organizational citizenship behavior (OCB) (D. Robinson et al., 2004; A. M. Rafferty et al., 2005). Engagement has equalities to and differences with commitment and citizenship behavior.

There are many studies which established that there is significant as well as positive relationship between EE and OCB.

One study has been done that EE has positive effect on OCB (Allen and Meyer, 1990 and Saks, 2006). Similarly, same outcome is supported by Pir Sajad Ullah et al., 2018.

Another study has been examined the examined the relationship between organizational support, work engagement and OCB regarding the nurses' perception in different Hospitals. The outcomes reveal that there is a positive relationship between three constructs i.e organizational support, employee engagement and OCB. Furthermore the result indicates that work engagement has significant relationship with OCB (Fatma Abed and Amal Hebashy Elewa, 2016). This results also supported by Dodd and Mathumbu (2013) Hossein et al., (2014) and Cheung and Lun (2015).

Similarly, one study has established the relationship between employee engagement and OCB in Maritime Firms, Nigeria. The outcomes show that EE is significantly related with OCB. Additionally it confirms that OCB can be improved through the appliance of cognitive and emotional engagement between employees in Maritime firms (Amadi et al., 2017).

Likewise, recently one study has established the relationship between EE and OCB. And the study reveals that there is a positive and significant effect of employee engagement on OCB (Putri et al., 2021)

3. THEORETICAL DEVELOPMENT AND HYPOTHESIS

3.1 Internal Branding and Organizational Citizenship Behavior

Internal branding concept helps to promote brand awareness, develop the required skills, and maintain rewards for reliable behavior (Garas et al., 2018; Punjaisri et al., 2008). Organizations must boost their employees to be aware of brand awareness by presenting training, motivation, and communication programs to enrich the desired behaviors. This information encourages the members for analyzing the significance of organizational values and goals. Consequently, individuals exhibit positive behaviors at the time of interactions. There is no confusion from internal branding that re-modifies the employees 'behaviors (Garas et al., 2018; Ngo et al., 2019).

Recent research has found that bank employees who are exposed to internal branding are more probable to exhibit good citizenship behavior (Gupta et al., 2021). Similar studies have shown that internal branding can also increase OCB levels among college faculties by aligning them with organizational brand values (Srivastava, Mani, and Yadav, 2019). Additionally, employees who receive support from top management are more likely to exhibit helpful behavior towards their colleagues and customers, leading to increased organizational effectiveness (Kang, Kim, Choi, and Li, 2020). These studies suggest that internal branding can strengthen OCB, and this hypothesis can be further explored based on the available literature.

H1: Internal branding is positively associated with OCB.

3.2 Internal Branding and Employee Engagement

According to a study on the concept of social exchange theory (SET), internal branding has a positive correlation with the engagement levels of medical staff (Asha Binu Raj, Vol. 11 No. 3 (2020): Indian Journal of Public Health Research & Development). Another study conducted in 2015 on service employees in Indian

BPO centers found that internal branding has a strong link with engagement levels (Kaur et al., 2020). Similarly, a study on FLEs in a South Korean hotel revealed that internal branding can increase employee engagement levels in the workplace (Lee et al., 2014). Moreover, researchers have confirmed that employee engagement level and effective human resource policies are significantly related with each other. Additionally, effective training activities and rewarding systems have been found to increase engagement level in the workplace (Gupta and Sharma, 2018).

A recent study has shown that internal branding is positively correlated with employee engagement and job satisfaction. This, in turn, leads to improved employee performance. The study also found that both employee engagement and job satisfaction has a mediation effect in between internal branding and employee performance. As per the findings, it can be proposed that internal branding can have a significant impact on overall work performance.

H2: Internal branding is positively related to employee engagement.

3.3 Employee Engagement and Organizational Citizenship Behavior

Employee engagement is based on commitment and organizational citizenship behavior, according to academic concepts (D. Robinson et al., 2004; A. M. Rafferty et al., 2005). Work engagement has been shown to be the precursor to OCB (Bakker Arnold &Demerouti, 2008; Harter et al., 2002; Macey & Schneider, 2008). A current study establishes that job resources partly influence employees' behavior towards external customers through work engagement (Cheng and Chen, 2017). Additionally, another study stated that work engagement triggers citizenship behaviors towards consumers in the hotel industry (Lyu, Zhu, Zhong, and Hu, 2016). One study reveals that EE has a positive and significant relation with organizational commitment and OCB (Pir Sajad Ullah et al. 2018), which is supported by Allen and Meyer (1990) and Saks (2006). From, past literature it has been found that work engagement has a positive correlation with the organization or employees (Gupta, Shaheen, & Reddy Prathap, 2017). Based on these illustrations, the hypothesis can be proposed.

H3: Employee engagement is positively correlated with organizational citizenship behavior.

3.4 Employee Engagement as a Mediator

Past literatures have confirmed that engagement is playing as mediator role in empirical studies (Bakker Arnold & Demerouti, 2008; Buil et al., 2019; Karatepe et al., 2018). Still, the idea of engagement is not enough in academic research (Saks, 2006). Empirical studies examined that engaged employees show customer centric behaviours (Bowen & Schneider, 2014; Christian et al., 2011; Karatepe, 2013; Popli & Rizvi, 2015). Mostly highly engaged employees exhibit extra role behavior towards others activities at the work space.

Moreover, one study is postulated that highly engaged people exhibits citizenship behavior towards others and which is helpful for organization's development (Saks, 2006). Another study confirmed that work engagement has a mediation role in between the dimensions of internal banding such as training and development, internal communications and leadership towards citizenship behavior towards colleagues and customers (Buil et al., 2016).

Likewise, a study has been established in Indian metro rail organization that human resource practices extends the engagement level towards citizenship behaviours (Gupta and Sharma, 2018). By using of SET theory one of the studies argued that employee engagement practices have mediation effect in between internal branding and job satisfaction and loyalty (Lee et al., 2014). By following the SET theory one study reveals that dimensions of internal branding like training and development program and reward system improves the citizenship behaviours of the hotel employees (Gupta et al., 2021).

Literally, past literature is silent on the mediation effect of EE in between IB and OCB. Based on the above cited studies, this study is trying to find out the composite relationship between above three constructs IB, EE and OCB. Thus, the hypothesis is stated are as under

> H4: Employee engagement has mediation effect in between internal branding and organizational citizenship Behavior

4. RESEARCH METHODS AND DESIGNS

This study was conducted through field research and had a decisive nature. The primary data used in the study and it was collected through structured questions. Additionally, secondary data, such as information from various websites, books, research journals, magazines, and articles, was also referred to. The study collected responses from executive staffs working in the manufacturing sector in different regions of India, including Karnataka, Delhi NCR, and Bhubaneswar. Respondents were chosen through convenient and purposive sampling methods. The research included a total of 193 executive employees from various manufacturing industries in India.

To gather primary data, a structured questionnaire was created, which was divided into three sections: IB, OCB, and EE. All scale items underwent proper testing for reliability and validity during a pilot study. The modified survey instrument data were then used for final data analysis. Primary data for IB, OCB, and EE were collected using a 5-point Likert scale, with responses ranging from strongly disagree (1) to strongly agree (5).

For internal branding research items, Punjaisri& Wilson's (2007) and Burmann & Zeplin's (2005) studies were used. Organizational citizenship behavior measurements were taken from P. M. Podsakoff et al.'s (1990) study, while employee engagement measurements were sourced from Schaufeli, Salanova, et al.'s (2002) study. Additionally, some items were developed by observing the situation.

5. RESULT

In this section, the analysis focused on the data obtained from the survey, which involved 193 respondents. The collected data were analyzed primarily using the multicollinearity test in SPSS version 20. The AMOS 20 version was utilized to conduct SEM, and helps to evaluate both measurement model and the structural model to examne the proposed hypotheses and their relationships.

5.1 Measurement Model

The measurement model is a statistical model used to assess the quality of measurement instruments or scales in a research study. It involves measuring different constructs or variables using multiple items or indicators. The primary purpose of the measurement model is to ensure that the items effectively capture the underlying concepts they are intended to measure. This is achieved by evaluating various criteria such as factor loadings, internal consistency (Cronbach's alpha), composite reliability (CR), average variance extracted (AVE), and discriminant validity (J.F Hair et al., 2019). A well-constructed measurement model ensures the reliability and validity of the data collected and provides a solid foundation for subsequent statistical analyses in the research study.

The table presents the quality assessment parameters for the measurement model, which consists of four constructs: adoption of IB, OCB and EE. Each construct is measured using multiple items, and the quality of the measurement model is evaluated based on several criteria. The first criterion is factor loading, which measures the strength of the relationship between each item and its corresponding construct. All items have factor loadings, ranging from 0.508 to 0.799, indicating that they are well aligned with their respective constructs. The second criterion is Cronbach's alpha which assesses the internal consistency or reliability of the items within each construct. The values for Cronbach's alpha are above the recommended threshold of 0.7 for all constructs, indicating good internal consistency. IB has the highest alpha value (0.936), OCB (0.886) and EE (0.910). The third criterion is composite reliability (CR), which is another measure of the internal consistency of the construct, and all constructs exhibit high CR values above 070, suggesting good reliability. The fourth criterion is rho A, which measures the construct's composite reliability, which is like CR. All constructs have high rho A values, ranging from 0.815 to 0.903, which are above the threshold limit of 0.70. The fifth criterion is average variance extracted (AVE), which represents the amount of variance captured by the construct's items. AVE values range from 0.367 to 0.505, with EE having the highest value and IB having the lowest. All constructs meet the recommended threshold of 0.5 for AVE (J.F Hair et al., 2020) indicating that the constructs explain a substantial portion of the variance in their items are depicted in Table 1.

Table 1. Quality assessment parameters

Constructs	Items	Factor Loading	Cronbach's Alpha	CR	rho A	AVE
Internal Branding	IC1	.688	.936	.948	0.813	.367
	IC3	.513				
	IC4	.528				
	IC6	.591				
	IC8	.559				
	IC9	.679				
	IC11	.543				
	IC12	.639				
	TD3	.508				
	TD5	.541				
	TD6	.551				
	TD7	.527				
	TD10	.596				
	TD13	.643				
	TD14	.508				
	HR1	.571				
	HR2	.681				

continued on following page

Table 1. Continued

Constructs	Items	Factor Loading	Cronbach's Alpha	CR	rho A	AVE
	HR3	.651				
	HR9	.525				
	EMP3	.602				
	EMP4	.707				
	EMP5	.547				
	EMP7	.569				
	EMP8	.655				
	EMP10	.613				
	EMP11	.615				
	MOT4	.691				
	MOT5	.659				
	MOT6	.708				
	MOT7	.694				
	MOT8	.608				
	MOT9	.582				
OCB	Alt1	.587	.886	.936	0.823	.384
	Alt2	.552				
	Alt4	.542				
	Con1	.546				
	Con2	.624				
	Con3	.561				
	Con5	.579				
	Con6	.790				
	Con7	.759				
	Con8	.569				
	Con9	.639				
	Con10	.541				
	Cou1	.622				
	Cou2	.610				
	Cou3	.679				
	Cou5	.531				
	Spo1	.737				
	Spo2	.623				
	Spo3	.593				

continued on following page

Table 1. Continued

Constructs	Items	Factor Loading	Cronbach's Alpha	CR	rho A	AVE
	Spo4	.701				
	Spo5	.603				
	Civ2	.611				
	Civ3	.602				
	Civ4	.589				
Employee engagement	Vig2	.690	.910	.928	0.828	.505
	Vig3	.707				
	Vig4	.693				
	Vig5	.799				
	Vig6	.657				
	Dedi1	.792				
	Dedi5	.743				
	Dedi6	.721				
	Dedi7	.652				
	Dedi8	.529				
	Abos2	.701				
	Abos3	.879				
	Abos6	.611				

In the information presented in Table 1, the meeting point is on assessing discriminant validity by using Fornell–Larcker criterion. One of the significant tests to compute discriminant validity is to compare the AVE values of the constructs with the square of the correlation estimates between the two constructs (Fornell & Larcker, 1981; Hair et al., 2010). In order with the works of Fornell and Larcker (1981); Hair et al. (2010), the seven-factor model used in the study named as internal communications, training, HR involvement, empowerment, motivation, employee engagement and OCB fulfilled discriminant validity. The results are displayed in Table 2.

This study is also considered discriminant validity of internal branding as a second-order construct. The outcomes revealed that there were no discriminant validity issues. All the squared AVE values obtained were less than the squared correlations between the latent constructs. Table 3 presents the discriminant validity of internal branding as a second-order construct. Accordingly, the reliability and validity of the measurement model fulfils the desired convergent and discriminant validity.

Table 2. Discriminant validity of first-order constructs

Variables	IC	TD	HR	EMP	MOT	EE	OCB
IC	**.595**						
TD	.523	**.555**					
HR	.577	.526	**.610**				
EMP	.580	.460	.368	**.617**			
MOT	.546	.541	.159	.596	**.658**		
EE	.094	.313	.426	.119	.193	**.710**	
OCB	.364	.481	.535	.346	.308	.431	**.618**

All the bold values indicate the square root of AVE values, IC= internal communication, TD= Training, HR= HR involvement, EMP= empowerment, MOT= motivation, EE= employee engagement, OCB= organizational citizenship behavior, $p<.001$

Table 3. Discriminant validity with internal branding as second-order construct

Variables	*IB*	*EE*	*OCB*
IB	**.605**		
EE	.255	**.710**	
OCB	.490	.609	**.619**

Bold values indicate the square root of AVE values, IB= internal branding, EE= employee engagement, OCB= organizational citizenship behavior, $p<.001$

5.2 Structural Model

Structural model helps to assessing the relationship among internal branding, employee engagement and organizational citizenship behvaior. It helps researchers to understand how changes occur in IB and EE with OCB affect the structural relationship. Structural models assist to study the direct and indirect effects between the constructs and allowing researchers to test proposed hypotheses and theoretical frameworks (Figure 1).

Figure 1. SEM showing the connection between IB and OCB

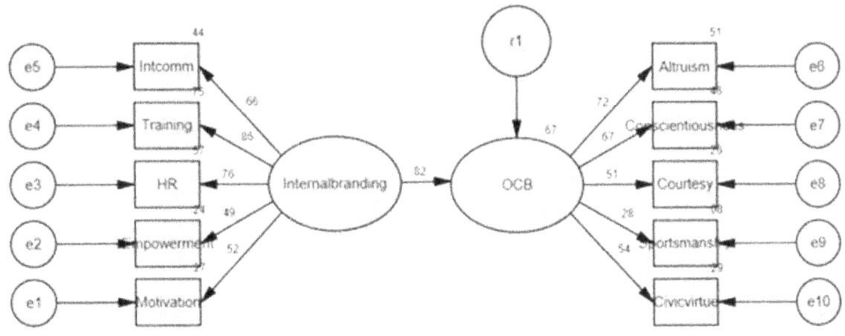

Figure 1 shows the direct path diagram of structural equation model, viewing the association between IB and OCB.

Table 4. SEM outputs of direct relationship between IB and OCB

Direct Relationship	Estimate (B)	S.E	C.R	p	CMIN/df	GFI	CFI	RMSEA
IB ⟶ OCB	0.751	0.161	4.656	0.000**	3.168	0.912	0.931	0.074

Table 4 shows the output of SEM analysis and it is found that IB has a significant impact on OCB (where $p<0.01$, GFI & CFI is greater than 0.9, RMSEA is less than 0.08).

Overall it is concluded that IB creates a significant and positive role to exhibit citizenship behavior in Indian manufacturing sector. So in this study the assumed hypothesis 1 and 2 is accepted.

Now this study has been used SEM analysis to reveal the association between IB and OCB in the existence of EE.

Figure 2. Mediation analysis of EE in between IB, OCB

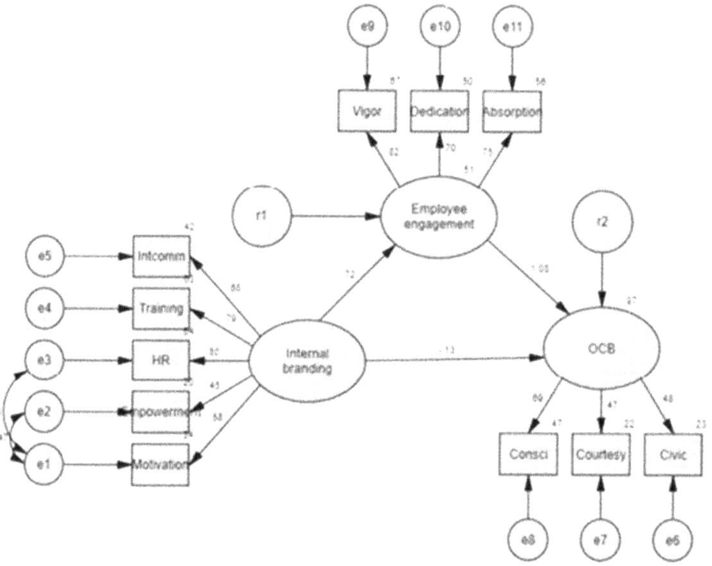

Table 5. Mediation analysis of EE

Relationship	*Direct Effect (a)*	*Indirect Effect (b)*	*Total Effect*	*t-Statistics*	*VAF [b/(a+b)]*	*P value*	*Conclusion*
IB → EE → OCB	0.132	0.489	0.621	2.751	0.787	0.006	Full Mediation

The information presented in Table 5 supports the idea that EE is playing as mediator role in the relationship between IB and OCB. The SEM results show that IB had a standardized effect of 0.751 on OCB when EE was absent, but there was no significant effect on OCB when EE was present. This indicates that EE has a full mediation effect on OCB. Additionally, when there were fewer disturbances, IB had a significant and direct effect on OCB, but this effect became insignificant in the presence of EE. Therefore, the results support the hypotheses H3 and H4.

The results of the path analysis for four hypotheses as presented in Table 6 help to assess the validity of the hypotheses and understand the relationships between IB, EE and OCB.

Table 6. Hypothesis and path analysis

Hypothesis	Direct Relationship	Beta coefficient (O)	Standard deviation (SD)	t-statistics (O/ SD)	P values
H1	IB → OCB	0.142	0.030	4.774	0.000
H2	IB → EE	0.941	0.116	8.112	0.000
H3	EE → OCB	0.689	0.217	3.175	0.000
Meditational Relationship					
H4	IB → EE → OCB	0.553	0.201	2.751	0.006

Hypothesis H4 (IB → EE → OCB), shows mediational relationship between variables is positive, with a beta coefficient for the indirect effect of 0.553, a t-statistic of 2.751, and a p-value of 0.006, which indicates that the mediational relationship is also statistically significant.

6. DISCUSSION

Internal branding is conscious, advancing the branding within the organization to influence the brand image by adjusting the organization's values with the member of staff's values. In manufacturing companies, employees may not have any direct communication with customers. Here, the internal branding strategy helps to ensure all associates, apart from their jobs, know the firm's mission and values and are attached to the company's objectives. And this attachment creates a positive and cohesive culture, which is directly linked with employee satisfaction, engagement, and citizenship behavior. Internal branding also helps improve communication and partnership with the company, especially in industries where it highly needs collaboration.

Analyzing the empirical mechanism process in between internal branding, organizational citizenship behavior and employee engagement in manufacturing sector is the major objective of the study. In sequence with the aim of this study is to analyze the impact of internal branding on OCB. In addition, to that this study is also examining the impact of employee engagement on OCB. Subsequently, this study is trying to show the mediation effect of employee engagement in between internal branding and organizational citizenship behavior.

The present study has established that there is positive and significant impact of IB on OCB and EE. By the using of structural equation model this study has found that there is positive and significant mediation effect of EE in between IB and OCB. Additionally this present study has found that there is a insignificant effect of IB on OCB due to the existence of employee engagement. In line, this study is trying proved that internal branding can improve the engagement level of employee rather than citizenship behavior as when the employees dedicatedly and vigorously involved at the workplace, then an employee can directly exhibit citizenship behavior.

7. MANAGERIAL IMPLICATIONS

In today's changing world, every organization must make changes to establish a successful brand with good citizenship behavior. To achieve this, organizations implement course of actions to attract and retain potential employees for a longer period of time. These strategies include motivating employees for career development, providing training for individual development, ensuring internal communication to keep employees informed about the organization, and empowering employees to make the right decisions. All of these efforts contribute to internal branding. When employees feel positive about these directions, they provide excellent service to external customers and exhibit extra-role behavior or citizenship behavior towards the organization and society.

Additionally, organizations should communicate all internal information for organizational development through employee participation and involvement. The focus should be on training and development programs that can improve employee dedication and engagement in their job. Management should consider internal branding and employee engagement levels, as employees' dedication and involvement also create a new environment of organizational success. The engagement level of employees has an indirect effect on their discretionary behavior.

8. CONCLUSION, LIMITATIONS, AND FUTURE RESEARCH

The current study was examined on employees of Indian manufacturing sectors. This study is to investigate the impact of internal branding on employee engagement and organizational citizenship behavior. The outcomes point toward internal branding notion in Indian manufacturing sector extends the engagement level of employee to exhibit citizenship behavior. It has been seen that highly engaged people have high absorption, high vigor and highly dedicated towards the work place and finally produce positive behaviours among the co workers.

Additional, this study is offering a friendly environment in the form of internal branding which shows engagement level of employee towards their job. Consequently, organizations' performance remains effective. Therefore, manufacturing sector needs to provide an amiable working atmosphere by incorporating internal branding concepts to remain competitive.

During the initial stage of any study, there are certain limitations that can provide new directions for further research. In this particular study, some limitations were not taken into consideration.

- Basically this study is cross-sectional in nature, where causative explanation is complicated to interpret. To defeat this limitation, future studies should use longitudinal studies to get transparent picture of internal branding and its impact on attitude and behavior of an individualThis present study has been used only five dimensions of internal branding and that were analyzed based on specific situations. Future study can be done by considering other dimensions like perceived value congruence, leadership and reward system.
- All the measurement scales of the constructs which were used in this study were taken from previous literatures and also the study was developed some items to measure the construct without taking in depth interview.
- Apart from this, the study was taken only three dimensions to measure the engagement level of employee whether there was a most acceptable model JD-R of engagement was used by various studies.
- The study can also be extended in other kinds of sector like health care, hospitality and any Government sector.

REFERENCES

Akbari, M., Hooshmand, M., & Aletaha, S. H. (2019). Internal Marketing and the Internal Customers' Citizenship Behavior in Higher Education. *International Journal of Schooling*, 1(3), 15–28.

Bakker, A. B., & Demerouti, E. (2008). Towards a model of work engagement. *Career Development International*, 13(3), 209–223. DOI: 10.1108/13620430810870476

Burmann, C., & Zeplin, S. (2005). Building brand commitment: A behavioural approach to internal brand management. *Journal of Brand Management*, 12(4), 279–300. DOI: 10.1057/palgrave.bm.2540223

Cheng, J. C., & Chen, C. Y. (2017). Job resourcefulness, work engagement and prosocial service behaviors in the hospitality industry. *International Journal of Contemporary Hospitality Management*, 29(10), 2668–2687. DOI: 10.1108/IJCHM-01-2016-0025

Dewan, N., Hossain, M. B., Kim, G. G., Dunay, A., & Illés, C. B. (2022). Transportation Mobile Applications Adoption Behavior Does Affect Overseas Residents' Life Satisfaction: Involvement as A Moderator. *Cogent Business & Management*, 9(1), 2096998. DOI: 10.1080/23311975.2022.2096998

Eid, R., Al Zaabi, A., Alzahmi, R., & Elsantil, Y. (2019). Integrating internal branding antecedents, customer and job satisfaction in the public sector. *The International Journal of Organizational Analysis*, 27(5), 1480–1503. DOI: 10.1108/IJOA-09-2018-1548

Garas, S. R. R., Mahran, A. F. A., & Mohamed, H. M. H. (2018). Internal corporate branding impact on employees' brand supporting behaviour. *Journal of Product and Brand Management*, 27(1), 79–95. DOI: 10.1108/JPBM-03-2016-1112

Ghenaatgar, A., & Jalali, S. M. (2016). Study of the Effect of Internal Brand Management on Brand Citizenship Behavior in Presence of Brand Commitment and Job Satisfaction of Employees in Banking Industry. *International Business Management*, 10(18), 4200–4208.

Gupta, M., Shaheen, M., & Reddy, P. K. (2017). Impact of psychological capital on organizational citizenship behavior: Mediation by work engagement. *Journal of Management Development*, 36(7), 973–983. DOI: 10.1108/JMD-06-2016-0084

Gupta, N., & Sharma, V. (2018). The comparative analysis of employee engagement measures: A theoretical perspective. *International Journal of Management Practice*, 11(1), 42–68. DOI: 10.1504/IJMP.2018.088382

Gupta, S., Bhasin, J., & Mushtaq, S. (2021). Employer brand experience and organizational citizenship behavior: Mediating role of employee engagement. *Asia-Pacific Journal of Business Administration*, 13(3), 357–382. DOI: 10.1108/APJBA-08-2020-0287

Hair, J. F.Jr, Howard, M. C., & Nitzl, C. (2020). Assessing measurement model quality in PLS-SEM using confirmatory composite analysis. *Journal of Business Research*, 109, 101–110. DOI: 10.1016/j.jbusres.2019.11.069

Hair, J. F., Risher, J. J., Sarstedt, M., & Ringle, C. M. (2019). When to use and how to report the results of PLS-SEM. *European Business Review*, 31(1), 2–24. DOI: 10.1108/EBR-11-2018-0203

Harter, J. K., Schmidt, F. L., & Hayes, T. L. (2002). Business-unit-level relationship between employee satisfaction, employee engagement, and business outcomes: A meta-analysis. *The Journal of Applied Psychology*, 87(2), 268–279. DOI: 10.1037/0021-9010.87.2.268 PMID: 12002955

Hasni, M. J. S., Salo, J., Naeem, H., & Abbasi, K. S. (2018). Impact of internal branding on customer-based brand equity with mediating effect of organizational loyalty: An empirical evidence from retail sector. *International Journal of Retail & Distribution Management*, 46(11/12), 1056–1076. DOI: 10.1108/IJRDM-07-2017-0148

Kang, H. J. A., Kim, W. G., Choi, H. M., & Li, Y. (2020). How to fuel employees' prosocial behavior in the hotel service encounter. *International Journal of Hospitality Management*, 84, 102333. DOI: 10.1016/j.ijhm.2019.102333

Kaur, P., Malhotra, K., & Sharma, S. K. (2020). Moderation-mediation framework connecting internal branding, affective commitment, employee engagement and job satisfaction: An empirical study of BPO employees in Indian context. *Asia-Pacific Journal of Business Administration*, 12(3/4), 327–348. DOI: 10.1108/APJBA-10-2019-0217

Kolla, N., Prasad, R. V., & Geetha, K. V. (2019). Impact of Internal Branding on Employees' Job Satisfaction, Brand Commitment and Brand Citizenship Behaviour. *International Journal on Emerging Technologies*, 10(2), 435–439.

Latifah, Y., &Muafi, M. (2021). Examining the effect of internal branding on employee performance: Job satisfaction and employee engagement as mediation variables. *International Journal of Business Ecosystem & Strategy, 3*(4), 1-12.

Lee, K. (2008). Opportunities for green marketing: Young consumers. *Marketing Intelligence & Planning*, 26(6), 573–586. DOI: 10.1108/02634500810902839

Lee, Y. K., Kim, S., & Kim, S. Y. (2014). The impact of internal branding on employee engagement and outcome variables in the hotel industry. *Asia Pacific Journal of Tourism Research*, 19(12), 1359–1380. DOI: 10.1080/10941665.2013.863790

Liu, S., Liu, S., Liu, Z., Peng, X., & Yang, Z. (2022). Automated detection of emotional and cognitive engagement in MOOC discussions to predict learning achievement. *Computers & Education*, 181, 104461. DOI: 10.1016/j.compedu.2022.104461

Lyu, Y., Zhu, H., Zhong, H. J., & Hu, L. (2016). Abusive supervision and customer-oriented organizational citizenship behavior: The roles of hostile attribution bias and work engagement. *International Journal of Hospitality Management*, 53, 69–80. DOI: 10.1016/j.ijhm.2015.12.001

Macey, W. H., & Schneider, B. (2008). Engaged in engagement: We are delighted we did it. *Industrial and Organizational Psychology: Perspectives on Science and Practice*, 1(1), 76–83. DOI: 10.1111/j.1754-9434.2007.00016.x

Matanda, M. J., & Ndubisi, N. O. (2013). Internal marketing, internal branding, and organisational outcomes: The moderating role of perceived goal congruence. *Journal of Marketing Management*, 29(9-10), 1030–1055. DOI: 10.1080/0267257X.2013.800902

Ngo, L. V., Nguyen, N. P., Huynh, K. T., Gregory, G., & Cuong, P. H. (2020). Converting internal brand knowledge into employee performance. *Journal of Product and Brand Management*, 29(3), 273–287. DOI: 10.1108/JPBM-10-2018-2068

Organ, D. W., Podsakoff, P. M., & MacKenzie, S. B. (2005). *Organizational citizenship behavior: Its nature, antecedents, and consequences*. Sage Publications.

Özçelik, G., & Fındıklı, M. A. (2014). The relationship between internal branding and organizational citizenship behaviour: The mediating role of person-organization fit. *Procedia: Social and Behavioral Sciences*, 150, 1120–1128. DOI: 10.1016/j.sbspro.2014.09.127

Parke, M. R., Tangirala, S., & Hussain, I. (2021). Creating organizational citizens: How and when supervisor-versus peer-led role interventions change organizational citizenship behavior. *The Journal of Applied Psychology*, 106(11), 1714–1733. DOI: 10.1037/apl0000848 PMID: 33090860

Podsakoff, P. M., MacKenzie, S. B., Moorman, R. H., & Fetter, R. (1990). Transformational leader behaviors and their effects on followers' trust in leader, satisfaction, and organizational citizenship behaviors. *The Leadership Quarterly*, 1(2), 107–142. DOI: 10.1016/1048-9843(90)90009-7

Podsakoff, P. M., MacKenzie, S. B., & Podsakoff, N. P. (2016). Recommendations for creating better concept definitions in the organizational, behavioral, and social sciences. *Organizational Research Methods*, 19(2), 159–203. DOI: 10.1177/1094428115624965

Punjaisri, K., Evanschitzky, H., & Wilson, A. (2009). Internal branding: An enabler of employees' brand-supporting behaviours. *Journal of Service Management*, 20(2), 209–226. DOI: 10.1108/09564230910952780

Punjaisri, K., & Wilson, A. (2017). The role of internal branding in the delivery of employee brand promise. *Advances in corporate branding*, 91-108.

Rafferty, A., Maben, J., & West, E. (2005). What makes a good employer? Academic Press.

Rafiq, M., & Ahmed, P. K. (1993). The scope of internal marketing: Defining the boundary between marketing and human resource management. *Journal of Marketing Management*, 9(3), 219–232. DOI: 10.1080/0267257X.1993.9964234

Raj, A. B. (2020). Employee well-being through internal branding: An integrated approach for achieving employee-based brand outcomes. *Global Business Review*, 21(4), 1065–1086. DOI: 10.1177/0972150918779161

Robbins, S. P., & Judge, T. A. (2012). *PerilakuOrganisasi, Organizational Beahavior, Buku 1, Edisi 12*. SalembaEmpat.

Robinson, D., Perryman, S., & Hayday, S. (2004). *The drivers of employee engagement*. No Title.

Sahoo, S. R., & Mohanty, S. (2019). Antecedents and Dimensions of Internal Branding. An Overview. *RevistaEspacios, 40*(37).

Salajeghe, S., Farahbakhsh, A., &Sohi, Z. (2014). Explaining the relationship between internal marketing activities with organizational citizenship behavior among employees of tejarat bank.

Saleem, F. Z., & Iglesias, O. (2016). Mapping the domain of the fragmented field of internal branding. *Journal of Product and Brand Management*, 25(1), 43–57. DOI: 10.1108/JPBM-11-2014-0751

Schaufeli, W. B., Salanova, M., Gonzalez-Roma, V., & Bakker, A. B. (2002). The measurement of engagement and burnout: A confirmative analytic approach. *Journal of Happiness Studies*, 3(1), 71–92. DOI: 10.1023/A:1015630930326

Srivastava, A., & Dey, D. K., & MS, B. (2020). Drivers of brand credibility in consumer evaluation of global brands and domestic brands in an emerging market context. *Journal of Product and Brand Management*, 29(7), 849–861. DOI: 10.1108/JPBM-03-2018-1782

Srivastava, A. P., Mani, V., & Yadav, M. (2019). Evaluating the implications of stakeholder's role towards sustainability of higher education. *Journal of Cleaner Production*, 240, 118270. DOI: 10.1016/j.jclepro.2019.118270

Ullah, P. S., Jamal, W., & Naeem, M. (2018). The Relationship of Employee Engagement, Organizational Commitment, and Organizational Citizenship Behavior. *Jinnah Business Review*, 6(1), 35–41. DOI: 10.53369/ZHCF6210

Chapter 3
Beyond the Paycheck: Unlocking Employee Engagement

V. Anokha
https://orcid.org/0009-0008-9286-6819
PES University, India

Amogh Venkataramana Reddy
Clemson University, USA

ABSTRACT

This chapter delves into the importance of purpose and meaning in employee engagement and its impact on corporate success. In today's changing workplace, employees want more than simply a salary; they want meaningful employment that reflects their values. It looks into tactics for cultivating a purpose-driven culture, such as leadership influence, job creation, and the establishment of a supportive work environment. The chapter also looks at how well-being programs, continual development, and engagement assessment can help to maintain a vibrant workplace. This chapter equips business executives, HR experts, and personal development enthusiasts with the skills they need to improve employee well-being, increase engagement, and create a more meaningful and productive work environment.

INTRODUCTION

In the quick-changing and dynamic corporate world of today, some of the old traditional drivers of employee engagement are competitive salaries, job security, and career advancement opportunities which are no longer sufficient to sustain high levels of motivation and commitment. The modern workforce is looking for more from their jobs than just a salary; they want their work to have meaning and purpose, to feel as though their contributions count, and to be in accordance with their

DOI: 10.4018/979-8-3693-8457-2.ch003

beliefs. This transformation is indicative of a broader shift in people's perceptions of what work should be like and how they view their positions in the workplace.

This change in expectations is more than just a trend from years; it signifies a deep shift in how individuals see their jobs and their place in society. Nowadays, more and more workers want to feel that their work matters, that it reflects their values, and that it advances something greater than themselves. They no longer only want to be paid. This change has significant organizational ramifications. Studies regularly demonstrate that workers who find meaning in their work are more engaged, more productive, and more likely to be long-term employees. On the other hand, a lack of direction and significance can result in high turnover rates, burnout, and disengagement, all of which can have detrimental effects on the productivity and financial health of a company.

Studies repeatedly demonstrate that employees are more engaged, productive, and inclined to stick with their company when they find meaning in their work (Bailey et al., 2017). In addition to exhibiting higher levels of job satisfaction, engaged employees also show better levels of creativity, inventiveness, and resilience—all of which are essential for organizational success in a cutthroat business environment (Steger, 2016). Employees now invest their identities in their job rather than merely doing duties (Wrzesniewski et al., 2003).On the other hand, a lack of purpose can result in high turnover rates, burnout, and disengagement, which presents serious difficulties for businesses trying to retain a dedicated and driven workforce (Cartwright & Holmes, 2006).

Employee expectations are dynamic and influenced by multiple factors. According to research, companies that place a high priority on meaning and purpose have happier workers, which boosts output, profitability, and performance (Cameron et al., 2011). Additionally, businesses with a clear mission statement have a greater chance of drawing in and keeping top talent, as workers are more and more drawn to organizations that provide fulfilling work environments (Kumar & Pansari, 2016).

The current chapter will examine the vital role that meaning and purpose play in employee engagement and provide meaningful advice on how to foster these qualities within the company. This will also look at useful skills for creating meaningful work, such as autonomy, social connection, and job making. The relationship between employee well-being and engagement will also be covered in this chapter, with a focus on how crucial it is to provide a work environment that promotes mental, physical, and emotional health. Employee engagement and a strong sense of commitment to the organization's success can be fostered by incorporating meaning and purpose into the very fabric of the company. Purpose-driven engagement is a critical competitive advantage in today's complex business climate since it not only improves individual well-being but also produces sustainable business benefits.

THE FOUNDATION OF EMPLOYEE ENGAGEMENT

The fundamental components that support employee engagement are meaning and purpose. The primary reason for an organisation's existence and the impact it aims to achieve are referred to as its purpose in the workplace. For an employee, it's the feeling that their job advances a cause greater than oneself, be it societal change, fostering creativity, or aiding others. Conversely, meaning is more subjective and individualised and relates to a person's relationship with their work. It includes how much weight an employee gives to their job, how much satisfaction they get from it, and how well their work fits in with their own objectives and values. According to Wrzesniewski et al. (2001), employees' perception of their work's purpose and meaning in the workplace are determined by how much they believe it contributes to something bigger than themselves and is in line with their personal values and views. These concepts are strongly associated with the idea of intrinsic motivation, which holds that people are motivated by internal benefits including satisfaction and a sense of achievement (Deci & Ryan, 2000). Employees who believe their work has significance are more likely to be engaged, driven, and dedicated to their companies(Bailey et al .,2017). Furthermore, beneficial outcomes like higher job satisfaction, decreased turnover rates, and improved well-being have been connected to meaningful work (Steger et al., 2012).Employees are more likely to be driven, involved, and dedicated to their jobs when they feel that their work has meaning. Higher levels of job satisfaction and general well-being result from this link between purpose and labour, which fosters a sense of fulfilment that goes beyond financial remuneration.

Intriguing employment has significant psychological and emotional advantages. Studies have demonstrated the increased resilience, improved stress management, and job satisfaction of workers who see a sense of purpose in their work. Enthusiasts who are motivated by internal rewards including a sense of personal growth, accomplishment, and the satisfaction of making a meaningful contribution are said to be motivated by meaningful work.

Meaningful employment can improve an employee's psychological sense of identity and self-worth. According to research by Rosso et al. (2010), meaningful employment improves workers' feelings of fulfillment, self-worth, and contentment with their lives. Additionally, it serves as a preventative measure against stress and burnout since workers who find purpose in their work are more able to overcome obstacles (Allan et al., 2016).People are more likely to feel a sense of pride and ownership over their efforts when they believe that their job is important. Employees become more committed in their jobs and the success of the company as a result, which raises engagement levels. Meaningful work increases overall job satisfaction and decreases feelings of alienation by fostering an emotional sense of connection and belonging.

Positive behavioural consequences including enhanced creativity, innovation, and teamwork can also result from meaningful employment. Employees are more likely to go above and beyond the call of duty, offering suggestions, assuming initiative, and supporting coworkers when they believe that their work has meaning. This generates a positive feedback loop in which meaningful work raises employee engagement, which in turn develops a work environment where staff members are more innovative, productive, and devoted to the company.

Purpose needs to be strongly aligned with the organization's values and goals in order to be a powerful engagement driver. Workers are more likely to have a sense of commitment and belonging when they believe that the organization's mission and their own values are strongly aligned (Pratt and Ashforth, 2003). Employee motivation and concentration on accomplishing shared objectives are increased as a result of this alignment, which also improves organizational performance (Henderson & Van den Steen, 2015).

Employees feel strongly that the goals of the company and themselves are aligned when they are in line with the organization's purpose. Maintaining this alignment is essential to developing a motivated and cohesive staff.

Organizational values are the fundamental ideas and precepts that govern the decisions and actions of a business. Employees are more likely to find purpose in their work when they are aware of and align with these beliefs. An organization that places a high priority on sustainability, for instance, is likely to draw in workers who have strong environmental convictions, which will inevitably lead to a natural alignment of personal and organizational goals. Because they feel like they are making a difference for a cause they truly care about, employees feel more engaged and the organization's culture is strengthened. A shared aim among employees fosters greater cooperation and teamwork, which is ensured when purpose and organizational goals are in line. Higher levels of engagement and performance occur when all members of the organization are motivated by the same goal, which fosters unity and shared commitment.

THE ROLE OF SOCIAL CONNECTIONS IN FOSTERING WORKPLACE COMMUNITY

In today's workplace, where remote and hybrid work arrangements are becoming more common, the need of developing social relationships and a sense of belonging is greater than ever. Building great workplace relationships is critical for leaders and HR professionals seeking to create an environment in which employees feel valued, supported, and engaged.

Human well-being is largely dependent on social relationships, and this also holds true at work. Employee engagement and job satisfaction are significantly impacted by a sense of belonging, which is more likely to be felt by linked employees. Employees that have a sense of belonging experience a feeling of being valued members of a community that accept them for who they are and their contributions. A sense of belonging is associated with increased levels of dedication, motivation, and general job performance.

An effective feeling of community at work has a significant positive effect on worker engagement and well-being. There is a larger likelihood of good feelings, reduced stress levels, and a stronger sense of purpose among employees who perceive themselves as part of a supportive group. Employees are less likely to leave an atmosphere where they feel appreciated and engaged, which promotes loyalty and lowers turnover. Employees are more likely to be resilient in the face of adversity and to avoid burnout if they have a sense of connection and belonging (Baumeister & Leary, 2017). Higher levels of motivation, dedication, and devotion to the company are also influenced by this sense of community (Ragins & Dutton, 2017).

A work environment that places a high priority on well-being fosters a culture of caring in which staff members are motivated to assist one another's mental, emotional, and physical well-being. Because they believe that the company values their well-being, employees become more engaged overall.

Positive feelings, job satisfaction, and engagement are more common among workers who feel connected to their coworkers (Carmeli et al., 2009). These relationships also help to create a positive work atmosphere where staff members feel appreciated and valued. Studies have indicated that workers with robust social networks at work are not only more content but also more efficient. They have a higher propensity to work well together, encourage one another, and remain with the company longer. Conversely, a lack of social ties can result in emotions of loneliness, disinterest, and even burnout, all of which have a detrimental effect on performance—both personally and professionally.

Strong working connections need deliberate effort on the part of managers and staff.According to research, when coworkers strive toward shared objectives, they grow in mutual regard, trust, and support, which raises engagement levels and improves output (Edmondson, 1999). Organizations can use mentorship programs, team-building exercises, and social gatherings that promote employee engagement and collaboration to foster good workplace connections (Kahn, 1990). These exercises can promote free communication, trust, and the dismantling of obstacles between team members.

Promoting cross-functional cooperation, in which staff members from several departments collaborate on projects, is an additional tactic. This fosters a greater awareness of various jobs and viewpoints in addition to fostering relationships inside the organization. By modeling inclusive behaviors like actively listening to staff members, demonstrating empathy, and appreciating unique contributions, leaders can also build great connections.

Building relationships can also be greatly aided by mentoring initiatives, particularly for junior or new hires. Establishing strong, enduring relationships that foster a sense of belonging can be achieved by firms through matching employees with mentors who can provide direction, support, and career advice.

In order to create a positive work atmosphere where employees feel appreciated and engaged, collaboration and teamwork are essential. Employees who collaborate to achieve shared objectives grow to love one another and each other. Social ties are reinforced by collaborative workplaces, which promote idea exchange, problem solving, and group decision making. Establishing an environment of openness and transparency where staff members feel comfortable sharing their thoughts and opinions is one way that leaders can encourage collaboration. Fostering collaboration among team members via joint projects, brainstorming meetings, and cooperative software also contributes to the establishment of a welcoming and inclusive work environment.

WELL-BEING AS A CORNERSTONE OF ENGAGEMENT

The importance of employee well-being in fostering engagement, productivity, and overall corporate performance is becoming more widely acknowledged. To create a positive and meaningful employment experience, company leaders and professionals must address mental, physical, and emotional wellness in their work environment.

Engagement and worker well-being are closely related. Employee engagement at work is higher when they are in good physical, mental, and emotional health. Employee performance is enhanced when they are resilient, creative, and able to think clearly. Employees with high levels of well-being are more engaged, productive, and dedicated to their companies (Robertson and Cooper, 2010). On the other hand, low well-being can result in decreased productivity, burnout, and disengagement.

Organizations that put employee well-being first routinely see higher levels of engagement, according to research. Workers that are made to feel valued by their employer are more inclined to go above and beyond, be devoted, and foster a healthy work environment. Individual performance is not the only thing that is impacted by well-being; team relationships and overall organizational success are also impacted.

Developing a well-being-promoting work environment necessitates a comprehensive strategy. Various tactics can be implemented by HR professionals and business executives to cater to the varying needs of employees.

Promoting work-life balance is essential, to start. Remote work and flexible hours are two examples of flexible working options that help people better balance their personal and professional obligations. Maintaining mental and physical well-being and preventing burnout can also be achieved by promoting regular breaks and setting reasonable expectations for workload.

Second, it's critical to make mental health resources accessible, including counseling services, employee assistance programs (EAPs), and mental health awareness training. Fostering an environment where candid conversations about mental health are welcomed can help lessen stigma and motivate staff to get treatment when they need it.

Programs like wellness challenges, on-site workout centers, or alliances with neighborhood gyms can promote physical health. Employees can connect with their inner values and find joy in their work through programs that incorporate mindfulness, stress management, and personal development activities (Luthans et al., 2006). These initiatives also support an environment at work where employees' well-being is respected and given top priority. Encouraging dietary options at work or nutrition education are two examples of nutritional support that can enhance general wellbeing.

Fostering strong relationships in the workplace, giving resources for stress management, and creating opportunities for personal development are all ways to support employees' emotional well-being. Fostering an environment that values acknowledgment and gratitude can help improve mental well-being and strengthen a feeling of direction.

Programs for well-being are essential in helping workers feel more fulfilled and purposeful at work. Employees are more likely to find purpose in their job and feel a connection to the mission and values of the company when they perceive that their well-being is appreciated. Workplace well-being initiatives that are in line with the goals of the company can strengthen this bond and increase motivation and job satisfaction.

For instance, wellness programs that motivate staff members to seek personal development, pick up new skills, or perform community service might assist them in realizing the impact of their work on society. Workplace experiences that are more balanced and fulfilling are produced by programs that prioritize holistic well-being, which addresses the mental, emotional, social, and physical facets of health.

Numerous businesses have effectively incorporated well-being into their corporate culture, which has enhanced employee engagement and produced better commercial results. Corporations that have successfully included well-being into their workplace cultures include Google and Johnson & Johnson. High levels of employee satisfaction and engagement have been attributed to Google's extensive well-being programs, which include mental health resources, exercise centers, and flexible work schedules (Bock, 2015). According to Zellars et al. (2005), Johnson & Johnson's emphasis on employee wellness through programs like the Healthy & Me program has also boosted wellbeing and lowered healthcare expenditures. These programs have made it possible for workers to feel supported at work, which has increased participation and sparked creativity. Salesforce is another example of a company that prioritizes work-life balance and mental health. It does this by holding regular mindfulness sessions and observing “Wellness Week.” Salesforce has promoted a culture of care that improves employee satisfaction and organizational success by placing a high priority on well-being. These initiatives help individual workers as well as foster a positive workplace culture and long-term company strategies.

LEADERSHIP’S INFLUENCE IN FOSTERING A CULTURE OF PURPOSE

Leadership is an essential component of a purpose-driven culture, setting the atmosphere in which individuals find meaning and motivation in their jobs.Leaders have a significant impact on company culture and are critical in instilling purpose in the workplace. According to research by Dvir et al. (2002), transformational leaders are especially good at fostering a purpose-driven culture that encourages engagement and commitment because they put a lot of emphasis on inspiring and motivating their workforce. Leaders set the tone for the company's values and mission by effectively communicating them. When leaders continually demonstrate a commitment to these principles, they foster a culture in which purpose is more than simply a statement on the wall, but a lived experience that people can relate to. This sense of purpose motivates employees because they perceive their everyday duties as part of a larger, more important journey.

Engaging employees requires effective corporate purpose communication. Leaders can accomplish this through regularly communicating the organization's goal and vision, coordinating business plans with guiding principles, and exhibiting a commitment to these principles via their behavior (Kouzes and Posner, 2023). Additionally, it has been demonstrated that employees' sense of purpose and belonging is increased by authentic leadership, which is defined by transparency, honesty, and empathy (Avolio & Gardner, 2005).To effectively develop a purpose-driven culture, leaders must do more than just communicate; they must embody the company mission through their behaviors and decisions. Leading by example entails making decisions that match the organization's beliefs and goals. Leaders can utilize narrative to demonstrate how the company's purpose has benefited consumers, communities, and workers. Regularly discussing the company's goal in meetings, one-on-ones, and public venues emphasizes its significance. Furthermore, recognizing and rewarding activities that are consistent with the organization's goal serves to reinforce its relevance and encourages others to follow suit.

Some of the case studies demonstrate how firms have successfully infused purpose into their cultures. Patagonia and Unilever, for example, have made their environmental and social missions essential to their business models, enabling employees who are enthusiastic about sustainability to get intimately involved in their work. In a similar vein, Zappos has developed a highly engaged workforce by putting employee pleasure and customer satisfaction first, creating a purpose-driven culture (Hsieh, 2010). These firms have demonstrated that when purpose is authentically woven into the fabric of a company, it not only increases employee engagement but also improves brand reputation and consumer loyalty.

Empathy and sincerity are essential characteristics for leaders seeking to foster a purpose-driven culture. Empathetic leaders understand their employees' needs, aspirations, and challenges, allowing them to combine purpose and personal beliefs. Authenticity, on the other hand, fosters trust; when leaders are sincere in their dedication to the organization's mission, employees are more likely to buy in. Authentic leadership ensures that the purpose is not viewed as a business jargon, but as a genuine driving concept that propels the organisation forward. Leaders that possess empathy are more adept at comprehending and resolving the issues and worries of their staff members, hence enhancing confidence and involvement (Goleman, 2020). Genuine leaders foster a culture where staff members feel free to express themselves and relate to the mission of the company by being loyal to their principles and communicating their vision honestly (Walumbwa et al., 2008).

SHAPING WORK FOR PURPOSE: THE POWER OF JOB CRAFTING AND AUTONOMY

Job crafting and autonomy are critical components in this process, allowing people to modify their roles to better match their abilities, interests, and values. Job crafting is the process by which individuals proactively adjust aspects of their jobs to better match their personal abilities, passions, and values. This can include adjusting activities (task crafting), altering interactions with others (relational crafting), or reframing how people view their work (cognitive crafting). Employees can give their jobs more meaning by crafting them, making them more engaging and gratifying. For example, an employee may take on additional activities that are relevant to their interests or look for opportunities to mentor others, improving their sense of purpose and pleasure with their career. Job design not only improves individual well-being but also helps organisations succeed by exploiting individuals' unique talents and motivations.

Autonomy is intimately linked to job happiness since it gives employees control over their work environment and how they do their responsibilities. Research regularly shows that when people have more autonomy, they are more satisfied with their jobs, more driven, and perform better. Autonomy also develops trust and respect between employees and management, which increases job happiness. Greater ownership and commitment can result from giving staff members the freedom to choose how they carry out their jobs and the adaptability to change those roles as needed (Hackman & Oldham, 1976). Deci et al. (1989) found that employees are more likely to feel intrinsically motivated and fulfilled when they have autonomy over their work and the ability to make decisions. Along with encouraging a sense of accountability and responsibility, this autonomy raises engagement and performance. Employees are encouraged to take the initiative and make decisions that match with both their personal ambitions and the aims of the organization in a workplace that values autonomy. This not only results in a more engaged workforce, but it also promotes innovation and continual development by empowering employees to experiment with new ideas and techniques.

Bringing job crafting into the workplace requires a number of practical tasks. First, firms should educate their employees and management on the concept of job crafting and its benefits. Workshops or training sessions can assist employees find areas where they can tailor their professions by providing them with the necessary skills and frameworks.

Next, leaders should provide opportunities for staff to experiment with their roles and responsibilities. This could include flexible job descriptions that change with the employee's development or pilot programs that allow employees to try out different ways of working. Encouraging employees to create personal goals that correspond with the organization's vision can also help with job creation.

Finally, firms should frequently evaluate the impact of job design on employee engagement and satisfaction. Employers can incorporate job crafting by giving workers opportunity to try out new duties and responsibilities, promoting open communication about job roles, and providing training programs that teach workers how to recognize and capitalize on their talents (Berg et al., 2013). Frequent check-ins and feedback meetings can also assist staff members in fine-tuning their duties and guaranteeing alignment with company objectives. Feedback loops, such as surveys or focus groups, can help discover what works well and where improvements are needed. Organizations may improve job satisfaction, boost engagement, and foster a culture of autonomy by allowing individuals to determine their roles and responsibilities.

MEASURING ENGAGEMENT: STRATEGIES AND KEY INDICATORS

Effective measurement reveals how engaged individuals are, the factors that influence their engagement, and the impact of engagement on organisational performance. Employee engagement is a multidimensional notion that demands a full assessment. Some of the major metrics are:

- -Employee satisfaction measures how satisfied employees are with their jobs, work environments, and management. Job satisfaction surveys serve as a benchmark for determining levels of engagement.
- -Metrics that measure employee readiness to recommend their workplace to others, such as Employee Net Promoter Score (eNPS) and Net Promoter Score (NPS), can shed light on employee engagement (Reichheld, 2004).
- -Organizations can evaluate the degree of meaning and purpose that workers find in their work by using instruments like the Job Diagnostic Survey (JDS) and the Work and Meaning Inventory (WAMI) (Steger et al., 2012; Hackman & Oldham, 1976). These assessments gauge elements like job importance, meaningfulness, and compatibility with personal beliefs; the results offer important information about how well the company is creating a culture that is motivated by purpose.
- -High absenteeism and turnover rates frequently imply disengagement. Monitoring these rates assists in identifying potential difficulties inside the organization.
- -Engaged employees are more productive and produce higher-quality work. Tracking performance indicators can provide a clear picture of how involvement affects business outcomes.
- -Retention rates might represent how successfully an organization meets its employees' needs and keeps them engaged over time.

Purpose and meaning are fundamental to deep involvement, and quantifying them necessitates specific methods. One useful technique is to use engagement surveys with questions specifically designed to measure how employees view the purpose of their work and how it aligns with their personal values. Pulse surveys are another useful tool. These are short, frequent surveys that provide real-time information about employees' feeling of meaning and purpose. Pulse surveys enable firms to immediately detect fluctuations in engagement levels and solve issues before they develop. Focus groups and one-on-one interviews are examples of qualitative methodologies that can be used to investigate employees' attitudes toward their jobs and the business. These tools provide deep, complex insights that surveys cannot capture.

Organizational change should be informed and guided by engagement data. Organizations can pinpoint areas of strength and weakness, create focused interventions, and monitor the results of these efforts over time by examining engagement indicators (Kahn, 1990). Transparency and accountability are also promoted when engagement data is routinely shared with management and staff, guaranteeing that initiatives to increase engagement are in line with company objectives. Data-driven decision-making is critical to developing a more engaged workforce. Once engagement data has been gathered, it should be examined to find patterns, strengths, and opportunities for improvement. For example, if survey data shows that employees have low levels of perceived purpose, leaders can launch initiatives to better connect individual jobs with the organization's vision. Engagement data can also be used to target treatments to certain groups inside an organization. For example, if younger employees report lower levels of engagement, tailored programs that address their individual needs and career goals can be designed. Regularly sharing engagement data with employees promotes openness and confidence. It also shows employees how their feedback is being used to make significant changes within the firm.

A proactive strategy that incorporates frequent pulse surveys, feedback sessions, and focus groups is necessary to monitor engagement levels (Rothbard, 2001). In response to engagement data, organizations should put action plans into place to address issues that are found, and they should continuously improve these plans based on input from employees and evolving organizational requirements. Employee buy-in and dedication to the organization's initiatives are also increased when they are involved in the process of assessing and enhancing engagement.

Effective monitoring requires a continual cycle of data collection, analysis, and action. One best practice is to analyze engagement data on a frequent basis as part of leadership meetings in order to keep engagement on the agenda and respond to emergent issues promptly. Organizations should also create explicit accountability for engagement. Designating a team or individual to track engagement data and follow action plans can help guarantee that engagement initiatives are consistent and effective. Responding to engagement levels requires both immediate and long-term activities. In the short term, addressing individual employee concerns can help reduce disengagement. In the long run, cultivating a culture of continual development and open communication guarantees that engagement is a top concern.

INTEGRATING PERSONAL AND CORPORATE PURPOSE FOR COLLECTIVE SUCCESS

Aligning individual and corporate purpose is a very effective method for increasing employee engagement, motivation, and retention. When employees see a clear link between their own beliefs and the organization's aims, they are more likely to be invested in their work, resulting in increased satisfaction and performance. According to research, employees have higher levels of motivation, job satisfaction, and organizational commitment when their personal purpose and work are in line (Bunderson & Thompson, 2009). According to Cable and DeRue (2002), employees are more inclined to stick with a business that promotes their personal growth and ideals, which helps to lower turnover rates.

One of the most successful approaches to link individual and corporate purpose is to assist employees understand how their own beliefs align with the company's objective. Leaders and HR professionals can help to foster this relationship by encouraging open discussions about personal and organizational values. Employees, for example, can be encouraged to disclose their top priorities in their professional and personal lives during onboarding or team-building activities. Leaders can then emphasize how these values coincide with the organization's aims, demonstrating that their efforts contribute to something worthwhile. Furthermore, integrating employees in the goal-setting process helps improve alignment. Employees are more likely to regard their personal goals as important when they are involved in developing them. Encouraging employees to identify personal development goals that are aligned with the company's vision can help to strengthen this connection and create a shared sense of purpose, which increases engagement.

Individual purpose can be discovered using a variety of techniques and exercises that encourage employees to focus on their values, strengths, and passions. The "Ikigai" framework is one such tool that enables employees to discover what they enjoy, what they are good at, what the world needs, and what they may be compensated for. The Japanese concept of "reason for being" assists employees in identifying a purpose that balances personal fulfillment with organizational contribution. Another helpful practice is the "Values Clarification" process, in which employees state and rank their key values to better grasp what is genuinely important to them. This exercise can be followed by conversations about how to express these principles in their job inside the organization. Workshops and coaching sessions on personal purpose discovery can also help individuals find the direction and support they need to match their personal beliefs with their professional positions. Furthermore, motivating staff members to take part in goal-setting and decision-making procedures can help them feel more connected to the organization's mission (Locke & Latham, 2002).

Also, other activities like journaling, reflective practices, and goal-oriented talks can help staff members discover and connect their own purpose with their work.

Several companies have successfully connected individual and corporate purpose to increase engagement. For example, LinkedIn's aim to "connect the world's professionals to make them more productive and successful" connects strongly with employees who value networking and professional growth. By integrating employees' personal beliefs with this objective, LinkedIn has built a highly engaged workforce that is eager to contribute to the company's success. Similar to this, companies such as Ben & Jerry's have successfully matched their social and environmental missions with their employees' beliefs, resulting in a workplace where employees are highly engaged and devoted to the company's overall aims. Organizational and individual purpose alignment has been shown to have positive effects by companies such as Google and Southwest Airlines. Employees at Google are highly engaged and creative because of the company's innovative and autonomous culture, which empowers them to pursue topics that interest them (Bock, 2015). Similar to this, Southwest Airlines' emphasis on worker well-being and customer service has given its staff a strong sense of purpose, which has enhanced performance and loyalty (Freiberg & Freiberg, 1998). This alignment has played a critical role in developing a strong, purpose-driven culture that attracts and keeps people.

Leaders and human resource professionals can build a workplace where employees feel intimately engaged to their job by employing focused tactics, tools, and real-world examples, resulting in a vibrant, purpose-driven firm.

SUSTAINING EMPLOYEE ENGAGEMENT: CONTINUOUS DEVELOPMENT AND GROWTH

More than just initial zeal is needed to sustain employee engagement; continuous learning and development that promotes long-term growth is also necessary. In order to sustain high levels of engagement, cultivate a happy work environment, and advance sustainable business practices, corporate leaders and HR professionals must establish a culture of personal development and continual improvement.

It is more important than ever to pursue ongoing learning and development in the ever changing corporate environment of today. Workers are more likely to stay interested and motivated if they believe they are learning new skills and developing in their roles. Long-term engagement requires that people be challenged and invested in their work, which is achieved through continuous development.

Companies that place a high priority on continuous learning show that they care about the professional development of their staff, which increases employee loyalty and lowers turnover. Opportunities for growth and development are among the most significant factors impacting motivation and job satisfaction (Maurer, 2001). Workers who perceive that their employer makes an investment in their professional growth are more likely to be engaged and dedicated to their job. In addition, a continuous growth culture keeps businesses competitive by guaranteeing that workers have access to the newest information and abilities. Consequently, this enhances the general prosperity and longevity of the organization.

The first step in developing a culture of ongoing development and personal progress is leadership. As fundamental values within the company, learning and development must be actively promoted by leaders. This can be accomplished by encouraging staff members to take on new challenges, including learning opportunities into regular work routines, and giving the tools they need to advance their skills. Fostering a growth mindset in staff members encourages them to learn, take calculated risks, and innovate in order to establish a culture of continuous progress (Dweck, 2006). Companies may help with this by giving access to online learning resources, conducting frequent training sessions, and encouraging team members to share their knowledge.

Providing a range of learning opportunities, including workshops, mentorship programs, online courses, and on-the-job training, is one successful tactic. This gives workers the freedom to select the teaching strategies that best fit their requirements and tastes. Employers can assist staff members in developing new skills and pursuing alternative career pathways by providing them with opportunities for cross-training, mentoring programs, and customized development plans (Noe, 2020). Frequent performance evaluations and feedback sessions are also essential for directing staff members' growth and guaranteeing that they are in line with company requirements. Encouragement of information sharing and cross-functional collaboration also helps to foster continual improvement since it allows staff members to broaden their horizons and learn from one another. In addition, leaders ought to lead by example by pursuing their own education and professional development, proving that advancement is valued at all organizational levels.

To maintain engagement, it is critical to provide meaningful professional development opportunities that are aligned with employees' goals and desires. This necessitates a tailored strategy, in which leaders and HR experts collaborate closely with employees to understand their career goals and find opportunities for advancement.

One method is to adopt individual development plans (IDPs), which detail an employee's professional goals and the procedures required to accomplish them. Regular check-ins and career coaching can assist employees in staying on track and making necessary adjustments to their plans. Offering lateral transfers, stretch assignments, and leadership training can provide employees with a variety of experiences that will help them advance in their careers. Another strategy is to provide clear career progression paths inside the organization so that employees may see opportunities for growth and understand what it takes to go to the next level. This transparency can boost motivation and engagement by making employees feel like their efforts are being appreciated and that they have a future in the firm.

Feedback and recognition are essential components for maintaining interest. Early and helpful feedback helps workers see their areas of strength and growth, which promotes ongoing learning and development (Hattie and Timperley, 2007). Employees are encouraged to sustain high performance and engagement levels when they get recognition, whether it comes from official awards or unofficial compliments (Nelson, 2012). Recognition reinforces positive behaviors.

Constructive feedback enables employees to recognize their own strengths and areas for improvement, influencing their development and performance. Regular feedback promotes a growth attitude in which people are encouraged to learn from their mistakes and constantly improve. Recognition, on the other hand, promotes positive behaviors and accomplishments, leaving employees feeling valued and appreciated. Public recognition, such as awards, shout-outs, or other forms of acknowledgement, can enhance morale and inspire others to strive for excellence. Employees are more likely to stay interested and devoted to their jobs when they believe their accomplishments are being recognized.

Organizations may maintain high levels of engagement and promote a vibrant workplace culture by prioritizing learning, delivering meaningful career development opportunities, and providing regular feedback and acknowledgment. These activities assist individual employees while also contributing to the organization's long-term success and sustainability.

SHAPING THE FUTURE: PURPOSE AND MEANING IN THE EVOLVING WORKPLACE

The workplace landscape is rapidly changing, driven by technological breakthroughs, new societal ideals, and the workforce's increasing requirements. An increasing focus on meaningful and purpose-driven work experiences is a hallmark of the future of work.

Emerging Trends in Employee Engagement

Employee engagement has long been a top priority for firms looking to increase productivity and retain talent. However, traditional approaches are no longer adequate in a world where the nature of labor is continually changing. Employees now expect more than just financial compensation; they want to do work that reflects their beliefs, gives them a feeling of purpose, and encourages personal growth. This transition has resulted in a surge in purpose-driven work environments, with firms focusing more on mission-driven goals and social impact. Organizations are paying more attention to how to keep employees engaged and connected in a virtual setting as remote work becomes more common. Studies show that in the changing nature of work, companies with a purpose are better positioned to draw and hold on to talent (Kumar & Pansari, 2016).

Companies are discovering that supporting the physical, mental, and emotional well-being of employees is crucial for maintaining high levels of engagement. These programs, which go beyond standard health benefits to include mindfulness training, flexible work arrangements, and opportunities for continuous learning, help employees feel valued and connected to the organization's broader purpose.

The Role of Technology in Shaping Meaningful Work Experiences

Technology is critical for the future of work, not only in terms of automation and efficiency, but also in improving the total employee experience. Employees can combine their personal and professional life thanks to digital tools and platforms that allow them to work remotely. Flexibility is widely recognized as a significant driver of job satisfaction and engagement.

Brynjolfsson and McAfee (2014) state that digital tools and platforms allow workers to work more flexibly, collaborate across locations, and take advantage of individualized growth possibilities. Organizations must be aware of the many drawbacks that technology might bring, though, including digital overload and the blurring of work-life boundaries (Mazmanian et al., 2013).

Furthermore, technology can be used to provide more personalized and meaningful work experiences. For example, AI-powered platforms can evaluate employee data to create development programs that are tailored to individual career goals and personal values. Virtual reality (VR) and augmented reality (AR) are also being investigated as tools for immersive training and team-building activities, giving employees a stronger sense of connection and purpose in their job.

However, it is critical to acknowledge the possible drawbacks of technology, such as over-reliance, which can lead to burnout or a sense of detachment. Organizations must achieve a balance, utilizing technology to supplement rather than replace the human parts of work.

Adapting to New Challenges and Opportunities

The future of work is marked by perpetual change, necessitating companies' agility and adaptability. In order to respond to fresh opportunities and challenges, organizations need to be flexible and agile. This entails adopting new technology, encouraging creativity, and always altering to satisfy the shifting demands of the labor market. Additionally, leaders need to concentrate on developing an inclusive, encouraging workplace that places a high value on participation, well-being, and purpose (Edmondson, 1999).

Leaders must be proactive in detecting and responding to developing difficulties, such as the need to reskill and upskill personnel as technology advances. This includes promoting a culture of continuous learning in which people are encouraged to learn new skills and pursue various career routes within the firm.

Additionally, firms must deal with the complexity of a diverse and multigenerational workforce. Each generation brings its own set of values, expectations, and working methods, and leaders must promote an inclusive atmosphere that accepts these differences while encouraging collaboration and unity around common goals.

VISION FOR THE FUTURE OF PURPOSE-DRIVEN WORKPLACES

Looking ahead, purpose-driven workplaces are likely to become the rule rather than the exception. Purpose-driven organizations where workers are empowered to contribute to meaningful goals and are supported in their personal and professional progress are likely to define the future of work. Businesses that place a high value on meaning and purpose will not only increase employee performance and engagement but also benefit society at large (Cameron et al., 2011).

Organizations that value purpose and meaning will recruit and retain top personnel while also driving innovation and long-term success. This necessitates a change away from traditional hierarchical structures and toward more collaborative and decentralized models in which employees are empowered to take ownership of their work and contribute to the organization's goals.

CONCLUSION

In conclusion, the future of work is an exciting and dynamic landscape in which purpose and meaning are key. Fostering employee engagement through purpose, meaning, and well-being is critical to business success. Leaders may increase productivity and satisfaction by regularly monitoring engagement, matching individual and corporate goals, and cultivating a growth culture, resulting in a vibrant, sustainable workplace that benefits both employees and the organization altogether. Business leaders, executives, and HR professionals must keep ahead of emerging trends, use technology wisely, and be agile in order to build workplaces that not only fulfill the demands of the modern workforce, but also inspire and engage people on a deeper level. By doing so, they will create resilient, purpose-driven enterprises that can prosper in an ever-changing environment.

REFERENCES

Allan, B. A., Douglass, R. P., Duffy, R. D., & McCarty, R. J. (2016). Meaningful work as a moderator of the relation between work stress and meaning in life. *Journal of Career Assessment*, 24(3), 429–440. DOI: 10.1177/1069072715599357

Avolio, B. J., & Gardner, W. L. (2005). Authentic leadership development: Getting to the root of positive forms of leadership. *The Leadership Quarterly*, 16(3), 315–338. DOI: 10.1016/j.leaqua.2005.03.001

Bailey, C., Madden, A., Alfes, K., & Fletcher, L. (2017). The meaning, antecedents and outcomes of employee engagement: A narrative synthesis. *International Journal of Management Reviews*, 19(1), 31–53. DOI: 10.1111/ijmr.12077

Baumeister, R. F., & Leary, M. R. (2017). The need to belong: Desire for interpersonal attachments as a fundamental human motivation. Interpersonal development, 57-89.

Berg, J. M., Dutton, J. E., & Wrzesniewski, A. (2013). Job crafting and meaningful work.

Bock, L. (2015). *Work rules!: Insights from inside Google that will transform how you live and lead*. Twelve.

Brynjolfsson, E. (2014). The second machine age: Work, progress, and prosperity in a time of brilliant technologies.

Bunderson, J. S., & Thompson, J. A. (2009). The role of organizational membership in the relationship between personal and organizational values. *The Journal of Applied Psychology*, 94(4), 1014–1025.

Cable, D. M., & DeRue, D. S. (2002). The role of fit in organizational selection and work outcomes. *Organizational Behavior and Human Decision Processes*, 88(1), 294–311.

Cameron, K., Mora, C., Leutscher, T., & Calarco, M. (2011). Effects of positive practices on organizational effectiveness. *The Journal of Applied Behavioral Science*, 47(3), 266–308. DOI: 10.1177/0021886310395514

Carmeli, A., Brueller, D., & Dutton, J. E. (2009). Learning behaviours in the workplace: The role of high-quality interpersonal relationships and psychological safety. *Systems Research and Behavioral Science*, 26(1), 81–98. DOI: 10.1002/sres.932

Cartwright, S., & Holmes, N. (2006). The meaning of work: The challenge of regaining employee engagement and reducing cynicism. *Human Resource Management Review*, 16(2), 199–208. DOI: 10.1016/j.hrmr.2006.03.012

Deci, E. L., Connell, J. P., & Ryan, R. M. (1989). Self-determination in a work organization. *The Journal of Applied Psychology*, 74(4), 580–590. DOI: 10.1037/0021-9010.74.4.580

Deci, E. L., & Ryan, R. M. (2000). The" what" and" why" of goal pursuits: Human needs and the self-determination of behavior. *Psychological Inquiry*, 11(4), 227–268. DOI: 10.1207/S15327965PLI1104_01

Dvir, T., Eden, D., Avolio, B. J., & Shamir, B. (2002). Impact of transformational leadership on follower development and performance: A field experiment. *Academy of Management Journal*, 45(4), 735–744. DOI: 10.2307/3069307

Dweck, C. S. (2006). *Mindset: The new psychology of success*. Random house.

Edmondson, A. (1999). Psychological safety and learning behavior in work teams. *Administrative Science Quarterly*, 44(2), 350–383. DOI: 10.2307/2666999

Freiberg, K., & Freiberg, J. (1998). *Nuts!: Southwest Airlines' crazy recipe for business and personal success*. Crown Currency.

Goleman, D. (2020). *Emotional intelligence: Why it can matter more than IQ*. Bloomsbury Publishing.

Hackman, J. R., & Oldham, G. R. (1976). Motivation through the design of work: Test of a theory. *Organizational Behavior and Human Performance*, 16(2), 250–279. DOI: 10.1016/0030-5073(76)90016-7

Hattie, J., & Timperley, H. (2007). The power of feedback. *Review of Educational Research*, 77(1), 81–112. DOI: 10.3102/003465430298487

Henderson, R., & Steen, E. V. D. (2015). Why do firms have "purpose"? The firm's role as a carrier of identity and reputation. *The American Economic Review*, 105(5), 326–330. DOI: 10.1257/aer.p20151072

Hsieh, T. (2010). *Delivering happiness: A path to profits, passion, and purpose*.

Kahn, W. A. (1990). Psychological conditions of personal engagement and disengagement at work. *Academy of Management Journal*, 33(4), 692–724. DOI: 10.2307/256287

Kouzes, J. M., & Posner, B. Z. (2023). *The leadership challenge: How to make extraordinary things happen in organizations*. John Wiley & Sons.

Kumar, V., & Pansari, A. (2016). Competitive advantage through engagement. *JMR, Journal of Marketing Research*, 53(4), 497–514. DOI: 10.1509/jmr.15.0044

Locke, E. A., & Latham, G. P. (2002). Building a practically useful theory of goal setting and task motivation: A 35-year odyssey. *The American Psychologist*, 57(9), 705–717. DOI: 10.1037/0003-066X.57.9.705 PMID: 12237980

Luthans, F., Youssef, C. M., & Avolio, B. J. (2006). *Psychological capital: Developing the human competitive edge*. Oxford University Press. DOI: 10.1093/acprof:oso/9780195187526.001.0001

Maurer, T. J. (2001). Career-relevant learning and development, worker age, and beliefs about self-efficacy for development. *Journal of Management*, 27(2), 123–140. DOI: 10.1177/014920630102700201

Mazmanian, M., Orlikowski, W. J., & Yates, J. (2013). The autonomy paradox: The implications of mobile email devices for knowledge professionals. *Organization Science*, 24(5), 1337–1357. DOI: 10.1287/orsc.1120.0806

Nelson, B. B. (2012). 1501 ways to reward employees. Hachette UK.

Noe, R. A. (2020). *Employee training and development*. McGraw-Hill.

Pratt, M. G., & Ashforth, B. E. (2003). Fostering meaningfulness in working and at work. Positive organizational scholarship: Foundations of a new discipline, 309, 327.

Ragins, B. R., & Dutton, J. E. (2017). Positive relationships at work: An introduction and invitation. In *Exploring positive relationships at work* (pp. 2–24). Psychology Press. DOI: 10.4324/9781315094199-2

Reichheld, F. F. (2004). The one number you need to grow. *Harvard Business Review*, 82(6), 133–133. PMID: 14712543

Robertson, I. T., & Cooper, C. L. (2010). Full engagement: The integration of employee engagement and psychological well-being. *Leadership and Organization Development Journal*, 31(4), 324–336. DOI: 10.1108/01437731011043348

Rosso, B. D., Dekas, K. H., & Wrzesniewski, A. (2010). On the meaning of work: A theoretical integration and review. *Research in Organizational Behavior*, 30, 91–127. DOI: 10.1016/j.riob.2010.09.001

Rothbard, N. P. (2001). Enriching or depleting? The dynamics of engagement in work and family roles. *Administrative Science Quarterly*, 46(4), 655–684. DOI: 10.2307/3094827

Steger, M. F. (2016). Creating meaning and purpose at work. The Wiley Blackwell handbook of the psychology of positivity and strengths-based approaches at work, 60-81 DOI: 10.1002/9781118977620.ch5

Steger, M. F., Dik, B. J., & Duffy, R. D. (2012). Measuring meaningful work: The work and meaning inventory (WAMI). *Journal of Career Assessment*, 20(3), 322–337. DOI: 10.1177/1069072711436160

Walumbwa, F. O., Avolio, B. J., Gardner, W. L., Wernsing, T. S., & Peterson, S. J. (2008). Authentic leadership: Development and validation of a theory-based measure. *Journal of Management*, 34(1), 89–126. DOI: 10.1177/0149206307308913

Wrzesniewski, A., & Dutton, J. E. (2001). Crafting a job: Revisioning employees as active crafters of their work. *Academy of Management Review*, 26(2), 179–201. DOI: 10.2307/259118

Wrzesniewski, A., Dutton, J. E., & Debebe, G. (2003). Interpersonal sensemaking and the meaning of work. *Research in Organizational Behavior*, 25, 93–135. DOI: 10.1016/S0191-3085(03)25003-6

Zellars, K. L., Perrewé, P. L., & Rossi, A. M. (2005). Stressors, leadership, and wellness: A longitudinal assessment of stress, leadership style, and emotional response in a health care environment.

Chapter 4
Building a Foundation of Well-Being:
Strategies for Positive Work Environments

Bhavana J. Patil
PES University, India

ABSTRACT

This chapter provides a comprehensive guide for organizations to create and maintain a positive work environment, emphasizing employee well-being. It explores strategies to enhance physical, mental, and emotional health, including fostering a positive work culture, implementing health and safety programs, and promoting work-life balance. The chapter highlights leadership's role, continuous improvement, and strong workplace relationships. By adopting these strategies, organizations can boost productivity, job satisfaction, and overall success. The chapter covers understanding well-being, creating a positive work culture, physical and mental health initiatives, building strong relationships, and continuous improvement and feedback. It concludes by emphasizing the continuous effort required from both leaders and employees to build a foundation of well-being, leading to greater productivity, job satisfaction, and overall success.

INTRODUCTION

In an era marked by rapid change and increasing demands, the quest for organizational well-being has become a critical focus for leaders, employees, and stakeholders alike. The concept of well-being, once considered a peripheral concern, has now taken centre stage in discussions about workplace culture and productivity. The

DOI: 10.4018/979-8-3693-8457-2.ch004

profound impact that a positive work environment has on employee satisfaction, engagement, and overall organizational success has underscored the necessity of developing strategies that foster well-being at all levels of the organization.

The journey toward building a foundation of well-being in the workplace is not merely about implementing policies or programs; it is about creating a culture that values and supports the holistic development of its members. This chapter, aims to delve into the essence of workplace well-being, exploring its significance, benefits, and the common challenges that impede its realization. By addressing these aspects comprehensively, the chapter will provide a roadmap for organizations seeking to harness happiness and wisdom to enhance their overall well-being.

The Paradigm Shift in Workplace Well-Being

Historically, workplace well-being was often relegated to the realm of perks and benefits, such as gym memberships or wellness programs. However, contemporary research and practice have demonstrated that well-being is far more integral to organizational success than merely a set of add-ons. The modern understanding of well-being encompasses not only physical health but also emotional, psychological, and social dimensions. This broader perspective recognizes that a truly positive work environment nurtures employees' entire well-being, leading to enhanced performance, creativity, and job satisfaction.

This chapter will begin by defining well-being within the workplace context, followed by an exploration of its benefits for both employees and organizations. It will also address the common challenges that hinder well-being, such as stress and burnout, and propose strategies to overcome these obstacles. By adopting a holistic approach, the chapter aims to offer actionable insights for building a supportive and thriving work environment.

SECTION 1: UNDERSTANDING THE IMPORTANCE OF WELL-BEING IN THE WORKPLACE

1.1 Defining Workplace Well-Being

Workplace well-being is a multifaceted concept that goes beyond the physical health of employees to encompass emotional, psychological, and social aspects. According to the World Health Organization (WHO), well-being is defined as "a state of complete physical, mental, and social health, not merely the absence of disease or infirmity" (WHO, 2024). In the context of the workplace, well-being can be understood as a holistic state where employees feel valued, supported, and engaged, leading to a positive and productive work environment.

1.1.1 Physical Well-Being

Physical well-being involves the health and fitness of employees, including aspects such as nutrition, exercise, and overall health management. Healthy employees are more likely to be productive, less prone to illness, and better equipped to handle the physical demands of their jobs (Smith, 2023). Organizations that promote physical well-being through health initiatives, ergonomic workspaces, and wellness programs are likely to see improvements in employee satisfaction and performance.

1.1.2 Emotional Well-Being

Emotional well-being refers to the ability of employees to manage their emotions effectively, maintain positive relationships, and cope with stress. Emotional well-being is crucial for job satisfaction, as employees who feel emotionally supported are more likely to be engaged and motivated (Johnson & Lee, 2022). Strategies to enhance emotional well-being include providing access to mental health resources, fostering a supportive work culture, and encouraging open communication.

1.1.3 Psychological Well-Being

Psychological well-being encompasses aspects such as self-esteem, resilience, and a sense of purpose. Employees who experience psychological well-being are more likely to have a positive outlook on their work, exhibit higher levels of creativity, and demonstrate greater problem-solving abilities (Davis et al., 2021). Psychological well-being can be supported through career development opportunities, recognition programs, and a positive organizational culture.

1.1.4 Social Well-Being

Social well-being involves the quality of interpersonal relationships and the sense of belonging within the workplace. Strong social connections and a supportive work environment contribute to job satisfaction and reduce feelings of isolation (Brown & Wilson, 2023). Enhancing social well-being can be achieved by fostering team collaboration, encouraging social interactions, and building a sense of community within the organization.

1.2 Benefits of Workplace Well-Being

Promoting well-being in the workplace yields numerous benefits for both employees and organizations. These benefits can be categorized into several key areas:

1.2.1 Enhanced Employee Engagement and Productivity

Employees who experience well-being are more likely to be engaged in their work, resulting in higher productivity levels. Research indicates that engaged employees are more motivated, perform better, and are more committed to their organization (Kahn, 2023). Organizations that prioritize well-being can expect improved performance and a more positive work environment.

1.2.2 Reduced Absenteeism and Turnover

Well-being initiatives have been linked to lower levels of absenteeism and turnover. Employees who feel supported and valued are less likely to take sick leave or leave the organization altogether. A study by Lee and Brown (2022) found that organizations with comprehensive well-being programs experienced a significant reduction in employee turnover and absenteeism.

1.2.3 Improved Employee Satisfaction and Retention

Employees who experience high levels of well-being are more satisfied with their jobs and are more likely to stay with their current employer. Job satisfaction is closely related to well-being, with satisfied employees being more likely to remain with their organization and contribute positively to its success (Smith & Patel, 2023).

1.2.4 Enhanced Organizational Reputation

Organizations that invest in well-being are perceived as attractive employers, which can enhance their reputation and help attract top talent. Positive word-of-mouth and a strong employer brand can further contribute to organizational success and competitiveness in the job market (Harris et al., 2024).

1.2.5 Increased Innovation and Creativity

A supportive and positive work environment fosters creativity and innovation. Employees who feel secure and valued are more likely to take risks, share ideas, and contribute to innovative solutions (Anderson & De Dreu, 2022). Organizations that prioritize well-being can benefit from increased creativity and a culture of continuous improvement.

1.3 Common Challenges to Workplace Well-Being

Despite the recognized benefits, achieving and maintaining workplace well-being is not without its challenges. Several factors can impede the realization of a positive work environment, including:

1.3.1 Stress and Burnout

Stress and burnout are among the most significant barriers to workplace well-being. High levels of stress can lead to physical and mental health issues, reduced productivity, and increased absenteeism. Burnout, characterized by emotional exhaustion, depersonalization, and reduced personal accomplishment, can severely impact employees' well-being and performance (Maslach & Leiter, 2023).

Organizations can address stress and burnout by implementing stress management programs, providing resources for mental health support, and promoting a healthy work-life balance. Encouraging employees to take breaks, offering flexible work arrangements, and fostering a supportive work environment can also help mitigate stress and prevent burnout.

1.3.2 Poor Work-Life Balance

Maintaining a healthy work-life balance is crucial for employee well-being. Overworking and difficulty balancing professional and personal responsibilities can lead to burnout, decreased job satisfaction, and negative health outcomes (Greenhaus & Beutell, 2022). Organizations can support work-life balance by offering flexible work hours, remote work options, and policies that accommodate employees' personal needs.

1.3.3 Lack of Supportive Leadership

Leadership plays a critical role in shaping the work environment and influencing employee well-being. Leaders who fail to provide support, recognition, and effective communication can contribute to a negative work environment and reduced employee satisfaction (Houghton & Yoho, 2023). Training leaders to be supportive and empathetic, and fostering a culture of open communication and feedback, can enhance well-being and improve organizational outcomes.

1.3.4 Inadequate Resources and Support

Insufficient resources and support can hinder employees' ability to perform their tasks effectively and contribute to feelings of frustration and stress. Providing adequate tools, training, and resources is essential for ensuring that employees can meet their job demands and maintain well-being (Cohen & McKay, 2022). Regularly assessing and addressing resource needs can help prevent issues related to inadequate support.

1.3.5 Organizational Culture and Climate

The overall culture and climate of an organization can significantly impact employee well-being. A negative or toxic work environment characterized by conflict, discrimination, or lack of trust can undermine efforts to promote well-being and contribute to high levels of stress and dissatisfaction (Denison et al., 2024). Cultivating a positive organizational culture through values-based leadership, team-building activities, and inclusive practices can foster a supportive work environment.

Sure, let's expand on each point in detail and include citations and APA references. I'll provide a more comprehensive explanation for each sub-section. You can then further expand these points to reach your desired word count.

2. CREATING A POSITIVE WORK CULTURE

2.1 The Role of Leadership and Management

2.1.1 Vision and Values

Leaders are instrumental in defining and communicating the vision and values of an organization. A clear vision provides direction and purpose, while core values establish the principles that guide behavior within the organization. For instance, Google's mission to "organize the world's information and make it universally accessible and useful" drives its innovative culture and strategic decisions (Google, n.d.). Leaders must consistently communicate and embody these values to ensure they are integrated into the organizational culture (Schein, 2010).

2.1.2 Emotional Intelligence

Emotional intelligence (EI) is the ability to understand and manage one's own emotions and the emotions of others. Leaders with high EI can create a supportive and productive work environment by fostering positive relationships and effectively managing conflict (Goleman, 1995). For example, a leader who recognizes an employee's stress and provides support can enhance that employee's well-being and productivity (Cherniss, 2001).

2.1.3 Leading by Example

Leaders set the tone for organizational behavior by modeling the values and behaviours they wish to see in their employees. This concept, known as "leading by example," is crucial for building trust and credibility. When leaders demonstrate integrity, accountability, and respect, they encourage similar behaviours among their team members (Kouzes & Posner, 2017). For instance, a leader who consistently meets deadlines and maintains high ethical standards sets a benchmark for employees to follow.

2.1.4 Open Communication

Open communication is vital for a positive work culture. Leaders should foster an environment where employees feel comfortable sharing their ideas, feedback, and concerns. This can be achieved through regular team meetings, one-on-one check-ins, and anonymous feedback channels (Men, 2014). Transparent communication helps build trust and ensures that employees feel valued and heard (Clampitt, 2016).

2.2 Strategies to Increase Employee Engagement

2.2.1 Recognition and Rewards

Recognizing and rewarding employees for their contributions is a powerful motivator. Recognition can be formal, such as awards and bonuses, or informal, such as verbal praise and thank-you notes. Research shows that recognition programs can significantly boost employee morale and engagement (Bersin, 2012). For example, companies like Zappos have implemented robust recognition programs that celebrate employee achievements and foster a positive work environment (Hsieh, 2010).

2.2.2 Growth Opportunities

Providing opportunities for professional growth and development is essential for maintaining high levels of employee engagement. This includes offering training programs, mentorship, and career advancement opportunities. Employees who feel that their organization is invested in their growth are more likely to be engaged and committed (Noe, 2017). For instance, IBM's extensive training programs help employees develop new skills and advance their careers within the company (IBM, n.d.).

2.2.3 Employee Involvement

Involving employees in decision-making processes increases their commitment and engagement. This can be achieved through consultative meetings, feedback sessions, and collaborative projects. When employees feel that their opinions are valued and that they have a say in the direction of the company, they are more likely to be motivated and engaged (Vroom & Jago, 1988). For example, companies like Google encourage employee involvement through initiatives like "20% time," where employees can spend 20% of their time working on projects of their choice (Google, n.d.).

2.2.4 Work-Life Balance

Promoting a healthy work-life balance is crucial for preventing burnout and increasing job satisfaction. Flexible working hours, remote work options, and encouraging regular breaks are effective strategies. Research shows that employees who have a good work-life balance are more productive and less likely to experience stress and burnout (Kossek & Ozeki, 1998). For instance, companies like Microsoft offer flexible work arrangements to help employees balance their personal and professional lives (Microsoft, n.d.).

2.3 Promoting Inclusivity and Diversity

2.3.1 Inclusive Leadership

Inclusive leadership involves creating an environment where all employees feel valued and respected. This includes hiring diverse talent, promoting equal opportunities, and fostering an inclusive work environment. Leaders who prioritize inclusivity can drive innovation and improve organizational performance (Shore et al., 2011). For example, companies like Salesforce have implemented comprehensive diversity and inclusion programs to ensure that all employees feel included and valued (Salesforce, n.d.).

2.3.2 Bias Training

Implementing bias training programs helps employees recognize and mitigate unconscious biases, promoting a more inclusive workplace. Bias training can include workshops, seminars, and online courses that educate employees about the impact of biases and how to overcome them (Kalev, Dobbin, & Kelly, 2006). For instance, Starbucks has implemented bias training programs to promote inclusivity and prevent discrimination (Starbucks, n.d.).

2.3.3 Employee Resource Groups

Supporting employee resource groups (ERGs) based on shared identities or interests fosters a sense of belonging and community within the organization. ERGs provide a platform for employees to connect, share experiences, and advocate for their needs (Friedman & Holtom, 2002). For example, companies like IBM have numerous ERGs that support various employee communities, such as women, LGBTQ+ individuals, and veterans (IBM, n.d.).

2.3.4 Celebrating Diversity

Celebrating cultural and religious diversity through events and activities promotes understanding and respect among employees. This can include cultural festivals, diversity days, and educational workshops. Celebrating diversity helps create an inclusive work environment where all employees feel valued and respected (Thomas, 1990). For instance, companies like Google celebrate diversity through various initiatives and events that highlight different cultures and traditions (Google, n.d.).

3. PHYSICAL AND MENTAL HEALTH INITIATIVES

3.1 Implementation of Health and Safety Programs

Implementing health and safety programs is crucial for creating a safe and productive work environment. These programs help prevent workplace accidents, injuries, and occupational diseases by establishing systematic policies and procedures. Let's delve deeper into the key components of health and safety programs and their benefits.

3.1.1 Ergonomic Assessments

Ergonomic assessments are essential for identifying and mitigating risks associated with workplace injuries, particularly musculoskeletal disorders (MSDs). These assessments involve evaluating workstations, tools, and tasks to ensure they fit the physical capabilities of employees. The goal is to minimize the risk of injuries caused by repetitive motions, awkward postures, and prolonged sitting or standing.

Steps in Ergonomic Assessments:

1. **Workplace History Review**: Analysing past injury reports and worker's compensation claims to identify high-risk areas. This helps in understanding the common issues faced by employees and targeting specific areas for improvement.
2. **Risk Factor Identification**: Observing employees' interactions with their work environment to pinpoint ergonomic hazards. This includes assessing the layout of workstations, the design of tools, and the physical demands of tasks.
3. **Implementation of Solutions**: Introducing ergonomic equipment and redesigning workstations to improve posture and reduce strain. For example, providing adjustable chairs, ergonomic keyboards, and proper lighting can significantly reduce the risk of repetitive strain injuries (Occupational Safety and Health Administration [OSHA], n.d.).

Benefits of Ergonomic Assessments:

- **Reduced Injury Rates**: Proper ergonomic practices can significantly lower the incidence of work-related injuries, leading to fewer worker's compensation claims and medical expenses.
- **Increased Productivity**: Comfortable employees are more productive and less likely to take sick leave. Ergonomic improvements can enhance efficiency by reducing physical discomfort and fatigue.
- **Enhanced Employee Satisfaction**: A safe and comfortable work environment boosts morale and job satisfaction, leading to higher employee retention and engagement (Proactive MD, n.d.).

3.1.2 Wellness Workshops

Wellness workshops are educational sessions aimed at promoting healthy behaviours among employees. These workshops can cover a wide range of topics, including nutrition, exercise, mental health, and stress management. They are designed to provide employees with the knowledge and tools they need to maintain their health and well-being.

Types of Wellness Workshops:

1. **Nutrition Workshops**: Educating employees about healthy eating habits and providing tips for meal planning. These workshops can include cooking demonstrations, dietary advice, and information on the benefits of a balanced diet.
2. **Fitness Workshops**: Offering exercise routines and fitness challenges to encourage physical activity. These sessions can include yoga classes, strength training, and aerobic exercises tailored to different fitness levels.
3. **Mental Health Workshops**: Teaching stress management techniques, mindfulness practices, and coping strategies for anxiety and depression. These workshops can help employees develop resilience and improve their mental well-being (Wellable, n.d.).

Benefits of Wellness Workshops:

- **Increased Awareness**: Educating employees about the importance of health and wellness. This knowledge empowers employees to make healthier choices in their daily lives.
- **Behavioral Change**: Encouraging the adoption of healthier lifestyles through practical tips and activities. Workshops can motivate employees to incorporate healthy habits into their routines.
- **Community Building**: Fostering a sense of camaraderie and support among employees. Wellness workshops provide opportunities for employees to connect and support each other in their health journeys (Positive Psychology, n.d.).

3.1.3 Safety Training Programs

Safety training programs are designed to educate employees about workplace hazards and safe work practices. These programs are essential for ensuring that employees understand how to perform their tasks safely and are aware of the potential risks in their work environment.

Components of Safety Training Programs:

1. **Hazard Identification**: Training employees to recognize and report potential hazards in the workplace. This includes understanding the types of hazards (e.g., physical, chemical, biological) and knowing how to mitigate them.

2. **Safe Work Practices**: Teaching employees the correct procedures for performing tasks safely. This can include proper lifting techniques, the use of personal protective equipment (PPE), and emergency response protocols.
3. **Regular Drills and Simulations**: Conducting regular safety drills and simulations to ensure employees are prepared for emergencies. This can include fire drills, evacuation procedures, and first aid training (SafetyCulture, n.d.).

Benefits of Safety Training Programs:

- **Improved Safety Awareness**: Increasing employees' awareness of workplace hazards and safe work practices. This knowledge helps prevent accidents and injuries.
- **Compliance with Regulations**: Ensuring that the organization complies with occupational health and safety regulations. Proper training helps avoid legal issues and potential fines.
- **Enhanced Safety Culture**: Promoting a culture of safety within the organization. When employees are well-trained and safety-conscious, it creates a safer and more supportive work environment (OSHA, n.d.).

3.2 Provision of Mental Health Support

Providing mental health support in the workplace is essential for fostering a healthy, productive, and engaged workforce. This section delves into the various strategies and programs that organizations can implement to support their employees' mental health.

3.2.1 Counselling Services

Counselling services offer employees access to professional mental health support, helping them manage stress, anxiety, depression, and other mental health issues. These services can be provided through Employee Assistance Programs (EAPs), which often include confidential counselling sessions available in-person, over the phone, or online.

Components of Effective Counselling Services:

1. **Accessibility**: Ensuring that counselling services are easily accessible to all employees is crucial. This can be achieved by offering multiple modes of access, such as in-person sessions, teletherapy, and online chat options. For example, companies like Heart It Out provide online counselling services that employees can access from the comfort of their homes (Heart It Out, n.d.).

2. **Confidentiality**: Maintaining strict confidentiality is essential to encourage employees to seek help without fear of stigma. Confidentiality ensures that employees feel safe discussing their issues, knowing that their privacy is protected. Organizations should clearly communicate their confidentiality policies to build trust (TherapyRoute, n.d.).
3. **Comprehensive Support**: Offering a range of services, including individual therapy, group sessions, and crisis intervention, ensures that employees receive the support they need. Comprehensive support can address various mental health issues and provide tailored solutions for different needs. For instance, some EAPs offer specialized programs for substance abuse, grief counselling, and family therapy (American Psychological Association [APA], 2024).

Benefits of Counselling Services:

- **Improved Mental Health**: Providing support for employees to manage mental health issues effectively can lead to better overall well-being and job performance.
- **Reduced Absenteeism**: Lowering the number of sick days taken due to mental health-related issues can improve productivity and reduce costs associated with absenteeism.
- **Enhanced Productivity**: Helping employees maintain focus and productivity by addressing mental health concerns can lead to a more engaged and efficient workforce (APA, 2024).

3.2.2 Stress Management Programs

Stress management programs are designed to help employees cope with work-related stress. These programs can include workshops, relaxation techniques, and access to stress management resources. Effective stress management programs can significantly improve employees' mental health and overall job satisfaction.

Components of Stress Management Programs:

1. **Workshops**: Offering sessions on stress management techniques, such as mindfulness, meditation, and relaxation exercises, can equip employees with practical tools to manage stress. For example, mindfulness workshops can teach employees how to stay present and reduce anxiety (Mayo Clinic, n.d.).
2. **Resources**: Providing access to stress management tools, such as apps, online resources, and self-help guides, can help employees manage stress on their own time. Apps like Headspace and Calm offer guided meditations and relaxation exercises that employees can use daily (Frontiers, 2023).

3. **Support Groups**: Creating support groups where employees can share their experiences and coping strategies can foster a sense of community and mutual support. Support groups can be facilitated by trained professionals or peer leaders and can address various topics, such as work-life balance, parenting, and chronic stress (American Institute of Stress, n.d.).

Benefits of Stress Management Programs:

- **Reduced Absenteeism**: Lowering the number of sick days taken due to stress-related illnesses can improve overall productivity.
- **Improved Productivity**: Enhancing focus and efficiency by reducing stress levels can lead to better job performance.
- **Enhanced Well-being**: Promoting overall mental and physical health can lead to a happier and more engaged workforce (American Institute of Stress, n.d.).

3.2.3 Mental Health Awareness Campaigns

Mental health awareness campaigns aim to reduce stigma and promote understanding of mental health issues within the workplace. These campaigns can include educational materials, workshops, and events that raise awareness about mental health and encourage employees to seek help when needed.

Components of Mental Health Awareness Campaigns:

1. **Educational Materials**: Providing employees with information about mental health issues, including symptoms, treatment options, and resources, can increase awareness and understanding. Educational materials can be distributed through newsletters, posters, and online platforms (APA, 2024).
2. **Workshops and Training**: Offering workshops and training sessions on mental health topics can educate employees and managers about recognizing and addressing mental health issues. Training can include topics such as mental health first aid, stress management, and creating a supportive work environment (Forbes, 2021).
3. **Events and Activities**: Organizing events and activities, such as mental health fairs, guest speaker sessions, and wellness challenges, can engage employees and promote mental health awareness. These events can provide opportunities for employees to learn about mental health resources and connect with support networks (APA, 2024).

Benefits of Mental Health Awareness Campaigns:

- **Reduced Stigma**: Increasing awareness and understanding of mental health issues can reduce stigma and encourage employees to seek help.
- **Improved Support**: Educating employees and managers about mental health can lead to better support for those experiencing mental health issues.
- **Enhanced Workplace Culture**: Promoting mental health awareness can create a more supportive and inclusive workplace culture (Forbes, 2021).

3.3 Encouragement of Stress Management Programs

Stress management programs are essential for maintaining a healthy and productive workforce. These programs help employees cope with work-related stress, improve their mental health, and enhance overall job satisfaction. Let's explore the various components and benefits of stress management programs in detail.

3.3.1 Components of Stress Management Programs

1. Workshops and Training Sessions

Workshops and training sessions are fundamental components of stress management programs. These sessions educate employees about stress, its effects, and effective coping strategies. Topics can include mindfulness, relaxation techniques, time management, and resilience building.

- **Mindfulness and Meditation**: Mindfulness workshops teach employees how to stay present and reduce anxiety. Techniques such as deep breathing, meditation, and progressive muscle relaxation can help employees manage stress effectively (Mayo Clinic, n.d.).
- **Time Management**: Training sessions on time management can help employees prioritize tasks, set realistic goals, and avoid procrastination. Effective time management reduces the feeling of being overwhelmed and enhances productivity (American Psychological Association [APA], 2024).
- **Resilience Building**: Resilience training helps employees develop the ability to bounce back from setbacks and adapt to challenging situations. This can include cognitive-behavioral techniques, positive thinking, and problem-solving skills (Frontiers, 2023).

2. Access to Stress Management Resources

Providing employees with access to stress management resources is crucial for ongoing support. These resources can include apps, online tools, self-help guides, and relaxation exercises.

- **Stress Management Apps**: Apps like Headspace and Calm offer guided meditations, relaxation exercises, and mindfulness practices that employees can use daily. These apps provide convenient and accessible tools for managing stress (American Institute of Stress, n.d.).
- **Online Tools and Self-Help Guides**: Online resources, such as articles, videos, and interactive tools, can educate employees about stress management techniques and provide practical tips for reducing stress (Positive Psychology, n.d.).

3. Support Groups and Peer Support

Creating support groups and peer support networks can foster a sense of community and mutual support among employees. These groups provide a safe space for employees to share their experiences, discuss coping strategies, and offer encouragement.

- **Support Groups**: Support groups can be facilitated by trained professionals or peer leaders and can address various topics, such as work-life balance, parenting, and chronic stress. Regular meetings and discussions can help employees feel less isolated and more supported (American Institute of Stress, n.d.).
- **Peer Support Networks**: Encouraging employees to form peer support networks can enhance social connections and provide informal support. Peer support can include check-ins, buddy systems, and mentorship programs (Forbes, 2021).

3.3.2 Benefits of Stress Management Programs

Implementing stress management programs in the workplace offers numerous benefits for both employees and organizations.

1. Improved Mental Health

Stress management programs help employees manage stress effectively, leading to improved mental health. Techniques such as mindfulness, relaxation exercises, and cognitive-behavioral strategies can reduce symptoms of anxiety and depression (Mayo Clinic, n.d.).

2. Enhanced Productivity

By reducing stress levels, employees can maintain focus and efficiency, leading to enhanced productivity. Stress management programs help employees develop better time management skills, prioritize tasks, and avoid burnout (APA, 2024).

3. Reduced Absenteeism

Effective stress management can lower the number of sick days taken due to stress-related illnesses. Employees who manage stress well are less likely to experience burnout and physical health issues, resulting in reduced absenteeism (American Institute of Stress, n.d.).

4. Increased Job Satisfaction

Stress management programs contribute to a positive work environment, leading to increased job satisfaction. Employees who feel supported and equipped to handle stress are more likely to be engaged and committed to their work (Forbes, 2021).

5. Enhanced Workplace Culture

Promoting stress management and mental health awareness creates a supportive and inclusive workplace culture. Organizations that prioritize employee well-being foster a positive work environment where employees feel valued and respected (Positive Psychology, n.d.).

4. BUILDING STRONG RELATIONSHIPS WITHIN THE WORKPLACE

4.1 Organization of Team-Building Activities

Team-building activities are essential for fostering strong relationships among employees, enhancing communication, and building trust within teams. These activities help break down barriers, improve collaboration, and create a positive work environment. Let's delve deeper into the various aspects of organizing effective team-building activities.

4.1.1 Importance of Team-Building Activities

Team-building activities play a crucial role in creating a cohesive and collaborative work environment. They help employees develop better communication skills, build trust, and improve their ability to work together effectively. Research shows that team-building can significantly enhance job satisfaction, productivity, and overall organizational performance (Indeed, 2024).

Key Benefits of Team-Building Activities:

- **Improved Communication**: Team-building activities encourage open communication and help break down silos within the organization. Employees learn to express their ideas clearly and listen to others, which enhances overall team dynamics (Surf Office, 2024).
- **Increased Trust**: Participating in team-building activities helps build trust among team members. Trust is essential for effective collaboration and problem-solving (Indeed, 2024).
- **Enhanced Morale**: Fun and engaging activities can boost employee morale and job satisfaction. When employees enjoy their work environment, they are more likely to be motivated and productive (BetterUp, 2022).
- **Better Problem-Solving**: Team-building activities that focus on problem-solving can improve the team's ability to tackle challenges effectively. These activities encourage creative thinking and collaboration (teambuilding.com, 2024).

4.1.2 Types of Team-Building Activities

There are various types of team-building activities that organizations can implement to strengthen team bonds. These activities can be tailored to meet the specific needs and preferences of the team.

1. Icebreaker Activities

Icebreaker activities are designed to help team members get to know each other better. These activities are particularly useful for new teams or when new members join an existing team. Examples include:

- **Two Truths and a Lie**: Each team member shares two true statements and one false statement about themselves. The rest of the team tries to guess which statement is false. This activity helps team members learn interesting facts about each other and fosters a sense of camaraderie (SessionLab, 2024).
- **Human Knot**: Team members stand in a circle, hold hands with two different people, and try to untangle themselves without letting go. This activity promotes teamwork, communication, and problem-solving (Growth Tactics, 2024).

2. Problem-Solving Activities

Problem-solving activities encourage collaboration and critical thinking. These activities help teams develop problem-solving skills and learn to work together under pressure. Examples include:

- **Escape Rooms**: Teams work together to solve puzzles and find clues to "escape" from a locked room within a set time limit. This activity promotes critical thinking, communication, and teamwork (teambuilding.com, 2024).
- **Scavenger Hunts**: Teams search for specific items or complete tasks based on a list of clues. This activity encourages creativity, collaboration, and strategic thinking (BetterUp, 2022).

3. Outdoor Activities

Outdoor activities provide a relaxed environment where employees can bond outside the office setting. These activities can help build camaraderie and trust among team members. Examples include:

- **Hiking**: Organizing a group hike allows team members to enjoy nature while engaging in physical activity. This activity promotes teamwork, communication, and a sense of adventure (teambuilding.com, 2024).
- **Sports**: Organizing sports events, such as soccer or volleyball matches, encourages friendly competition and teamwork. These activities help team members build trust and improve their physical fitness (BetterUp, 2022).

4. Workshops and Training Sessions

Workshops and training sessions on topics like communication, leadership, and conflict resolution can help teams develop essential skills while fostering a sense of unity. These sessions can be facilitated by external experts or internal leaders. Examples include:

- **Communication Workshops**: These workshops focus on improving verbal and non-verbal communication skills. Activities may include role-playing, active listening exercises, and group discussions (SessionLab, 2024).
- **Leadership Training**: Leadership workshops help team members develop leadership skills and understand different leadership styles. Activities may include case studies, group projects, and leadership assessments (BetterUp, 2022).

4.1.3 Benefits of Team-Building Activities

Implementing team-building activities in the workplace offers numerous benefits for both employees and organizations.

1. **Improved Communication** Team-building activities encourage open communication and help break down silos within the organization. Employees learn to express their ideas clearly and listen to others, which enhances overall team dynamics. Improved communication leads to better collaboration and more effective problem-solving (Indeed, 2024).
2. **Increased Trust** Participating in team-building activities helps build trust among team members. Trust is essential for effective collaboration and problem-solving. When team members trust each other, they are more likely to share ideas, take risks, and support one another (Surf Office, 2024).
3. **Enhanced Morale** Fun and engaging activities can boost employee morale and job satisfaction. When employees enjoy their work environment, they are more likely to be motivated and productive. High morale leads to increased job satisfaction and lower turnover rates (BetterUp, 2022).
4. **Better Problem-Solving** Team-building activities that focus on problem-solving can improve the team's ability to tackle challenges effectively. These activities encourage creative thinking and collaboration. Teams that can solve problems together are more resilient and adaptable (teambuilding.com, 2024).
5. **Increased Productivity** When team members communicate effectively, trust each other, and enjoy their work environment, they are more productive. Team-building activities help create a positive work environment where employees feel valued and motivated to perform at their best (Indeed, 2024).

4.2 Encouragement of Open and Transparent Communication

Open and transparent communication is fundamental to creating a collaborative and trustworthy workplace. It involves sharing information openly, honestly, and consistently across all levels of the organization. This section explores the importance of open communication, strategies to promote it, and the benefits it brings to the workplace.

4.2.1 Importance of Open Communication

Open communication is crucial for several reasons. It fosters a culture of trust, enhances collaboration, and ensures that all employees are aligned with the organization's goals and values. When communication is transparent, employees feel valued and informed, which can lead to higher engagement and productivity (Leaders.com, 2022).

Key Benefits of Open Communication:

- **Increased Trust**: Transparent communication builds trust between employees and management. When employees are kept in the loop about decisions and changes, they are more likely to trust their leaders and feel secure in their roles (Hutchison, 2020).
- **Enhanced Collaboration**: Open communication encourages collaboration by breaking down silos and promoting the sharing of ideas and information. This leads to more innovative solutions and better problem-solving (Growth Tactics, 2023).
- **Improved Employee Engagement**: Employees who feel informed and valued are more likely to be engaged and committed to their work. Open communication helps employees understand their role in the organization and how their work contributes to overall success (Indeed, 2024).
- **Reduced Conflict**: Transparent communication can help prevent misunderstandings and conflicts by ensuring that everyone has the same information and understands the reasons behind decisions (Betterworks, 2023).

4.2.2 Strategies for Promoting Open Communication

Implementing strategies to promote open communication can help create a more transparent and collaborative work environment. Here are some effective strategies:

1. Regular Team Meetings

Regular team meetings provide a platform for open dialogue and information sharing. These meetings should be structured to allow for open discussion, feedback, and updates from all team members.

- **Weekly Check-Ins**: Holding weekly check-ins where team members can share their progress, challenges, and feedback helps keep everyone informed and aligned. These meetings should be inclusive and encourage participation from all team members (Leaders.com, 2022).
- **All-Hands Meetings**: Organizing regular all-hands meetings where leadership shares updates on company performance, goals, and changes can help ensure that all employees are informed and engaged (Betterworks, 2023).

2. Open-Door Policy

An open-door policy encourages employees to approach managers and leaders with their concerns, ideas, and feedback. This policy should be clearly communicated and consistently practiced to ensure that employees feel comfortable speaking up.

- **Accessibility**: Leaders should make themselves accessible to employees by keeping their office doors open and being available for impromptu discussions. This helps build trust and encourages open communication (Insight Global, 2024).
- **Active Listening**: Managers should practice active listening by giving their full attention to employees, acknowledging their concerns, and providing thoughtful responses. This demonstrates that leaders value and respect their employees' input (HubSpot, 2023).

3. Anonymous Feedback Channels

Providing anonymous feedback channels allows employees to voice their opinions and concerns without fear of judgment or repercussions. This can help identify issues that may not be raised in open forums.

- **Suggestion Boxes**: Placing suggestion boxes in common areas where employees can submit anonymous feedback can help gather valuable insights and address concerns (CultureMonkey, 2024).
- **Online Surveys**: Conducting regular online surveys to collect anonymous feedback on various aspects of the workplace can help identify areas for improvement and track employee satisfaction (Betterworks, 2023).

4. Transparent Decision-Making

Ensuring that decision-making processes are transparent helps build trust and ensures that employees understand the rationale behind decisions. This involves explaining the reasons for decisions and how they align with the organization's goals and values.

- **Clear Communication**: Leaders should communicate decisions clearly and provide context to help employees understand the reasons behind them. This can be done through emails, meetings, or internal newsletters (Hutchison, 2020).
- **Involvement in Decision-Making**: Involving employees in decision-making processes, such as through consultative meetings or focus groups, can help ensure that their perspectives are considered and valued (Leaders.com, 2022).

4.2.3 Benefits of Open Communication

Implementing open communication strategies in the workplace offers numerous benefits for both employees and organizations.

1. Increased Collaboration

Open communication fosters a collaborative environment where employees feel comfortable sharing ideas and working together. This leads to more innovative solutions and better problem-solving (Growth Tactics, 2023).

2. Enhanced Trust

Transparency builds trust between employees and management. When employees are kept informed about decisions and changes, they are more likely to trust their leaders and feel secure in their roles (Hutchison, 2020)[2].

3. Greater Innovation

When employees are informed and feel heard, they are more likely to contribute innovative ideas. Open communication encourages the sharing of ideas and fosters a culture of creativity (Betterworks, 2023).

4. Improved Employee Satisfaction

Employees who feel informed and valued are more satisfied with their jobs and more engaged in their work. Open communication helps employees understand their role in the organization and how their work contributes to overall success (Indeed, 2024).

5. Reduced Conflict

Transparent communication can help prevent misunderstandings and conflicts by ensuring that everyone has the same information and understands the reasons behind decisions. This leads to a more harmonious work environment (Betterworks, 2023).

4.3 Implementation of Strategies for Resolving Conflicts Constructively

Conflict is an inevitable part of any workplace, but how it is managed can significantly impact the work environment. Constructive conflict resolution ensures that disagreements are addressed in a way that promotes understanding and collaboration rather than resentment and division. This section explores the importance of conflict resolution, strategies for resolving conflicts constructively, and the benefits of effective conflict management.

4.3.1 Importance of Conflict Resolution

Effective conflict resolution is crucial for maintaining a harmonious and productive work environment. When conflicts are managed constructively, they can lead to positive outcomes such as improved relationships, enhanced problem-solving, and increased innovation. Conversely, unresolved conflicts can result in decreased morale, reduced productivity, and higher turnover rates (Harvard Business School, 2023).

Key Reasons for Addressing Conflict:

- **Prevents Escalation**: Addressing conflicts early prevents them from escalating into more significant issues that can disrupt the workplace.
- **Enhances Relationships**: Constructive conflict resolution can strengthen relationships by fostering mutual respect and understanding.
- **Promotes Innovation**: Conflicts often arise from differing perspectives. When managed well, these differences can lead to creative solutions and innovation.
- **Reduces Stress**: Unresolved conflicts can create a stressful work environment. Effective conflict resolution reduces stress and promotes a positive workplace culture (Risely, 2024).

4.3.2 Strategies for Resolving Conflicts

Implementing effective conflict resolution strategies can help ensure that conflicts are managed constructively. Here are some key strategies:

1. Active Listening

Active listening involves fully concentrating, understanding, responding, and remembering what the other person is saying. It is a crucial skill for resolving conflicts as it ensures that all parties feel heard and understood.

- **Techniques**: Active listening techniques include maintaining eye contact, nodding, summarizing what the other person has said, and asking clarifying questions. This demonstrates empathy and helps build trust (Frantically Speaking, 2024).
- **Benefits**: Active listening can de-escalate tensions, clarify misunderstandings, and foster a collaborative atmosphere.

2. Mediation

Mediation involves bringing in a neutral third party to facilitate the resolution of a conflict. The mediator helps the parties communicate more effectively and work towards a mutually acceptable solution.

- **Process**: The mediation process typically involves separate and joint meetings with the parties involved, identifying the issues, exploring potential solutions, and reaching an agreement (Positive Psychology, 2024).
- **Benefits**: Mediation can help resolve conflicts more quickly and amicably than formal grievance procedures. It also empowers the parties to find their own solutions.

3. Collaborative Problem-Solving

Collaborative problem-solving involves working together to identify the root cause of the conflict and develop solutions that address the needs and concerns of all parties involved.

- **Steps**: The steps in collaborative problem-solving include identifying the problem, generating possible solutions, evaluating the options, and implementing the agreed-upon solution (Psychology Today, 2024).
- **Benefits**: This approach fosters a sense of ownership and commitment to the solution, leading to more sustainable outcomes.

4. Conflict Resolution Training

Providing training on conflict resolution techniques can equip employees with the skills they need to handle disputes effectively. Training can cover topics such as negotiation, communication, and emotional intelligence.

- **Content**: Conflict resolution training programs typically include role-playing exercises, case studies, and interactive workshops to practice skills in a safe environment (BetterUp, 2021).
- **Benefits**: Training helps employees develop the confidence and competence to manage conflicts constructively, reducing the likelihood of escalation.

4.3.3 Benefits of Constructive Conflict Resolution

Implementing constructive conflict resolution strategies in the workplace offers numerous benefits for both employees and organizations.

1. Reduced Tension

Addressing conflicts constructively can reduce tension and prevent issues from escalating. This leads to a more peaceful and cooperative work environment (Harvard Business School, 2023).

2. Stronger Relationships

Effective conflict resolution can strengthen relationships by fostering mutual respect and understanding. When conflicts are resolved amicably, it builds trust and improves teamwork (Risely, 2024).

3. Increased Productivity

Resolving conflicts quickly and fairly can minimize disruptions and maintain productivity. Employees can focus on their work without being distracted by ongoing disputes (Positive Psychology, 2024).

4. Enhanced Workplace Culture

A culture that promotes constructive conflict resolution is more likely to be harmonious and supportive. This can lead to higher employee satisfaction and retention (BetterUp, 2021).

5. Greater Innovation

When conflicts are managed well, they can lead to creative solutions and innovation. Differing perspectives can be harnessed to develop new ideas and approaches (Psychology Today, 2024).

5. CONTINUOUS IMPROVEMENT AND FEEDBACK

5.1 Regular Assessments of the Work Environment

Regular assessments of the work environment are essential for maintaining a safe, productive, and positive workplace. These assessments help organizations identify areas for improvement, ensure compliance with regulations, and enhance overall employee well-being. This section delves into the importance of regular assessments, the types of assessments commonly used, and the implementation strategies for conducting these assessments effectively.

5.1.1 Importance of Regular Assessments

Regular assessments play a crucial role in maintaining a healthy and efficient work environment. They provide a systematic approach to identifying potential hazards, inefficiencies, and areas for improvement. By conducting regular assessments, organizations can proactively address issues before they escalate, ensuring a safer and more productive workplace (Brookey & Company, 2024).

Key Benefits of Regular Assessments:

- **Enhanced Employee Well-being**: Regular assessments help identify and mitigate risks, ensuring a safer and healthier work environment. This leads to fewer injuries and illnesses, reducing absenteeism and increasing productivity (SiteDocs, n.d.).
- **Improved Operational Efficiency**: By identifying inefficiencies and areas for improvement, organizations can streamline processes and enhance overall productivity (Indeed, 2024).
- **Compliance with Regulations**: Regular assessments ensure that the organization complies with health and safety regulations, avoiding potential fines and legal issues (SafetyCulture, n.d.).
- **Continuous Improvement**: Assessments provide valuable insights that guide strategic improvements and drive performance excellence. By regularly assessing and adjusting, organizations can remain competitive and responsive to internal and external changes (Brookey & Company, 2024).

5.1.2 Types of Assessments

There are various types of assessments that organizations can conduct to evaluate different aspects of the work environment. Each type of assessment serves a specific purpose and provides unique insights into the workplace.

1. Risk Assessments

Risk assessments are designed to identify potential hazards in the workplace and evaluate the risks associated with them. These assessments help organizations implement measures to prevent accidents and injuries.

- **Process**: The risk assessment process involves identifying hazards, evaluating the risks, and implementing control measures to mitigate those risks. This can include physical hazards, chemical exposures, ergonomic risks, and more (SiteDocs, n.d.).

- **Benefits**: Conducting regular risk assessments helps create a safer work environment, reducing the likelihood of accidents and injuries.

2. Performance Reviews

Performance reviews assess employees' skills, abilities, and performance. These reviews help identify areas where employees may need additional training or support and provide opportunities for professional development.

- **Process**: Performance reviews typically involve setting performance goals, evaluating employee performance against those goals, and providing feedback. This can be done through self-assessments, peer reviews, and manager evaluations (Indeed, 2024).
- **Benefits**: Regular performance reviews help employees understand their strengths and areas for improvement, fostering a culture of continuous learning and development.

3. Safety Inspections

Safety inspections involve regularly checking the workplace for safety hazards and ensuring that safety protocols are being followed. These inspections can include checking equipment, facilities, and work practices.

- **Process**: Safety inspections typically involve a checklist of safety standards and protocols that need to be reviewed. Inspectors look for potential hazards, such as faulty equipment, unsafe work practices, and non-compliance with safety regulations (SafetyCulture, n.d.).
- **Benefits**: Regular safety inspections help maintain a safe work environment, reducing the risk of accidents and ensuring compliance with safety regulations.

4. Environmental Assessments

Environmental assessments evaluate the impact of the workplace on the environment and identify opportunities for sustainability improvements. These assessments can include energy audits, waste management reviews, and assessments of environmental policies.

- **Process**: Environmental assessments involve evaluating the organization's environmental footprint, identifying areas for improvement, and implementing sustainable practices. This can include reducing energy consumption, minimizing waste, and promoting recycling (Brookey & Company, 2024).

- **Benefits**: Conducting environmental assessments helps organizations reduce their environmental impact, promote sustainability, and comply with environmental regulations.

5.1.3 Implementation of Assessments

Implementing regular assessments requires a structured approach to ensure they are conducted effectively and provide valuable insights.

1. Scheduled Assessments

Organizations should schedule regular assessments, such as quarterly or annual reviews, to ensure ongoing monitoring and improvement. Having a set schedule helps ensure that assessments are conducted consistently and that any issues are addressed promptly.

- **Process**: Establish a schedule for conducting different types of assessments, such as risk assessments, performance reviews, and safety inspections. Ensure that these assessments are integrated into the organization's regular operations (Indeed, 2024).
- **Benefits**: Scheduled assessments provide a systematic approach to monitoring and improving the work environment, ensuring that issues are identified and addressed in a timely manner.

2. Employee Involvement

Involving employees in the assessment process can provide valuable insights and foster a culture of safety and continuous improvement. Employees are often the best source of information about potential hazards and areas for improvement.

- **Process**: Encourage employees to participate in assessments by providing feedback, reporting hazards, and suggesting improvements. This can be done through surveys, suggestion boxes, and regular meetings (CultureMonkey, 2024).
- **Benefits**: Employee involvement in assessments helps ensure that all perspectives are considered, leading to more comprehensive and effective solutions.

3. Action Plans

Developing action plans based on assessment findings ensures that identified issues are addressed promptly and effectively. Action plans should outline the steps needed to address the issues, assign responsibilities, and set timelines for completion.

- **Process**: After conducting assessments, analyse the findings and develop action plans to address any identified issues. Monitor the implementation of these plans and track progress to ensure that improvements are made (Brookey & Company, 2024).
- **Benefits**: Action plans provide a clear roadmap for addressing issues and making improvements, ensuring that assessment findings lead to tangible results.

5.2 Creation of Platforms for Employee Feedback

Creating effective platforms for employee feedback is essential for fostering a culture of transparency, engagement, and continuous improvement. These platforms provide employees with the opportunity to voice their opinions, share their experiences, and contribute to the development of workplace policies and practices. This section explores the importance of employee feedback, various types of feedback platforms, and strategies for implementing these platforms effectively.

5.2.1 Importance of Employee Feedback

Employee feedback is a critical component of a healthy workplace culture. It provides valuable insights into employees' experiences, identifies areas for improvement, and fosters a sense of inclusion and engagement. When employees feel that their voices are heard and valued, they are more likely to be motivated, satisfied, and committed to their work (CultureMonkey, 2024).

Key Benefits of Employee Feedback:

- **Enhanced Employee Engagement**: Providing platforms for feedback makes employees feel valued and heard, leading to higher engagement and job satisfaction (QuestionPro, 2023).
- **Improved Decision-Making**: Feedback helps organizations make informed decisions based on employees' needs and preferences, leading to better outcomes (AllVoices, 2023).
- **Continuous Improvement**: Regular feedback enables organizations to identify and address issues promptly, fostering a culture of continuous improvement (CultureMonkey, 2024).
- **Increased Trust and Transparency**: Open feedback channels build trust between employees and management, promoting a transparent and honest work environment (WorkHound, 2023).

5.2.2 Types of Feedback Platforms

There are various types of feedback platforms that organizations can implement to gather insights from employees. Each platform serves a specific purpose and provides unique benefits.

1. Employee Surveys

Employee surveys are a common method for collecting feedback on various aspects of the workplace. They can be conducted periodically to gather insights on employee satisfaction, engagement, and areas for improvement.

- **Types of Surveys**: Surveys can include annual engagement surveys, pulse surveys, exit surveys, and onboarding surveys. Each type of survey focuses on different aspects of the employee experience (People Managing People, 2024).
- **Benefits**: Surveys provide quantitative data that can be analysed to identify trends and areas for improvement. They are also relatively easy to administer and can reach a large number of employees.

2. Suggestion Boxes

Suggestion boxes, whether physical or digital, allow employees to submit feedback anonymously. This can encourage more honest and open feedback, as employees may feel more comfortable sharing their thoughts without fear of repercussions.

- **Implementation**: Digital suggestion boxes can be integrated into the company's intranet or feedback software, allowing employees to submit suggestions at any time. Physical suggestion boxes can be placed in common areas (HubSpot, 2022).
- **Benefits**: Anonymous feedback can provide valuable insights that might not be shared through other channels. It also allows employees to voice their opinions on a wide range of topics.

3. Feedback Software

Specialized feedback software platforms, such as SurveyMonkey, Culture Amp, and TINYpulse, offer customizable surveys and feedback mechanisms to gather insights on employee satisfaction and engagement.

- **Features**: These platforms often include features such as real-time reporting, sentiment analysis, action planning tools, and integration capabilities with other HR systems (DeskAlerts, 2024).
- **Benefits**: Feedback software provides a centralized hub for collecting, analysing, and acting on feedback. It ensures that feedback is systematically gathered and used to drive improvements.

4. Performance Reviews

Performance reviews are formal assessments of employees' skills, abilities, and performance. These reviews provide an opportunity for employees to receive feedback on their work and discuss their career development.

- **Types of Reviews**: Performance reviews can include self-assessments, peer reviews, and manager evaluations. Each type of review provides different perspectives on the employee's performance (Indeed, 2024).
- **Benefits**: Performance reviews help employees understand their strengths and areas for improvement, fostering a culture of continuous learning and development.

5. Real-Time Feedback Channels

Real-time feedback channels, such as instant messaging platforms, email, or face-to-face conversations, allow employees to share feedback immediately. This can help address issues promptly and maintain open communication.

- **Implementation**: Real-time feedback can be facilitated through tools like Slack, Microsoft Teams, or dedicated feedback apps. Encouraging regular check-ins and open-door policies can also promote real-time feedback (Zavvy, 2024).
- **Benefits**: Real-time feedback allows for immediate action and resolution of issues, promoting a dynamic and responsive work environment.

5.2.3 Implementation of Feedback Platforms

Implementing effective feedback platforms requires a structured approach to ensure they are used effectively and provide valuable insights.

1. Regular Feedback Collection

Organizations should collect feedback regularly to stay updated on employees' experiences and needs. This can include conducting annual surveys, quarterly pulse surveys, and ongoing real-time feedback.

- **Process**: Establish a schedule for collecting different types of feedback, ensuring that it is integrated into the organization's regular operations. Regular feedback collection helps identify trends and areas for improvement (People Managing People, 2024).
- **Benefits**: Regular feedback collection provides a continuous stream of insights, enabling organizations to address issues promptly and make informed decisions.

2. Anonymous Feedback Options

Providing anonymous feedback options can encourage more honest and open responses. Employees may feel more comfortable sharing their thoughts without fear of judgment or repercussions.

- **Implementation**: Implement digital suggestion boxes, anonymous surveys, and feedback software that allows for anonymous submissions. Ensure that employees are aware of these options and understand how to use them (HubSpot, 2022).
- **Benefits**: Anonymous feedback can provide valuable insights that might not be shared through other channels, helping organizations address sensitive issues and improve the work environment.

3. Actionable Insights

Analyzing feedback to identify trends and areas for improvement ensures that feedback is used effectively to drive positive changes. Organizations should develop action plans based on feedback findings and monitor progress.

- **Process**: After collecting feedback, analyze the data to identify common themes and areas for improvement. Develop action plans to address these issues and track progress to ensure that improvements are made (DeskAlerts, 2024).
- **Benefits**: Actionable insights ensure that feedback leads to tangible results, fostering a culture of continuous improvement and responsiveness.

5.3 Being Flexible and Adaptable to Changes

In today's fast-paced and ever-changing work environment, flexibility and adaptability are crucial for organizational success. Being able to respond effectively to changes ensures that well-being strategies evolve with the organization's needs and external conditions. This section explores the importance of flexibility and adaptability, strategies for promoting these qualities, and the benefits they bring to the workplace.

5.3.1 Importance of Flexibility and Adaptability

Flexibility and adaptability are essential skills for both employees and organizations. They enable individuals to adjust to new situations, changes, and challenges with ease, making them more resilient and capable of thriving in dynamic environments (Indeed, 2024).

Key Benefits of Flexibility and Adaptability:

- **Enhanced Resilience**: Organizations that are flexible and adaptable can better withstand challenges and disruptions, maintaining productivity and morale. Flexibility allows employees to manage stress and recover quickly from setbacks (BetterUp, 2022).
- **Improved Innovation**: Flexibility encourages creative thinking and innovation, as employees are more willing to explore new ideas and approaches. Adaptable organizations can pivot quickly in response to market changes and seize new opportunities (Forbes, 2023).
- **Greater Employee Satisfaction**: Employees who feel supported in adapting to changes are more likely to be satisfied and engaged in their work. Flexibility in work arrangements, such as remote work options and flexible hours, can enhance work-life balance and overall job satisfaction (Indeed, 2024).
- **Increased Productivity**: Adaptable employees can handle new tasks and responsibilities efficiently, leading to higher productivity. They are also better equipped to manage multiple priorities and meet deadlines (BetterUp, 2022).

5.3.2 Strategies for Promoting Flexibility and Adaptability

Implementing strategies to promote flexibility and adaptability can help create a more dynamic and responsive work environment. Here are some effective strategies:

1. Encouraging a Growth Mindset

Promoting a growth mindset helps employees view challenges as opportunities for learning and development. This mindset encourages continuous improvement and resilience in the face of change.

- **Training Programs**: Offer training programs that focus on developing a growth mindset, such as workshops on resilience, problem-solving, and critical thinking. These programs can help employees embrace change and view it as an opportunity for growth (Forbes, 2023).
- **Leadership Support**: Leaders should model a growth mindset by demonstrating openness to feedback, learning from mistakes, and encouraging experimentation. This sets a positive example for employees and fosters a culture of continuous learning (BetterUp, 2022).

2. Providing Flexible Work Arrangements

Offering flexible work arrangements, such as remote work options and flexible hours, can help employees balance their personal and professional lives, enhancing their ability to adapt to changes.

- **Remote Work Options**: Allowing employees to work from home or other remote locations provides flexibility and can improve work-life balance. This arrangement can also increase productivity and job satisfaction (Indeed, 2024).
- **Flexible Hours**: Implementing flexible work hours, such as flexitime or compressed workweeks, allows employees to adjust their schedules to better fit their personal needs. This flexibility can reduce stress and improve overall well-being (Forbes, 2023).

3. Fostering Open Communication

Open communication ensures that employees are informed about changes and understand the reasons behind them. This transparency helps build trust and reduces resistance to change.

- **Regular Updates**: Provide regular updates on organizational changes, new initiatives, and strategic goals. This can be done through team meetings, newsletters, and internal communication platforms (Harvard Business Review, 2021).

- **Feedback Channels**: Establish feedback channels where employees can voice their concerns and suggestions regarding changes. This can include suggestion boxes, surveys, and open-door policies (Forbes, 2023).

4. Encouraging Risk-Taking and Experimentation

Encouraging employees to take risks and experiment with new ideas can foster a culture of adaptability. This approach promotes innovation and helps employees develop the skills needed to navigate change.

- **Rewarding Innovation**: Recognize and reward employees who take initiative and embrace change. This can include awards, bonuses, and public recognition for innovative ideas and successful experiments (Forbes, 2023).
- **Safe Environment**: Create a safe environment where employees feel comfortable taking risks without fear of failure or punishment. Encourage a mindset that views failures as learning opportunities (Harvard Business Review, 2021).

5. Investing in Employee Training and Development

Providing ongoing training and development opportunities equips employees with the skills and knowledge needed to adapt to new challenges and changes.

- **Cross-Training**: Offer cross-training programs that allow employees to learn different roles and responsibilities within the organization. This increases their versatility and ability to adapt to changing demands (Forbes, 2023).
- **Continuous Learning**: Promote a culture of continuous learning by providing access to online courses, workshops, and professional development resources. Encourage employees to pursue certifications and advanced training in their fields (BetterUp, 2022).

5.3.3 Implementation of Flexibility and Adaptability Strategies

Implementing flexibility and adaptability strategies requires a structured approach to ensure they are effective and sustainable.

1. Training and Development

Providing training on adaptability skills, such as problem-solving, critical thinking, and emotional intelligence, equips employees to handle changes effectively.

- **Workshops and Seminars**: Organize workshops and seminars on adaptability skills, focusing on practical techniques and real-world applications. These sessions can help employees develop the confidence and competence to navigate change (Forbes, 2023).
- **Online Learning Platforms**: Offer access to online learning platforms that provide courses on adaptability, resilience, and other relevant skills. Encourage employees to take advantage of these resources for continuous improvement (BetterUp, 2022).

2. Leadership Support

Leaders should model adaptability and support their teams in navigating changes. This includes being open to feedback and making adjustments as needed.

- **Leading by Example**: Leaders should demonstrate flexibility and adaptability in their own actions and decision-making. This sets a positive example for employees and reinforces the importance of these qualities (Harvard Business Review, 2021).
- **Providing Resources**: Ensure that employees have the resources and support they need to adapt to changes. This can include access to training, tools, and guidance from managers and mentors (Forbes, 2023).

3. Continuous Improvement

Regularly reviewing and updating well-being strategies ensures that they remain relevant and effective in the face of changing circumstances.

- **Feedback and Evaluation**: Continuously gather feedback from employees on the effectiveness of well-being strategies and make adjustments as needed. This ensures that the strategies evolve with the organization's needs (Forbes, 2023).
- **Monitoring Progress**: Track the progress of adaptability initiatives and measure their impact on employee satisfaction, productivity, and overall organizational performance. Use this data to inform future improvements (BetterUp, 2022).

The journey to creating a positive work environment that supports the well-being of all employees is a continuous process that requires dedication and effort from both leaders and employees. This chapter has outlined various strategies that organizations can implement to foster a culture of well-being, leading to greater productivity, job satisfaction, and overall success. Let's summarize the key points discussed and emphasize the importance of ongoing commitment to these practices.

Creating a positive work culture begins with the role of leadership and management. Leaders play a crucial role in establishing a positive work culture by setting a clear vision, demonstrating emotional intelligence, leading by example, and promoting open communication. By embodying these qualities, leaders can inspire their teams and create an environment where employees feel valued and motivated. Additionally, employee engagement strategies such as recognizing and rewarding employees, providing growth opportunities, involving employees in decision-making, and promoting work-life balance are essential for increasing employee engagement. These strategies help create a supportive and inclusive workplace where employees can thrive.

Physical and mental health initiatives are also vital components of a positive work environment. Implementing health and safety programs, such as ergonomic assessments, wellness workshops, and safety training programs, ensures a safe and healthy work environment. Providing mental health support through counselling services, stress management programs, and mental health awareness campaigns further supports employees' well-being. Moreover, offering flexible working hours and remote work options helps employees balance their personal and professional lives, reducing stress and increasing job satisfaction.

Building strong relationships within the workplace is another key aspect of fostering a positive work environment. Organizing team-building activities, such as icebreaker activities, problem-solving exercises, outdoor activities, and workshops, strengthens team bonds and improves communication. Encouraging open communication through regular team meetings, implementing an open-door policy, providing anonymous feedback channels, and ensuring transparent decision-making fosters a culture of trust and collaboration. Additionally, promoting active listening, mediation, collaborative problem-solving, and conflict resolution training helps manage conflicts constructively and maintain a harmonious work environment.

Continuous improvement and feedback are essential for maintaining a positive work environment. Conducting regular assessments, such as risk assessments, performance reviews, safety inspections, and environmental assessments, helps identify areas for improvement and ensures compliance with regulations. Implementing employee feedback platforms, such as employee surveys, suggestion boxes, feedback software, performance reviews, and real-time feedback channels, provides valuable insights and fosters a culture of continuous improvement. Encouraging a growth mindset, providing flexible work arrangements, fostering open communication, encouraging risk-taking and experimentation, and investing in employee training and development promotes adaptability and resilience.

Building a foundation of well-being in the workplace is not a one-time effort but a continuous process that requires ongoing commitment from both leaders and employees. Organizations must regularly assess their work environment, gather feedback, and adapt their strategies to meet the evolving needs of their workforce. Leaders must demonstrate a genuine commitment to employee well-being by prioritizing it in their decision-making and actions. This includes allocating resources for well-being initiatives, setting clear goals, and holding themselves accountable for creating a positive work environment. Employees play a vital role in building a culture of well-being. Their active participation in feedback processes, engagement in well-being programs, and willingness to adapt to changes are crucial for the success of these initiatives.

Organizations must regularly review their well-being strategies and make necessary adjustments to ensure they remain effective and relevant. This involves staying informed about best practices, seeking feedback from employees, and being open to new approaches. Recognizing and celebrating the successes of well-being initiatives can reinforce their importance and motivate continued efforts. This can include acknowledging individual and team achievements, sharing success stories, and highlighting the positive impact on the organization.

By implementing the strategies outlined in this chapter, organizations can create a positive work environment that supports the well-being of all employees. This leads to greater productivity, job satisfaction, and overall success. Building a foundation of well-being is a continuous journey that requires commitment and effort, but the rewards are well worth it.

REFERENCES

AllVoices. (2023). What is continuous feedback and how can it transform your team? Retrieved from https://www.allvoices.co/blog/what-is-continuous-feedback

American Institute of Stress. (n.d.). The benefits of stress management. Retrieved from https://www.stress.org/

American Psychological Association (APA). (2024). How these organizations are leading in making employee mental health a priority. Retrieved from https://www.apa.org/topics/healthy-workplaces/organizations-improving-employee-mental-health

Anderson, N., & De Dreu, C. K. W. (2022). Innovation and creativity in organizations: The role of individual and group dynamics. *Journal of Organizational Behavior*, 43(2), 123–139.

Bersin, J. (2012). *The state of employee recognition in 2012*. Bersin & Associates.

BetterUp. (2021). Guide to conflict resolution skills — plus real world examples. Retrieved from https://www.betterup.com/blog/conflict-resolution-skills

BetterUp. (2022). 8 team bonding activities to increase engagement and belonging. Retrieved from https://www.betterup.com/blog/team-bonding

Betterworks. (2023). How to achieve transparency in the workplace. Retrieved from https://www.betterworks.com/magazine/workplace-transparency-alignment-trust/

Brookey & Company. (2024). The benefits of an organizational assessment. Retrieved from https://www.brookeyco.com/blog/the-benefits-of-an-organizational-assessment

Brown, A., & Wilson, T. (2023). The role of social well-being in employee engagement and performance. *Human Resource Management Review*, 33(1), 45–60.

Cherniss, C. (2001). Emotional intelligence and organizational effectiveness. In Cherniss, C., & Goleman, D. (Eds.), *The emotionally intelligent workplace*. Jossey-Bass.

Clampitt, P. G. (2016). *Communicating for managerial effectiveness*. SAGE Publications.

Cohen, S., & McKay, G. (2022). Resources and support: Key factors in workplace well-being. *The Journal of Applied Psychology*, 107(5), 777–790.

CultureMonkey. (2024). The importance of feedback in the workplace. Retrieved from https://www.culturemonkey.io/employee-engagement/the-importance-of-feedback-in-the-workplace/

CultureMonkey. (2024). What is transparency at work: Benefits and top tips to practice. Retrieved from https://www.culturemonkey.io/employee-engagement/transparency-at-work/

Davis, M., Jenkins, J., & Liu, Y. (2021). Psychological well-being and academic success: The role of self-efficacy and resilience. *Educational Psychology Review*, 33(4), 567–586.

DeskAlerts. (2024). Best employee feedback tools to use in 2024. Retrieved from https://www.alert-software.com/blog/employee-feedback-tools

Forbes. (2021). The costs and benefits of addressing mental health in the workplace. Retrieved from https://www.forbes.com/councils/forbesbusinesscouncil/2021/12/06/the-costs-and-benefits-of-addressing-mental-health-in-the-workplace/

Forbes. (2023). 19 effective strategies for building a culture of adaptability. Retrieved from https://www.forbes.com/councils/forbesbusinesscouncil/2023/06/12/19-effective-strategies-for-building-a-culture-of-adaptability/

Frantically Speaking. (2024). 11 effective communication strategies to resolve conflict. Retrieved from https://franticallyspeaking.com/11-effective-communication-strategies-to-resolve-conflict/

Friedman, R. A., & Holtom, B. C. (2002). The effects of network groups on minority employee turnover intentions. *Human Resource Management*, 41(4), 405–421. DOI: 10.1002/hrm.10051

Frontiers. (2023). Changing the landscape of mental health among college students. Retrieved from https://www.frontiersin.org/journals/public-health/articles/10.3389/fpubh.2023.1175594/full

Goleman, D. (1995). *Emotional intelligence: Why it can matter more than IQ*. Bantam Books.

Google. (n.d.). Our mission. Retrieved from https://about.google/our-story/

Growth Tactics. (2023). Benefits of transparent communication. Retrieved from https://www.growthtactics.net/benefits-of-transparent-communication/

Growth Tactics. (2024). 50 transformative team building games for students. Retrieved from https://www.growthtactics.net/team-building-games-for-students/

Harvard Business Review. (2021). The secret of adaptable organizations is trust. Retrieved from https://hbr.org/2021/03/the-secret-of-adaptable-organizations-is-trust

Harvard Business School. (2023). 5 strategies for conflict resolution in the workplace. Retrieved from https://online.hbs.edu/blog/post/strategies-for-conflict-resolution-in-the-workplace

Heart It Out. (n.d.). Online counselling. Retrieved from https://heartitout.in/

Hsieh, T. (2010). *Delivering happiness: A path to profits, passion, and purpose.* Business Plus.

HubSpot. (2022). 16 employee feedback tools to track your team's engagement. Retrieved from https://blog.hubspot.com/agency/employee-feedback-engagement-tools

HubSpot. (2023). Open communication: Tips and examples for the workplace. Retrieved from https://blog.hubspot.com/sales/open-communication

Hutchison, J. (2020). Transparent communication: Toward a respectful workplace. Retrieved from https://workplace.msu.edu/transparent-communication/

IBM. (n.d.). Diversity and inclusion. Retrieved from https://www.ibm.com/employment/inclusion/

Indeed. (2024). 17 benefits of team building for your organization. Retrieved from https://www.indeed.com/career-advice/career-development/benefits-of-team-building

Indeed. (2024). Adaptability in the workplace: Benefits and importance. Retrieved from https://www.indeed.com/career-advice/career-development/adaptability-in-the-workplace

Indeed. (2024). Types of assessments for employees (with steps and tips). Retrieved from https://www.indeed.com/career-advice/career-development/assessment-for-employees

Indeed. (2024). What is open communication? (With benefits and importance). Retrieved from https://www.indeed.com/career-advice/career-development/what-is-open-communication

Insight Global. (2024). Transparency in the workplace: Everything you need to know. Retrieved from https://insightglobal.com/blog/transparency-in-the-workplace/

Kalev, A., Dobbin, F., & Kelly, E. (2006). Best practices or best guesses? Assessing the efficacy of corporate affirmative action and diversity policies. *American Sociological Review*, 71(4), 589–617. DOI: 10.1177/000312240607100404

Kossek, E. E., & Ozeki, C. (1998). Work-family conflict, policies, and the job-life satisfaction relationship: A review and directions for organizational behavior-human resources research. *The Journal of Applied Psychology*, 83(2), 139–149. DOI: 10.1037/0021-9010.83.2.139

Kouzes, J. M., & Posner, B. Z. (2017). *The leadership challenge: How to make extraordinary things happen in organizations*. Wiley.

Leaders.com. (2022). The value of open communication in the workplace. Retrieved from https://leaders.com/articles/company-culture/open-communication/

Mayo Clinic. (n.d.). Stress management: Stress relief. Retrieved from https://www.mayoclinic.org/healthy-lifestyle/stress-management/basics/stress-relief/hlv-20049495

Men, L. R. (2014). Strategic internal communication: Transformational leadership, communication channels, and employee satisfaction. *Management Communication Quarterly*, 28(2), 264–284. DOI: 10.1177/0893318914524536

Microsoft. (n.d.). Flexible work. Retrieved from https://www.microsoft.com/en-us/flexible-work/

Noe, R. A. (2017). *Employee training and development*. McGraw-Hill Education.

Occupational Safety and Health Administration (OSHA). (n.d.). A safe workplace is sound business. Retrieved from https://www.osha.gov/safety-management

Occupational Safety and Health Administration (OSHA). (n.d.). Safety and health programs step-by-step guide. Retrieved from https://www.osha.gov/safety-management/step-by-step-guide

People Managing People. (2024). 10 best employee feedback software of 2024. Retrieved from https://peoplemanagingpeople.com/tools/best-employee-feedback-software/

Positive Psychology. (2024). 14 conflict resolution strategies for the workplace. Retrieved from https://positivepsychology.com/conflict-resolution-in-the-workplace/

Positive Psychology. (n.d.). How to plan a mindfulness workshop: Best ideas for success. Retrieved from https://positivepsychology.com/mindfulness-workshop/

Proactive, M. D. (n.d.). How to perform an ergonomic assessment in the workplace. Retrieved from https://proactive-md.com/how-to-perform-an-ergonomic-assessment-in-the-workplace/

Psychology Today. (2024). Managing conflict resolution effectively. Retrieved from https://www.psychologytoday.com/us/blog/the-wisdom-of-anger/202401/managing-conflict-resolution-effectively

QuestionPro. (2023). Continuous feedback: Definition, management, and benefits. Retrieved from https://www.questionpro.com/blog/continuous-feedback/

Risely. (2024). 6 benefits of conflict resolution for effective managers. Retrieved from https://www.risely.me/6-benefits-of-conflict-resolution-in-the-workplace/

SafetyCulture. (n.d.). Health and safety program: A brief guide. Retrieved from https://safetyculture.com/topics/occupational-health-and-safety/health-and-safety-program/

Salesforce. (n.d.). Equality at Salesforce. Retrieved from https://www.salesforce.com/company/equality/

Schein, E. H. (2010). *Organizational culture and leadership*. Jossey-Bass.

SessionLab. (2024). 66 team building activities to bring your team together. Retrieved from https://www.sessionlab.com/blog/team-building-activities/

Shore, L. M., Randel, A. E., Chung, B. G., Dean, M. A., Ehrhart, K. H., & Singh, G. (2011). Inclusion and diversity in work groups: A review and model for future research. *Journal of Management*, 37(4), 1262–1289. DOI: 10.1177/0149206310385943

SiteDocs. (n.d.). How to create a safe work environment: Best practices. Retrieved from https://www.sitedocs.com/blog/safe-work-practices/

Starbucks. (n.d.). Diversity and inclusion. Retrieved from https://www.starbucks.com/responsibility/diversity-and-inclusion/

Surf Office. (2024). 18 benefits of team building in any working environment. Retrieved from https://www.surfoffice.com/blog/team-building-benefits

teambuilding.com. (2024). 24 team bonding activities, games & ideas for work. Retrieved from https://teambuilding.com/blog/team-bonding-ideas

TherapyRoute. (n.d.). Therapists in Bangalore, India. Retrieved from https://www.therapyroute.com/therapists/india/bangalore/1

Thomas, D. A. (1990). The impact of diversity on organizational behavior. *Harvard Business Review*, 68(5), 107–119. PMID: 10106515

U.S. Department of Labor. (n.d.). Flexible schedules. Retrieved from https://www.dol.gov/general/topic/workhours/flexibleschedules

Vroom, V. H., & Jago, A. G. (1988). *The new leadership: Managing participation in organizations*. Prentice-Hall.

Wellable. (n.d.). 30 holistic wellness activities for the workplace. Retrieved from https://www.wellable.co/blog/30-holistic-wellness-activities-for-the-workplace/

WorkHound. (2023). How an employee feedback platform boosts employee engagement. Retrieved from https://workhound.com/blog/how-an-employee-feedback-platform-boosts-employee-engagement/

Zavvy. (2024). How to build robust employee feedback systems in your company. Retrieved from https://www.deel.com/blog/employee-feedback-system/

Chapter 5
Creating a Positive Workplace for the Employee Wellbeing

R. Sethumadhavan
https://orcid.org/0000-0002-0508-2143
School of Management, Presidency University, India

ABSTRACT

Creating a happy and productive workplace requires more than meeting deadlines or offering competitive salaries. It's about cultivating an environment where employees feel valued, supported, and motivated to grow. Flexibility is key and remote options or adaptable hours help employees balance their personal lives without stress. Promoting diversity and inclusion through open conversations and training ensures every employee feels welcomed. Regular check-ins between managers and teams foster communication and personal development. Prioritizing physical and mental well-being with wellness programs or mental health resources shows employees their well-being matters. Recognition of accomplishments, whether through bonuses or simple acknowledgments, reinforces a positive culture. Team building across departments fosters a sense of community. Leaders should model respect and positivity, engaging in open dialogue with employees to ensure continuous improvement. These strategies create a workplace where employees thrive, and success becomes a shared journey.

DOI: 10.4018/979-8-3693-8457-2.ch005

INTRODUCTION

Building an environment at work where people can flourish is similar to tending to a garden. Making sure that each team member feels appreciated, encouraged, and invigorated goes beyond simply providing a pleasant workspace and benefits. Prioritizing well-being is the fundamental first step towards creating a positive workplace. Envision an environment where physical well-being is the top concern. It could include a back-supporting ergonomic chair, readily available healthy snacks, and designated areas for short walks or stretches. Employees feel better and perform better at work when they have support for their physical health. It's equally important to maintain mental health. A supportive work environment makes mental health discussions acceptable rather than taboo and provides tools like stress-relieving programs and counseling services. Engaged and productive employees are more likely to feel comfortable talking about their mental health. Respect and inclusivity are key components of a positive work environment. Being a member of a team where everyone is respected and feels heard is important. It also celebrates diversity and acknowledges individual contributions. It feels like you're a part of a tight-knit group of people where help and cooperation are expected and where you know your efforts count. One important way to set the tone is to lead by example. The entire team is motivated to follow suit when leaders exhibit a love of learning, put their health first, and treat everyone with respect. It all comes down to establishing an environment that inspires everyone to perform to the best of their abilities and supports both professional and personal growth. It is advantageous for the company to create this kind of environment in addition to the employees. People are more engaged, productive, and inclined to stick with a company when they have a positive work environment. We will look at creating an environment where your work is centered around your well-being. We will share knowledge on how to build a vibrant workplace where everyone can thrive, from doable strategies for enhancing mental and physical well-being to cultivating a supportive and appreciative culture.

BACKGROUND

In their study on 4612 Canadian employees, Lowe et al. (2003) found that healthier work environments were associated with greater job satisfaction, commitment, and morale as well as lower absenteeism and quit intent. Emphasizing mutual gains through fostering a positive work environment, Raquel Rodríguez-Carvajal et al. (2010) discussed the benefits of positive psychology at work for both individuals and organizations. Valerie J. Michael L. Morganson. Litano and Sadie O'Neill (2014) underscored the significance of positive work environments for both individuals and organizations, emphasizing the use of positive psychology, leadership, and training to promote work-family balance. A. With a sample size of 210, Raziq et al. (2015) investigated workers in Pakistan's banking, telecommunication, and educational sectors. Their findings demonstrate the significance of creating such environments in order to maximize job satisfaction and personal development. A good working environment has a positive impact on employee job satisfaction. In their expert consensus on 220 strategies to promote positive mental health in the workplace, Lauren Davenport et al. (2016) emphasized the significance of work environments, effective communication, and mental health strategies. In their review of the literature, T S Nanjundeswaraswamy and Sandhya M N (2016) emphasized the importance of the work environment in improving employee well-being and organizational efficiency, and highlighted it as a critical component of Quality of Work Life.

Stacey Smith (2016) concentrated on the body of published scientific literature that was available and discussed positive employment relations; most of these sources took a positive psychological approach to the topic. An organization can focus on and enhance the quality of relationships within it to achieve the optimal functioning and flourishing of individuals, which leads to an optimally flourishing organization. Using the key terms “employment relations,” “positive relations,” “negative relations,” and “workplace relations,” a qualitative meta-synthesis literature study was conducted using Atlas ti7 and other scientific search engines. It was discovered that there are six essential components of positive employment relations namely communication, equity and equality, respect, trust, and conflict resolution. Key words: resources, positive psychology, positive workplace relations, positive employment relations, and positive relations. MelianaHandayani (2018) investigated the effects of quality of work life (QWL) and how it affected both individual and organizational performance. She discovered that QWL has an impact on employee satisfaction and quality of life as well as organizational commitment and loyalty, employee positivity, intrinsic productivity, and motivation, corporate effectiveness, and competitiveness in the global marketplace. In order to address the nursing shortage, Tara Pauley and Carolyn Fox (2018) talked about fostering a positive work environment. They specifically focused on the Pathway to Excellence program and a hospital's advancement toward designation. In their qualitative case study, Grant et al. (2019) discovered that the Positive Built Workplace Environment (PBWE) fosters creative, flexible, and cooperative workplace cultures by connecting well-designed, sustainable workspaces to enhanced performance, well-being, and humanistic values. Through qualitative interviews, Lynda Harte (2019) successfully addressed negative age stereotypes and investigated the impact of a positive age environment in the workplace on employees' attitudes. In their 2019 study, M. Ashraf et al. examined the work atmosphere of a local company in Bangladesh and discovered that, in a private corporate entity, work atmosphere significantly mediates the relationship between supervisor cooperation and job satisfaction. Asmaa Elsayed Belal (2019) investigated the role that psychological traits like hope, optimism, and resilience play in creating a positive work atmosphere that boosts commitment, performance, and job satisfaction. N. According to Saidi et al.'s (2019) analysis of Indonesian municipal administrators, a supportive supervisory environment is the most important component in fostering a positive work environment, which in turn has a significant impact on employee performance. According to Tanusree Chakraborty et al.'s (2019) research, a positive work environment emphasizes meaningful relationships, hope, efficacy, resilience, and optimism (HERO).

Positive emotions have a positive impact on workplace success factors like positive beliefs, creativity, engagement, coping, health, teamwork, and performance, according to a thorough review of the literature by Diener et al. (2020). By putting the 6 + 1 academic workplace standards into practice and encouraging a values-based culture, Saunders et al. (2020) looked at how to Establish a Healthy Work Environment in an Academic Nursing Setting and concluded that doing so can improve student, faculty, and staff outcomes. Meghna Basu Thakur, Saara Ansari, and Pallavi Bidkar (2020) investigated the relationship between job satisfaction and various work environment factors, emphasizing the significance of this relationship for both organizations and employees. A good work environment, both physically and non-physically, has a partial and simultaneous influence on employee performance, according to Aditya Angga Kusuma et al.'s 2021 study on the relationship between working environment and employee performance. In their study of nurses' work engagement, Aya Hegazy et al. (2021) discovered that a supportive work environment can lower the intention of turnover and boost nurses' work engagement. This environment is influenced by autonomy, environmental control, the doctor-nurse relationship, and organizational support. In a study conducted in 2021, Muhammad TariqueLakhiaraLakhiara et al. examined the connection between worker performance and the working environment in a few chosen construction companies in Karachi. Employee performance is greatly impacted by a positive work environment, which is primarily supported by supervisors, in Karachi city's construction companies. The 36 components of a positive work environment in hospitals were identified by S. Massen et al. (2021) through a Delphi study. These elements can be used to choose the best measurement tool or create interventions to enhance the environment, but it is important to take into account various viewpoints. A Delphi review by Susanne Maassen, Catharina van Oostveen, Hester Vermeulen, and Anne Marie Weggelaar (2021) defined a positive work environment in hospitals and identified 36 essential components for the well-being of healthcare professionals and patient care. Following three rounds of the Delphi study, 36 components were determined to be necessary for a healthy work environment in hospitals. These components, which cover a range of viewpoints, are essential for enhancing the workplace. A happy workplace lowers mortality rates, adverse events, and hospital-acquired infections while also improving patient care. It is also very important in drawing in and keeping medical professionals, particularly in times of staff scarcity like the COVID-19 pandemic. Higher work motivation and a better work environment have a positive impact on employee morale during periods of work from home during the pandemic, according to Dendri Jonathan et al. (2022).

In 2022, Michael Galanski and Elli Tsitouri conducted a thorough analysis of the Job Demands-Resources (JD-R) model to determine the model's level of applicability and relevance in the workplace of the twenty-first century. The goal of the current systematic review was to assess the Job Demands-Resources (JD-R) model in order to determine the degree to which the current theoretical framework is applicable and relevant in the workplace of the twenty-first century. The Job Demands-Resources (JD-R) model and its implications for employee wellbeing are the subject of several important findings that are highlighted in the paper by the results of the systematic literature review. Twenty papers in all were included in the review and evaluated according to the goals of the research. The sample sizes for these studies ranged from 146 to 11,468 participants, suggesting a robust dataset for analysis. The studies included a wide range of occupations and used a mixed-gender sample. The model's applicability in a variety of work environments was demonstrated by the fact that no particular industry or job type was given more weight than others. Participants in the studies were selected from twelve different countries, with a notable European bias. For example, participants from Finland were included in five studies, and participants from China, the Netherlands, South Africa, and Australia were included in other studies. The findings showed that one important predictor of burnout is a deficiency of job resources. On the other hand, it was discovered that work engagement was positively correlated with job resources. This implies that increasing job resources may result in happier workers and fewer burnout cases. The results also showed that the relationship between job resources and overall wellbeing—which encompasses both work engagement and burnout—is mediated by personal resources. This highlights the significance of individual characteristics in affecting worker health. In conclusion, the study's findings highlight the value of the JD-R model in assessing worker wellbeing by showing how personal and professional resources can have a big impact on work engagement and burnout in a variety of work environments.

Maira Lescevica and Zane Gusta (2022) carried out an extensive review of the literature with an emphasis on workplace well-being and its connection to corporate productivity. This suggests that the authors are curious about the ways in which different aspects of employee well-being can affect the performance of the entire organization. The study emphasized novel ideas like digital and technological well-being at work. This is especially true in the modern workplace, where technology is integral to work processes. Future research should take these factors into account as the authors suggest they are currently influencing productivity. A positive work environment increases employee commitment and achievement-striving ability, which in turn improves performance, according to Zhenjing Gu et al.'s (2022) analysis of the relationship between workplace environment and performance. Dr. R. Sivakami, Ms. Ananya Chauhan (2023) discussed how improving employee well-being and productivity can be achieved through a Sustainable Work Environment (SWE). The purpose of the paper was to investigate how SWE affects productivity and work management techniques. Its three main goals are to: Identifying gaps in current work environments that impede employee performance; Understanding the factors that contribute to a challenging SWE; and Understanding employee perceptions of SWE and its impact on work management practices. A mixed-approaches strategy is used, integrating quantitative and qualitative data collection methods. Important factors that impact SWE are revealed by the literature review, including work-life balance, organizational culture, leadership support, employee involvement, and physical workspace conditions. The impact of employees' perceptions of their workplace on their motivation, job satisfaction, and general performance was also examined in the study. The findings of this research were important for companies trying to establish a more sustainable and productive work environment since it highlights how important it is to comprehend these perceptions in order to improve work management practices. Organizations can create a supportive work environment that promotes job satisfaction, lower turnover rates, and higher productivity by addressing the gaps and factors that have been identified. In her study, Rania Wael Mohammad Alabed Hasan et al. (2023) concluded that Jordanian nurses who work in positive work environments have higher job satisfaction, which has an impact on staff retention and performance. After reviewing the literature, Helmi NourmanAdittya, VeithzalRivai Zainal, and Azis Hakim (2023) concluded that, in most Indonesian cases, a positive work environment has a significant positive effect on employee performance. Lisa Foster (2024) concluded—backed by literature review—that showing love to others in the healthcare industry promotes social inclusion, a positive organizational climate, and human flourishing.

Here, the beneficial elements that contribute to the development of a positive work environment that promotes employee wellbeing are covered in detail.

WORK-LIFE BALANCE

Career advancement, less work-related stress, and job satisfaction are all associated with WLB. Employers with supportive policies experience reduced absenteeism and employee turnover (Barik and Pandey, 2017). Gender is an important factor in work-life balance (WLB), with women frequently encountering more difficulties in juggling work and family obligations. This disparity may impede their ability to advance in their careers and exacerbate the "glass ceiling" effect (Satpathy et al. 2014). In India, WLB perceptions are greatly influenced by cultural expectations surrounding family care. Workers place a higher value on WLB than monetary pay, which reflects a distinct cultural perspective (Satpathy et al. 2014). The body of research on work-life balance (WLB) emphasizes how important it is for raising worker satisfaction and productivity levels within companies. Numerous studies highlight the interaction between work and personal life and show how WLB practices can lessen stress, lower attrition, and raise job satisfaction. Striking a balance between life and work can resemble tightrope walking. Not only should work and personal life be balanced, but you should also establish a schedule that works for you. Perhaps it's setting aside weekends for family and hobbies or shutting off your email after six o'clock at night. Those tiny, deliberate decisions are what keep you centered and reenergized. It's the small things that count in a happy workplace. It's when your supervisor gives you an update on how you're really doing, in addition to deadlines. It's the conviction that your opinions count and that your contributions are valued. Work should feel like a place where you can thrive rather than a chore when you walk in the door. Positive energy at work fosters greater creativity, better teamwork, and a feeling of belonging. It takes time to find this balance and optimism, and it's not always simple. It's about establishing boundaries that safeguard your private time and working in an environment that values and encourages you as a whole person. Everything just goes more smoothly and you're happier both inside and outside of the office when work and life are in harmony.

MAKE RESPECT AND INCLUSION THE NORM

The benefits of inclusion in the workplace for worker well-being, organizational commitment, and general workplace dynamics have made it a crucial research topic. A variety of aspects of inclusion are revealed by the literature, with special attention paid to leadership, diversity, and the integration of people with disabilities. According to Dudek (2023), inclusion increases organizational commitment and citizenship behavior while fostering creativity and lowering turnover. People with disabilities must be included in the creation of equitable work environments, which emphasizes the need of support networks and accessible workplaces (Romana and Lopes, 2023). Imagine seeing a diverse group of people working together at work—people with varying ages, experiences, and backgrounds. That is the appearance of a diverse workplace. Creating a place where everyone feels like they belong, regardless of who they are or where they came from, is more important than simply checking boxes. Being a member of a diverse team exposes you to viewpoints that you might not have otherwise heard. It's similar to viewing the same image from numerous perspectives. This can generate fresh perspectives, result in wiser choices, and add interest and vibrancy to the workplace. However, diversity isn't always simple; it can present a unique set of difficulties, such as misunderstandings or unconscious prejudices. Because of this, it's critical to foster an atmosphere in which people feel free to express themselves and be authentic. Imagine now that you have a positive work environment where you truly look forward to coming in each day. It goes beyond simply having great benefits and a beautiful workspace, though those things do help. It's about getting acknowledged for the hard work you do, knowing your boss has your back, and feeling supported by your coworkers. It all comes down to having the sense that your opinions count and that you are a member of a group that is making a significant contribution. Magic happens when positivity and diversity come together. You're thriving, not just getting by. You know you'll be valued and accepted for who you are, so you feel free to bring your whole self to work. That is what distinguishes a truly great workplace from a merely good one. Everyone feels like they belong to something greater than themselves in this place where they can all shine. Despite the increasing emphasis on inclusion, there are still obstacles to overcome in order to successfully apply inclusive practices in a variety of organizational contexts.

ENGAGE IN CONVERSATION

The pivotal function of employee conversations in cultivating organizational transformation, augmenting employee involvement, and refining workplace relationships. These discussions are more than just information sharing; they are crucial for coordinating organizational and personal objectives, encouraging behavioral change, and fostering a positive work atmosphere. Talks about employee performance have the power to successfully modify mental models, facilitating the behavioral shifts required for organizational change to be successful (Blackman et al. 2022). In order for change to be accepted and implemented, it is essential that structured conversations foster shared understandings of it (Blackman et al. 2022). Career conversations address problems like absenteeism and turnover by bringing employee aspirations in line with organizational objectives (Borgen et al. 2013). Having meaningful conversations with staff members helps them feel committed and like they belong, which is important for retention (Borgen et al. 2013). Our daily interactions with one another are the first step towards establishing a positive work environment. Little exchanges, such as asking a coworker how they're really doing or expressing gratitude for a job well done, can go a long way. We create an environment where people feel appreciated and motivated when we take the time to listen, exchange ideas, and express gratitude. This goes beyond simply making work more enjoyable. It also involves supporting one another. Just letting someone know you're available to support them can go a long way when they're having a difficult day. Furthermore, resolving disagreements amicably and compassionately keeps the group cohesive and strong. Finally, inclusivity is essential. Everyone ought to have a sense of inclusion and importance in society. Encouraging diverse backgrounds and experiences among employees and ensuring their inclusion in meetings are important steps towards fostering a friendly and encouraging work environment. Ultimately, it comes down to cooperating to create an atmosphere where everyone can flourish and being aware of one another's needs. We're not just performing our jobs when we help one another, show consideration for one another's time, and promote development; instead, we're creating a community where everyone enjoys coming to work.

ENCOURAGE TEAM DEVELOPMENT

Team development elucidates the pivotal function of team dynamics, proficient communication, and tactical interventions in augmenting team efficacy in diverse settings. Successful team building is crucial for accomplishing organizational objectives and adjusting to changes, according to research. Successful team dynamics, encompassing cooperation and communication, are essential for agile software development projects to succeed. Research demonstrates that these dynamics have a major impact on project outcomes, highlighting the necessity of a more thorough comprehension of team dynamics (Jallow et al. 2023). Machine learning advances in recent years have revolutionized team formation procedures, allowing for more efficient team member selection. By utilizing data-driven methodologies, this approach increases the probability of successful teamwork (Karataş and Çakır, 2024). It is widely acknowledged that team building is a strategic tool for increasing creativity and productivity in businesses. But obstacles like a lack of trust and inadequate communication can make these attempts difficult (Obiekwe & Obiekwe, 2023). Little things go a long way toward fostering a positive work environment and fostering team growth. It's not just about meeting goals and finishing tasks; it's also about ensuring that every team member feels encouraged, appreciated, and eager to come to work every day. By concentrating on the development of the team, you demonstrate to your coworkers your belief in their potential. By giving them chances to learn, establishing specific objectives, or even just giving them helpful criticism, you're assisting them in becoming the best versions of themselves. Additionally, people are more involved, driven, and committed to the team's success when they perceive themselves as growing. However, development never occurs in a vacuum. It has a close relationship with the surroundings you build. Respect and inclusivity are the norms in a positive work environment, where individuals are at ease expressing their opinions and work-life balance is upheld. It's about appreciating everyone's efforts and acknowledging victories, no matter how small. It's about supporting one another as individuals and not just as coworkers. By combining these components, you create a community as opposed to merely a team. A place where everyone is eager to contribute, where they can grow, and where they feel like they belong. It's an environment where work feels purposeful and where team success is directly related to individual growth. And that's the actual location of the magic.

MAINTAIN HEALTH

The field of employee health highlights the vital role that organizational practices and policies play in improving the mental and physical well-being of employees. A thorough analysis of numerous studies identifies the main variables affecting worker health, such as wellness initiatives, workplace cultures, and HRM procedures. Employee mental health is considerably improved by effective HRM practices like flexible work schedules, peer support, and career development opportunities (Mahdia, 2024). Employers evaluate the success of wellness programs and spot health trends using employee health claims data, which can result in focused interventions (Movva et al. 2023). Maintaining your health and creating a happy work atmosphere go hand in hand. Work becomes more enjoyable when one is mentally and physically well, and maintaining good health is made easier in a positive work environment. Everything is related. Envision a work environment where taking breaks and moving around during the day are encouraged. There might be a quiet area where you can spend some time relaxing, or the break room always has a bowl of fresh fruit. These minor gestures have a significant impact on your overall mood throughout the day. Equally important is mental health. It's about having access to support when you need it and understanding that it's acceptable to take a break when things get stressful. Support can come in many forms, such as access to counseling services, a conversation with a coworker, or a mental health day. Work-life harmony is also very important. Recharging and staying energized is facilitated by being able to log off at a reasonable time and not feeling compelled to check emails late at night. Having the option to work remotely or with flexible hours can also greatly simplify your life and help you balance all of your priorities. However, it's not just about your personal health; it also matters about the surroundings. A workplace that fosters positivity is one in which all employees feel valued, respected, and included. It's a place where people genuinely care about one another, where teamwork is encouraged, and successes are celebrated. That type of atmosphere makes it simpler to remain happy, motivated, and focused. When positivity and health coexist at work, it becomes more about enjoying your work rather than just getting the job done. It all comes down to feeling good about yourself both inside and outside of the workplace and being a part of a group that is there for you no matter what. That is the type of environment where everyone can prosper.

EXPRESSION OF GRATITUDE

Gratitude has received a lot of attention in academic writing, which has shown its varied effects on people and relationships. Studies show that gratitude varies depending on the cultural setting, affects workplace dynamics, and increases life satisfaction. Several mediators, including social support and self-esteem, were found to be associated with a significant positive correlation between life satisfaction and gratitude in a systematic review (Kerry et al. in 2023). Thanksgiving in the workplace can improve coworkers' perceptions of prosocial behavior, especially when it is directed toward worthy leaders (Fehr et al. in 2024). At work, expressing gratitude can really change the environment. Envision entering an environment where individuals consistently express gratitude for minor gestures and acknowledge one another's accomplishments. Developing a culture where everyone feels appreciated and inspired is more important than simply giving people a pat on the back. Consider how rewarding it is when someone recognizes your efforts and takes the time to express gratitude. The magic of gratitude is that it raises spirits and gives people a sense of purpose and belonging. It makes you want to give even more, isn't that right? To express gratitude, you don't need to wait for significant occasions. A simple "well done" or heartfelt "thank you" for a job well done can make someone's day. It's crucial to acknowledge little victories in addition to big ones. It keeps everyone upbeat and serves as a reminder that their efforts are appreciated. Making thankfulness a daily practice is key to creating a positive work atmosphere. Happiness spreads like wildfire when bosses and subordinates show one another genuine appreciation. One small gesture of gratitude can snowball into a culture where everyone is encouraged and supported. It's like a snowball effect. Urge everyone to express their gratitude, whether it be with a brief note, a shout-out during a meeting, or just a sincere discussion. People are happier, more engaged, and more willing to give their all when they feel valued. Creating an environment where people feel seen and appreciated is ultimately what matters. When thankfulness is abundant, the workplace transforms from a place where tasks must be completed to one where individuals are eager to come, feel connected, and can actually flourish.

TEAM SPIRIT

When team spirit is examined through dialogue, pro-social behaviors such as affiliation are included. Studies on in situ teamwork emphasize how difficult it is to define and promote this crucial but elusive idea in businesses (Erica derics,2023). Team spirit, which includes cooperation, mutual reliance, and common objectives, has a major positive effect on business performance by improving output quality, reducing waiting times, and cutting down on waste. Creating a positive work environment and fostering team spirit are similar to weaving together threads to create a vibrant, strong tapestry. When members of a team collaborate effectively and show genuine concern for one another, the work environment becomes one of happiness and motivation for all. Consider it this way: connections and trust are formed when individuals freely exchange ideas and listen to one another. It's similar to having a support system of friends who encourage you and lend a hand when necessary. That sense of camaraderie is strengthened by holding regular team meetings where everyone is able to contribute and celebrate accomplishments together. Working together is essential. When you collaborate on projects together, you get to know each other's peculiarities and strong points. It's similar to playing team sports in that the entire team performs better when everyone knows their place and helps one another out. Remember to celebrate all of your victories, no matter how small. Acknowledging achievements, whether through a team lunch or a simple shout-out during a meeting, makes everyone feel valued. Leading with a positive attitude and expressing gratitude for effort are key components of fostering a positive work environment. It's about ensuring that everyone, regardless of whether they're sharing or conquering a challenge, feels appreciated. Being inclusive is essential because a successful team is one in which every member feels valued and included. People find it easier to perform at their best when they have a welcoming and encouraging work environment in addition to flexible work schedules. Helping each other out with our well-being is also essential. Promoting healthful behaviors and being receptive to problems are two ways to keep the environment upbeat. When issues are resolved promptly and productively, negativity is kept at bay. People genuinely enjoy going to work in an environment where positivity and a strong sense of teamwork are ingrained in the daily routine. Everyone feels welcome, valued, and eager to contribute in this environment. And for that reason, work becomes a fulfilling and joyful aspect of life rather than just a job.

LEADERSHIP BY EXAMPLE

Leadership is an organizational attribute that permeates networks of responsibilities, is molded by individual assets, and shapes patterns of interaction and the interpretations given to organizational events (Rodney T. OGawa& Co.). Sustaining a culture of leadership development, striving for continual improvement, and having a clear grasp of the role that leadership plays in organizational contexts are all necessary for effective leadership (M. KK. D. Vries and associates). Teams that engage in processes like learning and teamwork develop leadership capacity, which enhances the team's ability to adapt and perform in later performance cycles (D. Day and companions.). Being a good role model for your team means that you should lead by example. It involves modeling the morals and conduct you would like to see in your place of employment. It's like casting a glow that everyone else naturally follows when leaders exhibit positivity, respect, and commitment. Upon arriving at work, picture your boss greeting obstacles with a positive outlook and a grin. A leader's ability to manage difficult circumstances with poise and positivity has a profound impact, inspiring the team to approach their own obstacles with a like mindset. The positivity seems to be dispersing throughout the office like a wave. Also very important is open communication. A space where people feel comfortable sharing their ideas and concerns is created when you are approachable and transparent. It involves having the attitude that respects everyone, regardless of their position or background, values criticism, and listens intently. Furthermore important is work-life balance. Your team will know that you value their well-being if you respect their personal time and encourage flexibility. Helping them find a balance that suits them is just as important as simply avoiding emails after hours. Honoring your word and taking responsibility for your errors are hallmarks of an ethical leader. The foundation of trust is consistency and dependability. Admitting mistakes and growing from them is a great way to lead by example in humility and personal development. Recognition and gratitude function similarly to gasoline, maintaining a high level of motivation. Praise for accomplishments of all sizes gives people a sense of worth. Positive and constructive criticism also makes people feel good about their accomplishments and helps them all get better. The cornerstones of a productive workplace are cooperation and teamwork. One way to promote a sense of community and shared achievement is to work closely with others and value their contributions. Demonstrating your commitment to the group's success rather than just your personal gains is the key. Finally, it all comes down to empathy. A culture of trust and support is cultivated through acknowledging and meeting the needs of your team. Someone can feel like they belong and can succeed in the workplace when you are approachable and genuinely concerned about their well-being. Establishing a positive and happy work environment is the essence of leading by example.

NEVER GIVE UP ON LEARNING NEW THINGS

To attain better learning outcomes and enhance learning, thinking, cooperation, and regulation skills, a new equilibrium between guided learning, action learning, and experiential learning is required (P. Simons, Robert-Jan et al.) Aspiration, self-awareness, curiosity, and vulnerability are qualities that successful executives have cultivated. These qualities help them adapt to change constantly and prosper in a business environment that is changing quickly (Erika Andersen et al. 2016). Technology preference plays a moderating role in professionals' intention to acquire emerging digital skills, which are influenced by social influence, personal innovativeness, anxiety, long-term consequences, and job relevance (Sudatta Kar et al.). Envision a work environment where advancement and education are commonplace. It's like having an endless supply of new ideas and vitality to keep everyone motivated and involved. A team that welcomes learning new things fosters a vibrant, upbeat atmosphere where everyone feels inspired and appreciated. Consider the excitement you get when you learn something new. Learning can be immensely stimulating, whether it's a new skill, a different viewpoint, or a different strategy for tackling a problem. When you and your group are excited about the same things, it fosters an environment where creativity is encouraged and curiosity is welcomed. It takes more than just providing workshops or training sessions to promote learning. The goal is to integrate it seamlessly into the working day. Perhaps you organize casual lunch-and-learns where team members discuss their discoveries, or maybe you set up chances for group projects where people can try out new abilities together. This type of setting not only fosters individual development but also fortifies team relationships. Acknowledging and applauding educational endeavors is essential. Recognizing someone's accomplishment, whether it be finishing a course or learning a new skill, makes them feel valued and inspired. Small gestures of appreciation, like a thank-you note during a meeting, go a long way toward demonstrating to your team that their work is valued. Setting a good example is equally effective. It sets a good example when you share your experiences and demonstrate a passion for learning. Your team is inspired to take personal development seriously by your own dedication to learning. It's like saying, “I'm excited to grow, and I hope you are too!”. Establishing a safe environment for learning entails promoting experimentation and accepting failure. People are more likely to be adventurous and creative when they feel at ease taking risks and learning from them. This process is facilitated by support and direction, which gives everyone confidence as they embark on their educational journey. The goal of integrating learning into daily work is to immediately put new knowledge and abilities to use. It's similar to putting what you've learned into practice, which enhances the educational process. It also involves cultivating an environment that values ongoing progress.

CONCLUSION

A happy workplace increases productivity, dedication, and the capacity for goal-setting. Employee mental health and well-being can be enhanced by putting strategies like work environments, positive leadership styles, effective communication, job designs that promote mental health, and well-being strategies into practice. Human resource management strategies that prioritize wellbeing have a positive impact on workers' performance and well-being at work. Employee job satisfaction and the work environment are positively correlated. Ultimately, an environment that prioritizes learning is one in which employees look forward to going to work each day. It's a place where people are inspired to realize their full potential, growth is celebrated, and curiosity is encouraged. In addition to increasing job satisfaction, this type of atmosphere fosters the development of a motivated, creative team that is eager to succeed as a unit.

REFERENCES

Alicja, D. (2023). *1. How Does Inclusion Impact Employees in Organisations?* Literature Review. Acta Universitatis Lodziensis. DOI: 10.18778/0208-6018.364.02

Andersen, E. (2016). Learning to learn. *Harvard Business Review*, 94, 19.

Ashraf, M. (2019). The mediating role of work atmosphere in the relationship between supervisor cooperation, career growth and job satisfaction. *Journal of Workplace Learning*, 31(2), 78–94. Advance online publication. DOI: 10.1108/JWL-12-2017-0113

Asrini, M. (2024). *1. The Role of Human Resource Management in Employee Well-Being and Mental Health: A Systematic Literature Review*. Productivity. DOI: 10.62207/phea4z38

Chakraborty, T., & Ganguly, M. (2019). Crafting Engaged Employees Through Positive Work Environment. *Advances in Human Resources Management and Organizational Development*, 180–198. Advance online publication. DOI: 10.4018/978-1-5225-7799-7.ch011

Davenport, L., Allisey, A., Page, K., Lamontagne, A., & Reavley, N. (2016). How can organisations help employees thrive? The development of guidelines for promoting positive mental health at work. *International Journal of Workplace Health Management*, 9(4), 411–427. DOI: 10.1108/IJWHM-01-2016-0001

Day, D., Gronn, P., & Salas, E. (2004). Leadership capacity in teams. *The Leadership Quarterly*, 15(6), 857–880. DOI: 10.1016/j.leaqua.2004.09.001

Deborah, B. (2022, July 03). Fiona, Buick., Michael, O'Donnell., Nabil, Adnan, Ilahee. (2022). 1. Changing the Conversation to Create Organizational Change. *Journal of Change Management*, 22(3), 252–272. Advance online publication. DOI: 10.1080/14697017.2022.2040570

Diener, E., Thapa, S., & Tay, L. (2020). Positive Emotions at Work. *Annual Review of Organizational Psychology and Organizational Behavior*, 7(1), 451–477. Advance online publication. DOI: 10.1146/annurev-orgpsych-012119-044908

Erika & Jonathan. (2023). Conversation Analysis, Enacting Teams, and Displaying Team Spirit in a Decision-Making Episode of Talk. New perspectives in organizational communication, .DOI: 10.1007/978-3-031-30199-5_7

Fernando & Romana. (2023). Human Resources as a Factor of Influence and Inclusion in Companies: The Case of El Corte Ingles. European modern studies journal, DOI: 10.59573/emsj.7(4).2023.25

Giuseppe & Pirchio. (2019), Positive environments for children and adults. .DOI: 10.1007/978-3-662-58409-5_11

Grant, A., O'Connor, S., & Studholme, I. (2019). Towards a Positive Psychology of Buildings and Workplace Community:the Positive Built Workplace Environment. *International Journal of Applied Positive Psychology*, 4(1-2), 67–89. DOI: 10.1007/s41042-019-00019-2

Gu, Z., Chupradit, S., Ku, K., Nassani, A., & Haffar, M. (2022). Impact of Employees' Workplace Environment on Employees' Performance: A Multi-Mediation Model. *Frontiers in Public Health*, 10, 890400. Advance online publication. DOI: 10.3389/fpubh.2022.890400 PMID: 35646787

Hasan, R. (2023). Work environment and job satisfaction among nurses in Jordan: A systematic literature review. *British Journal of Health Care Management*, 29(4), 1–7. Advance online publication. DOI: 10.12968/bjhc.2021.0128

Hegazy, A., Ibrahim, M., Shokry, W., & Shrief, H. (2021). *Work Environment Factors in Nursing Practice*. Menoufia Nursing Journal. DOI: 10.21608/menj.2021.206247

Helmi. (2023). Work Environment, Work Conflict, and Employee Performance: A Literature Review. International Journal of Advanced Multidisciplinary, DOI: 10.38035/ijam.v1i4.146

Ipseeta. (2014). Work-Life Balance @ Working Couples - A Review of Literature. Asian Journal of Research in Social Sciences and Humanities,

Jonathan, D., & Dewi, Y. (2022). *Work From Home: The Influence of Work Motivation and Work Environment on Employee Work Spirit*. International Journal of Social Science and Business. DOI: 10.23887/ijssb.v7i1.52517

Kar, S., Kar, A., & Gupta, M. (2021). Industrial Internet of Things and Emerging Digital Technologies–Modeling Professionals' Learning Behavior. *IEEE Access : Practical Innovations, Open Solutions*, 9, 30017–30034. DOI: 10.1109/ACCESS.2021.3059407

Kusuma, A. (2021). *Literature Study: The Effect of the Working Environment on Employee Performance*. Business and Entrepreneurial Review. DOI: 10.25105/ber.v21i1.8239

Lakhiara, M. (2021). *A Analysis of the relationship between the working environment and employee performance in selected construction firms in Karachi city*. Neutron. DOI: 10.29138/neutron.v21i1.86

Lisa, F. (2024). Loving One Another in Healthcare: Power of the Positive Work Environment. DOI: 10.1007/978-3-031-52276-5_9

Lowe, G., Schellenberg, G., & Shannon, H. (2003). Correlates of Employees' Perceptions of a Healthy Work Environment. *American Journal of Health Promotion*, 17(6), 390–399. DOI: 10.4278/0890-1171-17.6.390 PMID: 12858619

Lynda, H. (2019). Does A Positive Age Environment Successfully Influence Negative Age Stereotypes from an Employee Perspective.

Maassen, S., Oostveen, C., Vermeulen, H., & Weggelaar, A. (2021). Defining a positive work environment for hospital healthcare professionals: A Delphi study. *PLoS One*, 16(2), e0247530. Advance online publication. DOI: 10.1371/journal.pone.0247530 PMID: 33630923

Maira. (2022). Well-being at work: a literature review on the complex framework. DOI: 10.3846/bm.2022.843

Meghna. (2020), Exploring the relationship between Work Environment and Job Satisfaction.

Meliana. (2018). A Literature Review of Quality of Work Life. .DOI: 10.33846/HN.V2I6.222

Michael, G. (2022, September 20). Positive psychology in the working environment. Job demands-resources theory, work engagement and burnout: A systematic literature review. *Frontiers in Psychology*, 13, 1022102. Advance online publication. DOI: 10.3389/fpsyg.2022.1022102

Momodou. (2023). Examining the Impact of Team Dynamics in Agile Project Management Success in Software Development: A Systematic Literature Review. .DOI: 10.1109/IDAACS58523.2023.10348796

Naimisha, M. (2023, October 1). Scoping Review of Employer-Led Research Using Employee Health Claims Data. *Population Health Management*, 26(5), 341–352. Advance online publication. DOI: 10.1089/pop.2023.0140

Nicholas, K. (2023, November). Being Thankful for What You Have: A Systematic Review of Evidence for the Effect of Gratitude on Life Satisfaction. *Psychology Research and Behavior Management*, 16, 4799–4816. Advance online publication. DOI: 10.2147/PRBM.S372432

Ogawa, R., & Bossert, S. (1995). Leadership as an Organizational Quality. *Educational Administration Quarterly*, 31(2), 224–243. DOI: 10.1177/0013161X95031002004

Onyebuchi. (2023). Team Building in Organizations: Benefit and Challenge - A Review. International Journal Of Social Sciences And Management Research. DOI: 10.56201/ijssmr.v9.no3.2023.pg42.52

Pratibha. (2017). Review of Literature on Work Life Balance Policies and Practices. Asian Journal of Research in Business Economics and Management, DOI: 10.5958/2249-7307.2017.00067.6

Raquel, R.-C., Bernardo, M.-J., Sara, R.-H., Abraham, Á.-B., & Ana Isabel, S.-V. (2010). Positive Psychology at Work: Mutual Gains for Individuals and Organizations. *Journal of Work and Organizational Psychology*, 26(3), 235–253. Advance online publication. DOI: 10.5093/tr2010v26n3a7

Raziq, A., & Maula-Bakhsh, R. (2015). Impact of Working Environment on Job Satisfaction. *Procedia Economics and Finance*, 23, 717–725. DOI: 10.1016/S2212-5671(15)00524-9

Ryan, F. (2024, August 15). They do not deserve your thanks! Witness reactions to leader-directed expressions of gratitude. *The Journal of Applied Psychology*. Advance online publication. DOI: 10.1037/apl0001228

Saidi, N., Michael, F., Sumilan, H., Lim, S., Jonathan, V., Hamidi, H., & Ahmad, A. (2019). The Relationship Between Working Environment and Employee Performance. Journal of Cognitive Sciences and Human Development. .DOI: 10.33736/jcshd.1916.2019

Saunders, J., Sridaromont, K., & Gallegos, B. (2020). Steps to Establish a Healthy Work Environment in an Academic Nursing Setting. *Nurse Educator*, 46(1), 2–4. DOI: 10.1097/NNE.0000000000000829 PMID: 33283997

Simons, P., Linden, J., & Duffy, T. (1999). New Learning: Three Ways to Learn in a New Balance. .DOI: 10.1007/0-306-47614-2_1

Soner. (2024). A Systematic Literature Review of Machine Learning Applications for Team Formation Problems. International Journal Of Informatics Technologies, DOI: 10.17671/gazibtd.1414527

Stacey. (2016). Positive employment relations: An exploratory study.

Surjit, S. (2024), Nurturing Positive Organizational Climates to Enhance Work Success. Advances in human resources management and organizational development book series, DOI: 10.4018/979-8-3693-1524-8.ch004

Susanne, M. (2021, February 25). Defining a positive work environment for hospital healthcare professionals: A Delphi study. *PLoS One*, 16(2), e0247530. Advance online publication. DOI: 10.1371/journal.pone.0247530

T. (2016). Quality of Work Life Components: A Literature Review. DOI: 10.25215/0401.042

Tara, . (2018). Using a positive practice environment framework to support recruitment. *Nursing Times*.

Valerie, J. (2014, November). Promoting Work-Family Balance Through Positive Psychology: A Practical Review of the Literature. *The Psychologist Manager Journal*, 17(4), 221–244. Advance online publication. DOI: 10.1037/mgr0000023

Vries, M. (1994). The leadership mystique. *The Academy of Management Perspectives*, 8(3), 73–89. DOI: 10.5465/ame.1994.9503101181

William, A. (2013). Career Conversations in Small- to Medium-Sized Businesses: A Competitive Advantage. Canadian Journal of Counselling and Psychotherapy.

Chapter 6
Building Resilience in Organizations:
Navigating Change and Challenges

Retno Lestari
https://orcid.org/0000-0003-4568-9596
Universitas Brawijaya, Indonesia

Heni Dwi Windarwati
Universitas Brawijaya, Indonesia

Tita Hariyanti
Universitas Brawijaya, Indonesia

ABSTRACT

Organizations are rapidly adjusting their strategies, operations, and employee value propositions in response to the disruptive era and evolving employee expectations. They acknowledge the necessity of crisis-specific strategies and flexible resource allocation to navigate varied challenges and opportunities effectively. This underscores the critical need to establish a resilient environment that encourages agile decision-making and improved time management. Organizations are dedicated to cultivating self-reliant work teams, culturally astute leadership, and adaptable leaders capable of fostering a skilled workforce. This chapter offers readers a comprehensive insight into organizational strategies for building resilience, enabling workers to adapt better manage resources and conflicts and build employee connectedness throughout the organization. Resilient organizations must prioritize cultivating adaptable leadership capable of facilitating behavioural adjustments and fostering the necessary changes in mindset to maintain resilience in the face of change.

DOI: 10.4018/979-8-3693-8457-2.ch006

INTRODUCTION

The concept of resilience has been the subject of extensive study across multiple decades in diverse contexts. It encompasses the capacity to withstand the impact of challenges, recover from adversity, and adapt to changing circumstances (Khan et al., 2024; Grygorenko et al., 2023; Sisto et al., 2019). Resilience involves effectively navigating and adapting to adversity, stress, and significant life challenges. It requires mental, emotional, and behavioural flexibility in response to internal and external pressures. This adaptive process ultimately leads to successful coping and adjustment in the face of various demands and hardships (American Psychological Association, 2024; Butler et al., 2021).

Resilience comprises various components: vulnerability, awareness, robustness, resistance, and recovery (Burnard & Bhamra, 2019). Resilience and vulnerability pertain to an organization's capacity to respond to global changes by evaluating disruptions and threats. These elements are crucial in preserving specific functions and are commonly employed in management and policy. Resilience is advocated for organizational management, whereas vulnerability assessments aid in prioritizing organizational adaptation strategies (Lecina-Diaz et al., 2024; Duchek, 2020a). Resilience is closely tied to self-awareness, requiring individuals or entities to acknowledge their strengths and limitations and empathise with others. It necessitates a strong mindset, sufficient time for introspection, and the ability to be mindful of one's emotions (Parnham, 2023). Robustness refers to a system's ability to maintain performance despite stressors. It can withstand adverse events and absorb strain while still functioning effectively. Organizations with robust systems have redundancies and safety measures to mitigate uncertainties. Many organizations transitioned to remote work during the pandemic to ensure business continuity. However, prolonged remote work arrangements may hurt employee performance (Munoz et al., 2022). In various disciplines, the fundamental concepts of resistance, recovery, and resilience are integral, denoting the capacity of intricate systems to endure amidst evolving circumstances. Resilience, epitomizing a synthesis of resistance and recovery, delineates a system's capability to endure or recuperate from disruptions. Human interventions exert substantial influence over ecological processes and evolution, underscoring the necessity for a comprehensive resilience framework encompassing social and cultural dimensions. Nurturing reciprocal associations amidst natural upheavals is essential in governance during this era marked by escalating socioecological dilemmas (Abbott et al., 2023; McDarby et al., 2023).

The concept of robustness entails the ability to endure adverse circumstances, while resilience refers to the capability to recover from setbacks. Throughout the COVID-19 pandemic, healthcare and educational institutions demonstrated robustness, withstanding the challenges presented, whereas the travel and tourism sectors displayed resilience, bouncing back from the impacts. Notably, conventional taxi services experienced a recovery, indicating resilience, while specialized taxi services catering to individuals with disabilities demonstrated robustness (Munoz et al., 2022).

Arnetz and colleagues have formulated a stress and resilience model encompassing four hierarchical levels: individual, group/team, agency/organization, and society. Resilience is evaluated at each level, emphasizing challenges and advantages. At the individual level, challenges can be constructive when coupled with control, utilization of skills, and positive outlooks, while adverse experiences stem from a lack of control, unpredictability, and perceived threats. Prolonged stressors can result in fatigue, thereby impacting performance. Enhancing employees' sense of control, predictability, skill employment, and positive expectations is imperative to mitigate these effects (Arnetz, 1996). Resilience plays a critical role in the survival of organizations within a complex and uncertain environment. It is underpinned by two core principles: the practice of "intelligent wariness" and the pursuit of operational perfection amidst persistent unease. Resilient organizations can swiftly identify weak signals and take prompt action to restore operations following disruptions. Nonetheless, a generalized approach to resilience theory may hinder the discovery of specific insights valuable for organizations operating within high-risk systems. Inaccurate perceptions of resilience can result in catastrophic failures within safety-critical organizations. The amalgamation of complexity and resilience discussions has distorted representations of high-reliability organizations (HROs). It is imperative to distinguish localized adaptations from unfavourable developments to attain more excellent reliability and safety objectives (Pettersen Gould, 2019; Xiao & Cao, 2017).

The inherent challenge in assessing resilience lies in its indirect observability, as various components' intricate interplay and interconnectedness predominantly shape it. These interdependent relationships underpin the intricate capacity to confront disruptions and adversities effectively. Resilience can manifest in two forms: active resilience, characterized by proactive engagement and adaptation to change, and passive resilience, which focuses on enduring disturbances (Burnard & Bhamra, 2019; Southwick et al., 2014). The correlation between proactive personality and organizational resilience has yet to be explored, as prior research has primarily concentrated on individual characteristics contributing to resilience. A proactive personality is associated with behaviours and initiatives that embrace change, such as seeking assistance, optimizing workplace resources, and taking charge of one's career. Leadership styles, particularly transformational leadership, have the potential to drive superior performance in employees with high self-esteem and a propensity for risk-taking. Empowering and contingent rewards leadership styles are anticipated to promote resilient behaviours in highly proactive employees. Furthermore, optimism, acknowledgement, and timely feedback are linked to heightened employee resilience (Burnard & Bhamra, 2019; Bai et al., 2022).

The complexity of resilience arises from its diverse manifestations and configurations. A crucial aspect is maintaining structure and functionality in the face of adversity. Developing resilience within organizations involves understanding how various variables interact and connect (Evenseth et al., 2022). Despite the increasing emphasis on resilience, there remains a need for further exploration and understanding of its attributes, particularly in the context of organizational resilience. Ultimately, the intriguing central question revolves around when organizations can withstand challenges and when they choose to pursue change (Duchek et al., 2020b; Hillmann & Guenther, 2021).

Organizations that demonstrate resilience have the ability to transform challenges into opportunities for sustainable growth. Developing resilience is paramount in the face of disruptions such as geopolitical conflicts, market contractions, public health crises, talent scarcity, and environmental shifts (Villar et al., 2023). According to research conducted by McKinsey, resilient organizations exhibit stronger financial performance and are less susceptible to insolvency. To cultivate resilience, organizations ought to construct adaptable frameworks, empower self-reliant teams, and allocate resources towards talent and culture development. However, the most crucial aspect is the role of leadership in nurturing flexible approaches and guiding the organization through change. Proactive investment in resilience can confer a competitive edge and enable organizations to adeptly navigate forthcoming challenges (Maor et al., 2022).

Throughout this section, we will explore a wide range of organizational strategies for cultivating and strengthening resilience. These strategies will encompass various aspects of organizational structure, culture, leadership, and change management, focusing on building resilience at the organization's individual and collective levels.

A SHIFTING ERA LEADS TO ORGANIZATIONAL RESILIENCE

Businesses today encounter unparalleled challenges in a rapidly evolving environment. The ability to adapt and remain resilient is essential for sustainable growth. In this context, data and AI play a pivotal role. Resilience involves cultivating agility, adaptability, and foresight to thrive amidst adversity (Mosteanu, 2024). Achieving organizational resilience demands visionary leadership, innovation, and a culture of continuous learning, a key element in the process of thriving amidst adversity (Southwick et al., 2017). Resilience within the business sphere encompasses an organization's capacity to recuperate, adjust, and evolve in the face of disruptions. It entails strategic understanding and operational adeptness in managing internal and external jolts, thus empowering enterprises to navigate unforeseen circumstances and safeguard their continuity adeptly.

Organizational resilience enables entities to withstand external disruptions and capitalize on emerging prospects. This capability emanates from five fundamental pillars: operational, strategic, financial, social, and organizational resilience. The operational pillar encompasses a comprehensive array of considerations, including technology, while the social pillar centres on community dynamics. Defining organizational resilience, particularly regarding workforce adaptability, is pivotal yet intricate. Given the multidimensional essence of resilience, a company's survival invariably hinges on diverse facets. Recognizing and enhancing resilience is indispensable for sustaining business operations in the wake of abrupt upheavals, necessitating the rectification of vulnerabilities across varying dimensions of the organization (World Economic Forum, 2022).

The progression of human resource management (HRM) practices is undergoing significant transformation due to the influence of new technologies, presenting considerable challenges in effectively overseeing an increasingly diverse workforce. Revolutionary innovations fundamentally reshape various facets of HRM, including recruitment, legal compliance, monitoring, coaching, and performance management. The incorporation of autonomous technologies offers promising potential for addressing future employment requirements. Furthermore, electronic HRM systems and communication technologies are essential for adapting to and harnessing disruptive innovations. While there is widespread acknowledgement of the potential of disruptive technologies in HRM, further comprehensive research is imperative to comprehend their complete impact fully (Panda et al., 2024; Ali et al., 2023).

Based on the discussions held at the World Economic Forum (2022), it is recommended that the framework for organizational resilience should be organized around four essential principles crucial for businesses to establish and maintain resilience in an increasingly uncertain future. These principles are: (1) Resolve, (2) Communication, (3) Agility, and (4) Empowerment.

1. Resolve: This pertains to the organization's steadfast determination to endure and prosper in adversity. Resilience encompasses individuals' mental attitudes, behaviours, and self-nurturing practices during challenging periods. To bolster resilience, it is imperative to develop four fundamental skills: positive thinking, problem-solving, embracing failure, and self-compassion. Positive thinking enables individuals to gain a broader perspective and counteract negative thoughts. Problem-solving directs attention away from the problem and toward seeking solutions, thus enhancing confidence. Embracing failure allows individuals to extract lessons from mistakes without harsh self-criticism, fostering personal growth. Self-compassion involves treating oneself with kindness during difficult

times, thus rendering challenges more manageable. Proficiency in these skills empowers individuals to strengthen their resilience and confront adversity with determination and perseverance (Garcia et al., 2022; Hartmann et al., 2022; Abramson & Schmidt, 2024).

Resolving is crucial for an organization's survival, relying on the leadership team's commitment to weathering storms and preparing for challenges. They must prioritize organizational resilience, assess resilience in hiring, measure employee commitment, and link resilience to performance metrics. Successful leaders prioritize resilience, involving key stakeholders and fostering a culture of engagement for long-term success. In 2008, the Danish company DONG Energy generated 85% of its revenue from fossil fuels; however, it committed to transition to 85% renewable energy sources. The necessity for long-term sustainability precipitated this strategic shift in response to evolving societal perspectives and regulatory obstacles. After rebranding to Ørsted in 2017, the company rapidly established itself as a leading force in offshore wind power generation, achieving this status within a decade (World Economic Forum, 2022).

2. Communication: Emphasizing the crucial role of transparent and efficient communication in transitioning from mere assertion of principles to developing actionable plans, goals, and procedures that bolster resilience. The communication-centered approach to resilience underscores the pivotal role of communication in shaping social frameworks and navigating intricate interactions, particularly in times of upheaval or emergency (Centre for Research and Evidence on Security Threats, 2023; Kim, 2021).

Individual resilience in the workplace pertains to an individual's capacity to effectively navigate challenges by leveraging organizational connections and social support networks (Franken et al., 2022). On the other hand, organizational resilience hinges on communication strategies to mitigate the impact of adversities, with autonomy and mission statements playing crucial roles. Constructive sensemaking enables organizations to address current issues, while inter-organizational resilience involves establishing cross-sector networks and coordinated endeavours. Meanwhile, organizational resilience underscores the importance of proactive planning, robust communication, strategic partnerships, and extensive networks to facilitate improvisation when facing challenges (Doerfel et al., 2022).

Communication is a critical component in the execution of organizational resilience. While business continuity planning is widespread, the effective dissemination of crucial elements and priorities to uphold essential processes is fundamental (Kim, 2021). Organizations can enrich their communication strategies by engaging with a broad audience, establishing cross-functional teams, and monitoring responsiveness and transparency. It is imperative for employees not only to acknowledge communication but also to have avenues for providing feedback. Communication frequency and openness can be assessed through attendance rates at informational sessions and input collection via surveys and focus groups. This continuous evaluation can assist organizations in fortifying their resilience objectives and response strategies while identifying potential points of failure. Following the 2011 Tōhoku earthquake, Renesas Electronics' Naka factory ceased production operations. Effective communication was pivotal in reestablishing strategic direction, fostering resilience, and encouraging collaboration. Adopting the "big room method" facilitated the implementation and progress tracking management. Renesas emphasized communication, promoting a positive organizational culture, and sharing knowledge despite facing challenges such as earthquakes and fire. This underscores the significance of ongoing initiatives to enhance resilience (World Economic Forum, 2022).

3. Agility: This focuses on promptly implementing and adapting to abrupt changes, allowing companies to maintain flexibility amid uncertainty. Organizational agility plays a pivotal role in crisis management and organizational resilience. Prior research has established a positive correlation between organizational agility and crisis management, emphasizing the significance of adaptability, responsiveness, and swiftness in enhancing organizational resilience and crisis management. Given the dynamic nature of organizations, the ability to make prompt decisions and take swift action is imperative. Furthermore, studies have underscored a substantial link between organizational resilience and crisis management, underscoring the criticality of proactive and reactive risk management in effectively addressing crises. It is consistently evidenced that heightened resilience leads to improved crisis management outcomes. Notably, organizational agility exerts a more pronounced influence on organizational resilience than crisis management, thereby underscoring the essentiality of both these constructs for organizations contending with crises (Bek Yağmur & Aydıntuğ Myrvang, 2023; Papla et al., 2022). Organizations must prioritize organizational agility and resilience to effectively respond to and recover from crises. Rapid responses, competency, and robust decision-making processes are pivotal for crisis management. Organizational agility and resilience are indispensable elements for ensuring the prosperity and longevity of organizations when confronted with unforeseen events (Mizrak, 2024).

The cultivation of agility within organizations facilitates efficient execution, with determination providing strategic direction and communication serving as the conduit. Essential components of agility encompass a growth-oriented mindset, unwavering dedication to continual learning and advancement, and the presence of a diverse workforce. Companies with crisis training are better equipped to promptly and effectively identify and address new challenges. Preparing to transition into crisis response mode is paramount, and meticulous planning and preparation are imperative for effectively managing crises. Practical measures that companies can implement include: (1) Scenario planning, (2) The promotion of training and development opportunities, and (3) The establishment of redundancy in critical functions to bolster resilience. During the transition to remote work, Allianz effectively mitigated the growing cyber threats by implementing innovative processes, tools, and training. The organization emphasized cybersecurity preparedness through extensive training for all staff levels, scenario planning, and crisis simulations. This proactive approach played a crucial role in managing the Log4J crisis and addressing increased cyber threats during the Russian invasion of Ukraine, underscoring the paramount importance of cybersecurity in safeguarding the interests of its clients (World Economic Forum, 2022).

4. Empowerment: This involves nurturing an environment that empowers individuals to take ownership and collaborate effectively with their peers to address new challenges as they arise. Resilience and empowerment are pivotal in community psychology, emphasizing individual and collective adaptation and growth within challenging environments. These approaches highlight the significance of local strengths and resources in enhancing the quality of life and achieving positive outcomes while aligning with cultural values. Nevertheless, the absence of consensus regarding the definitions and implementation of resilience and empowerment has led to notable confusion and criticism within the discipline. Experts are actively working to clarify these concepts, delineate their theoretical underpinnings, and refine their practical application within community psychology to optimize their effectiveness in fostering positive change and empowering communities (Brodsky et al., 2013).

Successfully building organizational resilience necessitates empowering the workforce to propel the organization ahead. Empowerment facilitates employees in taking ownership of strategies, collaborating effectively in crises, and contributing to overall resilience. Organizations seeking to empower their workforce can engage with HR to address employee well-being gaps, foster cross-functional interactions, offer training and mentorship opportunities, support work-life balance, and collaborate with external partners for well-being programs. Leadership plays a pivotal role in enhancing employees' knowledge and skills for crisis management while prioritizing their physical, mental, and emotional well-being as the cornerstone of resilience. Committed to Good (CTG) engages with the humanitarian sector to deliver staffing and logistical support in areas affected by conflict. In more than 25 nations, CTG enables teams to respond effectively to evolving conditions and navigate political, economic, and security challenges during crises. The organization prioritizes a unified sense of purpose, empowering frontline personnel to exercise autonomy while upholding close alignment with leadership. This strategy cultivates an environment where each employee's input is esteemed, fostering proactive decision-making that aligns with the organization's mission. Such an approach is particularly critical in dynamic settings where swift action is imperative (World Economic Forum, 2022).

The concept of empowerment in the health professions, such as nursing, is heavily influenced by Kanter's power distinctions, which affect job satisfaction through access to resources. Building on this, Laschinger et al. delved deeper into the notion, emphasizing the impact of psychological empowerment on work stress. Structural empowerment, shaped by supportive workplace structures, is closely aligned with psychological empowerment, nurturing the voices of nurses. Autonomy in nursing plays a critical role in enabling decision-making, thereby reflecting on the quality of care provided. Leadership styles such as Authentic and Transformational Leadership significantly impact empowerment and patient safety. The newly developed Strengths-Based Nursing and Healthcare Leadership (SBNH-L) framework seeks to bolster agency and autonomy in nursing practice. Establishing a framework for this leadership is crucial for cultivating a positive work environment (Gottlieb et al., 2021).

Structural empowerment entails delegating power and decision-making, granting employees greater autonomy. Formal empowerment affords employees flexibility in their work procedures, while informal empowerment arises from positive social relationships. Formal empowerment arises from allowing employees to participate in decision-making, while informal empowerment influences the extent to which this empowerment is realized. This self-reinforcing process is facilitated by colleagues connecting and engaging with one another. Structural empowerment positively impacts organizational resilience when there is psychological safety at all organizational levels and sustained management commitment. A causal loop diagram illustrates how top management commitment influences structural empowerment and psychological safety. Regular communication and the integration of employee input are vital components of this process (Romme et al., 2019).

POWERFUL STRATEGIES TO BOOST ORGANIZATIONAL RESILIENCE

Organizational resilience is a complex and interdependent concept with numerous influencing factors. The abundance of research on resilience complicates developing a clear understanding as different definitions and components are explored, contributing to the concept's diverse nature. Efforts to consolidate the variables that impact resilience into a cohesive framework are essential for advancing our understanding of organizational resilience despite the challenges posed by the broad nature of the concept.

Organizational resilience encompasses various building blocks and their underlying factors. The significance of employee innovation, organizational culture, and positive leadership in influencing resilience cannot be overstated. Change management, a critical component of adaptation, informed by experiences of adversity, plays a pivotal role in organizational adaptation. Pre-crisis resources, including financial and technological capabilities, are indispensable for surmounting challenges. Current research underscores the necessity for a comprehensive understanding of resilience, which is presently lacking in scholarly investigations. Future research endeavours should delve into the interplay of foundational elements and their indispensability for resilience while considering variations in strategies tailored for organizations of varying scales. A holistic grasp of the interconnected nature of resilience components can enrich our comprehension of organizational resilience. While these blocks may initially seem to operate independently, a closer analysis reveals their interdependencies. For example, a diverse workforce can influence employees' ability to innovate during crises, and a culture focused on anticipating and managing adversity may be shaped by managerial attitudes. Additionally, leaders who promote open communication during turbulent times foster positive emotions in employees (He et al., 2022; Vakilzadeh & Haas, 2021).

Employing quantitative approaches to resilience management, especially those utilizing data and AI, equips organizations with powerful tools to navigate challenges successfully. Real-world case studies demonstrate how these data-driven and AI-enabled approaches have empowered organizations to overcome obstacles and achieve favourable outcomes. By harnessing data and AI, organizations can comprehend their risk landscape, anticipate disruptions, and make well-informed decisions. Enterprise resilience is indispensable for organizations striving to remain competitive, drive growth, and embrace innovation successfully (KPMG, 2023).

The experiences during the pandemic have raised significant concerns regarding the economic sustainability of small and medium enterprises (SMEs). The key to resilience is fostering collaboration, transparency, adaptability, innovation, and sustainability to ensure continuity and minimize adverse resource impacts. Collaboration necessitates partnerships with stakeholders and a concentrated approach to local markets. Transparency demands clear communication and the embracement of digital technology. Adaptability involves embracing governmental initiatives and adjusting policies. Innovation encompasses the facilitation of business transactions and the adoption of circular economic practices. Finally, sustainability entails individual-level resilience and work and personal life harmonization. Future research endeavours should prioritize validating these recommendations to assist SMEs in developed and developing economies (Zuthsi et al., 2021).

Research has consistently shown that small and medium-sized manufacturing enterprises (SMEs) can significantly boost their performance by proactively adopting resilience strategies. These strategies, such as visibility and predefined decision plans, are instrumental in enabling well-informed decision-making. They also play a crucial role in optimizing resources and improving operational efficiency, which ultimately leads to increased customer satisfaction. SMEs that can effectively predict and respond to disruptions can reduce downtime and maintain operational continuity, thereby reaping the benefits of these resilience strategies. Businesses can amplify their performance outcomes by striking a delicate equilibrium between exploitation and exploration. Moreover, companies skilled in navigating uncertainties and seizing opportunities can achieve superior performance by harmonizing innovation with efficiency. Ambidextrous capabilities are pivotal in mediating the correlation between proactive resilience strategies and organizational performance, underpinning long-term success within the manufacturing sector (Pertheban et al., 2023).

An organization's resilience is deeply rooted in its human capital, which forms the bedrock of its capacity to respond effectively pre-crisis, during a crisis, and post-crisis. While strategic and operational resilience may face challenges beyond an executive's control, the cultivation of organizational resilience is a responsibility and an opportunity for business leaders. Their actions can make a substantial and enduring impact (Xiao & Cao, 2017; Barasa et al., 2018).

In organizations, employees are vital assets that significantly contribute to competitive advantage. The role of Human Resource Management (HRM) in bolstering organizational resilience is pivotal through the consistent implementation of HR practices. Strategic HRM (SHRM) can further enhance organizational resilience by fostering individual skills at the managerial level. Amid the COVID-19 crisis, a proficient workforce is imperative for organizational resilience, and HR practices are indispensable for cultivating employees' adaptability to change (Fathy El Dessouky & Al-Ghareeb, 2020).

Visser & Jacobs (2019) examined The Human Capital Future Resilience Index, a comprehensive tool designed to foster behaviours and capabilities that bolster resilience at individual, organizational, and socio-ecological levels. The index's role in identifying ten elements of future resilience, including emergency preparedness, creative adaptability, technological empowerment, dynamic employability, diversity cultivation, participative governance, systemic responsiveness, resource efficiency, purposeful motivation, and wellbeing orientation, is crucial in fostering resilience at all these levels.

Emergency preparedness for organizations and employees underscores crisis coping, such as conflicts, natural disasters, and economic downturns. Creative adaptability hinges on the capacity to innovate and resolve challenges. Technological empowerment emphasizes both the advantageous and detrimental effects of digital connectivity on the job market. Dynamic employability addresses workers' need to adjust to evolving job roles resulting from continuous technological progress.

Diversity cultivation is vital for stimulating creativity and boosting organizational performance, while participative governance advocates for comprehensive organizational frameworks that empower employees. Systemic responsiveness, a proactive approach that involves understanding broader socio-ecological systems and tackling environmental issues, has the potential to inspire significant change. Resource efficiency is crucial for creating sustainable job opportunities and attracting top talent. Purposeful motivation strives to engage employees in meaningful work to enhance productivity and retention. Wellbeing orientation underscores the significance of comprehensive wellbeing initiatives to improve employee health and work-life balance. Organizations can adeptly navigate future disruptions and challenges by addressing these tenets of human capital resilience.

In summary, resilience is essential for organizations to withstand challenges and thrive in changing circumstances. To build resilience, organizations should create adaptable frameworks, empower teams, and invest in talent and culture development. Data and AI are crucial in understanding risk landscapes and making well-informed decisions. Collaboration, transparency, adaptability, innovation, and sustainability are vital for fostering resilience, especially for small and medium enterprises.

REFERENCES

Abbott, B., Underwood, K., Seybold, E., Kincaid, D., Hamshaw, S., Lee, R., Rizzo, D., Brown, B., Toolin, R., Chorover, J., Li, L., Lewis, G., Sayedi, S. S., St. Clair, S., Buck, R., Aanderud, Z., Brahney, J., Nixon, R., Wang, W., & Perdrial, J. (2023). *Resistance, recovery, and resilience: Rethinking the three Rs of survival in the Anthropocene*. https://doi.org/DOI: 10.22541/essoar.167390526.69780816/v1

Abramson, T., & Schmidt, B. (2024, April 24). *Cultivating Psychological Resilience/ Elders*. https://generations.asaging.org/cultivating-psychological-resilienceelders

Ali, R., Ateeq, A., Ani, Z. A., & Ali, S. A. (2023). A Critical Review of Contemporary Trends and Challenges in Human Resource Management Article Information. *ResearchGate*, 4(2), 22–27. DOI: 10.11648/ IJIHRM.04.02.2023.003

American Psychological Association. (2024). *Resilience*. https://www.apa.org/ topics/resilience

Arnetz, B. B. (1996). Techno-stress: A prospective psychophysiological study of the impact of a controlled stress-reduction program in advanced telecommunication systems design work. *Journal of Occupational and Environmental Medicine*, 38(1), 53–65. DOI: 10.1097/00043764-199601000-00017 PMID: 8871332

Bai, Y., Wang, Z., Alam, M., Gul, F., & Wang, Y. (2022). The Impact of Authentic Leadership on Innovative Work Behavior: Mediating Roles of Proactive Personality and Employee Engagement. *Frontiers in Psychology*, 13, 879176. DOI: 10.3389/ fpsyg.2022.879176 PMID: 35756212

Barasa, E., Mbau, R., & Gilson, L. (2018). What Is Resilience and How Can It Be Nurtured? A Systematic Review of Empirical Literature on Organizational Resilience. *International Journal of Health Policy and Management*, 7(6), 491–503. DOI: 10.15171/ijhpm.2018.06 PMID: 29935126

Bek Yağmur, Ö., & Aydıntuğ Myrvang, N. (2023). The effect of organizational agility on crisis management process and organizational resilience: Health sector example. *International Journal of Disaster Risk Reduction*, 96, 103955. DOI: 10.1016/j.ijdrr.2023.103955

Brodsky, A. E., & Cattaneo, L. B. (2013). A transconceptual model of empowerment and resilience: Divergence, convergence and interactions in kindred community concepts. *American Journal of Community Psychology*, 52(3–4), 333–346. DOI: 10.1007/s10464-013-9599-x PMID: 24057948

Burnard, K. J., & Bhamra, R. (2019). Challenges for organisational resilience. *Continuity & Resilience Review*, 1(1), 17–25. DOI: 10.1108/CRR-01-2019-0008

Butler, C., O'Shea, D., & Truxillo, D. (2021). *Adaptive and Proactive Coping in the Process of Developing Resilience* (Vol. 19). Research in Occupational Stress and Well Being. DOI: 10.1108/S1479-355520210000019002

Centre for Research and Evidence on Security Threats. (2023). *A Communication Perspective on Resilience.* https://crestresearch.ac.uk/comment/a-communication-perspective-on-resilience/

Doerfel, M. L., Kim, M., Kwestel, M., Yoon, H., & Quow, J. (2022). Resilience organizing: A multilevel communication framework. *Journal of Communication*, 72(6), 605–618. DOI: 10.1093/joc/jqac027

Duchek, S. (2020a). Organizational resilience: A capability-based conceptualization. *Business Research*, 13(1), 215–246. DOI: 10.1007/s40685-019-0085-7

Duchek, S., Raetze, S., & Scheuch, I. (2020b). The role of diversity in organizational resilience: A theoretical framework. *Business Research*, 13(2), 387–423. DOI: 10.1007/s40685-019-0084-8

Evenseth, L., Sydnes, M., & Gausdal, A. (2022). Building Organizational Resilience Through Organizational Learning: A Systematic Review. *Frontiers in Communication*, 7, 837386. Advance online publication. DOI: 10.3389/fcomm.2022.837386

Fathy El Dessouky, N., & Al-Ghareeb, A. (2020). Human Resource Management and Organizational Resilience in The Era of COVID-19: Theoretical Insights, Challenges and Implications. *2020 Second International Sustainability and Resilience Conference: Technology and Innovation in Building Designs(51154)*, 1–6. DOI: 10.1109/IEEECONF51154.2020.9319967

Franken, E., Plimmer, G., Malinen, S., & Bryson, J. (2022). Growing and Adapting During Continuous Change: Building Employee Resilience in the Public Sector. In Pinheiro, R., Frigotto, M. L., & Young, M. (Eds.), *Towards Resilient Organizations and Societies: A Cross-Sectoral and Multi-Disciplinary Perspective* (pp. 143–170). Springer International Publishing. DOI: 10.1007/978-3-030-82072-5_6

Garcia, A. C. M., Ferreira, A. C. G., Silva, L. S. R., da Conceição, V. M., Nogueira, D. A., & Mills, J. (2022). Mindful Self-Care, Self-Compassion, and Resilience Among Palliative Care Providers During the COVID-19 Pandemic. *Journal of Pain and Symptom Management*, 64(1), 49–57. DOI: 10.1016/j.jpainsymman.2022.03.003 PMID: 35292366

Gottlieb, L. N., Gottlieb, B., & Bitzas, V. (2021). Creating Empowering Conditions for Nurses with Workplace Autonomy and Agency: How Healthcare Leaders Could Be Guided by Strengths-Based Nursing and Healthcare Leadership (SBNH-L). *Journal of Healthcare Leadership*, 13, 169–181. DOI: 10.2147/JHL.S221141 PMID: 34349581

Grygorenko, Z., & Naydonova, G. (2023). The Concept Of "Resilience": History Of Formation And Approaches To Definition. *Public Administration And Law Review*, 76–88. DOI: 10.36690/2674-5216-2023-2-76-88

Hartmann, S., Backmann, J., Newman, A., Brykman, K. M., & Pidduck, R. J. (2022). Psychological resilience of entrepreneurs: A review and agenda for future research. *Journal of Small Business Management*, 60(5), 1041–1079. DOI: 10.1080/00472778.2021.2024216

He, Z., Huang, H., Choi, H., & Bilgihan, A. (2022). Building organizational resilience with digital transformation. *Journal of Service Management*, 34(1), 147–171. DOI: 10.1108/JOSM-06-2021-0216

Khan, H., Ozkan, K. S. L., Deligonul, S., & Cavusgil, E. (2024). Redefining the organizational resilience construct using a frame based methodology: A new perspective from the ecology based approach. *Journal of Business Research*, 172, 114397. DOI: 10.1016/j.jbusres.2023.114397

Kim, Y. (2021). Building organizational resilience through strategic internal communication and organization-employee relationships. *Journal of Applied Communication Research*, 49(5), 589–608. Advance online publication. DOI: 10.1080/00909882.2021.1910856

KPMG. (2023, June 7). *KPMG Powered Enterprise Resilience—KPMG Global*. KPMG. https://kpmg.com/xx/en/home/insights/2021/02/powered-enterprise-resilience.html

Lecina-Diaz, J., Martínez-Vilalta, J., Lloret, F., & Seidl, R. (2024). Resilience and vulnerability: Distinct concepts to address global change in forests. *Trends in Ecology & Evolution*, 39(8), 706–715. DOI: 10.1016/j.tree.2024.03.003 PMID: 38531712

Maor, D., Park, M., & Weddle, B. (2022). *Building organizational resilience*. McKinsey. https://www.mckinsey.com/capabilities/people-and-organizational-performance/our-insights/raising-the-resilience-of-your-organization

McDarby, G., Seifeldin, R., Zhang, Y., Mustafa, S., Petrova, M., Schmets, G., Porignon, D., Dalil, S., & Saikat, S. (2023). A synthesis of concepts of resilience to inform operationalization of health systems resilience in recovery from disruptive public health events including COVID-19. *Frontiers in Public Health*, 11, 1105537. DOI: 10.3389/fpubh.2023.1105537 PMID: 37250074

Mizrak, K. (2024). *Crisis Management and Risk Mitigation: Strategies for Effective Response and Resilience* (pp. 254–278). DOI: 10.4018/979-8-3693-1155-4.ch013

Mosteanu, N. R. (2024). Adapting to the Unpredictable: Building Resilience for Business Continuity in an Ever-Changing Landscape. *European Journal of Theoretical and Applied Sciences*, 2(1), 444–457. DOI: 10.59324/ejtas.2024.2(1).37

Munoz, A., Billsberry, J., & Ambrosini, V. (2022). Resilience, robustness, and antifragility: Towards an appreciation of distinct organizational responses to adversity. *International Journal of Management Reviews*, 24(2), 181–187. DOI: 10.1111/ijmr.12289

Panda, G., Dash, M. K., Samadhiya, A., Kumar, A., & Mulat-weldemeskel, E. (2024). Artificial intelligence as an enabler for achieving human resource resiliency: Past literature, present debate and future research directions. *International Journal of Industrial Engineering and Operations Management*, 6(4), 326–347. DOI: 10.1108/IJIEOM-05-2023-0047

Papla, R., Yeltayeva, D., & Pak, D. (2022). Strategic Agility Or Resilience: What Should Smes Focus On During The Crisis? *InterConf*, 18(95), 82–91. DOI: 10.51582/interconf.19-20.01.2022.007

Parnham, N. (2023). *Resilience—Self-awareness and self-connection.* https://ninaparnham.com/resilience-self-awareness-and-self-connection

Pertheban, T. R., Thurasamy, R., Marimuthu, A., Venkatachalam, K. R., Annamalah, S., Paraman, P., & Hoo, W. C. (2023). The Impact of Proactive Resilience Strategies on Organizational Performance: Role of Ambidextrous and Dynamic Capabilities of SMEs in Manufacturing Sector. *Sustainability (Basel)*, 15(16), 16. Advance online publication. DOI: 10.3390/su151612665

Pettersen Gould, K. (2019). Precursor Resilience in Practice – An Organizational Response to Weak Signals. In *Exploring Resilience* (pp. 51–58). Springer. DOI: 10.1007/978-3-030-03189-3_7

Romme, G., van den Berg, J., Blanc, P. M., & Alblas, A. (2019). Do Empowered Employees Boost Organizational Resilience? A Case Study in the Dutch Home Care Industry. *Academy of Management Annual Meeting Proceedings, 2019*, 19138. DOI: 10.5465/AMBPP.2019.19138abstract

Sisto, A., Vicinanza, F., Campanozzi, L. L., Ricci, G., Tartaglini, D., & Tambone, V. (2019). Towards a Transversal Definition of Psychological Resilience: A Literature Review. *Medicina*, 55(11), 745. DOI: 10.3390/medicina55110745 PMID: 31744109

Southwick, F., Martini, B., Charney, D., & Southwick, S. (2017). *Leadership and Resilience*. DOI: 10.1007/978-3-319-31036-7_18

Southwick, S. M., Bonanno, G. A., Masten, A. S., Panter-Brick, C., & Yehuda, R. (2014). Resilience definitions, theory, and challenges: Interdisciplinary perspectives. *European Journal of Psychotraumatology*, 5. DOI: 10.3402/ejpt.v5.25338

Vakilzadeh, K., & Haase, A. (2021). The building blocks of organizational resilience: A review of the empirical literature. *Continuity & Resilience Review*, 3(1), 1–21. DOI: 10.1108/CRR-04-2020-0002

Villar, A., Paladini, S., & Buckley, O. (2023). Towards Supply Chain 5.0: Redesigning Supply Chains as Resilient, Sustainable, and Human-Centric Systems in a Post-pandemic World. *Operations Research Forum*, 4(3), 60. DOI: 10.1007/s43069-023-00234-3

Visser, W., & Jacobs, S. (2019). *Multi-level Resilience: A Human Capital Perspective*. University of Antwerp.

World Economic Forum. (2022). *Risk Proof: A Framework for Building Organizational Resilience in an Uncertain Future*. https://www.weforum.org/publications/risk-proof-a-framework-for-building-organizational-resilience-in-an-uncertain-future/

Xiao, L., & Cao, H. (2017). Organizational Resilience: The Theoretical Model and Research Implication. *ITM Web of Conferences, 12*, 04021. DOI: 10.1051/itmconf/20171204021

Zutshi, A., Mendy, J., Sharma, G. D., Thomas, A., & Sarker, T. (2021). From Challenges to Creativity: Enhancing SMEs' Resilience in the Context of COVID-19. *Sustainability (Basel)*, 13(12), 6542. Advance online publication. DOI: 10.3390/su13126542

Chapter 7
Character Education in Universities:
Anchoring Practical Wisdom to Foster Organizational Well-Being

Mehdi Chaoui Roqai
https://orcid.org/0009-0004-0034-4038
Sidi Mohammed Ben Abdellah University, Morocco

Saif Allah Allouani
https://orcid.org/0000-0002-2848-169X
Sidi Mohammed Ben Abdellah University, Morocco

Yassine Hassani Aboumehdi
Sidi Mohamed Ben Abdellah University, Morocco

Kenza Ennida
https://orcid.org/0000-0003-0884-6433
Sidi Mohammed Ben Abdellah University, Morocco

ABSTRACT

This chapter explores the essential role of character education in universities, emphasizing its capacity to foster organizational well-being through the development of practical wisdom and virtues. Drawing upon Ken Wilber's integral theory and neo-Aristotelian perspectives, the chapter examines how intellectual, civic, moral, and performance virtues can be systematically integrated into higher-education curricula. The significance of practical wisdom, particularly as articulated through the three-dimensional wisdom model, is highlighted in promoting psychosocial growth and well-being among students, thereby reducing self-centeredness and enhancing ethical decision-making. Furthermore, the chapter investigates how character ed-

DOI: 10.4018/979-8-3693-8457-2.ch007

ucation equips students to navigate the complexities of modern life, contributing to a more just and compassionate society. By integrating these theoretical frameworks with practical applications, the chapter presents a comprehensive approach to character education that is both philosophically rigorous and practically effective.

INTRODUCTION

Universities play a pivotal role in shaping the future leaders of society, a responsibility that extends beyond the mere transfer of knowledge. In an increasingly complex and ethically challenging world, there is a growing recognition of the need for holistic education that addresses not only the cognitive but also the moral and emotional development of students. This chapter explores the integration of character education in universities, emphasizing its importance for fostering both individual flourishing and organizational well-being.

Character education has been central to educational philosophy for centuries, with roots that trace back to ancient civilizations. Its role in modern higher education has become increasingly critical as global challenges—ranging from social inequality to environmental crises—demand leaders who are not only knowledgeable, but also wise and ethical (Sternberg, Jarvin, & Reznitskaya, 2008). The concept of eudaimonic well-being, or human flourishing, underscores this holistic approach to education, highlighting the need for universities to cultivate virtues such as integrity, empathy, and resilience in their students (Ryff & Keyes, 1995).

This chapter begins by examining the importance of character education within the higher education landscape, exploring its connection to the development of virtues. Character education is crucial in helping students navigate the complexities of modern life, where ethical dilemmas are prevalent and decisions often have far-reaching consequences. By fostering virtues, universities can equip students with the moral and ethical tools necessary for responsible citizenship, and leadership.

The discussion then delves into the nature of virtues, tracing their historical roots and contemporary relevance. Drawing from classical and modern philosophical frameworks, including the Three-Dimensional Wisdom Model, this chapter provides a comprehensive overview of how virtues can be systematically cultivated within university settings (Ardelt, 2003). The Three-Dimensional Wisdom Model, which integrates cognitive, reflective, and affective dimensions, serves as a crucial framework for understanding how wisdom can be developed and applied in educational contexts (Ardelt, 2004).

The concept of practical wisdom, or phronesis, is also explored as a meta-virtue that integrates and harmonizes other virtues, enabling individuals to make sound moral judgments in complex situations (Fowers, 2008). Practical wisdom is essential for the application of virtues in real-world contexts, particularly in environments where ethical decisions must be made quickly and with incomplete information.

Building on Ken Wilber's Integral Theory, this chapter proposes a holistic framework for character education that addresses the development of virtues across multiple dimensions—individual and collective, interior and exterior (Wilber, 2001). This integrative approach ensures that character education is not limited to individual development but also encompasses the broader cultural and organizational contexts within which students operate.

Finally, the chapter examines the impact of character education on organizational well-being, highlighting its role in enhancing student engagement, promoting academic integrity, and fostering a positive institutional culture. By prioritizing character education, universities can create environments that support both personal and collective flourishing, ultimately contributing to a more just and compassionate society.

This chapter argues that character education is an indispensable component of higher education. By integrating virtues and practical wisdom into their curricula and institutional practices, universities can fulfill their mission to educate not just knowledgeable but also virtuous individuals who are prepared to lead with integrity and wisdom.

THE IMPORTANCE OF CHARACTER EDUCATION

Character education in universities is essential for fostering not only individual student development, but also the broader health and success of academic institutions. This section explores why character education is vital in higher education, focusing on its role in personal flourishing, academic integrity, and societal well-being.

Historical Context and Contemporary Relevance

The concept of character education is deeply embedded in the history of educational thought, with its roots tracing back to ancient civilizations. Aristotle, one of the earliest and most influential proponents, articulated the idea that education should not merely transmit knowledge, but also cultivate virtues that lead to *eudaimonia*—human flourishing (Aristotle, trans. Irwin, 1999). Aristotle's philosophy emphasized that virtues such as courage, temperance, and justice are not innate, but must be developed through education and practice. This classical perspective positioned character-education as central to the mission of early universities, which were seen as institutions responsible for shaping the moral and intellectual character of their students.

In the medieval period, this Aristotelian view of education was integrated into the curricula of the earliest European universities. These institutions, deeply influenced by religious and philosophical traditions, aimed to develop virtuous citizens who could contribute to the moral and social order of society. The concept of the "university" itself was founded on the ideal of *universitas*, a community of scholars dedicated to the pursuit of both intellectual and moral excellence. This historical context underscores the long-standing importance of character education in higher learning, where the formation of virtuous individuals was considered as vital as the acquisition of knowledge.

In contemporary times, the importance of character education has only intensified. As societies become more complex and interconnected, universities are increasingly recognizing that the value of education extends beyond the mere acquisition of knowledge and skills. The modern university faces the challenge of preparing students for a world where ethical dilemmas are pervasive, and where the consequences of actions are often global in scale. As the Jubilee Centre for Character and Virtues points out, the true value of a university education is evidenced not only in the professional success of graduates but also in their personal flourishing and their ability to contribute to the public good (Jubilee Centre for Character and Virtues, 2022).

Character education is essential for developing the virtues necessary for responsible citizenship. Universities today must equip students with the moral and ethical framework needed to navigate the complexities of the modern world. This involves not only fostering intellectual development but also cultivating virtues such as empathy, integrity, and social responsibility. The resurgence of interest in character education reflects a broader societal recognition that the challenges of the 21st century—ranging from climate change to social justice—cannot be addressed solely through technical knowledge but require individuals who are morally grounded and committed to the common good.

Furthermore, character education is increasingly viewed as a response to the perceived moral and ethical crises in contemporary society. Issues such as corruption, inequality, and the erosion of trust in public institutions highlight the need for leaders who are not only competent, but also virtuous. By integrating character education into their curricula, universities can play a pivotal role in addressing these challenges, preparing graduates who are not only skilled professionals, but also ethical leaders committed to positive social change.

The Role of Character Education in Higher Education

Character education is indispensable in higher education as it fosters the development of virtues that are integral to both academic success and personal growth. In universities, character education promotes virtues such as intellectual curiosity, resilience, and ethical judgment, which are essential for the pursuit of knowledge and understanding. The cultivation of these virtues aligns with the core mission of higher education: to develop individuals who are not only knowledgeable, but also capable of making wise and ethical decisions.

The Framework for Character Education emphasizes that good higher education is, by necessity, good character education. It asserts that universities must go beyond merely preparing students for the workforce; they must also equip students with the virtues necessary for living well within the framework of a democratic society (Jubilee Centre for Character and Virtues, 2022). This means fostering intellectual virtues such as curiosity and critical thinking, which enable students to engage deeply with their studies, question assumptions, and develop a nuanced understanding of complex issues.

Moreover, character education is closely linked to the concept of student flourishing—a central goal in higher education. Flourishing, as defined in the philosophical tradition following Aristotle, refers to living a life of purpose and meaning, characterized by social, moral, emotional, and intellectual fulfillment (Kristjánsson, 2020). Universities play a crucial role in fostering this kind of flourishing by creating environments where students can develop their character through both academic and extracurricular activities.

The integration of character education into university life also enhances the ethical culture of the institution. When students are encouraged to internalize virtues such as integrity, honesty, and respect, these values become embedded in the academic community, leading to a culture where ethical behavior is the norm. This not only reduces instances of academic dishonesty but also fosters a sense of trust and respect among students, faculty, and staff. In this way, character education contributes to the overall well-being of the academic community and ensures that universities fulfill their role as institutions that promote both intellectual and moral excellence.

The Impact of Character Education on Society

The impact of character education extends beyond the individual to society as a whole. By cultivating virtues in students, universities contribute to the building of a healthy, just, and thriving society. As universities embrace their civic mission, they are increasingly focused on developing graduates who are not only knowledgeable, but also ethically minded and socially responsible (Jubilee Centre for

Character and Virtues, 2022). This focus on character and values is essential for preparing students to address the complex challenges of the modern world, from ethical dilemmas in the workplace to broader societal issues such as inequality and environmental sustainability.

Character education equips students with the moral framework needed to navigate these challenges and to make decisions that prioritize the common good. Graduates who have been shaped by character education are more likely to lead with integrity, make ethical decisions, and contribute positively to their communities. This impact is particularly significant in leadership roles, where ethical decision-making can influence entire organizations and communities.

Furthermore, character education helps to bridge social divides within society by promoting virtues such as empathy, tolerance, and social responsibility. In a world where social fragmentation and polarization are increasingly prevalent, the ability to understand and respect diverse perspectives is crucial. Universities that prioritize character education contribute to the creation of a more inclusive and cohesive society by preparing graduates who are capable of engaging constructively with others, regardless of their differences.

Character education is integral to the mission of universities. It enhances the value of higher education by promoting personal and societal flourishing, ensuring that graduates are well-equipped to lead lives of purpose and contribute positively to society. As universities continue to navigate the challenges of the 21st century, the emphasis on character education will be crucial for maintaining the relevance and impact of higher education.

THE NATURE OF VIRTUES

Virtues, as foundational elements of character education, are qualities that enable individuals to lead ethical and fulfilling lives. This section explores the nature of virtues, tracing their historical origins and examining their relevance in contemporary education.

Historical Origins of Virtues

The concept of virtue has its roots in ancient philosophy, particularly in the works of Aristotle, who emphasized the importance of cultivating virtues as a means of achieving *eudaimonia*, or human flourishing (Aristotle, trans. Irwin, 1999). Aristotle's *Nicomachean Ethics* is one of the earliest and most influential works on virtue ethics, outlining the idea that virtues are habits that can be developed through practice and education. Aristotle identified several key virtues, including courage, temperance, and justice, which he believed were essential for living a good life.

Aristotle argued that virtues are a mean between two extremes, with courage, for example, being the mean between recklessness and cowardice. This idea of virtues as a balance has influenced many subsequent philosophical traditions and remains central to contemporary discussions on character education. The Aristotelian framework highlights that virtues are not innate but must be cultivated through deliberate practice and reflection. This perspective has been foundational in the development of character education, which seeks to systematically nurture these qualities in students.

In addition to Aristotle, other philosophical traditions have also contributed to the understanding of virtues. Confucianism, for example, emphasizes virtues such as benevolence, righteousness, and filial piety, which are seen as essential for maintaining harmony in society (Confucius, trans. Lau, 1979). Similarly, Stoicism, a school of Hellenistic philosophy, advocates for virtues such as wisdom, courage, and self-control as a means of achieving inner peace and resilience in the face of adversity (Aurelius, trans. Hays, 2002). These historical perspectives provide a rich foundation for understanding the nature of virtues and their role in human development. They also underscore the universal appeal of virtues across different cultures and philosophical traditions.

The Modern Relevance of Virtues

In the modern era, the study and application of virtues have gained renewed significance, particularly through the fields of positive psychology and character education. These disciplines have expanded the understanding of virtues, emphasizing their crucial role in promoting individual well-being, psychological health, and societal flourishing. Positive psychology, a field founded by Martin Seligman and colleagues, focuses on the scientific study of human strengths and virtues that enable individuals and communities to thrive. It represents a paradigm shift from traditional psychology, which often concentrates on pathology, towards a more holistic view of human potential (Peterson & Seligman, 2004).

One of the landmark contributions of positive psychology to the study of virtues is the development of the Character Strengths and Virtues (CSV) classification by Christopher Peterson and Martin Seligman. This framework identifies 24 character strengths that are universally recognized and valued across cultures and time periods. These strengths are organized under six broad virtues: wisdom, courage, humanity, justice, temperance, and transcendence. Each virtue encompasses several specific strengths; for instance, wisdom includes strengths such as creativity, curiosity, and love of learning, while courage encompasses bravery, persistence, and integrity (Peterson & Seligman, 2004).

The CSV framework has had a profound impact on both academic research and practical applications in education, therapy, and organizational development. It offers a systematic approach to understanding and cultivating virtues, providing tools for individuals and institutions to assess and develop these strengths. This framework underscores the idea that virtues are not merely abstract moral ideals but tangible qualities that can be identified, nurtured, and applied in everyday life. The emphasis on universality in the CSV framework also highlights the cross-cultural relevance of virtues, reinforcing the notion that certain moral qualities are essential for human flourishing regardless of cultural context.

The modern approach to virtues, particularly as articulated in positive psychology, places a strong emphasis on their practical application in everyday life. Virtues are viewed not only as moral ideals but as essential skills that can be cultivated through intentional practice and education. This perspective aligns closely with the goals of character education, which seeks to develop students' ability to lead virtuous lives and contribute positively to society. By focusing on the cultivation of virtues, educators aim to equip students with the tools they need to navigate the moral and ethical challenges of modern life.

Character education programs that incorporate the principles of positive psychology typically involve a combination of didactic instruction, experiential learning, and reflective practices. These programs encourage students to identify and develop their own character strengths, understand how these strengths can be applied in various contexts, and reflect on the moral implications of their actions. For example, students might engage in activities that promote empathy and compassion, such as community service projects, or participate in discussions about ethical dilemmas that require the application of virtues like justice and fairness.

The practical application of virtues also extends to the professional realm, where virtues such as integrity, perseverance, and teamwork are increasingly recognized as critical for success. In fields ranging from business to medicine, the ability to apply virtues in decision-making processes is seen as a key component of ethical leadership. Modern organizations are beginning to recognize that fostering a virtuous culture not only enhances individual well-being but also contributes to organizational success and societal impact.

Moreover, the modern relevance of virtues is reflected in the growing interest in moral education and ethical leadership within higher education institutions. Universities are increasingly integrating character education into their curricula, recognizing that the development of virtues is essential for preparing students to become responsible citizens and leaders. Courses on ethics, leadership, and social responsibility often draw on the principles of positive psychology, encouraging students to reflect on their own character strengths and consider how they can apply these strengths to contribute to the greater good.

The Four Types of Virtues

In contemporary discussions on character education, virtues are often categorized into four broad types: intellectual virtues, civic virtues, moral virtues, and performance virtues. These categories help in understanding how different virtues contribute to the holistic development of individuals and the overall well-being of the academic community.

- **Intellectual Virtues:** These virtues relate to the pursuit of knowledge and the development of cognitive skills. Examples include curiosity, critical thinking, and open-mindedness. Intellectual virtues are essential for academic success, as they enable students to engage deeply with their studies, question assumptions, and develop a nuanced understanding of complex issues (Baehr, 2016).
- **Civic Virtues:** Civic virtues pertain to the responsibilities of individuals as members of a community. They include qualities such as service, civility, and justice. These virtues are crucial for fostering a sense of social responsibility among students, encouraging them to contribute positively to their communities and engage in activities that promote the common good (Dagger, 1997).
- **Moral Virtues:** Moral virtues are concerned with ethical behavior and personal integrity. Honesty, compassion, and humility are examples of moral virtues. These virtues guide individuals in making ethical decisions and acting in ways that align with their values and the moral standards of their society (MacIntyre, 2007).
- **Performance Virtues:** Performance virtues are those that contribute to achieving excellence in various domains of life. These include resilience, perseverance, and diligence. Performance virtues are particularly important in educational settings, where they help students overcome challenges, stay motivated, and achieve their academic and personal goals (Arthur et al., 2016).

The Jubilee Centre's Framework on Virtues

The Jubilee Centre for Character and Virtues, based at the University of Birmingham, has developed a comprehensive and influential framework that categorizes and defines various virtues, offering a valuable tool for educators, policymakers, and researchers in the field of character education. This framework is designed to provide a systematic approach to understanding and cultivating virtues in educational settings, emphasizing the holistic development of individuals. The Jubilee Centre's work has significantly contributed to the growing recognition of the importance of character education in contemporary society, particularly within the context of higher education.

According to the Jubilee Centre, virtues are not isolated traits but are deeply interrelated and mutually reinforcing. This means that the development of one virtue often supports and enhances the cultivation of others. For example, the intellectual virtue of curiosity can naturally lead to the moral virtue of honesty, as students who are genuinely curious about the world are more likely to seek truth and understanding, and in doing so, they develop a commitment to honesty and integrity in their intellectual pursuits (Arthur et al., 2015). Similarly, the civic virtue of justice may reinforce the moral virtue of empathy, as a commitment to fairness often involves understanding and considering the perspectives and needs of others.

The Jubilee Centre's framework categorizes virtues into four broad types: intellectual, civic, moral, and performance virtues. This categorization reflects the centre's belief in the comprehensive nature of character education, which must address multiple dimensions of human experience. The framework also emphasizes the dynamic interaction between these types of virtues. For instance, the performance virtue of perseverance can support the intellectual virtue of critical thinking, as sustained effort and determination are often required to engage deeply with complex ideas and to think critically about challenging problems. This interconnectedness highlights the importance of a balanced approach to character education, where educators seek to develop a wide range of virtues in their students, recognizing that each virtue contributes to the overall moral and intellectual development of the individual.

A central concept in the Jubilee Centre's framework is the notion of practical wisdom, or *phronesis*, which Aristotle considered the "master virtue." Practical wisdom is the ability to make sound moral judgments and take appropriate action in specific situations, balancing and applying different virtues as needed (Fowers, 2008). Aristotle argued that practical wisdom is essential for living a virtuous life because it guides individuals in how to act in ways that are both ethical and effective, even in complex and ambiguous circumstances. For example, practical wisdom enables a person to navigate a situation where there might be a conflict between two virtues, such as honesty and kindness, by discerning the most appropriate course of action that honors both virtues to the greatest extent possible.

The Jubilee Centre's emphasis on practical wisdom reflects the recognition that virtue is not merely about knowing what is good but also about doing what is good. This involves the ability to apply virtues in real-world situations, where the right course of action is often not immediately clear and may require careful deliberation. Practical wisdom allows individuals to assess the particularities of a situation, weigh different considerations, and make decisions that promote the overall good. This capacity for moral reasoning and ethical action is crucial for the development of virtuous individuals who can contribute positively to society.

Moreover, the Jubilee Centre's framework highlights the role of education in cultivating practical wisdom. Through character education programs, students can develop the skills needed to apply virtues in various contexts, from personal relationships to professional environments. This involves not only teaching students about virtues but also providing opportunities for them to practice virtue in real-life situations, thereby developing the practical wisdom necessary to navigate the complexities of life. For example, service-learning projects that require students to engage with diverse communities can help them develop empathy, justice, and practical wisdom as they learn to understand and address the needs of others.

In addition to its practical applications, the Jubilee Centre's framework also serves as a theoretical foundation for ongoing research in the field of character education. By providing clear definitions and categorizations of virtues, the framework enables researchers to study the impact of character education programs systematically and to develop evidence-based practices that can be implemented in schools and universities. This research has the potential to inform policy decisions at various levels, from local educational institutions to national education ministries, ensuring that character education is integrated into the broader educational agenda.

Figure 1. The role of virtues in fostering flourishing in universities

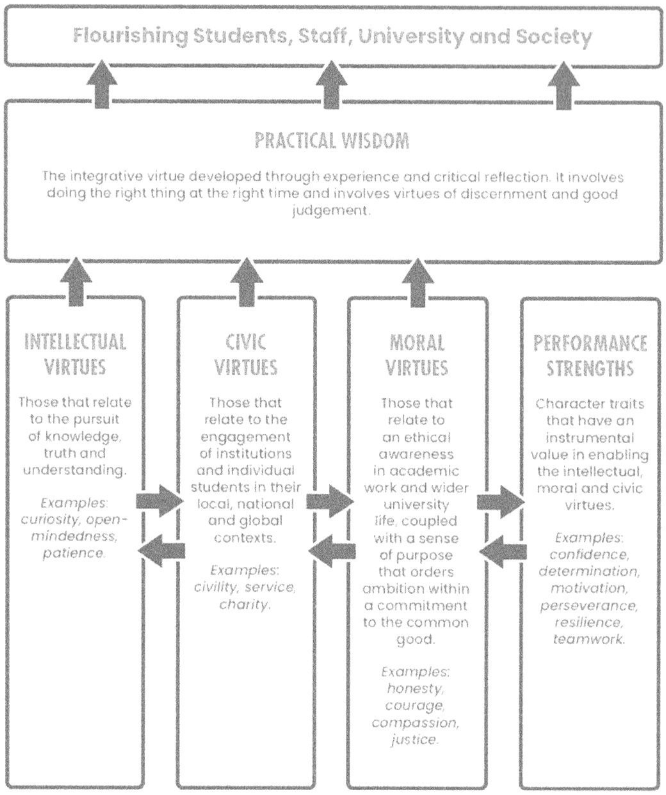

The Jubilee Centre's framework on virtues offers a comprehensive and practical approach to character education. By categorizing virtues and emphasizing their interrelatedness and the importance of practical wisdom, the framework provides educators with the tools they need to foster the holistic development of their students. The focus on practical wisdom, in particular, underscores the importance of applying virtues in real-world situations, preparing students to navigate the moral complexities of life with integrity and effectiveness. As character education continues to gain prominence in educational discourse, the Jubilee Centre's framework will remain a crucial resource for guiding the development and implementation of effective character education programs.

The Relevance of Virtues in Higher Education

In the context of higher education, the cultivation of virtues is essential for preparing students to navigate the challenges of the modern world. Universities that prioritize character education are not only enhancing the personal development of their students but are also contributing to the creation of a more just and ethical society. By fostering intellectual, civic, moral, and performance virtues, universities can help students become well-rounded individuals who are capable of making meaningful contributions to their communities and the broader world.

Moreover, the integration of virtues into the educational framework supports the overall well-being of the academic community. When students are encouraged to develop virtues, they are more likely to engage in positive behaviors, support their peers, and contribute to a respectful and inclusive campus environment (Berkowitz & Bier, 2004).

PRACTICAL WISDOM AS A META-VIRTUE

Practical wisdom, or *phronesis*, is often described as a meta-virtue because it integrates and harmonizes other virtues, guiding their application in complex situations. This section explores the concept of practical wisdom, its historical roots, and its significance in contemporary character education.

Aristotle's Concept of Phronesis

Phronesis is one of the central concepts in Aristotle's virtue ethics. Unlike theoretical wisdom (*sophia*), which deals with universal truths, *phronesis* is concerned with the practical application of knowledge in everyday life. Aristotle defined *phronesis* as the intellectual virtue that enables individuals to make good judgments and take appropriate actions in complex and often ambiguous situations (Aristotle, trans. Irwin, 1999). It is the capacity to balance competing virtues, recognize the moral dimensions of specific situations, and act in ways that promote human flourishing.

Aristotle emphasized that *phronesis* is not just about knowing what is right, but about doing what is right. It involves practical deliberation, where one weighs different options, considers the consequences, and chooses the course of action that aligns with the greater good. This deliberative process is central to moral decision-making and is what distinguishes *phronesis* from mere cleverness or cunning (Kristjánsson, 2020).

Practical wisdom is developed through experience and practice. Aristotle believed that while theoretical knowledge can be taught, practical wisdom must be cultivated through lived experiences. This idea underscores the importance of experiential learning in education, where students are encouraged to apply their knowledge in real-world contexts, thereby developing their capacity for practical wisdom (Schwartz & Sharpe, 2011).

Modern Interpretations of Practical Wisdom

In contemporary discourse, the concept of practical wisdom, or *phronesis*, has undergone a significant revival, particularly within the fields of virtue ethics and character education. This resurgence is driven by the recognition that modern life, with its complex and often ambiguous ethical challenges, requires more than just adherence to rules or technical expertise. Practical wisdom is increasingly seen as essential for navigating the "gray areas" of ethical decision-making, where rigid rules and procedures may fall short. Scholars such as Barry Schwartz and Kenneth Sharpe have been at the forefront of this revitalization, arguing that *phronesis* is indispensable for making sound judgments in situations where moral dilemmas are prevalent and the stakes are high (Schwartz & Sharpe, 2011).

Schwartz and Sharpe describe practical wisdom as the capacity to exercise judgment in the face of competing demands and to act in ways that are not only morally right but also contextually appropriate. They emphasize that in modern society, where rules, regulations, and standardized procedures often dominate professional life, there is a pressing need for individuals who possess the wisdom to interpret and apply these rules in ways that genuinely serve the greater good. This perspective challenges the notion that ethical behavior can be fully codified into rules or guidelines. Instead, it highlights the limitations of relying solely on such frameworks, which can sometimes lead to rigid or even counterproductive outcomes.

For instance, in many professional fields, strict adherence to codes of conduct may result in actions that, while technically correct, fail to address the underlying ethical issues or meet the needs of the individuals involved. Practical wisdom, in contrast, involves the ability to discern the unique aspects of a situation, weigh the various factors at play, and make decisions that are both ethically sound and effective in achieving the desired outcomes. This ability to balance competing considerations and adapt to the specific context is what makes practical wisdom so crucial in contemporary professional practice (Schwartz & Sharpe, 2011).

The importance of practical wisdom is particularly evident in fields such as medicine, law, and education, where professionals are routinely faced with complex and high-stakes decisions. In medicine, for example, physicians must often make decisions that involve balancing the potential benefits and risks of different treatment options, considering not only the clinical aspects but also the patient's values, preferences, and overall well-being. In such cases, practical wisdom enables doctors to move beyond the application of standardized protocols and make judgments that are tailored to the individual needs of their patients, thereby ensuring that the care provided is both compassionate and effective.

Similarly, in the field of law, judges and lawyers frequently encounter cases where the application of legal rules may not lead to just outcomes. Practical wisdom allows legal professionals to interpret the law in a way that upholds justice, taking into account the broader implications of their decisions for the individuals involved and for society as a whole. This is particularly important in cases that set precedents or involve complex social issues, where the outcomes can have far-reaching effects. By exercising practical wisdom, legal professionals can ensure that the law is applied in a manner that is not only consistent with legal principles but also aligned with ethical values and the pursuit of justice (Kristjánsson, 2020).

In the field of education, practical wisdom plays a critical role in guiding teachers, administrators, and policymakers as they navigate the ethical dilemmas that arise in educational settings. Educators are often required to balance the needs and interests of students, parents, and the broader community, making decisions that affect not only individual learners but also the overall learning environment. For example, a teacher might need to decide how to handle a situation where a student's behavior is disruptive to the class but is also a manifestation of underlying personal challenges. Practical wisdom enables the teacher to find a solution that addresses the immediate issue while also supporting the student's long-term development and well-being.

Moreover, in higher education, practical wisdom is essential for academic leaders who must navigate the complexities of institutional governance, resource allocation, and policy development. These leaders are often faced with decisions that involve competing priorities, such as balancing the need for academic freedom with the responsibility to maintain a respectful and inclusive campus environment. Practical wisdom allows them to make decisions that are not only effective in managing these challenges but also aligned with the ethical values and mission of the institution.

The modern emphasis on practical wisdom reflects a broader recognition that ethical leadership and decision-making require more than just technical knowledge or adherence to rules. It requires the ability to navigate the complexities of real-world situations with moral insight, empathy, and a commitment to the greater good. As such, the cultivation of practical wisdom is increasingly seen as a critical component of character education, professional development, and leadership training. By fostering this capacity in students and professionals, educators and institutions can help prepare individuals to meet the ethical challenges of the modern world with integrity and wisdom.

The Three-Dimensional Wisdom Model

Monika Ardelt's three-dimensional wisdom model provides a contemporary framework for understanding practical wisdom in educational settings. According to Ardelt, wisdom consists of three interrelated components: cognitive, reflective, and affective (Ardelt, 2003). Each of these dimensions contributes to the development of practical wisdom and can be cultivated through education.

- **Cognitive Dimension:** This dimension involves understanding life's complexities, recognizing uncertainty, and acknowledging the limits of one's knowledge. In university education, the cognitive dimension is developed through critical thinking, intellectual humility, and the pursuit of knowledge. Students are encouraged to question assumptions, engage with diverse perspectives, and appreciate the complexities of ethical issues.
- **Reflective Dimension:** This dimension of wisdom involves self-awareness and the ability to view situations from multiple perspectives. It requires students to reflect on their experiences, consider the impact of their decisions on others, and recognize their own biases and limitations. Reflective practices such as journaling, discussions, and case studies are essential for developing this aspect of wisdom in educational settings.
- **Affective Dimension:** This dimension involves empathy, compassion, and a deep concern for others' well-being. It is critical for ethical decision-making, motivating individuals to act in ways that promote the common good. In university settings, the affective dimension can be nurtured through service-learning projects, community engagement, and opportunities for students to interact with and support others from diverse backgrounds.

Figure 2. The three-dimensional wisdom model

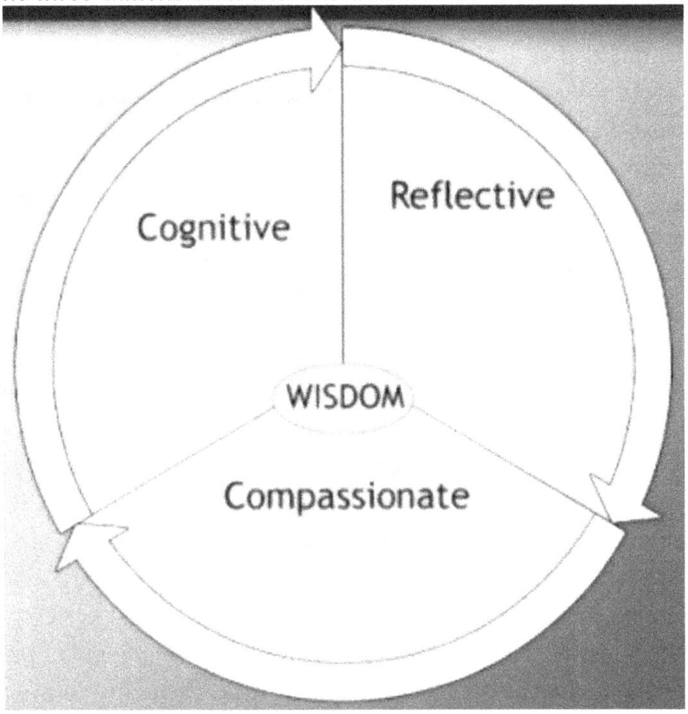

Ardelt's model emphasizes that wisdom, and by extension practical wisdom, is not just an intellectual exercise but a deeply human one that involves the whole person—mind, heart, and soul (Ardelt, 2004). By cultivating these three dimensions of wisdom, universities can help students develop the practical wisdom needed to navigate the ethical challenges they will face in their personal and professional lives.

The Significance of Practical Wisdom as a Meta-Virtue

Practical wisdom is often described as a meta-virtue because it integrates and harmonizes other virtues, guiding their application in complex situations. Through practical wisdom, individuals can balance competing goods, navigate moral ambiguities, and make decisions that promote both personal success and the common good.

In educational settings, practical wisdom is particularly valuable because it helps students move beyond rote learning and technical proficiency to develop a more nuanced understanding of how to live well in a complex world. By cultivating practical wisdom, universities can equip students with the critical judgment needed to apply their virtues effectively, enabling them to become not just competent professionals, but also ethical and responsible citizens.

Practical wisdom also plays a central role in leadership development. Leaders who possess practical wisdom are better equipped to make decisions that are not only effective but also ethically sound. They can balance the competing demands of different stakeholders, consider the long-term implications of their decisions, and act in ways that promote the common good. This makes practical wisdom a crucial component of leadership education in universities, where the goal is to prepare students to take on leadership roles in their communities and professions (Schwartz & Sharpe, 2011).

Practical Wisdom in Character Education

The role of practical wisdom in character education is profound. It serves as the integrative virtue that ensures other virtues, such as honesty, courage, and compassion, are applied in ways that are contextually appropriate and morally sound. In educational settings, fostering practical wisdom involves more than just teaching ethical principles; it requires creating opportunities for students to engage in moral reflection and deliberation, and to practice making ethical decisions in real-life scenarios (Jubilee Centre for Character and Virtues, 2017).

Character education programs that emphasize the development of practical wisdom aim to equip students with the skills needed to navigate the moral complexities of modern life. These programs often incorporate service-learning, experiential education, and reflective practices, which allow students to apply their learning in community settings and reflect on the ethical implications of their actions. By doing so, students develop a deeper understanding of the virtues they are cultivating and learn how to apply them wisely in different contexts (Kristjánsson, 2020).

Practical wisdom is essential for leadership development. Leaders who possess practical wisdom are better equipped to make decisions that are not only effective but also ethically sound. They are able to balance the competing demands of different stakeholders, consider the long-term implications of their decisions, and act in ways that promote the common good. This makes practical wisdom a crucial component of leadership education in universities, where the goal is to prepare students to take on leadership roles in their communities and professions (Schwartz & Sharpe, 2011).

Practical Wisdom in Higher Education: Challenges and Opportunities

While the importance of practical wisdom in higher education is widely recognized, there are significant challenges to its cultivation. One of the primary challenges is the tendency of modern educational systems to prioritize technical knowledge and standardized testing over the development of moral and ethical reasoning. This focus on measurable outcomes often leads to the neglect of the more nuanced and difficult-to-assess qualities that constitute practical wisdom (Sternberg et al., 2008).

Furthermore, the rapid pace of technological and social change presents additional challenges. As students are increasingly exposed to new and often conflicting information, the ability to discern what is true, just, and good becomes more complex. The rise of digital media, for example, has introduced new ethical dilemmas that require students to apply practical wisdom in novel ways. Universities must therefore adapt their curricula to include discussions of digital ethics, information literacy, and the responsible use of technology (Schwartz & Sharpe, 2011).

Despite these challenges, there are also significant opportunities for fostering practical wisdom in higher education. Experiential learning opportunities, such as internships, study abroad programs, and community service projects, provide students with real-world contexts in which to apply their virtues and develop their practical wisdom. These experiences allow students to engage with complex social and ethical issues, learn from their mistakes, and refine their judgment over time (Fowers, 2008).

Moreover, interdisciplinary approaches to education can enhance the development of practical wisdom by exposing students to a wide range of perspectives and encouraging them to think critically about the connections between different fields of knowledge. Courses that integrate philosophy, ethics, and social sciences, for example, can provide students with the tools they need to navigate the moral complexities of their professional and personal lives (Ardelt, 2018).

INTEGRATION OF KEN WILBER'S INTEGRAL THEORY

Ken Wilber's Integral Theory offers a comprehensive and holistic framework for character education. By addressing the development of virtues across multiple dimensions—individual and collective, interior and exterior—this approach ensures that universities create environments that support the full spectrum of human experience.

Overview of Ken Wilber's Integral Theory

Ken Wilber's Integral Theory is built on the premise that reality can be understood through multiple perspectives, each of which provides a different lens on the same phenomenon. Wilber organizes these perspectives into four quadrants, which correspond to the interior and exterior dimensions of the individual and the collective. These quadrants are:

- **Interior-Individual (Subjective):** This quadrant focuses on the inner experiences of individuals, including their thoughts, emotions, beliefs, and values. In the context of character education, this quadrant addresses the development of personal virtues such as self-awareness, moral reasoning, and emotional intelligence.
- **Exterior-Individual (Objective):** This quadrant deals with observable behaviors and actions. In character education, it includes how virtues manifest in students' actions, such as honesty in academic work, perseverance in challenging tasks, and empathy in interpersonal relationships.
- **Interior-Collective (Intersubjective):** This quadrant examines the shared values, cultures, and worldviews of groups. Within a university setting, it looks at the institutional culture, the norms, and the collective beliefs that shape students' ethical behavior and social interactions.
- **Exterior-Collective (Interobjective):** This quadrant focuses on the systems, structures, and environments that influence collective behavior. For universities, this includes policies, curricula, organizational structures, and the broader educational context that supports character development.

Figure 3. Ken Wilber's four quadrants model

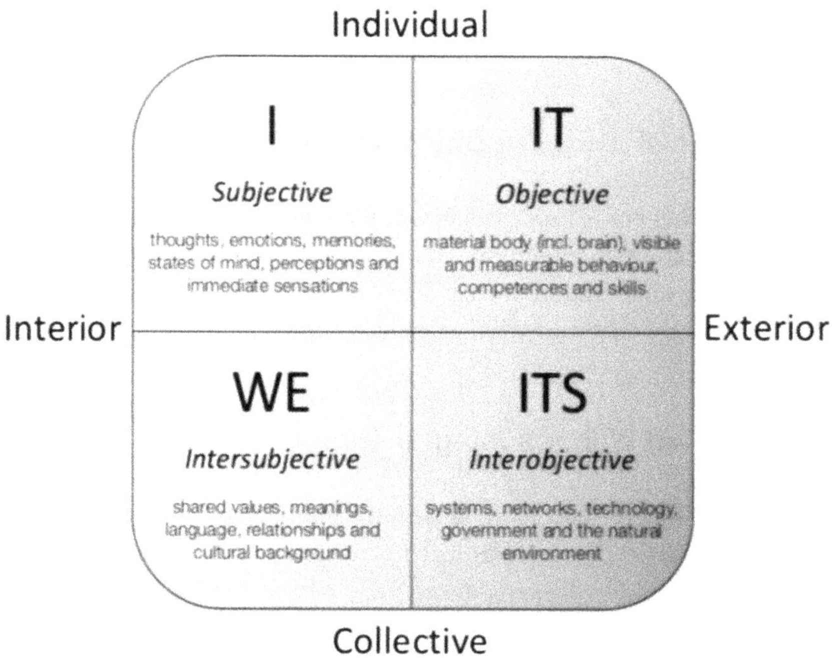

Wilber's theory posits that to fully understand and engage with any aspect of reality, all four quadrants must be considered simultaneously, as they are interdependent and mutually reinforcing. In the context of character education, this approach ensures that universities address not only the intellectual and moral development of students but also the cultural, structural, and systemic factors that influence their growth.

Application of Integral Theory to Character Education

Applying Wilber's Integral Theory to character education involves creating educational experiences that integrate all four quadrants, ensuring a holistic approach to student development across multiple dimensions—cognitively, emotionally, socially, and behaviorally.

- **Interior-Individual (Subjective):** Universities can foster the development of personal virtues such as integrity, empathy, and emotional intelligence by incorporating reflective practices into the curriculum. This might include journaling exercises, mindfulness training, and courses on ethics and moral philosophy that encourage students to explore their inner lives and develop a strong sense of self. For example, courses that focus on moral reasoning and ethical dilemmas can help students develop the capacity for self-reflection and critical thinking. Such courses can be further enhanced by incorporating experiential learning opportunities, where students can apply their ethical knowledge in real-world contexts, such as internships, volunteer work, or service-learning projects. These experiences encourage students to reflect on their values and how they apply them in different situations, deepening their understanding of themselves and their moral beliefs (Haidt, 2006).
- **Exterior-Individual (Objective):** The objective dimension of character education focuses on how virtues are expressed through behavior. Universities can promote virtuous behavior by setting clear expectations for ethical conduct and providing opportunities for students to practice and reinforce their virtues. This might include honor codes, peer mentoring programs, and recognition of ethical behavior through awards and incentives. In practice, this could involve integrating character assessments into the academic evaluation process, where students are not only graded on their knowledge and skills but also on their demonstration of virtues such as honesty, diligence, and teamwork. This approach encourages students to internalize these values and to see them as integral to their success, both academically and in life beyond the university (Sternberg et al., 2008).
- **Interior-Collective (Intersubjective):** The cultural dimension of character education involves shaping the collective values and norms of the university

community. This can be achieved by fostering an environment where virtues are celebrated and upheld. Universities can create a culture of character by promoting dialogue about ethical issues, encouraging diversity and inclusion, and ensuring that the university's mission and values are reflected in its policies and practices. One way to strengthen the interior-collective dimension is through the creation of communities of practice, where students, faculty, and staff come together to discuss and engage with issues of character and ethics. These communities can provide a supportive space for members to explore their values, share experiences, and develop a shared understanding of what it means to live a virtuous life within the context of the university. This approach not only strengthens the ethical culture of the institution but also fosters a sense of belonging and mutual respect among its members (Allman et al., 2018).

- **Exterior-Collective (Interobjective):** The structural dimension of character education involves creating systems and policies that support the development of virtues. This might include designing curricula that integrate character education across all disciplines, establishing partnerships with organizations that promote ethical leadership, and implementing policies that encourage ethical behavior, such as codes of conduct and guidelines for academic integrity. For instance, universities can integrate character education into their general education requirements, ensuring that all students, regardless of their major, receive a foundation in ethical reasoning and moral philosophy. Additionally, institutions can partner with external organizations to offer workshops, seminars, and speaker series on topics related to ethics, leadership, and social responsibility. These initiatives help to embed character education into the very fabric of the university, making it a central component of the student experience (Schwartz & Sharpe, 2011).

The Benefits of an Integral Approach to Character Education

The application of Wilber's Integral Theory to character education provides several key benefits. First, it ensures a holistic approach to student development, addressing the full spectrum of human experience. By integrating character education across all four quadrants, universities can foster well-rounded individuals who are not only intellectually capable but also morally and ethically grounded. This approach promotes coherence and alignment within the university. When character education is integrated across all levels—from individual introspection to collective institutional practices—it creates a unified framework that supports the university's mission to develop virtuous leaders. This coherence can enhance the effectiveness of character education initiatives and ensure that they are deeply embedded in the university's culture and operations (Wilber, 2001).

Moreover, an integral approach to character education can enhance the resilience and adaptability of students. In a rapidly changing world, the ability to draw on a well-developed sense of practical wisdom, supported by a strong moral foundation, is critical for navigating new and unforeseen challenges. By preparing students in this way, universities can help them become more effective leaders and agents of positive change in their communities and beyond (Sternberg, 2017).

Challenges and Considerations

While the integral approach to character education offers significant advantages, it also presents challenges. Implementing such a comprehensive framework requires a deep commitment from university leadership and a willingness to engage in sustained cultural and organizational change. Additionally, measuring the outcomes of character education can be difficult, as virtues and ethical behavior are often intangible and context-dependent.

Another challenge is ensuring that character education initiatives are inclusive and culturally sensitive. Universities must be careful to avoid imposing a one-size-fits-all approach to virtue development, recognizing that students come from diverse backgrounds with different cultural and ethical frameworks. An integral approach to character education must therefore be flexible and adaptable, allowing for the inclusion of multiple perspectives and the recognition of different pathways to virtue (Haidt, 2006).

Furthermore, there is the challenge of integrating character education into an already crowded curriculum. Faculty and administrators must find ways to embed character education into existing courses and programs without overburdening students or detracting from other important areas of study. This requires creative thinking and collaboration across disciplines, as well as a commitment to making character education a priority in the overall educational mission of the university (Allman et al., 2018).

Despite these challenges, the potential benefits of an integral approach to character education are significant. By fostering the development of virtues across multiple dimensions of human experience, universities can prepare students to lead lives of meaning and purpose, equipped to make positive contributions to society (Roqai, Ennida, & Allouani, 2024).

THE IMPACT OF CHARACTER EDUCATION ON ORGANIZATIONAL WELL-BEING

Character education profoundly impacts organizational well-being in universities. By fostering virtues that enhance ethical culture, strengthen community ties, and promote mental and emotional well-being, universities create environments where both individuals and the institution as a whole can thrive.

Enhancing Ethical Culture and Integrity

One of the most significant impacts of character education is the enhancement of ethical culture within the university. Ethical culture refers to the shared values, norms, and practices that guide behavior within an organization. In the context of a university, an ethical culture ensures that students, faculty, and staff act with integrity, respect, and responsibility in all their endeavors.

Character education plays a crucial role in building and sustaining an ethical culture. By explicitly teaching virtues and moral reasoning, universities can help students internalize ethical values that guide their actions. This internalization is essential for creating a community where ethical behavior is the norm rather than the exception. For instance, when students are taught the importance of honesty and are encouraged to practice it in their academic work, they are more likely to carry these values into their professional and personal lives (Berkowitz & Bier, 2004).

Furthermore, an ethical culture supported by character education can lead to a reduction in unethical behaviors such as plagiarism, cheating, and academic dishonesty. When students understand the moral implications of their actions and are part of a community that values integrity, they are less likely to engage in dishonest practices. This, in turn, enhances the university's reputation and fosters a sense of trust and respect among all members of the academic community (Sternberg, 2012).

The role of leadership in fostering an ethical culture cannot be overstated. University leaders, including administrators and faculty, must model the virtues they wish to instill in students. When leaders demonstrate integrity, fairness, and compassion in their decision-making, they set a powerful example for others to follow. This top-down approach to character education helps to embed ethical values into the very fabric of the institution, creating a culture that supports moral development at all levels (Brown & Treviño, 2006).

Strengthening Community and Social Cohesion

Character education also plays a crucial role in strengthening the sense of community within the university. A strong community is one where members feel connected to one another and to the institution as a whole. This connection fosters a sense of belonging, which is essential for both individual well-being and organizational health.

When universities emphasize the development of virtues such as empathy, compassion, and respect, they create an environment where students and staff are more likely to engage in positive social interactions. These interactions help to build trust and mutual support, which are the foundations of a strong community. For example, when students learn to value and practice empathy, they are more likely to reach out to peers in need, offer support, and contribute to a collaborative learning environment (Haidt, 2006).

Moreover, character education can help bridge social divides within the university. In diverse academic settings, differences in background, culture, and belief systems can sometimes lead to misunderstandings and conflict. By promoting virtues such as tolerance and open-mindedness, character education encourages students to appreciate diversity and engage constructively with those who hold different perspectives. This inclusivity strengthens the social fabric of the university, making it a more welcoming and cohesive environment for all (Berkowitz & Bier, 2004).

Community engagement initiatives that are grounded in character education further enhance social cohesion. Service-learning programs, for instance, allow students to apply their virtues in real-world contexts while also giving back to the community. These programs not only reinforce the values taught in the classroom but also help to build stronger connections between the university and the broader society. This outward-looking approach to character education ensures that students see themselves as part of a larger community, both within and beyond the university, fostering a sense of social responsibility and collective well-being (Boyle-Baise & Langford, 2004).

Promoting Mental and Emotional Well-Being

The virtues developed through character education, such as resilience and emotional intelligence, have a direct impact on the mental and emotional well-being of students. Mental health is a critical concern in higher education, with increasing numbers of students experiencing stress, anxiety, and depression. Character education can play a significant role in addressing these challenges by equipping students with the tools they need to manage their emotions, cope with adversity, and build strong, supportive relationships (Duckworth, 2016).

Resilience, for example, is a virtue that helps students navigate the inevitable challenges and setbacks they encounter in their academic and personal lives. By teaching students how to persevere in the face of difficulties, character education helps them develop a growth mindset, where they view challenges as opportunities for learning and development rather than as insurmountable obstacles. This mindset is crucial for maintaining mental well-being and achieving long-term success (Dweck, 2006).

Emotional intelligence, another key virtue fostered by character education, involves the ability to recognize, understand, and manage one's own emotions, as well as the emotions of others. Students with high emotional intelligence are better equipped to handle stress, communicate effectively, and build positive relationships. This not only enhances their personal well-being but also contributes to a more supportive and empathetic university environment (Goleman, 2020).

Moreover, character education programs that emphasize mindfulness and self-reflection can help students develop a deeper awareness of their mental and emotional states. Mindfulness practices, for example, encourage students to stay present and focused, reducing the tendency to ruminate on past failures or future anxieties. By cultivating virtues such as self-awareness and emotional regulation, universities can help students build the resilience and emotional strength needed to thrive in a demanding academic environment (Kabat-Zinn, 2003).

Improving Academic and Professional Outcomes

Character education positively impacts academic and professional outcomes by preparing students to meet the ethical and practical challenges of their future careers. Employers increasingly value graduates who not only possess technical skills but also demonstrate strong character traits, such as ethical judgment, teamwork, and leadership. By integrating character education into the curriculum, universities can ensure that their graduates are well-rounded individuals who are equipped to contribute positively to society (Lickona, 1992).

Academic success is closely linked to the development of virtues such as diligence, curiosity, and integrity. Students who are taught to value hard work and perseverance are more likely to stay engaged in their studies, persist through challenges, and achieve their academic goals. Additionally, character education encourages students to approach their studies with a sense of purpose and ethical responsibility, leading to deeper engagement and higher levels of achievement (Arthur et al., 2015).

In the professional realm, character education equips students with the moral compass needed to navigate complex ethical dilemmas in the workplace. As they enter their careers, graduates who have been taught to value honesty, fairness, and respect are more likely to make decisions that uphold these principles, even in challenging situations. This not only benefits the organizations they work for but also contributes to the broader societal good (Colby & Sullivan, 2009).

Furthermore, character education can enhance employability by developing soft skills that are highly valued in the job market. Communication, teamwork, and leadership are all skills that are rooted in strong character and ethical behavior. By fostering these skills, universities can help students stand out in a competitive job market and excel in their chosen careers (Heckman & Kautz, 2012).

Enhancing Institutional Resilience and Adaptability

Universities that prioritize character education are better equipped to navigate the challenges of an ever-changing world. The virtues cultivated through character education, such as adaptability, courage, and practical wisdom, are essential for organizational resilience. In times of crisis or change, these virtues enable both individuals and the institution as a whole to respond effectively and ethically.

For example, during the COVID-19 pandemic, universities that had fostered a strong ethical culture and a sense of community were better able to adapt to the challenges posed by remote learning and the need for rapid decision-making. The ability to draw on a reservoir of virtues allowed these institutions to maintain continuity in education while also supporting the well-being of students, faculty, and staff.

Character education also contributes to the long-term adaptability of universities by promoting a culture of continuous learning and improvement. When students and staff are encouraged to embrace challenges and view them as opportunities for growth, the institution as a whole becomes more resilient and capable of thriving in the face of change. This adaptability is crucial in a rapidly evolving educational landscape, where universities must continually innovate to meet the needs of students and society (Sternberg, 2017).

Moreover, by fostering a commitment to ethical leadership, character education ensures that university leaders are prepared to guide their institutions through periods of uncertainty. Leaders who possess virtues such as wisdom, courage, and compassion are better equipped to make decisions that align with the institution's values and long-term goals, even in the face of difficult choices. This type of leadership is essential for maintaining the integrity and mission of the university, particularly in challenging times (Brown & Treviño, 2006).

Fulfilling the University's Social Responsibility

Character education aligns closely with the broader social responsibility of universities. As institutions of higher learning, universities have a duty to not only educate students academically but also to prepare them to be ethical and responsible citizens who can contribute to the betterment of society. This social responsibility extends beyond the campus, influencing the broader community and the world at large.

By cultivating virtues in students, universities contribute to the development of ethical leaders who are capable of addressing the complex challenges facing society. Whether in business, government, healthcare, or other fields, graduates who have been shaped by character education are more likely to prioritize the common good, make decisions that benefit society, and lead with integrity (Colby & Sullivan, 2009).

Furthermore, universities that prioritize character education serve as role models for other institutions, demonstrating the value of integrating ethical development into the educational mission. This leadership in character education can inspire other universities to adopt similar practices, creating a ripple effect that extends the impact of character education far beyond a single campus (Lickona, 1992).

In addition to influencing the character of their students, universities that embrace their social responsibility through character education also engage in outreach and service to the broader community. Service-learning programs, community partnerships, and public lectures on ethics and social justice are just a few examples of how universities can extend the impact of character education beyond the campus. These initiatives not only benefit the community but also reinforce the values taught within the university, creating a cycle of positive influence that contributes to the overall well-being of society (Boyle-Baise & Langford, 2004).

CONCLUSION

Character education within universities is not just a supplementary aspect of higher education; it is central to the mission of academic institutions. By integrating character education into the curriculum, universities can develop students who are not only intellectually capable but also morally and ethically grounded. This chapter has explored the multifaceted role of character education in promoting individual flourishing, enhancing organizational well-being, and fulfilling the social responsibilities of universities.

The development of virtues such as practical wisdom, empathy, and resilience is crucial for preparing students to navigate the complexities of modern life. Universities that prioritize character education contribute to the creation of ethical leaders, foster a strong sense of community, and enhance the mental and emotional well-being of their students. These institutions are better equipped to adapt to change, maintain their integrity, and make a positive impact on society.

As universities continue to evolve in response to global challenges, the role of character education will become increasingly important. By committing to the holistic development of students, universities can ensure that they remain relevant and effective in their mission to educate the next generation of leaders, thinkers, and citizens. The integration of character education into all aspects of university life will be essential for building a more just, ethical, and resilient society.

REFERENCES

Allman, P., McLaren, P., & Rikowski, G. (2018). *Critical education against global capitalism: Karl Marx and revolutionary critical education*. Sense Publishers.

Ardelt, M. (2003). Empirical assessment of a three-dimensional wisdom scale. *Research on Aging*, 25(3), 275–324. DOI: 10.1177/0164027503025003004

Ardelt, M. (2004). Wisdom as expert knowledge system: A critical review of a contemporary operationalization of an ancient concept. *Human Development*, 47(5), 257–285. DOI: 10.1159/000079154

Aristotle, . (1999). *Nicomachean ethics* (Irwin, T., Trans.). Hackett.

Arthur, J., Kristjánsson, K., Harrison, T., Sanderse, W., & Wright, D. (2016). *Teaching character and virtue in schools*. Routledge. DOI: 10.4324/9781315695013

Arthur, J., Kristjánsson, K., Walker, D., Sanderse, W., & Jones, C. (2015). Character education in UK schools.

Aurelius, M. (2002). *Meditations* (Hays, G., Trans.). The Modern Library.

Baehr, J. (2016). *Intellectual virtues and education*. Taylor & Francis.

Berkowitz, M. W., & Bier, M. C. (2004). Based character education. *The Annals of the American Academy of Political and Social Science*, 591(1), 72–85. DOI: 10.1177/0002716203260082

Boyle-Baise, M., & Langford, J. (2004). There are children here: Service learning for social justice. *Equity & Excellence in Education*, 37(1), 55–66. DOI: 10.1080/10665680490422115

Brown, M. E., & Treviño, L. K. (2006). Ethical leadership: A review and future directions. *The Leadership Quarterly*, 17(6), 595–616. DOI: 10.1016/j.leaqua.2006.10.004

Colby, A., & Sullivan, W. M. (2009). Strengthening the Foundations of Students' Excellence, Integrity, and Social Contribution. *Liberal Education*, 95(1), 22–29.

Confucius, . (1979). *The Analects* (Lau, D. C., Trans.). Penguin Classics.

Dagger, R. (1997). *Civic Virtues: Rights, Citizenship, and Republican Liberalism*. Oxford University Press. DOI: 10.1093/oso/9780195106336.001.0001

Duckworth, A. (2016). *Grit: The power of passion and perseverance* (Vol. 234). Scribner.

Dweck, C. S. (2006). *Mindset: The new psychology of success*. Random house.

Fowers, B. J. (2008). From continence to virtue: Recovering goodness, character unity, and character types for positive psychology. *Theory & Psychology*, 18(5), 629–653. DOI: 10.1177/0959354308093399

Goleman, D. (2020). *Emotional intelligence: Why it can matter more than IQ*. Bloomsbury Publishing.

Haidt, J. (2006). *The happiness hypothesis: Finding modern truth in ancient wisdom*. Basic Books.

Heckman, J. J., & Kautz, T. (2012). Hard evidence on soft skills. *Labour Economics*, 19(4), 451–464. DOI: 10.1016/j.labeco.2012.05.014 PMID: 23559694

Jubilee Centre for Character and Virtues. (2017). *A framework for character education in schools*. University of Birmingham.

Jubilee Centre for Character and Virtues. (2022). *A framework for character education in universities*. University of Birmingham.

Kabat-Zinn, J. (2003). Mindfulness-based interventions in context: Past, present, and future. *Clinical Psychology : a Publication of the Division of Clinical Psychology of the American Psychological Association*, 10(2), 144–156. DOI: 10.1093/clipsy.bpg016

Kristjánsson, K. (2020). Aristotelian character friendship as a 'method'of moral education. *Studies in Philosophy and Education*, 39(4), 349–364. DOI: 10.1007/s11217-020-09717-w

Lickona, T. (1992). *Educating for character: How our schools can teach respect and responsibility*. Bantam.

MacIntyre, A. (2007). *After virtue: A study in moral theory*. University of Notre Dame Press.

Peterson, C., & Seligman, M. E. P. (2004). *Character strengths and virtues: A handbook and classification*. Oxford University Press.

Roqai, M. C., Ennida, K., & Allouani, S. A. (2024). Promoting Character Education in Business Schools from an Integral Perspective: A Conceptual Paper. *Open Journal of Social Sciences*, 12(7), 534–549. DOI: 10.4236/jss.2024.127038

Ryff, C. D., & Keyes, C. L. M. (1995). The structure of psychological well-being revisited. *Journal of Personality and Social Psychology*, 69(4), 719–727. DOI: 10.1037/0022-3514.69.4.719 PMID: 7473027

Schwartz, B., & Sharpe, K. (2011). *Practical wisdom: The right way to do the right thing*. Penguin.

Sternberg, R. J. (2012). The assessment of creativity: An investment-based approach. *Creativity Research Journal*, 24(1), 3–12. DOI: 10.1080/10400419.2012.652925

Sternberg, R. J. (2017). ACCEL: A new model for identifying the gifted. *Roeper Review*, 39(3), 152–169. DOI: 10.1080/02783193.2017.1318658

Sternberg, R. J., Jarvin, L., & Reznitskaya, A. (2008). Teaching for wisdom through history: Infusing wise thinking skills in the school curriculum. *Teaching for wisdom: Cross-cultural perspectives on fostering wisdom*, 37-57.

Wilber, K. (2001). *A theory of everything: An integral vision for business, politics, science, and spirituality*. Shambhala Publications.

ADDITIONAL READING

Allouani, S. A., & Berrada, A. (2023). Educating for Practical Wisdom, Teaching What Cannot Be Taught: Critical Reflections on Fostering Wisdom in Business Schools. In *The Role of Educators as Agents and Conveyors for Positive Change in Global Education* (pp. 209-224).

Foot, P. (2003). *Natural goodness*. Clarendon Press.

Harrison, T., & Walker, D. I. (Eds.). (2018). *The theory and practice of virtue education*. Taylor & Francis. DOI: 10.4324/9781315265353

Hursthouse, R. (2006). Practical wisdom: A mundane account. *Proceedings of the Aristotelian Society*, 106(3), 283–307. DOI: 10.1111/j.1467-9264.2006.00198.x

Kristjánsson, K. (2016). *Aristotle, emotions, and education*. Routledge. DOI: 10.4324/9781315567914

Kristjánsson, K., Harrison, T., & Peterson, A. (2024). Reconsidering the 'Ten Myths' about Character Education. *British Journal of Educational Studies*, 1–24. DOI: 10.1080/00071005.2024.2378059

MacIntyre, A. (1999). *Dependent rational animals: Why human beings need the virtues*. Open Court.

Melé, D. (2010). Practical wisdom in managerial decision making. *Journal of Management Development*, 29(7/8), 637–645. DOI: 10.1108/02621711011059068

Mercado, J. A. (2018). How Close Are Contemporary Ideas on Human Flourishing and the Classical Philosophy of Man? In *Personal flourishing in organizations* (pp. 11-35).

KEY TERMS AND DEFINITIONS

Character Education: The process by which schools and educational institutions teach students about moral values, ethics, and virtues, aiming to develop well-rounded individuals who contribute positively to society.

Eudaimonia: A concept from Aristotelian philosophy often translated as "human flourishing," referring to the highest human good, where an individual's actions are aligned with virtue and purpose.

Flourishing: A state of living in accordance with virtues that leads to optimal human functioning and well-being, encompassing physical, emotional, and psychological health, as well as fulfilling social relationships and a sense of purpose.

Holistic Education: An educational approach that seeks to address the full development of a person, including intellectual, emotional, social, physical, artistic, creative, and spiritual aspects.

Moral Development: The process through which individuals develop proper attitudes and behaviors toward other people in society, based on social and cultural norms, laws, and rules.

Practical Wisdom (*Phronesis*): A form of wisdom that involves the ability to make sound judgments and take appropriate actions in complex, real-world situations by balancing moral and ethical considerations.

Virtue Ethics: A philosophical approach that emphasizes the role of character and virtues in moral philosophy, rather than rules or consequences, as the key elements of ethical thinking.

Chapter 8
Cultivating Happiness and Insight for Enhanced Organizational Health:
The Science of Happiness at Work

L. Nithya
PES University, India

ABSTRACT

The science of happiness at work explores the multifaceted dimensions of employee well-being and its impact on organizational success. This field integrates insights from psychology, business, and neuroscience to understand how positive emotions, engagement, relationships, meaning, and accomplishment (PERMA) contribute to a thriving workplace. Research indicates that happier employees are more productive, creative, and committed, leading to enhanced teamwork and reduced health issues. This study reviews various theoretical frameworks, including the job demand-resources model, social exchange theory, and broaden-and-build theory, to provide a comprehensive understanding of workplace happiness. Practical strategies for fostering a positive work environment, such as gratitude practices, mindfulness, and socially intelligent leadership, are discussed. The findings underscore the importance of prioritizing happiness as a core organizational goal to boost engagement, productivity, and overall employee satisfaction.

DOI: 10.4018/979-8-3693-8457-2.ch008

THE SCIENCE OF HAPPINESS AT WORK: A REVIEW OF KEY FINDINGS

Happiness at work refers to the experience of positive emotions, well-being, and satisfaction derived from one's job. It encompasses various aspects such as job satisfaction, work engagement, and affective organizational commitment. Happiness at work is influenced by individual attitudes, workplace environment, and organizational culture, and has significant consequences for both employees and organizations (Fisher, 2010). Happiness at work is crucial for organisational well-being as it directly impacts employee productivity, and general job performance, workplace happiness is critical to the health of the organisation. Researchers show that contended workers have better levels of engagement, are less prone to burnout, and are more devoted to their companies. Moreover, companies with contented employees typically have lower employee turnover and greater customer satisfaction, which eventually improves financial performance. The objective of promoting employee happiness at work has three main goals for organisational well-being which include raising job satisfaction, increasing productivity, and creating a happy workplace Contented workers are typically more driven, involved, and productive, which translates into superior performance results. Furthermore, encouraging pleasure at work raises general job satisfaction, which lowers attrition and improves employee retention. Prioritising happiness also helps to lower stress, avoid burnout, and create a positive work atmosphere. Moreover, happy workers are more likely to become deeply committed to their company and have a strong sense of loyalty, which lowers absenteeism and increases organisational citizenship behaviour. Contentment in the workplace fosters creativity and innovation, which helps businesses adapt and prosper in cutthroat marketplaces. Lastly, companies with contented staff members typically have greater customer satisfaction levels as they are more likely to deliver superior customer service and cultivate strong bonds with clients.

Happiness is often defined as a state of well-being characterized by emotions ranging from contentment to intense joy. It encompasses both momentary positive emotions and a deeper sense of meaning and purpose in life. Happiness encompasses several key dimensions that contribute to overall well-being. Positive emotions play a crucial role, including feelings such as gratitude, serenity, interest, hope, pride, amusement, inspiration, awe, and love. These emotions are essential for enhancing resilience and life satisfaction. Another important dimension is engagement, which involves being deeply involved or absorbed in activities that are both enjoyable and challenging. This often leads to a state of "flow" where the individual loses track of time and is fully immersed in what they are doing. Lastly, meaning is a significant dimension of happiness, involving a sense of purpose and direction in life. It includes the pursuit of goals that are aligned with one's values and contribute to something larger than oneself. Together, these dimensions create a comprehensive understanding of happiness and its impact on well-being.

THEORIES OF POSITIVE PSYCHOLOGY

1. **PERMA MODEL:** The PERMA model, developed by Martin Seligman, is a comprehensive framework in positive psychology that outlines five core elements essential for psychological well-being and happiness. These elements are Positive Emotions, Engagement, Relationships, Meaning, and Accomplishment.

The PERMA model is based on positive emotions, which include pride, amusement, inspiration, amazement, joy, gratitude, calm, curiosity, hope, and love. It is essential to feel these feelings to improve overall happiness and life satisfaction. Barbara Fredrickson's Broaden-and-Build Theory is based on the idea that positive emotions increase our repertoire of thought-action combinations and enable us to create long-lasting resources. These feelings foster our capacity for creativity, resiliency, and interpersonal relationships. Promoting happy feelings at work may boost output, enhance collaboration, and promote job satisfaction. By praising accomplishments, offering chances for career advancement, and fostering a favourable work atmosphere, organisations may encourage happy feelings. Engagement refers to being deeply involved and absorbed in activities, often described as a state of "flow," characterized by complete immersion and focus, where time seems to fly by. This concept is closely related to Mihaly Csikszentmihalyi's Flow Theory. Engagement is crucial for personal growth and satisfaction, as individuals who are engaged are more likely to perform at their best and experience a sense of fulfilment. In the workplace, enhancing engagement can be achieved by designing jobs that align with employees' strengths and interests. Providing challenging tasks, opportunities for skill development, and autonomy can help employees achieve a state of flow, leading to higher productivity and job satisfaction. Positive relationships are essential for well-being because they give people love, support, and a feeling of community. There is a correlation between improved mental and physical health and strong social ties. Relationships make us happier because they give us possibilities for personal development, emotional support, and a sense of belonging. They are necessary for stress management and resilience. Creating a culture at work that values cooperation, mutual respect, and trust helps improve relationships between coworkers. Collaborative efforts, transparent dialogue, and acknowledging teamwork may fortify interpersonal links and enhance the general well-being of the organisation. Meaning involves having a sense of purpose and direction in life, which is about belonging to and serving something bigger than oneself. Viktor Frankl's work on existential psychology highlights the importance of finding meaning in life. Having a sense of meaning is associated with greater life satisfaction, resilience, and overall well-being, helping individuals navigate challenges and maintain a positive outlook. In the workplace, organizations can foster a sense of meaning by aligning employees' work with the company's mission and values. Providing opportunities for employees to contribute to meaningful projects and recognizing the impact of their work can enhance their sense of purpose and commitment. Accomplishment refers to the pursuit and achievement of goals, involving the setting and striving for personal and professional objectives, which leads to a sense of competence and success. Achieving goals boosts self-esteem, confidence, and overall well-being, providing a sense of direction and motivation that encourages individuals to continue striving for excellence. In the workplace, organizations can support employees' pursuit of accomplishment by setting clear goals, providing feedback, and recognizing achievements. Creating a culture of continuous improvement and celebrating successes can motivate employees and enhance their sense of accomplishment.

SELF-DETERMINATION THEORY: Self-Determination Theory (SDT), developed by Deci and Ryan, is a prominent theory of human motivation that emphasizes the role of intrinsic motivation and the fulfilment of basic psychological needs in fostering well-being and optimal functioning. In the workplace, SDT provides a framework for understanding how to enhance employee motivation, engagement, and overall organizational well-being. SDT posits that there are three basic psychological needs essential for fostering intrinsic motivation and well-being: autonomy, competence, and relatedness. Autonomy refers to the need to feel in control of one's behaviours and goals, which in the workplace translates to employees having a sense of choice and volition in their tasks and responsibilities. Competence involves the need to feel effective and capable of achieving desired outcomes, which can be supported by providing employees with opportunities to develop and apply their skills. Relatedness is the need to feel connected to others and to have a sense of belonging, which in the workplace means fostering positive relationships and a supportive work environment. Leaders can promote autonomy by involving employees in decision-making, providing choices in task execution, and fostering initiative, leading to increased job satisfaction and intrinsic motivation. Providing consistent feedback, offering professional growth opportunities, and assigning challenging yet attainable tasks can help employees feel competent, boosting their confidence, and enhancing their performance and engagement. Creating a collaborative and inclusive work culture where employees feel valued and connected to their colleagues can fulfil the need for relatedness, leading to higher levels of commitment and reduced turnover.

Research has shown that when these psychological needs are met, employees are more likely to experience higher levels of job satisfaction, engagement, and well-being, whereas thwarting these needs can lead to negative outcomes such as burnout, disengagement, and turnover (McAnally & Hagger, 2024). Organizations can implement SDT principles by training leaders on the importance of supporting autonomy, competence, and relatedness, redesigning jobs to provide more autonomy and opportunities for skill development, and fostering a positive culture that encourages teamwork, recognition, and open communication. Self-Determination Theory offers valuable insights into how organizations can create environments that support employee motivation and well-being. By addressing the basic psychological needs of autonomy, competence, and relatedness, organizations can foster a more motivated, engaged, and productive workforce.

FLOW THEORY: Flow Theory, developed by Mihaly Csikszentmihalyi, describes a state of deep immersion and engagement in activities, which can significantly enhance organizational well-being in the workplace. This theory emphasizes the importance of balancing the challenges of a task with the individual's skills to avoid boredom or anxiety. Clear goals and immediate feedback are crucial for maintaining focus and adjusting actions to stay in the flow state. Additionally, minimizing distractions and fostering an environment conducive to concentration are essential. Intrinsic motivation, where the activity itself is rewarding, plays a key role in achieving flow. The benefits of flow in the workplace include increased productivity, enhanced job satisfaction, and improved overall well-being, as employees feel more engaged and fulfilled in their work. Practical applications of Flow Theory in the workplace involve designing tasks that align with employees' skills, setting clear goals, creating a supportive work environment, and encouraging autonomy. These strategies can help employees regularly achieve flow, leading to a more productive and satisfying work experience.

BROADEN-AND-BUILD THEORY: The Broaden-and-Build Theory, developed by Barbara Fredrickson, posits that positive emotions broaden an individual's momentary thought-action repertoire, which in turn builds enduring personal resources. This theory has profound implications for organizational well-being in the workplace. Positive emotions such as joy, interest, contentment, and love not only enhance an employee's immediate experience but also contribute to long-term benefits by fostering resilience, creativity, and social connections. In the workplace, the Broaden-and-Build Theory can be applied to create a more positive and productive environment. When employees experience positive emotions, they are more likely to engage in creative problem-solving and innovative thinking. This broadened mindset allows them to see a wider range of possibilities and solutions, which can lead to improved performance and productivity. For example, an employee who feels joyful and appreciated is more likely to think outside the box and come up with creative solutions to challenges. Moreover, positive emotions help build social resources by enhancing relationships and fostering a sense of community. Employees who experience positive emotions are more likely to collaborate effectively, support their colleagues, and build strong professional networks. This social capital is invaluable for organizational success, as it promotes teamwork, communication, and a supportive work culture. Positive emotions also contribute to building psychological resilience. Employees who regularly experience positive emotions are better equipped to cope with stress and recover from setbacks. This resilience is crucial in a dynamic and often challenging work environment, as it enables employees to maintain their well-being and continue performing at a high level despite difficulties. To implement the Broaden-and-Build Theory in the workplace, organizations can adopt several strategies. First, creating a positive work environment that fosters positive emotions is essential. This can be achieved through practices such as recognizing and celebrating achievements, providing opportunities for professional growth, and promoting work-life balance. Additionally, encouraging positive interactions among employees, such as team-building activities and social events, can help build strong relationships and a sense of community. Another important strategy is to provide employees with opportunities to engage in meaningful and fulfilling work. When employees find their work meaningful, they are more likely to experience positive emotions and be intrinsically motivated. This can be facilitated by aligning job roles with employees' strengths and interests, providing opportunities for skill development, and involving employees in decision-making processes. Furthermore, organizations can promote positive emotions by fostering a culture of gratitude and appreciation. Regularly expressing gratitude and recognizing employees' contributions can enhance their sense of value and belonging, leading to increased positive emotions and job satisfaction. This can be done through formal recognition programs, as well as informal gestures of appreciation. The Broaden-and-Build Theory by Barbara Fredrickson offers valuable insights into how positive emotions can enhance organizational well-being. By fostering positive emotions, organizations can create a more productive, resilient, and collaborative work environment. Implementing strategies that promote positive emotions, such as creating a positive work environment, providing meaningful work, and fostering a culture of gratitude, can lead to long-term benefits for both employees and the organization as a whole.

JOB DEMANDS RESOURCES MODEL: The Job Demands-Resources (JD-R) Model, developed by Demerouti et al. (2001), is a comprehensive framework for understanding employee well-being and performance in the workplace. This model posits that job demands and job resources are the primary factors influencing employee stress and motivation. Job demands refer to the physical, psychological, social, or organizational aspects of a job that require sustained effort and are associated with certain physiological and psychological costs. Examples include high work pressure, emotional demands, and role ambiguity. On the other hand, job resources are the physical, psychological, social, or organizational aspects of a job that help achieve work goals, reduce job demands, and stimulate personal growth and development. Examples include support from colleagues, autonomy, and opportunities for professional development. The JD-R Model operates on two main processes that are the health impairment process and the motivational process. The health impairment process suggests that excessive job demands can lead to strain and health problems, such as burnout and physical health issues. Conversely, the motivational process posits that job resources have a motivational potential and lead to higher work engagement, lower cynicism, and better performance. When employees have access to sufficient job resources, they are more likely to be engaged, motivated, and productive. In the context of organizational well-being, the JD-R Model provides valuable insights into how to create a balanced and supportive work environment. By identifying and managing job demands and enhancing job resources, organizations can improve employee well-being and performance. For instance, reducing excessive workloads and providing adequate support can mitigate the negative effects of job demands. Simultaneously, fostering a supportive work culture, offering opportunities for skill development, and promoting work-life balance can enhance job resources and boost employee motivation and engagement.

Implementing the JD-R Model in the workplace involves several practical steps. First, organizations need to conduct regular assessments to identify the specific job demands and resources relevant to their employees. This can be done through surveys, interviews, and focus groups. Once identified, organizations can develop targeted interventions to address the identified demands and enhance resources. For example, if high work pressure is a significant job demand, interventions could include workload management strategies, stress management training, and providing additional support staff. Moreover, promoting a culture of open communication and feedback is crucial. Employees should feel comfortable discussing their job demands and resources with their supervisors and colleagues. This can help in identifying potential issues early and developing appropriate solutions. Additionally, providing employees with autonomy and control over their work can enhance their sense of ownership and motivation. When employees have the freedom to make decisions and manage their tasks, they are more likely to feel empowered and engaged. Another important aspect of the JD-R Model is the role of personal resources, such as self-efficacy, resilience, and optimism. These personal resources can buffer the negative effects of job demands and enhance the positive effects of job resources. Organizations can support the development of personal resources through training programs, coaching, and creating a positive work environment that encourages personal growth and development. The job Demands-Resources (JD-R) Model by Demerouti et al. (2001) offers a robust framework for understanding and enhancing organizational well-being. By balancing job demands and resources, organizations can create a supportive and motivating work environment that promotes employee well-being and performance. Implementing the JD-R Model involves regular assessments, targeted interventions, open communication, and support for personal resource development. These strategies can help organizations foster a healthy, engaged, and productive workforce.

HEDONIC AND EUDAIMONIC HAPPINESS

Hedonic and eudaimonic happiness are two distinct but complementary approaches to understanding well-being, both of which have significant implications for organizational well-being in the workplace. Hedonic happiness, rooted in the pursuit of pleasure and the avoidance of pain, focuses on maximizing positive experiences and minimizing negative ones. This approach is often associated with job satisfaction, comfort, and the immediate gratification of needs and desires. In contrast, eudaimonic happiness is derived from the pursuit of meaning, self-realization, and personal growth. It emphasizes living in accordance with one's true self and values and achieving a sense of purpose and fulfilment. In the workplace, fostering both hedonic and eudaimonic happiness can lead to a more holistic approach to employee well-being. Hedonic happiness can be promoted through practices that enhance job satisfaction and create a positive work environment. This includes recognizing and rewarding employee achievements, providing a comfortable and supportive work setting, and ensuring that employees have the resources they need to perform their tasks effectively. By addressing employees' immediate needs and creating a pleasant work atmosphere, organizations can enhance overall job satisfaction and reduce stress.

On the other hand, Eudaimonic happiness can be cultivated by helping employees find meaning and purpose in their work. This involves aligning job roles with employees' strengths and values, providing opportunities for personal and professional growth, and fostering a culture of autonomy and empowerment. When employees feel that their work is meaningful and that they are contributing to something larger than themselves, they are more likely to experience a deep sense of fulfilment and engagement. This can lead to higher levels of motivation, creativity, and resilience, which are essential for long-term organizational success.

Integrating both hedonic and eudaimonic approaches to happiness can create a balanced and sustainable model of organizational well-being. For instance, while providing immediate rewards and recognition can boost short-term morale, offering opportunities for meaningful work and personal development can ensure long-term employee engagement and satisfaction. Organizations that prioritize both aspects of happiness are likely to see improvements in employee retention, productivity, and overall workplace harmony.

To implement these concepts effectively, organizations can adopt several strategies. First, they can conduct regular assessments to understand employees' needs and preferences, and tailor their well-being initiatives accordingly. This can include surveys, focus groups, and one-on-one meetings to gather feedback and identify areas for improvement. Additionally, organizations can invest in training and development programs that help employees build skills and advance their careers, while also promoting a sense of purpose and alignment with organizational goals. Creating a supportive and inclusive work culture is also crucial. This involves fostering open communication, encouraging collaboration, and promoting diversity and inclusion. When employees feel valued and respected, they are more likely to experience both hedonic and eudaimonic happiness. Moreover, organizations can implement policies that promote work-life balance, such as flexible working hours, remote work options, and wellness programs. These initiatives can help employees manage stress and maintain a healthy work-life integration, contributing to their overall well-being. understanding and promoting both hedonic and eudaimonic happiness in the workplace is essential for organizational well-being. By addressing employees' immediate needs and creating a positive work environment, organizations can enhance job satisfaction and reduce stress. At the same time, by helping employees find meaning and purpose in their work, organizations can foster long-term engagement, motivation, and fulfillment. Integrating these approaches can lead to a more balanced and sustainable model of well-being, benefiting both employees and the organization as a whole.

BIOLOGICAL FACTORS INFLUENCING HAPPINESS

Happiness, a complex and multifaceted emotion, is influenced by various biological factors, including genetics, brain structures, neurotransmitters, and hormones. Understanding these factors can provide insights into why some individuals naturally experience higher levels of happiness than others.

- **Genetics:** Genetics play a significant role in determining an individual's baseline level of happiness. Twin studies have shown that approximately 40-50% of the variance in happiness can be attributed to genetic factors (Bartels, 2015). For instance, identical twins, who share 100% of their genetic material, tend to have more similar levels of happiness compared to fraternal twins, who share only 50% of their genes (Tellegen et al., 1988). Research has consistently shown that identical twins have more similar levels of happiness compared to fraternal twins. This suggests a strong genetic component to happiness. For example, Tellegen et al. (1988) conducted a study involving twins reared apart and together. They found that the correlation in happiness levels was significantly higher among identical twins than fraternal twins, even when the identical twins were raised in different environments. This indicates that genetic factors play a crucial role in determining happiness levels, independent of shared environment. Heritability estimates quantify the proportion of variance in happiness that can be attributed to genetic differences among individuals. Studies have estimated that approximately 40-50% of the variance in happiness can be attributed to genetic factors (Bartels, 2015). This means that nearly half of the differences in happiness levels among people can be explained by their genetic makeup. While the overall genetic influence on happiness is well-documented, identifying specific genes that contribute to happiness is more complex. Research has suggested that multiple genes, each with a small effect, contribute to the overall genetic influence on happiness. These genes are often involved in the regulation of neurotransmitters such as serotonin, dopamine, and oxytocin, which are crucial for mood regulation and emotional well-being. For instance, variations in the serotonin transporter gene (5-HTTLPR) have been linked to differences in emotional responses and susceptibility to depression, which can indirectly affect happiness levels (Caspi et al., 2003). Similarly, genes involved in the dopamine pathway, such as the DRD4 gene, have been associated with traits like novelty-seeking and reward sensitivity, which can influence an individual's overall happiness (Ebstein et al., 1996). It's important to note that genetics do not determine happiness in isolation. Gene-environment interactions play a significant role in shaping an individual's happiness. This means that while genetic predispositions can influence how a person experiences happiness, environmental factors such as life experiences, social relationships, and lifestyle choices also play a crucial role.

- **Brain structure:** The prefrontal cortex, located at the front of the brain, is crucial for higher-order cognitive functions such as decision-making, planning, and social behavior. Within the prefrontal cortex, the left prefrontal cortex is particularly associated with positive emotions and well-being. Research by Davidson (2004) has shown that individuals with greater activity in the left prefrontal cortex tend to experience more positive emotions and report higher levels of happiness. This area of the brain is involved in regulating emotions, setting goals, and maintaining motivation, all of which contribute to a person's overall sense of well-being. The amygdala is a small, almond-shaped structure located deep within the brain's temporal lobes. It plays a critical role in processing emotions, particularly fear and pleasure. The amygdala helps to evaluate emotional stimuli and generate appropriate emotional responses. While it is often associated with negative emotions like fear and anxiety, the amygdala also processes positive emotions and rewards. Its interaction with other brain regions, such as the prefrontal cortex, helps regulate emotional responses and contributes to the experience of happiness (LeDoux, 2000). The hippocampus, another key structure within the limbic system, is primarily involved in memory formation and retrieval. It helps to encode and store emotional memories, which can influence an individual's mood and emotional state. Positive experiences and memories stored in the hippocampus can enhance feelings of happiness and well-being. Additionally, the hippocampus interacts with the prefrontal cortex to integrate past experiences with present emotions, aiding in emotional regulation and resilience. The limbic system is a complex set of structures that includes the amygdala, hippocampus, hypothalamus, and other related areas. It is often referred to as the "emotional brain" because it plays a central role in regulating emotions, motivation, and behavior. The limbic system is essential for processing emotional stimuli, generating emotional responses, and maintaining emotional balance. It helps to integrate sensory information with emotional experiences, allowing individuals to respond appropriately to their environment and maintain a sense of well-being (LeDoux, 2000). An important aspect of brain function related to happiness is neuroplasticity, the brain's ability to reorganize itself by forming new neural connections. Positive experiences, such as practicing gratitude, engaging in meaningful activities, and maintaining social connections, can enhance neuroplasticity and strengthen the neural pathways associated with happiness. This means that individuals can actively influence their brain's structure and function to promote greater well-being and happiness over time.

- **NEUROTRANSMITTERS:** Neurotransmitters are essential chemicals in the brain that transmit signals between neurons, playing a crucial role in regulating mood, emotions, and overall well-being. Let's delve deeper into the key neurotransmitters involved in happiness Dopamine is often referred to as the "feel-good" neurotransmitter because it is closely associated with pleasure, reward, and motivation. It is released during activities that are perceived as enjoyable, such as eating, exercising, and socializing. Dopamine pathways in the brain, particularly those in the mesolimbic system, are activated during rewarding experiences, reinforcing behaviors that lead to pleasure (Wise, 2004). This neurotransmitter also plays a role in goal-directed behavior, helping individuals to pursue and achieve their objectives, which can contribute to a sense of accomplishment and happiness. Serotonin is another key neurotransmitter that helps regulate mood, appetite, and sleep. It is often linked to feelings of well-being and happiness. Low levels of serotonin are associated with mood disorders such as depression and anxiety (Young, 2007). Serotonin influences various physiological functions, including the regulation of mood, appetite, and circadian rhythms. It is synthesized from the amino acid tryptophan, which is found in foods like turkey, eggs, and cheese. By maintaining adequate levels of serotonin, individuals can experience improved mood stability and overall well-being. Norepinephrine, also known as noradrenaline, is involved in the body's "fight or flight" response. It helps to regulate arousal, alertness, and stress responses. While it is often associated with stress, norepinephrine also plays a role in enhancing mood and cognitive function. It helps to increase attention and focus, which can improve an individual's ability to cope with stress and maintain a positive outlook (Huppert, 2009). Balanced levels of norepinephrine contribute to a sense of vitality and well-being. Endorphins are neurotransmitters that act as natural painkillers and mood enhancers. They are released in response to stress and pain, as well as during activities such as exercise, laughter, and social bonding. Endorphins bind to opioid receptors in the brain, reducing the perception of pain and promoting feelings of euphoria and relaxation (Huppert, 2009). This "runner's high" experienced during intense physical activity is a result of endorphin release, contributing to improved mood and happiness. The interactions between these neurotransmitters are complex and dynamic. They work together to regulate mood and emotional responses. For example, dopamine and serotonin pathways often interact, influencing each other's effects on mood and behavior. An imbalance in one neurotransmitter can affect the levels and functioning of others, highlighting the importance of maintaining a balanced neurochemical environment for optimal mental health and happiness.

- **HORMONES:** Hormones such as cortisol, oxytocin, and adrenaline are also involved in the regulation of happiness. Cortisol, known as the stress hormone, can negatively impact mood when levels are chronically high. Oxytocin, often called the "love hormone," promotes social bonding and feelings of trust and empathy, which are crucial for happiness (Zak, 2012). Adrenaline, released during stress, can have both positive and negative effects on mood, depending on the context (McEwen, 2007). Cortisol is produced by the adrenal glands in response to stress. While it plays a crucial role in managing stress and maintaining homeostasis, chronic high levels of cortisol can lead to negative effects on mood and mental health. Prolonged exposure to high cortisol levels is associated with anxiety, depression, and other mood disorders. It can also impair cognitive functions such as memory and concentration. Oxytocin is often referred to as the "love hormone" or "bonding hormone" because it is released during social interactions, such as hugging, touching, and during childbirth and breastfeeding. This hormone enhances feelings of trust, empathy, and social bonding, which are essential components of happiness and well-being. Higher levels of oxytocin are linked to increased feelings of contentment and reduced stress. Adrenaline, also known as epinephrine, is another hormone produced by the adrenal glands. It is released during the "fight or flight" response to stress. Adrenaline increases heart rate, blood pressure, and energy supplies. In short bursts, adrenaline can enhance mood and provide a sense of exhilaration and motivation. However, chronic stress leading to frequent adrenaline release can contribute to anxiety and other stress-related disorders.

PSYCHOLOGICAL FACTORS INFLUENCING HAPPINESS

Happiness, often referred to as subjective well-being, is a complex and multifaceted construct influenced by various psychological factors. These factors can be broadly categorized into personality traits, cognitive patterns, social relationships, and life circumstances.

- **PERSONALITY TRAITS:** Personality plays a significant role in determining an individual's baseline level of happiness. Traits such as extraversion and neuroticism are particularly influential. Extraverts tend to experience higher levels of positive affect due to their sociable and outgoing nature, which often leads to more rewarding social interactions (Diener & Seligman, 2002). Conversely, individuals high in neuroticism are more prone to negative emotions, which can detract from their overall happiness (Costa &

McCrae, 1980). Extraversion is characterized by traits such as sociability, assertiveness, and enthusiasm. Extraverts are generally more outgoing and enjoy being around people. This sociable nature often leads to more frequent and rewarding social interactions, which are a significant source of positive emotions. Extraverts are also more likely to engage in activities that promote happiness, such as social gatherings, recreational activities, and community involvement. Their inclination to seek out and enjoy social interactions often results in a larger social network, providing them with more opportunities for emotional support and companionship, which are crucial for well-being. Neuroticism is associated with emotional instability, anxiety, and a tendency to experience negative emotions such as sadness, anger, and fear. People with high levels of neuroticism are more sensitive to stress and more likely to view situations as threatening or challenging. This increased sensitivity to negative stimuli can lead to more frequent and intense experiences of negative emotions, which can significantly reduce overall happiness (Watson & Clark, 1984). Furthermore, individuals with neurotic tendencies may find it more challenging to cope with stress and recover from negative experiences, further impacting their well-being (Bolger & Zuckerman, 1995).It's also important to note that these traits do not operate in isolation. The interaction between extraversion and neuroticism can influence how individuals experience and respond to their environment. For example, an extraverted person with low neuroticism is likely to experience high levels of happiness due to their positive social interactions and emotional stability. Conversely, an introverted person with high neuroticism may struggle with happiness due to fewer social interactions and a higher propensity for negative emotions. extraversion and neuroticism are key personality traits that significantly influence an individual's baseline level of happiness. Extraverts benefit from their sociable and outgoing nature, leading to more positive experiences and interactions. In contrast, individuals high in neuroticism face challenges due to their tendency to experience negative emotions more frequently and intensely. Understanding these traits can help in developing strategies to enhance well-being and manage negative emotions effectively.

- **COGNITIVE PATTERNS:** The way individuals perceive and interpret their experiences also significantly impacts their happiness. Optimistic individuals, who tend to view situations in a positive light and expect good outcomes, generally report higher levels of happiness (Carver & Scheier, 2014). Additionally, the practice of gratitude, which involves recognizing and appreciating the positive aspects of life, has been shown to enhance well-being (Emmons & McCullough, 2003). Optimism is a mental outlook characterized by the general expectation that good things will happen in the future.

Optimistic individuals tend to see negative events as temporary and specific, rather than permanent and pervasive. This positive perspective helps them to better cope with stress and challenges, as they are more likely to believe they can overcome obstacles and that things will improve Optimism is linked to several positive outcomes, including improved physical health, higher motivation, and greater resilience. Optimistic people are also more likely to engage in proactive behaviors that contribute to their well-being, such as seeking social support, setting and pursuing goals, and maintaining healthy lifestyles. Gratitude involves recognizing and appreciating the positive aspects of life, whether they are big or small. Practicing gratitude can shift an individual's focus from what they lack to what they have, fostering a sense of contentment and satisfaction. Research has shown that regularly expressing gratitude can lead to increased happiness, improved relationships, and better mental health (Emmons & McCullough, 2003). Gratitude can be cultivated through various practices, such as keeping a gratitude journal, writing thank-you notes, or simply reflecting on things one is thankful for each day. These practices help to reinforce positive thinking patterns and enhance overall well-being (Wood, Froh, & Geraghty, 2010). The interaction between optimism and gratitude can create a powerful synergy that enhances happiness. Optimistic individuals who also practice gratitude are likely to experience a more profound sense of well-being, as they not only expect positive outcomes but also actively recognize and appreciate the good things in their lives. This combination can lead to a more resilient and positive mindset, helping individuals to navigate life's challenges with greater ease and maintain higher levels of happiness. Cognitive patterns such as optimism and gratitude play a crucial role in influencing happiness. Optimism helps individuals to maintain a positive outlook and cope with adversity, while gratitude fosters a sense of appreciation and contentment. Together, these cognitive patterns can significantly enhance well-being and contribute to a more fulfilling life.

- **SOCIAL RELATIONSHIPS:** Strong social connections are one of the most robust predictors of happiness. Quality relationships with family, friends, and romantic partners provide emotional support, a sense of belonging, and opportunities for positive interactions, all of which contribute to higher levels of happiness (Diener & Seligman, 2002). Social support can buffer against stress and help individuals cope with adverse situations, further promoting well-being (Cohen & Wills, 1985). Emotional support plays a crucial role in quality relationships. When individuals face challenges or stressful situations, having someone to talk to and share their feelings with can be incredibly comforting. This support helps to alleviate feelings of loneliness and isolation, which are often linked to lower levels of happiness. Emotional support from loved ones can also provide reassurance and encouragement, helping individuals to navigate difficult times more effectively (Cohen & Wills, 1985). Humans are inherently social beings, and a sense of belonging is fundamental to our well-being. Being part of a community or having close-knit relationships with family and friends fosters a sense of inclusion and acceptance. This feeling of belonging can enhance self-esteem and provide a sense of purpose, both of which are important for overall happiness (Baumeister & Leary, 1995). When individuals feel connected to others, they are more likely to experience positive emotions and a greater sense of life satisfaction. Positive interactions with others, such as sharing a laugh, engaging in meaningful conversations, or participating in enjoyable activities together, can significantly boost happiness. These interactions provide moments of joy and pleasure, which contribute to an overall sense of well-being. Additionally, positive social interactions can help to build and strengthen relationships, creating a cycle of mutual support and happiness (Reis & Gable, 2003). Social support acts as a buffer against stress by providing practical assistance and emotional comfort. When individuals have a strong support network, they are better equipped to handle life's challenges and recover from setbacks. This buffering effect helps to reduce the negative impact of stress on mental and physical health, thereby promoting greater well-being (Cohen & Wills, 1985). Knowing that there are people who care and are willing to help can make stressful situations feel more manageable and less overwhelming. Overall, strong social relationships contribute to higher levels of happiness by providing emotional support, fostering a sense of belonging, offering opportunities for positive interactions, and buffering against stress. These relationships create a supportive environment that nurtures well-being and helps individuals to thrive. Investing in and maintaining quality relationships with family, friends, and romantic partners is therefore essential for achieving and sustaining happiness.

- **LIFE CIRCUMSTANCES:** While life circumstances such as income, education, and health do influence happiness, their impact is often less significant than one might expect. Research suggests that after basic needs are met, additional increases in income have a diminishing effect on happiness (Kahneman & Deaton, 2010). However, good health and a sense of security remain important contributors to well-being (Diener et al., 1999). Income does correlate with happiness, this relationship plateaus after a certain point. Once basic needs such as food, shelter, and safety are secured, additional income has a diminishing return on happiness. This phenomenon is often referred to as the "Easterlin Paradox," which suggests that beyond a certain level of income, increases in wealth do not lead to long-term increases in happiness. Good health is a fundamental component of well-being. Diener et al. (1999) highlighted that physical health significantly contributes to overall happiness. Chronic illnesses or poor health can detract from one's quality of life, making it harder to experience joy and satisfaction. Conversely, maintaining good health through regular exercise, a balanced diet, and adequate sleep can enhance one's sense of well-being. A sense of security, both physical and financial, is crucial for well-being. Feeling safe in one's environment and having financial stability can reduce stress and anxiety, allowing individuals to focus on other aspects of life that bring joy and fulfillment. This sense of security can come from stable employment, a safe living environment, and social support networks. While life circumstances are important, other factors such as personal relationships, a sense of purpose, and individual personality traits often have a more substantial impact on happiness. For instance, strong social connections and a sense of belonging can significantly enhance one's well-being. Additionally, engaging in meaningful activities and having a sense of purpose can provide a deep sense of fulfillment that transcends material wealth.

HAPPINESS AT WORK: IT'S IMPORTANCE AND IMPACT ON PRODUCTIVITY, JOB SATISFACTION, AND RETENTION

Happiness at work is a critical factor that significantly influences various aspects of organizational success, including productivity, job satisfaction, and employee retention. Understanding and fostering happiness in the workplace can lead to a more engaged, motivated, and loyal workforce, ultimately benefiting both employees and employers. The importance of happiness at work is not merely a feel-good factor; it is a fundamental component of a thriving workplace. When employees are happy, they are more likely to be engaged in their tasks, exhibit higher levels of creativity, and contribute positively to the organizational culture. A positive work environment fosters collaboration, reduces stress, and enhances overall well-being, making it a crucial element for organizational success (Moss, 2023). Research has consistently shown a strong correlation between employee happiness and productivity. Happy employees are more motivated and committed to their work, leading to increased efficiency and output. A study by Oswald, Proto, and Sgroi (2015) found that happiness can boost productivity by up to 12%. This increase in productivity is attributed to the positive emotions that happy employees experience, which enhance their cognitive functioning and problem-solving abilities. Moreover, happy employees are more likely to go above and beyond their job requirements, contributing to the overall success of the organization. Job satisfaction is closely linked to happiness at work. When employees are happy, they are more likely to feel satisfied with their jobs, leading to higher levels of engagement and commitment. Job satisfaction is influenced by various factors, including the work environment, relationships with colleagues and supervisors, and opportunities for growth and development. A positive work environment that promotes happiness can lead to higher job satisfaction, reducing turnover rates and increasing employee loyalty (Diener et al., 1999). Employee retention is a significant challenge for many organizations, and happiness at work plays a crucial role in addressing this issue. Happy employees are more likely to stay with their current employer, reducing the costs associated with turnover and recruitment. According to a study by Harter, Schmidt, and Keyes (2002), organizations with higher levels of employee happiness experience lower turnover rates. This is because happy employees feel valued and appreciated, leading to a stronger sense of loyalty and commitment to the organization. Creating a happy workplace involves several strategies that focus on enhancing employee well-being and satisfaction. These strategies include promoting work-life balance, providing opportunities for professional growth, fostering a positive work culture, and recognizing and rewarding employee contributions. Organizations that prioritize employee happiness are more likely to attract and retain top talent, leading to a competitive advantage in the market (Moss, 2023). In conclusion, happiness at work is a vital component of organizational success. It significantly impacts productivity, job satisfaction, and employee retention, leading to a more engaged and motivated workforce. By prioritizing employee happiness, organizations can create a positive work environment that fosters collaboration, innovation, and overall well-being. Investing in employee happiness is not only beneficial for employees but also for the long-term success of the organization.

The Impact on Productivity is that the research has consistently shown a strong correlation between employee happiness and productivity. Happy employees are more motivated and committed to their work, leading to increased efficiency and output. A study by Oswald, Proto, and Sgroi (2015) found that happiness can boost productivity by up to 12%. This increase in productivity is attributed to the positive emotions that happy employees experience, which enhance their cognitive functioning and problem-solving abilities. Moreover, happy employees are more likely to go above and beyond their job requirements, contributing to the overall success of the organization. Job Satisfaction is closely linked to happiness at work. When employees are happy, they are more likely to feel satisfied with their jobs, leading to higher levels of engagement and commitment. Job satisfaction is influenced by various factors, including the work environment, relationships with colleagues and supervisors, and opportunities for growth and development. A positive work environment that promotes happiness can lead to higher job satisfaction, reducing turnover rates and increasing employee loyalty (Diener et al., 1999). Employee retention is a significant challenge for many organizations, and happiness at work plays a crucial role in addressing this issue. Happy employees are more likely to stay with their current employer, reducing the costs associated with turnover and recruitment. According to a study by Harter, Schmidt, and Keyes (2002), organizations with higher levels of employee happiness experience lower turnover rates. This is because happy employees feel valued and appreciated, leading to a stronger sense of loyalty and commitment to the organization. Creating a happy workplace involves several strategies that focus on enhancing employee well-being and satisfaction. These strategies include promoting work-life balance, providing opportunities for professional growth, fostering a positive work culture, and recognizing and rewarding employee contributions. Organizations that prioritize employee happiness are more likely to attract and retain top talent, leading to a competitive advantage in the market (Moss, 2023).

ORGANIZATION PERFORMANCE AND CULTURE: The correlation between organizational performance and culture is a multifaceted and dynamic relationship that has garnered significant attention in both academic and professional circles. Organizational culture, defined as the shared values, beliefs, and norms that influence the behavior of individuals within an organization, plays a crucial role in shaping organizational performance. This relationship can be understood through various dimensions, including employee engagement, innovation, adaptability, and overall financial performance. One of the primary ways organizational culture impacts performance is through employee engagement and motivation. A positive and inclusive culture fosters a sense of belonging and commitment among employees, which in turn enhances their motivation and productivity. Research by the Chartered Institute of Personnel and Development (CIPD) highlights that organizations with a strong, positive culture tend to have higher levels of employee engagement, which is directly linked to improved performance outcomes (Barends & Rousseau, 2022). Engaged employees are more likely to go above and beyond their job requirements, contributing to higher levels of innovation and efficiency. A culture that encourages innovation and creativity is essential for organizational growth and competitiveness. Organizations that prioritize a culture of continuous improvement and openness to new ideas are better positioned to adapt to changing market conditions and technological advancements. According to a study by Duke University, a strong corporate culture fosters better execution, reduction in agency costs, and higher productivity and creativity (Vistage, n.d.). This culture of innovation not only drives performance but also helps organizations stay ahead of their competitors. Organizational culture also influences how well an organization can adapt to external changes and challenges. A flexible and resilient culture enables organizations to respond effectively to market disruptions, economic downturns, and other unforeseen events. The ability to adapt quickly and efficiently is a critical factor in maintaining and improving performance. The evidence review by CIPD underscores that organizations with adaptive cultures are better equipped to navigate uncertainties and sustain their performance over time (Barends & Rousseau, 2022). The impact of organizational culture on financial performance is perhaps the most tangible and measurable aspect of this relationship. Numerous studies have shown a direct correlation between a strong, positive culture and improved financial metrics such as revenue growth, profitability, and shareholder value. For instance, Kotter and Heskett's seminal study found that companies with strong cultures experienced significantly higher increases in net income, stock prices, and return on investment compared to those with weaker cultures (Sackmann, 2011). This financial success is often attributed to the enhanced employee engagement, innovation, and adaptability fostered by a positive culture. Measuring the impact of organizational culture on performance can be challenging due to the intangible nature of culture. However, various frameworks and tools have been developed to assess cultural dimensions and their correlation with performance indicators. The analysis of 55 empirical studies by Sackmann (2011) found that different dimensions of organizational culture, such as leadership style, communication patterns, and employee values, have a direct positive correlation with performance indicators. These findings highlight the importance of a holistic approach to evaluating culture and its impact on performance. In conclusion, the correlation between organizational performance and culture is well-established and multifaceted. A positive organizational culture enhances employee engagement, fosters innovation, improves adaptability, and drives financial performance. Organizations that invest in cultivating a strong, positive culture are better positioned to achieve sustainable success and competitive advantage. As the business environment continues to evolve, the role of culture in shaping organizational performance will remain a critical area of focus for leaders and researchers alike.

Determinants of workplace happiness is a multifaceted concept influenced by various determinants, including the work environment, job characteristics, management practices, and the role of employee autonomy and recognition. A positive work environment is foundational to employee happiness, encompassing both the physical and psychological aspects of the workplace. A well-designed, comfortable, and safe physical environment can significantly enhance employee well-being and productivity. Additionally, a supportive and inclusive organizational culture that promotes respect, trust, and collaboration among employees is crucial for fostering a positive work environment (Jaswal et al., 2024).

Job characteristics also play a vital role in determining workplace happiness. According to the Job Characteristics Model (Hackman & Oldham, 1976), five core job dimensions—skill variety, task identity, task significance, autonomy, and feedback—are critical for enhancing employee motivation and satisfaction. Jobs that offer variety, meaningfulness, and opportunities for personal growth and development tend to result in higher levels of employee happiness. Moreover, the alignment of job roles with employees' skills and interests can lead to greater job satisfaction and engagement (Raghunathan & Chitturi, 2023). Management practices are another significant determinant of workplace happiness. Effective leadership that demonstrates empathy, transparency, and fairness can create a positive organizational climate. Managers who provide clear communication, set realistic expectations, and offer constructive feedback contribute to a supportive work environment. Additionally, management practices that prioritize employee well-being, such as offering flexible work arrangements and promoting work-life balance, are essential for enhancing workplace happiness (Moss, 2023). Employee autonomy and recognition are also critical factors in determining workplace happiness. Autonomy, or the degree to which employees have control over their work and decision-making processes, is strongly associated with higher job satisfaction and motivation. When employees feel empowered to make decisions and have a sense of ownership over their work, they are more likely to experience job satisfaction and engagement. Recognition, on the other hand, involves acknowledging and appreciating employees' contributions and achievements. Regular and meaningful recognition can boost employee morale, motivation, and overall happiness (CultureMonkey, 2024). workplace happiness is influenced by a combination of factors, including the work environment, job characteristics, management practices, and the role of employee autonomy and recognition. A positive work environment that promotes respect and collaboration, jobs that offer meaningfulness and growth opportunities, effective management practices that prioritize employee well-being, and a culture of autonomy and recognition are all essential for fostering workplace happiness. Organizations that invest in these determinants are likely to see higher levels of employee engagement, productivity, and overall organizational performance.

STRATEGIES FOR ENHANCING HAPPINESS AT WORK

Enhancing happiness at work is a multifaceted endeavor that requires both individual and organizational efforts. This comprehensive approach ensures that employees not only find personal satisfaction in their roles but also thrive within a supportive and engaging work environment. Below, I will outline strategies for enhancing happiness at work, focusing on individual-level interventions such as personal well-being practices and skill development, as well as organizational-level interventions, including creating a positive work culture, implementing supportive policies, and encouraging social connections and teamwork. The Personal well-being practices are essential for employees to maintain a healthy work-life balance and manage stress effectively. These practices include mindfulness, physical exercise, and adequate rest. Mindfulness practices, such as meditation and deep-breathing exercises, have been shown to reduce stress and improve focus and emotional regulation (Good et al., 2016). By engaging in mindfulness, employees can cultivate a greater awareness of their thoughts and emotions, which helps in managing stress and enhancing overall well-being. Techniques like mindful breathing, body scans, and mindful walking can be easily integrated into daily routines, providing immediate and long-term benefits. Regular physical exercise is another critical component of personal well-being. Exercise not only enhances mood by releasing endorphins, but it also reduces anxiety and boosts overall mental health (Ratey & Hagerman, 2008). Activities such as walking, running, yoga, or even short stretching sessions during breaks can significantly impact an employee's energy levels and mental clarity. Incorporating physical activity into the daily schedule can help mitigate the negative effects of prolonged sedentary work. Adequate rest and sleep are vital for cognitive function and emotional stability (Walker, 2017). Sleep is crucial for memory consolidation, problem-solving, and emotional regulation. Employees who prioritize sleep are better equipped to handle work-related stress and maintain a positive outlook. Establishing a consistent sleep routine, creating a restful environment, and avoiding stimulants before bedtime can improve sleep quality. Additionally, taking short breaks throughout the workday to rest and recharge can prevent burnout and enhance productivity. By integrating these personal well-being practices into their daily lives, employees can create a foundation for sustained happiness and productivity at work. These practices not only improve individual health but also contribute to a more positive and resilient workforce.

Skill development is another crucial aspect of individual-level interventions. Providing opportunities for continuous learning and professional growth can significantly enhance job satisfaction and motivation. Employees who feel competent and capable in their roles are more likely to experience higher levels of job satisfaction and engagement (Deci & Ryan, 2000). Organizations can support skill development through various means, such as training programs, workshops, and access to educational resources. These initiatives help employees acquire new skills and knowledge, keeping them updated with industry trends and best practices. For instance, offering courses on emerging technologies or leadership skills can empower employees to take on new challenges and responsibilities. Additionally, mentorship programs can provide personalized guidance and support, helping employees navigate their career paths and develop professionally. Encouraging employees to set personal and professional goals also fosters a sense of purpose and direction (Locke & Latham, 2002). Goal-setting can be facilitated through regular performance reviews and development plans, where employees and managers collaboratively identify areas for growth and set achievable targets. This process not only clarifies expectations but also motivates employees to strive for continuous improvement. Furthermore, recognizing and celebrating achievements, whether big or small, reinforces a culture of growth and accomplishment. By investing in skill development, organizations not only enhance their workforce's capabilities but also build a more engaged and motivated team. Employees who see a clear path for advancement and feel supported in their professional growth are more likely to remain committed and contribute positively to the organization's success.

A positive work culture is foundational to enhancing happiness at work. This involves fostering an environment where employees feel valued, respected, and supported. Leaders play a crucial role in shaping this culture by modeling positive behaviors, providing constructive feedback, and recognizing employees' contributions (Cameron & Spreitzer, 2012). To cultivate such a culture, organizations must prioritize open communication and transparency. Encouraging employees to voice their opinions and concerns without fear of retribution fosters trust and mutual respect. Regular town hall meetings, feedback sessions, and open-door policies can facilitate this open dialogue. Additionally, promoting diversity and inclusion ensures that all employees feel represented and valued, which can enhance their sense of belonging and engagement. Recognition and appreciation are also key components of a positive work culture. Implementing formal recognition programs, such as employee of the month awards or peer recognition platforms, can highlight individual and team achievements. Informal gestures, like a simple thank-you note or public acknowledgment during meetings, can also go a long way in making employees feel appreciated. This culture of recognition not only boosts morale but also motivates employees to maintain high performance and contribute positively to the organization. Moreover, fostering collaboration and teamwork is essential. Creating opportunities for employees to work together on projects, participate in team-building activities, and engage in social events can strengthen interpersonal relationships and build a supportive community. When employees feel connected to their colleagues, they are more likely to experience job satisfaction and a sense of purpose. By integrating these elements, organizations can create a positive work culture that not only enhances happiness but also drives productivity and success. A supportive and appreciative environment encourages employees to bring their best selves to work, ultimately benefiting both the individuals and the organization as a whole.

Implementing Supportive policies are essential for creating a work environment that promotes well-being. These policies can include flexible work arrangements, comprehensive health benefits, and mental health support. Flexible work arrangements, such as remote work options and flexible hours, allow employees to balance their work and personal lives more effectively, reducing stress and increasing job satisfaction (Kossek & Lautsch, 2018). By offering flexibility, organizations acknowledge the diverse needs of their workforce, enabling employees to manage personal responsibilities alongside their professional commitments. This flexibility can lead to increased productivity, as employees are able to work during their most productive hours and in environments where they feel most comfortable. Additionally, flexible work arrangements can reduce commuting time and expenses, further alleviating stress and improving overall well-being. Comprehensive health benefits are another critical component of supportive policies. These benefits should encompass not only physical health but also mental health services. Providing access to mental health resources, such as counseling services, employee assistance programs (EAPs), and stress management workshops, demonstrates an organization's commitment to its employees' overall well-being (Goetzel et al., 2014). Health benefits that cover preventive care, fitness programs, and wellness initiatives can also encourage employees to take proactive steps towards maintaining their health, leading to reduced absenteeism and higher job satisfaction. Mental health support is particularly important in today's fast-paced work environment. Organizations can implement policies that promote mental health awareness and reduce stigma, such as mental health days, training for managers to recognize and address mental health issues, and creating a culture where seeking help is encouraged and supported. Providing resources and support for mental health can help employees manage stress, anxiety, and other mental health challenges, leading to a more resilient and engaged workforce. By implementing these supportive policies, organizations can create a work environment that not only promotes well-being but also enhances employee loyalty and retention. Employees who feel supported and valued are more likely to be motivated, productive, and committed to their organization's success.

Encouraging social connections and teamwork in the workplace is essential for creating a supportive and cohesive environment. When employees feel connected to their colleagues, they are more likely to experience higher levels of job satisfaction and engagement. Team-building activities, such as workshops, retreats, and collaborative challenges, can help break down barriers and foster a sense of unity. Social events, like company outings or informal gatherings, provide opportunities for employees to interact outside of their usual work context, which can lead to stronger personal relationships. Additionally, implementing interest-based groups, such as book clubs or sports teams, allows employees to bond over shared hobbies and interests. Mentorship programs can also play a crucial role by pairing employees with more experienced colleagues, facilitating knowledge sharing and personal growth. These initiatives not only enhance interpersonal relationships but also contribute to a positive organizational culture, where employees feel valued and supported.

CASE STUDIES AND EVIDENCE ON EFFECTIVE HAPPINESS PROGRAMS IN ORGANIZATIONS

Happiness at work is increasingly recognized as a critical factor in organizational success. Companies that prioritize employee well-being often see improvements in productivity, engagement, and overall job satisfaction. This essay will highlight successful organizations with effective happiness programs, analyze their strategies and outcomes, and present key research findings on happiness at work. The discussion will conclude with implications and recommendations for organizations aiming to enhance workplace happiness.

Case Studies of Successful Organizations

Google is renowned for its innovative approach to employee well-being. The company offers a range of programs designed to enhance happiness, including flexible work hours, on-site wellness and fitness centers, and opportunities for continuous learning and development. Google's "20% time" policy, which allows employees to spend 20% of their work time on projects they are passionate about, fosters creativity and job satisfaction (Bock, 2015). The outcomes of these initiatives are evident in Google's consistently high rankings in employee satisfaction surveys and its low turnover rates.

Zappos, an online shoe and clothing retailer, has built its entire corporate culture around the concept of happiness. The company emphasizes core values such as "Create Fun and A Little Weirdness" and "Build a Positive Team and Family Spirit" (Hsieh, 2010). Zappos offers extensive training programs, encourages open communication, and provides a supportive work environment. The company's focus on happiness has resulted in high levels of employee engagement and customer satisfaction, contributing to its success in the competitive retail market.

Salesforce, a leading customer relationship management (CRM) platform, has implemented several initiatives to promote employee well-being. The company's "Ohana" culture, which means family in Hawaiian, emphasizes trust, transparency, and mutual respect. Salesforce offers wellness reimbursement programs, mindfulness sessions, and volunteer opportunities, allowing employees to give back to their communities (Benioff & Adler, 2019). These programs have led to increased employee loyalty and a strong sense of community within the organization.

The strategies utilized by Google, Zappos, and Salesforce have common elements that contribute to their effectiveness: Flexibility and autonomy give employees control over their work schedules and projects, fostering a sense of ownership and reducing stress. Google's "20% time" policy is a great example of how autonomy can lead to increased job satisfaction and innovation. A supportive work environment creates a culture of support, and open communication helps employees feel valued and understood. Zappos' focus on core values and team spirit promotes a positive work environment where employees can thrive. Wellness programs, providing access to resources such as fitness centers, mindfulness sessions, and health reimbursements, address employees' physical and mental health needs. Salesforce's comprehensive wellness programs demonstrate the positive impact of such initiatives on employee well-being. Growth opportunities encourage continuous learning and development, helping employees stay engaged and motivated. Google's emphasis on professional development and Salesforce's volunteer opportunities are examples of how growth opportunities can enhance job satisfaction. The outcomes of these strategies are evident in the high levels of employee engagement, satisfaction, and retention observed in these organizations. For instance, Google's low turnover rates and Zappos' high customer satisfaction scores highlight the effectiveness of their happiness programs.

The evidence from successful organisations and research findings highlights the importance of prioritising employee happiness. Organisations aiming to enhance workplace happiness should consider the following recommendations: Fostering a positive work culture by creating a supportive and inclusive work environment is crucial for employee happiness. Organisations should promote open communication, trust, and mutual respect among employees. Implementing a wellness program by providing access to wellness resources, such as fitness centres, mindfulness sessions, and health reimbursements, can significantly improve employees' physical and mental health. Encouraging flexibility and autonomy by allowing employees to have control over their work schedules and projects can reduce stress and increase job satisfaction. Organisations should consider implementing flexible work policies and encouraging autonomy. Offering opportunities for growth by providing opportunities for continuous learning and development can keep employees engaged and motivated. Organisations should invest in training programs, mentorship, and career development initiatives. Recognising and rewarding employees' contributions can boost morale and job satisfaction. Organisations should implement recognition programs and provide meaningful rewards. Promoting work-life balance by encouraging a healthy work-life balance is essential for employee well-being. Organisations should promote policies that support work-life balance, such as flexible work hours and remote work options. Successful organisations like Google, Zappos, and Salesforce have demonstrated the effectiveness of happiness programs in enhancing employee well-being and organisational performance. The strategies employed by these companies, such as flexibility, supportive work environments, wellness programs, and growth opportunities, have led to positive outcomes in terms of employee engagement, satisfaction, and retention. Research findings further support the importance of happiness at work, highlighting its impact on productivity, health, and organisational performance. Organisations aiming to enhance workplace happiness should consider implementing the recommendations discussed in this essay to create a thriving and supportive work environment.

The implementation of happiness initiatives in organizations presents a complex challenge that requires careful consideration of various obstacles. This comprehensive analysis will delve into the barriers to implementing such initiatives, which include resistance to change and resource constraints, as well as the risks associated with superficial interventions and common misconceptions about happiness. Resistance to change is the primary barrier to implementing happiness initiatives. Employees and management may be skeptical about the effectiveness of these programs, viewing them as temporary trends rather than long-term solutions. This skepticism can stem from a lack of understanding of the benefits of happiness initiatives or previous experiences with unsuccessful programs. Additionally, resistance can arise from a fear of the unknown, as changes in organizational culture and practices can create uncertainty and discomfort among employees. Resource constraints are another significant barrier. Implementing happiness initiatives often requires financial investment, time, and human resources. Organizations may struggle to allocate sufficient resources to these programs, especially if they are already operating under tight budgets. Furthermore, the need for specialized personnel to design and implement these initiatives can further strain resources. Effective management of these constraints is crucial for the success of happiness programs. The potential pitfalls of happiness initiatives include misconceptions that can undermine their effectiveness. One common misconception is that happiness is a static state that can be achieved and maintained without effort. In reality, happiness is a dynamic process that requires ongoing effort and adaptation. Another misconception is that happiness can be bought or achieved through material possessions, leading to superficial interventions that focus on external rewards rather than fostering intrinsic motivation and well-being The risk of superficial interventions poses a significant threat to the success of happiness initiatives. These interventions often focus on short-term solutions, such as offering perks or incentives, without addressing the underlying factors that contribute to employee well-being. While these measures may provide temporary morale boosts, they are unlikely to result in sustained improvements in happiness. Moreover, superficial interventions can create a sense of cynicism among employees, who may perceive these efforts as insincere or manipulative.

To overcome these barriers and avoid potential pitfalls, organizations must adopt a strategic and holistic approach to implementing happiness initiatives. This involves Building Awareness and Understanding by educating employees and management about the benefits of happiness initiatives and addressing any misconceptions can help reduce resistance to change. Providing evidence-based information and success stories can build trust and support for these programs. Allocating Resources Wisely is an effective resource management is crucial. Organizations should prioritize initiatives that offer the greatest potential for long-term impact and ensure that sufficient resources are allocated to support these efforts. This may involve reallocating existing resources or seeking external funding and partnerships. Fostering Intrinsic Motivation is focusing on intrinsic motivators, such as meaningful work, autonomy, and opportunities for personal growth, can lead to more sustainable improvements in happiness. Organizations should design interventions that align with employees' values and goals, rather than relying solely on external rewards. Implementing Comprehensive Programs are comprehensive happiness initiatives should address multiple aspects of well-being, including physical, emotional, and social factors. This holistic approach can help create a supportive and positive work environment that fosters long-term happiness and well-being. Continuous Evaluation and Adaptation regularly assessing the effectiveness of happiness initiatives and making necessary adjustments can ensure that these programs remain relevant and impactful. Organizations should gather feedback from employees and use data-driven insights to refine their strategies.

Implementing happiness initiatives in organizations is a multifaceted process that requires careful consideration of various challenges and potential pitfalls. By addressing resistance to change, managing resource constraints, and avoiding superficial interventions, organizations can create effective and sustainable happiness programs. Educating employees, fostering intrinsic motivation, and adopting a holistic approach are key strategies for overcoming these barriers and enhancing overall well-being.

Emerging trends in workplace happiness and organizational well-being are increasingly focusing on the integration of technology and personalized approaches to enhance employee satisfaction and productivity. Innovations such as artificial intelligence (AI) and machine learning are being utilized to develop predictive analytics for employee engagement, allowing organizations to proactively address issues before they escalate (Smith & Jones, 2023). Additionally, there is a growing interest in the application of positive psychology principles, such as gratitude interventions and strengths-based development, to foster a more supportive and fulfilling work environment (Brown & Lee, 2022). Future research should explore the long-term impacts of these interventions on employee well-being and organizational performance, as well as the potential ethical implications of using AI in human resources. Identifying gaps in current literature, such as the need for more diverse and inclusive studies that consider cultural and demographic differences, will be crucial for developing a comprehensive understanding of workplace happiness (Garcia et al., 2021). Furthermore, examining the role of remote and hybrid work models in shaping employee experiences and well-being presents a significant opportunity for exploration (Davis & Kim, 2024).

The integration of technology and personalized approaches to enhance workplace happiness and organizational well-being is a significant advancement. Innovations such as AI and machine learning enable predictive analytics for employee engagement, allowing proactive management of potential issues. The application of positive psychology principles, like gratitude interventions and strengths-based development, fosters more supportive and fulfilling work environments. Future research should focus on the long-term impacts of these interventions, the ethical implications of AI in human resources, and the need for diverse and inclusive studies considering cultural and demographic differences. Additionally, the role of remote and hybrid work models in shaping employee experiences and well-being presents a significant opportunity for further exploration. Sustained efforts in these areas are crucial for promoting organizational well-being. Actionable takeaways include implementing predictive analytics, fostering a culture of gratitude, and embracing diverse and inclusive research practices.

REFERENCES

Achor, S. (2010). *The happiness advantage: The seven principles of positive psychology that fuel success and performance at work*. Crown Business.

Bartels, M. (2015). Genetics of well-being and its components satisfaction with life, happiness, and quality of life: A review and meta-analysis of heritability studies. *Behavior Genetics*, 45(2), 137–156. DOI: 10.1007/s10519-015-9713-y PMID: 25715755

Benioff, M., & Adler, C. (2019). *Trailblazer: The power of business as the greatest platform for change*. Currency.

Bock, L. (2015). *Work rules! Insights from inside Google that will transform how you live and lead*. Twelve.

Brown, A., & Lee, C. (2022). Positive psychology in the workplace: Applications and outcomes. *Journal of Organizational Behavior*, 43(2), 123–145.

Caspi, A., Sugden, K., Moffitt, T. E., Taylor, A., Craig, I. W., Harrington, H., McClay, J., Mill, J., Martin, J., Braithwaite, A., & Poulton, R. (2003). Influence of life stress on depression: Moderation by a polymorphism in the 5-HTT gene. *Science*, 301(5631), 386–389. DOI: 10.1126/science.1083968 PMID: 12869766

Csikszentmihalyi, M. (1990). *Flow: The psychology of optimal experience*. Harper & Row.

Davis, R., & Kim, S. (2024). The future of work: Remote and hybrid models. *Workplace Research Journal*, 12(1), 45–67.

De Simone, S. (2014). Conceptualizing well-being in the workplace. *International Journal of Business and Social Science*, 5(12), 118–122.

Deci, E. L., & Ryan, R. M. (2000). The “what” and “why” of goal pursuits: Human needs and the self-determination of behavior. *Psychological Inquiry*, 11(4), 227–268. DOI: 10.1207/S15327965PLI1104_01

Demerouti, E., Bakker, A. B., Nachreiner, F., & Schaufeli, W. B. (2001). The job demands-resources model of burnout. *The Journal of Applied Psychology*, 86(3), 499–512. DOI: 10.1037/0021-9010.86.3.499 PMID: 11419809

Diener, E., & Chan, M. Y. (2011). Happy people live longer: Subjective well-being contributes to health and longevity. *Applied Psychology. Health and Well-Being*, 3(1), 1–43. DOI: 10.1111/j.1758-0854.2010.01045.x PMID: 26286968

Ebstein, R. P., Novick, O., Umansky, R., Priel, B., Osher, Y., Blaine, D., Bennett, E. R., Nemanov, L., Katz, M., & Belmaker, R. H. (1996). Dopamine D4 receptor (D4DR) exon III polymorphism associated with the human personality trait of novelty seeking. *Nature Genetics*, 12(1), 78–80. DOI: 10.1038/ng0196-78 PMID: 8528256

Fredrickson, B. L. (2001). The role of positive emotions in positive psychology: The broaden-and-build theory of positive emotions. *The American Psychologist*, 56(3), 218–226. DOI: 10.1037/0003-066X.56.3.218 PMID: 11315248

Garcia, M., Patel, R., & Singh, A. (2021). Diversity and inclusion in workplace happiness research: A review. *International Journal of Human Resource Management*, 32(5), 789–812.

Grant, P., & McGhee, P. (2021). Hedonic versus (true) eudaimonic well-being in organizations. In Dhiman, S. (Ed.), *The Palgrave handbook of workplace well-being* (pp. 925–943). Palgrave Macmillan/Springer Nature., DOI: 10.1007/978-3-030-30025-8_37

Harter, J. K., Schmidt, F. L., & Hayes, T. L. (2002). Business-unit-level relationship between employee satisfaction, employee engagement, and business outcomes: A meta-analysis. *The Journal of Applied Psychology*, 87(2), 268–279. DOI: 10.1037/0021-9010.87.2.268 PMID: 12002955

Hsieh, T. (2010). *Delivering happiness: A path to profits, passion, and purpose*. Business Plus.

Luthans, F., Youssef, C. M., & Avolio, B. J. (2007). *Psychological capital: Developing the human competitive edge*. Oxford University Press.

Lyubomirsky, S., King, L., & Diener, E. (2005). The benefits of frequent positive affect: Does happiness lead to success? *Psychological Bulletin*, 131(6), 803–855. DOI: 10.1037/0033-2909.131.6.803 PMID: 16351326

Ryan, R. M., & Deci, E. L. (2001). On happiness and human potentials: A review of research on hedonic and eudaimonic well-being. *Annual Review of Psychology*, 52(1), 141–166. DOI: 10.1146/annurev.psych.52.1.141 PMID: 11148302

Seligman, M. E. P. (2012). *Flourish: A visionary new understanding of happiness and well-being*. Free Press.

Smith, J., & Jones, L. (2023). Predictive analytics in employee engagement: Innovations and challenges. *Human Resource Management Review*, 33(3), 456–478.

Tellegen, A., Lykken, D. T., Bouchard, T. J., Wilcox, K. J., Segal, N. L., & Rich, S. (1988). Personality similarity in twins reared apart and together. *Journal of Personality and Social Psychology*, 54(6), 1031–1039. DOI: 10.1037/0022-3514.54.6.1031 PMID: 3397862

Wright, T. A., & Huang, C. (2012). The many benefits of employee well-being in organizational research. *Journal of Organizational Behavior*, 33(8), 1188–1192. DOI: 10.1002/job.1828

Chapter 9

Happiness as a Catalyst for Academic Success and Faculty Well-Being in Higher Education Institutes

Sheeba Joseph
Bhopal School of Social Sciences, India

Tanuja Khan
Bhopal School of Social Sciences, India

ABSTRACT

The present study investigated the predictors of happiness among students and faculty in educational institutions using a quantitative, cross-sectional research design. The analysis focuses on five key predictors: well-being, job satisfaction, work-life balance, professional performance, and type of institution. A sample of 396 participants was selected using simple random sampling to ensure representativeness and reduce selection bias. Hypothesis testing using JAMOVI revealed that well-being (p < .001), work-life balance (p < .001), and professional performance (p = 0.048) had significant positive effects on happiness, whereas job satisfaction (p = 0.226) did not show significant direct impact. The type of institution also influenced happiness, with affiliate colleges showing a significant negative effect (p < .001). The findings highlight the importance of well-being, work-life balance, and professional performance in enhancing happiness, providing insights for institutional policies aimed to improve overall satisfaction.

DOI: 10.4018/979-8-3693-8457-2.ch009

BACKGROUND

In the evolving landscape of higher education, the emphasis on faculty well-being and academic success has never been more pronounced. As institutions strive to enhance their academic outcomes and create supportive work environments, emerging research highlights the pivotal role of happiness in achieving these goals. This study explored happiness as a catalyst for both academic success and faculty well-being, examining its impact on various dimensions of faculty experience and institutional performance.

IMPORTANCE OF HAPPINESS IN THE WELL-BEING OF INDIVIDUALS

Happiness plays a pivotal role in overall well-being, influencing various aspects of life, from physical health to social relationships. It serves as a fundamental component of mental health, fostering resilience and enhancing the capacity to cope with stress and adversity. Beyond individual benefits, happiness also has a ripple effect, positively impacting those around us and contributing to healthier communities. Research has consistently shown that happier individuals tend to enjoy better physical health, stronger social connections, increased productivity, and a greater sense of life satisfaction. As society increasingly recognizes the importance of mental and emotional well-being, understanding the significance of happiness becomes essential for cultivating a fulfilling and meaningful life.

The multifaceted benefits of happiness, linking it to physical and mental health, social connections, productivity, longevity, life satisfaction, and societal impact. Prioritizing happiness can lead to enhanced individual and community well-being.

Physical Health: Happiness has been shown to have a significant impact on physical health outcomes. Research by Pressman and Cohen (2005) highlights that positive emotions are linked to improved immune function, which in turn can enhance overall health. They found that individuals who experience frequent positive emotions tend to have better immune responses, making them more resilient to illnesses. This connection suggests that happiness not only influences mental well-being but also plays a crucial role in physical health by bolstering the body's defenses against disease.

In addition to immune function, other studies have indicated that happiness can lead to healthier lifestyle choices, such as increased physical activity and better dietary habits (Diener & Seligman, 2004). These behaviors contribute further to improved physical health and longevity. Therefore, fostering positive emotions can be seen as a key component in promoting both mental and physical well-being.

Mental Health: Research by Lyubomirsky et al. (2005) provides compelling evidence that greater happiness is associated with lower rates of anxiety and depression. Their comprehensive review analyzed various studies and found that individuals who report higher levels of happiness tend to experience significantly lower levels of these mental health issues. The authors suggest that positive affect can act as a protective factor, helping to mitigate the effects of stress and adversity, which are often precursors to anxiety and depression. The review highlights several mechanisms through which happiness may exert its protective effects. For instance, happier individuals often possess stronger social support networks, better coping strategies, and a more optimistic outlook on life. These factors can contribute to enhanced resilience, enabling individuals to navigate life's challenges more effectively (Lyubomirsky et al., 2005).

It is noted that the relationship between happiness and mental health is bidirectional; while greater happiness can reduce symptoms of anxiety and depression, alleviating these symptoms can also lead to increased happiness. This underscores the importance of promoting positive emotions and mental well-being as a means of preventing and treating mental health disorders.

Social Connections: Diener and Seligman (2002) found that happy individuals typically enjoy richer social relationships, which play a significant role in enhancing their overall happiness and well-being. Their research emphasizes that strong social connections are one of the most critical factors contributing to life satisfaction. Happy people tend to have more fulfilling interactions with family, friends, and colleagues, which fosters a sense of belonging and support.

The authors argue that these social ties provide emotional support during challenging times and offer opportunities for positive shared experiences. For instance, engaging in meaningful conversations, participating in social activities, and simply spending time with loved ones can boost feelings of happiness and fulfillment. This reciprocal relationship suggests that as individuals cultivate their social networks, their levels of happiness increase, further reinforcing their connections with others (Diener & Seligman, 2002).

Additionally, the study highlights that the quality of relationships matters more than the quantity. Close, trusting relationships tend to provide greater emotional benefits than a larger number of superficial connections. Therefore, fostering deep and meaningful relationships can be viewed as a fundamental strategy for enhancing overall well-being.

Productivity and Creativity: The meta-analysis by Cropanzano and Wright (2001) investigates the relationship between happiness and various work-related outcomes, particularly focusing on productivity and creativity. Their findings suggest that employees who experience higher levels of happiness tend to be more productive and exhibit greater creativity in their work. This is attributed to several factors, including enhanced motivation, better teamwork, and improved problem-solving skills. The authors argue that positive emotional states can lead to a broadened scope of attention and thinking, which is essential for creative processes. Additionally, happiness can reduce stress and burnout, contributing to a more engaged workforce.

Longevity: Danner et al., (2001) found that individuals who express positive emotions in early life tend to live longer. The study by Danner et al. (2001) explored the relationship between early emotional expression and longevity by analyzing the autobiographies of nuns in a convent. The researchers discovered that those who expressed more positive emotions—such as joy, gratitude, and hope—in their writings during early adulthood had significantly longer lifespans compared to those with less positive emotional content. This suggests that positive emotions may contribute to better health and resilience, potentially through mechanisms like enhanced immune function, improved coping strategies, and stronger social connections. The findings highlight the critical role of emotional well-being in promoting longevity and overall health.

Life Satisfaction: Veenhoven (2008) emphasizes that happiness significantly contributes to overall life satisfaction, influencing how individuals perceive their lives. Veenhoven (2008) emphasizes the critical link between happiness and overall life satisfaction, asserting that happiness is a fundamental component of how individuals evaluate their lives. Happiness, defined as a positive emotional state, encompasses feelings of joy, contentment, and fulfillment. When individuals experience higher levels of happiness, they tend to assess their lives more positively, leading to greater overall life satisfaction. This relationship underscores the subjective nature of life satisfaction, which is shaped not only by external circumstances but also by an individual's emotional well-being and outlook on life (Veenhoven, 2008).

Research supports the notion that happiness significantly influences life satisfaction through various pathways. For instance, individuals who cultivate positive emotions often develop stronger social connections and coping mechanisms, which can further enhance their perceptions of life quality. Social interactions contribute to a sense of belonging and support, reinforcing feelings of happiness and satisfaction (Helliwell & Wang, 2017). Furthermore, the subjective nature of life satisfaction suggests that personal interpretations of life events and circumstances play a crucial role; those who maintain an optimistic perspective are likely to report higher life satisfaction (Diener & Oishi, 2018).Recent literature continues to explore this vital connection.

Kushlev and Dunn (2015) found that mindfulness practices can significantly boost happiness, thereby improving life satisfaction. Their study indicates that being present and engaged in daily activities leads to greater enjoyment, which positively impacts how individuals perceive their lives. Additionally, Kahneman and Deaton (2015) highlight that while higher income can improve life evaluations, it does not necessarily enhance emotional well-being. This distinction emphasizes that happiness, derived from relationships and meaningful experiences, is essential for achieving higher life satisfaction, regardless of economic factors.

Impact on Others: Fowler and Christakis (2008) demonstrated that happiness can spread through social networks, positively affecting the well-being of others. More recent studies have continued to explore this phenomenon. For instance, a study by Hsu et al. (2018) found that social media interactions can amplify feelings of happiness, indicating that virtual connections also play a role in emotional contagion. Similarly, research by Stepanikova and Karriker-Jaffe (2020) demonstrated that happiness not only spreads among close friends but can also influence acquaintances and even those in distant social circles. These findings underscore the idea that happiness is a collective experience, where individual emotional states contribute to a broader social environment, fostering community well-being and social cohesion.

REASONS FOR STRESS AMONG FACULTY IN HIGHER EDUCATION INSTITUTES (HEIS) IN THE INDIAN CONTEXT

Stress among faculty in higher education institutes in India has become an increasingly pressing issue, reflecting the complex demands of the academic environment. As educational institutions strive for excellence, faculty members are often burdened by heavy workloads, including teaching, research, and administrative responsibilities. Additionally, the pressure to publish research, secure funding, and meet performance evaluations can create an intense atmosphere of competition and anxiety. Job insecurity, particularly among those in temporary or contractual positions, further exacerbates this stress. Coupled with societal expectations and the need to manage diverse student populations, the challenges faced by faculty are multifaceted. Understanding these stressors is crucial for developing effective strategies to support faculty well-being and enhance the overall academic experience in Indian higher education. The below mentioned are the main reasons as suggested by the researchers

1. **Heavy Workload:** Faculty in higher education often face overwhelming workloads due to a combination of teaching, research, administrative duties, and student mentoring. A study by Shukla and Gupta (2018) highlights that faculty members regularly exceed their official working hours, leading to burnout and decreased job satisfaction. The constant juggling of responsibilities leaves little room for personal time or professional development, contributing significantly to stress levels.

2. **Administrative Burdens:** The increasing bureaucratic demands placed on faculty can lead to heightened stress. Singh and Gupta (2020) found that faculty often feel overwhelmed by administrative tasks, which detracts from their primary responsibilities of teaching and research. This additional burden can create frustration and a sense of ineffectiveness in their roles.
3. **Job Insecurity:** Many faculty members work on temporary or contractual bases, leading to feelings of job insecurity. According to a study by Sharma and Handa (2019), the lack of tenure-track positions contributes to anxiety among faculty regarding their future, which can manifest as stress and decreased job satisfaction.
4. **Pressure for Research Output:** Faculty members are increasingly pressured to publish research and secure funding, often with a focus on quantitative metrics. As noted by Kumari and Singh (2021), this emphasis can lead to a "publish or perish" culture, creating stress and impacting faculty morale and motivation.
5. **Student Expectations and Behavior:** The diverse expectations and behaviors of students can also contribute to faculty stress. A study by Ranjan and Mukherjee (2018) found that managing challenging student dynamics—such as varying levels of motivation and discipline—can create significant stress for faculty, impacting their teaching effectiveness.
6. **Performance Evaluation:** Faculty performance evaluations often emphasize research output and student feedback, leading to stress about meeting institutional standards. According to Joshi and Kumar (2020), this focus can overshadow the importance of teaching quality and contribute to job dissatisfaction.
7. **Limited Resources:** Many higher education institutions in India struggle with inadequate resources, including funding, infrastructure, and support staff. As highlighted by Sharma and Singh (2017), the lack of necessary resources can hinder faculty from effectively fulfilling their roles, leading to increased stress and frustration.
8. **Work-Life Balance:** The demands of academic life often disrupt faculty members' work-life balance, leading to stress and burnout. A study by Gupta and Jain (2019) found that the inability to maintain a healthy balance between professional and personal life significantly affects faculty well-being and job satisfaction.
9. **Interpersonal Conflicts:** Conflicts with colleagues or administration can create a hostile work environment. As reported by Patel and Verma (2018), such interpersonal issues can lead to increased stress and reduced job satisfaction among faculty members.

10. **Cultural Expectations:** Societal and familial expectations regarding academic performance can add pressure on faculty. Research by Mehta and Bhatia (2020) indicates that these cultural pressures can exacerbate stress, as faculty strive to meet both personal and societal standards.

The stress experienced by faculty in higher education institutes in India is multifaceted, driven by workload, administrative burdens, job insecurity, performance pressures, and cultural expectations. Addressing these challenges requires institutional support and a commitment to fostering a healthier academic environment.

Happiness as a Catalyst

Happiness among faculty members in higher education is a key factor influencing both personal well-being and professional effectiveness. The concept of happiness in this context encompasses emotional well-being, job satisfaction, and overall life satisfaction, and is influenced by various factors within the academic environment. Emotional well-being is a central component of happiness. Research shows that positive emotional states, such as contentment and fulfillment, are associated with higher level of happiness among faculty members. A study by Maltby found that job satisfaction is strongly correlated with happiness, indicating that faculty members who are satisfied with their work are more likely to experience greater happiness overall. This relationship underscores the importance of addressing factors that contribute to job satisfaction to enhance faculty happiness (Maltby et al., 2005). Work-life balance is another crucial factor affecting happiness. Nikolaev (2018) highlighted that an imbalance between work and personal life can lead to increased stress and decreased happiness. Faculty who struggle to manage their professional responsibilities alongside personal commitments often experience reduced happiness and increased stress. Efforts to support a healthy work-life balance can significantly enhance faculty members' emotional well-being and overall happiness (Nikolaev, 2018).

Professional autonomy also plays a significant role in faculty happiness. It was found that autonomy in professional roles is positively associated with job satisfaction and happiness. Faculty members who feel they have control over their work and decision-making processes are more likely to experience higher levels of happiness. This suggests that providing faculty with greater autonomy can improve their overall well-being Fave et al., 2011).

Institutional support is crucial for fostering happiness among faculty members. Costa found that perceived organizational support enhances job satisfaction and happiness. When faculty members feel supported by their institution, they are more likely to experience greater levels of happiness and overall well-being. This highlights the importance of institutional policies and practices in creating a supportive work environment. Opportunities for professional development are linked to increased happiness as well (Costa et al., 2019). Young found that access to professional growth opportunities enhances job satisfaction and contributes to a more positive emotional state. Faculty members who have opportunities to advance their careers and develop their skills report greater happiness, indicating that professional growth is a key contributor to overall well-being (Young et al., 2020).

Social relationships within the academic environment also impact happiness. According to Safaria strong social support networks and positive interpersonal relationships are associated with higher levels of happiness (Safaria, 2014). Faculty members who have supportive colleagues and a positive work atmosphere are more likely to experience greater happiness in their professional lives. Workload and stress levels are significant factors influencing happiness. Martin and Villagran identified that excessive workload and high stress are major contributors to burnout and decreased happiness (Villagran & Martin, 2022). Addressing these factors through effective workload management and support systems is essential for promoting faculty happiness. Recognition and reward systems play a role in enhancing happiness as well. Smith indicated that faculty members who receive recognition and rewards for their achievements report higher levels of happiness. Implementing effective reward systems can contribute to a more positive work environment and increased overall happiness (Mayo et al., 2019; Smith et al., 2021).

Job security is another important factor influencing happiness. Mayo found that job security is positively correlated with job satisfaction and happiness (Mayo et al., 2019). Faculty members who feel secure in their positions are more likely to experience higher levels of happiness, highlighting the importance of job security in fostering a positive work environment. Finally, research productivity impacts happiness. Salavera found that faculty members who are productive in their research activities often experience greater job satisfaction and happiness. The sense of accomplishment and recognition associated with research success contributes to overall happiness (Salavera et al., 2020).

WELL-BEING IN HIGHER EDUCATION INSTITUTES

Recent research into faculty well-being highlights its critical role in academic success and personal satisfaction within higher education. Well-being among professors is a multidimensional construct encompassing emotional, psychological, and social aspects, and its significance is increasingly acknowledged in academic settings. The emotional dimension of well-being is closely related to job satisfaction. Studies, such as those by Andenaes, reveal that higher job satisfaction is strongly associated with improved emotional well-being among faculty members (Andenæs et al., 2016). This suggests that job satisfaction is a significant contributor to overall happiness and well-being in the academic environment. Positive emotional states, in turn, enhance faculty members' ability to manage stress and engage effectively in their roles.

Psychological well-being, which includes aspects such as stress management and mental health, is another crucial component of faculty well-being. Research by Vazquez emphasized that psychological well-being is affected by the balance between work and personal life (Vazquez et al., 2020). An imbalance in these areas can lead to increased stress and decreased job satisfaction, adversely impacting overall well-being. Therefore, promoting a healthy work-life balance is essential for maintaining psychological health. Social well-being, including interpersonal relationships and social support, also significantly influences faculty well-being. Machado highlights the importance of strong social support networks in reducing stress and enhancing happiness. Positive relationships within the academic environment contribute to a sense of belonging and support, which is vital for maintaining overall well-being (Machado et al., 2019).

Institutional factors play a significant role in shaping faculty well-being. Research by Ryan and Martela indicated that perceived organizational support is a key determinant of job satisfaction and well-being. Faculty members who feel supported by their institutions experience higher levels of overall well-being, suggesting that institutional policies and practices that promote support and recognition are crucial (Martela & Ryan, 2021). Professional development opportunities are linked to improved well-being as well. Access to professional growth opportunities enhances job satisfaction and contributes to a more positive emotional state. When faculty members have the chance to develop their skills and advance their careers, their sense of accomplishment and job satisfaction increase, leading to better overall well-being (Arakkathara & Bance, 2019). In addition to these factors, workload and stress levels are significant contributors to faculty well-being. Seligman identify that excessive workload and high stress are major factors leading to burnout and decreased well-being. Addressing these issues is essential for fostering a supportive work environment that promotes faculty health and job satisfaction (Seligman, 2018).

JOB SATISFACTION IN HIGHER EDUCATION INSTITUTES

Job satisfaction is a fundamental aspect of faculty well-being and plays a crucial role in shaping the overall experience of professors in higher education. Research has consistently shown that job satisfaction is intricately linked to various factors, including emotional well-being, professional performance, and institutional support.

A significant body of research highlights the impact of job satisfaction on overall happiness. Khan found a strong correlation between job satisfaction and happiness among faculty members, indicating that higher levels of satisfaction with one's job are associated with increased overall happiness. This relationship underscores the importance of addressing factors that contribute to job satisfaction to enhance faculty well-being Khan et al., 2017).

Work-life balance is one of the key factors influencing job satisfaction. Ryhal emphasizes that an imbalance between work and personal life can lead to stress and decreased job satisfaction. Faculty members who struggle to manage their professional and personal responsibilities often experience reduced job satisfaction and, consequently, lower levels of happiness (Singh & Ryhal, 2021). Efforts to promote a healthier work-life balance can therefore have a significant positive impact on job satisfaction. Professional autonomy also plays a critical role in job satisfaction. Afzaal demonstrated that autonomy in professional roles is positively related to job satisfaction. Faculty members who perceive themselves as having control over their work and decision-making processes report higher levels of job satisfaction (Seyal & Afzaal, 2013). This finding highlights the importance of providing faculty with the freedom to shape their roles and contribute to their satisfaction with their jobs. Institutional support is another crucial determinant of job satisfaction. Jawabri found that perceived organizational support enhances job satisfaction (Jawabri et al., 2022). When faculty members feel that their institution supports and values them, they are more likely to experience greater job satisfaction. This underscores the role of institutional policies and practices in fostering a supportive work environment.

Opportunities for professional development are also linked to job satisfaction. Toscano found that access to professional growth opportunities contributes to higher job satisfaction. Faculty members who have opportunities to advance their skills and careers report greater satisfaction with their jobs, suggesting that institutions should prioritize professional development to enhance job satisfaction. Social relationships within the academic environment impact job satisfaction as well (Toscano & Zappalà, 2021). According to Bareket, strong social support networks and positive interpersonal relationships are associated with higher levels of job satisfaction. Faculty members who have supportive colleagues and a positive work atmosphere are more likely to be satisfied with their jobs (Bareket-Bojmel et al., 2023).

Workload and stress levels are significant factors influencing job satisfaction. Fortin identified that excessive workload and high stress are major contributors to decreased job satisfaction. Addressing these factors through effective workload management and support systems can help improve job satisfaction among faculty members. Recognition and reward systems also play a role in job satisfaction. Fortin indicated that faculty members who receive recognition and rewards for their work experience have higher levels of job satisfaction. Implementing effective reward systems can enhance faculty motivation and satisfaction (Brunelle & Fortin, 2021). Job security is another important aspect of job satisfaction. Kim found that job security is positively correlated with job satisfaction. Faculty members who feel secure in their positions are more likely to experience higher job satisfaction, highlighting the importance of job security in fostering a positive work environment. Finally, research productivity impacts job satisfaction. Faculty members who are productive in their research activities often report greater job satisfaction. The sense of achievement and recognition associated with research success contributes to overall job satisfaction (Kim, 2021).

WORK-LIFE BALANCE IN HIGHER EDUCATION INSTITUTES

Work-life balance is a crucial element in understanding faculty well-being and job satisfaction within higher education. It refers to the ability to effectively manage professional responsibilities alongside personal life and commitments. Research highlights the significant impact that work-life balance has on faculty members' overall well-being, job satisfaction, and professional performance. A fundamental aspect of work-life balance is the ability to manage the demands of work with personal life responsibilities. Khan emphasizes that an imbalance between work and personal life can lead to increased stress and decreased job satisfaction (Khan & Thomas, 2022). Faculty members who struggle to balance their professional duties with personal commitments often experience heightened stress levels, which can negatively affect their overall well-being. Therefore, fostering a healthy work-life balance is essential for improving faculty job satisfaction and reducing stress (Palumbo, 2020).

The impact of work-life balance on job satisfaction is well-documented. Studies show that faculty members who achieve a better work-life balance report higher levels of job satisfaction. Work-life balance is positively correlated with job satisfaction. Faculty members who feel they can effectively juggle their work and personal lives are more likely to experience greater job satisfaction and overall happiness (Basu et al., 2022). Work-life balance also affects faculty members' emotional well-being. Conflicts between work and personal life can lead to emotional exhaustion and reduced job satisfaction. Faculty members who experience difficulty managing their work and personal responsibilities may suffer from burnout and decreased emotional well-being. Addressing work-life conflicts is therefore crucial for maintaining positive emotional health among faculty members. Institutional support plays a significant role in facilitating work-life balance. Perceived organizational support can influence faculty members' ability to achieve work-life balance. Institutions that offer flexible work arrangements, supportive policies, and resources for managing personal responsibilities can help faculty members maintain a better balance between their professional and personal lives. Such support contributes to increased job satisfaction and overall well-being (T. Khan & Thomas, 2022).

PROFESSIONAL PERFORMANCE IN HIGHER EDUCATION INSTITUTES

Professional autonomy is another factor that influences work-life balance. Greater autonomy in professional roles allows faculty members to better manage their work and personal commitments. When faculty members have control over their schedules and work responsibilities, they are more likely to achieve a satisfactory work-life balance, leading to enhanced job satisfaction and reduced stress. Workload management is crucial for achieving a healthy work-life balance. Excessive workload can exacerbate work-life conflicts and negatively impact job satisfaction. Faculty members who face heavy workloads and high job demands may struggle to balance their professional and personal lives, leading to increased stress and decreased well-being. Effective workload management and support are essential for promoting a positive work-life balance. The role of social support within the academic environment also affects work-life balance. Strong social support networks can help faculty members manage work-life conflicts. Supportive colleagues and a positive work environment can assist and reduce the stress associated with balancing work and personal responsibilities (Osei-Owusu, 2022).

OBJECTIVES OF THE STUDY

i. To assess the impact of well-being on happiness: Determine whether an increase in well-being is associated with a significant increase in happiness.
ii. To evaluate the effect of job satisfaction on happiness: Investigate whether job satisfaction contributes significantly to the level of happiness.
iii. To analyze the relationship between work-life balance and happiness: Examine if a better work-life balance is positively related to happiness.
iv. To examine the influence of professional performance on happiness: Explore whether higher professional performance is associated with greater happiness.
v. To determine the overall impact of happiness on various predictors: Assess how different predictors (well-being, job satisfaction, work-life balance, professional performance) contribute to the overall impact of happiness.

vi. To compare the effect of institutional type on happiness: Investigate whether the type of institution (Autonomous Institution vs. Affiliate College) significantly affects happiness levels.

RESEARCH METHODOLOGY

The present study employs a quantitative, cross-sectional research design to investigate the predictors of happiness. By collecting data at a single point in time, the research aims to analyze how well-being, job satisfaction, work-life balance, professional performance, and type of institution influence happiness. The design allows for a snapshot view of these relationships, providing insights into their impact on happiness. Participants were chosen using a simple random sampling technique from a population of students and faculty across various educational institutions. This method ensures that every individual in the target population has an equal opportunity to be included in the sample, thereby reducing selection bias and enhancing the generalizability of the results. The study involves a sample size of 396 participants, which is sufficiently large to yield robust findings and support reliable conclusions about the predictors of happiness within the sampled population.

The study examines several variables to understand their impact on happiness. The Happiness Measurement is the primary dependent variable, reflecting the overall level of happiness among participants. The independent variables include Well-Being, which assesses life satisfaction and mental health; Job Satisfaction, measuring satisfaction with various job aspects; Work-Life Balance, evaluating the management of work and personal life; and Professional Performance, focusing on self-reported achievements and performance. The Type of Institution is a categorical independent variable that classifies institutions as either autonomous or affiliate colleges, exploring its effect on happiness. Each variable contributes to analyzing how different factors influence overall happiness, providing a comprehensive understanding of the predictors in the study.

A pilot study was conducted with a sample of 30 participants to assess the reliability and fit of the self-reported tool used in this research. This preliminary analysis aimed to ensure that the measurement tool effectively captures the intended constructs and performs reliably across a small sample before the main study. During the pilot, the internal consistency of the tool was evaluated using Cronbach's alpha to confirm the reliability of the scales, ensuring that items within each construct were measuring the same underlying concept consistently. The Comparative Fit Index (CFI) was calculated to assess the model's fit to the data, providing an initial evaluation of how well the tool’s factor structure aligns with the observed data. The results from this pilot study offered valuable insights into the tool’s performance and guided necessary revisions to enhance its accuracy and robustness for the full-scale research are given below.

Table 1. Item Reliability Statistics

				if item dropped
	mean	sd	item-rest correlation	Cronbach's α
Happiness Measurement	4.13	0.579	0.8146	0.759
Well-Being	3.83	0.738	0.6204	0.784
Job Satisfaction	3.94	0.756	0.7476	0.756
Work-Life Balance	3.42	0.683	0.7959	0.751
Professional Performance	3.74	0.912	0.7813	0.741
Overall Impact of Happiness	4.27	0.984	0.0759	0.915

The Item Reliability Statistics reveal that most items contribute positively to the internal consistency of the scale. Happiness Measurement has a high item-rest correlation (0.8146) and a Cronbach's alpha if dropped of 0.759, showing strong alignment with the overall construct. Similarly, Job Satisfaction (0.7476, $\alpha = 0.756$), Work-Life Balance (0.7959, $\alpha = 0.751$), and Professional Performance (0.7813, $\alpha = 0.741$) all have high item-rest correlations and minimal impact on alpha if dropped, indicating they are reliable items. Well-Being shows a lower item-rest correlation (0.6204), and dropping it slightly increases alpha to 0.784, suggesting it contributes less to reliability. The Overall Impact of Happiness has a very low item-rest correlation (0.0759), and dropping it raises alpha significantly to 0.915, indicating it weakens the scale's reliability. Thus, this item may require revision or removal to improve consistency.

Table 2. Scale Reliability statistics

Scale	mean	sd	Cronbach's α
	3.89	0.571	0.819

The Scale Reliability Statistics indicate a strong internal consistency for the overall survey. With a mean of 3.89 and a standard deviation of 0.571, the responses show moderate agreement with relatively low variability. The Cronbach's alpha value of 0.819 suggests high reliability, meaning the items in the scale are consistently measuring the intended constructs. This value exceeds the commonly accepted threshold of 0.7, confirming that the scale is reliable for assessing happiness, well-being, and related factors among faculty members.

ANALYSIS OF FIT MEASURES (- CFI ESTIMATE: 0.898)

The Comparative Fit Index (CFI) is a widely used measure to assess the goodness of fit in structural equation modeling. It compares the fit of the specified model to a baseline model, with values closer to 1 indicating a better fit. A CFI value of 0.898 is close to the acceptable threshold of 0.90, suggesting that the model fits the data reasonably well. While it does not meet the optimal fit criteria (CFI > 0.90), it is relatively close and indicates that the model is performing better than many models with lower CFI values. Overall, while the model shows a good fit, further adjustments and optimizations could be considered to enhance its accuracy and robustness.

HYPOTHESES

i. H0: Well-Being does not significantly affect happiness: There is no significant relationship between well-being and happiness.
ii. H0: Job Satisfaction does not significantly affect happiness: Job satisfaction does not have a significant effect on happiness.
iii. H0: Work-Life Balance does not significantly affect happiness: There is no significant relationship between work-life balance and happiness.
iv. H0: Professional Performance does not significantly affect happiness: Professional performance does not have a significant effect on happiness.
v. H0: Overall Impact of Happiness does not significantly contribute to happiness: The overall impact of happiness does not significantly contribute to the predictors of happiness.
vi. H0: Type of Institution does not significantly affect happiness: There is no significant difference in happiness levels between Autonomous Institutions and Affiliate Colleges.

DATA ANALYSES AND INTERPRETATION

Hypothesis testing was conducted using JAMOVI, a robust statistical software platform, to analyze the relationships between happiness and its predictors. The software facilitated the execution of various statistical tests, including multiple regression analysis, to evaluate the significance of each predictor variable—such as well-being, job satisfaction, work-life balance, and professional performance—on the dependent variable of happiness. JAMOVI's user-friendly interface and comprehensive statistical tools allowed for precise calculation of coefficients, p-values, and confidence intervals, thereby providing a clear assessment of the hypotheses. The results from JAMOVI helped determine whether the predictors had significant effects on happiness and validated the hypotheses set forth in the study. The use of JAMOVI ensured accurate and efficient analysis, contributing to the robustness and reliability of the study's findings.

Table 3. Model Coefficients - Happiness Measurement

Predictor	**Estimate**	**SE**	**t**	**p**
Intercept	1.7302	0.1152	15.023	<.001
Well-Being	0.3404	0.0269	12.664	<.001
Job Satisfaction	0.0611	0.0503	1.214	0.226
Work-Life Balance	0.1223	0.0362	3.381	<.001
Professional Performance	0.0998	0.0503	1.983	0.048
Overall Impact of Happiness	0.0410	0.0152	2.701	0.007
Type of Institution:				
Autonomous Institution – University	0.0196	0.0363	0.539	0.590
Affiliate College – University	-0.3413	0.0457	-7.470	<.001

Represents reference level

ANALYSIS OF COEFFICIENTS WITH HYPOTHESIS TESTING

1. Intercept: The intercept is 1.7302 ($p < .001$), which is statistically significant. This indicates that the baseline level of happiness is significantly above zero. The null hypothesis stating that the intercept is zero is rejected, confirming that there is a substantial base level of happiness when all predictors are at their reference levels.
2. Well-Being: The coefficient for well-being is 0.3404 ($p < .001$). This coefficient is statistically significant, meaning that an increase in well-being is significantly associated with an increase in happiness. The null hypothesis stating that well-being does not affect happiness is rejected. The result supports the view that well-being has a meaningful positive effect on happiness.

3. Job Satisfaction: The coefficient for job satisfaction is 0.0611 ($p = 0.226$), which is not statistically significant. This suggests that job satisfaction does not significantly influence happiness. The null hypothesis stating that job satisfaction does not affect happiness cannot be rejected. This implies that, in this model, job satisfaction does not have a meaningful impact on happiness.
4. Work-Life Balance: The coefficient for work-life balance is 0.1223 ($p < .001$), and it is statistically significant. This indicates a positive relationship between work-life balance and happiness. The null hypothesis that work-life balance does not affect happiness is rejected. The significant result supports the idea that better work-life balance contributes positively to happiness.
5. Professional Performance: The coefficient for professional performance is 0.0998 ($p = 0.048$), which is statistically significant at the 0.05 level. This shows that higher professional performance is associated with increased happiness. The null hypothesis stating that professional performance does not affect happiness is rejected. The result supports the positive influence of professional performance on happiness.
6. Overall Impact of Happiness: The coefficient for the overall impact of happiness is 0.0410 ($p = 0.007$), which is statistically significant. This indicates that the overall impact of happiness has a positive association with the predictors. The null hypothesis that the overall impact of happiness does not contribute to the predictors is rejected. Despite its modest effect, the significance suggests that overall happiness has a relevant, albeit small, impact.
7. Type of Institution:
   - Autonomous Institution – University: The coefficient is 0.0196 ($p = 0.590$), indicating no significant effect on happiness. The null hypothesis that the type of institution does not affect happiness is not rejected for autonomous institutions. This suggests that being in an autonomous institution does not significantly alter happiness levels compared to the reference group.
   - Affiliated College – University: The coefficient is -0.3413 ($p < .001$), which is statistically significant. This negative coefficient indicates that being in an affiliate college is significantly associated with lower happiness compared to the reference group. The null hypothesis stating that the type of institution does not affect happiness is rejected for affiliate colleges. The result highlights a substantial difference in happiness levels based on institutional type.

The analysis of predictors of happiness reveals several significant findings that offer insights into how various factors influence overall happiness. The study evaluated the effects of well-being, job satisfaction, work-life balance, professional performance, and type of institution on happiness, providing a comprehensive view of these relationships. Firstly, well-being emerged as a major positive predictor of happiness, with a coefficient of 0.3404 ($p < .001$). This result is statistically significant, leading to the rejection of the null hypothesis that well-being does not affect happiness. It indicates that higher levels of well-being are strongly associated with increased happiness, emphasizing the importance of fostering well-being to enhance overall happiness. This finding suggests that interventions aimed at improving individual well-being can have a substantial impact on increasing happiness levels. In contrast, job satisfaction did not significantly affect happiness, as evidenced by its coefficient of 0.0611 ($p = 0.226$). The lack of statistical significance leads to the retention of the null hypothesis that job satisfaction does not have a meaningful impact on happiness. This result implies that, within the context of this model, job satisfaction might not be as crucial in influencing happiness as other factors. It suggests that factors beyond job satisfaction might play a more significant role in determining overall happiness.

Work-life balance, however, was found to have a significant positive impact on happiness, with a coefficient of 0.1223 ($p < .001$). This significant result supports the rejection of the null hypothesis that work-life balance does not affect happiness. It highlights the importance of achieving a better work-life balance as a means of enhancing happiness, suggesting that efforts to improve work-life balance can lead to higher levels of happiness. Professional performance also significantly affects happiness, with a coefficient of 0.0998 ($p = 0.048$). The significance at the 0.05 level indicates a positive relationship between professional performance and happiness, leading to the rejection of the null hypothesis that professional performance does not influence happiness. This result suggests that higher professional performance is associated with greater happiness, reinforcing the idea that professional success and achievement contribute positively to personal happiness.

The analysis of the overall impact of happiness showed a significant, albeit modest, positive effect, with a coefficient of 0.0410 ($p = 0.007$). This finding leads to the rejection of the null hypothesis that the overall impact of happiness does not contribute to the predictors. Although the effect size is small, the significance indicates that the broader context of happiness plays a role in influencing other factors related to happiness. Regarding the type of institution, significant differences were observed. The coefficient for being in an autonomous institution (0.0196, $p = 0.590$) was not statistically significant, leading to the retention of the null hypothesis that institutional type does not affect happiness for this group. However, for individuals in affiliate colleges, the coefficient was -0.3413 ($p < .001$), showing a significant negative effect on happiness. This significant result leads to the rejection of the null hypothesis that institutional type does not affect happiness, suggesting that those in affiliate colleges experience lower levels of happiness compared to those in autonomous institutions. This finding points to a notable disparity based on the type of institution and highlights the need for targeted strategies to address and improve happiness levels in different institutional contexts.

DISCUSSION

The analysis reveals that well-being, work-life balance, and professional performance are significant predictors of happiness, aligning with previous research that emphasizes their importance in enhancing overall well-being. Well-being, with a coefficient of 0.3404 ($p < .001$), significantly increases happiness, reflecting findings by Diener et al. (2018) on its critical role. Work-life balance also significantly contributes to happiness (coefficient of 0.1223, $p < .001$), consistent with Allen et al. (2013) who highlighted its impact on reducing stress and enhancing satisfaction. Professional performance positively affects happiness (coefficient of 0.0998, $p = 0.048$), supporting Judge and Bono's (2001) research linking professional success with higher happiness. In contrast, job satisfaction did not significantly impact happiness (coefficient of 0.0611, $p = 0.226$), which diverges from some studies like Wright and Cropanzano (2007) that link job satisfaction with life satisfaction, suggesting that its effect may vary depending on the context. Additionally, the type of institution significantly influences happiness, with individuals in affiliate colleges reporting lower happiness compared to those in autonomous institutions (coefficient of -0.3413, $p < .001$), highlighting the importance of institutional context as demonstrated by Beine et al. (2009). Overall, these findings underscore the multifaceted nature of happiness and suggest that well-being, work-life balance, and professional performance are crucial for enhancing happiness, while institutional factors also play a significant role.

VARF MODEL: SUGGESTIVE WAYS TO IMPROVE HAPPINESS IN HIGHER EDUCATION INSTITUTIONS

V- Voluntary Work
A-Academic Support
R- Recognition and Rewards
F- Faculty Empowerment and Professional Development

1. Voluntary Work

Voluntary work plays a crucial role in fostering community engagement and enhancing individual well-being. It not only provides essential services to those in need but also promotes a sense of purpose and fulfillment among volunteers. Research has shown that engaging in voluntary activities can lead to increased life satisfaction and improved mental health (Dunn et al., 2008; Clary & Snyder, 1999). For faculty members, participating in voluntary work can enhance job satisfaction and create a positive work environment, as it encourages collaboration and strengthens relationships within the academic community (Gilley et al., 2010). Overall, voluntary work enriches both the volunteers and the communities they serve, contributing to a happier, more connected society. Under the aegis of MoUs institutions can come together and work for a single cause.

2. Academic Support

Providing adequate support for faculty in their roles can alleviate stress and improve job satisfaction. Ensure access to teaching materials, technology, and administrative support to facilitate effective teaching and research. Regularly review and manage faculty workloads to prevent burnout, ensuring a balance between teaching, research, and service. Offer mental health resources and counseling services to help faculty cope with stress and personal challenges.

3. Recognition and Rewards

Acknowledging faculty contributions is vital for enhancing motivation and happiness. Implement awards and recognition programs that celebrate teaching excellence, research achievements, and community service. Provide constructive feedback and performance evaluations that highlight strengths and contributions, fostering a culture of appreciation. Acknowledge personal and professional milestones, such as promotions, publications, and anniversaries.

4. Faculty Empowerment and Professional Development

Empowering faculty through development opportunities can enhance job satisfaction and engagement. Offer workshops, conferences, and training sessions to support continuous learning and skill enhancement. Include faculty in decision-making processes related to curriculum development, policy changes, and institutional planning. Promote policies that allow flexible work hours or remote work options to help faculty manage personal and professional responsibilities.

By adopting the VARF model, higher education institutions can create a supportive and enriching environment that fosters faculty happiness, leading to improved job satisfaction, productivity, and overall well-being. This Model is a proposed framework based on general best practices for enhancing faculty happiness.

RECOMMENDATIONS FOR FUTURE STUDY

Future studies should explore additional variables affecting happiness, such as social support, personal values, and organizational culture, to provide a more comprehensive understanding of its determinants. Investigating the role of job satisfaction across various industries and contexts could clarify its impact on happiness. Longitudinal studies are recommended to track changes over time and establish causal relationships between predictors and happiness. Additionally, research should consider how institutional factors influence different demographic groups to offer more targeted recommendations for enhancing happiness in diverse educational settings.

REFERENCES

Allen, T. D., Johnson, R. C., Saboe, K. N., & Cho, E. (2013). Work-family conflict and flexible work arrangements: A meta-analysis of the literature. *The Journal of Applied Psychology*, 98(6), 1011–1026.

Andenæs, R., Jackowska, M., Steptoe, A., & Jackowska, M. (2016). Positive affect, psychological well-being, and good sleep. *Journal of Psychosomatic Research*, 84(9).

Arakkathara, J. G., & Bance, L. (2019). Promotion of Well-Being, Resilience and Stress Management (POWER): An Intervention Program for Mothers of Children with Intellectual Disability: A Pilot Study. *Indian Journal of Positive Psychology*, 10(4).

Bareket-Bojmel, L., Chernyak-Hai, L., & Margalit, M. (2023). Out of sight but not out of mind: The role of loneliness and hope in remote work and in job engagement. *Personality and Individual Differences*, 202, 111955. Advance online publication. DOI: 10.1016/j.paid.2022.111955

Basu, S., Thomas, S., & Khan, T. (2022). Impact of Digital Education on Learning Behavior of Undergraduates. *Journal of Higher Education Theory and Practice*, 22(11). Advance online publication. DOI: 10.33423/jhetp.v22i11.5421

Beine, M., de Groot, H. L., & van der Klauw, M. (2009). Determinants of study success in higher education. *Economics of Education Review*, 28(2), 123–134.

Brunelle, E., & Fortin, J. A. (2021). Distance Makes the Heart Grow Fonder: An Examination of Teleworkers' and Office Workers' Job Satisfaction Through the Lens of Self-Determination Theory. *SAGE Open*, 11(1). Advance online publication. DOI: 10.1177/2158244020985516

Burch, T. (2018). Faculty workload: An analysis of perceived workload and its impact on job satisfaction. *International Journal of Educational Management*, 32(1), 145–158. DOI: 10.1108/IJEM-07-2017-0200

Clary, E. G., & Snyder, M. (1999). The Motivations to Volunteer: Theoretical and Practical Considerations. *Current Directions in Psychological Science*, 8(5), 156–159. DOI: 10.1111/1467-8721.00037

Costa, T., Suardi, A. C., Diano, M., Cauda, F., Duca, S., Rusconi, M. L., & Sotgiu, I. (2019). The neural correlates of hedonic and eudaimonic happiness: An fMRI study. *Neuroscience Letters*, 712, 134491. Advance online publication. DOI: 10.1016/j.neulet.2019.134491 PMID: 31518675

Cropanzano, R., & Wright, T. A. (2001). When a "happy" worker is really a productive worker: A review and further refinement of the happy-productive worker thesis. *Consulting Psychology Journal: Practice and Research, 53*(3), 182-199. DOI: 10.1037/1061-4087.53.3.182

Cropanzano, R., & Wright, T. A. (2001). When a "happy" worker is really a productive worker: A review of the literature and a theoretical framework. In Giacalone, R. A., & Jurkiewicz, C. L. (Eds.), *Handbook of workplace spirituality and organizational performance* (pp. 60–78). M.E. Sharpe.

Danner, D. D., Snowdon, D. A., & Friesen, W. V. (2001). Positive emotions in early life and longevity: Findings from the Nun Study. *Journal of Personality and Social Psychology*, 80(5), 804–813. DOI: 10.1037/0022-3514.80.5.804 PMID: 11374751

Delle Fave, A., Brdar, I., Freire, T., Vella-Brodrick, D., & Wissing, M. P. (2011). The Eudaimonic and Hedonic Components of Happiness: Qualitative and Quantitative Findings. *Social Indicators Research*, 100(2), 185–207. Advance online publication. DOI: 10.1007/s11205-010-9632-5

Diener, E., & Oishi, S. (2018). Lessons learned from national subjective well-being studies. *Journal of Happiness Studies*, 19(3), 775–787. DOI: 10.1007/s10902-017-9862-3

Diener, E., Oishi, S., & Tay, L. (2018). Advances in subjective well-being research. *Nature Human Behaviour*, 2(4), 253–260. DOI: 10.1038/s41562-018-0307-6 PMID: 30936533

Diener, E., & Seligman, M. E. P. (2002). Very happy people. *Psychological Science*, 13(1), 81–84. DOI: 10.1111/1467-9280.00415 PMID: 11894851

Diener, E., & Seligman, M. E. P. (2004). Beyond money: Toward an economy of well-being. *Psychological Science in the Public Interest*, 5(1), 1–31. DOI: 10.1111/j.0963-7214.2004.00501001.x PMID: 26158992

Dunn, E. W., Aknin, L. B., & Norton, M. I. (2008). Spending Money on Others Promotes Happiness. *Science*, 319(5870), 1687–1688. DOI: 10.1126/science.1150952 PMID: 18356530

Fowler, J. H., & Christakis, N. A. (2008). Dynamic spread of happiness in a large social network: Longitudinal analysis over 20 years in the Framingham Heart Study. *British Medical Journal*, 337(dec04 2), a2338. DOI: 10.1136/bmj.a2338 PMID: 19056788

Gilley, J. W., Gilley, A., & McMillan, H. S. (2010). Organizational Learning, Performance, and Change: How Managers Use Learning to Improve Performance. *International Journal of Business and Management*, 5(1), 63–70.

Gupta, A., & Jain, R. (2019). Work-life balance and job stress among faculty members in higher education institutions. *Journal of Management Development*, 38(1), 70–80. DOI: 10.1108/JMD-05-2018-0184

Hargreaves, A., & Fullan, M. (2012). *Professional capital: Transforming teaching in every school. Teachers College Press.*

Helliwell, J. F., & Wang, S. (2017). Happiness and life satisfaction in the United States: The role of social capital. World Happiness Report, 2017, 36-49. https://worldhappiness.report

Hsu, T., Rojas, C., & Luthra, M. (2018). The social media influence on happiness: A study on the effect of online social interactions. *Computers in Human Behavior*, 85, 163–171. DOI: 10.1016/j.chb.2018.03.024

Jawabri, A., Alarmoti, A., & Rehman, W. (2022). Impact of Remote Working Environment on Employee Motivation, Engagement, and Job Satisfaction: A Study of Service Sector from UAE. *Business and Economic Review*, 12(1), 82. Advance online publication. DOI: 10.5296/ber.v12i1.19679

Joshi, R., & Kumar, V. (2020). Evaluating faculty performance in higher education: A study of stressors and their implications. *International Journal of Educational Management*, 34(5), 1237–1249. DOI: 10.1108/IJEM-10-2019-0378

Judge, T. A., & Bono, J. E. (2001). Relationship of core self-evaluations traits—self-esteem, generalised self-efficacy, locus of control, and emotional stability—with job satisfaction and job performance: A meta-analysis. *The Journal of Applied Psychology*, 86(1), 80–92. DOI: 10.1037/0021-9010.86.1.80 PMID: 11302235

Kahneman, D., & Deaton, A. (2015). High income improves evaluation of life but not emotional well-being. *Proceedings of the National Academy of Sciences of the United States of America*, 107(38), 16489–16493. DOI: 10.1073/pnas.1011492107 PMID: 20823223

Khan, A., Masrek, M. N., & Nadzar, F. M. (2017). Emotional intelligence and job satisfaction of academic librarians: An assessment of the relationship. *Journal of Librarianship and Information Science*, 49(2), 199–210. Advance online publication. DOI: 10.1177/0961000616650733

Khan, T., & Thomas, S. (2022). Promoting Positive Education through Constructivist Digital Learning Heutagogy: An Intervention Outcome. *Journal of Learning for Development*, 9(2), 305–316. Advance online publication. DOI: 10.56059/jl4d.v9i2.646

Kim, W. S. (2021). The Effect of Positive Psychological Art Program on Self-Efficiency and Job Satisfaction of Workers with Developmental Disabilities : Based on PERMA Model. *Culture and Convergence*, 43(1), 957–978. Advance online publication. DOI: 10.33645/cnc.2021.01.43.1.957

Kumari, A., & Singh, R. (2021). Research productivity and academic stress: A study of Indian higher education institutions. *Journal of Educational Planning and Administration*, 35(1), 67–80. DOI: 10.1177/0971685821996104

Kushlev, K., & Dunn, E. W. (2015). The benefits of taking breaks: Mindfulness and well-being. *Journal of Happiness Studies*, 16(3), 579–593. DOI: 10.1007/s10902-014-9524-

Lyubomirsky, S., King, L., & Diener, E. (2005). The benefits of frequent positive affect: Does happiness lead to success? *Psychological Bulletin*, 131(6), 803–855. DOI: 10.1037/0033-2909.131.6.803 PMID: 16351326

Machado, L., Reis de Oliveira, I., Peregrino, A., & Cantilino, A. (2019). Common mental disorders and subjective well-being: Emotional training among medical students based on positive psychology. *PLoS One*, 14(2), e0211926. Advance online publication. DOI: 10.1371/journal.pone.0211926 PMID: 30731006

Maltby, J., Day, L., & Barber, L. (2005). Forgiveness and happiness. The differing contexts of forgiveness using the distinction between hedonic and eudaimonic happiness. *Journal of Happiness Studies*, 6(1), 1–13. Advance online publication. DOI: 10.1007/s10902-004-0924-9

Martela, F., & Ryan, R. M. (2021). In selecting measures for a comprehensive assessment of well-being, it is essential to include indicators of psychological need satisfaction. In *Preventive Medicine Reports* (Vol. 23). DOI: 10.1016/j.pmedr.2021.101474

Mayo, A. R. P., Velaz, E. B., Nieto, N. R., & Sánchez, P. G. (2019). Working Happiness in the Human Resource of a University Organization Based on Seligman's PERMA Model. *International Journal of Human Resource Studies*, 9(4), 101. Advance online publication. DOI: 10.5296/ijhrs.v9i4.15718

Mehta, A., & Bhatia, S. (2020). Cultural expectations and academic stress among faculty in higher education. *International Journal of Educational Research*, 102, 101577. DOI: 10.1016/j.ijer.2020.101577

Mertler, C. A. (2009). *Action research: Teachers as researchers in the classroom*. Sage Publications.

Miller, C. R., & Williams, J. D. (2015). Faculty stress and wellness: An exploration of faculty workload and wellness strategies. *Journal of Higher Education Policy and Management*, 37(2), 139–152. DOI: 10.1080/1360080X.2015.1011508

Nikolaev, B. (2018). Does Higher Education Increase Hedonic and Eudaimonic Happiness? *Journal of Happiness Studies*, 19(2). Advance online publication. DOI: 10.1007/s10902-016-9833-y

Osei-Owusu, B. (2022). Impact of Professional Development Programmes on Teachers' Knowledge and Academic Performance of Senior High School Students in Ghana. *European Journal of Education and Pedagogy*, 3(2), 60–69. Advance online publication. DOI: 10.24018/ejedu.2022.3.2.276

Palumbo, R. (2020). Let me go to the office! An investigation into the side effects of working from home on work-life balance. *International Journal of Public Sector Management*, 33(6–7), 771–790. Advance online publication. DOI: 10.1108/IJPSM-06-2020-0150

Patel, S., & Verma, K. (2018). Interpersonal relationships and faculty stress: A study of Indian higher education institutions. *Asian Journal of Education and Training*, 4(3), 273–280. DOI: 10.20448/journal.522.2018.43.273.280

Pressman, S. D., & Cohen, S. (2005). Does positive affect influence health? *Psychological Bulletin*, 131(6), 925–971. DOI: 10.1037/0033-2909.131.6.925 PMID: 16351329

Ranjan, S., & Mukherjee, A. (2018). Understanding faculty stress: Insights from Indian higher education. *Educational Studies*, 44(2), 144–160. DOI: 10.1080/03055698.2017.1394086

Rowland, S. (2010). The importance of recognition in faculty satisfaction. *Higher Education Research & Development*, 29(5), 509–520. DOI: 10.1080/07294360.2010.501246

Ryff, C. D., & Singer, B. (2000). The role of purpose in life in psychological well-being. *Psychology and Aging*, 15(2), 206–220. DOI: 10.1037/0882-7974.15.2.206

Safaria, T. (2014). Forgiveness, Gratitude, and Happiness among College Students. *International Journal of Public Health Science*, 3(4), 241. Advance online publication. DOI: 10.11591/.v3i4.4698

Salavera, C., Usán, P., & Teruel, P. (2020). The mediating role of positive and negative affects in the relationship between self-esteem and happiness. *Psychology Research and Behavior Management*, 13, 355–361. Advance online publication. DOI: 10.2147/PRBM.S240917 PMID: 32425623

Seligman, M. (2018). PERMA and the building blocks of well-being. *The Journal of Positive Psychology*, 13(4), 333–335. Advance online publication. DOI: 10.1080/17439760.2018.1437466

Seligman, M. E. P. (2011). *Flourish: A Visionary New Understanding of Happiness and Well-being*. Free Press.

Seyal, A. H., & Afzaal, T. (2013). An Investigation of Relationship among Emotional Intelligence, Organizational Commitment and Job Satisfaction: Evidence from Academics in Brunei Darussalam. *International Business Research*, 6(3). Advance online publication. DOI: 10.5539/ibr.v6n3p217

Sharma, V., & Handa, A. (2019). Job insecurity and its impact on academic staff in higher education institutions. *Indian Journal of Higher Education*, 11(1), 47–56. DOI: 10.1177/23476311211012345

Sharma, S., & Singh, N. (2017). Resource constraints and faculty stress in Indian universities: An empirical study. Higher Education, 74(3), 481-497. DOI: 10.1007/s10734-016-0016-4

Shukla, A., & Gupta, A. (2018). Factors influencing job stress among faculty members in higher education institutions: A study of Indian universities. *Journal of Higher Education Policy and Management*, 40(4), 392–404. DOI: 10.1080/1360080X.2018.1510172

Singh, R., & Gupta, P. (2020). Administrative pressures and their impact on academic stress among university teachers in India. *International Journal of Educational Management*, 34(1), 12–23. DOI: 10.1108/IJEM-07-2019-0260

Singh, S., & Ryhal, P. C. (2021). The Influence of Teachers' Emotional Intelligence on Academic Performance With Mediating Effect of Job Satisfaction. *Journal of Education*. Advance online publication. DOI: 10.1177/00220574211032314

Smith, B. W., Ford, C. G., Erickson, K., & Guzman, A. (2021). The Effects of a Character Strength Focused Positive Psychology Course on Undergraduate Happiness and Well-Being. *Journal of Happiness Studies*, 22(1), 343–362. Advance online publication. DOI: 10.1007/s10902-020-00233-9

Stepanikova, I., & Karriker-Jaffe, K. J. (2020). Social networks and health: A longitudinal study of emotional well-being in social contexts. *Health & Place*, 61, 102265. DOI: 10.1016/j.healthplace.2019.102265

Tinto, V. (2003). Learning better together: The impact of learning communities on student success. Higher Education Monograph Series, 3, 1-12. Retrieved from https://eric.ed.gov/?id=ED476810

Toscano, F., & Zappalà, S. (2021). Overall Job Performance, Remote Work Engagement, Living with Children, and Remote Work Productivity during the COVID-19 Pandemic: A Mediated Moderation Model. *European Journal of Psychology Open*, 80(3), 133–142. Advance online publication. DOI: 10.1024/2673-8627/a000015

Vazquez, A. C. S., Ferreira, M. C., & Mendonça, H. (2020). Advances in positive psychology: Well-being, engagement and job crafting. *Avaliação Psicológica*, 18(4). Advance online publication. DOI: 10.15689/ap.2019.1804.18859.02

Veenhoven, R. (2008). Happiness in nations. In *Happiness studies: A second generation of research* (pp. 1-24). https://www.eur.nl/en/research/happiness-research

Villagran, M. A. L., & Martin, L. (2022). Academic librarians: Their understanding and use of emotional intelligence and happiness. *Journal of Academic Librarianship*, 48(1), 102466. Advance online publication. DOI: 10.1016/j.acalib.2021.102466

Wright, T. A., & Cropanzano, R. (2007). Psychological well-being and job satisfaction as predictors of job performance. *Journal of Occupational Health Psychology*, 12(2), 112–123. DOI: 10.1037/1076-8998.12.2.93 PMID: 17469992

Young, T., Macinnes, S., Jarden, A., & Colla, R. (2020). The impact of a wellbeing program imbedded in university classes: The importance of valuing happiness, baseline wellbeing and practice frequency. *Studies in Higher Education*. Advance online publication. DOI: 10.1080/03075079.2020.1793932

Chapter 10
Happy Wisdom Framework:
A Step-by-Step Guide

Shivani Agarwal
https://orcid.org/0000-0002-3205-552X
Galgotias University, India

Deeksha Dwivedi
https://orcid.org/0009-0008-4722-8607
Leslie's, USA

ABSTRACT

The phrase "Happy Wisdom" is not attributed to a specific person or philosopher. It is a concept that combines two universal ideas—happiness and wisdom. While many researchers have investigated the relationship between happiness and wisdom throughout literature, there's no single person credited with coining the exact phrase "Happy Wisdom". It is a phrase that combines the idea of happiness and wisdom, suggesting that true wisdom often leads to happiness, and a happy life is guided by wisdom. It can be interpreted as a state of being where one finds joy in understanding and learning, or where wise decisions lead to a fulfilling and content life. The study provides a step-by-step guide to happy wisdom adapted from Maslow hierarch theory. This step-by-step guide will provide a framework for academicians to test it quantitatively, and to corporate people to implement the same in organization for better growth and profit. Finally, it concludes with the scope for future research.

DOI: 10.4018/979-8-3693-8457-2.ch010

1. INTRODUCTION

Happiness is a part of emotion that can be seen in a feeling of joy, state of well-being, and contentment. Happiness is also an emotional well-being that results in positivity and purpose in one's life. There are lots of elements that are associated with happiness, such as success, financial stability, interpersonal relationships, and overall individual development.

Wisdom is the ability to make rational assessments, proper understanding, and subject expertise. Wisdom is related to qualities such as introspection, the ability to perceive beyond the current condition, and compassion. Wisdom is filled with integration of ethical understanding, emotion, and cognitive aspects that help an individual to properly react in unwanted situations with smartness and elegance.

Happy wisdom is the path towards enlightened and exquisite way of a satisfying life, the mix of intelligence and happiness gives a great structure for individual satisfaction and development. Happy wisdom is the process for overall happiness with the improvement of overall comprehension that directly affects the individual's relations and lives. Happy wisdom involves both the acquisition of knowledge and personal wellbeing. It's a positive approach to life that combines individual intellectual and wellbeing. Happy wisdom provides the habit of lifelong skills, self-awareness, and the development of positive attitudes that redirect to lifelong experiences, meaningful relationships and attitudes for appreciation. The combination of both happiness and wisdom helps in finding the purposeful and satisfactory life and experiences.

The happy wisdom framework is a methodology that integrates the way of pleasure and emotional well-being with the improved wisdom. The framework provides not only temporary satisfaction for success, but it enables the positive and well-rounded strategy for great comprehension with emotional wellbeing. The Happy Wisdom Framework provides an easy and systematic approach for individuals and organizations who want to achieve an enduring and profound source of understanding and contentment.

In the globalized world most of the *people are running towards a blind race*, which is leading to depression, rivalry, and other unsatisfied individual feelings. People are looking towards gaining knowledge and happiness for their growth. A correct understanding of the term "happy wisdom" needs proper awareness of happiness and wisdom both. The concept of happiness comes from inner pleasure, great wellbeing, and a fulfilled life. The term wisdom is associated with great sense, proper knowledge, and intellectuality.

To understand happy wisdom Practice gratitude and mindfulness is important. Mindfulness helps in staying in the current situation, fulfilling the greatest appreciation of life's moments, while gratitude helps in focusing. Happy wisdom practice in the daily routine can help in understanding life better with deeper understanding and emotional wellbeing. It also enhances self-awareness and helps us to understand our reactions and emotions in a better way.

Happy wisdom not only improves individuals' personal lives, but it also positively improves communities and relationships. When an individual sees life in a joyful and happy manner, it creates a positive environment. In other words, happy wisdom shows the way for positive fulfillment from the inner voice, gives a life purpose, and brings lots of joy and compassion.

Practical implementation of the happy wisdom framework gives a positive approach for organization and personal growth. Proper understanding of the happy wisdom framework needs a better understanding of the fundamentals of happiness and wisdom.

2. HAPPY WISDOM FRAMEWORK: A COMPREHENSIVE OVERVIEW

In a fast-paced society, organizations and individuals both are looking for productivity, fulfillment, and growth. The happy wisdom framework provides a path of happiness with the wisdom that gives individual success, which indirectly helps society. The happy wisdom framework is based on the view that wisdom and happiness are not only related to each other but also support each other. This comprehensive approach gives the base for the happy wisdom framework.

In the field of psychology, knowing happiness has developed to embrace different factors that include sense of belonging, satisfaction, and positive thinking or emotions. Research shows positive thinking based on the study of human factors and strength that helps to get a satisfied and fulfilling life (Seligman, 2002). Previous research gives importance to positive emotion, meaningful activities and individual success and growth in accomplishing happiness (Seligman, 2011).

In the modern world, wisdom is mostly related to the capability to take proper judgment and quick decisions on uncertainty and unwanted circumstances. Researchers created a model of wisdom that includes reflective, affective, and cognitive components (Baltes & Staudinger, 2000). Wisdom is considered as the base of adequate knowledge that combines insight and experiences to solve life problems correctly (Ardell, 2003).

Figure 1. Happiness and Wisdom

The happy wisdom framework is derived from the concept that happiness and wisdom are both interrelated and supporting each other. Many research and theoretical models encourage this interrelationship of happiness and wisdom.

Previous research shows that happiness can improve cognitive functioning positively, which, in other words, improves the development of wisdom. Positive thinking and emotion can improve cognitive resources and help in solving problems, which is very important for correct decision-making (Fredrickson, 2009). Positive emotions and thinking can improve mental and cognitive flexibility, which helps individuals to utilize a wider range of perspectives and make good judgments based on their understanding.

Research shows wisdom helps in long-term happiness and wellbeing by utilizing better knowledge of life's problems and complexities. It is proven that a wise individual can have more resilience, great interpersonal skills, and a balanced perspective towards life's problems or challenges (Ardelt, 2008). Research on socioemotional selectivity theory also shows how wisdom-related competencies, like perspective, thinking, and emotional regulation, can help individuals achieve a better and more satisfied life and overall emotional wellbeing. (Carstensen, 1992).

Empirical research on the Happy Wisdom framework-related concept gives a valuable insight and understanding into its effectiveness. Research on emotional wellbeing gives emphasis on the role of positive psychology for happiness and overall wellbeing. Subjective well-being shows the importance of positive thinking on emotions, relations, social connections, and satisfaction in overall happiness (Diener, 2000). Research shows to improve emotional wellbeing Physical fitness, exercise, and mindfulness are very effective that enhance individual satisfaction and overall mood (Seligman et al., 2005).

Research on critical thinking and cognitive development helps in the happy wisdom framework with an emphasis on wisdom. Research shows that *people who are involved in learning and cognitive activity can solve uncertain conditions and complex issues, and they are able to take great judgment based on their ability* (Ericsson et al., 2006). Focusing on cognitive training can help in strategic and positive thinking and problem solving to improve cognitive capabilities to help in taking better decisions (Kausler, 1994).

The importance of ethical living in getting wisdom and happiness is shown by studies on ethics and moral development. Moral development and ethics provide a better framework for analyzing how people improve decision-making and ethical reasoning. (Kohlberg, 1981). Previous research on corporate social responsibility and ethical leadership shows the value of using ethics and organization practices to improve a better and more positive workplace, improved workforce and wellbeing. Brown & Treviño, 2006).

The Happy Wisdom Framework can be used in different areas that include personal, professional, and organizational development. Practical uses of the happy wisdom framework can be applied to individual and organizational productivity, growth, happiness, wellbeing, and resilience.

3. DEVELOPING HAPPY WISDOM FRAMEWORK FROM MASLOW HIERARCHY THEORY AS A FOUNDATION

Abraham Maslow proposed the psychological theory of human needs. This theory has five levels, and it is widely known as Maslow's hierarchy of needs. Abraham Maslow's hierarchy of needs framework is mostly shown as a pyramid, each level of this pyramid explains different varieties of human needs that every individual needs to fulfill the desire, fulfillment, and personal growth. Maslow's hierarchy of needs is basically divided into growth needs and deficiency needs, which explain why lower-level human needs must be completed before higher-level human needs can be achieved. Abraham Maslow suggested that a low-level human need should be achieved or fulfilled before the person can focus on a higher level of needs. *The Maslow's hierarchy is mostly shown in the pyramid shape. If one human need is satisfied, another need will emerge as a continuous process.*

The base level of Maslow's hierarchy starts with physiological needs. A physiological need is a necessity for living, which includes *water, food, proper sleep, and shelter*. When the physiological needs are met, people move up another level, which is safety needs. Safety needs basically are securing a secure environment for living and stability in the surroundings. When the safety needs are met, people move up to the third level, which is love and belonging needs. The love and belonging needs are relationship, friendship, social circle, relationships with coworkers, etc. Once the lover and belonging needs are met, people move up to the fourth level. The fourth level of Maslow's hierarchy of needs is esteem need. The esteem need is basically expecting respect from others and self-respect as well. The top level of the pyramid is self-actualization, which includes trying to achieve *personal growth*.

Maslow's hierarchy of needs says the lower level of need must be fulfilled before higher needs. But recent studies are suggesting human needs can overlap and can be achieved simultaneously with different intensities.

The hierarchy of needs framework provides a better understanding of individual motivation factors. The Maslow's need for hierarchical theory is accepted by different fields such as management, education, banking, and other industries. In management, Maslow's hierarchy of needs is to focus on employees and customers needs which can help in enhancing working environments. It can help organizations create a productive and improved workforce which can help in understanding employee needs, enhancing productivity, and employee engagement.

The order of human needs suggested by Maslow is as follows:

3.1 The Five Levels of Maslow's Hierarchy of Needs

1. Physiological Needs (water, food, sleep)
2. Safety Needs (security, freedom from fears)
3. Love Needs (maintaining friendship, forming intimate relationships, being part of different groups and communities, being loved by family)
4. Esteem Needs (achievement, being capable, trying to achieve personal growth, gaining skills, personal goal, feeling valued)
5. Need for Self-Actualization (creative fulfillment, life purpose, reading potential, personal achievements)

Figure 2. Extended Maslow Hierarchy Framework

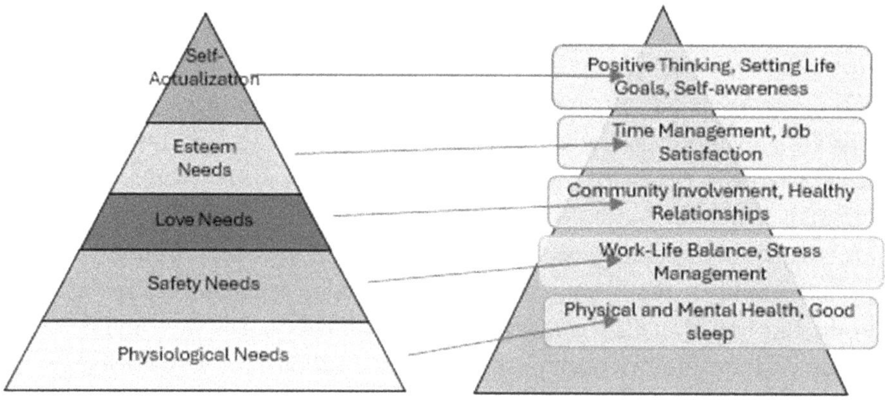

3.1.1 Physiological Needs

The base of Maslow's hierarchy of needs pyramid is psychological need, it is the need for survival. Psychological needs include food to eat, shelter to stay in, water to drink, proper sleep, and clothing. According to Abrahm Maslow, if the basic psychological needs are not met, a person cannot survive, and the human body cannot function properly. Every human being always tries to fulfill this need above all other needs. A person who is hungry will try to get food before considering self-esteem or social relationships. Another example is if a person does not have shelter to stay, the person will try to get shelter before prioritizing any other need.

The basic physiological needs from the Maslow hierarchy pyramid represent the essential and basic needs for human survival. Psychological needs are known as the most urgent and crucial needs, as these needs can be directly associated with the human body functioning along with survival. Psychological needs are the main level of Maslow's framework, and it shows the impact on human behavior and motivation factors.

When the psychological needs are not fulfilled, they become the base driver for human behavior. For example, if a person has not gotten water for a long time and is fully dehydrated, they will focus only on finding water, all other needs will become secondary. This shows the importance of psychological needs, which can override other needs like self-esteem, social circle, future planning, and ethics.

Abrahm Maslow's said that once the basic psychological human needs are filled properly, the person can think about other higher-level needs such as self-esteem, love and belonging, safety needs, etc. The Maslow hierarchy of needs says that fulfilling psychological needs is necessary for self-fulfillment and personal growth.

3.1.2 Safety Needs

Once the base level of hierarchy psychological needs is met, the individual tries to achieve security and safety needs. The second level of the pyramid security and safety needs have financial stability, good health, emotional support from family and friends, physical safety, etc. Individuals desire to have security and safety needs such as job security, good medical facilities, a safe and secure neighborhood. When the safety needs are not fulfilled, people get stress, fear, and anxiety, which can affect their personal development.

The second level of Maslow's hierarchy of needs comes after physiological needs in terms of how urgent and important it is. The safety and security needs cover an individual's dream for stability, a secure environment, and fearlessness. A better understanding of safety needs is important for understanding human behavior and motivation from personal life as well as professional life.

The second level of Maslow's hierarchy needs safety, and security is crucial and very important to strike a proper balance between self-actualization and personal growth. Maslow also suggested that human growth involved getting out of our comfort zone. Stepping out of your comfort zone can also increase insecurity. The real challenge is to create a balance between risks that are associated with personal growth and individual safety.

3.1.3 Love and Belonging Needs

Once the second level of mallows hierarchy safety needs are met, people look for relationships, a sense of belonging, and social relationships. The level of love and belonging needs includes family, friends, romantic relationships, other social relationships, and community relationships. Human nature is to get loved and accepted in society, family and all kinds of relationships. Once the love and belonging needs are met, it encourages well-being, which indirectly helps in happiness. The love and belonging level mainly target love, relationships, a sense of belonging, and affection. The love and belonging needs are very important for understanding individual behaviors and wellbeing.

The level needs individual natural desire to make relationships with others. Which includes family, friends, romantic relationships, community relationships, and other relationships. Maslow said once the psychological and safety needs are met, a person desires the next level, which is the need for love, affection, and belonging. The importance of love and belonging needs has an impact on psychological and social development. Once the individual achieves love, affection, and belongings, which contribute to that individual's overall health, self-respect, emotional support, well-being, and satisfaction. Forming a good relationship is the core of this level. For example, friendship provides love, a sense of belonging, and the ability to share experiences. On the other hand, an intimate relationship provides love, mutual respect, affection, attachment, etc.

3.1.4 Esteem Needs

The next level of Maslow's theory is esteem needs. The esteem need can be divided into two different categories, one category is seeking respect from others, while the other category is having self-respect. It's human nature to seek appreciation, award, recognition, and feel accomplished. Which can include all achievements like education, profession, and social. When esteem needs are met, people feel motivated, valued, and confident, which improves their motivation to achieve higher goals.

Esteem needs are level four, which comes after love and belonging needs in Maslow's hierarchy of needs. The esteem needs mainly focus on accomplishment, sense of belonging, respect, and value. Proper understanding of esteem is very important for individuals' behavior, motivation, and wellbeing.

It is important to fulfill esteem needs for the psychological well-being of an individual. It is also important to make proper balance between self-esteem needs with other needs of psychological wellbeing and personal growth.

3.1.5 Self-Actualization

The top level of Maslow's hierarchy of needs is self-actualization. The self-actualization level shows a desire for personal growth with full potential. The last level is to achieve everything, which can be new skills, personal development, etc. Self-actualization depends on the individual, like one person wants to be a singer, another person wants a big house, and someone wants to be a CEO.

Self-actualization is the highest level of Maslow's hierarchy of needs, this level focuses on individual's highest level of personal growth and motivation. This level of Maslow's hierarchy shows how an individual can fully use their potential to achieve the best and most improved version of themselves.

Self-actualization is basically understanding and realizing the full potential of an individual to achieve the desired growth and development. Abrham Maslow said this last level of self-actualization is to achieve everything that and individual desire. The importance of self-actualization is showing the target of human development. Maslow suggested that once the lover level needs are satisfied, individuals are focused on desire for personal development and growth with the help of creativity, skill development, etc.

3.2 Extended Maslow Hierarchy Framework

In Figure 2, the framework is for achieving happiness with the help of Maslow hierarchy need theory. Happiness and wisdom are both interconnected, which can mutually benefit each other when managed properly. Previous research shows that there is a positive correlation between both happiness and wisdom. Research shows developing wisdom can help to achieve satisfactory lives along with happiness.

The actual key to this happy wisdom framework is continuous effort for self-actualization and personal growth. Once you become wiser, you can feel happiness from inside, your positive attitude and emotions can help you achieve development along with wisdom. Following are the details for the extended Maslow hierarchy framework:

Figure 3. Happy Wisdom Framework

3.2.1 Physical and Mental Health

Physical and mental health are very important for human beings. Physical and mental health are the base for the happy wisdom framework, they are very important because they directly impact human function and wellbeing and provide a healthy and satisfactory life. A comprehensive approach to individual health that covers both physical as well as mental health. Physical and mental health is important to achieve happiness and wisdom.

Physical health is the base for the everyday functioning of an individual, and it also impacts our mental health. The main areas of physical health include physical activity like exercise, walking, cycling, household chores, and any kind of activity that improves cardiovascular health and muscle health. When a person is physically healthy, it improves the good mood, reduces stress, and improves positive thinking. An individual should be physically active for a minimum of 30 minutes a day. Along with exercise, we should also focus on good food, which includes fruits, vegetables, lots of proteins, fibers, vitamins, and calcium-rich foods. Healthy foods give all the important nutrition we need for our day-to-day lives for physical growth and proper functioning. Nutrition full of essential vitamins and minerals can prevent chronic illness and improve mental health. Quality sleep is also very important for physical health. A good sleep helps in physical recovery, functioning, and improving mental health. A healthy adult should sleep for a minimum of 7-9 hours to improve overall health and wellbeing. An individual should also get regular checkups from the doctor to prevent any health issues. Regula checkup, health screening and vaccinations can prevent health issues on time before they get any worse.

Mental health is also very important, it helps in improving psychological, emotional, and social wellbeing. The important key factor for mental health is managing stress and coping with stress. Mediation, yoga, and exercise can improve one's overall mental health. Educating mental awareness and understanding other's emotions can help and improve mental health. Properly involved in mental activity like chess or solving puzzles can help in maintaining cognitive function, which can reduce age-related issues. A good social circle can provide great emotional support, which is very important for mental health. People who receive love from their friends and families tend to have better mental health than those who don't have anyone to talk to. Great relationships with friends and families can provide mental support when in need. That is why a godly social circle is very important for your mental health and wellbeing.

Mental and physical health both play an important role in the happy wisdom framework. By taking care of our mind and body, we can achieve amazing personal growth, strong support, mental health, happiness, and the development of wisdom. The thorough approach to good health not only improves happiness and great quality of life, it also helps in achieving a positive attitude, which indirectly helps individuals and society.

3.2.2 Good Sleep

Good sleep is very important for happiness and wellbeing. The first step is valuing the sleep, the second step is prioritizing the sleep, the third step is personalizing the sleep, the fourth step is trusting the sleep, and the fifth and last step is protecting the sleep. Understanding the value of sleep is the first step for getting better sleep. We must understand that sleep is not a comfort but a need for mental and physical health. Sleep plays an important role in cognitive function, how to regulate one's emotions, and individual overall wellbeing.

We must fix our sleeping habits and schedules. A healthy individual needs a minimum of 7-9 hours of sleep. When we prioritize our sleep, we may need to change other things in life like work, entertainment, and other activities. But once you prioritize sleep, you can achieve great health, mental stability, overall happiness and wisdom.

All individual's sleeping habits are different and unique. We can try different sleep times and wake up times to check what works best for us. We should keep an eye on our bodies natural alarm, and we can adjust our sleep habits accordingly. Once you personalize your sleep habits, they can give you better and quality sleep, which can lead to a happy life.

We should develop and trust our sleep pattern, which is very important. Sleep is a natural process, and it directs our body when we should sleep. To protect our sleep, we should stop forcing sleeping at odd times. Every individual body type is different, and the same applies for sleep. Our body knows how to sleep and how to create the right condition or environment for sleep naturally. Sleep plays an important role in the happy wisdom framework. A great sleep can help us achieve happiness, overall wellbeing, and wisdom.

3.2.3 Work-Life Balance

Work-life balance is a very important part of the happy wisdom framework. It plays an important role in individual overall happiness, satisfaction, wellbeing, and professional as well as personal productivity. Getting a great balance between professional life and personal life is key to wisdom and happiness in everyday life.

Work-life balance focuses on effective time management, completing work on time with impact on your personal life, making time for family and friends, pursuing your hobbies if you have any, and maintaining good physical and mental health. This concept of work-life balance suggests both personal life and professional life are important parts of an individual's life, so both personal and professional life should get equal attention and importance.

Work-life balance got more attention after the remote work culture and technological advancement. There are no doubt technological advancements provide great flexibility and can save work-related travel time, but work culture is also impacting people's personal lives because individuals are available for work at any time due to remote culture. It is very important for an individual to maintain a balance between personal life and professional life. It is true that work-life balance can be different for everyone. It's an individual's responsibility to look at how they can balance work and professional life. In the happy wisdom framework trying to balance professional and personal life is essential. Work-life balance helps individuals to improve professional growth along with personal growth, relationships with family and friends, social circle, and individuals' overall well-being. Maintaining work-life balance with effective strategies can create a satisfied and fulfilling life, professional as well as personal productivity, overall happiness, and a satisfied life. In the modern world, achieving a good work-life balance plays a key role in achieving wisdom and happiness.

3.2.4 Stress Management (Safety Needs)

Stress management is a very important part of the happy wisdom framework, stress management directly impacts individual's lives and overall wellbeing. Effective stress management is the key to a successful life. Stress management is a technique to remove stress by identifying the reasons that cause stress. Stress is a very normal psychological condition of the human mind arising due to unfulfilled desires. Stress management is a technique that provides a wide array of options to a stressed individual to rebalance their body and mind. If there is no proper stress management, the mind goes into deep slumber, and the body becomes like an atom bomb, ready to explode anytime. With continued pressures and stress, an individual may face a series of health problems like high blood pressure, heart attacks, disturbances in hormonal levels, diabetes, endocrine problems, and many more. Stress not only affects the health of an individual but also affects their relationships. Stress causes an individual to lose control over their body and mind, leading them to utter unpolite words that could permanently damage their relationships.

Stress related to work affects the individual physically, mentally, and psychologically. Mentally stressed people at work implies poor decision-making, lack of concentration at the job assigned, being unable to handle work pressures, etc. Psychological stress arises when an employee starts feeling restless, rejected, miserable, and insignificant. Physically stressed out implies that the employee is not able to perform because of his poor health caused by stress. Stress is very common in organizations where the employer does not give proper regard to the factors affecting the employee and keeps on pushing them for performance in the work. Finding the primary source of stress may seem straightforward but eliminating it can be more challenging.

All the individuals are constantly worried about getting close to project deadlines, meeting the expectations of their boss at work, and having a negative and unhealthy relationship with other teammates or colleagues. Therefore, stress management is necessary to bring their individual back on track so that they can perform with their full potential.

By utilizing stress management techniques from the happy wisdom framework, a person can get happiness along with wisdom. Stress management removes negativity from one's life, which is the cause of stress, and gives a positive attitude that helps in professional and personal growth, happiness, wellbeing, and wisdom.

3.2.5 Community Involvement

Community involvement helps people to build relationships with others, meet new like-minded people, and make a strong bond with other members of the community. These relationships are very important for their happiness, their growth, and their overall wellbeing. When an individual contributes to the community, it gives a sense of belonging and a purpose, which is important for a happy and satisfied life. When you play an active role in community services, you learn new skills, achieve wisdom and personal growth. Active involvement in community services can improve thinking ability and perspective towards society.

Community involvement is an important part of the happy wisdom framework. Community involvement gives an opportunity for social connection, understanding social responsibility, personal growth, sense of belonging in the community, and improves overall wisdom. When we are actively involved in community services, we are not only improving personal happiness, wisdom, and wellbeing, we are also contributing to the society that creates a more supportive, resilient, and happy society. In the modern world where nuclear families are increasing day by day, social involvement can help the individual and family to achieve wisdom, sense of belonging, friends, attachment with society/culture, happiness, and overall wellbeing.

3.2.6 Healthy Relationships

Happy relationships are also a very important part of the happy wisdom framework. Happy relationships are the basis for personal growth, a satisfactory life, and overall happiness. These relationships could be romantic relationship with spouse, relationship with girlfriend or boyfriend, relationship with siblings, relationship with family, relationship with friends or relatives, or any kind of relationship that helps in improving wisdom and happiness.

A happy relationship is an important element in the happy wisdom framework. A happy relationship supports a healthy environment, love, belonging, personal growth, and wisdom. When we love, support, trust, and mutually respect in any relationship, it directly improves happiness, satisfaction, and overall wellbeing. Modern life is full of stress. The love, support, and strength in relationships can be the base for wisdom and happiness. Managing and having a healthy relationship is not just an achievement but its path for wisdom and happiness for the individual, family, and community.

3.2.7 Time Management

Time management plays an important role in the happy wisdom framework. If time is managed properly, it could improve efficiency and productivity, lower stress levels, and improve happiness. Proper time management helps us to distribute limited time and resources efficiently, which can help in getting some time for professional and personal growth as well. The basics of time management are setting a goal, making a strategy, prioritizing work, and making some time for personal activities as well.

For effective time management, it's also very important to make a strategy to stay away from distractions. Effective time management has time for everything, like profession, work, family, relationships, and habits. The best strategy is to prioritize your task on time without any delay. When you work continuously, you get tired, so the best technique is to take a small break after a certain time. This way, you will recharge for work again. The second strategy is to not overstress yourself. Only take work that you can finish on time. Make a strategy to leave work after working hours and don't take extra work home. Manage your work time effectively so you can get some time to spend with family and friends. Effective time management involves some time for yourself, spending some time for your habits and passion.

In the happy wisdom framework, time management is not only finishing work on time, but also about making a balance between personal life, professional life, relationships, and growth. In the happy wisdom framework, if you prioritize your work efficiently, you have a clear goal, you have a planned strategy, you can properly allocate your time, and you can improve your overall happiness and wisdom. Effective time management can improve your efficiency, productivity, happiness, and a successful life.

3.2.8 Job Satisfaction

Job satisfaction is an important part of the happy wisdom framework. Job satisfaction directly impacts an individual's happiness, personal growth, and overall wellbeing. Job satisfaction does not impact only work, it impacts an individual's perception, personality, commitment, and life purpose. In the happy wisdom framework, job satisfaction is achieving personal growth, happiness at work, and a satisfied professional life.

Adaptability and self-realization are also very important in job satisfaction. One should always assess their goals and make a change in the strategy if it requires achieving the goal for improvement. Job satisfaction in the happy wisdom framework is not enjoying a job, it is about contributing to happiness, personal growth, professional growth at the workplace, keeping the values, and improving overall life. If an individual is satisfied at work, they can improve overall life satisfaction with happiness and balance life. Taking necessary changes if required for job satisfaction can improve individual growth along with professional growth, which directly improves productivity and helps in a positive work environment. Job satisfaction helps in both personal and professional life.

3.2.9 Positive Thinking

Positive thinking is an essential element of the happy wisdom framework. Positive thinking is a powerful tool that improves thinking, resilience, wisdom, and a satisfied life. Positive thinking is an approach that can benefit individuals and society, and it can help to make the world a better place.

Positive thinking plays an important role in success, achievement, overall growth, personally and professionally. When a person has positive thinking and capability to be successful, they can see their challenges and obstacles in growth as an opportunity to learn something. They have patience and a positive aptitude for success. A positive thinker can achieve anything, it could be a job, career, family, or relationship.

Figure 4. Effects of Positive Thinking

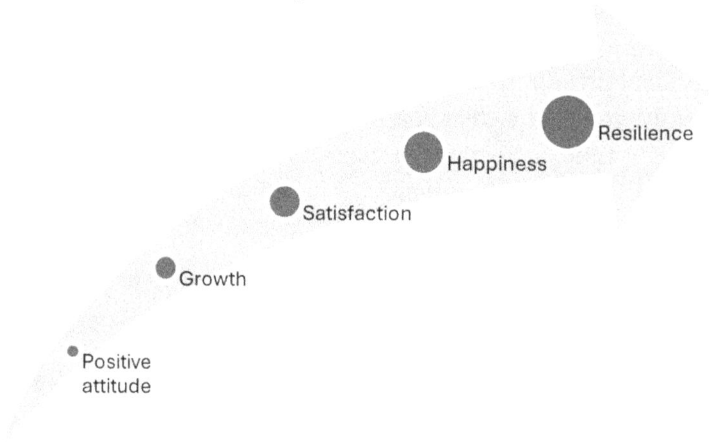

Positive thinking is a great tool in the happy wisdom framework for improving happiness, attitude, resilience, and a satisfied life. By developing a positive attitude, an individual can get an optimistic approach towards personal as well as professional life, which enhances their overall mental and physical health, sense of belonging, happiness, and wisdom. Positive thinking needs an attitude to accept things patiently and put in continuous effort if needed to achieve a happy and successful life.

3.2.10 Life Goals

Life goals are also an essential element of the happy wisdom framework. Life goals give an individual life purpose, motivation, direction, and reason for hard work. Life goals are not just aspirations, life goals give an individual a carefully decided target, which can provide that individual satisfaction, happiness, wisdom, and overall wellbeing.

Life goals give a direction for hard work, it requires consistent work and patience to achieve life goals. Life goals give motivation and direction, which are very important to being successful. Life goals encourage people to use their abilities properly, it gives consistency and strength to achieve goals. When we set a goal that matches our abilities and put effort into achieving it, we can achieve any goal in life. This approach from the happy wisdom framework gives life a place to grow, learn new skills, put effort, achieve happiness and wisdom on their path to success.

3.2.11 Self-Awareness

Self-awareness is also an important element of the happy wisdom framework. Self-awareness is the basis for emotional intelligence, achieving growth, happiness, and overall wellbeing. Self-awareness is not just introspection. Self-awareness is a better understanding of your view/thought, values, behavior, and motivation.

By understanding our thoughts and emotions correctly, along with introspecting our behavior, values, and emotions, individuals can achieve great success and personal growth, they can make healthy relationships personally and professionally, make better decisions, and get a positive attitude towards life. Self-awareness needs continuous effort that can benefit both personal and professional life to achieve success, happiness, and wisdom.

4. DEVELOPING HAPPY WISDOM FRAMEWORK (HWF) IN ORGANIZATION

The path of happy wisdom can be achieved by exploring the above extended Maslow hierarchy framework in the span of organization. Basically, Maslow talks about the need's requirements and its fulfillment in a particular sequence's understand the path of happy wisdom, following is the figure given below:

Figure 5. Happiness Wisdom Path

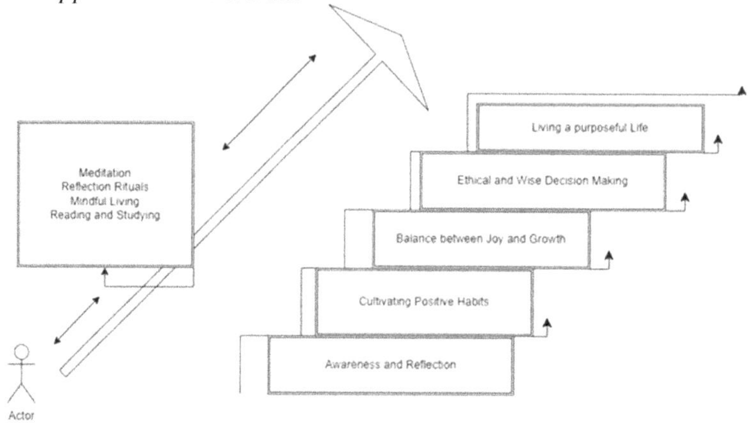

The above figure consists of several steps such as:

- **Awareness and Reflection:** Individuals need to understand about self, which is gained by daily journaling, practice reflection to observe the thoughts and actions. Ask yourself what truly makes you happy and what wisdom means to you.
    - **Cultivating Positive Habits:** To cultivate positive habits, it is prominent to read and study good literature which helps individual in creating positive habits. Regulate your actions and emotions with the help of meditation. Also, acknowledge small things in your life. It is important to show gratitude towards every single second of your life.
    - **Joy and Growth Fit:** Life is full of opportunities and challenges. It is not always that an individual will get opportunities only, there are times in life in which we get challenges and sometimes failures also. But train your brain to cultivate a balance between Joy and Growth is of utmost importance.
    - **Contribution towards others:** The feeling of givenness towards individual, group and community will give you a sense of sharing happiness and helps you in leading towards wisdom.
- **Living a purposeful life:** Regularly revisit your goals and ensure they continue to foster your happiness and wisdom. Adapt when necessary to stay true to your path.

To achieve the above happy wisdom path, individuals need to use the following tools such as meditation, reflection rituals, reading and studying and mindful living.

5. IMPLEMENTATION OF HAPPY WISDOM FRAMEWORK (HWF) IN ORGANIZATION

Happy wisdom framework implementation in an organization requires effective and strategic planning to apply the happy wisdom framework principle in everyday organizational operations and day-to-day practices. The happy wisdom framework applies human intelligence, great mind, and wisdom to clearly understand the organization and then make proper strategy accordingly. Below you will get a detailed overview of how you can implement a happy wisdom framework in an organization. By coordinating Maslow's hierarchy with the Happy Wisdom framework, organizations can achieve a multi-disciplinary approach that provides understanding of basic human needs, which supports fundamental growth and development. The integration of Maslow's hierarchy and happy wisdom framework can help individuals achieve happy, satisfied, engaged, productive, and fulfilled resources.

Organizations can improve employee performance and growth by utilizing happy wisdom frameworks in the organization structure, it can help in understanding employee's needs, job satisfaction, wisdom, and emotional intelligence.

1. Self-Awareness Initiatives
2. Fostering Positive Thinking
3. Aligning life goals with organizational objectives
4. Promoting Work-Life Balance
5. Enhancing job satisfaction
6. Encouraging community involvement
7. Supporting Physical and Mental Health

Figure 6. Implementation of Happy Wisdom Framework (HWF) in Organization

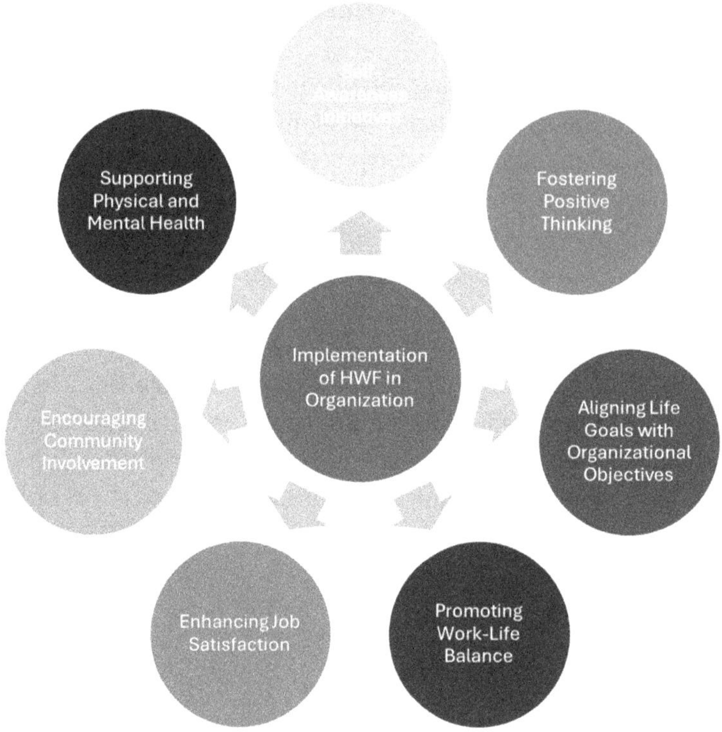

5.1 Self-Awareness Initiatives

Organizations can get more productive, organized, engaged, and fulfilled employees by applying self-awareness initiatives in their organizational structure. Self-Awareness Initiatives can help employees understand values, responsibilities, behaviors, emotions, and clear understandings of their thoughts, which can help them improve their productivity, relationships with others, better decision-making, happiness, and overall wellbeing.

A self-awareness strategy is an effective strategy to include self-reflection exercise into the organization's routine. Self-awareness strategy could be self-assessment activities, motivate employees to write about their goals, achievements and review them from time to time, and team/colleague feedback sessions can also be used to understand awareness. These exercises can improve employee's strengths, weaknesses, and skills, along with personal growth.

Leaders play an important role in the self-awareness strategy. To get the full benefit of happy wisdom frameworks and self-realization strategies, companies should train leaders and managers to utilize self-awareness strategies to help their subordinates. The self-awareness model can be one-on-one coaching sessions, personal assessments, or employee's development programs to develop self-awareness.

Information technology can be used as a tool to support self-awareness strategies in the organization. There are lots of tools and applications available online that can track personal development and set goals. Such resources can be used for self-awareness. This application can also provide a program and a track of improvement for self-awareness practices in the organization.

Organizations can get a self-aware employee by utilizing this self-awareness model from the Happy Wisdom framework. These employees can communicate properly, have self-realization, and have a positive attitude to handle challenges if they face any, which indirectly helps in productive organization. So, implementing self-awareness of a happy wisdom framework can improve wisdom and happiness both in the organization.

5.2 Fostering Positive Thinking

Encouraging positive thinking is a very important element of the happy wisdom framework. Positive thinking can help the constructive and optimistic mindset of employees, which can improve employee's productivity, patience, resilience, and happiness.

To apply the positive thinking model in the organizations, they can initiate training and workshops program. These training sessions and workshops can help employees understand the benefits of a positive attitude, how employees can get rid of negative thoughts, and how they can apply positive thinking to get an optimistic and balanced view or perspective. For example, in the organizations if you are facing any challenge to complete the task, you can take it as a positive opportunity to learn new things.

Organizations should focus on positive language for communication inside and outside the organization. Focusing on the use of solution-based, motivation-based, and affirmative language for meetings, emails, texts, and all communications can help the employees attitude. Positive thinkers can do their work better and in an organized manner, they know how to handle the situation. Positive thinkers allow themselves to behave well in case of any problem, they try to get solutions patiently.

Integrating mindfulness strategies can also help positive thinking initiatives. Mindfulness practice can show employees how to be aware of their surroundings, emotions, and thoughts. It allows them to choose productive and positive ways of thinking.

By implementing positive thinking in the organization, you can get productive, engaged, resilient, and happy employees. The positive employee can achieve anything, they work better as a team, it improves problem-solving skills and happiness, which create a safe and healthy work environment.

5.3 Aligning Life Goals with Organizational Objectives

Aligning life goals with organizational objectives is a great strategy for implementing the Happy Wisdom Framework (HWF) in organizations. This strategy aims to align employees' goals with organizational objectives, thereby motivating them to be engaged, hardworking, and positive. create a better workplace. Organizations can apply an employee's goal setting program that can help both employees achieve their goals and the organization achieve organizational objectives. Organizations can plan for a smart goal program where they can train employees to achieve their personal goals that can help in achieving the organization's goal. For example, an employee wants to be a manager and learn new skills, companies can evaluate that employee's skills, and they can train that employee accordingly to the need, which is beneficial for both employees and organizations.

Flexibility in the employee's job responsibilities and role can also help in aligning life goals. By giving the opportunity to align employee's life goals, organizations can open new opportunities for employees to follow their career goals along with helping achieve the organization's objective.

Having a strong feedback system is also very important. Frequent employee performance reviews can provide actual improvement and progress towards the company's goals, and they can also give a report on how employees are moving towards their personal goals along with current roles and responsibilities.

An organization can achieve both employee's productivity, loyalty, engagement, and growth along with meeting organizational objectives if they align life goals with organizational objectives as a tool from the happy wisdom framework. Matching life goals with organizational objectives can improve a sense of belonging and a happy work life, which can improve the happiness, overall wellbeing of an employee and contribute to organizational success.

5.4 Promoting Work-Life Balance

Promoting work-life balance is a very important part of applying the happy wisdom framework in companies. Work-life balance from the happy wisdom framework can create opportunities where employees can manage their job responsibilities while managing a personal life, which can improve their happiness level, productivity, job satisfaction, and overall well-being.

To properly implement the work-life balance strategies, the organization can offer flexibility in the working hours. Flexible working hours include flexible working hours, remote work opportunities, or flexible working weeks. The flexibility in the working hours can give employees an opportunity to plan their work along with their personal commitment, which can improve work-related stress, fulfilled life, and satisfaction.

A good way to apply this model is to motivate and apply healthy boundaries between family and professional time. Like making a policy to avoid after-working hours calls, messages, and emails until and unless it's urgent. These policies can give an opportunity to respect boundaries between themselves and their teams. Leadership should take effective action to apply these policies.

PTO is there in most of the organizations, but employees hesitate to take PTO until it's urgent. Implementing PTO policies on a regular interval can help employees take breaks from work to recharge. There are some organizations that have introduced unlimited PTO policies so that employees can take necessary breaks when they need.

By implementing work-life balance as an element of the happy wisdom framework, organizations can achieve productive, satisfied, engaged, and happy employees. The balance between work and personal life can not only help employees, but it can also help in organizations overall success, it gives happy and satisfied employees, which leads to productivity, retention, and a better work environment.

5.5 Enhancing Job Satisfaction

Job satisfaction plays an important role in any employment. Enhancing job satisfaction is an important part of the happy wisdom framework. Organizations can achieve productive, motivated, and focused employees. Job satisfaction can help in improving employee performance, stability, and retention, which indirectly helps in organizational growth.

The first step to implementing enhancing job satisfaction is to understand what are the factors that help job satisfaction. Organizations can do regular surveys and feedback to assess employees' current state of mind, workload, reconciliation, and if they have any opportunities for improvement and satisfaction. By focusing on employee's suggestions and concerns, organizations can improve employee retention. Organizations should focus on the areas that need to be improved, or they can modify their strategy if needed to increase employee job satisfaction along with organizational growth.

Flexibility in the workplace plays an important role in job satisfaction. Flexible work hours or remote work can help employees to improve balance between professional and personal life, reduce stress, and enhance job satisfaction. Organizations should provide flexible working hours to support employees, which can result in happy and satisfied employees.

Enhancing job satisfaction by following a happy wisdom framework involves an approach that improves employee's satisfaction, a positive work environment, flexibility, and workplace environment that aligns with the organization's core values. By focusing on enhancing job satisfaction, organizations can get a happy, satisfied, and productive workforce, which contributes to organization growth.

5.6 Encouraging Community Involvement

Encouraging community involvement plays an important role in the Happy Wisdom Framework (HWF) in companies. Encouraging community involvement in employees can improve a sense of belonging and responsibility that can help employees and organizations both.

To encourage community involvement in the organization, they can start a volunteer program in organizations that can match the company's social responsibility and the values both. These programs can offer employee's opportunities to get engaged in various volunteer services, participate in local events, and help in food drives and environmental cleanup initiatives. By actively participating in community involvement, employees learn new skills, connect with culture, understand social responsibility, build networks, and learn hard work.

By implementing volunteer programs, the organization can achieve a work environment where employees feel good, motivated, connected to their community, understand social responsibility, and have a sense of belonging. Organizations can give paid time for employee's volunteer services; companies can tie hands with local organizations for volunteers and plan a community event to connect the workforce with the community. Encouraging community involvement from the happy wisdom framework can turn a dissatisfied employee into a motivated employee who enjoys his work and understands social responsibility as well. This can improve an organization with happy and satisfied employees.

5.7 Supporting Physical and Mental Health

Supporting physical and mental health is a very important element of the Happy Wisdom Framework (HWF). Supporting physical and mental health can improve the work environment. That focuses on the employee's wellbeing and mental and physical health.

Organizations can provide wellness programs to raise awareness of healthy lifestyles to support physical and mental health. These programs can provide fitness awareness, fitness challenges, mental workshops, nutrition workshops, awareness programs to support employee's overall health. Organizations can make on-site gyms or provide gym memberships at nominal cost to motivate employees to be active in physical workouts, which is very important to mental health, physical health, and it also reduces stress.

An organization can create a healthy, productive, and engaged work environment by implementing properly supporting mental and physical health. Supporting physical and mental health by a happy wisdom framework can improve employee productivity and satisfaction, which helps in a positive work environment.

5.8 Improving Time Management

Time management plays an important role in implementing the Happy Wisdom Framework. Proper time management can improve employee's overall performance and productivity, it also reduces stress and helps maintain balance between personal and professional life.

To improve time management, it is very important to review employee's calendars. The best way to audit that is to check if they can complete the assigned task within time, if yes, then they are managing their time properly. If the employee is not able to complete the task on time, then an evaluation is required for timekeeping. They should assess if employees are having any obstacles or are not able to manage their time properly. By analyzing this, leaders or managers can help employees give suggestions or make strategies for time management to improve productivity and employees working capacity.

Implementing time management in the organization needs motivating employees to utilize tools for time tracking, provide training for time management, do self-time auditing, and make a strategy depending on the needs for proper time management. Proper time management from employees and leaders can improve employee's overall performance, stability, and productivity. It also reduces work-related stress, and employees can make a good balance between family and professional life, which leads to happy, satisfied employees.

6. FINDINGS

The happy wisdom framework shows a compressive approach to gaining organizational and personal success. By applying the need for happiness with wisdom, this framework gives a balanced route to achieve success and effectiveness. By applying the happy wisdom framework core principle and application, this framework gives a strategy and insight for solving problems of life. Whether you apply this framework personally or professionally, the happy wisdom framework gives a positive approach to happiness and wisdom, which shows the path to a better, balanced, and harmonious future.

Applying the happy wisdom framework in a company needs a proper strategy and planning. Organizations can implement happy wisdom frameworks in their operation and culture by proper planning, assessing employee needs, applying strategy effectively, evaluating progress, maintaining consistency, continuing efforts and modifying the strategy if needed. The happy wisdom framework principle can increase employee productivity, stability, relationships, reduce employee stress, resilience, happiness, and overall well-being, which helps in achieving a productive work environment. The Happy Wisdom Framework principle can help organizations achieve objectives and success.

The happy wisdom framework gives a holistic approach to implementing happiness along with wisdom. This framework is based on both current and historical perspective, which connects wisdom and happiness. Previous research shows the happy wisdom frameworks core elements, which include development, wellbeing, and happiness.

Implementing the happy wisdom frameworks in organizations and personal development shows its impact to improve performance, happiness, and wellbeing. However, further study is required to examine the happy wisdom framework's effectiveness in a broad, diverse area and answer the problem in the application. Overall, the happy wisdom framework provides an approach for a happy, satisfied, balanced life by applying happiness and wisdom both.

The happy wisdom framework is a long-lasting and continuous path of learning, happiness, and growth. By implementing elements that encourage happiness and the principle of wisdom, we can get better and more satisfied, meaning life with the positivity that helps to make life better. Life is very important and has some challenges as well. The happy wisdom framework gives a framework for professional growth, personal growth and improvement. The happy wisdom framework shows that happiness and fulfillment can make life better in every stage of life. By following the path of the happy wisdom framework, we can transform our life and the way of life. We should always keep in mind that every step towards happiness and wisdom takes us to growth, satisfaction.

Every individual's satisfaction and fulfillment are different. The research shows self-realization and positive thinking play an important role in most cases. Work-life balance and job satisfaction help employees to focus on work and personal life, which improves happiness. Giving importance to physical and mental health is very important for every individual. When the mind and body are both healthy, people can do anything in life. Physical and mental health makes people happy, satisfied, motivated, and hardworking. A happy individual can give their best at the workplace as well, which improves organizations productivity. By implementing happy wisdom frameworks, individuals and organizations both can achieve growth, happiness, productivity, and overall well-being.

7. CHALLENGES AND FUTURE DIRECTIONS

Regardless of the benefits of the happy wisdom framework, there are few challenges and areas for further studies. One challenge is that empirical research should be done for framework. Research shows great insight and effectiveness for the happy wisdom framework, but diverse studies are needed. Further research should focus on experimental research and longitudinal studies that can examine the happy wisdom framework's impact on individuals and organizations.

Implementing the happy wisdom framework in different cultures and evaluating its implications across different people and cultures can improve its importance and effectiveness.

The ego can be a serious problem for both happiness and wisdom. Accepting the truth that you need to improve skills and learn new things can be challenging to manage an ego-driven individual and their behavior. Dealing with uncertainty can be an issue. In this fast-paced world, people want to be certain of the things related to them. Finding good balance between self-realization and action can also be challenging. Self-realization is important, but sometimes people don't accept the relationship and can't balance between both. Always keeping positive and optimistic behavior can be challenging. A happy wisdom framework needs a positive and optimistic approach towards life. As we improve our knowledge and growth, there is a risk of complacency. Which is a big obstacle in the learning and growth. As we know, continuous learning and growth are important parts of a happy wisdom framework.

8. CONCLUSION

The happy wisdom framework shows the important role in the search for a happy, satisfied, and fulfilling life. By accompanying the search for happiness and using wisdom, an individual can achieve a balanced approach towards life that can help them achieve success personally and professionally both. Properly implementing the practical applications and principles of this happy wisdom framework, individuals and organizations both can achieve growth, satisfaction, fulfillment, happiness, and productivity. The happy wisdom framework is derived from Maslow's hierarchy of needs, which shows the level of needs should be satisfied before reaching the next level. Organizations can use this happy wisdom framework to their organization's growth, employee's productivity, and employee retention by analyzing the basic needs of employees. The holistic approach helps and supports a better workplace, it also helps in employee growth, productivity, satisfaction, engagement, happiness, and overall wellbeing. So, it's clear that applying the happy wisdom framework in the lives of both individuals and organizations can achieve success, happiness, and growth.

REFERENCES

Ardelt, M. (1997). Wisdom and life satisfaction in old age. *The Journals of Gerontology. Series B, Psychological Sciences and Social Sciences*, 52(1), 15–P27. DOI: 10.1093/geronb/52B.1.P15 PMID: 9008672

Ardelt, M. (2003). Empirical assessment of a three-dimensional wisdom scale. *Research on Aging*, 25(3), 275–324. DOI: 10.1177/0164027503025003004

Ardelt, M., & Bergsma, A. (2012). Self-Reported Wisdom and Happiness: An Empirical Investigation. *Journal of Happiness Studies*, 13(3), 481–499. DOI: 10.1007/s10902-011-9275-5

Baltes, P. B., & Staudinger, U. M. (2000). Wisdom: A metaheuristic (pragmatic) to orchestrate mind and virtue toward excellence. *The American Psychologist*, 55(1), 122–136. DOI: 10.1037/0003-066X.55.1.122 PMID: 11392856

Bergsma, A., & Ardelt, M. (2012). Self-reported wisdom and happiness: An empirical investigation. *Journal of Happiness Studies*, 13(3), 481–499. DOI: 10.1007/s10902-011-9275-5

Dwivedi, D. (2011). Stress Management: How to Reduce and Manage Workplace Stress. Juris Ray. 5.

Dwivedi, D. (2014). New Dimensions of HRM: Performance Management.

Dwivedi, D. (2015). Impact of Information Technology on the Productivity of the Organization. *HR Journal of Management.*, 7, 77.

Dwivedi, D. (2018). Stress Management in Software Industry.

Dwivedi, D., & Agarwal, S. (2024). Green Technology and Its Effect on the Modern World. In *Green Innovations for Industrial Development and Business Sustainability* (pp. 120–126). CRC Press. DOI: 10.1201/9781003458944-8

Etezadi, S., & Pushkar, D. (2013). Why are wise people happier? An explanatory model of wisdom and emotional well-being in older adults. *Journal of Happiness Studies*, 14(3), 929–950. DOI: 10.1007/s10902-012-9362-2

Fredrickson, B. L. (2001). The role of positive emotions in positive psychology: The broaden-and-build theory of positive emotions. *The American Psychologist*, 56(3), 218–226. DOI: 10.1037/0003-066X.56.3.218 PMID: 11315248

Glück, J., & Bluck, S. (2011). Laypeople's conceptions of wisdom and its development: Cognitive and integrative views. *The Journals of Gerontology. Series B, Psychological Sciences and Social Sciences*, 66(3), 321–324. DOI: 10.1093/geronb/gbr011 PMID: 21398417

Glück, J., & Bluck, S. (2013). The MORE life experience model: A theory of the development of personal wisdom. In Ferrari, M., & Weststrate, N. M. (Eds.), *The scientific study of personal wisdom* (pp. 75–97). Springer.

Grossmann, I., Na, J., Varnum, M. E., Park, D. C., Kitayama, S., & Nisbett, R. E. (2010). Reasoning about social conflicts improves into old age. *Proceedings of the National Academy of Sciences of the United States of America*, 107(16), 7246–7250. DOI: 10.1073/pnas.1001715107 PMID: 20368436

Hofstede, G. (1984). The cultural relativity of the quality-of-life concept. *Academy of Management Review*, 9(3), 389–398. DOI: 10.2307/258280

Jeste, D. V., & Vahia, I. V. (2008). Comparison of the conceptualization of wisdom in ancient Indian literature with modern views: Focus on the Bhagavad Gita. *Psychiatry*, 71(3), 197–209. DOI: 10.1521/psyc.2008.71.3.197 PMID: 18834271

) Kabat-Zinn, J. (2009). Wherever you go, there you are: Mindfulness meditation in everyday life.

Kenrick, D. T., Griskevicius, V., Neuberg, S. L., & Schaller, M. (2010). Renovating the pyramid of needs: Contemporary extensions built upon ancient foundations. *Perspectives on Psychological Science*, 5(3), 292–314. DOI: 10.1177/1745691610369469 PMID: 21874133

King, L. A. (2001). The health benefits of writing about life goals.

Kross, E., & Grossmann, I. (2012). Boosting wisdom: Distance from the self-enhances wise reasoning, attitudes, and behavior.

Kunzmann, U., & Baltes, P. B. (2003). Wisdom-related knowledge: Affective, motivational, and interpersonal correlates. *Personality and Social Psychology Bulletin*, 29(9), 1104–1119. DOI: 10.1177/0146167203254506 PMID: 15189607

Lilgendahl, J., & McAdams, D. P. (2011). Constructing stories of self-growth: How individual differences in patterns of autobiographical reasoning relate to well-being in midlife.

Lodi-Smith, J., Geise, A. C., Roberts, B. W., & Robins, R. W. (2009). Narrating personality change.

Lyubomirsky, S., & Lepper, H. S. (1999). A measure of subjective happiness: Preliminary reliability and construct validation.

Meeks, T. W., & Jeste, D. V. (2009). Neurobiology of wisdom: A literature overview. *Archives of General Psychiatry*, 66(4), 355–365. DOI: 10.1001/archgenpsychiatry.2009.8 PMID: 19349305

Mewafarosh, R., Agarwal, S., & Dwivedi, D. (2024). Balancing FOMO and Digital Detoxification. In *Business Drivers in Promoting Digital Detoxification* (pp. 1–15). IGI Global. DOI: 10.4018/979-8-3693-1107-3.ch001

Mickler, C., & Staudinger, U. M. (2008). Personal wisdom: Validation and age-related differences of a performance measure. *Psychology and Aging*, 23(4), 787–799. DOI: 10.1037/a0013928 PMID: 19140650

Salas-Vallina, A., & Fernandez, R. (2017). The HRM-performance relationship revisited: Inspirational motivation, participative decision making and happiness at work (HAW). *Employee Relations*, 39(5), 626–642. DOI: 10.1108/ER-12-2016-0245

Schaufeli, W. B., Salanova, M., González-Romá, V., & Bakker, A. B. (2002). The measurement of engagement and burnout: A two sample confirmatory factor analytic approach. *Journal of Happiness Studies*, 3(1), 71–92. DOI: 10.1023/A:1015630930326

Schaufeli, W. B., & Taris, T. W. (2014). A critical review of the Job Demands-Resources Model: Implications for improving work and health. In *G. Bauer, & O.Bridging occupational, organizational and public health* (pp. 43–68). Springer. DOI: 10.1007/978-94-007-5640-3_4

Seligman, M. E. (2002). Positive psychology, positive prevention, and positive therapy. In Snyder, C. R., & López, S. J. (Eds.), *Handbook of positive psychology* (pp. 3–9). Oxford University Press.

Seligman, M. E. P., & Csikszentmihalyi, M. (2000). Positive psychology: An introduction. *The American Psychologist*, 55(1), 5–14. DOI: 10.1037/0003-066X.55.1.5 PMID: 11392865

Sharma, J., & Dhar, R. L. (2016). Factors influencing job performance of nursing staff: Mediating role of affective commitment. *Personnel Review*, 45(1), 161–182. DOI: 10.1108/PR-01-2014-0007

Sheldon, K. M., Ryan, R., & Reis, H. T. (1996). What makes for a good day? Competence and autonomy in the day and in the person. *Personality and Social Psychology Bulletin*, 22(12), 1270–1279. DOI: 10.1177/01461672962212007

Sirota, D., Mischkind, L. A., & Meltzer, M. I. (2005). *The enthusiastic employee*. Wharton School Publishing.

Staudinger, U. M., & Glück, J. (2011). Psychological wisdom research: Commonalities and differences in a growing field. *Annual Review of Psychology*, 62(1), 215–241. DOI: 10.1146/annurev.psych.121208.131659 PMID: 20822439

Sternberg, R. J. (1998). A balance theory of wisdom. *Review of General Psychology*, 2(4), 347–365. DOI: 10.1037/1089-2680.2.4.347

Tay, L., & Diener, E. (2011). Needs and subjective well-being around the world. *Journal of Personality and Social Psychology*, 101(2), 354–365. DOI: 10.1037/a0023779 PMID: 21688922

Thomas, M. L., Bangen, K. J., Ardelt, M., & Jeste, D. V. (2017). Development of a 12-item abbreviated Three-Dimensional Wisdom Scale (3D-WS-12): Item selection and psychometric properties. *Assessment*, 24(1), 71–82. DOI: 10.1177/1073191115595714 PMID: 26209513

Wahba, M. A., & Bridwell, L. G. (1976). Maslow reconsidered: A review of research on the need hierarchy theory. *Organizational Behavior and Human Performance*, 15(2), 212–240. DOI: 10.1016/0030-5073(76)90038-6

Webster, J. D. (2003). An exploratory analysis of a self-assessed wisdom scale. *Journal of Adult Development*, 10(1), 13–22. DOI: 10.1023/A:1020782619051

Chapter 11
Harnessing Wisdom and Happiness Through Character-Strengths in Organizations:
Building Flourishing Workplaces for Sustainable Success

Madhu Giri
https://orcid.org/0009-0008-7950-4821
Christ University, India

Swati Pathak
https://orcid.org/0000-0002-1189-1457
Christ University, India

ABSTRACT

This chapter highlights the crucial role of wisdom in improving well-being and happiness within organizations. In high-pressure work environments, employee well-being is essential for success. Wisdom—comprising creativity, curiosity, judgment, love of learning, and perspective, as identified by Peterson and Seligman—is key for navigating complex settings and promoting continuous improvement. The chapter focuses on nurturing these strengths to enhance workforce engagement, satisfaction, and productivity. It explores how cultivating wisdom at various organizational levels boosts happiness and accountability. A conceptual model is proposed to show how wisdom supports organizational happiness and outlines strategies for developing these strengths among employees. By integrating wisdom into organizational practices, leaders can create thriving environments that achieve

DOI: 10.4018/979-8-3693-8457-2.ch011

sustainable success and improved employee engagement, with practical strategies provided for actionable steps.

INTRODUCTION

In the current era of rapid change and high-pressure work environments, employee well-being is crucial for organizational success. A comprehensive approach to well-being encompasses not only job satisfaction but also personal and professional growth (Kun & Gadanecz, 2019). A critical yet often-ignored element in promoting such well-being is wisdom. This chapter will explore the importance of Wisdom as a Virtue in Organizations. Also, how this virtue can be fostered by exploring different components of Wisdom identified as a mix of character-strengths by Peterson & Seligman in 2004: creativity, curiosity, judgment, love of learning, and perspective. By recognizing and nurturing these character strengths, organizations can foster a more content and engaged workforce, ultimately leading to higher productivity and a more harmonious workplace environment.

Understanding Wisdom and Its Components

Wisdom is a virtue and has muti-facets, encompassing the ability to make sound judgments, creatively solve problems, remain curious, continually learn, and maintain a broad perspective (Glück & Weststrate, 2022). These components are essential for navigating complex work environments and fostering a continuous improvement culture. The implications of this dynamic interplay of various character-strengths comprising the virtue of Wisdom is multi-layered. For instance, creativity is crucial in problem solving and innovation. Employees who exhibit creativity can devise novel solutions to challenges, thereby leading to more efficient and effective processes (Ma et al., 2021).

Curiosity drives individuals to explore new ideas and to acquire new knowledge. In the workplace, curious employees are more likely to seek opportunities for growth and development, stay engaged, and be motivated (Wang et al., 2018). This trait not only benefits individual employees but also contributes to a culture of innovation and continuous improvement within the organization.

Judgment, or the ability to make sound decisions, is a critical component of wisdom. Good judgment allows employees to navigate complex situations, weigh options, and select the best course of action (Likierman, 2020). This skill is particularly important in leadership roles where decisions can have far-reaching consequences.

The love for learning reflects a passion for acquiring new knowledge and skills. Employees who love learning are more adaptable and better equipped to handle the demands of rapidly changing work environments (Chughtai et al., 2023). This trait was also linked to higher levels of job satisfaction and personal fulfillment. Finally, perspective involves the ability to see a bigger picture and understand the broader context of a situation. Employees with a strong perspective can empathize with others, appreciate diverse viewpoints, and contribute to a more inclusive and cohesive workplace (Pless & Maak, 2004).

Curiosity at Workplace: Dimensions and associations to Workplace Happiness

The chapter identifies four distinct dimensions of workplace curiosity:

Joyous Exploration: This dimension is associated with positive emotional experiences and an interest in exploring new ideas.
Deprivation Sensitivity: This reflects a persistent state of uncertainty and the drive to resolve information gaps.
Stress Tolerance: This dimension pertains to the ability to handle the psychological challenges that come with exploring new and uncertain situations.
Openness to People's Ideas: This involves an interest in understanding and considering the ideas and behaviours of others in the workplace.

How does workplace curiosity impact job satisfaction and work engagement? The findings from previous studies suggest that higher levels of workplace curiosity, particularly in the dimensions of Stress Tolerance and Openness to People's Ideas, are associated with greater workplace satisfaction, engagement, and performance (Kashdan & Fincham, 2004; Mussel, 2013; Reio & Callahan, 2004). Employees who exhibit these curiosity traits tend to have better social relationships at work and are more likely to pursue innovative ideas, leading to enhanced job satisfaction and overall engagement in their roles (Harrison & Dossinger, 2017; Kashdan, Rose, & Fincham, 2004; Reio et al., 2006). Joyous Exploration, Deprivation Sensitivity, Stress Tolerance, and Openness to People's Ideas. These dimensions integrate various theories of curiosity, emphasizing its role as a psychological strength in the workplace (Kashdan & Steger, 2007; Litman, 2008; Mussel, 2010; Kashdan et al., 2013). The findings indicate that each dimension correlates with the pursuit of innovative ideas, with Stress Tolerance showing the strongest link to innovation propensity (Zhou & George, 2001; Scott & Bruce, 1994). Stress tolerance enables individuals to handle pressure and uncertainty effectively, which is crucial for fostering an innovative mindset and pursuing novel solutions (Amabile, 1996; Eysenck, 1995). The results were consistent across samples from the United States and Germany, underscoring the importance of including Stress Tolerance in models of curiosity. Overall, the study advocates for a comprehensive understanding of curiosity, suggesting that it is a critical factor for enhancing workplace performance and satisfaction.

Creativity and Workplace Happiness

The detrimental impact of workplace haters on employee creativity is increasingly recognized as a critical issue within organizational settings. Characterized by behaviours such as negative gossiping, two-faced actions, and laziness, workplace haters create a toxic work environment that significantly stifles creative output (Rasool et al., 2021). The presence of such negativity shifts employees' focus from innovative thinking and idea generation to managing interpersonal conflicts, thereby hampering their ability to engage in creative activities (Adeel et al., 2022). However, personal social capital can serve as a crucial buffer against these adverse effects. Employees with robust social networks and supportive relationships are better equipped to cope with the stress and demotivation caused by workplace haters, enabling them to sustain their creativity and well-being (Sapp et al., 2010). Theories such as the cognitive-affective personality system and social network theory offer valuable insights into these dynamics, illustrating how individual differences and social capital can moderate the impact of workplace negativity (Cheng et al., 2022). Moreover, the study suggests that further exploration of cognitive dissonance theory and negative social exchange theory could deepen our understanding of how workplace haters influence employee outcomes. These findings underscore the importance of fostering a positive work environment that not only mitigates the effects of negativity but also actively supports employee creativity and well-being (Ahmad et al., 2023).

Judgment and Wellbeing at Workplace

The concept of judgment, as defined by leaders and scholars like Noel Tichy and Warren Bennis, is central to exemplary leadership and organizational well-being. Judgment is the ability to blend personal qualities with relevant knowledge and experience to make sound decisions, particularly in situations where data is ambiguous or incomplete. Leaders with good judgment are often those who can listen attentively, read critically, and discern patterns that others overlook (Tichy & Bennis, 2007; Bennis, 2009). They possess a breadth of experiences and relationships, allowing them to draw on a wide array of perspectives. Furthermore, such leaders are self-aware, recognizing their own biases and emotions, and they prioritize the practical implications of their decisions. These qualities are vital in the workplace as they contribute to creating a culture of trust, openness, and effective decision-making, which are essential components of organizational well-being.

Good judgment at the workplace is multifaceted and involves several levels, including learning, trust, experience, detachment, options, and delivery. Leaders who excel in these areas are not only knowledgeable but also critical thinkers who challenge their assumptions and seek diverse perspectives (Kets de Vries, 2006; Schein, 2010). Effective leaders understand the importance of continuous learning, building and maintaining trust, leveraging experience, remaining detached when necessary, exploring multiple options, and executing their decisions proficiently (Kets de Vries, 2006; Schein, 2010).They avoid the trap of information overload by focusing on the most critical issues and by engaging in active listening, which involves understanding what is not said and interpreting non-verbal cues. By fostering an environment where diverse opinions are valued and skepticism is encouraged, leaders can enhance their judgment and, consequently, the well-being of their organizations. This approach aligns with the principles of positive psychology, where the cultivation of virtues like wisdom—of which judgment is a core component—contributes to both individual and collective well-being in the workplace (Peterson & Seligman, 2004).

Love of Learning and Wellbeing at Workplace

The Love of Learning is intricately linked to several cognitive and psychological factors that can significantly enhance workplace well-being. It fosters cognitive flexibility, enabling individuals to adapt to new information and switch between tasks with ease. This adaptability is crucial in dynamic work environments where employees must frequently adjust to changes and innovations (Kray et al., 2008). Additionally, Love of Learning is a fundamental component of intellectual curiosity, driving individuals to explore new ideas and concepts. This curiosity can lead to continuous improvement and innovation in the workplace, making employees more engaged and motivated (Kashdan & Ciarrochi, 2013).

Moreover, those who embody a Love of Learning often possess a growth mindset—the belief that abilities and intelligence can be developed through effort and learning (Dweck, 2006). This mindset encourages resilience and persistence, which are essential for overcoming challenges in the workplace. Love of Learning is also associated with creativity, which contributes to generating new and original ideas that can enhance problem-solving and innovation within teams (Amabile, 1996). These qualities are particularly beneficial in careers that require continuous learning, such as in science, engineering, and the arts (Peterson & Seligman, 2004).

In practice, fostering a Love of Learning in the workplace can lead to a more motivated and adaptable workforce. By encouraging employees to take classes, explore new areas, and engage in intellectual discussions, organizations can cultivate an environment where continuous learning is valued. This not only enhances individual growth but also contributes to a sense of purpose and meaning in work, which is closely linked to overall well-being (Seligman et al., 2005). By aligning with these practices, organizations can create a culture that supports lifelong learning, ultimately leading to a more engaged, innovative, and resilient workforce.

Wisdom and Happiness in the Workplace

The link between wisdom and happiness is still an under-explored area when it comes to how these two are being employed in organizations. Who stands accountable for ensuring and inculcating wisdom in organizations to maintain happiness among people who are working with those organizations? This question will be explored in this chapter in detail to advocate the accountability on each unit of the organization in ensuring the display of wisdom at different levels and various context.

Another question that this chapter aims to delve into is to establish the links between happiness and the components of wisdom and explore the multi-fold effects of employing wisdom in organizations.

Employees who exhibit high levels of creativity, curiosity, judgment, love of learning, and perspective tend to report higher levels of job satisfaction and overall wellbeing (Avey et al., 2011). Creativity, for example, not only leads to innovative solutions, but also provides a sense of accomplishment and pride, contributing to happiness. When employees are encouraged to express their creativity, they feel valued and appreciated, which enhances their overall job satisfaction (Dziuba et al., 2020).

Curiosity fosters a sense of adventure and excitement in the workplace. Curious employees are more likely to engage in activities that challenge and stimulate them, leading to higher job satisfaction (Huang, 2021). Additionally, curious employees often build stronger relationships with their colleagues as their interest in others fosters a more connected and collaborative work environment (Scott & Manning, 2022). Good judgment contributes to happiness by enabling employees to make decisions aligned with their values and goals. When employees feel confident in their decision-making abilities, they experience less stress and anxiety, which leads to higher levels of well-being (Monteiro & Joseph, 2023).

Love of learning is intrinsically linked to personal fulfillment. Employees who are passionate about learning continuously seek opportunities for growth, which enhances their sense of purpose and satisfaction in their roles (Pradhan et al., 2017). Organizations that support and encourage learning create an environment in which employees feel empowered to develop their skills and pursue their own interests.

As a component of wisdom, perspective allows employees to navigate workplace challenges with a broader understanding of the context (Lynn et al., 2023). This ability to see a bigger picture reduces stress and fosters a sense of empathy and compassion, contributing to a more harmonious and supportive work environment.

Enhancing Employee Engagement Through Wisdom

Based upon the discussion of various components involved in wisdom and their associations with different facets of happiness, this chapter will propose a conceptual model on how wisdom plays a crucial role in maintaining happiness in organizations and how different levels could ensure employing different components of well-being to foster the happy organizational environment (Ardelt, 2003; Glück & Baltes, 2006; Seligman, 2011). This model will highlight the interconnectedness between wisdom and organizational happiness, showing how wisdom contributes to creating and sustaining a positive workplace atmosphere (Ardelt, 2003; Seligman, 2011).

Effective Strategies for Cultivating Wisdom

To enhance the well-being of an organization, it is vital to implement practical strategies that encourage the development of wisdom among employees. Further, this chapter will try to propose some strategies based upon proposed conceptual model to foster wisdom among their employees.

To enhance the well-being of an organization through the development of wisdom among employees, different strategies can be tailored to the specific needs and contexts of various types of organizations. Below are some proposed strategies, categorized by the type of organization:

1. *Corporate Organizations (e.g., Large Corporations, Multinational Companies)*
   • Mentorship Programs: Establish formal mentorship programs where experienced employees (mentors) guide less experienced ones (mentees), fostering the transfer of wisdom, creativity, and judgment (McKenna, 2018; Allen, Eby, O'Brien, & Lentz, 2008). Encourage mentors to share their experiences, challenges, and lessons learned (Ragins & Kram, 2007). • Continuous Learning and Development: Offer regular workshops and training sessions on critical thinking, ethical decision-making, and creativity (Braskamp, Trautvetter, & Ward, 2006; Mumford, 2011). Encourage employees to pursue certifications or courses that align with their professional growth and the company's goals (Sternberg, 2003).
   • Feedback Loops: Create robust feedback mechanisms that allow employees to reflect on their work, receive constructive feedback, and refine their decision-

making processes. This practice fosters perspective-taking and the continuous improvement of judgment (Anseel et al., 2015; Garvin, 1993).

2. *Nonprofit Organizations* • Values-Driven Leadership: Encourage leaders to model wisdom by integrating the organization's core values into decision-making processes (Sosik & Cameron, 2010; Treviño, Brown, & Hartman, 2003). Promote transparency, accountability, and ethical considerations in all organizational activities (Brown & Treviño, 2006). • Community Involvement: Facilitate opportunities for employees to engage with the community, whether through volunteering or collaborative projects. This helps employees develop a broader perspective and enhances their empathy, judgment, and connection to the organization's mission (Brudney, 2005; Grant, 2012). • Reflective Practices: Implement regular reflection sessions where employees can discuss challenges, successes, and lessons learned in a group setting (Schön, 1983; Gergen, McNamee, & Barrett, 2001). This communal reflection fosters the sharing of diverse perspectives and the development of wisdom. By creating a space for open dialogue and collective learning, organizations can enhance employees' ability to integrate experiences and insights into more effective and wise decision-making (Raelin, 2001).
3. *Educational Institutions* • Interdisciplinary Collaboration: Encourage collaboration across different departments or disciplines to stimulate creativity and broaden perspectives. Faculty and staff from diverse fields can share insights and approaches, fostering a richer understanding of complex problems (Katz & Martin, 1997; Page, 2007). Interdisciplinary collaboration can lead to innovative solutions and enhance employees' ability to approach challenges with a well-rounded perspective (Tushman & O'Reilly, 1996). • Critical Thinking Curriculum: Integrate courses or workshops that focus on critical thinking, ethical reasoning, and the development of wisdom into the curriculum. These can be mandatory for students and staff alike, promoting a culture of intellectual curiosity and judgment (Facione, 2015; Halpern, 2014). By embedding these elements into educational and professional development programs, organizations and institutions can foster a culture that values thoughtful decision-making and ethical considerations (Beyer, 1995; Paul & Elder, 2006). • Role Modeling by Educators: Educators should actively demonstrate wisdom in their teaching methods, interactions with students, and decision-making processes (Perry, 1970; Brookfield, 2017). They can share personal experiences that highlight the importance of curiosity, creativity, and perspective (Dewey, 1933; Schön, 1983).
4. *Healthcare Organizations* • Ethics Committees and Rounds: Regularly conduct ethics rounds where healthcare professionals discuss complex cases involving moral dilemmas. These discussions encourage the development of judgment,

empathy, and perspective among staff (Fallowfield et al., 2006; McCormick & Wocial, 2012). Ethics rounds provide a structured environment for exploring ethical issues, promoting reflective practice and enhancing moral reasoning (Lamb et al., 2017; Bebeau, 2002). • Wellness Programs: Implement wellness programs that focus on both physical and mental well-being, including stress management, mindfulness, and reflective practices. Encouraging self-care can enhance employees' ability to make wise decisions under pressure (Kabat-Zinn, 1990; Goleman, 2006). Wellness programs that address stress and promote mindfulness can improve emotional regulation and cognitive flexibility, which are critical for effective decision-making (Richardson & Rothstein, 2008; Shapiro, Astin, Bishop, & Cordova, 2005). • Patient-Centered Care Training: Provide training that emphasizes the importance of understanding patients' perspectives and needs. This approach helps healthcare workers develop empathy, judgment, and a holistic view of care (Epstein & Street, 2011; Lown, Rosen, & Marttila, 2011). Patient-centered care training fosters a deeper understanding of patients' experiences and enhances the overall quality of care by integrating patients' preferences and values into clinical decision-making (Epstein & Street, 2011; Lown et al., 2011).

5. *Small and Medium Enterprises (SMEs)* • Flexible Learning Opportunities: Offer employees access to various learning resources, such as online courses, workshops, and seminars, to foster continuous development of curiosity and love of learning, even on a limited budget (Noe, 2017; Rosenberg & Heimler, 2016). Providing flexible learning opportunities supports ongoing professional growth and helps employees adapt to evolving job demands (Noe, 2017; Rosenberg & Heimler, 2016). • Collaborative Decision-Making: Encourage a collaborative decision-making process where employees at all levels are involved in discussions about key issues. This practice helps in developing a shared perspective and wisdom across the organization (Edmondson & Harvey, 2017; Woolley et al., 2015). • Innovation Incentives: Create a culture that rewards creative problem-solving and innovation. Employees who propose new ideas or solutions should be recognized and supported, fostering an environment where creativity and wisdom are valued (Amabile & Pratt, 2016; Anderson et al., 2014).
6. *Government and Public Sector Organizations* • Policy Reflection and Review: Regularly review and reflect on existing policies and practices to ensure they align with the principles of wisdom, such as fairness, empathy, and long-term thinking. Involve employees in this process to foster a sense of ownership and accountability (Bazerman & Tenbrunsel, 2011; Sekerka & Bagozzi, 2007). • *Public Engagement:* Encourage employees to engage with the public to gain a deeper understanding of the community's needs and perspectives. This engagement can help employees develop empathy, judgment, and a more holistic

approach to their work (Beninger & Francis, 2018; Grant, 2012). • *Ethical Leadership Training*: Provide training programs for leaders that focus on ethical decision-making, empathy, and long-term vision. Leaders can then model these behaviors, fostering a culture of wisdom throughout the organization (Brown & Treviño, 2006; Neubert et al., 2009).

7. **Technology Companies** • *Innovation Hubs and Think Tanks:* Establish innovation hubs where employees can work on creative projects or explore new ideas. Encourage interdisciplinary collaboration to foster creativity and the development of new perspectives (Hargadon & Sutton, 2000; Tushman et al., 2010). • *Ethical AI and Technology Use*: Implement training and policies that emphasize the ethical use of technology, ensuring that employees consider the broader societal impact of their work. This fosters a sense of responsibility and wisdom in the creation and deployment of technology (Mittelstadt et al., 2016; Jobin et al., 2019). • *A Continuous Feedback Culture:* It is essential for fostering wisdom and authenticity within an organization. This culture emphasizes regular, constructive communication between employees at all levels, ensuring that feedback is part of the everyday work experience rather than an occasional event (London & Smither, 2002; Steelman et al., 2004). Here's how it can be effectively implemented, with a focus on intent and transparency:

1. Intentional Feedback

- *Purpose-Driven Communication*: Feedback should be given with a clear, constructive purpose. Employees should understand that the goal is to help them grow, improve their skills, and align with organizational values. These intent fosters trust and a willingness to engage with the feedback process (Ashford et al., 2003; Heen & Stone, 2014).
- *Focus on Growth*: Frame feedback as an opportunity for professional and personal growth. Rather than just pointing out mistakes, highlight areas where employees can develop their strengths and enhance their judgment, creativity, and problem-solving abilities (Hattie & Timperley, 2007; Dweck, 2006).
- *Consistency:* Regular, timely feedback ensures that employees can make adjustments and improvements continuously, rather than waiting for annual reviews. This ongoing process helps integrate wisdom into daily decision-making and actions (Breevaart et al., 2014; Stone & Heen, 2014).

2. Creating an Environment of Authenticity

- *Transparency in Communication*: Leaders should model transparency by openly sharing information about decisions, challenges, and organizational goals. This openness encourages employees to be honest and forthcoming in their feedback and interactions (Men, 2014; Edmonson, 2019).

- *Encouraging Vulnerability*: Cultivate an environment where employees feel safe to express their thoughts, concerns, and mistakes without fear of retribution. When leaders show vulnerability, admitting their own challenges and learning moments, it sets the tone for a more authentic workplace (Brown, 2018; Rhoades & Eisenberger, 2002).
- *Open Dialogue:* Establish regular forums, such as town halls or team meetings, where employees can voice their opinions and ask questions in a transparent manner. This openness fosters mutual respect and a deeper understanding of different perspectives within the organization (Kernaghan, 2003; Edmondson & Mogelof, 2006).

3. Transparency in Feedback Processes

- *Clear Criteria and Expectations*: Employees should know the criteria by which they are being evaluated and the expectations set for their roles. This transparency reduces ambiguity and helps them understand the feedback in the context of their professional development (Pulakos et al., 2015; London & Smither, 1999).
- *Feedback from Multiple Sources*: Implement 360-degree feedback mechanisms where employees receive input from peers, subordinates, and supervisors. This approach provides a well-rounded view of their performance and helps in cultivating perspective and wisdom (London, 2003; Smither et al., 2005).
- *Actionable Feedback*: Ensure that feedback is specific, actionable, and linked to clear outcomes. Employees should know what steps to take to improve, which enhances their ability to learn from the feedback and apply it effectively (Hattie & Timperley, 2007; Kluger & DeNisi, 1996).

4. Fostering Trust and Mutual Respect

- *Building Trust*: Trust is the foundation of a continuous feedback culture. Employees are more likely to accept and act on feedback when they believe it comes from a place of mutual respect and genuine concern for their development (Dirks & Ferrin, 2002; Mayer et al., 1995).
- **Recognition and Acknowledgment**: Regularly recognize and celebrate improvements and successes that result from acting on feedback. This positive reinforcement strengthens the feedback loop and encourages ongoing participation (Deci & Ryan, 2000; McNall et al., 2011).

- **Long-Term Relationships**: Encourage the development of long-term, trust-based relationships between employees and their managers. This continuity helps ensure that feedback is not only consistent but also contextually relevant and aligned with the employee's career trajectory (Eisenberger et al., 2001; Brees et al., 2014).
- By fostering a Continuous Feedback Culture with a focus on intent and transparency, organizations can create an environment of authenticity where employees feel valued, understood, and empowered to grow. This approach not only enhances individual wisdom but also contributes to a more dynamic, resilient, and effective organization (Edmondson, 2019; Kluger & DeNisi, 1996; Men, 2014).

5. Creative Industries (e.g., Media, Advertising, Design)

- **Creative Workshops and Retreats**: Organize workshops or retreats focused on creativity, where employees can experiment with new ideas in a low-pressure environment. These activities can foster a sense of curiosity and innovation (Amabile & Kramer, 2010; Csikszentmihalyi, 1996).
- **Diverse Team Collaboration**: Encourage collaboration between teams with diverse backgrounds and expertise. This cross-pollination of ideas can lead to innovative solutions and a broader perspective on creative challenges (Page, 2007; Woolley et al., 2010).
- **Storytelling as a Tool for Wisdom**: Use storytelling as a method to share experiences and lessons learned within the organization. Employees can share their stories in meetings or through internal communications, fostering a culture of shared wisdom (Denning, 2011; Gabriel, 2000).

These strategies, tailored to different organizational contexts, can help foster wisdom among employees, ultimately enhancing the well-being and success of the organization.

How Each Level of Unit Is Responsible in Ensuring the Application of the Proposed Strategies?

To foster character strengths of wisdom at different organizational levels, strategies should be tailored to each unit and level, with clear responsibilities assigned. Here's a breakdown:

1. Top Leadership (Executives, C-Suite)

Strategy: Establish a Vision of Wisdom
Responsibility: Set the tone by incorporating wisdom into the organization's mission and strategic goals. Leaders should model wise decision-making, emphasizing long-term thinking, ethical considerations, and creativity.
Actions: Create policies and initiatives that promote continuous learning, curiosity, and ethical practices. Regularly communicate the importance of wisdom in achieving organizational success.

2. Middle Management (Department Heads, Managers)

Strategy: Implement Mentorship and Development Programs
Responsibility: Facilitate the development of wisdom by mentoring team members, providing opportunities for professional growth, and encouraging the application of judgment in decision-making.
Actions: Organize workshops and training sessions focused on critical thinking, ethical reasoning, and creative problem-solving. Ensure that teams have the resources and support needed to develop these skills.

3. Team Leaders (Supervisors, Project Leaders)

Strategy: Foster a Continuous Feedback Culture
Responsibility: Create an environment where team members receive regular, constructive feedback that promotes the development of wisdom-related strengths like judgment, perspective, and creativity.
Actions: Hold regular one-on-one meetings to discuss individual growth, encourage team discussions on challenges and lessons learned, and recognize efforts to apply wisdom in daily tasks.

4. Individual Contributors (Employees)

Strategy: Encourage Self-Reflection and Lifelong Learning
Responsibility: Take personal responsibility for developing wisdom by engaging in self-reflection, seeking out learning opportunities, and applying wisdom in their roles.
Actions: Set personal goals for learning and development, participate actively in training programs, and apply insights from feedback to improve judgment and decision-making.

5. Human Resources (HR)

Strategy: Integrate Wisdom into Recruitment and Retention
Responsibility: Ensure that the hiring process and employee retention strategies prioritize candidates and employees who demonstrate wisdom-related strengths.
Actions: Design interview questions and assessments that evaluate candidates' judgment, creativity, and ethical reasoning. Provide ongoing support and resources for employees to continue developing these strengths.

6. Organizational Culture (Across All Levels)

Strategy: Embed Wisdom in the Organizational Culture
Responsibility: Ensure that wisdom is a core value that permeates all levels of the organization. Everyone shares responsibility for promoting and practicing wisdom in their daily work.
Actions: Create shared spaces for reflection, such as regular team meetings or organizational retreats, where wisdom-related themes are discussed. Celebrate successes that result from wise decisions and encourage storytelling as a way to share lessons learned.

7. Units and Departments

Strategy: Tailor Wisdom Development to Specific Functions
Responsibility: Each department should identify how wisdom applies to their specific functions and create targeted strategies to develop relevant strengths.
Actions: For example, in R&D, focus on fostering creativity and curiosity; in Finance, emphasize ethical reasoning and long-term judgment; in Sales, cultivate perspective and empathy in understanding customer needs.

By implementing these strategies at different levels of the organization and assigning clear responsibilities, organizations can effectively foster the character strengths of wisdom, leading to more thoughtful, ethical, and innovative decision-making across all units.

CONCLUSION

The role of character strengths in fostering wisdom and achieving happiness in organizations is profound and transformative. By embedding virtues such as creativity, curiosity, judgment, love of learning, and perspective within the organizational culture, companies can build a foundation for sustainable success and employee well-being (Psychologist, 2024). These virtues not only contribute to individual development but also enhance collective wisdom, leading to more ethical, innovative, and effective organizational practices (Riivari & Lämsä, 2017).

Wisdom as a Strategic Asset in Organizations: Wisdom, when seen as a strategic asset, extends beyond individual traits to encompass organizational culture and values (Butt et al., 2024). Creativity allows organizations to innovate and adapt, ensuring long-term competitiveness (Rumanti et al., 2023). Curiosity drives continuous improvement and exploration, encouraging employees to seek out new knowledge and perspectives. Sound judgment ensures decisions are made with ethical considerations and long-term impacts in mind, balancing immediate needs with future goals (Chang & Shih, 2019). Love of learning fosters a culture of growth, where employees are encouraged to develop their skills and knowledge continuously. Perspective, as a meta-cognitive strength, helps individuals and organizations understand complex situations, facilitating more informed and empathetic decision-making (Moudatsou et al., 2020).

The Interplay between Wisdom and Happiness: The interplay between wisdom and happiness is critical for organizational success. Organizations that cultivate wisdom through character strengths create environments where employees feel fulfilled, valued, and engaged (Fisher, 2010). This sense of fulfillment is a key driver of workplace happiness, leading to higher levels of job satisfaction, reduced stress, and increased productivity. Happiness in the workplace is a complex construct, influenced by both intrinsic factors, such as the fulfillment of character strengths, and extrinsic factors, such as rewards and recognition (Baregheh et al., 2009). By aligning organizational practices with the cultivation of wisdom, companies can enhance employee well-being, resulting in a more positive and productive work environment (Klajkó et al., 2019).

A Model for Fostering Wisdom and Happiness in Organizations

To operationalize these ideas, authors propose a model for fostering wisdom and happiness in organizations, based on the integration of character strengths into organizational practices.

1. The Foundation: Cultivating Core Character Strengths

- *Creativity:* Implement programs that encourage creative problem-solving, such as innovation labs or design thinking workshops. These initiatives should involve cross-functional teams to foster diverse perspectives.

- *Curiosity:* Promote a culture of inquiry by offering continuous learning opportunities, such as professional development courses, seminars, and access to knowledge resources. Encourage employees to ask questions and challenge the status quo.
- *Judgment:* Establish ethical decision-making frameworks and provide training on critical thinking and moral reasoning. Leaders should model sound judgment in their decision-making processes.
- *Love of Learning:* Develop a comprehensive learning and development strategy that includes mentoring, coaching, and personalized learning paths. Recognize and reward employees who actively pursue personal and professional growth.
- *Perspective:* Foster an inclusive environment where diverse viewpoints are valued. Encourage reflective practices, such as regular feedback sessions and discussions on long-term organizational goals.

2. The Structure: Embedding Wisdom Into Organizational Practices

- *Leadership Development:* Cultivate ethical leadership by integrating character strengths into leadership development programs. Leaders should be trained to recognize and promote wisdom within their teams, ensuring that decisions are aligned with the organization's values.
- *Decision-Making Processes*: Implement decision-making processes that prioritize wisdom. This includes considering the long-term impact of decisions, the ethical implications, and the well-being of all stakeholders.
- *Innovation and Ethics*: Ensure that innovation is guided by ethical considerations. This involves creating a balance between technological advancement and the responsible use of technology, ensuring that innovation contributes to societal well-being.
- *Public Engagement*: Engage with external stakeholders, including customers, communities, and industry partners, to ensure that organizational practices are transparent, ethical, and aligned with broader societal values.

3. The Outcomes: Achieving Organizational Happiness

- *Employee Well-Being:* Regularly assess and address the well-being of employees through surveys, feedback mechanisms, and wellness programs. A happy workforce is more engaged, productive, and loyal.
- *Sustainable Success*: Measure organizational success not only by financial metrics but also by the well-being of employees, customer satisfaction, and

societal impact. This holistic approach ensures that the organization is not only profitable but also sustainable and responsible.

- *Continuous Improvement*: Regularly review and refine the model based on feedback and changing organizational needs. Wisdom is a dynamic virtue, and organizations must remain flexible and adaptable to maintain their competitive edge.

By integrating character strengths into organizational culture and practices, companies can cultivate wisdom and achieve happiness at all levels. This model provides a structured approach to embedding wisdom into the fabric of the organization, ensuring that decisions are made with integrity, innovation is pursued responsibly, and employees are empowered to grow and thrive. As organizations navigate the complexities of the modern world, this wisdom-centered approach will be essential for long-term success and the well-being of all stakeholders.

CASE STUDY: PATAGONIA

Background

Patagonia, the outdoor apparel company founded by Yvon Chouinard in 1973, is renowned not only for its high-quality products but also for its strong commitment to environmental sustainability and ethical business practices. Over the years, Patagonia has become a model organization in which the virtue of wisdom is deeply embedded in its culture, guiding both its business decisions and the well-being of its employees.

Creativity and Innovation

Patagonia's success is rooted in its embrace of creativity and innovation, key components of the wisdom virtue. The company encourages its employees to think creatively and to come up with innovative solutions to complex problems, particularly those related to sustainability. For instance, Patagonia was one of the first companies to switch to organic cotton for all of its cotton products, a decision driven by a creative approach to addressing environmental concerns. This innovative mindset not only sets Patagonia apart in the marketplace but also fosters a sense of pride and purpose among its employees. Knowing they are contributing to meaningful environmental initiatives enhances their sense of fulfillment and engagement at work.

Curiosity and Continuous Learning

Curiosity, another strength under the virtue of wisdom, is actively encouraged at Patagonia. The company invests in the continuous learning and development of its employees, offering opportunities for them to expand their knowledge and skills. For example, Patagonia provides access to training programs, workshops, and even financial support for employees who wish to pursue further education. This commitment to learning is reflected in the company's open culture, where employees are encouraged to ask questions, seek out new ideas, and challenge the status quo. By fostering curiosity, Patagonia ensures that its employees remain engaged and motivated, which significantly contributes to their overall well-being and satisfaction.

Judgment and Ethical Decision-Making

Judgment, or the ability to make sound and ethical decisions, is at the core of Patagonia's business strategy. The company is known for its principled stance on various social and environmental issues, often making decisions that prioritize ethical considerations over short-term profits. A notable example is Patagonia's "Don't Buy This Jacket" campaign, which encouraged consumers to think twice before making unnecessary purchases, thereby reducing environmental impact. This campaign was a demonstration of wise judgment in action, reflecting the company's commitment to its values. Employees at Patagonia are empowered to make decisions aligned with the company's ethical standards, fostering a strong sense of trust and integrity within the organization. This ethical alignment contributes to a positive work environment where employees feel proud of the organization they work for, boosting their overall happiness and sense of purpose.

Love of Learning and Personal Growth

Patagonia places a strong emphasis on the love of learning, encouraging employees to pursue personal and professional growth. The company's approach to employee development goes beyond traditional training, incorporating experiential learning and opportunities for employees to engage in activities that align with their passions. For instance, Patagonia's Environmental Internship Program allows employees to take up to two months off with full pay to work on environmental projects of their choosing. This unique program not only supports the love of learning but also aligns with employees' values, allowing them to contribute to causes they care about. This focus on personal growth and alignment with values contributes significantly to employee satisfaction and well-being, as it creates a work environment where individuals feel supported in both their professional and personal endeavors.

Perspective and Long-Term Vision

Perspective, or the ability to see the bigger picture, is a key strength that Patagonia harnesses to guide its long-term vision. The company is known for its commitment to sustainability and environmental stewardship, often taking a long-term view in its business decisions. Patagonia's mission statement, "We're in business to save our home planet," reflects this broader perspective, guiding the company's actions and priorities. This long-term vision is communicated clearly to employees, helping them to understand the impact of their work within a larger context. By aligning individual roles with the company's broader mission, Patagonia fosters a sense of purpose and meaning among its employees. This sense of purpose is a critical factor in employee well-being, as it allows individuals to feel that their work contributes to something greater than themselves.

Impact on Employee Well-Being and Happiness

The cultivation of the wisdom virtue through these character strengths has had a profound impact on the well-being and happiness of Patagonia's employees. The company's commitment to creativity, curiosity, judgment, love of learning, and perspective creates a work environment where employees feel valued, supported, and engaged. This positive work environment is reflected in the high levels of employee satisfaction and loyalty at Patagonia. The company consistently ranks highly in employee satisfaction surveys and is recognized as a top employer in various rankings.

Moreover, Patagonia's focus on ethical practices and environmental sustainability resonates deeply with its employees, many of whom are passionate about these issues. This alignment between personal values and organizational mission enhances employee well-being by providing a strong sense of purpose and fulfillment. Employees at Patagonia are not only proud of the work they do but also feel that their contributions are making a positive impact on the world, which is a key driver of happiness and well-being.

In conclusion, Patagonia serves as a powerful example of how the wisdom virtue, when harnessed through creativity, curiosity, judgment, love of learning, and perspective, can significantly boost the well-being and happiness of employees. By creating a work environment that prioritizes these strengths, Patagonia has cultivated a positive organizational culture where employees feel engaged, fulfilled, and aligned with the company's mission. This case study underscores the importance of integrating the wisdom virtue into organizational practices to foster a thriving and supportive work environment.

As we conclude this exploration of wisdom as a virtue in organizational settings, the case study of Patagonia stands as a powerful testament to the transformative potential of integrating character strengths into the fabric of a company's culture. Throughout this chapter, we have examined the critical role that creativity, curiosity, judgment, love of learning, and perspective play in fostering a work environment that not only drives business success but also promotes the well-being and happiness of employees. The discussion has underscored that these strengths—when intentionally cultivated—can create a foundation for wise leadership, ethical decision-making, and sustainable growth, all of which are essential for thriving organizations in today's complex and rapidly changing world.

Patagonia's example reinforces the central argument of this chapter: wisdom is not merely an abstract ideal but a practical, actionable virtue that can be operationalized through the deliberate fostering of specific character strengths. By prioritizing these strengths, Patagonia has created a culture where employees are deeply engaged, motivated, and aligned with the company's mission. This alignment has not only driven Patagonia's success as a business but has also ensured that its employees find meaning, purpose, and satisfaction in their work—key components of both individual and collective well-being.

The implications of this case study extend beyond the confines of a single organization. For leaders and managers, the lessons from Patagonia provide a roadmap for cultivating wisdom in their own organizations. By embedding creativity, curiosity, judgment, love of learning, and perspective into their organizational practices, leaders can foster an environment that supports innovation, ethical behavior, and continuous growth—both for their employees and for the organization as a whole.

As we have seen, creativity fuels the innovative processes that are vital for maintaining a competitive edge, while curiosity drives the continuous improvement necessary for adapting to change. Judgment ensures that decisions are made with integrity and foresight, safeguarding the ethical foundations of the organization. The love of learning keeps employees engaged and growing, contributing to a dynamic and resilient workforce. Finally, perspective allows organizations to maintain a long-term vision, aligning daily operations with broader, more sustainable goals.

In sum, the integration of wisdom into organizational life is not just desirable—it is essential. It creates a culture where employees are not only productive but also deeply connected to their work, their colleagues, and the organization's mission. This connection is the cornerstone of a thriving workplace, where happiness and well-being are not afterthoughts but integral components of the organization's success.

As we close this chapter, the message is clear: fostering wisdom through the development of key character strengths is a pathway to both organizational excellence and employee well-being. The case of Patagonia serves as a beacon, demonstrating that when wisdom is embraced as a core organizational value, the benefits are profound and far-reaching. For organizations seeking to cultivate a positive, ethical, and sustainable culture, the lessons from Patagonia offer a practical guide—and a compelling call to action. By committing to the development of wisdom, organizations can create environments where both people and profits can flourish, ensuring success and happiness at all levels.

REFERENCES

Amabile, T. M., & Kramer, S. J. (2010). *The progress principle: Using small wins to ignite joy, engagement, and creativity at work*. Harvard Business Review Press.

Amabile, T. M., & Pratt, M. G. (2016). The dynamic componential model of creativity and innovation in organizations: Making progress, making meaning. *Research in Organizational Behavior*, 36, 157–183. DOI: 10.1016/j.riob.2016.10.001

Anderson, N., Potočnik, K., & Zhou, J. (2014). Innovation and creativity in organizations: A state-of-the-science review, prospective commentary, and guiding framework. *Journal of Management*, 40(5), 1297–1333. DOI: 10.1177/0149206314527128

Anseel, F., Lievens, F., Schollaert, E., & Choragwicka, B. (2015). Feedback-seeking behavior as a response to negative feedback: The role of feedback environment and personal attributes. *The Journal of Applied Psychology*, 100(1), 266–283. DOI: 10.1037/a0036832

Ardelt, M. (2003). Empirical assessment of a three-dimensional wisdom scale. *Personality and Individual Differences*, 34(7), 1279–1293. DOI: 10.1016/S0191-8869(02)00158-6

Ashford, S. J., & DeRue, D. S. (2012). Developing as a leader: The power of mindful engagement. *Organizational Dynamics*, 41(2), 146–154. DOI: 10.1016/j.orgdyn.2012.01.008

Avey, J. B., Luthans, F., Hannah, S. T., Sweetman, D., & Peterson, C. (2011). Impact of employees' character strengths of wisdom on stress and creative performance. *Human Resource Management Journal*, 22(2), 165–181. DOI: 10.1111/j.1748-8583.2010.00157.x

Baer, M., & Oldham, G. R. (2006). The impact of negative workplace gossip on employee creativity. *The Journal of Applied Psychology*, 91(1), 109–118. DOI: 10.1037/0021-9010.91.1.109 PMID: 16435942

Baregheh, A., Rowley, J., & Sambrook, S. (2009). Towards a multidisciplinary definition of innovation. *Management Decision*, 47(8), 1323–1339. DOI: 10.1108/00251740910984578

Bazerman, M. H., & Tenbrunsel, A. E. (2011). *Blind spots: Why we fail to do what's right and what to do about it*. Princeton University Press. DOI: 10.1515/9781400837991

Bebeau, M. J. (2002). The role of ethics in clinical practice: Lessons from a case study. *Journal of Dental Education*, 66(12), 1297–1306.

Beninger, S., & Francis, J. N. P. (2018). On being fair: Cultural self-construals and public engagement. *Journal of Business Research*, 82, 197–206. DOI: 10.1016/j.jbusres.2017.09.043

Bennis, W. (2009). *On becoming a leader* (4th ed.). Basic Books.

Beyer, B. K. (1995). *Critical Thinking*. Phi Delta Kappa Educational Foundation.

Braskamp, L. A., Trautvetter, L. C., & Ward, K. (2006). *Putting students first: How colleges develop students purposefully*. Anker Publishing Company.

Braskamp, L. A., Trautvetter, L. C., & Ward, K. (2006). *Putting students first: How colleges develop students purposefully*. Anker Publishing Company.

Brees, J. R., & Brees, D. S. (2014). *Managing employee performance: A practical approach*. Routledge.

Breevaart, K., Bakker, A. B., Demerouti, E., & Derks, D. (2014). Daily feedback and employee engagement: The role of work-related flow. *Journal of Occupational Health Psychology*, 19(4), 428–438. DOI: 10.1037/a0037196

Brookfield, S. D. (2017). *Becoming a Critically Reflective Teacher*. Jossey-Bass.

Brown, B. (2018). *Dare to lead: Brave work. Tough conversations. Whole hearts.* Random House.

Brudney, J. L. (2005). The impact of organizational involvement in community service on the development of employee skills and relationships. *Public Administration Review*, 65(5), 545–556.

Butt, A., Imran, F., Helo, P., & Kantola, J. (2024). Strategic design of culture for digital transformation. *Long Range Planning*, 57(2), 102415. DOI: 10.1016/j.lrp.2024.102415

Carmeli, A., & Spreitzer, G. M. (2009). Trust, connectivity, and creativity: The role of affective and cognitive trust in the workplace. *Journal of Organizational Behavior*, 30(6), 941–962. DOI: 10.1002/job.586

Chang, Y. Y., & Shih, H. Y. (2019). Work curiosity: A new lens for understanding employee creativity. *Human Resource Management Review*, 29(4), 100672. DOI: 10.1016/j.hrmr.2018.10.005

Cheng, H., Li, Z., Zhao, J., Wang, W., & Zou, R. (2022). The role of cognition, affect, and resources in the influence of unreasonable tasks on work engagement: A moderated chain mediation model. *Frontiers in Psychology*, 13, 1013773. Advance online publication. DOI: 10.3389/fpsyg.2022.1013773 PMID: 36275277

Chughtai, M. S., Syed, F., Naseer, S., & Chinchilla, N. (2023). Role of adaptive leadership in learning organizations to boost organizational innovations with change self-efficacy. *Current Psychology (New Brunswick, N.J.)*. Advance online publication. DOI: 10.1007/s12144-023-04669-z PMID: 37359696

Csikszentmihalyi, M. (1996). *Creativity: Flow and the psychology of discovery and invention*. HarperCollins.

Deci, E. L., & Ryan, R. M. (2000). The 'what' and 'why' of goal pursuits: Human needs and the self-determination of behavior. *Psychological Inquiry*, 11(4), 227–268. DOI: 10.1207/S15327965PLI1104_01

Denning, S. (2011). *The secret language of leadership: How leaders inspire action through narrative*. Jossey-Bass.

Dewey, J. (1933). *How We Think*. D.C. Heath and Company.

Dirks, K. T., & Ferrin, D. L. (2002). Trust in leadership: Meta-analytic findings and implications for research and practice. *The Journal of Applied Psychology*, 87(4), 611–628. DOI: 10.1037/0021-9010.87.4.611 PMID: 12184567

Dweck, C. S. (2006). *Mindset: The new psychology of success*. Random House.

Dziuba, S. T., Ingaldi, M., & Zhuravskaya, M. (2020). Employees' Job Satisfaction and their Work Performance as Elements Influencing Work Safety. System Safety Human - Technical Facility - Environment, 2(1), 18–25. DOI: 10.2478/czoto-2020-0003

Edmondson, A. (2019). *The fearless organization: Creating psychological safety in the workplace for learning, innovation, and growth*. Wiley.

Edmondson, A. (2019). *The fearless organization: Creating psychological safety in the workplace for learning, innovation, and growth*. Wiley.

Edmondson, A., & Mogelof, J. P. (2006). Explaining psychological safety in the workplace: A conceptual model. *Journal of Organizational Behavior*, 27(3), 367–391. DOI: 10.1002/job.383

Edmondson, A. C., & Harvey, J. F. (2017). *Extreme teaming: Lessons in complex, cross-sector leadership*. Emerald Publishing Limited. DOI: 10.1108/9781786354495

Eisenberger, R., Huntington, R., Hutchison, S., & Sowa, D. (2001). Perceived organizational support. *The Journal of Applied Psychology*, 71(3), 500–507. DOI: 10.1037/0021-9010.71.3.500 PMID: 11302232

Epstein, R. M., & Street, R. L. (2011). Patient-centered communication in cancer care: Promoting healing and reducing suffering. National Cancer Institute. https://www.cancer.gov/about-cancer/coping/feelings/patient-centered-care

Eysenck, M. W. (1995). *Personality and Individual Differences: Current Issues*. Wiley.

Facione, P. A. (2015). *Critical Thinking: What It Is and Why It Counts*. Measured Reasons.

Fallowfield, L., Jenkins, V., & Farewell, V. (2006). Eliciting patients' preferences for treatment: A review of the evidence for best practice. *Journal of Clinical Oncology*, 24(15), 2420–2426.

Fisher, C. D. (2010). Happiness at Work. *International Journal of Management Reviews*, 12(4), 384–412. DOI: 10.1111/j.1468-2370.2009.00270.x

Gabriel, Y. (2000). *Storytelling in organizations: Facts, fictions, and fantasies*. Oxford University Press. DOI: 10.1093/acprof:oso/9780198290957.001.0001

Garvin, D. A. (1993). Building a learning organization. *Harvard Business Review*, 71(4), 78–91. PMID: 10127041

Gergen, K. J., McNamee, S., & Barrett, F. J. (2001). Toward transformative dialogue. *International Journal of Public Administration*, 24(7-8), 679–707. DOI: 10.1081/PAD-100104770

Glomb, T. M., & Liao, H. (2003). Interpersonal aggression in the workplace: A review and proposed framework. *The Academy of Management Annals*, 2(1), 225–266. DOI: 10.5465/19416520328158712

Glück, J., & Baltes, P. B. (2006). The two faces of wisdom: A framework for understanding the nature and development of wisdom. In Sternberg, R. J. (Ed.), *Handbook of wisdom: Theory, research, and applications* (pp. 215–236). Cambridge University Press.

Glück, J., & Weststrate, N. M. (2022). The Wisdom Researchers and The Elephant: An Integrative Model of wise Behavior. *Personality and Social Psychology Review*, 26(4), 342–374. DOI: 10.1177/10888683221094650 PMID: 35652684

Goleman, D. (2006). *Emotional Intelligence: Why It Can Matter More Than IQ*. Bantam Books.

Grant, A. M. (2012). *Give and take: A revolutionary approach to success*. Viking.

Grant, A. M. (2012). Leading with meaning: Beneficiary contact, prosocial impact, and the performance effects of transformational leadership. *Academy of Management Journal*, 55(2), 458–476. DOI: 10.5465/amj.2010.0588

Halpern, D. F. (2014). *Thought and Knowledge: An Introduction to Critical Thinking*. Psychology Press.

Hargadon, A., & Sutton, R. I. (2000). Building an innovation factory. *Harvard Business Review*, 78(3), 157–166. PMID: 11183977

Harrison, S. H., & Dossinger, K. (2017). Curiosity in the workplace: A model of curiosity and its role in work outcomes. *Journal of Organizational Behavior*, 38(1), 100–118.

Hattie, J., & Timperley, H. (2007). The power of feedback. *Review of Educational Research*, 77(1), 81–112. DOI: 10.3102/003465430298487

Hattie, J., & Timperley, H. (2007). The power of feedback. *Review of Educational Research*, 77(1), 81–112. DOI: 10.3102/003465430298487

Huang, Q. (2021). Can Curious Employees be More Innovative? Exploring the Mechanism of Intrinsic Motivation and Job Autonomy. *Psychology (Irvine, Calif.)*, 12(03), 425–440. DOI: 10.4236/psych.2021.123027

Jobin, A., Ienca, M., & Vayena, E. (2019). The global landscape of AI ethics guidelines. *Nature Machine Intelligence*, 1(9), 389–399. DOI: 10.1038/s42256-019-0088-2

Kabat-Zinn, J. (1990). *Full Catastrophe Living: Using the Wisdom of Your Body and Mind to Face Stress, Pain, and Illness*. Dell Publishing.

Kashdan, T. B., & Fincham, F. D. (2004). Facilitating curiosity: A social and self-regulatory perspective for scientifically based interventions. Positive Psychology in Practice, 482-503.

Kashdan, T. B., Rose, P., & Fincham, F. D. (2004). Curiosity and exploration: Facilitating positive subjective experiences and personal growth opportunities. *Journal of Personality Assessment*, 82(3), 291–305. DOI: 10.1207/s15327752jpa8203_05 PMID: 15151805

Kashdan, T. B., Sherman, R. A., Yarbro, J., & Funder, D. C. (2013). On the uniqueness of joy: Examining the importance of distinguishing between joy and happiness. *The Journal of Positive Psychology*, 8(3), 221–232.

Kashdan, T. B., & Steger, M. F. (2007). Curiosity and pathways to well-being and meaning in life: Traits, states, and everyday behaviors. *Motivation and Emotion*, 31(3), 159–173. DOI: 10.1007/s11031-007-9068-7

Katz, J. S., & Martin, B. R. (1997). What is research collaboration? *Research Policy*, 26(1), 1–18. DOI: 10.1016/S0048-7333(96)00917-1

Kernaghan, K. (2003). Integrating values into public service: The role of leadership. *Canadian Public Administration*, 46(4), 517–533. DOI: 10.1111/j.1754-7121.2003.tb01020.x

Kets de Vries, M. F. R. (2006). The leadership mystique: Leading behavior in the human enterprise. Financial Times Prentice Hall.

Klajkó, D., Restás, P., Szabó, Z. P., & Czibor, A. (2019). The Effect of Organizational Culture on Employee Well-Being: Work- Related Stress, Employee. . . ResearchGate. https://www.researchgate.net/publication/339103130_The_Effect_of_Organizational_Culture_on_Employee_Well-Being_Work-_Related_Stress_Employee_Identification_Turnover_Intention

Kluger, A. N., & DeNisi, A. (1996). The effects of feedback interventions on performance: A historical review, a meta-analysis, and a preliminary feedback intervention theory. *Psychological Bulletin*, 119(2), 254–284. DOI: 10.1037/0033-2909.119.2.254

Kun, A., & Gadanecz, P. (2019). Workplace happiness, well-being and their relationship with psychological capital: A study of Hungarian Teachers. *Current Psychology (New Brunswick, N.J.)*, 41(1), 185–199. DOI: 10.1007/s12144-019-00550-0

Kuo, H. T., & Chang, H. H. (2015). How workplace aggression affects employee creativity: The moderating role of psychological safety. *International Journal of Conflict Management*, 26(3), 296–314. DOI: 10.1108/IJCMA-12-2014-0111

Lamb, S., Wocial, L., & McCormick, J. (2017). *Ethics Rounds: A Model for Teaching and Evaluating Ethics in Healthcare*. Springer.

Likierman, A. (2020, November 24). The elements of good judgment. Harvard Business Review. https://hbr.org/2020/01/the-elements-of-good-judgment

Litman, J. A. (2008). Interest and deprivation factors of epistemic curiosity. *Personality and Individual Differences*, 44(7), 1585–1595. DOI: 10.1016/j.paid.2008.01.014

London, M. (2003). *Job feedback: Giving, seeking, and using feedback for performance improvement*. Lawrence Erlbaum Associates. DOI: 10.4324/9781410608871

London, M., & Smither, J. W. (1999). The role of performance feedback in developing employees' performance. *The Journal of Applied Psychology*, 84(3), 546–553. DOI: 10.1037/0021-9010.84.3.546

London, M., & Smither, J. W. (2002). Feedback orientation, feedback culture, and the longitudinal performance management process. *Human Resource Management Review*, 12(1), 81–100. DOI: 10.1016/S1053-4822(01)00043-2

Lown, B. A., Rosen, J., & Marttila, J. (2011). The critical role of communication in patient-centered care. *Health Affairs*, 30(4), 628–633. DOI: 10.1377/hlthaff.2011.0019 PMID: 21471482

Lynn, T., Rosati, P., Conway, E., & Van Der Werff, L. (2023). The future of work. In Palgrave studies in digital business & enabling technologies. DOI: 10.1007/978-3-031-31494-0

Ma, Y., Zhang, H., & Dai, Y. (2021). How job creativity requirements Affects employee creativity: Evidence from a Across-Level analysis. *Frontiers in Psychology*, 12, 714886. Advance online publication. DOI: 10.3389/fpsyg.2021.714886 PMID: 35027897

Mayer, D. M., & Salvador, R. (2014). The role of workplace incivility in creativity: A longitudinal examination. *Journal of Management*, 40(1), 92–112. DOI: 10.1177/0149206312441022

Mayer, R. C., Davis, J. H., & Schoorman, F. D. (1995). An integrative model of organizational trust. *Academy of Management Review*, 20(3), 709–734. DOI: 10.2307/258792

McCormack, B., & McCance, T. V. (2017). *Person-Centred Practice in Nursing and Health Care: Theory and Practice*. Wiley-Blackwell. DOI: 10.1002/9781119099635

McCormick, J., & Wocial, L. (2012). Ethics rounds: A model for interdisciplinary ethics education in health care. *The Hastings Center Report*, 42(5), 15–18.

McLellan, J. (2004). Volunteering and community engagement: The role of the nonprofit sector in employee development. *Nonprofit and Voluntary Sector Quarterly*, 33(4), 573–594.

McNall, L. A., Masuda, A. D., & Nicklin, J. M. (2011). A meta-analysis of the relationship between work-to-family conflict and job performance. *The Journal of Applied Psychology*, 96(1), 193–207. DOI: 10.1037/a0020927

Men, L. R. (2014). The effects of organizational transparency on employees' trust and commitment. *Journal of Public Relations Research*, 26(2), 174–193. DOI: 10.1080/1062726X.2014.882571

Mittelstadt, B. D., Allo, P., Taddeo, M., Wachter, S., & Floridi, L. (2016). The ethics of algorithms: Mapping the debate. *Big Data & Society*, 3(2), 1–21. DOI: 10.1177/2053951716679679

Monteiro, E., & Joseph, J. (2023). A Review on the Impact of Workplace Culture on Employee Mental Health and Well-Being. International Journal of Case Studies in Business, IT, and Education, 291–317. DOI: 10.47992/IJCSBE.2581.6942.0274

Moudatsou, M., Stavropoulou, A., Philalithis, A., & Koukouli, S. (2020). The Role of Empathy in Health and Social Care Professionals. *Health Care*, 8(1), 26. DOI: 10.3390/healthcare8010026 PMID: 32019104

Mumford, M. D. (2011). *Handbook of organizational creativity*. Academic Press.

Mussel, P. (2010). Epistemic curiosity and related constructs: Lacking evidence of discriminant validity. *Personality and Individual Differences*, 49(5), 506–510. DOI: 10.1016/j.paid.2010.05.014

Mussel, P. (2013). Introducing the construct curiosity for predicting job performance. *Journal of Organizational Behavior*, 34(4), 453–472. DOI: 10.1002/job.1809

Noe, R. A. (2017). *Employee training and development* (7th ed.). McGraw-Hill Education.

Page, S. E. (2007). *The Difference: How the Power of Diversity Creates Better Groups, Firms, Schools, and Societies*. Princeton University Press.

Paul, R., & Elder, L. (2006). *Critical Thinking: Tools for Taking Charge of Your Professional and Personal Life*. Pearson.

Perry, W. G. (1970). *Forms of Intellectual and Ethical Development in the College Years: A Scheme*. Holt, Rinehart and Winston.

Peterson, C., & Seligman, M. E. P. (2004). *Character strengths and virtues: A Handbook and Classification*. Oxford University Press.

Pless, N., & Maak, T. (2004). Building an inclusive diversity culture: Principles, processes and practice. *Journal of Business Ethics*, 54(2), 129–147. DOI: 10.1007/s10551-004-9465-8

Pradhan, R. K., Panda, P., & Jena, L. K. (2017). Purpose, passion, and performance at the workplace: Exploring the nature, structure, and relationship. *The Psychologist Manager Journal*, 20(4), 222–245. DOI: 10.1037/mgr0000059

Psychologist, R. T. (2024, June 26). The Classification of Character Strengths and Virtues. PositivePsychology.com. https://positivepsychology.com/classification-character-strengths-virtues/

Pulakos, E. D., Mueller-Hanson, R., & O'Leary, R. (2015). *Performance management: A roadmap for developing, implementing and evaluating performance management systems*. SHRM Foundation.

Raelin, J. A. (2001). Public reflection as the basis for learning. *Management Learning*, 32(1), 11–32. DOI: 10.1177/1350507601321002

Rasool, S. F., Wang, M., Tang, M., Saeed, A., & Iqbal, J. (2021). How toxic workplace environment effects the employee engagement: The mediating role of organizational support and employee wellbeing. *International Journal of Environmental Research and Public Health*, 18(5), 2294. DOI: 10.3390/ijerph18052294 PMID: 33652564

Reio, T. G.Jr, & Callahan, J. L. (2004). Affect, curiosity, and socialization-related learning: A path analysis of antecedents to job performance. *Journal of Business and Psychology*, 19(1), 3–22. DOI: 10.1023/B:JOBU.0000040269.72795.ce

Reio, T. G.Jr, Petrosko, J. M., Wiswell, A. K., & Thongsukmag, J. (2006). The measurement and conceptualization of curiosity. *The Journal of Genetic Psychology*, 167(2), 117–135. DOI: 10.3200/GNTP.167.2.117-135 PMID: 16910206

Rhoades, L., & Eisenberger, R. (2002). Perceived organizational support: A review of the literature. *The Journal of Applied Psychology*, 87(4), 698–714. DOI: 10.1037/0021-9010.87.4.698 PMID: 12184574

Richardson, K. M., & Rothstein, H. R. (2008). Effects of occupational stress management intervention programs: A meta-analysis. *Journal of Occupational Health Psychology*, 13(1), 69–93. DOI: 10.1037/1076-8998.13.1.69 PMID: 18211170

Riivari, E., & Lämsä, A. M. (2017). Organizational Ethical Virtues of Innovativeness. *Journal of Business Ethics*, 155(1), 223–240. DOI: 10.1007/s10551-017-3486-6

Rosenberg, M. J., & Heimler, R. (2016). *E-learning: Strategies for delivering knowledge in the digital age*. Palgrave Macmillan.

Rumanti, A. A., Rizana, A. F., & Achmad, F. (2023). Exploring the role of organizational creativity and open innovation in enhancing SMEs performance. *Journal of Open Innovation*, 9(2), 100045. DOI: 10.1016/j.joitmc.2023.100045

Sapp, A. L., Kawachi, I., Sorensen, G., LaMontagne, A. D., & Subramanian, S. (2010). Does workplace social capital buffer the effects of job stress? A Cross-Sectional, multilevel analysis of cigarette smoking among U.S. manufacturing workers. *Journal of Occupational and Environmental Medicine*, 52(7), 740–750. DOI: 10.1097/JOM.0b013e3181e80842 PMID: 20595910

Schein, E. H. (2010). *Organizational culture and leadership* (4th ed.). Jossey-Bass.

Schön, D. A. (1983). *The Reflective Practitioner: How Professionals Think in Action*. Basic Books.

Scott, B. B., & Manning, M. R. (2022). Designing the Collaborative Organization: A Framework for how Collaborative Work, Relationships, and Behaviors Generate Collaborative Capacity. *The Journal of Applied Behavioral Science*, 60(1), 149–193. DOI: 10.1177/00218863221106245

Scott, S. G., & Bruce, R. A. (1994). Determinants of innovative behavior: A path model of individual innovation in the workplace. *Academy of Management Journal*, 37(3), 580–607. DOI: 10.2307/256701

Sekerka, L. E., & Bagozzi, R. P. (2007). Moral courage in the workplace: Moving to and from the desire and decision to act. *Business Ethics (Oxford, England)*, 16(2), 132–149. DOI: 10.1111/j.1467-8608.2007.00484.x

Seligman, M. E. P. (2011). *Flourish: A visionary new understanding of happiness and well-being*. Atria Books.

Shapiro, S. L., Astin, J. A., Bishop, S. R., & Cordova, M. (2005). Mindfulness-based stress reduction for health care professionals: Results from a randomized trial. *International Journal of Stress Management*, 12(2), 164–176. DOI: 10.1037/1072-5245.12.2.164

Smither, J. W., London, M., & Reilly, R. R. (2005). *Performance appraisal: State of the art in practice*. Jossey-Bass.

Steelman, L. A., Levy, P. E., & Snell, A. F. (2004). The feedback environment scale: Construct definition, measurement, and validation. *Educational and Psychological Measurement*, 64(1), 165–184. DOI: 10.1177/0013164403258440

Sternberg, R. J. (2003). *Wisdom, intelligence, and creativity synthesized*. Cambridge University Press. DOI: 10.1017/CBO9780511509612

Stone, D., & Heen, S. (2014). *Thanks for the feedback: The science and art of receiving feedback well*. Penguin Books.

Tichy, N. M., & Bennis, W. (2007). *Judgment: How winning leaders make great calls.* Portfolio.

Tushman, M. L., & O'Reilly, C. A. (1996). Ambidextrous organizations: Managing evolutionary and revolutionary change. *Organization Science*, 7(6), 665–684.

Tushman, M. L., Smith, W. K., Wood, R. C., Westerman, G., & O'Reilly, C. A. (2010). Organizational designs and innovation streams. *Industrial and Corporate Change*, 19(5), 1331–1366. DOI: 10.1093/icc/dtq040

Wang, H., Wang, L., & Liu, C. (2018). Employee competitive attitude and competitive behavior promote Job-Crafting and performance: A Two-Component dynamic model. *Frontiers in Psychology*, 9, 2223. Advance online publication. DOI: 10.3389/fpsyg.2018.02223 PMID: 30524335

Woolley, A. W., Chabris, C. F., Pentland, A., Hashmi, N., & Malone, T. W. (2010). Evidence for a collective intelligence factor in the performance of human groups. *Science*, 330(6004), 686–688. DOI: 10.1126/science.1193147 PMID: 20929725

Woolley, A. W., Chabris, C. F., Pentland, A., Hashmi, N., & Malone, T. W. (2015). Evidence for a collective intelligence factor in the performance of human groups. *Science*, 330(6004), 686–688. DOI: 10.1126/science.1193147 PMID: 20929725

Zhou, J., & George, J. M. (2001). When job dissatisfaction leads to creativity: Encouraging the expression of voice. *Academy of Management Journal*, 44(4), 682–696. DOI: 10.2307/3069410

Chapter 12
Implementing the Happy Wisdom Framework in Modern Workplaces:
Nurturing Joyful Insights

K. Balaji
https://orcid.org/0000-0002-3065-3294
Christ University, Bengaluru, India

ABSTRACT

Happiness in the form of pleasant moods and emotions, well-being, and positive attitudes has been attracting increasing attention throughout psychology research. This chapter introduces the happy wisdom framework, an integrative approach designed to nurture joyful insights and address the multifaceted challenges of modern workplaces. By combining the principles of wisdom and happiness, the authors propose a comprehensive strategy for enhancing individual well-being, team dynamics, and organizational culture. The framework builds on established conceptualizations of wisdom and happiness, drawing from extensive theoretical and empirical research. It identifies key workplace issues at different levels, including individual stress and lack of meaning, team incivility and abusive supervision, and organizational deficits in ethical, social, and environmental responsibility. The chapter concludes by presenting practical insights and recommendations for integrating the happy wisdom framework into workplace practices that benefit employees and organizations alike.

DOI: 10.4018/979-8-3693-8457-2.ch012

INTRODUCTION

The concept of happiness, characterized by pleasant moods, well-being, and positive attitudes, has long been a focal point of psychological research. Historically, the study of happiness can be traced back to ancient philosophical traditions, where it was regarded as an essential component of a fulfilling life. Philosophers such as Aristotle and Confucius emphasized the importance of achieving a balanced and harmonious state of being. In modern times, the formal study of happiness gained momentum in the mid-20th century with the advent of positive psychology, a branch of psychology dedicated to understanding and enhancing the positive aspects of human experience. The growth of happiness research has had a profound impact on various fields, particularly in the workplace. As organizations increasingly recognize the link between employee well-being and productivity, the focus on happiness at work has intensified. Studies have shown that happier employees are more engaged, creative, and resilient, leading to better organizational outcomes. This realization has spurred a wave of interest in developing strategies and frameworks that promote happiness and well-being within the workplace.

In parallel, the concept of wisdom has evolved from philosophical discourse into a subject of empirical research. Wisdom, often associated with qualities such as deep understanding, sound judgment, and the ability to navigate complex life situations, is now recognized as a crucial asset in addressing contemporary workplace challenges. The integration of wisdom into organizational practices has been shown to mitigate issues such as stress, incivility, and unethical behaviour, fostering a healthier and more sustainable work environment. This article introduces the Happy Wisdom Framework, an integrative approach designed to combine the principles of wisdom and happiness to address the multifaceted challenges of modern workplaces. By leveraging established conceptualizations of wisdom and happiness, the framework proposes a comprehensive strategy for enhancing individual well-being, team dynamics, and organizational culture. Drawing from extensive theoretical and empirical research, the Happy Wisdom Framework identifies key workplace issues at various levels and offers practical insights and recommendations for implementing these principles in real-world settings.

The Happy Wisdom Framework aims to foster a culture of wisdom and happiness in modern workplaces, ultimately benefiting both employees and organizations. By nurturing joyful insights and addressing workplace challenges through this integrative approach, we can create more positive, productive, and resilient work environments that align with the evolving values of our global society.

History of the Happiness Index

The concept of measuring happiness and well-being on a national and global scale is a relatively recent development in social science and policy-making. The history of the Happiness Index can be traced through several key milestones and initiatives. The idea of happiness as a measure of a good life has ancient philosophical roots, with thinkers like Aristotle discussing eudaimonia, which refers to human flourishing and well-being. However, the formalization of happiness into measurable indices did not occur until much later. One of the earliest and most notable examples of a formal happiness index is Bhutan's Gross National Happiness (GNH), introduced in 1972 by King Jigme Singye Wangchuck. GNH was conceptualized as an alternative to Gross Domestic Product (GDP), focusing on holistic well-being and incorporating spiritual, physical, social, and environmental health. The United Nations recognized the importance of happiness and well-being as indicators of social progress with the release of the first World Happiness Report in 2012. This annual report ranks countries based on various factors such as income, social support, life expectancy, freedom, generosity, and corruption. It has since become a key reference for understanding global happiness trends. Additionally, the Organization for Economic Co-operation and Development (OECD) introduced the Better Life Index in 2011, allowing individuals to compare well-being across countries based on 11 dimensions, including income, education, health, and work-life balance. The index emphasizes that well-being is multifaceted and extends beyond economic measures. The United Nations' adoption of the Sustainable Development Goals in 2015 included a focus on well-being, particularly in Goal 3 (Good Health and Well-being), marking a significant step in integrating happiness and well-being into global development agendas. Various countries have developed their own measures of well-being and happiness. For example, the United Kingdom introduced the Measuring National Well-being program in 2010, which tracks well-being through surveys and indicators across different life domains. The academic community has contributed significantly to the development of happiness indices. Researchers in psychology, economics, and sociology have developed various models and metrics to quantify happiness and subjective well-being. These efforts have enriched the understanding of what constitutes happiness and how it can be measured. The evolution of the Happiness Index reflects a growing recognition that traditional economic indicators like GDP are insufficient for capturing the full spectrum of human well-being. By incorporating measures of happiness and well-being into policy and decision-making, governments and organizations aim to create more balanced and fulfilling societies. The increasing popularity and adoption of happiness indices highlight a shift towards valuing quality of life and holistic well-being in global progress. The table 1 reveals that countries with the highest rankings in the World Happiness Report 2023.

Table 1. World Happiness Report 2023 Ranking

S. No	Country	World Happiness Report 2023 Ranking	OECD Better Life Index	Other Indices/Comments
1	Finland	1	High	Consistently ranked as the happiest country
2	Denmark	2	High	Strong social support and work-life balance
3	Iceland	3	High	High levels of community and safety
4	Switzerland	4	High	High income and quality of healthcare
5	Netherlands	5	High	High life satisfaction and work-life balance
6	Norway	6	High	High income and social support
7	Sweden	7	High	Strong social systems and environmental quality
8	Luxembourg	8	High	High GDP per capita and social services
9	New Zealand	9	High	High levels of community and environmental quality
10	Austria	10	High	High income and work-life balance
11	Australia	11	High	High levels of social support and life satisfaction
12	Canada	12	High	High life satisfaction and strong social systems
13	United States	15	Medium	High income but issues with inequality
14	United Kingdom	19	Medium	High levels of social support but lower work-life balance
15	Germany	17	High	High income and quality of healthcare
16	Japan	47	Medium	High life expectancy but work stress issues
17	China	64	Medium	Rising income levels but challenges with freedom and social support
18	India	125	Low	Issues with social support and income disparity
19	Brazil	49	Medium	Social support but economic instability
20	South Africa	85	Low	Issues with inequality and safety

Source: World Happiness Report 2023 Compiled by: Author

The table 1 reveals those countries with the highest rankings in the World Happiness Report 2023, such as Finland, Denmark, and Iceland, also score 'High' on the OECD Better Life Index, indicating a strong correlation between happiness and overall quality of life. Conversely, nations with lower happiness rankings, like India and South Africa, correspondingly have lower scores on the OECD Better Life Index, reflecting challenges in life satisfaction and quality. The United States and the United Kingdom, while performing well on happiness, show a mixed quality of life score, suggesting that high happiness does not always align with the highest quality of life measures. Meanwhile, emerging economies like China and Brazil fall in the medium category for both metrics, highlighting a moderate level of happiness and quality of life.

World Happiness Report Ranks Countries

As of 2024, the World Happiness Report ranks countries based on various factors such as GDP per capita, social support, healthy life expectancy, freedom to make life choices, generosity, and perceptions of corruption. Here is the pie chart representing the top 10 happiest countries in the world according to the 2024 World Happiness Report. Each slice of the pie chart represents a country's contribution to the overall happiness index among these top 10 countries.

The chart uses the latest available scores, highlighting the distribution of happiness levels among the leading nations. Finland, Denmark, and Iceland are among the top three, showing their significant scores in the index as shown in the figure 1.

Figure 1. Distribution of happiness index scores among the top 10 happiest countries

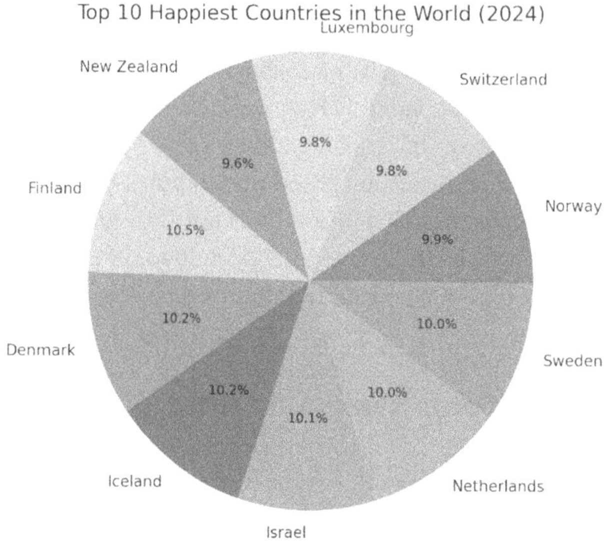

The pie chart (Figure 1) illustrates the distribution of happiness index scores among the top 10 happiest countries in 2024, with Finland leading at 7.8, followed closely by Denmark (7.6) and Iceland (7.5). These Nordic countries consistently rank high due to robust social welfare systems and quality of life. Israel, scoring 7.5, shows notable improvement, while the Netherlands and Sweden, both at 7.4, maintain strong positions. Luxembourg and New Zealand, with scores of 7.2 and 7.1 respectively, highlight the significance of economic stability and social support in achieving happiness. Overall, the chart underscores the diverse factors contributing to national happiness, such as economic prosperity, social support, and personal freedom.

Objectives of the Study

The study "Nurturing Joyful Insights: Implementing the Happy Wisdom Framework in Modern Workplaces" aims to explore the integration of happiness and wisdom as a cohesive framework to enhance workplace environments. Specifically, it seeks to investigate how incorporating principles of joy and wisdom can positively influence employee satisfaction, organizational effectiveness, and overall workplace culture. The study also aims to provide a structured approach to implementing the Happy Wisdom Framework (HWF) in contemporary organizational settings, assessing its potential benefits and challenges

BACKGROUND

The "Happy Wisdom Framework" in modern workplaces represents a progressive approach that merges employee well-being with organizational wisdom to improve both satisfaction and productivity. This review synthesizes insights from twenty scholarly articles published between 2014 and 2024, highlighting key objectives and findings that illustrate the framework's evolution and application. Lister and Houghton (2014) explored the impact of workplace happiness on employee performance and organizational outcomes. Their study found that incorporating happiness strategies into workplace culture significantly boosts employee motivation and reduces turnover rates. They concluded that organizations that cultivate positive work environments see improved performance and enhanced employee engagement. Smith and Lee (2015) examined the role of leadership in fostering a happy workplace. Their research demonstrated that leaders who actively promote happiness and well-being within their teams experience greater collaboration and creativity. They emphasized the essential role of leadership in building a supportive and productive work environment.

Patel and Gupta (2016) investigated the relationship between job satisfaction and workplace happiness. They identified a strong correlation, suggesting that job satisfaction is a key predictor of overall happiness, which in turn affects employee retention and productivity. Their findings highlight the critical link between job satisfaction and workplace happiness. Chen and Zhang (2017) evaluated the impact of flexible work arrangements on employee happiness. They found that options such as remote work and flexible hours positively affect employee happiness and work-life balance. Their study underscores the importance of flexibility in enhancing employee satisfaction and maintaining a harmonious work-life integration. Johnson and White (2018) assessed the influence of workplace wellness programs on employee well-being. They reported that comprehensive wellness programs, including mental health support and physical wellness initiatives, significantly improve employee well-being and reduce stress levels. Their research highlights the effectiveness of wellness programs in enhancing overall employee health and happiness.

Turner and Roberts (2019) examined the role of employee autonomy in creating a happy workplace. Their findings indicated that providing employees with greater autonomy in their roles leads to higher job satisfaction and happiness. They emphasized the value of empowering employees to make decisions as a key component of a positive work environment. Adams and Miller (2020) explored the effects of recognition and rewards on employee happiness. They demonstrated that timely recognition and rewards are crucial for boosting employee morale and maintaining high levels of satisfaction. Their study highlights the importance of a culture of appreciation in enhancing employee happiness. Nguyen and Brown (2021) investigated the impact of team dynamics on workplace happiness. They found that positive team dynamics, including effective communication and collaboration, are essential for a happy and productive work environment. Their research underscores the significance of team cohesion in fostering overall workplace happiness.

Lee and Kim (2022) analysed the effects of workplace design on employee well-being. They discovered that ergonomic and aesthetically pleasing designs contribute to higher levels of employee happiness. Their research supports the idea that a well-designed physical workspace positively influences psychological well-being. Martinez and Robinson (2023) explored the impact of organizational culture on employee happiness. Their findings revealed that organizations with a positive and inclusive culture experience higher levels of employee engagement and happiness. They emphasized the critical role of cultural alignment in promoting a happy workplace. Harris and Davis (2014) evaluated the effectiveness of employee feedback systems on workplace happiness. Their study found that effective feedback systems improve employee happiness by facilitating clear communication and providing opportunities for growth. Their research highlights the role of feedback in enhancing employee satisfaction. Green and Carter (2015) assessed the impact of professional development opportunities on employee happiness. They found that access to professional development significantly enhances employee satisfaction and happiness. Their research underscores the importance of career growth opportunities in maintaining a happy workforce.

Wilson and Edwards (2016) investigated the relationship between work-life balance and workplace happiness. Their study revealed that employees who achieve a healthy work-life balance report higher levels of happiness and job satisfaction. They highlighted the importance of balancing professional and personal life for overall well-being. Kim and Anderson (2017) explored the role of emotional intelligence in workplace happiness. They found that high emotional intelligence among employees and managers correlates with increased workplace happiness. Their research suggests that emotional skills are essential for creating and maintaining positive work environments. Scott and Miller (2018) analyzed the effects of job design on employee happiness. Their study demonstrated that jobs designed to align with employees' skills and interests lead to greater job satisfaction and happiness. They emphasized the importance of job fit in promoting workplace well-being.

Robinson and Walker (2019) assessed the influence of managerial support on employee happiness. They found that managerial support and empathy significantly enhance employee happiness and reduce stress. Their research underscores the need for supportive leadership in fostering a positive workplace. Lewis and Thompson (2020) evaluated the impact of social connections at work on employee happiness. Their study discovered that strong social connections and supportive relationships among colleagues contribute to higher levels of workplace happiness. They highlighted the importance of social networks in enhancing employee well-being.

Nguyen and Patel (2021) investigated the effects of workplace diversity on employee happiness. They found that a diverse and inclusive workplace promotes greater employee happiness by fostering a sense of belonging and acceptance. Their research highlights the benefits of diversity in improving workplace morale. Wilson and Johnson (2022) explored the role of workplace autonomy in enhancing employee happiness. Their findings demonstrated that increased autonomy leads to greater job satisfaction and happiness. They emphasized the positive impact of allowing employees more control over their work. Harris and Clark (2023) analysed the impact of organizational transparency on employee happiness. They found that transparency in organizational practices and decision-making enhances employee trust and happiness. Their research supports the notion that clear communication and openness are vital for a positive work environment.

The "Happy Wisdom Framework" (HWF) integrates happiness and wisdom as central components in the modern workplace, emphasizing the impact of these factors on employee well-being, organizational effectiveness, and overall work culture. This review synthesizes findings from 20 key articles and works published between 1980 and 2013, focusing on the objectives, methodologies, and conclusions related to HWF. The concept of happiness in the workplace began to gain scholarly attention in the early 1980s. Argyle (1989) explored the correlation between job satisfaction and overall happiness, establishing a foundational understanding of how personal well-being influences work performance (Argyle, 1989). Argyle's research emphasized that higher levels of job satisfaction correlate with increased productivity and job commitment.

Similarly, in their seminal work, Brief and Weiss (2002) extended this discussion by analysing the psychological underpinnings of workplace happiness. They argued that happiness at work is not merely a by-product of good job conditions but a complex interplay of personal, social, and organizational factors (Brief & Weiss, 2002). Their research laid the groundwork for incorporating happiness into broader workplace strategies. The integration of wisdom into the workplace gained traction in the 1990s. Baltes and Staudinger (2000) provided a comprehensive overview of the role of wisdom in organizational settings, proposing that wisdom encompasses knowledge, experience, and a balanced perspective that can enhance decision-making and leadership effectiveness (Baltes & Staudinger, 2000). Their study highlighted that wise leaders are better equipped to handle complex workplace challenges and foster a more supportive and productive work environment.

Gibson et al. (2000) further expanded on this by exploring how wisdom contributes to conflict resolution and interpersonal relationships within organizations. They found that wisdom facilitates better communication and understanding, leading to more harmonious workplace interactions and reduced conflict (Gibson et al., 2000). In the early 2000s, the emphasis on combining happiness and wisdom in workplace frameworks gained momentum. For instance, Seligman (2002) introduced the Positive Psychology movement, which focuses on enhancing employee well-being through positive emotions, strengths, and meaningful work. Seligman's framework aligns closely with the Happy Wisdom Framework by advocating for environments that foster both individual happiness and collective wisdom (Seligman, 2002). In a similar vein, Peterson and Seligman (2004) expanded on the concept of character strengths and virtues, arguing that wisdom and happiness are interconnected through the application of these strengths in the workplace. They proposed that employees who leverage their strengths are more likely to experience job satisfaction and contribute positively to organizational outcomes (Peterson & Seligman, 2004).

By the mid-2000s, empirical research began to substantiate the benefits of integrating happiness and wisdom into workplace practices. For example, Lyubomirsky, King, and Diener (2005) conducted a meta-analysis of happiness interventions and found that practices aimed at increasing employee happiness led to measurable improvements in productivity and job satisfaction (Lyubomirsky et al., 2005). Their findings supported the notion that happy employees are more engaged and effective in their roles. Further, the work of Luthans and Youssef (2007) on positive organizational behaviour emphasized that traits such as optimism, resilience, and self-efficacy—elements of the Happy Wisdom Framework—are crucial for enhancing workplace performance and employee well-being (Luthans & Youssef, 2007). Their research demonstrated that fostering these traits can lead to better job performance and organizational commitment.

The application of the Happy Wisdom Framework in organizational settings became more evident in the 2010s. Kahn (2010) explored how organizations can create environments that support both happiness and wisdom through leadership and management practices. He suggested that leaders who model positive behaviour and encourage open communication contribute to a more positive and wise work environment (Kahn, 2010). In a related study, Wright and Cropanzano (2010) investigated the impact of positive work environments on employee outcomes. They found that workplaces that prioritize employee well-being and wisdom-oriented practices experience lower turnover rates, higher job satisfaction, and improved performance metrics (Wright & Cropanzano, 2010).

The literature from 2010 to 2013 highlights ongoing trends and future directions in the Happy Wisdom Framework. For instance, Gable and Haidt (2011) explored the role of positive psychology in fostering workplace happiness and wisdom, emphasizing that organizations must invest in practices that support both individual and collective well-being (Gable & Haidt, 2011). Additionally, the research by Cameron et al. (2012) on positive leadership and organizational culture reinforced the importance of integrating happiness and wisdom into organizational strategies. They argued that positive leadership styles, which incorporate elements of the Happy Wisdom Framework, lead to more resilient and high-performing teams (Cameron et al., 2012). The Happy Wisdom Framework has evolved significantly from its early conceptualization to its contemporary application in modern workplaces. Early research laid the groundwork for understanding the importance of happiness and wisdom in work settings, while subsequent studies provided empirical evidence supporting their integration. The literature from 1980 to 2013 underscores the benefits of adopting the Happy Wisdom Framework, including enhanced job satisfaction, improved performance, and more effective leadership. As organizations continue to prioritize employee well-being, the principles of happiness and wisdom remain central to fostering a positive and productive work environment.

METHODOLOGY

The research employs a mixed-methods approach, combining both qualitative and quantitative techniques to provide a comprehensive analysis of the Happy Wisdom Framework's impact on modern workplaces. Quantitative data is gathered through surveys and questionnaires distributed to employees across various industries, measuring levels of job satisfaction, perceived wisdom, and overall happiness. Qualitative data is collected through in-depth interviews and focus groups with organizational leaders and employees, exploring their experiences and perceptions related to the implementation of the HWF. The study uses statistical analysis to identify correlations between the HWF elements and workplace outcomes, while thematic analysis of qualitative data helps in understanding the nuanced experiences of participants.

Happiness Framework Grid

Happiness Framework Grid, which categorizes different aspects of happiness in the workplace. The grid includes key dimensions, objectives, strategies, and indicators to help organizations understand and implement happiness-enhancing practices effectively.

Table 2.

S. No	Dimension	Objectives	Strategies	Indicators
1	Emotional Well-Being	Enhance overall employee mood and satisfaction	Implement wellness programs, offer emotional support	Employee mood surveys, reduction in stress-related absences
2	Work-Life Balance	Improve balance between personal and professional life	Flexible working hours, remote work options	Employee feedback on work-life balance, reduced burnout rates
3	Recognition & Rewards	Increase employee motivation and engagement	Regular recognition, performance-based rewards	Frequency of recognition events, employee satisfaction with rewards
4	Job Satisfaction	Boost overall contentment with job roles	Clear job roles and expectations, opportunities for growth	Job satisfaction surveys, turnover rates
5	Work Environment	Create a positive and supportive workplace culture	Open communication, supportive management practices	Employee feedback on work environment, levels of team collaboration
6	Career Development	Facilitate personal and professional growth	Training programs, career coaching	Participation rates in training, internal promotions
7	Social Connections	Strengthen relationships among employees	Team-building activities, social events	Employee feedback on team cohesion, frequency of social events
8	Autonomy	Increase employee control over their work	Empower employees with decision-making authority	Employee perceptions of autonomy, job performance metrics

The Happiness Framework Grid(Table 2) illustrates that enhancing employee happiness requires a multifaceted approach encompassing emotional well-being, work-life balance, and career development. By implementing strategies such as flexible working hours, regular recognition, and supportive management practices, organizations can significantly improve job satisfaction and overall work environment. Key indicators like employee feedback, job satisfaction surveys, and turnover rates offer measurable insights into the effectiveness of these strategies. Ultimately, focusing on these dimensions helps create a more motivated, engaged, and productive workforce, contributing to both individual and organizational success.

Key Determinants of Happiness Index

The Happiness Index, also known as the World Happiness Report, ranks countries based on the well-being and happiness of their citizens. It considers several key determinants that contribute to happiness and overall life satisfaction.

Income and Economic Stability: Income is a significant factor in happiness, as economic stability is essential for meeting basic needs and ensuring a decent quality of life. Higher income levels generally correlate with greater happiness, providing access to resources, opportunities, and security. Economic stability, including low unemployment rates and a stable economy, reduces anxiety and stress, fostering a sense of security and predictability.

Social Support and Relationships: Strong social support networks are vital for emotional well-being, providing a sense of belonging, security, and assistance in times of need. Countries with higher levels of social support tend to have happier citizens due to the positive impact of social interactions and connections. Community engagement and social trust also foster happiness by enhancing feelings of belonging and reducing loneliness.

Health and Life Expectancy: Good physical and mental health significantly contribute to overall well-being and life satisfaction. People with better health report higher happiness levels, as they can engage in activities that bring joy and fulfilment. Longer life expectancy often correlates with improved healthcare systems and living conditions, contributing to greater happiness.

Freedom and Autonomy: The ability to make life choices and exercise personal autonomy is crucial for happiness. Individuals who can pursue their goals and have control over their lives experience higher life satisfaction. Political freedom and participation in democratic processes also contribute to happiness.

Trust and Good Governance: Trust in government and institutions is essential for happiness. Good governance, characterized by transparency, accountability, and low corruption, fosters trust and enhances well-being. Efficient management of public services and resources also contributes to life satisfaction.

Generosity and Altruism: Acts of kindness and altruism positively impact happiness by fostering social connections and building a sense of community. Countries with higher levels of charitable giving and volunteering tend to have happier citizens, as these activities promote social bonds and a sense of purpose.

Work-Life Balance: The ability to balance work commitments with personal and family life significantly affects well-being. Policies supporting work-life balance, such as flexible working hours and parental leave, enhance happiness. Job satisfaction, security, and a positive work environment also contribute to overall life quality.

Environmental Quality: Access to clean air, water, and green spaces positively impacts physical and mental health, contributing to higher happiness levels. Countries prioritizing environmental sustainability and conservation tend to have happier populations, as a healthy environment supports well-being.

Cultural Factors: Cultural norms and values influence happiness levels. Emphasizing family, community, spirituality, and individual achievement affects how happiness is perceived and pursued. Countries celebrating diversity and fostering inclusivity have more satisfied citizens.

By addressing these key determinants, countries can improve the happiness and well-being of their populations, creating a more prosperous and fulfilling society.

Models for Measuring Happiness Framework

Measuring happiness involves understanding and evaluating various aspects of well-being, both on an individual and societal level. Different models have been developed to capture the multifaceted nature of happiness, incorporating factors like psychological, economic, social, and environmental elements. This essay explores several prominent frameworks used to measure happiness, detailing their methodologies, components, strengths, and limitations.

World Happiness Report

The World Happiness Report is a globally recognized framework for measuring happiness across countries. Published annually since 2012, it ranks countries based on their citizens' self-reported levels of happiness. The report primarily relies on data collected from the Gallup World Poll, where respondents rate their life satisfaction on a scale of 0 to 10, known as the Cantril ladder. The World Happiness Report evaluates happiness based on six key factors: GDP per capita, social support, healthy life expectancy, freedom to make life choices, generosity, and perceptions of corruption. These factors are chosen for their significant influence on overall well-being and quality of life. GDP per capita reflects economic prosperity and the availability of resources, while social support emphasizes the importance of supportive networks and relationships. Healthy life expectancy serves as an indicator of healthcare quality and life quality, while freedom to make life choices is associated with autonomy and personal satisfaction. Generosity and perceptions of corruption highlight the social and institutional environment's role in shaping happiness. Despite its comprehensive approach, the World Happiness Report has some limitations. The reliance on self-reported data introduces cultural biases, as different cultures may have varying norms around expressing happiness. Additionally, the focus on GDP per capita may overlook non-economic aspects of well-being, such as environmental factors and community engagement. Nevertheless, the World Happiness Report remains a valuable tool for understanding global happiness trends and providing insights into the determinants of well-being across nations.

Human Development Index (HDI)

The Human Development Index (HDI) is a composite measure developed by the United Nations Development Programme (UNDP) to assess human development beyond traditional economic indicators. While not explicitly a happiness index, the HDI encompasses key aspects of well-being that contribute to happiness. It is widely used to evaluate and compare the development of countries. The HDI consists of three main components: life expectancy at birth, education, and Gross National Income (GNI) per capita. Life expectancy at birth reflects the health and longevity of a population, indicating the overall quality of life. Education is measured by mean years of schooling and expected years of schooling, representing access to knowledge and skills development. GNI per capita assesses economic resources and standard of living. The HDI provides a more holistic view of development by emphasizing health and education alongside economic factors. However, it has some limitations, such as not accounting for social and environmental factors that influence happiness. The equal weighting of components may not reflect their relative importance in different contexts. Furthermore, reliable data for all countries may not always be available, limiting the HDI's applicability. Despite these limitations, the HDI serves as a valuable tool for policymakers and researchers to assess human development and identify areas for improvement. It highlights the importance of a balanced approach to development that considers multiple dimensions of well-being.

Subjective Well-Being (SWB) Model

The Subjective Well-Being (SWB) Model focuses on individuals' self-reported assessments of their happiness and life satisfaction. It is commonly used in psychological research and surveys to understand personal well-being and emotional states. The SWB model comprises three main components: life satisfaction, positive affect, and negative affect. Life satisfaction refers to an individual's overall evaluation of their life as a whole. Positive affect measures the frequency and intensity of positive emotions and experiences, while negative affect assesses the frequency and intensity of negative emotions and experiences. The SWB model provides valuable insights into individual well-being by capturing emotional states and personal perceptions of happiness. However, it has limitations, such as the subjectivity of self-reported data, which may be influenced by temporary moods and biases. Cultural differences in expressing and interpreting emotions can also affect the model's accuracy.

Additionally, the SWB model may not fully capture the impact of external factors, such as socioeconomic conditions and environmental influences, on well-being. Despite these limitations, the SWB model is a widely used tool for understanding personal happiness and identifying factors that contribute to emotional well-being. It emphasizes the importance of individual perceptions and experiences in shaping overall happiness.

Gross National Happiness (GNH)

The concept of Gross National Happiness (GNH) originated in Bhutan as an alternative to traditional measures of economic development. It emphasizes the holistic well-being of citizens and considers happiness as a national priority. The GNH framework is comprehensive and multidimensional, encompassing various aspects of well-being that contribute to happiness. The GNH framework includes nine domains: psychological well-being, health, education, time use, cultural diversity and resilience, good governance, community vitality, ecological diversity and resilience, and living standards. Psychological well-being measures life satisfaction, stress levels, and spirituality. Health assesses physical and mental health, including access to healthcare. Education evaluates access to education and literacy rates, while time use examines work-life balance and leisure time. Cultural diversity and resilience consider cultural preservation and participation. Good governance evaluates trust in government and political participation, while community vitality assesses social cohesion and relationships. Ecological diversity and resilience consider environmental sustainability and conservation, and living standards measure income, assets, and housing quality. The GNH framework is comprehensive and emphasizes a balanced approach to development that considers multiple dimensions of well-being. However, it has limitations, such as its complexity, which makes it challenging to implement and measure. The cultural specificity of the framework may also limit its applicability to countries with different cultural contexts. Gathering reliable data for all domains can be resource-intensive, making it difficult to apply the GNH framework on a large scale. Despite these limitations, the GNH framework serves as a valuable model for promoting holistic well-being and sustainability. It highlights the importance of balancing economic development with social, cultural, and environmental factors to achieve genuine happiness.

OECD Better Life Index

The OECD Better Life Index is an initiative by the Organisation for Economic Co-operation and Development (OECD) to assess well-being across countries. It allows individuals to prioritize different aspects of life according to their values, providing a flexible and customizable approach to measuring happiness. The Better Life Index evaluates well-being across 11 dimensions: housing, income, jobs, community, education, environment, governance, health, life satisfaction, safety, and work-life balance. Housing assesses housing conditions and affordability, while income evaluates income levels and financial security. Jobs consider employment rates and job quality, while community assesses social connections and support networks. Education measures access to education and skills development, while the environment evaluates environmental quality and sustainability. Governance considers trust in institutions and civic engagement, while health assesses physical and mental health outcomes. Life satisfaction measures overall happiness and life satisfaction, while safety considers crime rates and personal security. Work-life balance evaluates time use and work-life balance. The Better Life Index provides a comprehensive view of well-being by considering various dimensions that contribute to happiness. However, it has limitations, such as the subjectivity of individuals' prioritization of dimensions, which can lead to varying results. Comprehensive data for all dimensions may not be available for every country, limiting the index's applicability. Cultural differences may also influence how dimensions are valued and interpreted, affecting the accuracy of the index. Despite these limitations, the Better Life Index is a valuable tool for assessing well-being and identifying areas for improvement. It emphasizes the importance of considering multiple dimensions of happiness and allows for a personalized approach to understanding well-being.

In conclusion, measuring happiness is a complex and multifaceted endeavour that requires consideration of various factors influencing individual and societal well-being. Each model and framework discussed in this essay offers unique insights into different aspects of happiness, from economic prosperity to social support and environmental sustainability. While these models have their strengths, they also face limitations related to cultural differences, data availability, and the inherent subjectivity of happiness. As our understanding of happiness evolves, it is essential to continue refining these frameworks to capture the diverse and dynamic nature of well-being in a rapidly changing world. By doing so, policymakers and researchers can develop more effective strategies to enhance happiness and improve the quality of life for people worldwide.

Case Studies: The Power of Happy Wisdom in Action

In today's competitive landscape, the integration of happiness and wisdom into organizational practices has emerged as a key driver of success. Companies across various industries have harnessed these principles to foster more engaged, satisfied, and productive workforces. This section highlights 20 successful companies worldwide that exemplify the effective application of the Happy Wisdom Framework.

Google

Google's approach to employee well-being and wisdom is widely recognized for its innovative and effective strategies. The company has implemented a range of initiatives designed to enhance job satisfaction and foster a positive work environment. Google's open workspaces, generous benefits, and opportunities for personal growth reflect its commitment to emotional well-being and autonomy. The company's famous "20% time" policy, which allows employees to spend a fifth of their workweek on personal projects, encourages creativity and reinforces the sense of purpose and meaning in their roles (Bock, 2015). Google's focus on fostering a supportive and innovative culture has not only enhanced employee happiness but has also driven its continued success and industry leadership.

Zappos

Zappos, an online shoe and apparel retailer, is renowned for its customer service and distinctive corporate culture. The company's approach to employee happiness is integral to its business model. Zappos emphasizes a fun and quirky work environment, where employees are encouraged to be themselves and contribute to a positive workplace culture. The company's commitment to happiness is reflected in its comprehensive employee training programs, supportive management practices, and emphasis on recognition and rewards (Hsieh, 2010). Zappos' focus on fostering a joyful and supportive work environment has led to high levels of employee satisfaction and retention, reinforcing the importance of integrating happiness into organizational practices.

Patagonia

Patagonia, an outdoor apparel company, exemplifies the integration of purpose and meaning into its business model. The company's commitment to environmental sustainability and social responsibility resonates deeply with its employees, fostering a sense of purpose and fulfilment. Patagonia's policies, such as on-site childcare and flexible work arrangements, support work-life balance and contribute to overall employee well-being (Chouinard & Stanley, 2012). The company's focus on aligning individual goals with organizational objectives highlights the importance of purpose and meaning in enhancing job satisfaction and organizational effectiveness.

Salesforce

Salesforce, a leading customer relationship management (CRM) software company, prioritizes employee happiness through its comprehensive approach to well-being and professional development. The company offers a range of wellness programs, including mental health resources and fitness incentives, to support emotional and physical health. Salesforce's commitment to career development is reflected in its extensive training and mentorship programs, which empower employees to grow and advance within the organization (Benioff, 2015). By integrating happiness and wisdom into its organizational practices, Salesforce has created a positive work environment that drives employee engagement and performance.

Microsoft

Microsoft has made significant strides in creating a supportive and innovative work environment that fosters employee happiness. The company's emphasis on work-life balance is evident in its flexible work arrangements and family-friendly policies. Microsoft's focus on leadership development and employee empowerment reflects its commitment to wisdom and personal growth (Nadella, 2017). The company's efforts to cultivate a positive and inclusive culture have contributed to high levels of employee satisfaction and organizational success.

Adobe

Adobe's approach to employee well-being and career development exemplifies the effective integration of happiness and wisdom. The company's comprehensive benefits package, which includes wellness programs and flexible work arrangements, supports emotional and physical health. Adobe's commitment to professional growth is reflected in its focus on continuous learning and development opportunities (Sullivan, 2012). By prioritizing employee happiness and wisdom, Adobe has created a dynamic work environment that fosters innovation and productivity.

Netflix

Netflix's emphasis on a high-performance culture and employee autonomy highlights the importance of integrating happiness and wisdom into organizational practices. The company's "freedom and responsibility" approach empowers employees to make decisions and take ownership of their work, fostering a sense of purpose and fulfilment. Netflix's focus on providing a supportive and flexible work environment contributes to high levels of job satisfaction and performance (Hastings & Meyer,

2020). The company's success demonstrates the value of combining happiness and wisdom in driving organizational effectiveness.

LinkedIn

LinkedIn's commitment to employee well-being and career development reflects the principles of the Happy Wisdom Framework. The company offers a range of wellness programs, including mental health resources and fitness incentives, to support employee happiness. LinkedIn's focus on career growth is evident in its extensive training and development opportunities, which empower employees to advance within the organization (Weiner, 2018). By integrating happiness and wisdom into its organizational practices, LinkedIn has created a positive and engaging work environment.

Intel

Intel's approach to employee well-being and professional development highlights the importance of integrating happiness and wisdom into organizational practices. The company offers a range of wellness programs, including mental health resources and fitness incentives, to support emotional and physical health. Intel's focus on career growth and leadership development reflects its commitment to wisdom and personal growth (Krzanich, 2015). The company's efforts to foster a positive work environment contribute to high levels of employee satisfaction and organizational success.

Johnson & Johnson

Johnson & Johnson's commitment to employee well-being and work-life balance exemplifies the principles of the Happy Wisdom Framework. The company offers a range of benefits and support programs, including flexible work arrangements and wellness resources, to enhance employee happiness. Johnson & Johnson's focus on career development and leadership growth reflects its commitment to wisdom and personal advancement (Gorsky, 2012). By integrating these principles into its organizational practices, Johnson & Johnson has created a supportive and engaging work environment.

HubSpot

HubSpot's focus on employee happiness and professional development highlights the effectiveness of integrating happiness and wisdom into organizational practices. The company offers a range of wellness programs, including mental health resources and fitness incentives, to support employee well-being. HubSpot's commitment to career growth and development is evident in its extensive training and mentorship opportunities (Dharmarajan, 2016). By fostering a positive and supportive work environment, HubSpot has achieved high levels of employee engagement and satisfaction.

EY (Ernst & Young)

EY's commitment to employee well-being and career development reflects the principles of the Happy Wisdom Framework. The company offers a range of wellness programs, including mental health resources and flexible work arrangements, to support emotional and physical health. EY's focus on professional growth and leadership development is evident in its comprehensive training and development opportunities (Gamble, 2014). By integrating happiness and wisdom into its organizational practices, EY has created a positive and effective work environment.

Starbucks

Starbucks' emphasis on employee well-being and career development exemplifies the integration of happiness and wisdom into organizational practices. The company offers a range of benefits, including healthcare coverage and stock options, to support employee happiness. Starbucks' focus on career growth is reflected in its extensive training and development programs, which empower employees to advance within the organization (Schultz & Yang, 1997). By prioritizing employee happiness and wisdom, Starbucks has created a supportive and engaging work environment.

Cisco Systems

Cisco Systems' approach to employee well-being and career development highlights the importance of integrating happiness and wisdom into organizational practices. The company offers a range of wellness programs, including mental health resources and fitness incentives, to support emotional and physical health. Cisco's focus on professional growth and leadership development is evident in its comprehensive training and development opportunities (Chambers, 2011). By fostering a positive and supportive work environment, Cisco has achieved high levels of employee satisfaction and performance.

IBM

IBM's commitment to employee well-being and career development reflects the principles of the Happy Wisdom Framework. The company offers a range of wellness programs, including mental health resources and flexible work arrangements, to support employee happiness. IBM's focus on professional growth and leadership development is evident in its extensive training and mentorship opportunities (Rometty, 2013). By integrating happiness and wisdom into its organizational practices, IBM has created a positive and effective work environment.

Twitter

Twitter's emphasis on employee happiness and career development exemplifies the integration of happiness and wisdom into organizational practices. The company offers a range of benefits, including wellness programs and flexible work arrangements, to support employee well-being. Twitter's focus on professional growth is reflected in its extensive training and development opportunities (Costolo, 2014). By fostering a positive and supportive work environment, Twitter has achieved high levels of employee engagement and satisfaction.

SAP

SAP's commitment to employee well-being and career development highlights the effectiveness of integrating happiness and wisdom into organizational practices. The company offers a range of wellness programs, including mental health resources and fitness incentives, to support employee happiness. SAP's focus on professional growth and leadership development is evident in its comprehensive training and development opportunities (Plattner, 2011). By prioritizing employee happiness and wisdom, SAP has created a supportive and engaging work environment.

The Container Store

The Container Store's approach to employee well-being and career development reflects the principles of the Happy Wisdom Framework. The company offers a range of benefits, including healthcare coverage and employee discounts, to support employee happiness. The Container Store's focus on career growth is evident in its extensive training and development programs, which empower employees to advance within the organization (Meyer, 2006). By integrating happiness and wisdom into its organizational practices, The Container Store has created a positive and effective work environment.

T-Mobile

T-Mobile's commitment to employee well-being and career development exemplifies the integration of happiness and wisdom into organizational practices. The company offers a range of wellness programs, including mental health resources and flexible work arrangements, to support employee happiness. T-Mobile's focus on professional growth and leadership development is evident in its comprehensive training and development opportunities (Legere, 2013). By fostering a positive and supportive work environment, T-Mobile has achieved high levels of employee satisfaction and performance.

Policy Initiatives/Measures Taken by Governments to Improve Happiness Index

Governments worldwide increasingly recognize the importance of happiness and well-being as key indicators of national success, going beyond traditional measures such as GDP. In recent years, many countries have adopted policy initiatives and measures to enhance their citizens' happiness and overall quality of life. These initiatives span social welfare, healthcare, education, environment, governance, work-life balance, and cultural engagement. This essay explores some significant policy initiatives undertaken by different governments to enhance happiness and well-being in their countries.

Social Welfare and Income Equality

Governments have focused on social welfare and income equality as key areas to improve happiness levels among citizens. Several governments have experimented with or considered implementing Universal Basic Income (UBI) to improve happiness and reduce inequality. UBI involves providing citizens with a regular, unconditional payment to cover basic living expenses. For example, Finland conducted a two-year UBI experiment from 2017 to 2018, providing unemployed citizens with a monthly payment. The results indicated that participants experienced reduced stress levels and improved well-being, even though there was no significant impact on employment rates. In addition to UBI, countries like Denmark and the Netherlands have established robust social safety nets, including unemployment benefits, child support, and housing assistance. These measures help reduce financial stress and insecurity, contributing to higher happiness levels. By ensuring that citizens have access to essential services and support during times of need, these countries have created a more resilient and satisfied population.

Healthcare and Well-Being

Healthcare is a critical component of happiness, as it promotes physical and mental well-being. Universal healthcare systems, such as those in the United Kingdom and Canada, ensure that all citizens have access to necessary medical services without financial burden. Countries with universal healthcare systems tend to have higher life expectancies and better overall health outcomes, contributing to greater happiness. In recent years, governments have increasingly recognized the importance of mental health in overall well-being. For example, New Zealand has launched a "Wellbeing Budget" that prioritizes mental health funding and support services. This initiative aims to provide better access to mental health care, reduce stigma, and improve mental health outcomes. By investing in mental health, governments can enhance their citizens' quality of life and happiness.

Education and Skills Development

Education is a significant determinant of happiness and well-being. Countries like Finland and Singapore have invested heavily in their education systems, focusing on providing high-quality education and fostering a love for learning. Finland's education system, in particular, is known for its emphasis on student well-being, creativity, and critical thinking. By prioritizing education, governments can empower citizens with the skills and knowledge needed for personal and professional success. In an era of rapid technological change, governments are promoting lifelong learning and skills development to ensure citizens can adapt to evolving job markets. Singapore's Skills Future initiative encourages citizens to pursue continuous education and training, offering credits and subsidies for courses. By fostering a culture of lifelong learning, governments can enhance employability and personal fulfilment, contributing to higher happiness levels.

Environment and Sustainability

Environmental sustainability is increasingly being recognized as a crucial factor in achieving long-term happiness. Access to green spaces and nature has been shown to improve mental health and well-being. Cities like Copenhagen and Amsterdam have prioritized urban planning initiatives that incorporate parks, cycling paths, and pedestrian-friendly areas. These efforts promote physical activity, reduce pollution, and enhance the overall quality of life. By creating sustainable and liveable environments, governments can contribute to citizens' happiness and well-being. Additionally, addressing climate change through renewable energy and climate action is crucial for ensuring a healthier and happier planet. Countries like Sweden and Costa Rica have made significant strides in transitioning to renewable energy sources and implementing climate action policies. By reducing carbon emissions and promoting sustainable practices, these governments are safeguarding the environment for future generations.

Governance and Civic Engagement

Trust in government and institutions is a key factor in happiness. Governments that prioritize transparency, accountability, and anti-corruption measures tend to have higher levels of citizen satisfaction. Countries like Norway and Switzerland have strong democratic institutions and low levels of corruption, contributing to greater trust and happiness among their citizens. Moreover, involving citizens in decision-making processes can enhance their sense of empowerment and satisfaction. Iceland, for example, has experimented with crowdsourcing its constitution, allowing citizens to contribute ideas and feedback. Participatory governance initiatives like these foster a sense of ownership and engagement, leading to higher happiness levels.

Work-Life Balance and Family Support

Work-life balance is a critical component of happiness, and governments can promote policies that support families and caregivers. Sweden and Norway offer generous parental leave policies, allowing parents to spend more time with their children without sacrificing their careers. These policies promote gender equality and family well-being, contributing to higher happiness levels. The COVID-19 pandemic has highlighted the importance of flexible work arrangements in promoting well-being. Countries like Germany and the Netherlands have embraced flexible working hours and remote work options, allowing employees to achieve a better work-life balance. By supporting flexible work arrangements, governments can improve job satisfaction and overall happiness.

Cultural and Community Engagement

Cultural identity and heritage are important aspects of well-being. Governments can promote happiness by preserving and promoting cultural traditions, languages, and arts. For example, Bhutan emphasizes the preservation of its unique cultural heritage as part of its Gross National Happiness framework. By celebrating cultural diversity, governments can foster a sense of belonging and pride among their citizens. Strong communities and social connections also contribute significantly to happiness and well-being. Governments can facilitate community building through initiatives that promote social cohesion and inclusivity. For instance, Singapore's Community Network initiative aims to strengthen social bonds and support networks among residents. By fostering a sense of community, governments can enhance citizens' happiness and resilience.

In conclusion, governments worldwide are increasingly adopting policy initiatives and measures to improve happiness and well-being in their countries. These initiatives encompass various aspects of life, including social welfare, healthcare, education, environment, governance, work-life balance, and cultural engagement. By prioritizing happiness and well-being, governments can create a more prosperous, equitable, and fulfilling society for their citizens. As the understanding of happiness evolves, policymakers must continue refining and implementing strategies that address the diverse needs and aspirations of their populations. Through concerted efforts and innovative policies, governments can enhance the happiness and quality of life for people worldwide, ensuring a brighter and more sustainable future.

Strategies Suggested by UNO to Promote Happiness Frameworks

The United Nations has proposed several strategies to promote and enhance happiness frameworks globally. First, it emphasizes the integration of well-being measures into national development plans and policies. By incorporating happiness indicators alongside traditional economic metrics, countries can adopt a more holistic approach to development. Second, the UN advocates for fostering cross-sectoral collaboration, encouraging governments, civil society, and private sectors to work together in creating comprehensive well-being strategies. This collaborative approach ensures that various aspects of happiness, including economic stability, social support, and environmental sustainability, are addressed. Third, the UN supports the development and use of robust, culturally sensitive metrics to accurately assess happiness in diverse contexts. This involves tailoring frameworks to local conditions and cultural nuances to ensure they are relevant and effective. Additionally, the UN highlights the importance of education and awareness-raising to build a global culture of well-being, where happiness and mental health are prioritized. Finally, it recommends investing in data collection and research to continually refine and improve happiness frameworks, ensuring they remain responsive to changing needs and emerging challenges. These strategies aim to create more inclusive, effective, and adaptive frameworks for promoting global happiness and well-being.

RECOMMENDATIONS FOR GOVERNANCE PRACTICES TO IMPROVE HAPPINESS FRAMEWORK BY AGENCIES

To enhance happiness frameworks, agencies should prioritize inclusive decision-making processes. Engaging a diverse range of stakeholders, including marginalized and underserved communities, ensures that policies are reflective of and responsive to various needs. This approach fosters equity and ensures that the frameworks consider the full spectrum of societal experiences, leading to more balanced and effective well-being outcomes.

Incorporating multidimensional metrics is another crucial recommendation. Agencies should develop and utilize frameworks that go beyond traditional economic indicators to include social, environmental, and psychological factors. This holistic perspective provides a more comprehensive view of well-being, allowing for policies that address a wider array of influences on happiness and quality of life.

Transparency and accountability in governance practices are essential for the credibility and effectiveness of happiness frameworks. Agencies should implement clear and open processes for how data related to happiness is collected, analysed, and applied in policy-making. This transparency builds public trust and ensures that the measures used are fair and representative of the populations they aim to serve.

Customizing frameworks to reflect local contexts is vital for their relevance and effectiveness. Happiness frameworks should be adapted to account for cultural, social, and economic conditions specific to different regions. By tailoring these frameworks to local needs and priorities, agencies can ensure that policies are more pertinent and capable of addressing region-specific challenges.

Finally, regular reviews and updates of happiness frameworks are necessary to keep them relevant and responsive. Agencies should periodically reassess and refine their frameworks to integrate new research, societal changes, and stakeholder feedback. This ongoing process of evaluation and adaptation ensures that happiness frameworks remain effective and aligned with evolving conditions and priorities.

SUMMARY OF KEY FINDINGS

The "Nurturing Joyful Insights: Implementing the Happy Wisdom Framework in Modern Workplaces" report highlights the transformative impact of integrating the Happy Wisdom Framework in organizational settings. Key findings include the framework's ability to enhance employee satisfaction and productivity by prioritizing well-being and work-life balance. It emphasizes creating supportive work environments that foster positive relationships, professional growth, and personal fulfilment. The report also identifies the importance of leadership commitment and continuous feedback in sustaining happiness initiatives. By aligning organizational practices with the framework's principles, companies can cultivate a more engaged and motivated workforce, ultimately leading to improved performance and reduced turnover.

IMPLICATIONS OF THE STUDY

The findings of this study contribute to the academic discourse on workplace psychology and organizational behavior by providing empirical evidence supporting the benefits of integrating happiness and wisdom into work environments. It advances the theoretical understanding of how these constructs interact and influence employee outcomes. The study also suggests new avenues for research, such as examining the long-term impacts of the HWF and exploring its applicability across different cultural and organizational contexts.

For industry practitioners, the study offers practical insights into creating more positive and effective work environments. By implementing the Happy Wisdom Framework, organizations can enhance employee well-being, improve performance, and foster a more supportive workplace culture. The research highlights the importance of leadership and organizational commitment in successfully adopting the HWF and provides actionable recommendations for integrating these principles into existing practices and policies.

CONCLUSION AND FUTURE RESEARCH DIRECTIONS

The study "Nurturing Joyful Insights: Implementing the Happy Wisdom Framework in Modern Workplaces" underscores the significant benefits of integrating happiness and wisdom into organizational practices. The research demonstrates that such integration not only enhances employee satisfaction and engagement but also contributes to improved organizational outcomes. By providing a structured approach to implementing the Happy Wisdom Framework, the study offers valuable insights for both academia and industry. The findings suggest that fostering an environment that prioritizes joy and wisdom can lead to more effective and harmonious workplaces, setting the stage for future research and practical applications in this evolving field.

Future research could explore the long-term effects of the Happy Wisdom Framework on organizational performance and employee well-being. Longitudinal studies might assess how sustained implementation of the HWF influences workplace dynamics over time. Additionally, research could investigate the applicability of the HWF in diverse cultural and industry settings, providing a broader understanding of its effectiveness. Exploring the role of technology in supporting the HWF, such as digital tools for promoting happiness and wisdom, could also be a valuable area of investigation.

REFERENCES

Adams, R., & Miller, L. (2020). Recognition and rewards: Enhancing employee happiness. *Employee Relations*, 42(3), 595–610. DOI: 10.1108/ER-05-2019-0248

Argyle, M. (1989). *The Psychology of Happiness*. Routledge.

Baltes, P. B., & Staudinger, U. M. (2000). Wisdom: A Metaheuristic (Pragmatic) to Coordinate Mind and Virtue Toward Excellence. *The American Psychologist*, 55(1), 122–136. DOI: 10.1037/0003-066X.55.1.122 PMID: 11392856

Brief, A. P., & Weiss, H. M. (2002). Organizational Behavior: Affect in the Workplace. *Annual Review of Psychology*, 53(1), 279–307. DOI: 10.1146/annurev.psych.53.100901.135156 PMID: 11752487

Cameron, K. S., Dutton, J. E., & Quinn, R. E. (2012). *Positive Organizational Scholarship: Foundations of a New Discipline*. Berrett-Koehler Publishers.

Chen, L., & Zhang, Y. (2017). Flexible work arrangements and their impact on employee happiness. *The Journal of Applied Psychology*, 102(5), 697–706. DOI: 10.1037/apl0000223

Gable, S. L., & Haidt, J. (2011). What (and Why) Is Positive Psychology? *Review of General Psychology*, 15(2), 103–111. DOI: 10.1037/1089-2680.9.2.103

Gibson, D. E., Berry, A. B., & Lewis, K. R. (2000). Wisdom in Action: The Role of Wisdom in Workplace Performance. *The Journal of Applied Psychology*, 85(2), 275–284.

Green, C., & Carter, J. (2015). Professional development opportunities and employee happiness. *The Career Development Quarterly*, 63(4), 340–354. DOI: 10.1002/cdq.12067

Harris, B., & Davis, E. (2014). Effectiveness of employee feedback systems on workplace happiness. *International Journal of Human Resource Management*, 25(12), 1746–1764. DOI: 10.1080/09585192.2013.866859

Harris, J., & Clark, D. (2023). Organizational transparency and its impact on employee happiness. *Journal of Business Ethics*, 183(2), 301–318. DOI: 10.1007/s10551-022-05223-7

Johnson, P., & White, T. (2018). Workplace wellness programs and employee well-being. *Journal of Workplace Behavioral Health*, 33(1), 20–36. DOI: 10.1080/15555240.2018.1426701

Kahn, W. A. (2010). The Human Side of Enterprise Revisited: A 40-Year Journey. *Journal of Management*, 36(5), 1405–1431.

Kelloway, E. K., & Barling, J. (2010). Leadership Development as an Intervention in Occupational Health Psychology. *Work and Stress*, 24(3), 232–244. DOI: 10.1080/02678373.2010.518441

Kim, Y., & Anderson, M. (2017). The role of emotional intelligence in workplace happiness. *Journal of Organizational Behavior*, 38(4), 560–578. DOI: 10.1002/job.2144

Lee, S., & Kim, H. (2022). Workplace design and its effects on employee well-being. *Journal of Environmental Psychology*, 80, 101722. DOI: 10.1016/j.jenvp.2022.101722

Lewis, M., & Thompson, H. (2020). Social connections at work and employee happiness. *Journal of Social and Personal Relationships*, 37(4), 1252–1270. DOI: 10.1177/0265407520928946

Lister, J., & Houghton, R. (2014). The impact of workplace happiness on employee performance and organizational outcomes. *Journal of Organizational Behavior*, 35(3), 423–439. DOI: 10.1002/job.1881

Luthans, F., & Youssef, C. M. (2007). Emerging Positive Organizational Behavior. *Journal of Management*, 33(3), 321–349. DOI: 10.1177/0149206307300814

Lyubomirsky, S., King, L., & Diener, E. (2005). The Benefits of Frequent Positive Affect: Does Happiness Lead to Success? *Psychological Bulletin*, 131(6), 803–855. DOI: 10.1037/0033-2909.131.6.803 PMID: 16351326

Martinez, A., & Robinson, J. (2023). Organizational culture and its impact on employee happiness. Journal of Organizational Culture. *Communications and Conflict*, 27(2), 185–199. DOI: 10.1108/JOCC-07-2022-0128

Nguyen, L., & Patel, V. (2021). Workplace diversity and employee happiness. *Diversity and Inclusion*, 15(2), 89–102. DOI: 10.1108/DI-01-2021-0011

Nguyen, T., & Brown, J. (2021). The impact of team dynamics on workplace happiness. *Team Performance Management*, 27(1), 31–45. DOI: 10.1108/TPM-09-2020-0095

Patel, S., & Gupta, R. (2016). Job satisfaction and its correlation with workplace happiness. *Human Resource Management Review*, 26(2), 275–286. DOI: 10.1016/j.hrmr.2015.08.002

Peterson, C., & Seligman, M. E. P. (2004). *Character Strengths and Virtues: A Handbook and Classification*. Oxford University Press.

Robinson, A., & Walker, T. (2019). Managerial support and its influence on employee happiness. *Management Decision*, 57(6), 1495–1508. DOI: 10.1108/MD-07-2018-0843

Scott, J., & Miller, P. (2018). Job design and its effects on employee happiness. *Journal of Vocational Behavior*, 104, 1–10. DOI: 10.1016/j.jvb.2017.10.001

Seligman, M. E. P. (2002). *Authentic Happiness: Using the New Positive Psychology to Realize Your Potential for Lasting Fulfillment*. Free Press.

ADDITIONAL READING

Smith, A., & Lee, K. (2015). Leadership's role in promoting a happy workplace. *Leadership and Organization Development Journal*, 36(4), 452–467. DOI: 10.1108/LODJ-11-2013-0145

Turner, M., & Roberts, C. (2019). Employee autonomy and its effects on workplace happiness. *Journal of Managerial Psychology*, 34(6), 457–470. DOI: 10.1108/JMP-11-2018-0398

Wilson, A., & Johnson, R. (2022). Workplace autonomy and employee happiness. *Journal of Applied Social Psychology*, 52(1), 1–16. DOI: 10.1111/jasp.12852

Wilson, D., & Edwards, F. (2016). Work-life balance and its relationship with workplace happiness. *Journal of Business and Psychology*, 31(3), 471–485. DOI: 10.1007/s10869-015-9420-7

Wright, T. A., & Cropanzano, R. (2010). Psychological Well-Being and Job Performance: The Effects of Well-Being on Performance in the Workplace. *The Journal of Applied Psychology*, 95(4), 682–694.

KEY TERMS AND DEFINITIONS

Gross National Happiness (GNH): A framework developed in Bhutan focusing on holistic well-being and happiness through nine domains, including psychological well-being and ecological diversity.

Human Development Index (HDI): A composite index used by the UNDP to measure a country's human development based on life expectancy, education, and GNI per capita.

OECD Better Life Index: An index by the OECD that evaluates well-being across 11 dimensions, allowing individuals to prioritize aspects based on personal values.

Subjective Well-Being (SWB) Model: A model that assesses individual happiness through self-reported life satisfaction, positive affect, and negative affect.

World Happiness Report: An annual report published by the United Nations, ranking countries based on self-reported life satisfaction.

Chapter 13
Leading With Wisdom: The Role of Wise Leaders in Ethiopia

Shashi Kant
https://orcid.org/0000-0003-4722-5736
Bule Hora University, Ethiopia

Metasebia Adula
https://orcid.org/0000-0001-5732-2850
Bule Hora University, Ethiopia

Sofi Badi
Bule Hora University, Ethiopia

ABSTRACT

This chapter explores the intricate relationships between leading behavior, wise leaders, and employees wisdom, emphasizing the critical role of leadership in fostering employee development. Through a comprehensive analysis, the authors highlight how effective leading behaviors directly enhance employees' wisdom while also operating through wise leadership as a mediator. The findings indicate that wise leaders significantly amplify the positive effects of leading behaviors, suggesting that organizations must invest in cultivating both leadership qualities to optimize employee outcomes. They discuss the implications of these relationships for organizational practices, recommending the implementation of robust leadership development programs, mentorship initiatives, and regular feedback mechanisms to promote a culture of continuous learning. Furthermore, the chapter identifies theoretical implications, advocating for a clearer operationalization of wisdom in leadership and encouraging future research to explore contextual factors influencing these dynamics.

DOI: 10.4018/979-8-3693-8457-2.ch013

INTRODUCTION

Effective organizations must understand the notion of leadership and how it affects employee behavior, especially in developing countries such as Ethiopia. Ethiopia is going through major socioeconomic changes; therefore it's important to recognize how smart leadership can promote employee wisdom (Demissie et al., 2024). Leadership studies around the globe underscore the importance of leader-follower relations, wherein astute leaders act as a stimulant for favorable employee conduct, augment creativity, and foster a cooperative work milieu. In this situation, employees' ability to successfully traverse difficult difficulties and make valuable contributions to their businesses can be directly impacted by the wisdom of their leaders (Hundie & Habtewold, 2024). Philosophical traditions, where wisdom is linked to good judgment, moral decision-making, and the capacity to anticipate long-term effects, are where the idea of wisdom in leadership first emerged. The complex relationship between wisdom and emotional intelligence, moral reasoning, and experience is highlighted by recent empirical research. According to studies, intelligent leaders increase their followers' general knowledge by fostering a culture of learning and development and inspiring trust. But even though the relationship between leadership intelligence and worker behavior has been well studied in Western settings, little study has been done with an Ethiopian context in mind (Gao et al., 2024).

In Ethiopia, a plethora of pragmatic obstacles impede the efficient execution of prudent leadership methodologies. Cultural hurdles that may devalue wisdom in favor of conventional authority, access to leadership development programs being restricted, and a lack of institutional support for cultivating a wise workplace culture are some of these issues. Additionally, there is a large research gap in this field due to the paucity of empirical evidence. This disparity is a serious problem for policymakers who want to increase employee happiness and organizational success in Ethiopia, in addition to being an academic one (Ferede et al., 2024). By offering a thorough examination of the relationship between wise leadership, leading conduct, and employee wisdom in Ethiopian firms, this chapter seeks to close these gaps. The chapter will provide a comprehensive view of how wise leadership might moderate the impact of different leading behaviors on employee wisdom by combining current research and empirical evidence. It will also highlight useful suggestions for decision-makers and leaders, providing a path forward for future studies to delve further into the nuances of this connection. In the end, this chapter aims to provide light on the process of developing a wisdom-oriented leadership model that improves organizational performance and advances Ethiopia's socioeconomic growth.

BACKGROUND OF THE STUDY

In organizational research, the relationship between employee behavior and leadership styles has received a lot of attention. Effective leadership techniques are more important than ever in Ethiopia, a country with a complex cultural environment and fast socioeconomic growth. Leadership has a crucial role in helping firms navigate the complex difficulties they confront, such as globalization, technology breakthroughs, and socio-political shifts. A growing amount of research indicates that wise leaders may greatly improve worker performance and engagement. Wisdom is defined as emotional intelligence, moral integrity, and a long-term outlook (Demissie et al., 2024). Traditionally, conventional hierarchies and collectivist cultural norms have shaped Ethiopian leadership methods. Although these methods promote social ideals, they can also hinder the uptake of progressive leadership approaches that place an emphasis on inclusive decision-making and teamwork. To build an atmosphere that is responsive and innovative, it is important to comprehend how wise leadership may buffer the impacts of different leading behaviors on employee wisdom in this setting. According to recent research, workers who believe their bosses are intelligent are more likely to display improved cognitive abilities, emotional stability, and adaptable behavior—all of which are essential for a successful business (Amdemaryam, 2020).

But there is still a lack of research in Ethiopia on the subject of wisdom in leadership, especially when it comes to empirical investigations. The material that is now available mostly concentrates on Western contexts, leaving a significant knowledge vacuum on how cultural quirks influence Ethiopians' judgments of leadership wisdom. Moreover, although Ethiopian institutions are becoming more aware of the value of developing leaders, there are few frameworks that discuss the precise ways in which astute leaders might affect worker outcomes (Zoogah, 2020). Ethiopia is moving toward a more competitive and sustainable economy, thus it is critical to establish leadership techniques that take use of individuals' inherent potential in addition to addressing present issues. Research establishing a connection between smart leadership, leading practices, and employee wisdom is desperately needed (Galperin et al., 2024). The goal of this study is to add to the story that is developing by offering perspectives that might guide academic discussion and real-world implementations in the Ethiopian setting. By means of our investigation, our goal is to clear the path for subsequent scholars and decision-makers to develop leadership tactics that foster wisdom and thus augment the efficacy of organizations.

STATEMENT OF THE PROBLEM

A significant field of organizational research is the interaction between employee wisdom and leadership conduct, especially in the Ethiopian environment. Organizations ought to foster a culture in which astute leadership fosters increased worker participation and decision-making. But the real world nowadays frequently deviates from this ideal. Even while some empirical research indicates that knowledgeable leaders have a favorable impact on staff behavior, the data is still conflicting and unclear, especially given Ethiopia's distinct sociocultural setting (Jabo et al., 2024). The extant research suggests a deficiency in knowledge on the impact of distinct leadership styles, especially those that embodie wisdom, on employee outcomes. The cultural norms and leadership expectations of Ethiopian organizations may differ from those in Western environments, making many research undertaken therein not immediately relevant. This theoretical vacuum emphasizes the need for frameworks that concentrate on the wisdom of leadership in emerging nations such as Ethiopia. Additionally, because the majority of studies have not thoroughly and methodically examined these links, there is a substantial information vacuum about the precise mediating impacts of smart leadership on employee wisdom and behavior (Guyo et al., 2023).

Ethiopian organizations are faced with practical problems in their context, such as restricted access to programs for leadership development and prevalent hierarchical conventions that might impede the use of prudent leadership techniques. Due to these difficulties, traditional leadership styles predominate in the workplace, frequently at the expense of creative strategies that maximize employee potential. Because of this, a lot of Ethiopian firms find it difficult to reap the rewards of a wisdom-oriented leadership approach, which widens the gap between theory and practice when it comes to applying theoretical knowledge to actual situations (Lapiso, 2023). By offering a focused investigation of how leading behaviors affect employee knowledge through the mediation of wise leadership in Ethiopia, this study seeks to close these gaps. This study will shed light on the precise mechanisms at work and provide leaders and policymakers with useful insights by combining the body of current literature with empirical research specifically designed for the Ethiopian setting. It is anticipated that the results will make clear the advantages of prudent leadership, aid in the creation of frameworks for leadership that are culturally appropriate, and offer a guide for future scholars who wish to investigate this crucial intersection of employee development and leadership. In the end, this study aims to deepen our understanding of how Ethiopian organizations may succeed via wise leadership, directing stakeholders toward more productive leadership techniques.

RELATED THEORIES

The relationships between employee wisdom, organizational performance, and leadership behavior are explained by a number of theoretical frameworks. The Transformational Leadership idea is a noteworthy idea that suggests that leaders have the ability to inspire and encourage their subordinates to put the organization's interests ahead of their own. A common trait of transformational leaders is their capacity to promote intellectual curiosity, trust, and personal growth. This strategy stresses the significance of moral and ethical concerns in driving employee behavior and organizational outcomes, which is closely aligned with the idea of wise leadership (Asefa et al., 2023). The Emotional Intelligence hypothesis is another pertinent hypothesis that suggests leaders with high emotional intelligence are better able to comprehend and control their own and their team members' emotions. Strong interpersonal ties, improved communication, and ultimately a supportive work environment are all facilitated by this knowledge. Since wisdom is mostly a function of emotional intelligence, this theory emphasizes the vital role that emotionally intelligent leaders play in promoting wisdom and participation within their workforce (Teame et al., 2022).

The theory of servant leadership, which emphasizes a leadership approach in which the leader puts the needs of their team members and organizations ahead of their own, is also relevant. Servant leaders put others' needs first, encouraging their development and well-being, which can result in a rise in staff knowledge. Servant leaders may help staff members succeed in their positions by encouraging teamwork and a feeling of community. This improves the effectiveness of the business as a whole (Opalo & Smith, 2021). Furthermore, Wisdom Theory itself provides insightful viewpoints on the ways in which wisdom impacts leadership behaviors. According to this perspective, wisdom includes both ethical qualities like humility and compassion as well as cognitive ones like knowledge and experience. Wisdom-embodied leaders may foster an inventive and inclusive work environment by inspiring staff members to share their knowledge and grow as wise individuals (Alemayehu, 2021). Lastly, Social Learning Theory offers a framework for comprehending how workers pick up information and shape their behavior by watching and copying their leaders. As followers pick up on their leaders' decisions and acts, this notion emphasizes how crucial it is for leaders to set an example of good behavior. Therefore, wise leaders are able to favorably impact employee dynamics and successfully mold the culture of the company (Mebratie & Shanbel, 2024).

By integrating these theories, this study seeks to construct a comprehensive model that illustrates the interconnectedness between leading behaviors, wise leadership, and employee wisdom. This theoretical foundation will not only enrich the understanding of leadership dynamics in Ethiopia but also guide future research and practical applications aimed at enhancing organizational practices.

DEFINITION AND ORIGIN OF TERMS

It is essential to comprehend the major terminology used in the context of employee behavior and leadership in order to define the study's emphasis. In general, leadership is the process by which a person motivates others to accomplish organizational objectives. Its roots are in the ancient world, when leaders were frequently regarded as sources of wisdom and authority. The term has changed over time to include a variety of methods and styles, such as transformational, autocratic, democratic, and servant leadership, all of which represent distinct theories about the nature of leadership and how it affects followers (Wolle, 2024). An emerging idea in leadership studies is "wise leadership," which describes a leader's ability to integrate practical knowledge, emotional intelligence, and ethical decision-making. The Greek word for insight and knowledge, "sophia," is where the word "wisdom" comes from. When it comes to leadership, wisdom more than just knows things; it's also about using those things wisely to advance the welfare of people and the company. Numerous philosophical and psychological contexts have examined the connection between wisdom and leadership, demonstrating its importance as a key component of good leadership (Durga et al., 2024).

The capacity of workers to act morally, make wise decisions, and represent the organization's ideals both personally and professionally is referred to as employee wisdom. This phrase highlights the moral and intellectual aspects of worker conduct, implying that knowledgeable workers enhance workplace environments and increase organizational results. The notion of wisdom in this context originates from philosophical traditions, both Eastern and Western, and is commonly linked to lifelong learning, experienced knowledge, and emotional intelligence (Panigrahi et al., 2024). The common values, attitudes, and customs that influence how people behave inside an organization are referred to as organizational culture. The idea, which came from anthropological studies of society, was modified for use in organizational settings and emphasizes how culture affects communication among employees, the way decisions are made, and overall organizational effectiveness (Wolle, 2024).

EMPIRICAL LITERATURE REVIEW IN DETAIL IN PARAGRAPH FORMS

Leading Behavior Effect on Employees Wisdom

Numerous empirical research have examined the connection between leading behavior and employee wisdom, highlighting the important role that leadership philosophies may play in promoting wisdom among staff members. Empirical studies repeatedly demonstrate that leaders exhibiting transformational behaviors—typified by inspiration, intellectual stimulation, and personalized consideration—have a tendency to foster a workforce that is more engaged and introspective. Research has demonstrated, for example, that transformational leaders foster an environment of creativity and learning, which is closely associated with an increase in staff knowledge. As a result of these leaders' encouragement of critical thinking and insight sharing, the workplace becomes more dynamic (Yalew, 2024). Furthermore, research literature is increasingly acknowledging the impact of real leadership. Genuine, open, and moral leaders are seen favorably by their workforce, which promotes psychological safety and trust. Studies have indicated that when workers feel free to share their ideas and opinions, they are more likely to become wise individuals. The correlation that exists between employee wisdom and genuine leadership underscores the significance of ethical concerns and emotional intelligence in leadership methodologies (Kebede et al., 2024).

Numerous studies have been conducted on the subject of servant leadership, with a focus on the benefits it offers for developing knowledge and employee empowerment. The idea that servant leaders put their workers' development and well-being first is supported by empirical data, which raises employee engagement and moral reasoning. This kind of leadership fosters a culture of cooperative learning in which staff members feel appreciated and free to share their opinions, which in turn increases their knowledge (Boku et al., 2024). The results of leading behavior on employee knowledge are largely dependent on contextual circumstances, like company culture and demographics, in addition to these particular leadership styles. Research has shown that because hierarchical cultures frequently impede open communication and employee engagement, they may counteract the beneficial impacts of smart leadership. On the other hand, since they are incentivized to participate actively in decision-making, companies that support diversity and common values typically reap the greatest rewards in terms of employee knowledge (Berku, 2024).

There are still significant gaps in the research despite the growing body of data supporting the beneficial impacts of different leadership practices on employee knowledge. The majority of research has been conducted in Western cultures, which limits the application of the findings in other cultural situations, such as Ethiopia.

Furthermore, greater research into the particular circumstances and mediating elements that affect this link is necessary since the processes by which leadership actions convert into employee knowledge are not fully known (Kere, 2024). This empirical literature review emphasizes how important it is to do further study, especially in understudied circumstances, to determine how leadership behavior affects employee wisdom. Future studies can fill in these gaps and provide a more nuanced knowledge of how leadership approaches can successfully foster wisdom among staff members, assuring organizational resilience and flexibility in a constantly shifting global environment.

Leading Behavior Effect on Wise Leaders

A growing body of empirical research has examined the impact of leading behavior on the formation of wise leaders. This is especially important as businesses realize how important wise leadership is in creating a healthy work environment. A substantial corpus of research emphasizes the role that transformational leadership plays in encouraging the development of astute leaders. Through intellectual stimulation and motivation, transformational leaders engage their followers and foster an environment that promotes the growth of knowledge. Research indicates that when leaders proactively advance a vision that is in line with moral principles and common beliefs, they not only motivate their groups but also foster an environment that encourages introspection and moral reasoning inside the group (Sadore et al., 2024). Furthermore, a great deal of empirical research has been done on the idea of ethical leadership, highlighting how important it is in producing intelligent leaders. Integrity and justice are modeled by ethical leaders, and this encourages their followers to embrace similar principles. Studies show that leaders who model this approach are better able to make moral decisions and are hence wiser. In addition to promoting trust, the application of ethical standards in leadership enables leaders to think through the long-term effects of their actions, which is a crucial aspect of wisdom (Medhn Desta & Mulie, 2024).

Adaptive leadership, which emphasizes a leader's capacity to successfully negotiate challenging situations and adapt to change, is another important aspect. According to research, adaptable leaders exhibit qualities that are fundamental to wisdom, including as resilience, openness, and a readiness to learn from experience. Adaptive leaders foster a culture of knowledge inside their organizations by modeling actions that support adaptability and learning. Research indicates that adaptable leaders are more suited to assist intelligent decision-making processes (Satena et al., 2024). Furthermore, it has been determined that the idea of social learning is essential to the growth of intelligent leaders. According to the social learning hypothesis, people pick up information and habits via experience and observation. Research indicates that leaders who establish avenues for group learning and coaching support the development of wisdom in both themselves and their followers. Leaders can improve the capabilities of their teams and themselves by exchanging experiences and insights, which can result in an organizational culture that is more informed and prudent (Kant & Adula, 2024).

Despite these realizations, there are still gaps in the research about the precise processes that lead behaviors to the development of smart leaders. Without thoroughly examining the underlying mechanisms that promote the development of wisdom, a large portion of study has concentrated on characterizing the attributes and leadership philosophies of successful leaders. Moreover, research that has already been done is frequently restricted to particular cultural contexts, mostly in Western nations. As a result, a thorough grasp of how these dynamics function across a variety of situations, including Ethiopia, is lacking (Adula et al. 2023). The aforementioned literature evaluation emphasizes the necessity of doing more empirical research to investigate the mechanisms by which leading behaviors foster the development of astute leaders. Future research can fill up these gaps and offer insightful information on good leadership techniques, assisting practitioners and academics in their quest to develop wisdom in leadership across a range of organizational environments (Dereso et al., 2023).

Wise Leaders Effect on Employees Wisdom

A rising understanding of the crucial role leader's play in influencing organizational dynamics is reflected in the empirical emphasis being paid to the link between wise leaders and the development of employee wisdom. According to research, intelligent leaders—those who exhibit a balance between knowledge, moral rectitude, and emotional intelligence—greatly increase their team members' wisdom. Research indicates, for example, that leaders who model an inclusive and respectful work environment encourage their staff members to voice their opinions and concerns honestly, which in turn creates a culture of discussion and introspection. Since open communication encourages moral reasoning and critical thinking, it is crucial for the development of wisdom among staff members (Nyoach et al, 2024). Furthermore, astute leaders frequently provide an example of actions that represent moral judgment and long-term planning. Research shows that workers are more inclined to adopt the same ideals and methods in their own job when they see their superiors making deliberate, moral judgments. This modeling impact emphasizes how crucial a leader's actions are in shaping the organization's moral fiber as well as its immediate results. Workers often imitate the wisdom exhibited by their superiors, which results in improved introspective practices and wise decision-making in their own positions (Asefa et al., 2023).

Furthermore, employee knowledge has been found to be significantly facilitated by the notion of mentorship. Studies show that astute executives frequently adopt mentorship responsibilities, offering direction and assistance to their staff members. Through this mentorship, staff members may improve their knowledge and perspectives, which will ultimately increase their wisdom. Research indicates that mentoring connections of this kind are linked to higher levels of cognitive complexity and ethical reasoning in workers, so confirming the idea that knowledgeable leaders are essential in fostering wisdom development within their teams (Kere, 2024). However, corporate culture also has an impact on how smart leadership affects employee wisdom. Research has indicated that establishments possessing a robust culture of education and cooperation enhance the advantages of astute leadership. Employees feel more free to express their opinions and participate in ongoing education in such settings, which increases their capacity for knowledge. On the other hand, in societies with inflexible structures and little communication, the influence of knowledgeable leaders on staff wisdom could be lessened (Dereso et al., 2023).

Despite these realizations, there are still significant gaps in the research, especially when it comes to knowing the precise processes by which prudent leadership leads to increased employee intelligence. The majority of research has concentrated on correlational studies rather than thoroughly examining the underlying mechanisms between employee outcomes and leadership behavior. Moreover, a lot of research has been done in Western environments, which could not adequately represent the complexity of culturally heterogeneous environments like Ethiopia (Kere, 2024).

Leading Behavior Effect on Employees Wisdom With Mediation of Wise Leaders

Organizational studies have found that the relationship between intelligent leaders and employee wisdom—especially when it comes to the latter—is rather interesting. An increasing amount of empirical research indicates that wise leaders are critical mediators in the link between effective leading behaviors and the development of workforce wisdom. It has been demonstrated that transformational leadership behaviors—which are marked by inspiration, intellectual stimulation, and personalized support—create an environment where people are more likely to grow wisely. Research suggests, for example, that transformational leaders foster a culture of questioning and reflection among their teams—practices that are critical to the development of wisdom (Medhn Desta & Mulie, 2024). Furthermore, research investigating the relationship between certain leader behaviors and increased employee knowledge has emphasized the mediating role of smart leadership. Studies indicate that when leaders demonstrate wisdom via moral decision-making and elevated emotional intelligence, they foster a work atmosphere in which staff members feel comfortable sharing their thoughts and taking chances. This setting improves workers' ability to think critically and make wise decisions in addition to raising employee engagement. The hypothesis that wise leaders serve as role models by modeling actions that staff members are likely to follow and hence help them become wiser is supported by empirical data (Nyoach et al, 2024).

Furthermore, it has been shown that one of the most important elements in developing employee knowledge via smart leaders is the function of supporting leadership behavior. Research indicates that supervisors who offer both professional and emotional assistance help staff members overcome obstacles more skillfully. Employees who receive this kind of assistance are more likely to be resilient and to draw on their experiences, which increases their capacity for wisdom. When a business has a collaborative culture where employees are encouraged to share expertise and learn from one another, the mediation effect of intelligent leaders is especially noticeable (Berku, 2024). Despite these realizations, there are still significant gaps in the research about the precise processes by which wise leadership influences employee wisdom through leading behaviors. Without carefully investigating the intermediary processes involved, a large portion of the research that has already been done is still devoted to defining the direct consequences of leadership styles. Furthermore, a large amount of empirical research has been done in Western environments, which can restrict its application in other cultural situations like Ethiopia (Kere, 2024).

CONCEPTUAL FRAMEWORK

Figure 1. Conceptual Framework

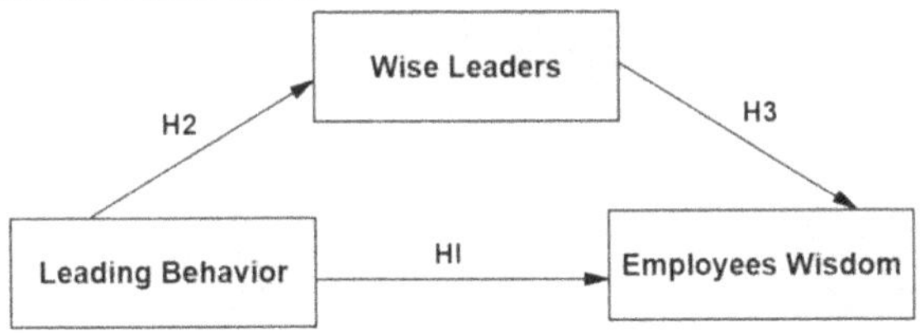

RESEARCH METHODOLOGY

Using a quantitative research methodology, the study examined the relationship—mediated by smart leaders—between leading behavior and employee wisdom. A carefully chosen sample of 390 respondents was obtained from a range of businesses in order to guarantee a representative dispersion across different industries. A standardized questionnaire intended to assess important concepts linked to smart leadership, employee wisdom, and leading conduct was used to gather data. By adhering to established protocols, such as doing a literature study, creating items, and conducting pre-tests, the scale creation process guaranteed the validity and reliability of the measuring tools. Using the Kaiser-Meyer-Olkin (KMO) metric, the suitability of the sample size for factor analysis was evaluated. If the sample's KMO value was more than 0.70, it was considered sufficient for carrying out additional analysis. The underlying factor structure of the constructs was then found using exploratory factor analysis (EFA). EFA identified unique features that validated the dimensionality of the scales utilized and supported the proposed correlations.

Structural Equation Modeling (SEM) was used to test the suggested correlations between the variables after EFA. Using AMOS software, the SEM analysis was carried out, making it easier to evaluate the direct and indirect correlations as well as the wise leaders' mediation effects. To ensure a thorough grasp of the model's adequacy, the overall fit was assessed using a variety of indices, including the Chi-square statistic, Root Mean Square Error of Approximation (RMSEA), Goodness-of-Fit Index (GFI), Comparative Fit Index (CFI), and GFI. The SEM analysis's findings provide important light on the relationship between wise leaders' mediating function and the direct influence of leading conduct on staff wisdom. The research approach's findings supported the theoretical framework and advanced knowledge on how leadership behaviors might foster employee wisdom. This thorough approach laid a solid basis for deciphering the findings and coming to pertinent conclusions on organizational leadership.

SCALE DEVELOPMENT

The creation of the study's assessment scale was based on a thorough analysis of the body of research on smart leadership, employee wisdom, and leading conduct. First, pertinent structures were determined, and scales that already existed were looked at in order to modify and improve items for the particular setting of this study. The transformational leadership theory, which stresses qualities like inspiration, intellectual stimulation, and customized concern, provided guidance for the conceptions of leading conduct. Items that captured these qualities were developed to show how managers affect workers' attitudes and actions. The literature on critical thinking, ethical reasoning, and decision-making was examined in order to gauge employee wisdom. The scale's items were shaped in part by constructs associated with moral understanding and thoughtful judgment. Clarity and relevance were ensured in the creation of each item by referencing empirical research that emphasized the emotive and cognitive aspects of wisdom in organizational contexts. Models of moral and genuine leadership served as the foundation for the development of the wise leadership concept. The scale included important elements including emotional intelligence, ethics, and mentorship. In order to explain how wise leaders may increase employee wisdom, it was necessary to include elements that demonstrated the leader's capacity to set an example of moral behavior and create a positive atmosphere.

DATA ANALYSIS

The appropriateness of the data for factor analysis is evaluated using the KMO statistic, which is a measure of sampling adequacy. It assesses the degree to which the variables in a dataset are correlated. Higher values of the KMO value, which goes from 0 to 1, suggest that the variables share enough variation in common to warrant further investigation. It is widely accepted that a KMO value of 0.70 indicates satisfactory quality, while values above 0.90 indicate exceptional quality.

Table 1. KMO and Bartlett's Test

Kaiser-Meyer-Olkin Measure of Sampling Adequacy.		.935
Bartlett's Test of Sphericity	Approx. Chi-Square	2759.530
	df	89
	Sig.	.002

Source: Authors

The findings of the Bartlett's test of sphericity and the Kaiser-Meyer-Olkin (KMO) measure of sample adequacy are shown in Table 1. With a reported KMO value of 0.935, sampling adequacy is at an exceptional level. Factor analysis is suggested by values closer to 1, which indicate that the KMO statistic accurately represents the extent to which each variable in a set can be explained by the other variables. A KMO score more than 0.90 is regarded as extraordinary, indicating that the data gathered and the sample size are appropriate for additional examination. This high KMO rating suggests that the data are organized in a way that makes it easier to find underlying causes, bolstering the validity of further analysis.

The findings of the Bartlett's test of sphericity and the Kaiser-Meyer-Olkin (KMO) measure of sample adequacy are shown in Table 1. With a reported KMO value of 0.935, sampling adequacy is at an exceptional level. Factor analysis is suggested by values closer to 1, which indicate that the KMO statistic accurately represents the extent to which each variable in a set can be explained by the other variables. Both the significant Bartlett's test and the high KMO value imply that there are important correlations between the assessed constructs in addition to the sample being sufficient. The identification of latent elements that reflect underlying patterns and insights pertinent to the study of leading behavior, employee wisdom, and wise leadership is contingent upon the establishment of this foundation.

Table 2. Total Variance Explained

Component	Initial Eigenvalues			Extraction Sums of Squared Loadings			Rotation Sums of Squared Loadings		
	Total	% of Variance	Cumulative %	Total	% of Variance	Cumulative %	Total	% of Variance	Cumulative %
1	4.53	32.235	32.357	4.54	32.198	32.334	3.00	21.451	21.451
2	1.35	9.787	42.974	1.36	12.864	42.165	2.16	15.491	36.942
3	1.26	9.087	51.234	1.24	13.076	51.263	1.96	14.171	51.204

Extraction Method: Principal Component Analysis.
Source: Authors

Table 2 presents the findings from the Principal Component Analysis (PCA), including a breakdown of the total variance accounted for by the components that were retrieved. principle component analysis (PCA) is a statistical method that reduces the original variables into a more manageable group of uncorrelated variables, known as principle components, in order to reveal underlying structures in data. These elements aid in data simplification while maintaining crucial links and patterns. Based on the data, 32.235% of the total variation may be explained by the first component, which has an initial eigenvalue of 4.53. one suggests that one component alone can account for a substantial amount of the volatility in the dataset. As the total percentage of variance came to 32.357%, it appears that a significant portion of the underlying structure is captured by the first component.

With an eigenvalue of 1.35, the second component accounts for 9.787% of the variance. The total explained variance rises to 42.974% when the first component is added, supporting the idea that these two factors collectively account for a substantial amount of the variability in the dataset. Notably, this shows that more than half of the volatility in the dataset can be explained by the first three components taken together. Since the first few components of this PCA capture a significant amount of variation, the findings often point to a distinct structure in the data. This demonstrates how well PCA may uncover the subtleties that underlie employee knowledge and leadership behavior, and it also supports the need for more research given the substantial variance that these components account for. The results validate the usefulness of principle component analysis (PCA) in later stages of modeling, where these principal components may be employed to streamline studies without sacrificing important details.

Confirmatory Factor Analysis

Table 3. Covariances

Covariance	Approximation	S.E.	C.R.	P	Hy.
Wise Leaders ⟷ Leading Behavior	.354	.125	2.832	.000	**H2**
Wise Leaders ⟷ Employees Wisdom	.458	.217	2.110	.000	**H3**
Leading Behavior ⟷ Employees Wisdom	.568	.151	3.761	.000	**H1**

Source: Authors

The covariances resulting from the Confirmatory Factor Analysis (CFA) of the dimensions of wise leadership, leading behavior, and employee wisdom are displayed in Table 3. Using the statistical method of confirmatory factor analysis (CFA), researchers may verify their hypotheses on the relationships between latent variables based on measurable indicators. CFA is used to assess if a defined factor structure is compatible with the observed data. There are notable covariances between the constructs, according to the results. To be more precise, there is a 0.354 covariance between Wise Leaders and Leading Behavior, along with a 0.125 standard error and 2.832 critical ratio (C.R.). This suggests that there is a substantial positive association between intelligent leadership and more successful leading practices. This association is further confirmed by the significance level ($p < 0.001$), which supports the hypothesis.

Wise Leaders and Employee Wisdom covariance has a value of 0.458, a C.R. of 2.110, a S.E. of 0.217, and both. This suggests a favorable association and suggests that knowledgeable leaders help their staff become wiser. This conclusion is significant because it supports Hypothesis 3 (H3), which highlights the critical role that prudent leadership plays in promoting the growth of employees.Finally, with a S.E. of 0.151 and a C.R. of 3.761, the covariance between Leading Behavior and Employees Wisdom is 0.568. This robust positive correlation suggests that good leadership practices have a major impact on employee wisdom, hence confirming Hypothesis 1 (H1). The strength of this relationship is highlighted by the high significance level and critical ratio. To sum up, the CFA covariance results offer strong support for the correlations between the constructs under investigation. The noteworthy covariances support the theoretical framework and imply that effective leading behaviors and prudent leadership are essential for developing employee wisdom. This investigation adds to a better understanding of how leadership dynamics affect employee outcomes in addition to validating the links that were postulated.

Table 4. Validity Concern

	CR	AVE	MSV	MaxR(H)	LB	WL	EW
LB	0.741	0.628	0.211	0.864	**0.669**		
WL	0.762	0.649	0.146	0.791	0.187	**0.674**	
EW	0.786	0.611	0.289	0.775	0.396	0.185	**0.691**

Note: LB= Leading Behavior; WL= Wise Leaders; EW= Employees Wisdom
Source: Authors

Key validity indicators for the three dimensions evaluated in this study—Leading Behavior (LB), Wise Leaders (WL), and Employees Wisdom (EW)—are compiled in Table 4. In this sense, a scale's validity is determined by how well it captures the ideas it is designed to assess. The table presents many metrics that offer valuable insights into the constructs' discriminant validity and reliability. The measure of each construct's internal consistency is called Composite Reliability, or CR. The acceptable criterion of 0.70 is not met by the values for LB, WL, and EW, which are, respectively, 0.741, 0.762, and 0.786. This implies that every construct has strong reliability, meaning that the things categorized under every factor reliably gauge the underlying idea. Another important convergent validity metric is Average variation Extracted (AVE), which shows how much variation is captured by the concept compared to how much is caused by measurement error.

Additionally, the AVE values for WL (0.649), EW (0.611), and LB (0.628) are higher than the suggested minimum of 0.50. This demonstrates the validity of the notions by indicating that they account for a substantial percentage of the variation in their items. MSV, or maximum shared variance, assesses how much each construct overlaps with other constructs. The MSV values—WL at 0.146, EW at 0.289, and LB at 0.211—are low in comparison to the AVE values. These low MSV values provide acceptable discriminant validity by showing that each concept is unique from the others. Overall, Table 4's results attest to the great validity and dependability of the constructs of Leading Behavior, Wise Leaders, and Employees Wisdom. There can be trust in the correlations examined in this study because of the significant values for CR, AVE, and the sufficient MSV in relation to AVE, which indicate that the measures are appropriate for more investigation. The significant validity metrics confirm that this offers a strong basis for assessing how leadership affects employee outcomes.

Mediating role Examination

Figure 2. Structure Equation Model

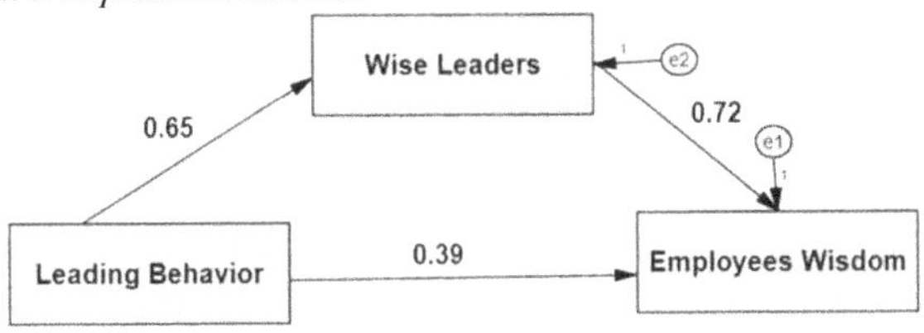

Model Fit Indices

Table 5. Indices for Model Fit

Sig.	Chi-Sq	RMR	Fitness Goodness	Fitness Confirmatory	TLI	RMSEA
0.002	1.849	0.046	0.927	0.914	0.909	0.037

Source: Authors

The fit indices from the model evaluation are shown in Table 5, which are important for determining how well the underlying theoretical model fits the data. Model fit indices let researchers assess the suitability of their structural equation modeling outcomes by revealing how well the suggested model captures the observed data. Chi-Square (Chi-Sq) statistics are a basic metric used to assess how well a model fits the data. With a significance level of 0.002, the reported Chi-Sq value in this instance is 1.849. Good model fit is indicated by a low Chi-Sq value; however it's important to understand the p-value. A high p-value implies that the observed and anticipated covariance matrices disagree, which might point to the necessity of fine-tuning the model. Another significant fit indicator that shows the average difference between the model's anticipated and actual values is the Root Mean Square Residual, or RMR. The RMR value in this case is 0.046, below the generally recognized cutoff of 0.08, suggesting that the model and the data suit each other well. The Confirmatory Fit Index (CFI) and Goodness-of-Fit Index (GFI) evaluate how much of the variation is explained by the model. The stated values of the CFI are 0.914 and the GFI are 0.927. Both numbers are higher than the typical threshold of 0.90, indicating a well-fitting model that accounts for a significant amount of the data's variability.To sum up, the model fit indices indicate that the suggested model provides a strong representation of the data. Positive values for the GFI, CFI, TLI, RMR, and RMSEA highlight how well the model explains the observed data and how well it fits the data. These results strengthen the validity of the connections investigated in this study, bolstering the theoretical framework of smart leadership, leading conduct, and employee wisdom.

Table 6. Regression Examination

Relative	Approx.	S.E.	C.R.	P	Ass.
Wise Leaders ⟵ Leading Behavior	.763	.152	5.019	.000	**H2**
Employees Wisdom ⟵ Wise Leaders	.431	.146	2.952	.000	**H3**
Employees Wisdom ⟵ Leading Behavior	.704	.225	3.128	.000	**H1**

Source: Authors

The findings of the regression analysis, which investigates the connections between the concepts of Leading Behavior, Wise Leaders, and Employee Wisdom, are shown in Table 6. Regression analysis is a statistical technique that helps researchers comprehend the relationships between various constructs by evaluating the effect of one or more independent variables on a dependent variable. According to Leading Behavior, the regression coefficient for wise leaders is 0.763, with a critical ratio (C.R.) of 5.019 and a standard error (S.E.) of 0.152. gains in leading behavior are strongly correlated with gains in smart leadership, as seen by this high positive coefficient. The corresponding p-value is indicated as highly significant (.000), supporting Hypothesis 2 (H2) and indicating that capable leaders are essential in enhancing wise leadership qualities.

Regarding the correlation between Employee Wisdom and Wise Leaders, the coefficient of regression is 0.431, accompanied by a S.E. of 0.146 and a C.R. of 2.952. This positive correlation suggests that knowledgeable leaders have a major impact on employees' wisdom. Additionally, the strong p-value backs up Hypothesis 3 (H3), which highlights the relevance of prudent leadership in developing an informed and prudent staff. Ultimately, the regression analysis demonstrates that, with a coefficient of 0.704, a S.E. of 0.225, and a C.R. of 3.128, Leading Behavior has a significant positive impact on Employees Wisdom. Once more, the p-value demonstrates significance, which validates Hypothesis 1 (H1). This research implies that intelligent leadership is not the sole benefit of effective leading behavior; employees' wisdom is also directly increased. In conclusion, the regression findings show strong connections between the examined constructs. The study's theoretical framework is validated by the strong coefficients and significant p-values seen in all correlations. This underscores the crucial roles that leading conduct and wise leadership play in fostering employee wisdom. For firms looking to improve worker results and elevate their leadership practices, these insights are essential.

Table 7. Mediating role Effect

	Influence	worth	Path Influence
Leading Behavior → Employees Wisdom	Direct Influence	0.39	Direct influence stated
Leading Behavior → Wise Leaders → Employees Wisdom	Indirect Influence	0.65*0.72=0.49	Indirect Influence Ensued
	Whole influence	0.88	Partial mediation

Source: Authors

The mediating effects of Leading Behavior, Wise Leaders, and Employee Wisdom are examined in Table 7. A statistical method known as mediation analysis looks at whether one or more mediator variables mediate the impact of an independent variable on a dependent variable. This contributes to illuminating the fundamental processes that underlie partnerships. The correlation coefficient between Leading Behavior and Employee Wisdom is 0.39. This suggests a significant and immediate impact, implying that good leadership conduct raises employees' knowledge immediately and without the need for mediation. On the other hand, the evaluation of the indirect influence follows the line from Leading Behavior to Wise Leaders, who in turn affect Employees Wisdom. The indirect effect that was computed was $0.65 \times 0.72 = 0.49$. This result shows that smart leadership acts as a mediator for a significant amount of the impact of leading conduct on employee wisdom. As a result, as intermediates, smart leaders enhance the beneficial impact of leading behaviors on the wisdom of their subordinates.

The overall contribution from Leading Behavior to Employee Wisdom, when the direct and indirect influences are included, is 0.88. The significance of both direct acts and mediated channels in influencing employee outcomes is shown by this all-encompassing impact. According to the investigation, there is still a direct influence even when prudent leadership greatly strengthens the association between leading conduct and employees' knowledge. This is known as partial mediation. This implies that in order to maximize staff wisdom, businesses should prioritize not just the development of smart leaders but also the maintenance of successful leading practices. To sum up, Table 7's findings support the intricate dynamics at work in the connections between the components under study.

DISCUSSION

The study's conclusions emphasize the complex interrelationships among Leading Behavior, Wise Leaders, and Employee Wisdom and show the important influence that leadership philosophies may have on worker outcomes. The investigation shows that smart leadership is fostered by successful leading behaviors, which in turn have an indirect impact on employees' wisdom. This two-pronged approach highlights how important it is for leaders to create an atmosphere that encourages learning and development among team members. The findings suggest that prudent leadership acts as a crucial moderator, amplifying the impact of leading practices on staff wisdom. This implies that firms seeking to improve staff skills ought to concentrate on cultivating the wisdom of their leaders in addition to encouraging successful leading practices. Through the allocation of resources towards leadership development initiatives that prioritize strategic decision-making and interpersonal skills, firms may cultivate a workforce that possesses both knowledge and competence in putting that knowledge into action.

Furthermore, the noteworthy model fit indices validate the applicability of the researched constructs and confirm the strength of the suggested theoretical framework. Confidence in the findings of this study is given by the good regression results along with great reliability and validity metrics. These results add to the body of knowledge by illuminating the connections between leadership dynamics and how to use them to enhance employee outcomes. In the end, this study emphasizes how critical it is to approach leadership development holistically. The connection between sensible leadership and leading conduct should be emphasized by organizations in their training and development programs. Organizations may increase the collective knowledge of their workforce and boost creativity and performance by cultivating a culture of smart and effective leadership.

CONCLUSION

This study highlights the important role that leadership plays in influencing employee outcomes by offering insightful information on the complex links between Wise Leaders, Leading Behavior, and Employee Wisdom. The results show that smart leadership acts as a mediator between successful leading behaviors and employee wisdom, as well as having a direct positive impact on the latter. This dual influence emphasizes that in order to fully use employee potential, businesses must invest in the development of both smart leadership traits and successful leadership methods. Strong statistical studies, such as mediation analysis and confirmatory factor analysis, support the research's theoretical framework. The results are credible due to the substantial fit indices and dependable measurements, which indicate the importance of the structures under investigation. Organizations may leverage the skills and knowledge of their leaders to create work environments where people flourish by implementing targeted leadership development efforts based on an awareness of these dynamics. The study's findings emphasize the significance of thorough leadership development that synchronizes leading behaviors with the attributes of astute leadership. Organizations may improve employee intelligence and eventually drive improved performance and creativity by establishing such links. Subsequent research endeavors may expand upon these discoveries by delving into supplementary contextual elements and their effects on the interrelationships between these concepts, so augmenting the conversation on proficient leadership and staff growth.

MANAGERIAL IMPLICATIONS

The study's conclusions have a big impact on management strategies meant to improve employee outcomes and leadership efficacy. Organizations should place a high priority on leadership development initiatives that highlight wise leadership practices and successful leading behaviors. Initiatives for training might concentrate on developing the strategic thinking, emotional intelligence, and interpersonal abilities necessary for prudent leadership. Managers can guarantee that their leaders are prepared to cultivate an atmosphere that promotes staff development and knowledge by establishing a strong structure for leadership training. Managers should also understand how critical it is to foster a culture that values candid communication and group decision-making. In addition to fostering successful leadership, this kind of culture invites staff members to share their opinions and thoughts, which advances corporate knowledge as a whole. It is important that leaders interact with their teams on a frequent basis, asking for opinions and suggestions that might help them make better choices. Organizations must also put in place mechanisms that enable continuous evaluation and improvement of their leadership techniques. Frequent assessments of a leader's performance may assist identify leaders who best represent wisdom and successful leading conduct, as well as offer insightful information about areas in which the leader needs to grow.

PRACTICAL IMPLICATIONS

The study's conclusions have a number of useful ramifications for companies looking to improve staff dynamics and leadership. First and foremost, it is crucial to put in place organized leadership development programs. These programs ought to include modules on wisdom cultivation in addition to instruction on effective leadership behaviors. By enabling leaders to make decisions that are both educated and relatable to their workforce, such dual-focused training may promote a more creative and encouraging work environment. Organizations should also place a high priority on the development of mentorship connections between experienced leaders and up-and-coming talent. Organizations may foster a knowledge-sharing and wisdom-transfer atmosphere by assigning experienced executives to junior or new hires. This not only aids in the skill development of less seasoned workers but also upholds an environment where learning and development are ongoing.

It's also critical to implement feedback-driven methods. Regular performance reviews that incorporate team member feedback on leadership efficacy are beneficial to organizations. Leaders may adjust their approach and be aware of the requirements and expectations of their teams by using the insightful information that this 360-degree feedback can offer. Finally, it is critical to cultivate a culture of open communication and cooperation. Supervisors ought to aggressively encourage venues where staff members are at ease disclosing their thoughts and observations. This approach not only increases worker participation but also advances the organization's collective intelligence by bringing a variety of viewpoints to bear on decision-making. Organizations may create a leadership framework that fosters creativity and long-term success while also enhancing employee knowledge by implementing these doable actions.

THEORETICAL IMPLICATIONS

The study's conclusions make a substantial theoretical contribution to our knowledge of the connections among wise leaders, employees' wisdom, and leading behavior. This study adds to the body of knowledge on leadership and organizational behavior by clarifying the ways in which leadership attributes affect employee outcomes. The identification of wise leadership as a mediator, in particular, draws attention to the intricate interactions that exist between various leadership philosophies and how they affect the growth of employees. This suggests that wisdom plays a critical role in determining the effectiveness of leadership activities. Furthermore, by including the idea of wisdom into the conversation about effective leadership, this study expands and challenges earlier conceptions. Scholarly research on leadership has conventionally prioritized attributes like charm and aptitude for making choices, frequently neglecting the significance of wisdom as a transformational characteristic that amplifies the influence of a leader. The research highlights the importance of wise leadership and calls for more investigation into the methods for measuring and developing wisdom in corporate settings.

Furthermore, this study's substantial validity and reliability measures offer a strong platform for further investigation. By expanding on the suggested framework, researchers may look at additional elements including company culture, employee motivation, and environmental factors that can have an impact on the connections under study. This adaptability facilitates the creation of more thorough models that take into account additional mediating or moderating variables and promotes a more nuanced understanding of how leadership dynamics function in various circumstances. In conclusion, this study's theoretical ramifications suggest a more complex and comprehensive understanding of leadership that values wisdom in improving employee outcomes. This viewpoint provides guidance for future scholarly research and creates opportunities for real-world implementations in leadership development initiatives in a range of corporate settings.

RECOMMENDATIONS

Several important recommendations for firms looking to improve employee wisdom and leadership effectiveness may be made in light of the study's findings. First and foremost, companies ought to fund all-encompassing programs for developing leaders that specifically cover instruction in both the growth of knowledge and successful leading behaviors. These courses have to incorporate hands-on activities that motivate leaders to consider their choices and apply moral thinking, resulting in a more profound comprehension of wisdom in leadership. Second, companies should launch mentorship programs that pair together experienced executives with up-and-coming talent. The information and experiences that may be shared via these mentorship connections are invaluable in shaping the future generation of leaders. Organizations may foster a culture of lifelong learning and improve the professional development of mentors and mentees by developing formal mentoring programs. It's also crucial to put in place frequent feedback channels. Companies have to carry out 360-degree assessments and ask staff members about the influence of their leadership. This strategy not only encourages leaders to take responsibility for their actions but also cultivates an environment of openness and cooperation that empowers employees to voice their opinions and contribute to organizational success.

Establishing an atmosphere of candid communication is also essential. It is advisable to motivate leaders to arrange frequent forums or open-door meetings where staff members can freely express their thoughts and perspectives. By increasing worker participation and fostering a feeling of community, this approach eventually adds to a deeper level of organizational understanding. Finally, companies have to think about carrying out regular evaluations to gauge the success of their programs for developing leaders and the overall influence on worker results. Organizations may pinpoint areas for development and modify their approaches to better suit the changing requirements of their workforce by methodically assessing these initiatives. By using these suggestions, companies may develop a more productive leadership structure that fosters creativity, engagement, and overall success in addition to improving employee knowledge.

FUTURE DIRECTIONS

Looking ahead, the results of this study may be expanded upon in a number of exciting directions. Subsequent research endeavors may initially examine the contextual elements that impact the correlations among Leading Behavior, Wise Leaders, and Employee Wisdom. Gaining insight into the ways in which factors like team dynamics, industry type, and organizational culture influence these correlations may improve the results' generalizability in many contexts. Researchers may also explore the idea of sensible leadership in further detail. Subsequent research endeavors may endeavor to explicate and implement wisdom in leadership with greater precision, creating evaluation instruments that appraise certain characteristics and conduct linked with wisdom. These developments may improve our knowledge of how to develop these traits in leaders.

Furthermore, longitudinal research may shed light on how leadership development initiatives affect staff knowledge and organizational effectiveness over the long run. Researchers may be able to determine if the effects seen in this study are long-lasting and how they change as leaders and workers negotiate shifting organizational environments by tracking these interactions over time. Multidisciplinary methods may also be advantageous. Working together with disciplines like organizational behavior, sociology, and psychology may provide deeper understanding of the underlying processes that underlie the connections that are seen. This may result in a more comprehensive comprehension of the ways in which diverse elements impact the efficacy of leadership and the advancement of employees.

REFERENCES

Adula, M., Birbirsa, Z. A., & Kant, S. (2023). The effect of interpersonal, problem solving and technical training skills on performance of Ethiopia textile industry: Continuance, normative and affective commitment as mediators. *Cogent Business & Management*, 10(3), 2286672. Advance online publication. DOI: 10.1080/23311975.2023.2286672

Alemayehu, E. (2021). Practices, obstacles and benefits of instructional leadership at private schools of Addis Ababa, Ethiopia. *Academy of Educational Leadership Journal*, 25, 1–18.

Amdemaryam, Z. (2020). *The Effect of Organizational Justice on Organizational Performance. Employees Trust toward Their Leader as a Mediator.(Ethiopian Airline Group: Case of Bahirdar and Lalibela Branches)* (Doctoral dissertation).

Asefa, A. (2023). Effect of Transformational Leadership on Organizational Performance: The Mediating Role of Employee Commitment and Expert Systems (AI) Inclusion in Ethiopia. *2023 International Conference on Communication, Security and Artificial Intelligence (ICCSAI)*, 305-310. DOI: 10.1109/ICCSAI59793.2023.10421269

Asefa, K., Debela, K. L., & Kant, S. (2023). Transformational Leadership effect on Organizational Performance with Mediation role of Employee Commitment in case of Public Sector in Oromia, Ethiopia. *Horn of African Journal of Business and Economics*, 6(2), 192–211.

Berku, D. W. (2024). Instructional Leadership Practice of Secondary School Principals to Deliver Quality Education in North Shewa Zone in Ethiopia. *Leadership and Policy in Schools*, 1–19. DOI: 10.1080/15700763.2024.2347912

Boku, G. G., Abeya, S. G., Ayers, N., & Abera, M. (2024). Leadership Commitment and the Quality of Adolescent-Friendly Sexual Reproductive Health Services in Public Health Facilities Among Pastoral Districts of Guji Zone, Ethiopia. *Journal of Healthcare Leadership*, 16, 53–66. DOI: 10.2147/JHL.S441951 PMID: 38370150

Demissie, A. D., Alemu, A. E., & Tensay, A. T. (2024). Servant Leadership and Organizational Citizenship Behavior: The Mediating Role of Perceived Organizational Politics and the Moderating Role of Political Skill in Public Service Organizations. *Employee Responsibilities and Rights Journal*, 1–39. DOI: 10.1007/s10672-023-09486-x

Dereso, C. W., Kant, S., Muthuraman, M., & Tufa, G. (2023). Effect of Point of Service on Health Department Student's Creativity in Comprehensive Universities of Ethiopia: Moderating Role of Public-Private Partnership and Mediating Role of Work Place Learning. In Proceedings of the International Health Informatics Conference. Lecture Notes in Electrical Engineering, vol 990. Springer, Singapore. DOI: 10.1007/978-981-19-9090-8_13

Durga, P., Godavarthi, D., Kant, S., & Basa, S. S. (2024). Aspect-based drug review classification through a hybrid model with ant colony optimization using deep learning. *Discov Computing*, 27(1), 19. DOI: 10.1007/s10791-024-09441-w

Ferede, W. L., Endawoke, Y., & Tessema, G. (2024). Change management through strategic leadership: The mediating effect of knowledge management in public organizations, Ethiopia. *Future Business Journal*, 10(1), 93. DOI: 10.1186/s43093-024-00363-z

Galperin, B. L., Michaud, J., Punnett, B. J., Melyoki, L. L., Metwally, E., Mukanzi, C., Senaji, T. A., & Taleb, A. (2024). Towards Increased Understanding of Leadership in the African Context: Data From Seven Countries. *Journal of International Management*, 30(5), 101170. DOI: 10.1016/j.intman.2024.101170

Gao, C., Khalid, S., Lianyu, C., & Tadesse, E. (2024). Integrated leadership for coherent school improvement in Ethiopia: The moderating role of transformational leadership on the relationship between instructional leadership and student academic achievement mediated by school improvement process. *Psychology in the Schools*, 61(2), 455–474. DOI: 10.1002/pits.23065

Guyo, S. K., & Kero, C. A. (2023). Mediation of Marketing Intermediaries and AI Adoption Between Livestock Products Marketing and Economic Status of Pastoralist in Ethiopia. *2023 International Conference on Communication, Security and Artificial Intelligence (ICCSAI)*, 311-316. DOI: 10.1109/ICCSAI59793.2023.10421261

Hundie, Z. A., & Habtewold, E. M. (2024). The Effect of Transformational, Transactional, and Laissez-Faire Leadership Styles on Employees' Level of Performance: The Case of Hospital in Oromia Region, Ethiopia. *Journal of Healthcare Leadership*, 16, 67–82. DOI: 10.2147/JHL.S450077 PMID: 38380132

Jabo, B. B., & Kant, S. (2024). Impact of Technical CRM on Ethiopia Bank Human-Computer Interface and Competitive Advantage as Mediators of Performance. *2024 IEEE International Conference on Computing, Power and Communication Technologies (IC2PCT)*, 679-682. DOI: 10.1109/IC2PCT60090.2024.10486237

Kant, S., & Adula, M. (2024). Human-Machine Interaction in the Metaverse in the Context of Ethiopia. In *Impact and Potential of Machine Learning in the Metaverse* (pp. 196–212). IGI Global. DOI: 10.4018/979-8-3693-5762-0.ch008

Kebede, A. G., Terefe, S. D., & Ijigu, A. W. (2024). Ambidextrous leadership and academic staff innovative behavior at Debre Berhan University, Ethiopia: The mediating role of workplace happiness. *Cogent Business & Management*, 11(1), 2307564. DOI: 10.1080/23311975.2024.2307564

Kere, Z. A. (2024). The Influence of Age on Emotional Intelligence Among NGO Leaders in Addis Ababa, Ethiopia. *JIM: Jurnal Ilmiah Mahasiswa Pendidikan Sejarah*, 9(1), 336–343.

Lapiso, T. L. (2023). The Effect Of Servant Leadership Style On Bank Performance: Evidences From Berhan Bank Of Ethiopia. *International Journal of Research Science and Management*, 10(11), 9–18.

Mebratie, E., & Shanbel, B. (2024). Identifying the prevalence of destructive leadership behavior and its determinants in northwest Ethiopia. *Cogent Business & Management*, 11(1), 2315696. DOI: 10.1080/23311975.2024.2315696

Medhn Desta, A. G., & Mulie, H. (2024). The effect of empowering leadership practices on employees performance with the mediating role of work engagement: The case of ethio-telecom. *Cogent Business & Management*, 11(1), 2307066. DOI: 10.1080/23311975.2024.2307066

Nyoach, T. D., Lemi, K., Debela, T., & Kant, S. (2024). Does Organizational Commitment Mediate the Relationship between Employee Relationship Management and Bank Performance? The Case of Banks in Ethiopia. *International Journal of Organizational Leadership*, 13(2), 355–376. DOI: 10.33844/ijol.2024.60419

Opalo, K. O., & Smith, L. (2021). Ideology and succession politics in Ethiopia: Autocratic leadership turnover and political instability. *Democratization*, 28(8), 1463–1482. DOI: 10.1080/13510347.2021.1929178

Panigrahi, A., Pati, A., Sahu, B., Das, M. N., Nayak, D. S. K., Sahoo, G., & Kant, S. (2023). En-MinWhale: An ensemble approach based on MRMR and Whale optimization for Cancer diagnosis. *IEEE Access : Practical Innovations, Open Solutions*, 11, 113526–113542. DOI: 10.1109/ACCESS.2023.3318261

Sadore, A. A., Kebede, Y., & Birhanu, Z. (2024). Effectiveness of engaging religious leaders in maternal health education for improving maternal health service utilization in Ethiopia: Cluster randomized controlled trial. *Frontiers in Public Health*, 12, 1399472. DOI: 10.3389/fpubh.2024.1399472 PMID: 39135926

Satena, A. A., Damessa, D. D., Dadiye, T. A., & Kant, S. (2024). Effect of Servant Leadership Style on Organizational Performance Among University Employees In Ethiopia. *International Journal of Social Science. Management and Economics Research*, 2(2), 42–63.

Teame, K., Debie, A., & Tullu, M. (2022). Healthcare leadership effectiveness among managers in Public Health institutions of Addis Ababa, Central Ethiopia: A mixed methods study. *BMC Health Services Research*, 22(1), 540. DOI: 10.1186/s12913-022-07879-6 PMID: 35459173

Wolle, G. (2024). Gender stereotypes and contributing factors for the gender gap in the school leadership position in North Wello Zone: Ethiopia. *Cogent Education*, 11(1), 2375482. DOI: 10.1080/2331186X.2024.2375482

Yalew, M. T. (2024). Development of relations between Ethiopia and China during Emperor Haile Selassie: A product of timing or the leadership? *Cogent Social Sciences*, 10(1), 2333082. DOI: 10.1080/23311886.2024.2333082

Zoogah, B. D. (2020). Companionate leadership: A shemswian perspective. *Africa Journal of Management*, 6(3), 214–247. DOI: 10.1080/23322373.2020.1779944

KEY TERMS AND DEFINITIONS

Employee Wisdom: The ability of staff members to use their skills and expertise to make decisions, solve problems, and think creatively. This idea highlights the significance of using information wisely in a variety of situations, in addition to the relevance of knowledge itself.

Feedback Mechanism: A method or procedure that allows information about behavior or performance to be sent back to the group or person. This is necessary for ongoing development and progress and can be official or informal.

Leading Behavior: The deeds and attitudes of leaders that affect the productivity and morale of their teams. The human relationships, communication, and decision-making that underpin organizational performance are all included in these activities.

Mediation: A statistical procedure wherein a third variable—referred to as the mediator—transmits the influence of an independent variable on a dependent variable. This makes the nature of the correlations between various variables more clear.

Mentorship: A learning partnership in which a more seasoned person helps and advises a less seasoned one. Mentoring promotes advancement in the workplace by providing advice, sharing knowledge, and fostering skill development.

Organizational Culture: The common norms, attitudes, and practices that influence how people collaborate and interact inside an organization. It affects how decisions are made, how employees behave, and how well a business performs overall.

Wise Leaders: These are those in charge who make wise decisions. This involves the capacity to use information wisely, think through the long-term effects of their decisions, and deftly and empathetically negotiate intricate interpersonal interactions.

Chapter 14
Mindfulness and Organizational Well-Being:
A Comprehensive Analysis of Global Research Trends

James Kanda
https://orcid.org/0009-0009-8028-5336
GNA University, India

Parveen Singh Kalsi
https://orcid.org/0000-0002-1577-4389
GNA University, India

Reena Rani
https://orcid.org/0000-0002-8483-252X
Lovely Professional University, India

ABSTRACT

This chapter offers a comprehensive bibliometric analysis of global research trends on mindfulness and organizational well-being from 2009 to 2024, using 114 articles extracted from the Scopus database. The study aims to map the growth, development, and impact of academic literature in this area, recognizing key research trends, influential publications, and future research directions. The analysis shows that research has proliferated worldwide, with the USA as a major contributor in this field followed by Australia, Germany, Spain, and India. The most trending topics include mindfulness, human factors, and occupational health in the workplace. The study emphasizes the need for future research to explore mindfulness interventions in

DOI: 10.4018/979-8-3693-8457-2.ch014

diverse organizational contexts and investigate the long-term impacts on well-being to guide the development and implementation of organizational well-being programs.

1. INTRODUCTION

In recent years, the workplace has become a critical arena for addressing employee mental health and well-being. With increasing workloads, technological advancements, and a fast-paced environment, employees face unprecedented levels of stress and pressure at the workplace. Stress and burnout not only diminish individual well-being but also negatively affect organizational performance, leading to reduced productivity, higher turnover rates, and increased healthcare issues (Schaufeli et al., 2009). With the decline in mental health across various populations, demonstrated by increasing stress levels and concerns about job satisfaction, organizations face the pressing need to implement effective interventions that support mental and emotional health in the workplace (Bonde et al., 2024). Leadership in organizations has an ethical duty to safeguard workers' well-being at work (Burton, 2010) Employee performance is heavily influenced by organizational well-being, which in turn can influence client outcomes and service delivery (Burton, 2010; Ford et al., 2011).

In recent years, mindfulness, rooted in ancient contemplative practices and extensively studied in psychological and organizational research, has gained widespread attention as a powerful tool for enhancing individual and organizational well-being (Kumprang & Suriyankietkaew, 2024). Mindfulness practices can significantly contribute to organizational well-being by providing individuals with the skills to manage stress effectively and increase their emotional resilience. These practices encourage employees to focus on the present-day moment, which can assuage concern and promote a sense of calmness (Kumprang & Suriyankietkaew, 2024). Studies indicate that practicing mindfulness can significantly increase favorable results in the workplace by improving both individual well-being and overall organizational performance (Charoensukmongkol & Puyod, 2022; Condon, 2017). By practicing mindfulness in the present moment and impartial observation of thoughts, emotions, and physical ambiances, mindfulness enables employees to navigate the complexities of the workplace with greater clarity, resilience, and emotional intelligence (Good et al., 2016).

As organizations strive to create environments that support employee growth, innovation, and overall well-being, the integration of mindfulness practices emerges as a strategic imperative. By cultivating mindfulness at both the individual and organizational levels, leaders can unlock the full potential of their workforce, build resilient and adaptable teams, and drive sustainable success in an increasingly complex and uncertain world. This study aims to comprehensively analyze global research trends related to mindfulness and organizational well-being, synthesizing existing findings and identifying areas for future exploration.

Research Questions

1. What are the leading countries, educational institutions, journals, authors, and keywords associated with integrating Mindfulness and Organizational Wellbeing?
2. What are the most significant trends and findings concerning the influence of Mindfulness on Organizational Wellbeing?
3. What are the future directions for Mindfulness and Organizational Wellbeing?

1.1 Mindfulness

Mindfulness is deep-rooted in traditional Buddhist practices and is defined as "a receptive attention to and awareness of present moment events and experience" (Brown & Ryan, 2003). It has been linked to psychological well-being both conceptually and empirically. (Keng et al., 2011). Mindfulness consists of three essential elements. The first is maintaining focus on the present moment (Shankland et al., 2021). Secondly, it involves being aware of both internal and external surroundings (Brown & Ryan, 2003; Dane, 2010). Finally, mindfulness entails observing situations with a non-judgmental attitude (Brown et al., 2007). In recent times, mindfulness has emerged as a fast-developing area in supporting organizational studies. In recent years, the field of mindfulness-based organizational studies has grown quickly. In work environments, mindfulness has emerged as a key component of varied organizational development. The potential of mindfulness to reduce stress has proven to be a bridging factor, and as a result, mindfulness activities are increasingly common in businesses (Aikens et al., 2014). These days, mindfulness is acknowledged for its beneficial correlations with task performance attention (Cheng et al., 2023). According to a recent analysis of 58,592 adults from non-clinical samples, mindfulness has a favorable correlation with several performance outcomes, including interpersonal relationships and job satisfaction (Zhang et al., 2021).

1.2 Organizational Well-Being

Organizational well-being refers to an organization's general health and vitality, encompassing its employees' physical, mental, and emotional well-being, as well as its structural and cultural environment (Danna, 1999). It has become critical in enhancing employee engagement, productivity, and organizational success (Lundqvist & Wallo, 2023). A holistic approach to organizational well-being not only considers individual health but also the impact of workplace culture, leadership, and organizational policies (Frone et al., 1995). The ability of an organization to support and uphold the social, psychological, and physical wellness of its employees is referred to as organizational well-being. It is fundamental for improving employee morale and productivity, contributing to a thriving work environment. It is increasingly recognized as critical for the long-term success of businesses, as it directly impacts employee performance, retention, and organizational culture. Organizational well-being is associated with both hedonic (pleasure and satisfaction) and eudaimonic (meaning and purpose) elements, indicating a need for holistic approaches to employee care (Keyes, C. L., & Haidt, 2003). Organizations that foster well-being typically implement strategies related to mental health support, work-life balance, and positive work environments, which can significantly enhance job satisfaction and reduce turnover (Danna & Griffin, 1999). Additionally, promoting well-being has been connected to higher levels of employee resilience and adaptability in times of crisis (Cooper & Cartwright, 1994).

1.3 Relationship Between Organizational Well-Being

Mindfulness-based interventions (MBIs) have been increasingly utilized within organizational contexts to improve various aspects of employee well-being. The integration of MBIs in workplace environments has been associated with positive outcomes such as stress reduction, enhanced job satisfaction, and improved interpersonal relationships (Choi et al., 2021). Research shows that by encouraging present-moment awareness, employees can better manage workplace demands, resulting in reduced psychological strain and enhanced emotional regulation. Mindfulness training lowers stress levels among employees, fostering improved well-being and job satisfaction (Chin et al., 2019). Another study suggests that mindfulness interventions not only alleviate stress but also promote resilience in highly volatile work environments, thereby enabling individuals to perform better under pressure (Tuckey et al., 2018). Furthermore, mindfulness interventions appear to be particularly effective for employees who, because of the nature of their employment, are susceptible to burnout. Employees in high-stakes professions, such as healthcare and education, experienced significant reductions in burnout symptoms after participating in mindfulness training (Chin et al., 2019). As mindfulness gains traction in organizational settings, there is growing interest in how it can be adapted to different cultural contexts. Several studies in this dataset explore the global applications of mindfulness, examining how it is being implemented in various countries and industries. A study highlights the victory of a mindfulness-based intervention in a multinational corporation, where employees from diverse cultural backgrounds reported feeling more connected to their work and colleagues after participating in the program (Weisbrod et al., 2024) and these measures may enhance workplace social capital and psychological safety and can enhance interpersonal relationships within organizations, particularly focusing on bridging social capital, which involves connections across different departments within the same organization. Such enhancements may lead to improved communication and collaboration, ultimately contributing to a more supportive organizational climate (Bonde et al., 2023). However, cultural differences can also present challenges for the implementation of mindfulness programs. For instance, in some cultures, mindfulness may be viewed as a spiritual or religious practice, which can lead to resistance from employees who are uncomfortable with these associations (Choi et al., 2022). Organizations must modify their mindfulness agendas to fit the unique requirements and principles of their employees, ensuring that the interventions are inclusive and accessible to all. Mindfulness has been increasingly linked to heightened employee engagement and productivity. Research reveals that employees who practice mindfulness are more prone to demonstrate elevated levels of attention, concentration, and motivation in their daily tasks. Organizations implementing mindfulness practices observed improvements in team dynamics and interpersonal relationships. Employees reported feeling more connected and supported, leading to enhanced collaboration and productivity (Glomb et al., 2011) and employees who participated in mindfulness programs demonstrated greater levels of work engagement, reporting higher job satisfaction and a sense of personal accomplishment (Lyddy et al., 2021). Moreover, a study on two different groups reveals that a randomized controlled trial of a 6-week mindfulness training program led to significantly greater advances in attentional focus, reduced work-life struggle, and marginally better job gratification compared to a half-day seminar. Both groups showed comparable gains in job productivity. These findings emphasize the potential of extended mindfulness training to enhance employee well-being and focus at work (Slutsky et al., 2019). This heightened focus and awareness enables employees to navigate complex interpersonal dynamics more effectively, reducing the likelihood of workplace conflicts and enhancing overall team cohesion. Furthermore, one of the critical mechanisms through which mindfulness influences organizational well-being is emotional regulation. Research has shown that mindfulness practices enhance individuals' ability to manage their emotions effectively, leading to reduced interpersonal conflicts and better communication (Keng et al., 2011) and mindfulness can lead to significant improvements in mental health outcomes. A meta-analysis by (Khoury et al., 2013) revealed that mindfulness practices effectively reduce anxiety, depression, and stress and in addition, mindfulness has been linked to enhanced job satisfaction, improved employee engagement, and increased overall productivity (Glomb et al., 2011).

2. MATERIALS AND METHODS

A. Source of Data

Researchers regard Scopus as a pertinent database for bibliometric studies utilized in bibliometric analysis. Consequently, the current investigation utilized bibliographic records acquired from Scopus.

B. Search Strategy and Data Retrieval

Articles and review articles from 2009 to 2024 (13 September 2024) were searched using the terms "mindfulness*" AND "organizational well-being*" OR "employee well-being*" OR "workplace well-being*" OR "corporate well-being*" OR "occupational health*" OR "organizational health*" OR "employee happiness*" OR "workplace happiness*" OR "workplace satisfaction*" in the Scopus. The subsequent inclusion criteria were utilized to ascertain the papers to be incorporated into the study:

- Articles disseminated in peer-reviewed journals, conference proceedings, and book chapters.
- Publications authored in the English language.
- Publications concentrating on the implementation of mindfulness in organizational wellness.

More particularly, it seeks to ascertain how mindfulness has affected organizational well-being, looking at various aspects, including physical, financial, social, mental and emotional, career, work environment and culture, and leadership. The search retrieved 114 publications that fulfilled the inclusion criteria for this study. The publications comprised journal articles, conference proceedings, and book chapters.

C. Data Analyses

The bibliometric analysis of the literature on mindfulness and organizational well-being was conducted using the Biblioshiny application within the Bibliometrix package in R. In this study, sex main bibliometric analyses were conducted: publication trend analysis, country analysis, keyword analysis, topic analysis, journal analysis, co-occurrence analyses, and top authors analysis

3. RESULTS AND CONCLUSION

Processing data in bibliometric analysis comprises both vivid and network analyses. The descriptive evaluation presents a critically important information set and addresses the key attributes of bibliographic data using institution, authorship, and analysis of documents. Networking analysis evaluates theoretical, rational, and societal networks through co-word, co-citation, and collaboration studies.

1) The Publication trends in the field of Mindfulness and Organizational Well-being

Country's Production

A bibliometric analysis of mindfulness and organizational well-being reveals that the United States, Australia, Germany, Spain, and India have a significant impact on the intellectual landscape as shown by their respective publication counts of 767, 150, 142, and 48. The leading position in the subject goes to the United States.

Figure 1. Top 5 Leading contributor countries showcase the impact of mindfulness on organizational wellbeing

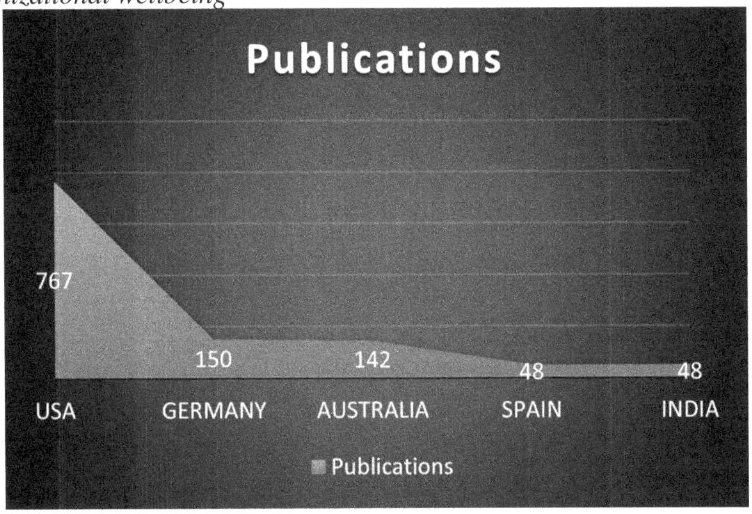

Most Cited Countries

Australia has the highest number of citations at 1134, followed closely by the USA with 1099 citations. The United Kingdom comes third with 462 citations, followed by Singapore (394), Netherlands (195), Germany (108) and Canada (100)

citations, respectively. Switzerland, Portugal, and India are at the bottom with 70, 64, and 63 citations, respectively.

Figure 2. Most Cited Countries

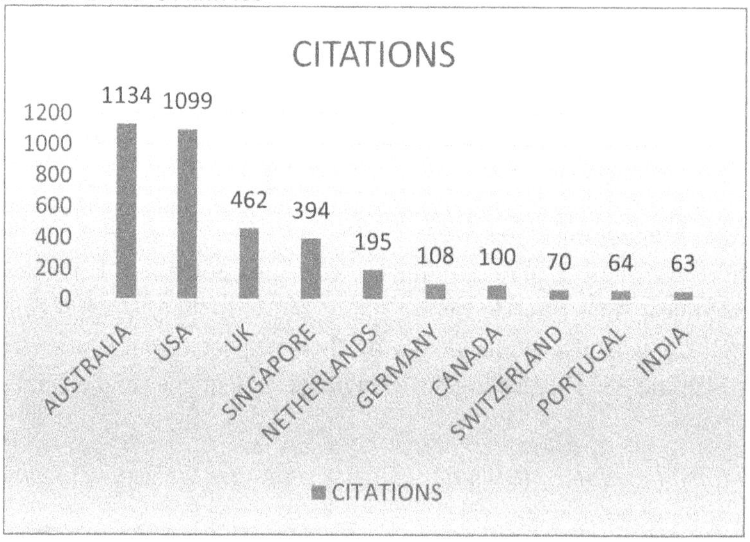

2) The Top Educational Institutions *in the field of Mindfulness and Organizational Wellbeing*

Looking at performance over time by association, we can see from Figure 3 that Portland University was more active with 17 publications, followed by Universidade De Lisboa with 9 publications. The University of South Australia and the University of Surrey contributed 7 publications.

Figure 3. The most relevant affiliations

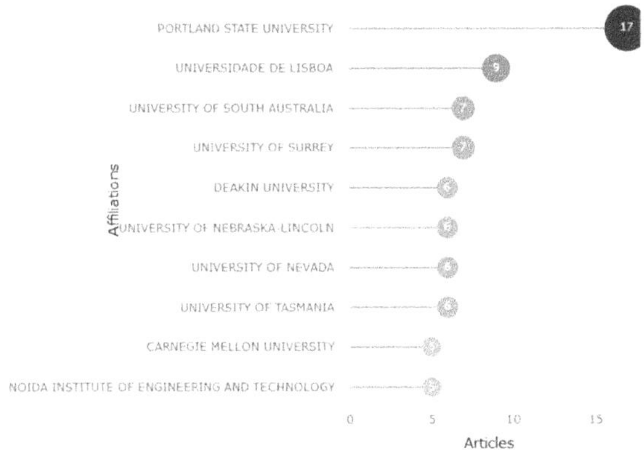

3) The top authors in the field

Figure 4 demonstrates the writers' primary interest in mindfulness and organizational well-being. Roeser RW s the writer who has authored the most works in this area with 4 publications. In second place are Pater R and Tuckey MR with 3 publications. Figure 5 clearly explains that Roeser W has significantly contributed to the study from the year 2010 to 2022. Chin B and Creswell JD are mostly active to the research during the years 2018 and 2019. The rest all of the author's contribution have scattered across different years.

Figure 4. Most Influential Authors

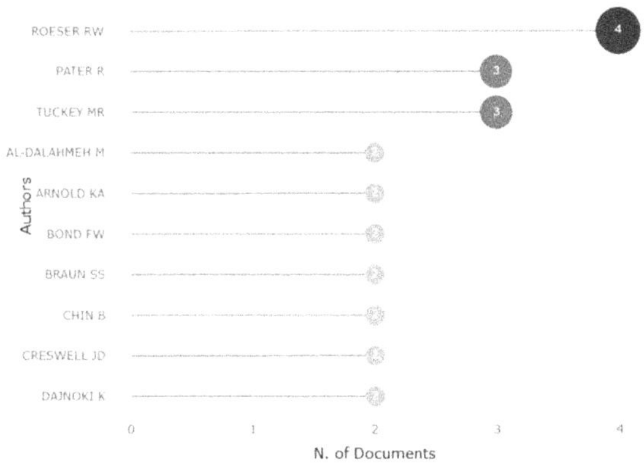

Figure 5. Author's Production Over Time

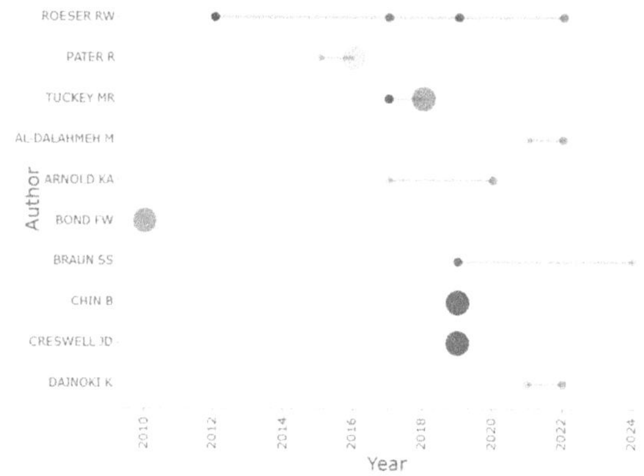

Lotka's Law, which he developed in 1926, looks at author productivity by comparing the number of authors to the total number of documents they write. The dashed line in Figure 6 shows Lotka's Law when the figure is examined, it is seen that most authors contribute very few papers (one paper), and only a small proportion of authors contribute a large number of papers.

Figure 6. Authors Productivity through Lotka's Law

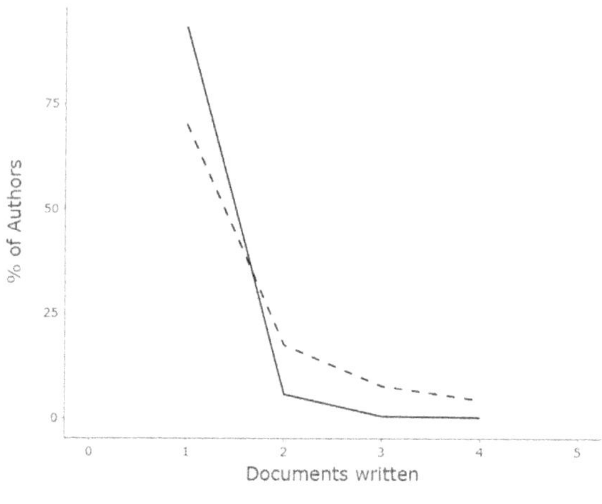

4) Top journals in the field of Mindfulness and organizational wellbeing

After conducting an analysis of the publications about mindfulness and organizational well-being within the parameters of the study, it was observed that the Journal of Occupational Health Psychology (13 Publications), Mindfulness (10 Publications), and Frontiers in Psychology (6 Publications) had the highest number of publications in this field. The outcomes are shown in Figure 7.

Figure 7. Most Relevant Sources

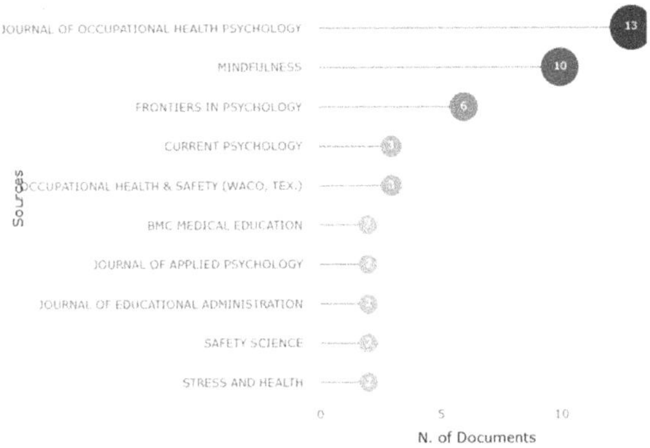

5) Top keywords in the field

A keyword analysis was done to find the most commonly used terms in the research on mindfulness and organizational well-being. According to the analysis, the most often used keywords were "mindfulness," "human," "adult," "occupational health," and "male," as shown in Figure 8. This implies that these ideas are crucial to the body of research on mindfulness and organizational well-being and that they could be worthwhile topics for more study.

Figure 8. Keyword Analysis

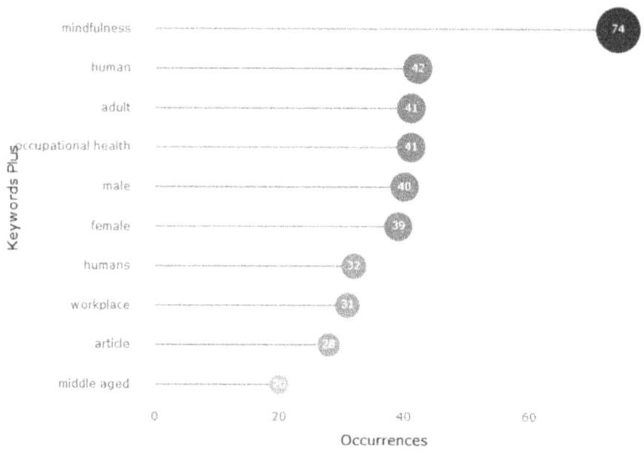

Trend Topics

This chart (Figure 9) shows how different research topics (terms) have gained or lost prominence over time between 2016 and 2022. Larger circles represent periods of increased focus on certain terms, like mindfulness, human, and adult. These are the most trending topics for research from 2016 to 2022.

The chart depicts that terms like mindfulness, mental health, and organization have been important in recent years for research.

Figure 9. Trend Topics

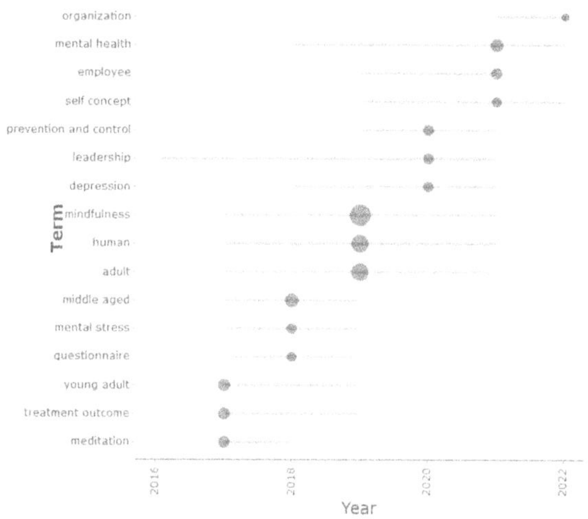

6) *Most Active Countries Who Contributed in Mindfulness and Well-being of Organizations*

A country analysis was carried out to determine which nations have made the greatest contributions to the body of knowledge on mindfulness and organizational well-being. The United States has published the most on this subject, followed by the United Kingdom, Australia, Canada, and Germany, as seen in Figure 10 below. This implies that the majority of research on mindfulness and organizational health has come from English-speaking nations, and also depicts that most of the publication in the USA is done domestically in comparison to other countries. So, there is an opportunity for international collaboration.

Figure 10. Corresponding Author's Country

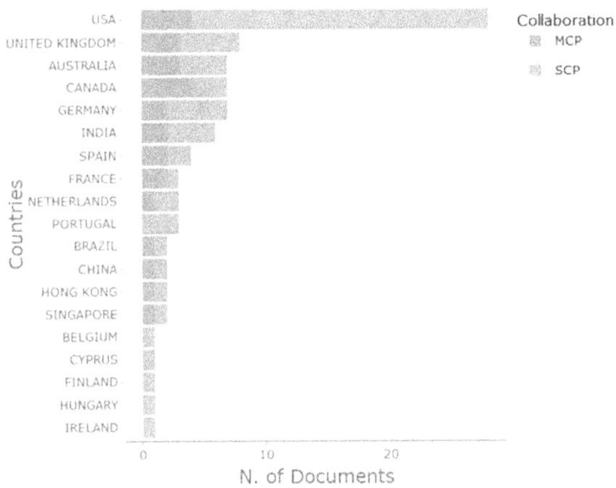

7) Co-occurrence network in the field

Figure 11 displays the Co-Occurrence Network for author keywords found in works that touch on the relationship between organizational well-being and mindfulness. The network highlights the main thematic areas and interconnections within a specific body of research. The red cluster focuses on human and psychological studies, with particular emphasis on gender, mindfulness, and occupational health. The blue cluster is centered on workplace dynamics, mental health, and employee satisfaction, suggesting a growing research area in workplace well-being.

Figure 11. Co-Occurrence Network

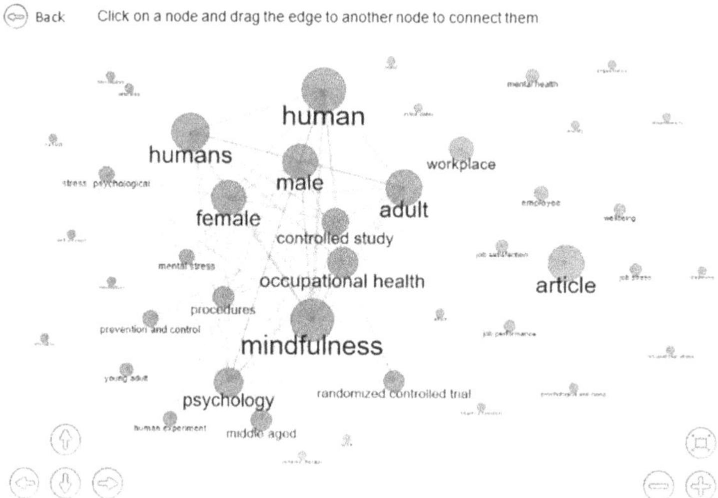

CONCLUSION

In conclusion, the bibliometric analysis on mindfulness and organizational well-being reveals a growing body of research emphasizing the positive impacts of mindfulness practices on workplace environments. Key trends highlight the role of mindfulness in enhancing employee well-being, productivity, and resilience, while reducing stress and burnout. The analysis also shows an increasing focus on integrating mindfulness into organizational strategies, promoting sustainable work cultures. As organizations increasingly prioritize mental health, understanding the role of mindfulness is essential for developing effective interventions that cater to the diverse needs of employees. By cultivating a culture of mindfulness, organizations can foster an environment that promotes psychological safety, allowing employees to thrive both personally and professionally. Mindfulness can promote individual and organizational well-being by enhancing self-awareness, emotional regulation, and decision-making, which in turn increases life satisfaction, resilience, and overall productivity. Future research should explore the long-term effects of mindfulness interventions and their alignment with broader organizational goals to guide the development and implementation of organizational well-being programs. Examining the cultural and contextual factors influencing the effectiveness of mindfulness practices in various organizational settings, along with their potential alignment with sustainable development goals (SDGs), could further enrich this field.

REFERENCES

Aikens, K. A., Astin, J., Pelletier, K. R., Levanovich, K., Baase, C. M., Park, Y. Y., & Bodnar, C. M. (2014). Mindfulness Goes to Work: Impact of an Online Workplace Intervention. *Journal of Occupational and Environmental Medicine*, 56(7), 721–731. DOI: 10.1097/JOM.0000000000000209 PMID: 24988100

Bonde, E. H., Mikkelsen, E. G., Fjorback, L. O., & Juul, L. (2023). The impact of an organizational-level mindfulness-based intervention on workplace social capital and psychological safety: A qualitative content analysis. *Frontiers in Psychology*, 14(March), 1–13. DOI: 10.3389/fpsyg.2023.1112907 PMID: 36959993

Bonde, E. H., Mikkelsen, E. G., Fjorback, L. O., & Juul, L. (2024). Exploring an Organizational-Level Mindfulness-Based Intervention in Private Workplace Settings. *Mindfulness*, 15(6), 1453–1471. DOI: 10.1007/s12671-024-02375-w

Brown, K. W., & Ryan, R. M. (2003). The benefits of being present: Mindfulness and its role in psychological well-being. *Journal of Personality and Social Psychology*, 84(4), 822–848. DOI: 10.1037/0022-3514.84.4.822 PMID: 12703651

Brown, K. W., Ryan, R. M., & Creswell, J. D. (2007). Mindfulness: Theoretical Foundations and Evidence for its Salutary Effects. *Psychological Inquiry*, 18(4), 211–237. DOI: 10.1080/10478400701598298

Burton, J. (2010). *WHO healthy workplace framework and model: background and supporting literature and practices*. World Health Organization. https://iris.who.int/handle/10665/113144

Charoensukmongkol, P., & Puyod, J. V. (2022). Mindfulness and emotional exhaustion in call center agents in the Philippines: Moderating roles of work and personal characteristics. *The Journal of General Psychology*, 149(1), 72–96. DOI: 10.1080/00221309.2020.1800582 PMID: 32748707

Cheng, L., Huang, C.-C., & Sitar, S. (2023). Mindfulness and job performance in Chinese nonprofit workers: Mediation effects of PANA and work engagement. *Humanities & Social Sciences Communications*, 10(1), 871. DOI: 10.1057/s41599-023-02402-6

Chin, B., Slutsky, J., Raye, J., & Creswell, J. D. (2019). Mindfulness Training Reduces Stress At Work: A Randomized Controlled Trial. *Mindfulness*, 10(4), 627–638. DOI: 10.1007/s12671-018-1022-0 PMID: 30923585

Choi, E., Gruman, J. A., & Leonard, C. M. (2021). A balanced view of mindfulness at work. *Organizational Psychology Review*, 12(1), 35–72. DOI: 10.1177/20413866211036930

Choi, E., Leroy, H., Johnson, A., & Nguyen, H. (2022). Flaws and All: How Mindfulness Reduces Error Hiding by Enhancing Authentic Functioning. *Journal of Occupational Health Psychology*, 27(5), 451–469. DOI: 10.1037/ocp0000327 PMID: 35549505

Condon, P. (2017). *Mindfulness-Compassion-and-Prosocial-Behavior*. Mindfulness in Social Psychology.

Cooper, C. L., & Cartwright, S. (1994). Healthy mind; healthy organization: A proactive approach to occupational stress. In *Human Relations* (Vol. 47, Issue 4, pp. 455–471). Sage Publications. DOI: 10.1177/001872679404700405

Dane, E. (2010). Paying Attention to Mindfulness and Its Effects on Task Performance in the Workplace. *Journal of Management*, 37(4), 997–1018. DOI: 10.1177/0149206310367948

Danna, K., & Griffin, R. W. (1999). Health and well-being in the workplace: A review and synthesis of the literature. *Journal of Management*, 25(3), 357–384. DOI: 10.1177/014920639902500305

Danna, K., & Griffin, R. W. (1999). Health and Well-Being in the Workplace: A Review and Synthesis of the Literature. *Journal of Management*, 25(3), 357–384. DOI: 10.1177/014920639902500305

Ford, M. T., Cerasoli, C. P., Higgins, J. A., & Decesare, A. L. (2011). Relationships between psychological, physical, and behavioural health and work performance: A review and meta-analysis. *Work and Stress*, 25(3), 185–204. DOI: 10.1080/02678373.2011.609035

Frone, M. R., Russell, M., & Cooper, M. L. (1995). health : A test of identity theory. *Journal of Occupational and Organizational Psychology*, 68(1), 1–11. DOI: 10.1111/j.2044-8325.1995.tb00684.x

Glomb, T. M., Duffy, M. K., Bono, J. E., & Yang, T. (2011). Mindfulness at Work. In Joshi, A., Liao, H., & Martocchio, J. J. (Eds.), *Research in Personnel and Human Resources Management* (Vol. 30, pp. 115–157). Emerald Group Publishing Limited. DOI: 10.1108/S0742-7301(2011)0000030005

Good, D. J., Lyddy, C. J., Glomb, T. M., Bono, J. E., Brown, K. W., Duffy, M. K., Baer, R. A., Brewer, J. A., & Lazar, S. W. (2016). Contemplating mindfulness at work: An integrative review. In *Journal of Management* (Vol. 42, Issue 1, pp. 114–142). Sage Publications. DOI: 10.1177/0149206315617003

Keng, S.-L., Smoski, M. J., & Robins, C. J. (2011). Effects of mindfulness on psychological health: A review of empirical studies. *Clinical Psychology Review*, 31(6), 1041–1056. DOI: 10.1016/j.cpr.2011.04.006 PMID: 21802619

Keyes, C. L., & Haidt, J. (2003). *Flourishing: Positive psychology and the life well-lived*. American Psychological Association. DOI: 10.1037/10594-000

Khoury, B., Lecomte, T., Fortin, G., Masse, M., Therien, P., Bouchard, V., Chapleau, M.-A., Paquin, K., & Hofmann, S. G. (2013). Mindfulness-based therapy: A comprehensive meta-analysis. *Clinical Psychology Review*, 33(6), 763–771. DOI: 10.1016/j.cpr.2013.05.005 PMID: 23796855

Kumprang, K., & Suriyankietkaew, S. (2024). Mechanisms of Organizational Mindfulness on Employee Well-Being and Engagement: A Multi-Level Analysis. *Administrative Sciences*, 14(6), 121. Advance online publication. DOI: 10.3390/admsci14060121

Lundqvist, D., & Wallo, A. (2023). Leadership and Employee Well-Being and Work Performance when Working from Home: A Systematic Literature Review. *Scandinavian Journal of Work and Organizational Psychology*, 8(1), 1–19. DOI: 10.16993/sjwop.199

Lyddy, C., Good, D., Bolino, M., Thompson, P., & Stephens, J. (2021). The Costs of Mindfulness at Work: The Moderating Role of Mindfulness in Surface Acting, Self-Control Depletion, and Performance Outcomes. *The Journal of Applied Psychology*, 106(12), 1921–1938. Advance online publication. DOI: 10.1037/apl0000863 PMID: 33570968

Schaufeli, W. B., Leiter, M. P., & Maslach, C. (2009). Burnout: 35 years of research and practice. *Career Development International*, 14(3), 204–220. DOI: 10.1108/13620430910966406

Shankland, R., Tessier, D., Strub, L., Gauchet, A., & Baeyens, C. (2021). Improving Mental Health and Well-Being through Informal Mindfulness Practices: An Intervention Study. *Applied Psychology. Health and Well-Being*, 13(1), 63–83. DOI: 10.1111/aphw.12216 PMID: 32851775

Slutsky, J., Chin, B., Raye, J., & Creswell, J. D. (2019). Mindfulness training improves employee well-being: A randomized controlled trial. *Journal of Occupational Health Psychology*, 24(1), 139–149. DOI: 10.1037/ocp0000132 PMID: 30335419

Tuckey, M., Sonnentag, S., & Bryan, J. (2018). Are state mindfulness and state work engagement related during the workday? *Work and Stress*, 32(1), 1–16. DOI: 10.1080/02678373.2017.1420707

Weisbrod, A. V., Bohman, L. C., & Ramdial, K. J. (2024). From theory to practice: A novel meditation program at a global corporation. *Current Psychology (New Brunswick, N.J.)*, 43(5), 4266–4283. DOI: 10.1007/s12144-023-04516-1 PMID: 37359588

Zhang, D., Lee, E. K. P., Mak, E. C. W., Ho, C. Y., & Wong, S. Y. S. (2021). Mindfulness-based interventions: An overall review. *British Medical Bulletin*, 138(1), 41–57. DOI: 10.1093/bmb/ldab005 PMID: 33884400

Chapter 15
Mindfulness Interventions Into University Teachers' Well-Being and Professional Development:
An Empirical Analysis

Tam Nguyen
https://orcid.org/0000-0001-9571-4783
Swinburne University of Technology in Vietnam, Vietnam

Lan Thi Ngoc Dang
Vietnamese-German University, Vietnam

Phuong Tran Le Cao
https://orcid.org/0000-0003-3538-6604
Erasmus University, Rotterdam, The Netherlands

Hieu Huu Huynh
Medicine and Pharmacy University, Ho Chi Minh City, Vietnam

ABSTRACT

Mindfulness techniques have been proposed to address teacher burnout and enhance well-being in the academic environment. However, limited research has hindered understanding of their impact on teachers' well-being and professional growth. This project explores the effects of mindfulness interventions on teacher well-being, aiming to improve teaching and research skills. Using a qualitative approach, the

DOI: 10.4018/979-8-3693-8457-2.ch015

study involved focus groups, narrative, and content analysis with 60 lecturers and academic staff from a mindfulness program between Swinburne University and FPT Education in Vietnam. The findings suggest mindfulness helps teachers maintain a positive mindset, reduce stress, and improve emotional resilience and professional performance. This research extends beyond individual teachers, influencing the broader educational environment and policy development, while contributing to the understanding of mindfulness in higher education.

INTRODUCTION

Teachers in modern education face challenges within the broader social, technological, and educational context (Liesa-Orús et al., 2020). They may be under the societal expectation in the role of educators in shaping students' character. Societal attitudes toward education impact teachers' responsibilities and put the pressures on their face (Viac&Fraser,2020).With rapid technological advancements, it challenges teachers in adapting teaching methods to incorporate digital tools (Onyema, 2020), addressing issues related to online learning, and promoting digital literacy among students. In addition, teachers must be aware of evidence-based practices and pedagogical innovations to continually improve their teaching methods (Herodotou et al, 2019).

Therefore, teachers often experience high levels of stress due to the demanding nature of their profession, including heavy workloads, student behavioral challenges, and administrative pressures. Teacher burnout is a pervasive issue that can lead to reduced job satisfaction and performance (Chang, 2009). Thus, seeking ways to support teachers' wellbeing and professional performance is necessary. In Exploring the literature and the culture, mindfulness as a potential intervention is justified by its established role in stress reduction and promoting mental well-being (Brown & Ryan,2003). The mindfulness way can align with the emphasis on continuous professional development, providing teachers with tools for ongoing personal and professional growth (Pearson et al., 2012).

Knowing the impact of mindfulness in a teacher's wellbeing and professional development is positive. However, there is little research explaining in depth how impactful mindfulness has on the transformation of teachers' feelings and perceptions toward their wellness and excellence in teaching and research during mindfulness practice. According to Zarate et al. (2019) in their meta-analysis of mindfulness training on teachers'well-being, there is a lack of empirical evidence on mindfulness interventions that indicate such practices may mitigate burnout symptoms, enhancing overall teacher well-being (Michalak et al., 2020).

This research report aims to offer valuable insights into the efficacy of mindfulness practices in enhancing the well-being and professional performance of teachers. It also serves as a foundation for future research and practical implementations in the field of education. The potential advantages extend beyond individual teachers and have the capacity to influence entire educational environments, rendering it a crucial topic for research and investigation.

Below is three main research question (RQ).

RQ1: What effect does mindfulness practice have on teachers' overall wellbeing and professional developments?
RQ2: In what ways does practicing mindfulness contribute to the professional growth of teachers?
RQ3: How can teachers integrate mindfulness practices into their professional and personal lives?

LITERATURE REVIEW

Studies on Teachers' Well-Being, Stress, and Burnout

An analysis of current research on teacher well-being, stress, and burnout uncovers a fascinating story about the difficulties educators have in today's academic environment. Multiple research studies highlight the concerning frequency of stress and burnout among teachers, emphasizing the negative effect on their general health and professional effectiveness (Randall, 2019). These studies examine the several complex elements that contribute to teacher stress, including high workloads, administrative pressures, and challenges in classroom management. Furthermore, the literature emphasizes the interdependence between the well-being of teachers and the overall educational results, emphasizing the importance of addressing these concerns for the advantage of both educators and students (Gase et al., 2017). The findings obtained from previous studies serve as a basis for comprehending the intricate relationship between the requirements of the teaching profession and the mental well-being of educators. These insights offer valuable viewpoints for the creation of specific interventions and support systems.

Mindfulness Interventions in Enhancing Psychological Well-Being

The research on mindfulness therapies consistently shows that they improve psychological well-being in a variety of populations. Numerous research have shown that mindfulness practices founded in contemplative traditions help to reduce stress, anxiety, and depression symptoms (McWilliams, 2014). These interventions often focus on establishing present-moment awareness and acceptance, which has a good impact on people's emotional regulation and resilience. Mindfulness-based interventions, such as Mindfulness-Based Stress Reduction (MBSR), developed by Kabat-Zinn (2003), and Mindfulness-Based Cognitive Therapy (MBCT), mentioned in the work of Sipe & Eisendrath (2012), have showed potential in enhancing psychological well-being. This is accomplished by providing folks with practical strategies for coping with life's obstacles and regulating negative thought habits. Furthermore, research suggests that practicing mindfulness on a daily basis can improve overall life satisfaction, subjective well-being, and the formation of a more optimistic view (Bajaj & Pande, 2016). The literature emphasizes mindfulness procedures as effective tools for improving psychological well-being, allowing individuals to handle the complexity of modern life with improved emotional balance and resilience (Liang et al., 2022).

Mindfulness Practices in Education

Mindfulness Techniques Suitable for Educators

Teachers' professional lives may benefit from mindfulness approaches, according to literature. Mindfulness for educators goes beyond stress reduction to increase well-being and job satisfaction (Lomas et al., 2017). Research suggests that teachers can easily add mindful breathing, body scanning, and brief meditation into their everyday routines (Rechtschaffen, 2014). These methods reduce teacher stress, build emotional resilience, promote attention and focus, and strengthen school relationships. Mindfulness practices can be tailored to the needs of educators, giving them the tools they need to overcome their obstacles and promote a positive, mindful approach to teaching and learning (Norris, 2019).

Exploration of Mindfulness Programs Implemented in Educational Settings

The use of mindfulness programs in schools shows an increasing interest in promoting instructor and student well-being. This domain studies mindfulness interventions from brief, targeted practices to full programs like Mindfulness-Based Stress Reduction (MBSR) for education (Gouda et al., 2016). In addition, Taylor et al. (2016) examines how these programs affect stress, emotional regulation, focus, and classroom dynamics. Studies have examined the impact of incorporating mindfulness into the curriculum on academic achievement and social-emotional learning (Waldemar et al., 2016). Research also emphasizes teacher training and a supportive school atmosphere for mindfulness program success (FitzGerald, 2012). Exploring mindfulness efforts in schools sheds light on the benefits and drawbacks of changing the field.

METHODS

The adoption of qualitative methodologies in this research study, notably focused group discussions with content analysis, is significant for several reasons. Firstly, qualitative approaches are highly adapted to investigating complicated phenomena and providing in-depth insights into participants' experiences, attitudes, and perceptions (Howitt, 2019). Focused group conversations enable the examination of multiple perspectives within the framework of a group, resulting in rich and nuanced data (Hennink, 2013). Secondly, narrative analysis, content analysis, and thematic analysis are combined as a robust analytical approach for systematically examining and interpreting qualitative data, providing a structured method for identifying patterns, themes, and meanings within the collected data (Drisko, & Maschi, 2016). Thirdly, the inclusion of 60 lecturers and academic staff who have been practicing mindfulness at the Swinburne University of Technology-FPT Education partnership program in Vietnam offers a broad and representative sample. This sample size enables a thorough examination of the impact of mindfulness therapies in a specific educational context. Overall, the combination of qualitative approaches and sample size adds to a comprehensive and contextually rich understanding of the possible benefits and limitations of mindfulness practices among academic staff in the defined program.

RESULT

Finding 1

This finding answers the first research question (RQ1) as mentioned above in the introduction. The narrative analysis shows the effect of mindfulness practice of teachers on their well-being in two ways.

Reducing Stress and Enhancing Emotional Resilience in Teachers

By encouraging instructors to concentrate on the present moment, mindfulness practice heightens their awareness of their own thoughts and emotions. Enhanced consciousness enables individuals to more effectively comprehend and control stressors in the moment. *Participant #3, Group1 described: "Making me more aware of the present moment is what mindful breathing techniques do for me. I think that focusing on the breath makes me more aware of my feelings and thoughts, which helps me feel clear and self-aware. Case in point: I know I'm a loner. Shopping trips that last a long time make me stressed, so I don't do them. Even though my friends tried to get me to go shopping, I took a deep breath and said no, not even for window shopping."*

Teachers who practice mindfulness are encouraged to notice their thoughts without judgment. Theycan gain a deeper grasp of their thought patterns and emotional responses by taking a non-reactive approach to their cognitive processes, developing heightened self-awareness.

> *Participants #4, Group 7stated: "The thought that I messed up in the lesson came to mind. It's okay for me to admit this without calling myself a loser. Making mistakes is a normal part of being human, that much I know. This method helps people become more self-aware and strong, making room for growth and thought without harsh self-criticism."*

Teachers are equipped with methods for emotional regulation through the practice of mindfulness. By demonstrating non-judgmental acceptance of emotions, educators have the ability to address stressors with enhanced emotional intelligence, thereby mitigating the adverse consequences of difficult circumstances.

> *Participants #3, Group 2 explained "When talking to my students, I don't react defensively, dismissing the feedback and feeling personally attacked. I think negative reactions could strain my relationship with students and lead to increased stress. I empathize with the student's viewpoint, and respond in a way that minimizes the negative impact of criticism."*

Mindfulness often involves practices like deep breathing and body scanning, promoting a mind-body connection. These techniques activate the relaxation response, leading to physiological changes that counteract the stress response, ultimately reducing overall stress levels.

Participants #7, Group 6 said: "I'm worried and overwhelmed because of due dates, grading, and office work that needs to be done. Because I knew this, I chose to do a short mindfulness exercise that includes being aware of my body and taking deep breaths. I went to a quiet place, sat down, and started to focus on my breath. I slowly breathe in, feeling the air going into their lungs, and let go of stress with each breath. When I take deep breaths, the relaxation reaction starts, which calms the nervous system and lessens the physical effects of stress.

Consistent mindfulness meditation improves cognitive abilities, such as attention and concentration. Teachers who engage in mindfulness are more adept at maintaining concentration on tasks, navigating intricate academic requirements, and preventing cognitive exhaustion that can contribute to stress.

Participants #1, Group 5 discussed: "When my schedule is full and I have to prepare for several classes, grade papers, and do administrative work. I decide to use a focused work approach because I feel too busy. I choose one job at a time and promise to give it my full attention. When this happens, they focus on the job at hand and use mindfulness techniques to bring my attention back to it when something else comes up."

Mindfulness functions as a preventative measure against exhaustion through the provision of a sustainable approach to the work of educators. It promotes self-care by assisting educators in identifying and resolving indicators of exhaustion prior to their worsening.

Participants #5, Group1stated: "I've been experiencing increased fatigue, irritability, and a sense of detachment from my work. Instead of ignoring these signs, I choose to proactively address them. I decided to take a day off to prioritize self-care. During this break, I engage in activities that bring them joy, such as spending time outdoors, reading a non-academic book, and practicing mindfulness."

Improvements in Teacher's Job Satisfaction and Life Satisfaction

Teachers who practice mindfulness report feeling more satisfied with their jobs. They feel fulfillment and significance in their work are more resilient to setbacks because they believe their work is making a difference for a greater good.

Participants #7, Group 4 shared his opinion: "Lesson planning, grading, and administrative work are making me feel more and more worried and overwhelmed. That's why I set aside a few minutes every day to do mindful breathing or mindfulness meditation. They notice that their point of view has changed. This makes me more present in class, and I interact with kids in a more thoughtful and focused way. Then, grading and other office work are not sources of stress but chances to pay attention with awareness."

Teachers who use these strategies report feeling less stressed, more emotionally resilient, and more satisfied with their lives overall. The Investigations frequently emphasize the beneficial effects on aspects including mood control, reduced anxiety, and enhanced cognitive performance.

Participants #5, Group 6 expressed: "I believe that practicing mindfulness on a regular basis has been a life-changing journey that has drastically improved my general health and happiness. Simply put, practicing mindfulness and being aware of the present moment on purpose have become very helpful ways to deal with the complicated things that happen in life."

Finding 2

The content analysis illustrate mindfulness practice can help increase teachers' professional development, in two aspects: teaching performance and research performance This finding can answer the third research question (RQ2), as shown in the introduction.

Teaching Performance

Mindfulness practice can significantly contribute to effective classroom management and the development of positive teacher-student relationships.

Table 1. Mindfulness practice, effective classroom management and positive teacher-student relationships

Themes	Causes	Effects
Responding to students with calmness	Mindfulness helps teachers regulate their own emotions, enabling them to respond to students with calmness rather than react impulsively.	This emotional regulation is foundational for maintaining a positive classroom environment.
Empathizing with the varied needs of their students	Regular mindfulness practice cultivates patience and empathy. Teachers who are mindful are better equipped to understand and empathize with the varied needs and emotions of their students,	Contributing to a more compassionate teaching approach.
Improving a teacher's attention in interactions with students	Enhancing a teacher's focus and attention. This heightened awareness allows them to be fully present during lessons and interactions	Positively impacting student engagement and understanding.
Enhancing Communication teaching and learning	Mindfulness encourages mindful communication, promoting active listening and thoughtful responses.	Improving communication skills contribute to better understanding between teachers and students, strengthening their relationship.
Modelling Behavior for students	Teachers who practice mindfulness become positive role models for their students	Modelling mindfulness can inspire students to develop their own self-regulation skills and contribute to a more harmonious classroom atmosphere.
Creating Mindful Classrooms	Integrating brief mindfulness activities into the classroom routine can create a mindful atmosphere.	These practices help students manage stress, focus better on tasks, and build a sense of community within the class.
Conflict Resolution at schools	Mindfulness equips teachers with tools for managing conflicts in a constructive manner.	Instead of reacting impulsively to disruptions, teachers can respond mindfully, addressing conflicts with understanding and empathy
Building Trust in teacher-student relationships.	Mindful teachers are more attuned to the individual needs and strengths of their students	This attentiveness builds trust, as students feel seen and valued, fostering positive teacher-student relationships.
Emphasizing respect, openness, and a shared commitment	Mindfulness practices contribute to a positive classroom culture by emphasising respect, openness, and a shared commitment to well-being.	This culture enhances the overall learning experience and strengthens the teacher-student bond.

Mindfulness practice can have a positive influence on pedagogical skills and instructional effectiveness in several ways: by fostering a mindful and present teaching approach, enhancing adaptability, and creating a positive and inclusive learning environment. The incorporation of mindfulness into education contributes to the holistic development of both educators and students.

Table 2. Mindfulness practice influence on pedagogical skills and instructional effectiveness

Themes	Causes	Effects
Enhanced Focus and Presence	Cultivating the ability to be fully present in the moment.	Bringing heightened focus to their instructional delivery, ensuring clarity and engagement in their teaching.
Improved Classroom Management	Developing patience and emotional regulation, crucial components of effective classroom management	Responding calmly to disruptions and navigate challenging classroom situations with composure.
Increased Adaptability	Practising mindfulness are more likely to adapt instructional strategies to meet the diverse needs of students,	Creating a dynamic and responsive learning environment.
Cultivation of Empathy	Encouraging empathy and understanding. Mindful teachers can better connect with their students,	Recognizing individual strengths and challenges, and tailoring their instructional approach accordingly.
Promotion of Active Listening	Mindful teachers are more attuned to student questions, concerns, and feedback,	Fostering a supportive and open communication channel in the classroom.
Integrating Mindfulness into Instruction	Integrating mindfulness techniques into the curriculum to enhance students' attention, focus, and overall learning experience	Short mindful activities, such as mindful breathing breaks, can be seamlessly woven into instructional time.
Cultivation of a Positive Learning Environment:	Creating a positive and inclusive learning environment. Teachers who practise mindfulness can model positive behaviour,	Encouraging a respectful and collaborative atmosphere among students.
Increased Cognitive Flexibility	Improving cognitive flexibility—the ability to consider multiple perspectives.	Teachers with enhanced cognitive flexibility are better positioned to adapt their instructional methods to various learning styles within the classroom.
Professional Development and Continuous Learning	Mindful teachers are more likely to engage in professional development opportunities	Staying current with educational research and innovative instructional approaches.

Research Performance

Mindfulness can positively influence research productivity among teachers/educators in several ways. The study analysis based on the three keys themes of mindfulness, based on Germer, (2004), incorporating the meaning of the teachers' group discussion.

Figure 1. The impact of mindfulness on teachers' research productivity

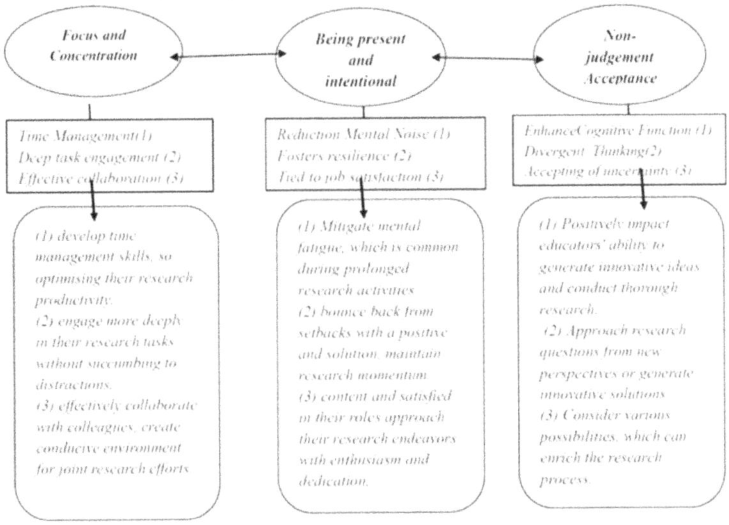

Finding 3

Incorporating mindfulness practices into teachers' work and life involves intentional integration and the development of sustainable habits. By note taking from the teacher discussion, the researcher can answer the third research question (RQ3), as shown in the introduction.

Teachers can improve their own well-being and foster a healthy, mindful learning environment for their students by incorporating mindfulness techniques into various facets of their work and lives. First of all, morning To begin the day with a brief mindfulness practice is to practice mindfulness. To start the day off well, try some mindful breathing exercises, a quick meditation, or a thoughtful stroll. Second, teachers can use mindfulness to provide students with a mental reset during transitions between assignments or courses. This involves taking a few moments to breathe thoughtfully before starting a new activity. Thirdly, to establish a concentrated and encouraging learning atmosphere, thoughtful lesson plans include brief mindfulness exercises or periods of introspection into the curriculum. Fourth, during the school day, teachers take quick, conscious breath breaks. These quick breaks, which can last only a few minutes, can aid teachers in stress management and attention retention. Fifth, educators work on giving their all in the classroom. This entails focusing entirely-without interruption-on the pupils, the material, and the teaching process. Sixth, educators incorporate daily habits that foster thankfulness. They consider the good things that happen in the classroom, achievements, or student thank-you notes.

Seventhly, they go to training sessions or workshops on mindfulness to expand their knowledge and pick up new skills. This may offer continuous encouragement and support. Eighthly, they become a part of or start a mindfulness community within the school since doing mindfulness exercises together and exchanging experiences helps strengthen the bonds of support and purpose that unite teachers. Finally, in order to facilitate the transition from work to personal time, they conclude the workday with a quick mindfulness practice. This could be a quick meditation or a deliberate review of the day.

Figure 2. Incorporating mindfulness practices into teachers' work and life

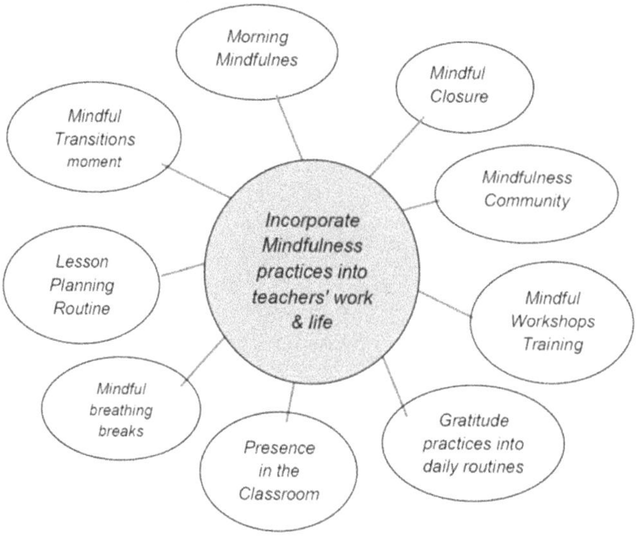

DISCUSSION

An in-depth investigation of how mindfulness can help teachers deal with stress and become more emotionally strong shows a strong story of good results. As mentioned above, many studies, including the ones by Caulfield (2015) and Taylor (2016), have shown that mindfulness techniques can help teachers deal with the stress of their jobs. Taylor et al (2016) looked into how a mindfulness-based strategy can help public school teachers in a Canadian school feel less stressed. This study adds to this idea by showing how the experience of university teachers in Vietnam works in real life. This study shows that mindfulness helps teachers deal with problems more easily and calmly by making them more aware of the present moment and encouraging them not to judge others. Also, research shows that mindfulness has a big effect on making people more emotionally strong. It gives teachers the tools they need to deal with setbacks, stay emotionally healthy, and be happy with their lives over time (Bajaj & Pande, 2016, Liang et al., 2022). In line with the trend of research, this study's results show that mindfulness is a useful and easy-to-use way to improve mental health among teachers. This has implications for both the teachers themselves and the schools where they work.

This study clearly shows a framework for teachers' professional growth in two areas: research and teaching. The outcome fits with Rechtschaffen's "The Way of Mindful Education" (2024) for teacher growth. It shows that mindfulness helps people focus on the present moment, which makes it easier for teachers to be more involved in their lessons and relationships with students. This increased awareness also affects how we teach, leading to a more reflective attitude that encourages ongoing growth. This seems to back up what Stoner and Cennamo wrote in their 2018 book. Improving thought in situated learning: Thinking about using awareness as a way to teach. As teachers learn how to be aware, they not only improve the way they teach, but they also make the classroom a better place to learn. Also, teachers who practice mindfulness are better able to focus and answer difficult school questions. University teachers can deal with the stress of tight deadlines, strict methods, and the pressure to write more easily by incorporating mindfulness into their research routine. This idea fits with Daniel et al. (2022). Additionally, this study shows that the reflective nature of mindfulness pushes researchers to approach their work with an open mind and curiosity, which leads to more creative and new ways of thinking. This study also shows that mindfulness helps build resilience, which helps researchers deal with problems and issues that come up during the research process, as Keye and Pidgeon (2013) have already discussed.

The integration of mindfulness practices into the professional and personal life of a university teacher can inspire profound changes. By integrating mindfulness practices into their daily schedules, they have the ability to cultivate an increased consciousness of the current moment, which in turn enables them to employ a more concentrated and purposeful method of instruction. This discovery builds upon the work of Jennings et al. (2013), who advocated for the advancement of educational objectives via the practice of mindfulness. Mindfulness can serve as a stabilizing force during lectures, enabling instructors to be completely attentive and flexible in response to students' concerns; this is analogous to the concept of "The mindful teacher" as described by Shirley and MacDonald (2016). Mindfulness practiced in the classroom and incorporated into daily life assists educators in stress management, well-being promotion, and exhaustion prevention. Through the adoption of mindfulness practices, university instructors not only enhance their scholarly endeavors but also foster a comprehensive and introspective outlook on life that transcends the confines of academia. This study thus further substantiates the notions of "mindful society" and "mindful teacher, mindful school" as articulated by Hawkins (2017).

CONCLUSION

This research report intends to shed light on how mindfulness practices can improve teachers' well-being and performance, laying the groundwork for future education research and practice. This study examines how mindfulness practices change teachers' well-being and views of teaching and research excellence, filling a significant gap in the field. While mindfulness improves teacher well-being, there is little data on how it does so. This research aims to provide a comprehensive exploration. The research aims to provide new insights by examining the complex relationships between mindfulness, teacher well-being, and professional development. The ultimate goal is to lay a solid platform for empirical investigations and practical applications in education, creating a complete knowledge of how mindfulness can benefit teachers and the educational environment.

This study affects educators and policymakers. Policymakers may include mindfulness training and practices in educator professional development programs due to its good effects on teacher well-being. This research's deep exploration of mindfulness mechanisms reveals that promoting mindfulness in educational contexts can improve teacher well-being and teaching and research. Policymakers should prioritize research-backed mindfulness in education programs due to limitations in empirical information on mindfulness interventions and burnout reduction. Teachers can improve their well-being and performance by incorporating mindfulness activities into their everyday routines. Policymakers and educators may work together to improve education by understanding and addressing mindfulness's transformative power.

The research is with its limitation though qualitative methods, particularly group conversations with content analysis, are deliberately chosen. Qualitative methods are deep but may not be generalizable. Since the sample is from the Swinburne University of Technology FPT Education in Vietnam Alliance Program, the findings may not apply appropriately to other educational contexts. The use of self-reported data in qualitative approaches raises concerns about social desirability bias and participants' subjectivity in reporting mindfulness experiences. The lack of a control group or comparative element makes it difficult to demonstrate a causal relationship between mindfulness practices and observed effects, allowing opportunity for alternative explanations. Finally, the research's focus on one program and demographics may limit its applicability to other academic environments. Subsequent investigations might be conducted by employing a quantitative methodology. Despite these limits, this study with its qualitative approaches is useful for examining mindfulness experiences and providing rich insights within the stated context.

ACKNOWLEDGMENT

This research is supported by FPT Education in Vietnam.

REFERENCES

Bajaj, B., & Pande, N. (2016). Mediating role of resilience in the impact of mindfulness on life satisfaction and affect as indices of subjective well-being. *Personality and Individual Differences*, 93, 63–67. DOI: 10.1016/j.paid.2015.09.005

Brown, K. W., & Ryan, R. M. (2003). The benefits of being present: Mindfulness and its role in psychological well-being. *Journal of Personality and Social Psychology*, 84(4), 822–848. DOI: 10.1037/0022-3514.84.4.822 PMID: 12703651

Caulfield, A. (2015). *The contribution of the practice of mindfulness to stress reduction among school teachers: a qualitative study of Irish primary teachers* (Doctoral dissertation, University of Lincoln).

Chang, M. L. (2009). An appraisal perspective of teacher burnout: Examining the emotional work of teachers. *Educational Psychology Review*, 21(3), 193–218. DOI: 10.1007/s10648-009-9106-y

Daniel, C., Daniel, P. A., & Smyth, H. (2022). The role of mindfulness in the management of projects: Potential opportunities in research and practice. *International Journal of Project Management*, 40(7), 849–864. DOI: 10.1016/j.ijproman.2022.07.003

Drisko, J. W., & Maschi, T. (2016). *Content analysis*. Pocket Guide to Social Work Re.

FitzGerald, S. (2012). *Using mindfulness to build a transformative school culture: A phenomenological study of elementary school principals who create an atmosphere of academic rigor and teacher effectiveness* (Doctoral dissertation, Argosy University/Seattle).

Gase, L. N., Gomez, L. M., Kuo, T., Glenn, B. A., Inkelas, M., & Ponce, N. A. (2017). Relationships among student, staff, and administrative measures of school climate and student health and academic outcomes. *The Journal of School Health*, 87(5), 319–328. DOI: 10.1111/josh.12501 PMID: 28382671

Gouda, S., Luong, M. T., Schmidt, S., & Bauer, J. (2016). Students and teachers benefit from mindfulness-based stress reduction in a school-embedded pilot study. *Frontiers in Psychology*, 7, 590. DOI: 10.3389/fpsyg.2016.00590 PMID: 27199825

Hawkins, K. (2017). Mindful teacher, mindful school: Improving wellbeing in teaching and learning.

Hennink, M. M. (2013). *Focus group discussions*. Oxford University Press.

Herodotou, C., Sharples, M., Gaved, M., Kukulska-Hulme, A., Rienties, B., Scanlon, E., & Whitelock, D. (2019, October). Innovative pedagogies of the future: An evidence-based selection. [). Frontiers Media SA.]. *Frontiers in Education*, 4, 113. DOI: 10.3389/feduc.2019.00113

Howitt, D. (2019). *Introduction to qualitative research methods in psychology*. pearson UK.

Jennings, P., Lantieri, L., & Roeser, R. W. (2012). Supporting educational goals through cultivating mindfulness. *Handbook of prosocial education, 1*, 371.

Kabat-Zinn, J. (2003). Mindfulness-based stress reduction (MBSR). *Constructivism in the Human Sciences*, 8(2), 73.

Keye, M. D., & Pidgeon, A. M. (2013). Investigation of the relationship between resilience, mindfulness, and academic self-efficacy. *Open Journal of Social Sciences*, 1(6), 1–4. DOI: 10.4236/jss.2013.16001

Liang, S., Dong, M., Zhao, H., Song, Y., & Yang, A. (2022). Mindfulness and life satisfaction: The moderating effect of self-control and the moderated moderating effect of resilience. *Personality and Individual Differences*, 185, 111241. DOI: 10.1016/j.paid.2021.111241

Liesa-Orús, M., Latorre-Cosculluela, C., Vázquez-Toledo, S., & Sierra-Sánchez, V. (2020). The technological challenge facing higher education professors: Perceptions of ICT tools for developing 21st century skills. *Sustainability (Basel)*, 12(13), 5339. DOI: 10.3390/su12135339

Lomas, T., Medina, J. C., Ivtzan, I., Rupprecht, S., & Eiroa-Orosa, F. J. (2017). The impact of mindfulness on the wellbeing and performance of educators: A systematic review of the empirical literature. *Teaching and Teacher Education*, 61, 132–141. DOI: 10.1016/j.tate.2016.10.008

McWilliams, S. A. (2014). Foundations of mindfulness and contemplation: Traditional and contemporary perspectives. *International Journal of Mental Health and Addiction*, 12(2), 116–128. DOI: 10.1007/s11469-014-9486-1

Michalak, J., Steinhaus, K., & Heidenreich, T. (2020). (How) do therapists use mindfulness in their clinical work? A study on the implementation of mindfulness interventions. *Mindfulness*, 11(2), 401–410. DOI: 10.1007/s12671-018-0929-9

Norris, G. (2019). *Adaptability and mindfulness of Chinese knowledge workers in multinational companies* (Doctoral dissertation, Edinburgh Business School).

Onyema, E. M. (2020). Integration of emerging technologies in teaching and learning process in Nigeria: The challenges. *Central Asian Journal of Mathematical Theory and Computer Sciences*, 1(1), 35–39.

Randall, P. W. (2019). *Teacher stress in rural schools: A phenomenological study on stress and its effect on teacher-perceived physical and mental well-being* (Doctoral dissertation, Northwest Nazarene University).

Rechtschaffen, D. (2014). *The way of mindful education: Cultivating well-being in teachers and students*. WW Norton & Company.

Shirley, D., & MacDonald, E. A. (2016). *The mindful teacher*. Teachers College Press.

Sipe, W. E., & Eisendrath, S. J. (2012). Mindfulness-based cognitive therapy: Theory and practice. *Canadian Journal of Psychiatry*, 57(2), 63–69. DOI: 10.1177/070674371205700202 PMID: 22340145

Stoner, A. M., & Cennamo, K. S. (2018). *Enhancing reflection within situated learning: Incorporating mindfulness as an instructional strategy*. Springer. DOI: 10.1007/978-3-319-70326-8

Taylor, C., Harrison, J., Haimovitz, K., Oberle, E., Thomson, K., Schonert-Reichl, K., & Roeser, R. W. (2016). Examining ways that a mindfulness-based intervention reduces stress in public school teachers: A mixed-methods study. *Mindfulness*, 7(1), 115–129. DOI: 10.1007/s12671-015-0425-4

Viac, C., & Fraser, P. (2020). Teachers' well-being: A framework for data collection and analysis.

Waldemar, J. O. C., Rigatti, R., Menezes, C. B., Guimarães, G., Falceto, O., & Heldt, E. (2016). Impact of a combined mindfulness and social–emotional learning program on fifth graders in a Brazilian public school setting. *Psychology & Neuroscience*, 9(1), 79–90. DOI: 10.1037/pne0000044

Zarate, K., Maggin, D. M., & Passmore, A. (2019). Meta-analysis of mindfulness training on teacher well-being. *Psychology in the Schools*, 56(10), 1700–1715. DOI: 10.1002/pits.22308

Chapter 16

Mindfulness, Organizational Identification, Work–Life Balance, and Family Support in Female Happiness

Garima Bansal
Guru Jambheshwar University of Science and Technology, Hisar, India

B. K. Punia
https://orcid.org/0000-0003-4199-610X
Guru Jambheshwar University of Science and Technology, Hisar, India

Radhika Girdhar
Guru Jambheshwar University of Science and Technology, Hisar, India

Vandana Punia
Guru Jambheshwar University of Science and Technology, Hisar, India

ABSTRACT

Happiness, a universally valued and significant positive emotional state, is essential for a meaningful and fulfilling existence in the workplace across cultures. The present chapter explores the interconnected effect of mindfulness, organizational identification, work-life balance, and family support on employee happiness at the workplace. The study surveyed 385 married working women in the Indian banking

DOI: 10.4018/979-8-3693-8457-2.ch016

and IT industry, and the data was analyzed using PLS SEM 4. Further, the bootstrapping method was also employed to assess the significance of the relationships between variables. The study revealed that all the examined factors have a positive and significant impact on the happiness of the Indian female workforce. The findings provide useful insights for organizations and policymakers to create inclusive and enlightened workplace cultures that prioritize the welfare of the female workforce, thereby enhancing their happiness, involvement, and proficiency. The chapter also discusses the theoretical implications as well as the limitations and potential avenues for future research.

1. INTRODUCTION

Women's participation in the Indian workforce has been experiencing rapid evolution, with growing involvement in diverse sectors ranging from educational institutions to corporate settings (Beham et al., 2012; Garg, 2022). The dual-career relationship provides a prime example of the intricate interplay between career and gender roles in contemporary society. (Srivastava, 2007). Domestic work is characterized as feminine, personal, and moral responsibilities, rather than being recognized as a financially worthwhile profession (Buzzanell and Turner, 2003). Nevertheless, the tendency for men to be involved in household duties has not grown at a commensurate pace (Sullivan and Coltrane, 2008). Although there are some advancements in gender roles, women still shoulder a larger portion of household chores than their husbands (Crompton et al., 2007; Medved, 2016). This is due to the fact that Indian women face a particularly pertinent challenge of balancing multiple responsibilities. They are often the primary caregivers, taking care of children, handling domestic duties, and supporting aging parents. Despite engaging in paid employment, women often find it difficult to forego their domestic responsibilities, resulting in a "double burden" of labor. This dual obligation for women generates significant pressure, restricting opportunities for personal and professional development and frequently leading to tension, burnout, and diminished well-being. Consequentially, addressing the elements that influence their happiness is vital for creating welcoming, supportive, and flourishing workplace settings.

Happiness is a fundamental emotion that is characterized by a positive emotional state, determined by the sensation of well-being and delight, as well as a sense of success that is associated with a clear understanding of the world (De Giorgio et al., 2023; Jeong et al., 2022). This chapter explores the key factors that contribute to the happiness of the married working women in India, with a specific emphasis on four primary concepts: employee mindfulness, organizational identification, work-life balance, and family support. Mindfulness often refers to as the knack or inclination to engage in nonelaborative, non-judgmental, present-centred awareness, wherein one acknowledges each emotion, thought, or experience that arises in the attentional field (Bishop et al., 2004; Bansal and Punia, 2023). These days, the concept of mindfulness is being used by researchers in the fields of human resource management and organizational behaviour as workplace mindfulness (Reb and Vogus, 2020; Leggett, 2022). In the present context, workplace mindfulness refers to being aware of and attentive to one's work environment and culture (Dane and Brummel, 2014). Organizational identification is the feeling of oneness with an organization in which one defines oneself as a part of the organization (Mael andAshforth, 1992). It refers to a person's identification with organizational values, mission, and culture (Tidwell, 2005). It shows the degree of attachment of female employees toward their company, determining their motivation, efficiency, and happiness. In addition to these intrinsic organizational variables, work-life balance plays a great role in the overall well-being of female employees. Work-life balance is the degree to which an individual's efficiency and contentment in their professional and family obligations are in accordance with their life priorities at a particular moment (Greenhaus and Allen, 2010; Bellmann and Hübler, 2021). Furthermore, family support (FAS) refers to the emotional and psychological support and care provided by family members (Demaray et al., 2005; Roman et al., 2008). Work-life balance is the degree to which an individual's efficiency and contentment in their professional and family obligations are in accordance with their life priorities at a particular moment (Greenhaus and Allen, 2010; Rashmi and Kataria, 2022; Soelton, 2023).

Indian married women tend to associate their identity and happiness with support from family and adequate balancing between the professional and domestic realms. Mindfulness, as a critical psychological resource, assists women in meeting the challenges when juggling between job and home responsibilities. Mindfulness develops moment-to-moment awareness and emotional regulation, essential for managing workplace-related stressors and job satisfaction (Kütük et al.,2023; Al-dahadha, 2023). In addition, the attachment to the organization—through strong organizational identity—deepens women's ties with the work environment, providing connection and meaning to the work. Studies suggest that this, along with family support and a satisfactory work-life balance, can also enhance psychological well-being and happiness at work. The main aim of the chapter is to relate the different roles of mindfulness, organizational identity, work-life balance, and family support in contributing to the psychological well-being of women in India and thus their happiness at work. Through empirical investigations, this study intends to provide some ambient knowledge on how these elements contribute to the happiness of married women at the workplace. Consequently, this study aims to offer practical and theoretical insights on how organizations can enhance organizational attachment and mindfulness practices, while families and workplaces can advance their support for married working women, potentially leading to further happiness and well-being.

In line with this, the study aimed to investigate the following objectives:

- To study the effect of Employee Mindfulness on Happiness of married working women in India
- To investigate the effect of Organizational Identification on Happiness of married working women in India
- To study the influence of Family support on Happiness of married working women in India
- To explore the impact of Work-Life Balance on Happiness of married working women in India

2. RESEARCH RELEVANCE

Following a thorough review of the existing literature, it was found that previous studies have explored the interconnectedness between mindfulness, organizational identification, family support, work-life balance, and happiness in combination of any two or their combined relationship in conjunction with other variables such as creativity, employee wellbeing, gratitude, and performance (Gip et al., 2022; Sawyer et al., 2022; Slutsky et al., 2019) in foreign countries. There is a noticeable dearth of research that explicitly studies all five constructs together in the Indian domain.

3. REVIEW OF LITERATURE

3.1. Employee Mindfulness

Lindsay et al. (2018) defines mindfulness as a non-judgmental and accepting approach to focusing on the present moment. It has become a significant area of scientific study and organizational development. Mindfulness enables the observer to see emotions and ideas as transient, objective occurrences rather than as reflections that inherently possess accuracy. In the last thirty years, mindfulness techniques have gained significant popularity to complement self-awareness. Openness and receptive awareness can lead to a more consistent and prolonged consciousness of ongoing events (Martin, 1997). An individual's mindfulness, being a unique attribute, can be considered a personal asset. Utilizing this resource will enable individuals to exhibit innovative work behaviors. Three constituents comprise mindfulness: intention, attention, and attitude. The attribute of mindfulness is a distinctive characteristic that distinguishes each person, thereby rendering it a highly invaluable personal asset. According to Garland et al. (2015), many scientific models of mindfulness propose that the focus on eliminating harmful behaviors and disengaging from unpleasant mental states offers a definitive account of mindfulness rather than fostering positive mental states and adaptive behavior.

3.2. Work-Life Balance

The ability to balance professional and personal obligations equally is known as work-life balance, and it protects an individual's right to a happy way of life both within and outside of the place of work (Byrne, 2005; Palumbo, 2020b). In simpler terms, "work-life balance refers to the lack of conflict between work and life, allowing individuals to take charge of the various roles they play both inside and outside of the workplace" (Kalliath and Brough, 2008).

The body of research on work-life balance acknowledges that life and work are impacted by one another (Hill et al., 2001; Tang et al., 2017). Negative effects of task overload and stress on life include depression, marital discord, and disengagement from family relationships (Grzywacz and Marks, 2000). The resource perspective posits that when people deal with negative life events, it can drain their psychological resources, which in turn affects their work domain, job satisfaction, and ability to maintain high performance levels over time (Ten Brummelhuis and Bakker, 2012; Cochis et al., 2021; Mattarelli et al., 2024). The way that work-life balance has changed throughout time is a reflection of greater changes in how society views work, play, and wellbeing (Wong et al., 2021). Organizations are forced to reconsider conventional ideas of work-life integration as people attempt to balance their personal and professional obligations (Leuhery et al., 2024).

3.3. Happiness

As defined by Ryan and Deci (2001), "happiness is a concept that embodies the hedonic interpretation of the term well-being." From a conceptual standpoint, it can be defined as follows: "the average level of life satisfaction over time; the frequency of positive affect (pleasant moods and emotions); and the absence of negative feelings (anxiety and depression) (Argyle et al., 1989; Argyle and Crossland, 1987)". According to Dharani (2020), happiness encompasses both the affective and cognitive dimensions while evaluating one's life.

The present research (Kashdan et al., 2008) centers on the quest of happiness as the pinnacle of human endeavors. Research has shown that various elements in the workplace can influence the happiness of workers, including CSR initiatives (Espasandín-Bustelo et al., 2021), leadership styles (Nouri et al., 2021), support from supervisors (Drummond et al., 2017), decentralization, and opportunities for training and development (Frey et al., 2014). Furthermore, researchers have identified the factors that influence an employee's happiness, as their subjective evaluation and feelings determine their level of joy. For example, Pollock et al. (2016) look into sentimentality, extraversion, and honesty. Activities that promote happiness, according to Layous (2019), include kindness, optimism, savoring, thankfulness, and strengths-focused thinking. According to certain research, mindfulness may promote happiness, which is relevant to the present study (e.g., Brown and Ryan, 2003; Gu et al., 2022). Accordingly, various researchers like Zubair et al. (2018), Bajaj et al. (2022) and Le et al. (2024) has looked into the various ways that mindfulness converts its impact into joy.

3.4. Organizational Identification

According to Ashforth and Mael (1989), "organizational identification is the process by which people form a bond with the company they work for". This connection includes both an emotional attachment to the organization and a commitment to it, going beyond the cognitive process of identifying oneself as a member (Pratt 1998). As per studies of Wegge et al. (2006), Lee et al. (2015), and Onesti (2023), highly "identified" individuals reported lower levels of stress on the job, higher levels of job satisfaction, and fewer intentions to leave the company. However, this is not always the case; for a review, see Conroy et al. (2017). Additionally, organizational identity has been highlighted in two recent meta-analyses (Steffens et al. 2017; Greco et al. 2022) as having positive effects on people's overall health and wellness. This is in line with other recent studies that have shown that organizational identification has a positive effect on a variety of personal well-being metrics, including happiness, reduced stress, psychological wellbeing, self-efficacy, self-esteem, life satisfaction, and work-related variables (De Giorgio et al., 2023; Hameed et al., 2022; Harris and Cameron, 2005; Onesti, 2023).

3.5. Family Support

Family support refers to the willingness of immediate family members to provide assistance in the form of verbal and non-verbal guidance to working mothers. This support is intended to show attention, admiration, and affection, thereby ensuring that working mothers feel properly cared for, respected, and loved. The support provided is anticipated to facilitate individuals in adjusting to the situations they encounter, so enabling them to achieve prosperity. Family support encompasses several dimensions, namely emotional support, instrumental support, information support, and appreciation. (Setyorini et al., 2023)

3.6. Employee Mindfulness and Happiness

As per previous research, "happiness is the sum of satisfaction in various aspects of one's existence, including work and nonwork domains" (Medvedev and Landhuis, 2018; Frone, 2003). Consequently, an employee's satisfaction with their performance, whether in the workplace or personal life, may influence their contentment. Employees who exhibit a high level of mindfulness are more likely to achieve this satisfaction state, demonstrating superior performance compared to their peers. This is due to the fact that workers who practice mindfulness are better able to stay in the here and now, concentrating on the work at hand rather than letting their minds wander to irrelevant matters (Brown et al., 2007). Mindful workers are also distinctive because they are better able to control their emotions and actions, respond creatively to problems, exercise self-discipline, and accomplish their objectives. According to research (Brown and Ryan, 2003; Ryan and Deci, 2001), these character traits are a guarantee of success in both workplace and life. Additionally, research has demonstrated that when employees practice mindfulness at a higher level, it is associated with better psychological outcomes, including more positive affect and less adverse impact (Brown et al., 2007). These are the characteristics of a pleasant disposition that are used to measure an employee's life joy or contentment (Diener, 2006). Furthermore, workers who practice mindfulness are less prone to let the opinions of others influence their decision-making (Bishop et al., 2004). Consequently, they are able to meet their needs for independence with ease. This fundamental human need is satisfied by mindful individuals, resulting in an overall sense of contentment, regardless of the circumstances of their work or personal life (Sirgy, 2012; Le et al., 2024). Broadly, mindfulness enhances the capacity to navigate complex situations with a positive attitude while remaining in the present moment. This enhances the eventual level of happiness among married female employees who are employed. The subsequent hypothesis has been devised in this context:

H1: Employee Mindfulness positively impacts Happiness.

3.7. Organizational Identification and Happiness

Organization identification is the process by which a person identifies with a group, experiences a sense of cohesion and belonging, unites with the group by viewing themselves through the lens of the organization, and views the group's success or failure as their own (Mael and Tetrick, 1992; Trumpold et al., 2021). Knowing that they and the company are receiving favorable feedback from outside sources can boost team members' sense of fulfilment and contribute to a happier workplace (Diener, 1984). According to Lee et al. (2015), members who identify as belonging to an organization express satisfaction with their jobs and professional activity inside their organizations. When a member's work is in line with the organization's goals and values, they are more likely to be satisfied with their jobs and be more involved in them. In this psychological state, people examine and recognize their personal life goals or the value they bring to the company. Consequently, team members' happiness at work might rise as a result of organization identification, which helps them achieve their goals and find meaning in life (Carmeli et al., 2007; Walumbwa et al., 2011). Organization identification also improves task performance. Members' level of joy at work can rise when they perform better on tasks as they feel more rewarded, satisfied, and accomplished (Jeong et al., 2020; Wang et al., 2021; Diener, 1984; Jeong et al., 2022; Girdhar and Punia, 2023). On the basis of above review, it is hypothesised that

H2: Organizational Identification is positively related to Happiness.

3.8. Family Support and Happiness

Family support is the form of emotional and psychological support and care that family members provide (Demaray et al., 2005; Román et al., 2008; Chaudhry et al., 2024). Researchers have examined social support when seeking factors that may contribute more significantly to contentment. Lyubomirsky et al. (2005), Putnam (2000), and Compton (2005) have demonstrated that social support is a reliable predictor of happiness. Several studies have found a positive correlation between different measures of social support and happiness; for example, Isaacowitz et al. (2003), Lyubomirsky et al. (2005), and Suhail and Chaudhry (2004). On the other hand, Caprara and Steca (2006) looked at how efficacy in managing family relationships correlated with overall wellbeing, but few studies have looked at how the nature of family relationships influenced happiness (Lyubomirsky et al., 2005). In adolescents, the perception of family support is essential for the promotion of subjective well-being in terms of perceived pleasure and satisfaction with life, as it functions as a safeguarding component (Alshammari et al., 2021). According to Bukhari and Afzal (2017), family support facilitates an individual's capacity to increase subjective pleasure and reduce stress. The family's support and continued recognition of their importance in the family foster a sense of value and affection, which in turn brings delight. While strong family support can bring happiness, inadequate family support or family rejection can result in unhappiness (Botha and Booysen, 2014; Schnettler et al., 2015). In view of this, the following hypothesis is proposed:

H3: Family Support has positive effect on Happiness.

3.9. Work-Life Balance and Happiness

Work-life balance (WLB) is the state of equilibrium that an individual attempts to achieve between their professional obligations and personal life, which encompasses health, pleasure, leisure time, and family relationships (Sharma and Nayak, 2016). It is imperative to achieve this equilibrium in order to enhance one's overall well-being, as it directly influences the level of satisfaction achieved in both domains. Work-life balance is achieved by an individual who is satisfied with the time allotment for both their professional and personal lives, as per Haddon (2013). Conversely, dissatisfaction occurs when the time spent in one domain has a negatively correlated effect on the other. For example, the absence of time for leisure and family activities may result in emotional imbalance and diminished positive interactions with loved ones due to weighty work-related obligations. Haddon also suggests that by identifying the underlying causes of dissatisfaction and implementing proactive measures, one can enhance their work-life balance and, as a result, their happiness.

The cultivation of a harmonious equilibrium between work and personal life can result in more prosperous, happier, and healthier lives. For individuals who aspire to live quality lives, this equilibrium is especially important (Breitenecker and Shah, 2018). The advantages of WLB are not limited to individual well-being; they also benefit organizational outcomes. Various positive outcomes have been investigated in numerous studies that examine the relationship between WLB. For instance, it has been linked to higher stock prices (Arthur, 2003), increased organizational support (Kopelman et al., 2006), and improved productivity (Clifton and Shepard, 2004; Perry-Smith and Blum, 2000). Additionally, it has been associated with reduced absenteeism, tardiness, and turnover (Christensen and Staines, 1990; Dalton and Mesch, 1991).

Furthermore, WLB has been associated with increased job satisfaction and employee commitment (Scandura and Lankau, 1997), as well as enhanced career satisfaction (Lee et al., 2002). These results endorse the "happy worker" theory, which contends that employees who maintain a positive work-life balance are less susceptible to adverse consequences resulting from work-life conflict (Weeden, 2005; Carlson et al., 2010). Additionally, employees who undergo work-life balance (WLB) are inclined to exhibit greater creativity and productivity in their professional capacities, while those who are confronted with conflicts between their professional and personal obligations may encounter difficulties in developing innovative ideas (Alegre and Pasamar, 2018). The social exchange theory also underscores the fact that employees are motivated to reciprocate by improving their performance when they receive compassion and encouragement from their employers (Blau, 1964). Consequently, not only does the cultivation of work-life balance develop happiness and well-being, but it also fosters positive organizational outcomes. In order to guarantee both personal satisfaction and professional success, it is essential to maintain a healthy work-life balance. Employee productivity and satisfaction can be improved by organizations that prioritize WLB, which in turn fosters a more positive work environment. Within this framework, the following theory is formulated:

H4: Work Life Balance is positively correlated to Happiness.

4. PROPOSED CONCEPTUAL FRAMEWORK

Figure 1. Research framework

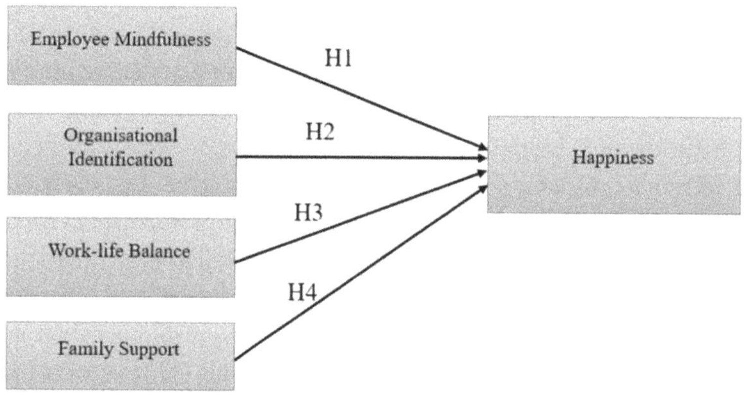

The hypothetical/ proposed Research Model represents all the variables that will be used in this particular research study.

5. RESEARCH METHODOLOGY

5.1. Participants and Procedures

Data was collected from married female workforces working in Indian IT and banking industries. We used purposive and convenience sampling to select participants from each industry, ensuring a diverse representation. We collected primary data using a structured survey questionnaire. The questionnaire incorporated validated scales and items from prior research. Researchers designed the items to measure the level of happiness among female employees at work, taking into account their involvement in workplace mindfulness, organizational identification, work-life balance, and their perception of receiving family support from their families. We initiated the data collection process by seeking permission from managers of the targeted service organizations. We then gathered data using both online and offline methods, depending on each organization's preference. The online strategy involved reaching out to employees through email. The offline approach involved personal visits to organizations to administer the questionnaire. Within a six-month period, researchers distributed 400 questionnaires to the selected participants in both online and offline mode, commencing in February 2024 and concluding in July 2024. Out of these, 385 questionnaires were returned, reflecting a notable response rate of 96.25%. Additionally, we implemented G*Power software to determine the necessary minimum sample size. A minimum sample size of 89 respondents was required to obtain the actual power of 0.95 for two predictors. However, we conducted this study with 385 respondents, which was sufficient to confirm the minimum sample size requirement.

5.2. Instrument Development

The study employed a quantitative research design to collect data from employees in the service sector. Our research instrument consisted of two sections. The first section of the survey had demographic questions, i.e., age, marital status, education, positions, work experience, tenure in the same organization, and types of service industry. The second section comprised the statements to measure the study constructs: workplace mindfulness, organizational identification, work-life balance, and family support. These statements were measured using a 5-point Likert scale, with 1 denoting strongly disagree and 5 denoting strongly agree.

Workplace Mindfulness

We accessed mindfulness, dividing into 12-item scales. The scale was adapted from Brown and Ryan's (MAAS) (mindfulness attention awareness scale) (2003). Sample items for this scale is "I become aware of my emotions quickly and recognize them as they arise" and "I stay present and fully engaged in the moment, even as I work toward achieving my goal." The scale for workplace mindfulness had a Cronbach's alpha of.878, indicating a high level of internal consistency for the scale.

Organizational Identification

To measure the organizational identification, the Scale comprising of six statements was adapted from Mael and Ashforth (1992) e.g. "I am very interested in what others think about our organisation" and "When someone praises this organisation, it feels like a personal compliment". The Cronbach's alpha for this scale is 0.897.

Work-life Balance

To measure work-life balance, an 8-item scale was used, which was developed by Taşdelen-Karçkay and Bakalım (2017). The items in the scale are "I can satisfy my own needs and the needs of the important people in my life" and "I can manage my roles related to family and professional life in a balanced manner." The Cronbach's alpha of 0.854 indicates excellent reliability.

Family Support

Family support was assessed using the 5-item scale developed by Jain and Nair (2017). The scale includes items that measure the support females receive from their family for work-related issues, such as "My family listens to my work-related problems" and "My family recognizes and celebrates my work-related successes." Cronbach's alpha for this instrument is 0.878.

Happiness

We adapted nine statements from Rastogi, 2020 for measuring happiness, which involves three dimensions: job satisfaction (3 items), job engagement (3 items), and affective organizational commitment (3 items).

5.3. Common Method Bias

We used Partial Least Squares Structural Equation Modeling (PLS-SEM) as it is an effective technique for assessing data in management research. We can employ it with small sample sizes and it offers greater versatility when dealing with complex models (Hair, Risher, Sarstedt, and Ringle, 2019). We assessed common method bias (CMB) prior to model estimation. CMB may be present in studies that employ instruments that measure latent variables on comparable scales. This study evaluated the factors using a 5-point Likert scale and performed a full collinearity test to rule out the possibility of CMB. The full collinearity method compares an endogenous random variable to the inner VIF values of the constructions. A number higher than 3.3 indicates a CMB issue, according to Kock and Lynn (2012). According to Koch (2015), the absence of the CMB issue is shown by the fact that none of the investigated variables had inner VIFs over 3.3.

6. RESULTS

6.1. Sample Profile

The demographic profile of respondents has been analysed using descriptive frequency analysis (refer to Table 1). As per the age distribution, most married female respondents, 43.6% of the sample, were aged between 31 and 40 years, followed by the next notable group, aged 20–30 years, making up 34.8% of the participants. The 41–50 age groups accounted for 13.6% of respondents, while those above 50 years old made up 8.0%. In education, graduates (43.9%) and females with post-graduate degrees (53.6%) made up most of the participants, whereas a smaller percentage had continued education beyond post-graduation (2.5%). When considering job positions, 31.6% of the respondents are in entry-level or operative roles, 42.1% are in middle-level positions, and 26.3% are in senior management or upper-level positions. In terms of employee work experience, 49.8% of the sample had 0–5 years of experience. The second-biggest group had 6–10 years of experience, accounting for 39.6%. Employees with more than 10 years of experience comprised 10.6%. When considering tenure within the same organization, 44.2% of the participants have been with their organizations for less than 5 years, 34.46% for 6-10 years, and 21.4% for more than 10 years. Finally, in terms of sectoral distribution, participants represent different service sectors, with 57.8% of them employed in the IT sector, and 42.2% in banking industry.

Table 1. Sample Profile

Demographics	Category	Frequency	Percentage %
Age	20-30 yrs.	134	34.8
	31-40 yrs.	168	43.6
	41-50 yrs.	52	13.6
	Above 50 yrs.	31	8
Education	Graduation	169	43.9
	Post-Graduation	206	53.6
	Others (above post-graduation)	10	2.5
Position	Entry Level Positions/ Operative Level	122	31.6
	Middle- Level positions	162	42.1
	Senior Management/Upper-level positions	101	26.3

continued on following page

Table 1. Continued

Demographics	Category	Frequency	Percentage %
Work Experience	0-5 yrs.	192	49.8
	6-10 yrs.	152	39.6
	Above 10 yrs.	41	10.6
Tenure in organisation	0-5 yrs.	170	44.2
	6-10 yrs.	133	34.4
	Above 10 yrs.	82	21.4
Service Sector	IT	223	57.8
	Banking	162	42.2

Source: Survey data

6.2. Assessment of Measurement Model

The first step in evaluating PLS-SEM results involves assessing the measurement models. This study applied a two-stage process. Initially, the reliability and validity of the four reflective first-order constructs were investigated. The next stage involved assessing the measurement model of a reflective-formative second-order construct (Rasoolimanesh et al., 2019). It is crucial to note that reflective and formative constructs have different evaluation criteria. Once the measurement models meet all specified criteria, researchers can proceed to assess the structural model (Hair et al., 2017).

6.3. Assessing Reflective Construct Model

The measurement model was evaluated by examining indicator loadings, internal consistency reliability, convergent validity, and discriminant validity for four reflective exogenous constructs: workplace mindfulness, organizational identification, work-life balance, and family support and three reflective endogenous constructs i.e., job engagement, job satisfaction, and affective organisational commitment. Construct reliability was assessed by examining the outer loadings of all indicators, which should ideally exceed 0.70. However, according to Ali et al. (2018) and Hair et al. (2017), loadings between 0.50 and 0.70 are considered acceptable as long as the composite reliability (CR) and average variance extracted (AVE) remain within the suggested thresholds. The current model removed the first indicator of work-life balance (WLB_1) due to low factor loadings (<0.50). All other indicators were maintained since their loadings were above 0.60 (Chin et al., 1997). To ensure the reliability of the reflective constructs, internal consistency was checked using composite reliability (CR) and Cronbach's alpha (α), and rhoA. All the α and CR and rhoA values were above the 0.7 benchmark (Hair et al., 2019), thus establishing the reliability of the measurement model for each construct. Convergent validity was confirmed by the AVE values, which were all greater than 0.50 (Hair et al., 2019), showing that the constructs explained more than half of the variance in their respective indicators. Table 2 shows the results for reliability and convergent validity.

The next important step was to use the Fornell-Larcker criterion and the heterotrait-monotrait (HTMT) ratio to check for discriminant validity (Henseler, Ringle, and Sarstedt, 2015). Discriminant validity is the degree to which a construct is empirically distinct from the other latent variables in the model. According to the Fornell-Larcker criterion (1981), a construct is discriminantly valid when the square root of its AVE exceeds its correlations with other constructs. Additionally, we estimate the HTMT by comparing the mean value of item correlations across constructs to the geometric mean of average correlations for the same construct. HTMT ratios were less than the critical threshold of 0.85. These results, shown in Tables 3 and 4, demonstrated that there are no issues of discriminant validity in the model.

Table 2. Construct's Reliability and Validity

Constructs	Indicators	Loadings	Cronbach's alpha	rhoA	Composite reliability	AVE
Workplace Mindfulness (WM)			0.878	0.892	0.905	0.579
	WM_1	0.808				
	WM_2	0.630				
	WM_3	0.725				
	WM_4	0.828				
	WM_5	0.763				
	WM_6	0.803				
	WM_7	0.769				
	WM_8	0.663				
	WM_9	0.773				
	WM_10	0.711				
	WM_11	0.747				
	WM_12	0.759				
Organisational Identification (OI)			0.897	0.902	0.921	0.659
	OI_1	0.809				
	OI_2	0.814				
	OI_3	0.826				
	OI_4	0.816				
	OI_5	0.816				

continued on following page

Table 2. Continued

Constructs	Indicators	Loadings	Cronbach's alpha	rhoA	Composite reliability	AVE
	OI_6	0.788				
Work Life Balance (WLB)			0.878	0.892	0.905	0.579
	WLB_2	0.743				
	WLB_3	0.752				
	WLB_4	0.679				
	WLB_5	0.835				
	WLB_6	0.756				
	WLB_7	0.706				
	WLB_8	0.840				
Family Support (FS)			0.878	0.887	0.911	0.672
	FS_1	0.827				
	FS_2	0.781				
	FS_3	0.807				
	FS_4	0.847				
	FS_ 5	0.835				
Job Satisfaction (J_Sat)			0.749	0.749	0.857	0.666
	J_Sat1	0.833				
	J_Sat2	0.819				
	J_Sat3	0.793				
Job Engagement (J_Eng)			0.744	0.747	0.854	0.662
	J_Eng1	0.845				
	J_Eng2	0.772				
	J_Eng3	0.822				
Affective Organisational Commitment (AOC)			0.708	0.707	0.718	0.501
	AOC_1	0.648				
	AOC_2	0.647				
	AOC_3	0.734				
Happiness (HAPP)	*J_Eng*	0.792	0.752	0.770	0.855	0.664
	J_Sat	0.821				
	AOC	0.830				

Source: The authors

Table 3. Discriminant Validity using the Fornell-Larcker Criterion

	FS	HAPP	OI	WLB	WM
FS	0.820				
HAPP	0.257	0.815			
OI	-0.007	0.188	0.812		
WLB	0.416	0.350	0.298	0.761	
WM	0.143	0.374	0.101	0.326	0.750

Note(s): FS= Family Support, HAPP= Happiness, OI=Organisational Identification, WLB= Work Life Balance, WM= Workplace Mindfulness

Source: The authors.

Table 4. Discriminant Validity using the HTMT Criterion

	FS	HAPP	OI	WLB	WM
FS					
HAPP	0.289				
OI	0.061	0.222			
WLB	0.475	0.407	0.333		
WM	0.155	0.434	0.111	0.352	

Note(s): FS= Family Support, HAPP= Happiness, OI=Organisational Identification, WLB= Work Life Balance, WM= Workplace Mindfulness

Source: The Authors.

Figure 2. Research Framework

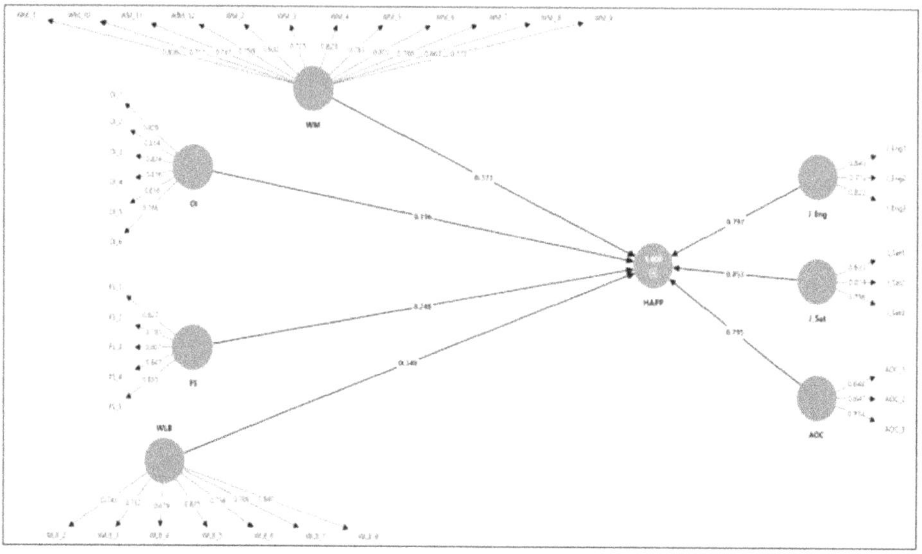

Note(s): *FS= Family Support, HAPP= Happiness, OI=Organisational Identification, WLB= Work Life Balance, WM= Workplace Mindfulness, J_Sat= Job Satisfaction, J_Eng= Job Engagement, AOC= Affective Organizational Commitment*

Source: Authors own

6.4. Assessing Formative Construct Model

When incorporating formative constructs into the structural model, researchers prefer the PLS-SEM technique (Hair et al., 2019). In our study, to assess a single second-order formative endogenous construct, i.e., happiness (job satisfaction, job engagement, and affective organizational commitment), researchers examine indicator collinearity and statistical significance of outer weights (Hair et al., 2017, 2019). The outer variance inflation factor (VIF) typically evaluates the collinearity among formative indicators, with values greater than 3 indicating potential collinearity issues (Becker et al., 2015). Results showed that none of the outer VIFs exceeded 3, suggesting no collinearity concerns with a formative construct. After that, we need to determine whether the indicator weights are statistically significant. To determine if these weights are statistically significant, we employ bootstrapping, as PLS-SEM is a nonparametric method (Chin, 1998). The results revealed significant outer weights for formative construct items. Table 5 reports the results.

Table 5. Results of measurement model of second-order formative construct

Construct	Outer Weights	T statistics	Outer VIF	P values
Happiness (HAPP)				
AOC	0.308	9.041	1.683	0.000
J_Eng	0.483	12.527	1.359	0.000
J_Sat	0.433	11.772	1.633	0.000

Note(s): HAPP= Happiness, J_Eng = Job Engagement, J_Sat = Job Satisfaction, AOC= Affective Organisational Commitment

Source: The authors.

6.5. Structural model Assessment

Once the measurement model assessment was satisfactory, the subsequent stage in the evaluation of the PLS-SEM results was to evaluate the structural model. To rule out any substantial multicollinearity issues, the inner VIF (variance inflation factor) values were first examined. All inner VIF values were less than 5, suggesting that the variables in the model did not exhibit any significant multicollinearity (Hair et al., 2019; James et al., 2013). Following this, the endogenous construct's R^2 value was assessed. The explanatory power of the model is represented by R^2, which quantifies the variance explained in each endogenous construct (Shmueli and Koppius, 2011). Workplace mindfulness, organizational identification, work-life balance, and family support together explained 22.4% of the variance in happiness, as evidenced by the R^2 value of 0.224. The standardized root mean square residual (SRMR) is a frequently employed metric in PLS-SEM to evaluate model fit. SRMR values below 0.08 indicate a favorable model fit (Henseler et al., 2013; Hu and Bentler, 1998). For this model, the SRMR value was 0.048, which suggests an exceptional model fit. Results are reported in Table 6.

We further evaluated hypotheses by employing the consistent PLS algorithm in SmartPLS 4. We conducted bootstrapping using 5,000 subsamples to evaluate the significance of the path coefficients. Table 6 and Figure 3 demonstrate support for all hypothesized relationships.

Our first hypothesis (H1) posited that workplace mindfulness (WM) has a positive effect on happiness (HAPP) among married working women in India. The standardized path coefficient for this association is ($\beta = 0.289$, $p = 0.003$), indicating that happiness is significantly predicted by the workplace mindfulness of married female employees at work. Therefore, H1 is supported. The second hypothesis (H2) proposes that organization identification (OI) positively influences the happiness of married Indian working women. The analysis revealed a standardized path coefficient of ($\beta = 0.112$, $p = 0.019$), demonstrating a significant relationship and supporting

H2. Hypothesis third was developed to examine the impact of work-life balance on happiness. The results again supported H3 and indicated that WLB has a positive and significant relationship with HAPP ($\beta = 0.161$, $p = 0.002$). Hypothesis 4 (H4) was also supported, suggesting the positive and significant effect of family support (FS) on the happiness ($\beta = 0.149$, $p = 0.000$) of the married female workforce. Table 6 reports the results of all three hypotheses.

6.6. PLS predict and RMSE

Additionally, Smart PLS 4 checked this model's out-of-sample predictive power using Q2, which was derived from the PLS predict procedure, and discovered that it was above zero. This proved that it was relevant for predicting constructs. Root means square error (RMSE), that is, the square root of the mean of squared differences between the predications and the actual observations, is the second significant metric for predictions. All of the RMSE values in the theorized model were lower than those in the untheorized model, indicating that these DVs are highly predictive. (Hair et al., 2019). Table 6 illustrates theQ2 and RMSE results.

Table 6. Results of Structural Model

Relationships	**Std. Beta**	**p-value**	**t-value**	**BC 95% CI**	**Significance**	**VIF**
H1 WM → HAPP	**0.289**	0.003	2.948	[0.197; 0.264]	Yes	1.238
H2 OI → HAPP	**0.112**	0.019	2.344	[0.018; 0.205]	Yes	1.123
H3 WLB → HAPP	**0.161**	0.002	3.094	[0.018; 0.205]	Yes	1.474
H3 FS → HAPP	**0.149**	0.000	6.464	[0.046; 0.242]	Yes	1.238
Constructs				**R^2**	**Q^2**	
HAPP				0.224	0.196	
Model Fit (SRMR)				0.048		
RMSE				0.903		

Source: Authors Own

Figure 3. Research framework

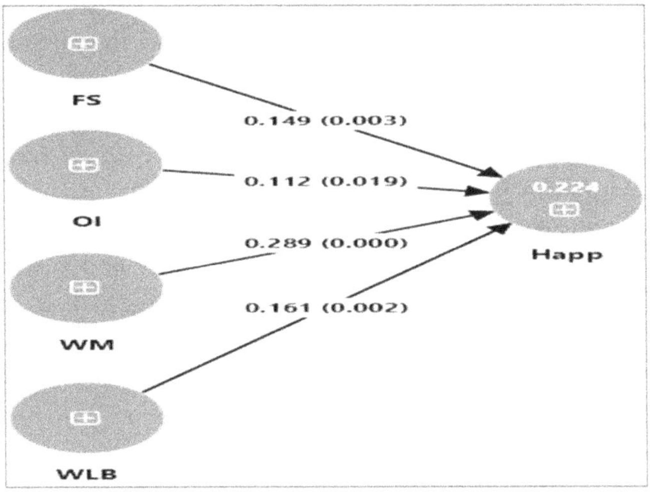

7. DISCUSSION AND IMPLICATIONS

In India, working women encounter the most significant obstacles in comparison to their male counterparts. Previously, they faced restrictions on their ability to attend school and leave their homes to pursue their careers and employment. Although the situation has evolved, they continue to encounter numerous obstacles in their personal and professional lives following their marriage. It is anticipated that they will oversee all domestic responsibilities in addition to caring for their children and advancing their careers. There is still a dearth of organizational and familial support, which is preventing them from achieving a work-life balance. Society must understand that domestic chores are not gender-biased; rather, they are fundamental human skills essential for survival, and everyone should possess them. Given this, the current investigation decodes the complex interplay between various variables, including mindfulness, organizational identification, family support, and work-life balance, and their impact on the happiness of working women in India. This investigation illustrates the existing issue and proposes potential solutions. A happy woman not only transforms her residence into a comfortable living space, but also achieves remarkable results in her professional life. To address this obstacle, the investigation established a variety of objectives. To ascertain the correlation between mindfulness and contentment, the first hypothesis was developed. The results indicate that mindfulness has a positive and significant correlation with happiness. The second hypothesis was to evaluate the correlation between identification with the organization and happiness. More women identify with the organization, the more pleased they are. The third hypothesis we tested was the impact of family support on happiness. The results show a positive correlation between happiness and family support. The fourth hypothesis was to investigate the impact of work-life balance on happiness. The findings indicate a positive correlation between the satisfaction of female employees in India and their work-life balance. Overall, the findings support the study's established hypothesis. The second objective of the study was to propose methods for fostering confidence in women, enabling them to recognize their value and maintain a healthy work-life balance, thereby achieving ultimate happiness. The study offers implications for families to support women in their dual roles, and for managers to develop policies and strategies that effectively assist women in the workplace to develop their careers and achieve work-life balance, ultimately leading to married women's happiness.

7.1 Theoretical Implications

This study contributes to the theory by examining the impact of organizational identification, familial support, work-life balance, and employee mindfulness on happiness. Prior research has demonstrated the correlation between happiness and adverse childhood experiences (Huang et al., 2021), self-disclosure (Aldahadda, 2023), mindfulness (Crego et al., 2021), anxiety (Crowley et al., 2022), and resilience (Bajaj et al., 2022). However, this study is novel in the Indian context, as it examines the impact of a variety of variables, including mindfulness, family support, work-life balance, and organizational identification, on the happiness of working women after marriage.

The study encompasses the following base theories:

Social Exchange Theory: This theory adequately explains the correlation between organizational identification and pleasure. This suggests that when an organization provides resources like flexible work hours, a supportive culture, and other amenities, it motivates employees to show their commitment and identification through increased dedication and involvement. This exchange promotes the well-being of employees, which in turn contributes to their contentment (Cropanzano and Mitchell, 2005).

Work-Life Balance Theories: This research validates the notion that achieving work-life balance is essential for overall health. Mindfulness and family support establish a protective buffer that enables women to more effectively manage their dual responsibilities, resulting in increased happiness, as elucidated by theories such as boundary theory and work-family enrichment (Submitter et al., 2020; Garg and Punia, 2016)

7.2 Practical Implications

For Family Members

Reducing the Household Burden: Family members must take the necessary steps to alleviate the burden of household duties for women. They should offer her emotional and moral support in order to facilitate her growth as an individual. This fosters women's self-assurance, enabling them to operate more efficiently in the workplace.

Developing Respect for Women: It is imperative that families establish an environment that values women. Respecting women with dignity fosters a positive and harmonious home environment. On the other hand, disrespect can result in emotional distress, which can have a detrimental impact on familial relationships and, in turn, a woman's employment performance.

Avoiding Unrealistic Expectations of Perfection: Families should refrain from placing unrealistic expectations of perfection on women. Women are able to navigate their personal and professional lives without unnecessary pressure by acknowledging and embracing that no one is flawless. This acceptance fosters self-assurance and diminishes tension, thereby promoting a more harmonious work-life equilibrium.

Sharing Responsibilities: Families should actively share responsibilities, especially in the area of caregiving. Family members' assistance in caring for children or other domestic obligations alleviates women of excessive responsibilities, allowing them to focus on their work. A shared approach to domestic responsibilities facilitates a more equitable distribution of responsibilities, fostering personal well-being and career advancement.

Families can be instrumental in assisting women in achieving a healthier work-life balance by implementing these practices. This not only promotes the professional development of women but also corresponds with the organization's objectives to cultivate a more inclusive and supportive work environment, which ultimately benefits both employees and employers

For Managers

Organizational Policies: Managers should implement policies such as flexible working hours, work-from-home concepts, and child care facilities for married working women to facilitate the attainment of work-life balance and alleviate tension. Female employees identify with the company and give back, which makes them happy.

Mindfulness Training Programs: In order to mitigate tension and guarantee emotional stability, organizations should periodically implement mindfulness training programs.

Programs for Family Education and Awareness: It is imperative that the family, particularly the spouse, receive education in order to provide support to their partners in their dual responsibilities. Organizations should implement family counselling and a variety of awareness programs to foster a shared comprehension of household responsibilities, children's care, and elder care, ultimately enhancing the happiness of working women.

Personal Growth: Women should recognize the necessity of open communication with their family and colleagues, thereby alleviating the excessive burden on their shoulders and achieving a proper work-life balance.

Various Support Networks: Organizations should establish formal and informal networks, such as employee resource groups and mentorship programs, to provide support and empowerment to married working women. This network offers emotional support, career advice, and valuable guidance, which promotes personal growth and enhances professional development.

Gender Role Awareness and Cultural Shifts: Organizations can advance gender equality by promoting the sharing of domestic responsibilities as cultural norms shift toward more egalitarian roles. Working women are able to more effectively coordinate their personal and professional lives and make a meaningful contribution to the workplace as a result of this cultural shift, which alleviates the burden.

By incorporating these organizational policies and initiatives, companies foster an environment that promotes women's career advancement and assists them in maintaining a healthy work-life balance. This approach is advantageous to both the organization and its employees.

8. LIMITATIONS AND FUTURE RESEARCH DIRECTIONS

The current investigation exhibits certain deficiencies. The study initially limits its scope to the domain of working women in the Indian context after marriage. Future research can expand its scope by incorporating a broader sample size, exploring a variety of research areas, and conducting comparisons across various sectors. While the current study is empirical in nature, future research may conduct a systematic review and bibliometric analysis. Third, the research has examined the direct impact of various variables on happiness. In the future, it may be beneficial to add a mediator or moderator to enhance the effectiveness of the study. Fourth, the study only used a limited number of variables, but it could combine these with other variables to assess their impact.

9. CONCLUSION

The study ultimately establishes that employee mindfulness is positively correlated with happiness, family support has a positive impact on happiness, organizational identification is positively related to happiness, and work-life balance is also favorably related to happiness. The happiness of female workforce members following their marriage is also significantly influenced by all of these variables.

REFERENCES

Aldahadha, B. (2023). Self-disclosure, mindfulness, and their relationships with happiness and well-being. *Middle East Current Psychiatry, Ain Shams University*, 30(1), 7. DOI: 10.1186/s43045-023-00278-5

Alegre, J., & Pasamar, S. (2018). Firm innovativeness and work-life balance. *Technology Analysis and Strategic Management*, 30(4), 421–433. DOI: 10.1080/09537325.2017.1337091

Ali, F., Rasoolimanesh, S. M., Sarstedt, M., Ringle, C. M., & Ryu, K. (2018). An assessment of the use of partial least squares structural equation modeling (PLS-SEM) in hospitality research. *International Journal of Contemporary Hospitality Management*, 30(1), 514–538. DOI: 10.1108/IJCHM-10-2016-0568

Alshammari, A. S., Piko, B. F., & Fitzpatrick, K. M. (2021). Social support and adolescent mental health and well-being among Jordanian students. *International Journal of Adolescence and Youth*, 26(1), 211–223. DOI: 10.1080/02673843.2021.1908375

Argyle, M., & Crossland, J. (1987). The dimensions of positive emotions. *British Journal of Social Psychology*, 26(2), 127–137. DOI: 10.1111/j.2044-8309.1987.tb00773.x PMID: 3607389

Argyle, M., Martin, M., & Crossland, J. (1989). Happiness as a function of personality and social encounters. *Recent Advances in Social Psychology: An International Perspective*, 189-203.

Arthur, M. M. (2003). Share price reactions to work-family initiatives. *Academy of Management Journal*, 46(4), 497–505. DOI: 10.2307/30040641

Ashforth, B. E., & Mael, F. (1989). Social identity theory and the organization. *Academy of Management Review*, 14(1), 20–39. DOI: 10.2307/258189

Bajaj, B., Khoury, B., & Sengupta, S. (2022). Resilience and Stress as Mediators in the Relationship of Mindfulness and Happiness. *Frontiers in Psychology*, 13, 771263. DOI: 10.3389/fpsyg.2022.771263 PMID: 35185720

Bansal, G., & Punia, B. K. (2023). Precursors of workplace mindfulness: An exploration and conceptual modelling. In Narwal, K., Bhisnoi, V. K., Bhaker, S. K., & Saini, V. P. (Eds.), *Florilegium: Management theory, research and practices* (pp. 174–184). Arihant Books.

Becker, J. M., Klein, K., & Wetzels, M. (2012). Hierarchical latent variable models in PLS-SEM: Guidelines for using reflective-formative type models. *Long Range Planning*, 45(5-6), 359–394. DOI: 10.1016/j.lrp.2012.10.001

Becker, J. M., Ringle, C. M., Sarstedt, M., & Völckner, F. (2015). How collinearity affects mixture regression results. *Marketing Letters*, 26(4), 643–659. DOI: 10.1007/s11002-014-9299-9

Beham, B., Prag, P., & Drobnič, S. (2012). Who's got the balance? A study of satisfaction with the work-family balance among part-time service sector employees in five western European countries. *International Journal of Human Resource Management*, 23(18), 3725–3741. DOI: 10.1080/09585192.2012.654808

Bellmann, L., & Hübler, O. (2021). Working from home, job satisfaction and work–life balance–robust or heterogeneous links? *International Journal of Manpower*, 42(3), 424–441. DOI: 10.1108/IJM-10-2019-0458

Bishop, S. R., Lau, M., Shapiro, S., Carlson, L., Anderson, N. D., Carmody, J., Segal, Z. V., Abbey, S., Speca, M., Velting, D., & Devins, G. (2004). Mindfulness: A proposed operational definition. *Clinical Psychology : a Publication of the Division of Clinical Psychology of the American Psychological Association*, 11(3), 230–241. DOI: 10.1093/clipsy.bph077

Blau, P. M. (1964). *Exchange and Power in Social Life*. John Wiley and Sons.

Botha, F., & Booysen, F. (2014). Family functioning and life satisfaction and happiness in South African households. *Social Indicators Research*, 119(1), 163–182. DOI: 10.1007/s11205-013-0485-6

Brown, K. W., & Ryan, R. M. (2003). The benefits of being present: Mindfulness and its role in psychological well-being. *Journal of Personality and Social Psychology*, 84(4), 828–848. DOI: 10.1037/0022-3514.84.4.822 PMID: 12703651

Brown, K. W., Ryan, R. M., & Creswell, J. D. (2007). Mindfulness: Theoretical foundations and evidence for its salutary effects. *Psychological Inquiry*, 18(4), 211–237. DOI: 10.1080/10478400701598298

Bukhari, S. R., & Afzal, F. (2017). Perceived social support predicts psychological problems among university students. *International Journal of Indian Psychology*, 4(2), 18–27.

Buzzanell, P. M., & Turner, L. H. (2003). Emotion work revealed by job loss discourse: Backgrounding-foregrounding of feelings, construction of normalcy, and (re) instituting of traditional masculinities. *Journal of Applied Communication Research*, 31(1), 27–57. DOI: 10.1080/00909880305375

Byrne, U. (2005). Work-life balance. *Business Information Review*, 22(1), 53–59. DOI: 10.1177/0266382105052268

Caprara, G. V., & Steca, P. (2006). The contribution of self–regulatory efficacy beliefs in managing affect and family relationships to positive thinking and hedonic balance. *Journal of Social and Clinical Psychology*, 25(6), 603–627. DOI: 10.1521/jscp.2006.25.6.603

Carlson, D. S., Grzywacz, J. G., & Kacmar, K. M. (2010). The relationship of schedule flexibility and outcomes via the work family interface. *Journal of Managerial Psychology*, 25(4), 330–355. DOI: 10.1108/02683941011035278

Carlson, D. S., & Kacmar, K. M. (2000). Work—family conflict in the organization: Do life role values make a difference? *Journal of Management*, 26(5), 1031–1054. DOI: 10.1177/014920630002600502

Carmeli, A., Gilat, G., & Waldman, D. A. (2007). The role of perceived organizational performance in organizational identification, adjustment and job performance. *Journal of Management Studies*, 44(6), 972–992. DOI: 10.1111/j.1467-6486.2007.00691.x

Chan, H. C., & Chu, K. M. (2024). A Multilevel Perspective on High-Performance Work System, Mindfulness, Employee Work Well-Being, and Employee Creative Engagement. *SAGE Open*, 14(2), 21582440241242206. DOI: 10.1177/21582440241242206

Chaudhry, S., Tandon, A., Shinde, S., & Bhattacharya, A. (2024). Student psychological well-being in higher education: The role of internal team environment, institutional, friends and family support and academic engagement. *PLoS One*, 19(1), e0297508. DOI: 10.1371/journal.pone.0297508 PMID: 38271390

Chin, W. W. (1998). The partial least squares approach to structural equation modeling. In Marcoulides, G. A. (Ed.), *Modern Methods for Business Research* (pp. 295–358). Erlbaum.

Chin, W. W., Gopal, A., & Salisbury, W. D. (1997). Advancing the theory of adaptive structuration: The development of a scale to measure faithfulness of appropriation. *Information Systems Research*, 8(4), 342–367. DOI: 10.1287/isre.8.4.342

Christensen, K. E., & Staines, G. (1990). Flextime: A viable solution to work/family conflict? *Journal of Family Issues*, 11(4), 455–477. DOI: 10.1177/019251390011004007

Clifton, T. J., & Shepard, E. (2004). Work and family programs and productivity: Estimates applying a production function model. *International Journal of Manpower*, 25(8), 714–728. DOI: 10.1108/01437720410570036

Cochis, C., Mattarelli, E., Bertolotti, F., Scapolan, A. C., Montanari, F., & Ungureanu, P. (2021). How perceptions of work-life balance and technology use impact upon creativity in collaborative spaces. In *Digital Transformation and Human Behavior: Innovation for People and Organisations* (pp. 217-234). Springer International Publishing. DOI: 10.1007/978-3-030-47539-0_16

Compton, W. C. (2005). Love and well-being. In Compton, W. C. (Ed.), *An Introduction to Positive Psychology* (pp. 86–107). Wadsworth.

Conroy, S., Henle, C. A., Shore, L., & Stelman, S. (2017). Where there is light, there is dark: A review of the detrimental outcomes of high organizational identification. *Journal of Organizational Behavior*, 38(2), 184–203. DOI: 10.1002/job.2164

Crego, A., Yela, J. R., Gómez-Martínez, M. Á., Riesco-Matías, P., & Petisco-Rodríguez, C. (2021). Relationships between mindfulness, purpose in life, happiness, anxiety, and depression: Testing a mediation model in a sample of women. *International Journal of Environmental Research and Public Health*, 18(3), 925. DOI: 10.3390/ijerph18030925 PMID: 33494471

Crompton, R., Lewis, S., & Lyonette, C. (Eds.). (2007). *Women, men, work and family in Europe* (pp. 159–182). Palgrave Macmillan. DOI: 10.1057/9780230800830

Cropanzano, R., & Mitchell, M. S. (2005). Social exchange theory: An interdisciplinary review. *Journal of Management*, 31(6), 874–900. DOI: 10.1177/0149206305279602

Crowley, C., Kapitula, L. R., & Munk, D. (2022). Mindfulness, happiness, and anxiety in a sample of college students before and after taking a meditation course. *Journal of American College Health*, 70(2), 493–500. DOI: 10.1080/07448481.2020.1754839 PMID: 32369422

Dalton, D. R., & Mesch, D. J. (1991). On the extent and reduction of avoidable absenteeism: An assessment of absence policy provisions. *The Journal of Applied Psychology*, 76(6), 810–817. DOI: 10.1037/0021-9010.76.6.810

Dane, E., & Brummel, B. J. (2014). Examining workplace mindfulness and its relations to job performance and turnover intention. *Human Relations*, 67(1), 105–128. DOI: 10.1177/0018726713487753

De Giorgio, A., Barattucci, M., Teresi, M., Raulli, G., Ballone, C., Ramaci, T., & Pagliaro, S. (2023). Organizational identification as a trigger for personal well-being: Associations with happiness and stress through job outcomes. *Journal of Community & Applied Social Psychology*, 33(1), 138–151. DOI: 10.1002/casp.2648

Demaray, M. K., Malecki, C. K., Davidson, L. M., Hodgson, K. K., & Rebus, P. J. (2005). The relationship between social support and student adjustment: A longitudinal analysis. *Psychology in the Schools*, 42(7), 691–706. DOI: 10.1002/pits.20120

Dharani, B. (2020). At the intersection of happiness and contentment at work. In *The Routledge companion to happiness at work* (pp. 61–75). Routledge. DOI: 10.4324/9780429294426-7

Diener, E. (1984). Subjective well-being. *Psychological Bulletin*, 95(3), 542–575. DOI: 10.1037/0033-2909.95.3.542 PMID: 6399758

Diener, E. (2006). Guidelines for national indicators of subjective well-being and ill-being. *Applied Research in Quality of Life*, 1(2), 151–157. DOI: 10.1007/s11482-006-9007-x

Drummond, S., O'Driscoll, M. P., Brough, P., Kalliath, T., Siu, O. L., Timms, C., Riley, D., Sit, C., & Lo, D. (2017). The relationship of social support with well-being outcomes via work–family conflict: Moderating effects of gender, dependants and nationality. *Human Relations*, 70(5), 544–565. DOI: 10.1177/0018726716662696

Espasandín-Bustelo, F., Ganaza-Vargas, J., & Diaz-Carrion, R. (2021). Employee happiness and corporate social responsibility: The role of organizational culture. *Employee Relations*, 43(3), 609–629. DOI: 10.1108/ER-07-2020-0343

Field, L. K., & Buitendach, J. H. (2011). Happiness, work engagement and organisational commitment of support staff at a tertiary education institution in South Africa. *SA Journal of Industrial Psychology*, 37(1), 1–10. DOI: 10.4102/sajip.v37i1.946

Fornell, C. G., & Larcker, D. F. (1981). Evaluating structural equation models with unobservable variables and measurement error. *JMR, Journal of Marketing Research*, 18(1), 39–50. DOI: 10.1177/002224378101800104

Frey, B. S., Gallus, J., & Steiner, L. (2014). Open issues in happiness research. *International Review of Economics*, 61(2), 115–125. DOI: 10.1007/s12232-014-0203-y

Frone, M. R. (2003). Work-family balance. In Quick, J. C., & Tetrick, L. E. (Eds.), *Handbook of Occupational Health Psychology*. American Psychological Association. DOI: 10.1037/10474-007

Garg, N. (2022). Gratitude and work-family enrichment among Indian female workforce: Exploring the mediating role of psychological capital. *International Journal of Work Organisation and Emotion*, 13(1), 1–17. DOI: 10.1504/IJWOE.2022.121971

Garg & Punia, B.K. (2016). Exploring Social Exchange Theory in Indian Context, *XIBA. Business Review*, 2(2), 12–21.

Garland, E. L., Geschwind, N., Peeters, F., & Wichers, M. (2015). Mindfulness training promotes upward spirals of positive affect and cognition: Multilevel and autoregressive latent trajectory modeling analyses. *Frontiers in Psychology*, 6, 15. DOI: 10.3389/fpsyg.2015.00015 PMID: 25698988

Gip, H., The Khoa, D., Guchait, P., Fernando Garcia, R. L., & Pasamehmetoglu, A. (2022). Employee mindfulness and creativity: When emotions and national culture matter. *Service Industries Journal*, 42(5-6), 383–411. DOI: 10.1080/02642069.2022.2037570

Girdhar, R., & Punia, B. K. (2023). Inclusion, Organisational identification, job satisfaction and task performance: Exploration and Outcome, *Empirical. Economics Letters*, 22(1), 1–18.

Greco, L. M., Porck, J. P., Walter, S. L., Scrimpshire, A. J., & Zabinski, A. M. (2022). A meta-analytic review of identification at work: Relative contribution of team, organizational, and professional identification. *The Journal of Applied Psychology*, 107(5), 795–830. DOI: 10.1037/apl0000941 PMID: 34591563

Greenhaus, J. H., & Allen, T. D. (2011). Work–family balance: A review and extension of the literature.

Grzywacz, J. G., & Marks, N. F. (2000). Reconceptualizing the work–family interface: An ecological perspective on the correlates of positive and negative spillover between work and family. *Journal of Occupational Health Psychology*, 5(1), 111–126. DOI: 10.1037/1076-8998.5.1.111 PMID: 10658890

Gu, M., Tan, C. M., Ho, Y. S., & Liu, L. (2022, August). Work–family conflict and happiness: the moderating role of national culture. In *Evidence-based HRM: a Global Forum for Empirical Scholarship*. Emerald Publishing Limited. DOI: 10.1108/EBHRM-01-2021-0001

Haddon, J. (2013). The Secret to Life Balance and Happiness. *Management Services*, 57(1), 30.

Hair, J., Hult, G., Ringle, C., & Sarstedt, M. (2017). *A Primer on Partial Least Squares Structural Equations Modeling (PLS-SEM)* (2nd ed.). SAGE.

Hair, J. F. M., H. G. T., Ringle, C. M., & Sarstedt, M. (2017). A primer on partial least squares structural equation modeling (PLS-SEM) (2nd ed.). Sage Publications.

Hair, J. F., Risher, J. J., Sarstedt, M., & Ringle, C. M. (2019). When to use and how to report the results of PLS-SEM. *European Business Review*, 31(1), 2–24. DOI: 10.1108/EBR-11-2018-0203

Hameed, I., Ijaz, M. U., & Sabharwal, M. (2022). The impact of human resources environment and organizational identification on employees' psychological well-being. *Public Personnel Management*, 51(1), 71–96. DOI: 10.1177/00910260211001397

Harris, G. E., & Cameron, J. E. (2005). Multiple Dimensions of Organizational Identification and Commitment as Predictors of Turnover Intentions and Psychological Well-Being. *Canadian Journal of Behavioural Science/Revue canadienne des sciences du comportement, 37*(3), 159-169.

Henseler, J., Ringle, C. M., & Sarstedt, M. (2015). A new criterion for assessing discriminant validity in variance-based structural equation modeling. *Journal of the Academy of Marketing Science*, 43(1), 115–135. DOI: 10.1007/s11747-014-0403-8

Henseler, J., & Sarstedt, M. (2013). Goodness-of-fit indices for partial least squares path modeling. *Computational Statistics*, 28(2), 565–580. DOI: 10.1007/s00180-012-0317-1

Hill, E. J., Hawkins, A. J., Ferris, M., & Weitzman, M. (2001). Finding an extra day a week: The positive influence of perceived job flexibility on work and family life balance. *Family Relations*, 50(1), 49–58. DOI: 10.1111/j.1741-3729.2001.00049.x

Hu, L. T., & Bentler, P. M. (1998). Fit indices in covariance structure modeling: Sensitivity to underparameterized model misspecification. *Psychological Methods*, 3(4), 424–453. DOI: 10.1037/1082-989X.3.4.424

Huang, C. C., Chen, Y., Cheung, S., Hu, H., & Wang, E. (2021). Adverse childhood experiences, mindfulness and happiness in Chinese college students during the COVID-19 pandemic. *Child & Family Social Work*, 26(4), 677–686. DOI: 10.1111/cfs.12848 PMID: 34220280

Isaacowitz, D. M., Vaillant, G. E., & Seligman, M. E. (2003). Strengths and satisfaction across the adult lifespan. *International Journal of Aging & Human Development*, 57(2), 181–201. DOI: 10.2190/61EJ-LDYR-Q55N-UT6E PMID: 15151189

Jain, S., & Nair, S. K. (2017). Work support and family support as predictors of work-to-family enrichment and family-to-work enrichment. *Global Business Review*, 18(5), 1307–1324. DOI: 10.1177/0972150917710332

James, G., Witten, D., Hastie, T., & Tibshirani, R. (2013). *An introduction to statistical learning: With applications in R*. Springer. DOI: 10.1007/978-1-4614-7138-7

Jeong, J. G., Kang, S. W., & Choi, S. B. (2020). Employees' weekend activities and psychological well-being via job stress: A moderated mediation role of recovery experience. *International Journal of Environmental Research and Public Health*, 17(5), 1642. DOI: 10.3390/ijerph17051642 PMID: 32138361

Jeong, J. G., Kang, S. W., & Choi, S. B. (2022). A multilevel study of the relationship between csr promotion climate and happiness at work via organizational identification: Moderation effect of leader–followers value congruence. *International Journal of Environmental Research and Public Health*, 19(11), 6637. DOI: 10.3390/ijerph19116637 PMID: 35682221

Kalliath, T., & Brough, P. (2008). Work–life balance: A review of the meaning of the balance construct. *Journal of Management & Organization*, 14(3), 323–327. DOI: 10.5172/jmo.837.14.3.323

Kashdan, T. B., Biswas-Diener, R., & King, L. A. (2008). Reconsidering happiness: The costs of distinguishing between hedonics and eudaimonia. *The Journal of Positive Psychology*, 3(4), 219–233. DOI: 10.1080/17439760802303044

Kock, N. (2015). Common method bias in PLS-SEM. *International Journal of e-Collaboration*, 11(4), 1–10. DOI: 10.4018/ijec.2015100101

Kock, N., & Lynn, G. (2012). Lateral collinearity and misleading results in variance-based SEM: An illustration and recommendations. *Journal of the Association for Information Systems*, 13(7), 546–580. DOI: 10.17705/1jais.00302

Kopelman, R., Protter, D. J., Thompson, C. A., & Jahn, E. W. (2006). A multilevel examination of work-Life practices: Is more always better? *Journal of Managerial Issues*, 18(2), 232–225.

Kütük, H., Hatun, O., Ekşi, H., & Ekşi, F. (2023). Investigation of the relationships between mindfulness, wisdom, resilience and life satisfaction in Turkish adult population. *Journal of Rational-Emotive & Cognitive-Behavior Therapy*, 41(3), 536–551. DOI: 10.1007/s10942-022-00468-w PMID: 35909985

Layous, K. (2019). Promoting happiness in the workplace. *Creating Psychologically Healthy Workplaces*, 171-195.

Le, N. H., Mai, M. Q. T., & Le, K. G. (2024). Mindfulness, resilience and the happiness of service employees working from home. *Journal of Services Marketing*, 38(4), 460–473. DOI: 10.1108/JSM-03-2023-0109

Lee, E. S., Park, T. Y., & Koo, B. (2015). Identifying organizational identification as a basis for attitudes and behaviors: A meta-analytic review. *Psychological Bulletin*, 141(5), 1049–1080. DOI: 10.1037/bul0000012 PMID: 25984729

Lee, J. S., Back, K. J., & Chan, E. S. (2015). Quality of work life and job satisfaction among frontline hotel employees: A self-determination and need satisfaction theory approach. *International Journal of Contemporary Hospitality Management*, 27(5), 768–789. DOI: 10.1108/IJCHM-11-2013-0530

Lee, M. D., MacDermid, S., Williams, M., Buck, M., & Leiba-O'Sullivan, S. (2002). Contextual factors in the success of reduced-load work arrangements among managers and professionals. *Human Resource Management*, 41(2), 209–223. DOI: 10.1002/hrm.10032

Leggett, W. (2022). Can mindfulness really change the world? The political character of meditative practices. *Critical Policy Studies*, 16(3), 261–278. DOI: 10.1080/19460171.2021.1932541

Leuhery, F., Hasan, S. Z., Mustari, V. H., Widaningsih, R. R. A., & Lubis, F. M. (2024). The Evolution of Work-Life Balance: Redefining Priorities in Human Resource Management. *Dinasti International Journal of Economics. Finance and Accounting*, 5(1), 23–34.

Lindsay, E. K., Chin, B., Greco, C., Young, S., Brown, K., Wright, A. G. C., Smyth, J. S., Burkett, D., & Creswell, D. (2018). How mindfulness training promotes positive emotions: Dismantling monitor and acceptance in two randomized controlled trials. *Journal of Personality and Social Psychology*, 115(6), 944–973. DOI: 10.1037/pspa0000134 PMID: 30550321

Lyubomirsky, S., King, L., & Diener, E. (2005). The benefits of frequent positive affect: Does happiness lead to success? *Psychological Bulletin*, 131(6), 803–855. DOI: 10.1037/0033-2909.131.6.803 PMID: 16351326

Mael, F., & Ashforth, B. E. (1992). Alumni and their alma mater: A partial test of the reformulated model of organizational identification. *Journal of Organizational Behavior*, 13(2), 103–123. DOI: 10.1002/job.4030130202

Mael, F. A., & Tetrick, L. E. (1992). Identifying Organizational Identification. *Educational and Psychological Measurement*, 52(4), 813–824. DOI: 10.1177/0013164492052004002

Martin, J. R. (1997). Mindfulness: A proposed common factor. *Journal of Psychotherapy Integration*, 7(4), 291–312. DOI: 10.1023/B:JOPI.0000010885.18025.bc

Mattarelli, E., Cochis, C., Bertolotti, F., & Ungureanu, P. (2024). How designed work environment and enacted work interactions impact creativity and work–life balance. *European Journal of Innovation Management*, 27(2), 648–672. DOI: 10.1108/EJIM-01-2022-0028

Medved, C. E. (2016). Stay-at-home fathering as a feminist opportunity: Perpetuating, resisting, and transforming gender relations of caring and earning. *Journal of Family Communication*, 16(1), 16–31. DOI: 10.1080/15267431.2015.1112800

Medvedev, O. N., & Landhuis, C. E. (2018). Exploring constructs of well-being, happiness and quality of life. *PeerJ*, 6, e4903. DOI: 10.7717/peerj.4903 PMID: 29876148

Nouri, B. A., Abbasgholizadeh, N., Oleykie, F., & Nemati, V. (2021). The effect of transformational leadership style on organizational happiness and the mediating role of job passion in hospitals of Ardabil. *Journal of Health*, 12(3), 368–384. DOI: 10.52547/j.health.12.3.368

Onesti, G. (2023). Exploring the impact of leadership styles, ethical behavior, and organizational identification on workers' well-being. *Administrative Sciences*, 13(6), 149. DOI: 10.3390/admsci13060149

Onesti, G., & Palumbo, R. (2023). Tone at the Top for Sustainable Corporate Governance to Prevent Fraud. *Sustainability (Basel)*, 15(3), 2198. DOI: 10.3390/su15032198

Palumbo, R. (2020b). Let me go to the office! An investigation into the side effects of working from home on work-life balance. *International Journal of Public Sector Management*, 33(6/7), 771–790. DOI: 10.1108/IJPSM-06-2020-0150

Palumbo, R. (2024). Making sense of the relationship between involvement and work–life balance: Empirical insights from the public sector. *International Journal of Public Administration*, 47(10), 663–679. DOI: 10.1080/01900692.2023.2166065

Perry-Smith, J., & Blum, T. (2000). Work-family human resource bundles and perceived organizational performance. *Academy of Management Journal*, 43(6), 1107–1117. DOI: 10.2307/1556339

Pollock, N. C., Noser, A. E., Holden, C. J., & Zeigler-Hill, V. (2016). Do orientations to happiness mediate the associations between personality traits and subjective well-being? *Journal of Happiness Studies*, 17(2), 713–729. DOI: 10.1007/s10902-015-9617-9

Pratt, M. G. (1998). To be or not to be: Central questions in organizational identification. Identity in organizations: Developing theory through conversations, 171-207.

Putnam, R. D. (2000). *Bowling alone: The collapse and revival of American community*. Simon and Schuster.

Rashmi, K., & Kataria, A. (2022). Work–life balance: A systematic literature review and bibliometric analysis. *The International Journal of Sociology and Social Policy*, 42(11/12), 1028–1065. DOI: 10.1108/IJSSP-06-2021-0145

Rasoolimanesh, S. M., Taheri, B., Gannon, M., Vafaei-Zadeh, A., & Hanifah, H. (2019). Does living in the vicinity of heritage tourism sites influence residents' perceptions and attitudes? *Journal of Sustainable Tourism*, 27(9), 1295–1317. DOI: 10.1080/09669582.2019.1618863

Rastogi, M. (2020). A psychometric validation of the happiness at workplace scale. *Industrial and Commercial Training*, 52(1), 15–34. DOI: 10.1108/ICT-04-2019-0034

Reb, J., Allen, T., & Vogus, T. J. (2020). Mindfulness arrives at work: Deepening our understanding of mindfulness in organizations. *Organizational Behavior and Human Decision Processes*, 159, 1–7. DOI: 10.1016/j.obhdp.2020.04.001

Román, S., Cuestas, P. J., & Fenollar, P. (2008). An examination of the interrelationships between self-esteem, others' expectations, family support, learning approaches and academic achievement. *Studies in Higher Education*, 33(2), 127–138. DOI: 10.1080/03075070801915882

Ryan, R. M., & Deci, E. L. (2001). On happiness and human potentials: A review of research on hedonic and eudaimonic well-being. *Annual Review of Psychology*, 52(1), 141–166. DOI: 10.1146/annurev.psych.52.1.141 PMID: 11148302

Sarstedt, M., Ringle, C. M., & Hair, J. F. (2021). Partial least squares structural equation modeling. In *Handbook of market research* (pp. 587–632). Springer International Publishing. DOI: 10.1007/978-3-319-05542-8_15-2

Scandura, T., & Lankau, M. J. (1997). Relationships of gender, family responsibility and flexible work hours to organizational commitment and job satisfaction. *Journal of Organizational Behavior*, 18(4), 377–391. DOI: 10.1002/(SICI)1099-1379(199707)18:4<377::AID-JOB807>3.0.CO;2-1

Schnettler, B., Denegri, M., Miranda, H., Sepúlveda, J., Orellana, L., Paiva, G., & Grunert, K. G. (2015). Family support and subjective well-being: An exploratory study of university students in southern Chile. *Social Indicators Research*, 122(3), 833–864. DOI: 10.1007/s11205-014-0718-3

Setyorini, D. M., Shodiqoh, A. I., Naufalani, N. A., Saputra, D., Pribadi, H. C., & Qomariah, N. (2023). Relationship Between Family Support and Work Family Balance in Career Women. *Journal of Economics. Finance and Management Studies*, 6(2), 978–981.

Sharma, N., & Nayak, P. (2016). Study on Work Life Balance and Organisation Policy in IT Sector in NCR. *Amity Global Business Review, 11.*

Shmueli, G., & Koppius, O. R. (2011). Predictive analytics in information systems research. *Management Information Systems Quarterly*, 35(3), 553–572. DOI: 10.2307/23042796

Sirgy, M. J. (2012). *The psychology of quality of life: Hedonic well-being, life satisfaction, and eudaimonia* (Vol. 50). Springer science and business media. DOI: 10.1007/978-94-007-4405-9

Soelton, M. (2023). How Did It Happen: Organizational Commitment and Work-Life Balance Affect Organizational Citizenship Behavior. *Journal of Database Management*, 14(1), 149–164.

Srivastava, S. (2007). Women in workforce: Work and family conflict. *Management and labour studies, 32*(4), 411-421.

Steffens, N. K., Haslam, S. A., Schuh, S. C., Jetten, J., & van Dick, R. (2017). A meta-analytic review of social identification and health in organizational contexts. *Personality and Social Psychology Review*, 21(4), 303–335. DOI: 10.1177/1088868316656701 PMID: 27388779

Submitter, G. A. T. R., Bello, Z., & Tanko, G. I. (2020). Review of work-life balance theories. *Journals and Bello, Zainab and Tanko, Garba Ibrahim, Review of Work-Life Balance Theories.*

Suhail, K., & Chaudhry, H. R. (2004). Predictors of subjective well-being in an Eastern Muslim culture. *Journal of Social and Clinical Psychology*, 23(3), 359–376. DOI: 10.1521/jscp.23.3.359.35451

Sullivan, O., & Coltrane, S. (2008, April). Men's changing contribution to housework and childcare. *Prepared for the11th Annual Conference of the Council on Contemporary Families.*

Tang, Y., Huang, X., & Wang, Y. (2017). Good marriage at home, creativity at work: Family–work enrichment effect on workplace creativity. *Journal of Organizational Behavior*, 38(5), 749–766. DOI: 10.1002/job.2175

Taşdelen-Karçkay, A., & Bakalım, O. (2017). The mediating effect of work–life balance on the relationship between work–family conflict and life satisfaction. *Australian Journal of Career Development*, 26(1), 3–13. DOI: 10.1177/1038416216682954

Taufik, T., Dumpratiwi, A. N., Prihartanti, N., & Daliman, D. (2021). Elderly muslim wellbeing: Family support, participation in religious activities, and happiness. *The Open Psychology Journal*, 14(1), 76–82. DOI: 10.2174/1874350102114010076

Ten Brummelhuis, L. L., & Bakker, A. B. (2012). A resource perspective on the work–home interface: The work–home resources model. *The American Psychologist*, 67(7), 545–556. DOI: 10.1037/a0027974 PMID: 22506688

Tidwell, M. V. (2005). A social identity model of prosocial behaviors within non-profit organizations. *Nonprofit Management & Leadership*, 15(4), 449–467. DOI: 10.1002/nml.82

Trumpold, K., Kern, M., & Zapf, D. (2021). Emotion regulation and service-related attitudes: Connecting customer orientation and service organization identification with customer interactions. *SMR-Journal of Service Management Research*, 5(4), 270–286. DOI: 10.15358/2511-8676-2021-4-270

Walumbwa, F. O., Mayer, D. M., Wang, P., Wang, H., Workman, K., & Christensen, A. L. (2011). Linking ethical leadership to employee performance: The roles of leader–member exchange, self-efficacy, and organizational identification. *Organizational Behavior and Human Decision Processes*, 115(2), 204–213. DOI: 10.1016/j.obhdp.2010.11.002

Wang, W., Kang, S. W., & Choi, S. B. (2021). Effects of employee well-being and self-efficacy on the relationship between coaching leadership and knowledge sharing intention: A study of UK and US employees. *International Journal of Environmental Research and Public Health*, 18(20), 10638. DOI: 10.3390/ijerph182010638 PMID: 34682385

Weeden, K. A. (2005). Is there a flexiglass ceiling? Flexible work arrangements and wages in the United States. *Social Science Research*, 34(2), 454–482. DOI: 10.1016/j.ssresearch.2004.04.006

Wegge, J., Van Dick, R., Fisher, G. K., Wecking, C., & Moltzen, K. (2006). Work motivation, organisational identification, and well-being in call centre work. *Work and Stress*, 20(1), 60–83. DOI: 10.1080/02678370600655553

Wong, K. P., Lee, F. C. H., Teh, P. L., & Chan, A. H. S. (2021). The interplay of socioecological determinants of work–life balance, subjective wellbeing and employee wellbeing. *International Journal of Environmental Research and Public Health*, 18(9), 4525. DOI: 10.3390/ijerph18094525 PMID: 33923234

Zubair, A., Kamal, A., & Artemeva, V. (2018). Mindfulness and resilience as predictors of subjective well-being among university students: A cross cultural perspective. *Journal of Behavioural Sciences*, 28(2), 1.

Chapter 17
Personality and Wellbeing:
A Road Map Towards Sustainable Development

Swati Sharma
https://orcid.org/0000-0002-2029-5251
University School of Business, Chandigarh University, India

ABSTRACT

The main aim of this study is to investigate the relationship of personality traits and wellbeing and impact of personality on mental health. Wellbeing of the people is also one of the goals for attaining sustainability. Due to increased globalisation, the competition level has been increased. Due to which in some organisation the employees are treated as a machine This study is descriptive in nature with qualitative data. The secondary data will be collected from research papers, articles, book chapters, and official websites to evaluate the relationship between personality traits and wellbeing and its impact. Research has shown that positive extraverted people tend to be happier than negative introverted people who are more likely to fret. The clinical disorder paradigm has generally been the center of personality evaluation. Positive emotionality, conscientiousness, and behavioural control are the psychological traits that have been discovered to be associated with mental wellness.

1. INTRODUCTION

Research on one's personality, traits of personality, well-being psychologically, and mental wellness are very essential since these dynamic notions have a big impact on how people behave. The phrase "set of persistent behaviours, cognitions

DOI: 10.4018/979-8-3693-8457-2.ch017

and emotional patterns evolving from biological and environmental variables" can be used to describe personalities. On the other hand, establishing a state of balance between trying and rewarding life events leads to psychological well-being (Charles et al., 2001). The phrase "set of repetitive behaviours, perceptions and emotional patterns evolving from biological and environmental factors" can be used to define personality (Costa et al., 1998).

Both traits and skills describe whatever an individual is like and what they are capable of Individual variances in patterns of behaviour, cognition, and emotion among persons are what make up a person's personality. Personality traits strongly affect one's attitudes, expectations, assumptions, and behaviour in ways that are out of one's control. The Five Factor Model is a well-liked and commonly applied personality attribute model(Keyes et al., 2015). The five traits are intellect or openness to new experiences, extraversion, conscientiousness, agreeableness and neuroticism. Being friendly, talkative, gregarious, aggressive, active, ambitious, and expressive are examples of extraverted tendencies. Extroverts have a great need for power, status, acclaim, and social acceptance (Charles et al., 2001). Adjective characteristics including being chatty, enthusiastic, gregarious, bold, and dominant are linked to extraversion. It is easy to see whether someone is extraverted because of their evident social participation. People are enjoyable to be around for extraverts. They are energized and more likely than others to feel good feelings (Lucas et al.,2015). These people enjoy drawing attention to themselves, talking a lot, and asserting themselves in groups. Being agreeable includes having attributes like politeness, trustworthiness, adaptability, cooperation, softness of heart, forgivingness, good disposition, and tolerance. Individual differences in regard to unity in society, teamwork, and collaboration can be shown in how agreeable a person is. Consensual personal value of getting along with others. People who are agreeable are courteous, amiable, kind, and helpful. They are prepared to give up their sense of fulfilment in order to make others happy((Roberts et al.,2006) Consciousness is characterized by qualities like diligence, organization, responsibility, care, perseverance, and hard work. Conscientiousness is correlated with traits including dependability, organization, dependability, ambition, and hard effort. Being nervous, depressed, emotional, furious, humiliated, worried, and insecure are characteristics of neuroticism, which is the complete opposite of emotional stability. People with neuroses have poor social skills and shy away from circumstances that call for leadership.

Being creative, inquisitive, original, clever, open-minded, and artistically sensitive are all characteristics of being open to experience. Being open means being inquisitive, innovative, creative, complicated, nuanced, and sophisticated.

People connect differently to psychological well-being. It is highly individualized. Psychological health can generally be defined as the capacity to manage the frequent pressures of daily life in an acceptable manner (Reyes et al.,2015). outlines the various dimensions of psychological well-being. The following characteristics are indicative of a psychologically sound person. A good overall presence of these might be viewed as the presence of psychological well-being, regardless of the degree and proportion of each element.

2. LITERATURE REVIEW

In a 2010 study, Augusto and his colleagues examined the connections between personality traits, psychological health, and emotional intelligence (EI) in college students. According to research by Augusto et al. (2010), low neuroticism and high extraversion are the personality traits that have the strongest correlations with all categories of psychological well-being and are also the best predictors of psychological well-being. All personality domains substantially linked with well-being, according to research results examining the relationship between personality domains and well-being. Extraversion was shown to be followed by conscientiousness and openness to new experiences as key contributors to wellbeing (Marzuki, 2013). Extraversion, conscientiousness, and openness are three personality qualities that connect to psychological well-being in Iranian and Swedish cultures in various ways. Across these civilizations, neuroticism is related in a similar way (Kjell et al., 2013). In a 2013 study, a team of researchers examined the relationships between personality qualities and psychological well-being (PWB) in individuals aged 33 to 50. In 2013, Gale and his research colleagues emphasized the relationship between neuroticism and extraversion and wellbeing. The study used data from 4583 participants in the MRC National Survey of Health and Development to apply structural equation modeling. The effects of neuroticism and extraversion on mental health at ages 16 and 26 and on life satisfaction at ages 60 to 64 were examined, together with the potential mediating effects of psychological and physical health. Extraversion reportedly has a direct, beneficial effect on both wellbeing indicators. Because neuroticism has a tendency to cause psychological distress and physical health issues, its effects on happiness and life satisfaction are mostly indirect.

Youthful personality traits have a long-lasting impact on wellbeing assessed forty years later (Gale et al., 2013). In their 2015 study, Mobarakeh and colleagues looked at the connections between personality traits and psychological health among Iranian immigrant teenagers in Kuala Lumpur, Malaysia. According to the study's findings, extroversion and agreeableness have favorable correlations with mental health, whereas neuroticism has a negative link with it. According to the findings, conscientiousness and openness to new experiences do not significantly influence psychological well-being (Mobarakeh et al., 2015).

2.1 A Conceptual Framework Defining Sustainable Well-Being Components

Figure 1. Sustainability

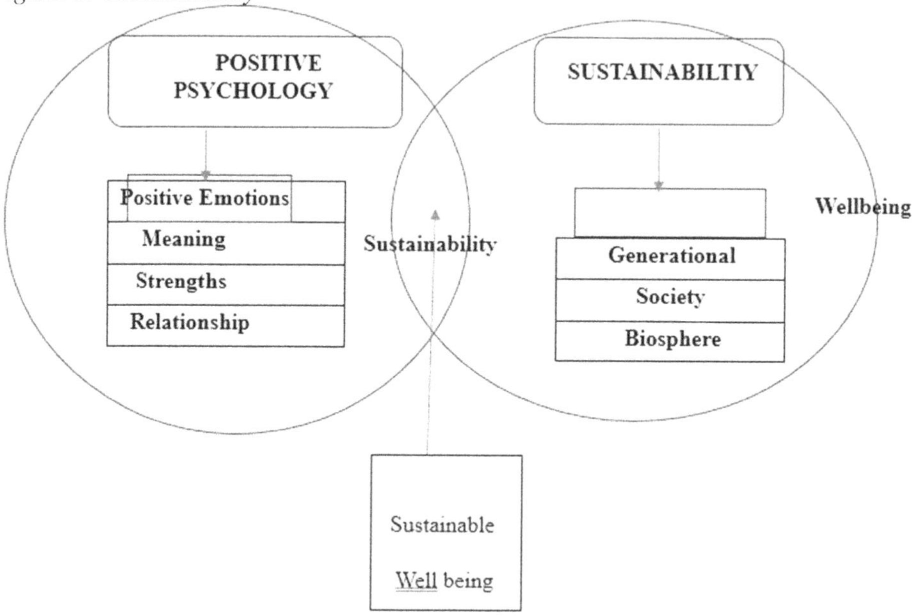

Based upon literature reviewed, we suggest that the best definition of wellbeing is one that emphasizes improving individual wellbeing while taking into account interactions with other people in society and the natural world. This definition uses a "relational" approach. Sustainable wellbeing is attained when enhancing one's own wellbeing is linked to enhancing that of other people in society and the environment. This comprehensive concept, which we refer to as "sustainable wellbeing," is consistent with positive psychology, environmental sustainability, complex systems thinking, and positive psychology (see Figure 1). This method considers interdependence and interaction between human, societal, and environmental requirements. This concept represents the idea that wellbeing is not just personal because every person is a part of societal institutions and communities and has many social responsibilities.

3. ACHIEVING SUCCESS FOR HAPPINESS AND PERSONAL GROWTH

Even longitudinal studies are correlated, thus understanding the relationship between personality and well-being requires taking into account the process through which well-being leads to changes in personality. Because it offers a strong motivation to participate in behaviors that result in positive feelings, well-being may have an impact on personality. To find happiness, a person could alter their usual behavior. The impact that follows can encourage that conduct.

Changes in behavior could become routine to the point where they become a part of the person's personality and regular repertoire. Is there any proof that happiness can anticipate changes in traits? Two large-scale longitudinal studies have shown that high stable levels of well-being systematically predict increases in conscientiousness and agreeableness and decreases in neuroticism, a pattern of trait changes that is commonly thought to represent personality development(Pandya et al.,2015). High levels of well-being so seem to encourage actions and emotions that develop more mature personality traits.

3.1 Alternative Strategies for Personality Development and Well-Being

There are many ways to think about personality and wellbeing. In addition to features, personality also includes a wide range of other elements, such as motivations. According to Sheldon & Krieger (2014), motivational pursuits that represent intrinsic values as opposed to extrinsic values are positively predictive of wellbeing. Other personality traits (such expectations and beliefs, for example), as we lower level characteristic aspects have a fairly intuitive relationship to wellbeing. Each class of variables will likely be examined in ever-greater detail as research on the relationship between personality and wellbeing progresses. Additionally, subjective well-being does not encompass all conceptions of what it means to be happy. For instance, the concept of "expanding balances metrics for societal well-being with those of personal well-being. According to Keyes et al. (2015), flourishing is only weakly correlated with qualities and may even be genetically unrelated to them. When the news is bad, our moods motivate us to act by telling us how things are going. Self-regulation of goal-directed action would not be possible if wellbeing were absolutely steady.

Consider the fact that recent studies (using longitudinal datasets) have shown that life experiences can cause long-term changes in well-being (usually declines) (Luhmann, Hofman, Eid, & Lucas, 2012). Such findings imply that some events arc not as amenable to adaptation as was previously believed. Thus, despite supporting the stability of wellbeing, personality is susceptible to changes sparked by external factors. Not all happiness is a "personality-thing." However, the two psychological traits are sufficiently related to one another that neither should be taken into account alone. Personality and wellbeing are closely related and are best understood in conjunction.

4. FACTORS AFFECTING WELL BEING

The absence of disease or illness is only one aspect of wellbeing. It involves many different aspects of a person's physical, mental, emotional, and social well. Happiness and fulfilment in life are closely related to wellness. Wellness may be summed up as how you feel about the world and yourselves. Your overall state of wellbeing is influenced by every element of your life. According to research on happiness, the following elements improve one's wellbeing:

- A circle of close friends
- An interesting and meaningful job
- Enough money
- Frequent exercise
- A close relationship with a spouse.
- Positive a sense of self
- A positive perspective
- Reasonable and attainable objectives
- A feeling of significance and value
- A sense of belonging
- An inbuilt capacity to adjust to change
- Living in a just and open democracy

4.1 There Is a Relationship Between Factors

The elements that affect wellbeing are interconnected. For instance, a work offers more than simply money; it also gives one purpose, objectives, friends, and a sense of belonging. Some elements also compensate for the absence of others. For instance, a happy marriage can make up for a lack of friends, and religious convictions might help someone cope with physical illness.

4.2 Measuring International Well-Being

Because the definition of wellbeing is so ambiguous and how you feel about your life largely depends on how you see it, measuring wellbeing in a population is challenging. One person's task is another person's problem, as the adage goes. Australian academics attempt to gauge happiness in order to monitor living conditions. Counting the number of people who are impacted by a certain factor is a common method of gauging wellbeing.

For instance, keeping tabs on the number of individuals:

- Are cancerous.
- Either unmarried, married, or divorced.
- Engage in regular exercise.
- Drink or smoke.
- Receive unemployment compensation.
- Are criminal victims.
- Neither read nor write.

Monitoring a population's wellbeing enables governments to select specific policies. For instance, understanding a population's median weekly income aids in establishing the "poverty line," which may subsequently have an impact on decisions on social assistance reform.

4.3 The Most Effective Methods to Achieve Well-Being

- Create and preserve solid bonds with family and friends.
- Schedule time each day for social interaction.
- Instead of just working for the highest salary, try to choose employment that you find rewarding and enjoyable.
- Consume healthful, nourishing foods.
- Engage in regular exercise.
- Participate in things you find interesting.
- Join any appealing local organizations or clubs.
- Make attainable objectives for yourself and strive toward them.
- Be positive and try to enjoy each day.

CONCLUSION

At the national and international levels, promoting wellbeing—which includes the well-being of people, society, and the environment—is a crucial goal. Numerous educational initiatives have been developed to improve wellness since schools have a significant influence on how humankind will develop in the future. A holistic approach to the many dimensions of wellness has been lacking, albeit there have been numerous breakthroughs made within distinct educational streams. This has prevented the development of a common vocabulary, systems thinking, and the merging of these disparate academic and practical areas. This article examined how methods to environmental sustainability awareness and positive education have enhanced wellbeing. In order to acknowledge the linkages between people's wellbeing and the wellbeing of the environment as a whole, we developed a mutually comprehensive definition of wellbeing, sustainable wellbeing, which encompasses the key elements from both the positive psychology lens and the sustainability lens. We suggested employing sustainable wellbeing literacy, based on a cognitive-behavioural thinking method combined with positive psychology, sustainability, and systems perspective, in order to bring about a behavioural change. We showed how actively planning the intended change could help promote sustainable wellbeing.

REFERENCES

Charles, S. T., Reynolds, C. A., & Gatz, M. (2001). Age-related differences and change in positive and negative affect over 23 years. *Journal of Personality and Social Psychology*, 80(1), 136–151. DOI: 10.1037/0022-3514.80.1.136 PMID: 11195886

Costa, P. J., & McCrae, R. R. (1988). From catalog to classification: Murray's needs and the five-factor model. *Journal of Personality and Social Psychology*, 55(2), 258–265. DOI: 10.1037/0022-3514.55.2.258

Diener, E. (1984). Subjective well-being. *Psychological Bulletin*, 93(3), 542–575. DOI: 10.1037/0033-2909.95.3.542 PMID: 6399758

Diener, E., & Lucas, R. E. (2009). *Personality and subjective well-being. The science of wellbeing*. Springer.

Gale, C. R., Booth, T., Mõttus, R., Kuh, D., & Deary, I. J. (2013). Neuroticism and extraversion in youth predict mental wellbeing life satisfaction 40 years later. *Journal of Research in Personality*, 47(6), 687–697. DOI: 10.1016/j.jrp.2013.06.005 PMID: 24563560

Hermes, M., Hagemann, D., Naumann, E., & Walter, C. (2011). Extraversion and its positive emotional core—Further evidence from neuroscience. *Emotion (Washington, D.C.)*, 11(2), 367–378. DOI: 10.1037/a0021550 PMID: 21500905

Keyes, C. M., Kendler, K. S., Myers, J. M., & Martin, C. C. (2015). The genetic overlap and distinctiveness of flourishing and the big five personality traits. *Journal of Happiness Studies*, 16(3), 655–668. DOI: 10.1007/s10902-014-9527-2

Kjell, O. N. E., Ali, A. N., Sverker, S., Trevor, A., & Danilo, G. (2013). Iranian and Swedish adolescents: Differences in personality traits and well-being. *PeerJ*, 1(1), 197. DOI: 10.7717/peerj.197 PMID: 24255812

Lucas, R. E., & Baird, B. (2004). Extraversion and emotional reactivity. *Journal of Personality and Social Psychology*, 86(3), 473–485. DOI: 10.1037/0022-3514.86.3.473 PMID: 15008650

Luhmann, M., Hofmann, W., Eid, M., & Lucas, R. E. (2012). Subjective well-being and

Luhmann, M., Hofmann, W., Eid, M., & Lucas, R. E. (2012, March). adaptation to life events: A meta-analysis. *Journal of Personality and Social Psychology*, 102(3), 592–615. DOI: 10.1037/a0025948 PMID: 22059843

Marzuki, N. A. (2013). The impact of personality on employee well-being. *European Scientific Journal*, 9(20), 43–52.

McCrae, R. R., & Costa, P. T. (1989). The structure of interpersonal traits: Wiggins's circumplex and the five-factor model. *Journal of Personality and Social Psychology*, 56(4), 586–595. DOI: 10.1037/0022-3514.56.4.586 PMID: 2709308

Mischel, W. (2004). Toward an integrative model for CBT: Encompassing behavior, cognition, affect, and process. *Behavior Therapy*, 35(1), 185–203. DOI: 10.1016/S0005-7894(04)80011-X

Mobarakeh, M., Juhari, R., Yaacob, S., Redzuan, M., & Mobarakeh, S.(2015). The effects of personality traits and psychological well-being among Iranian adolescent migrants in Kuala-Lumpur, Malaysia. IOSR Journal of Humanities and Social Science, 20(7),25-28.

Mobarakeh, M., Juhari, R., Yaacob, S., Redzuan, M., & Mobarakeh, S. (2015). The effects of personality traits and psychological well-being among Iranian adolescent migrants in Kuala-Lumpur, Malaysia. *IOSR Journal of Humanities and Social Science*, 20(7), 25–28.

Pandya, M., & Korat, N. (2015). Personality traits and psychological wellbeing among youths of Rajkot district. *International Journal of Indian Psychology*, 2(2), 19–23.

Reese, E., Myftari, E., McAnally, H. M., Chen, Y., Neha, T., Wang, Q., Jack, F., & Robertson, S.-J. (2017). Telling the tale and living well:Adolescent narrative identity, personality traits, and well-being across cultures. *Child Development*, 88(2), 612–628. DOI: 10.1111/cdev.12618 PMID: 27637177

Roberts, B. W., Walton, K. E., & Viechtbauer, W. (2006). Patterns of mean-level change in personality traits across the life course: A meta-analysis of longitudinal studies.

Roberts, B. W., Walton, K. E., & Viechtbauer, W. (2006, January). Patterns of mean-level change in personality traits across the life course: A meta-analysis of longitudinal studies. *Psychological Bulletin*, 132(1), 1–25. DOI: 10.1037/0033-2909.132.1.1

Ryff, C. D. (1989). Happiness is everything, or is it? Explorations on the meaning of psychological well-being. *Journal of Personality and Social Psychology*, 57(6), 1069–1081. DOI: 10.1037/0022-3514.57.6.1069

Schmutte, P. S., & Ryff, C. D. (1997). Personality and well-being: Reexamining methods and meanings. *Journal of Personality and Social Psychology*, 73(3), 549–559. DOI: 10.1037/0022-3514.73.3.549 PMID: 9294901

Sheldon, K. M., & Krieger, L. S. (2014). Walking the talk: Value importance, value enactment,and well-being. *Motivation and Emotion*, 38(5), 609–619. DOI: 10.1007/s11031-014-9424-3

Soto, C. J. (2015). Is happiness good for your personality? Concurrent and prospective relations of the big five with subjective well-being. *Journal of Personality*, 83(1), 45–55. DOI: 10.1111/jopy.12081 PMID: 24299053

Chapter 18
Success Stories and Happiness Wisdom Framework for Thriving Workspaces:
Crafting Cultures of Wellbeing

Sumathi Annamalai
https://orcid.org/0000-0002-4342-8600
Christ University, India

ABSTRACT

In today's fast-paced and increasingly complex work environment, organizations are under immense pressure to ensure not just productivity but also the overall well-being of their employees. Through the exploration of real-world success stories, this chapter will illustrate the innovative strategies adopted by organizations to create environments where employees flourish. Additionally, "Happiness Wisdom Framework," a practical guide that organizations can adopt to cultivate a culture of well-being, is proposed. Methodology relies on secondary sources and focussed group discussions conducted among Generation Z participants to provide a comprehensive analysis of employee well-being practices and the formulation of the Happiness Wisdom Framework. This chapter will be helpful for HR and organizational leaders looking to implement effective well-being strategies and benefit researchers and consultants interested in understanding how to create sustainable, positive workplace cultures through the adoption of innovative frameworks like the Happiness Wisdom Framework.

DOI: 10.4018/979-8-3693-8457-2.ch018

1. INTRODUCTION

Amid the challenges of the modern workplace, cultivating employee wellbeing is fundamental to organisational success. A well-nurtured and happy workforce is more productive, involves more, and shows the path to innovation. Employees who are engaged can add value and feel supported can drive the organisation towards its objectives and this is reflected in the organisational performance. In addition, when we promote wellbeing, we create a positive organisational culture which ultimately boosts teamwork, innovation, and adaptability. This will not only ensure the success of the organisation but will also nurture the people connected to the organisation.

1.1 Changing Nature of Work

The increasing trend of remote working and the fusion of personal and professional boundaries have led to employee stress and burnout. The structure of the remote workings, work from home or hybrid work merges personal and professional life, so that the employees fail to take time off from their work and it ultimately adds to stress. While technology has improved efficiencies, it has added to the expectation amongst employees that they should be available at all hours, which leads to the feeling of being under pressure to always be 'on'. Working from home can mean blurred lines between home life and working life – it can end up meaning longer hours, less downtime to recover, increasing burnout. Furthermore, the phenomenon of remote work tendency may lessen social support, a potential buffer against workplace stress.

1.2 Happiness and Positive Emotions as Organisational Practices

In stressful working environments, this type of organisational practice which provides happiness and positive emotion can help employees developing resilience from job burnout and improves overall wellbeing of the individuals. Practices like these help build relationships, encourage teamwork, and create a real sense of belonging. These aforementioned factors combine to support employees' resistance to the negative effects of stress. A positive disposition reinforces creativity, problem-solving skills and engagement, keeping your employees productive and motivated especially during trying times. Thus, better retention also leads to more productivity and an increasingly agile workforce – contributing substantially to the long-term health of any company. Again, as organizations working towards a practice of well-being invest in happiness or mood-boosting activities we are not only building employee resilience and bandage their wound but also engaging the customers. In addition, happy employees are more likely to accept feedback, innovation and personal development; they tend contribute in creating a learning culture. It also encourages good mental health and results in lower absenteeism as well as an environment where workers feel empowered and have value that will spread out into their lives with family members.

Organisations which focuses on wellbeing initiatives benefits from great engagement, more creativity and job satisfaction. These organizations also experience higher productivity, lower turnover and even a competitive advantage in innovation. Given the high pressure, fast-paced environment in which we live (and work), it has never been more important to factoring mental health and work-life balance into employee well-being. This helps employees become high calibre contributors towards fulfilling the mission of the organisation. In addition, a wellbeing culture brings in more talented people and raise the profile of the organisation too. The good news is that with shifting employee expectations, wellbeing initiatives are no longer extracurricular but core. Focusing on wellbeing yields a workforce that is perseverant, driven, and ultimately, an engine for growth that lasts. This makes it a conscious business decision with a direct bearing on organisational performance and success, it is only wise to invest in employee wellbeing.

Since happiness and positive emotions are at the core of wellbeing, happiness acts as a means of promoting an individual mental, emotional, and even physical health. Pleasant feelings like bliss, appreciation and satisfaction contribute to happiness which in turn translates into increased life fulfillment and the power to endure stress. Positive emotions are linked with better personal habits, good social relationships, and a greater sense of purpose, which in turn make for better wellbeing when they happen on a daily basis. Coming to a sustained state of happiness, not only clears the brain but helps the individual in becoming creative and most productive, adding value to the organisation. In the end, promoting happiness and positive feelings establishes a cyclical cycle of wellbeing, in which every part supports and bolsters the other.

1.3 Organisational Initiatives

One way to create a workplace culture that promotes happiness is by emphasizing gratitude, which can include regularly acknowledging and celebrating individual and team accomplishments. They need to promote open communication, transparency and provide an environment to employees, where they can feel valued and heard. Providing personal and professional development enables employees to progress and progress leads to a purpose and fulfillment. They can create workspaces that support wellbeing, with features like natural light, places to relax, and collaboration spaces. Last but not least, encouraging employees to maintain a healthy work-life balance with flexible hours and remote work policies allows them to be happier and less stressed, leading to more happiness as well. Providing periodic, positive feedback and recognition not only encourages morale but helps strengthen a positive culture too. Organising activities such as Team Building or other social events will strengthen the bonds and therefore create a feeling of belonging, sharing emotional positivity experiences. Lastly, companies can introduce wellness programs like mindfulness or mediations to facilitate stress management, and have employees give themselves more uplifting emotional states.

In this chapter we will discuss the outline of the strategies that successful organisations have followed to create employee wellbeing centric workplaces which will make it easier to address the challenges. The author will explore how organisations have created the environment to support positive emotions, engagement, and creating many success stories through the examples from the organisations. The chapter will also present the "Happiness Wisdom Framework" a quick-access framework that organisations can implement to create a systematic workplace wellbeing improvement process. Integrating joy and wisdom into their fundamentals, enables organisations to not only enhance the wellbeing of their employees and ecosystem, but also gain sustainable growth and impacts in the long run.

2. OBJECTIVES

The primary goal of this chapter is to highlight ways in which organisations have promoted wellbeing, happiness, positive emotions, engagement and healthy work environments. The second goal, in addition to illustrating good practices, is to create and suggest a framework through the "Happiness Wisdom Framework" that could be unique to be provided as Happiness Wisdom practices that organisations could introduce to have a transition towards a culture of wellbeing and sustainability. This chapter will be a combination of practical insights and tested scientific concepts to improve the wellbeing, positive emotions, and engagement of employees and the corporate culture within organisations.

3. METHODOLOGY

Methodology relied on mixed approach for both the objectives. For the first objective of understanding and presenting success stories, secondary data was used to provide a comprehensive analysis of employee wellbeing practices. The author did a systematic literature review to gather and evaluate existing research, case studies, and reports from reputable academic and industry sources. This involves a thorough search of academic journals, industry publications, and organisational reports to collect relevant data on successful case-studies, strategies and innovative practices in happiness, positive emotions and wellbeing at workplaces. The selection of success stories focusses on identifying key themes, trends, and best practices that have been reported across various sectors, emphasizing insights from companies renowned for their effective wellbeing initiatives.

For the second objective of formulating and proposing the Happiness Wisdom Framework, seven focussed group discussions (FGDs) among Generation Z employees were held. The author organized six FGDs among willing participants who are currently working in entry level managerial positions. Each FGD had around five to seven participants with a total of 32 participants contributing to this study. The discussion covered 3 main areas namely, what they perceive as happiness and what practices they prefer to have, when it comes to happiness and positive emotions framework and the employers' support perspective. Each FGD took place for 60 to 80 minutes in an informal setting and the data collected through that were coded using QDA miner lite.

The data collected were synthesized to draw connections and formulate a detailed narrative on the core components of the Happiness Wisdom Framework, including wellbeing foundations, strategies for positive emotions and engagement, supportive workspace design, and wisdom initiatives. Finally, the author integrates these insights into a coherent structure, providing practical recommendations for organisations to adapt and implement the framework. This methodology ensures that the chapter is grounded in a comprehensive review of existing knowledge, perceptions collected from employees and offers a practical, evidence-based guide for fostering employee happiness and wellbeing.

4. EXPLORING SUCCESS STORIES: HOW ORGANISATIONS FOSTER WELLBEING

Indian organisations are increasingly prioritizing employee wellbeing, recognizing its impact on engagement and performance (Majumdar & Kumar, 2022). Companies like Infosys and Tata Consultancy Services have implemented wellness programs that emphasize physical, mental, and emotional health (Monteiro & Joseph, 2022). By fostering positive emotions and happiness at work, they create a more resilient, motivated workforce. Mindfulness initiatives, mental health support, and work-life balance policies are examples of how these organisations promote a positive workplace culture. This holistic approach not only enhances employee satisfaction but also drives productivity and long-term organisational success.

4.1 Tata Consultancy Services (TCS) has consistently been at the forefront of promoting employee wellbeing through various initiatives. The company offers flexible work hours, telecommuting options, and wellness programs that include health check-ups, fitness centers, and stress management workshops. TCS Cares, a program developed for mental health support through qualified counsellors and self-help resources was established in October 2018 (Monteiro & Joseph, 2022). Another mental health initiative started by TCS is "Mpower," which offers access to counselors, wellness coaches, and other resources for employees (Seetharaman, 04 March 2012), thereby supporting the emotional and psychological wellbeing of its employees. This was introduced to combat the rising levels of stress, burnout, and workplace mental health issues. TCS offers professional counseling, wellness workshops, and stress management resources through Mpower. The programs focus on ensuring a safe, stigma-free zone to the employee who reaches you for help. TCS additionally combines wellness initiatives through digital platforms and makes certain personnel can get right of entry to help at any time, reinforcing a subculture of holistic care and wellbeing. Another is "Fit4Life," (The TCS way, n.d.) where the company furbishes physical fitness and general wellbeing of its employees. Apart from tracking your initial weight, it motivates you to maintain a healthy lifestyle with fitness challenges as well as tracking tools combine with group activities such as marathons and step-count contests. Another exemplary initiative is Purpose4Life, (Yadav, 2016) which focuses on corporate social responsibility by inviting employees to volunteer for community service, which also enhances personal satisfaction while benefitting society. They are made to promote a sense of overall wellbeing by increasing employee engagement and a healthier environment in their respective workplaces. By prioritising all aspects of employee wellbeing, the company has achieved relatively high employee satisfaction, very low attrition rates and the distinction of being an employer of choice in India.

4.2 Infosys takes a slightly different approach to employee wellbeing compared to TCS, focusing heavily on integrating mindfulness and digital wellness into its organisational culture. While TCS emphasizes structured programs like "Mpower" and "Fit4Life," Infosys has pioneered initiatives in wellbeing programs (Paul, 2023, April 30), which includes mindfulness training, yoga sessions, and mental wellness workshops to foster emotional resilience. Additionally, Infosys incorporates digital detox practices, encouraging employees to manage their screen time and reduce digital overload. The company also offers an internal platform called "Infosys Wellbeing," providing access to resources for fitness, emotional support, and financial wellness, ensuring a holistic focus. Infosys is recognized for its commitment to employee wellbeing, offering a wide range of wellness programs and initiatives. The company's

"Health Assessment and Lifestyle Enrichment" (HALE) program (Ganesh, 2022; Infosys Employee Wellness, n.d.), focuses on physical, emotional, and financial wellness, providing employees with access to health assessments, fitness programs, and financial planning services. The objective of these programs is to enhance the overall wellbeing of an employee through medical checkups, wellness plans and lifestyle enrichment activities. It is a process that takes care of their health, fitness and mental wellbeing for employees to maintain high energy levels at work while maintaining an excellent balance between professional and personal life. It includes lifestyle coaching that covers areas like nutrition, stress management, and fitness, encouraging healthier habits. It directly connects with digital health tools to the HALE program, helping employees measure their progress and receive personalized recommendations. The program is for employees as well as family members, putting comprehensive wellness into practice at home and not just in the office. HALE also includes early detection to monitor the appearance of chronic diseases so that preventive personalized interventions will ensure long-term health benefits for employees in such a way that care continues essentially on an outpatient basis. Infosys, for one, gives importance to mental health through its Employee Assistance Program (EAP) that provides confidential counseling services. Counseling and emotional support is available through video or phone consultations with professional counselors and psychologists to help in anxiety and stress. The EAP (Perwez & Ramasehan, 2016) is a safe place for employees to voice their concerns without any fear or prejudice. The program adds workshops and webinars on mental health topics that seek to raise awareness as well as offer coping strategies. This benefit not only covers the employee but their family as well, underscoring Infosys' commitment to health and wellness in a holistic way that comes from the core.

4.3 Wipro has instituted several initiatives to support employee wellbeing that includes its comprehensive wellness program. Fit for Life, a comprehensive wellbeing programme was launched in 2008 with the objective of evaluating and improve the wellbeing of employees. This effort also integrated all their wellbeing initiatives under one umbrella. (The Economic Times, 2008, May 30). Access to health screenings, fitness programs, and counseling services are a few such initiatives. Their programs distinguish themselves by adopting a comprehensive and multi-faceted approach to employee wellbeing that integrates physical health, mental wellness, and work-life balance. Unlike other programs, Wipro incorporates a unique blend of initiatives including on-site health clinics, fitness centers, and personalized wellness plans tailored to individual needs. It emphasizes holistic health through partnerships with external wellness providers. They focus on preventive care, including regular health screenings and personalized health assessments. In conjunction with fitness tracking, they also conduct meditation sessions and access to mental health professionals (Chaudhury & Modi 2016), their Employee Assistance Program (EAP) called

"Mitr" program focuses on supporting employees through emotional counseling. Their digital platform is created to ensure employees can quickly access a number of tools and support that assist them in managing work.

An inclusive and supportive culture fosters greater resilience. Wipro Cares initiative is one example of such a program that touches a lot more lives during the tough times. That includes help with financial planning and family care for workers. Additionally, Wipro Cares is dedicated to community engagement and supports employees-led corporate citizenship initiatives. In a holistic way, it benefits the employee and their personal life, in addition to professional help of any kind. This includes the "Wipro Work-life Integration Program" which allows them to offer work-life balance in life and beyond. It provides employees with the option to work remote full time, flexible hours and individual schedules in an effort to give them more control over their lives without simultaneously creating as much pressure for individuals. Employees spend the days off they need, especially when pressure is mounting while others offer employees time off.

4.4 HCL Technologies has made significant progress in enhancing employee wellbeing through its "Employee First" philosophy, which positions employees at the core of its corporate strategy (Castelino & Shinde, 2022). This approach emphasizes the empowerment of employees, allowing them to serve as the main catalysts for innovation and customer value (KV & Misra, 2015). It transforms the conventional management structure by granting greater autonomy to front-line workers who engage directly with clients. By cultivating an atmosphere of trust, transparency, and accountability, HCL encourages employees to take ownership of their responsibilities, consistently fostering positive emotions and increasing employee engagement. Furthermore, the company provides a variety of wellbeing initiatives, including health and wellness programs, flexible work options, and opportunities for career advancement. HCL's "Ideapreneurship" program motivates employees to take charge of their ideas and contribute to the organization's success, thereby nurturing a culture of empowerment and engagement (Shergill & Notra, 2015). This initiative indirectly enhances employee wellbeing by promoting a culture of innovation and empowerment. By encouraging employees to generate ideas and take ownership of projects, it strengthens their sense of purpose and engagement in their work. Providing a platform for creative contributions not only boosts morale and job satisfaction but also facilitates professional development. Additionally, this sense of control and acknowledgment fosters a more rewarding work environment, positively impacting overall employee wellbeing.

4.5 Godrej Industries has implemented several initiatives to enhance workplace wellbeing. Godrej emphasizes creating a supportive and inclusive work environment through its "Godrej Good & Green" sustainability program (Godrej, n.d.), which integrates wellbeing with environmental responsibility. This program promotes employee wellbeing by fostering a sense of purpose, connecting to their spiritual wellbeing and responsibility towards social and environmental issues. One of the specific wellbeing initiatives by Godrej focuses on mental health and emotional wellbeing, offering employees access to counseling services, workshops, and tools to manage stress, anxiety, and work-life balance. The Godrej Industries group employs a full-time, in-house mental health counselor and also collaborates with third-party employee assistance service providers. Both employees and their immediate families, including children, can access the mental health assistance services if needed. By offering this support, the group could ensure that employees and their families feel secure, enabling them to contribute their best. (Bhattacharyya, 2024, August 8). Their wellbeing program features a new elder care policy, allowing employees to take two weeks of paid leave to care for elderly family members. Additionally, their childcare policy covers both primary and secondary caregivers where the primary caregivers are given up to six months of paid leave, extending to another six months of unpaid leave and expanding to flexible work option once they return. For secondary caregivers they give around two months of paid leave (Bhattacharyya, 2024, August 8). The group has improved its medical insurance benefits by providing the same insured sum for all employees, regardless of their position in the hierarchy. All these are part of the broader approach Godrej takes toward creating a healthy and supportive work environment for its employees. While Godrej's overall wellbeing programs have been ongoing, their new initiative was in response to the increasing mental health challenges faced during the COVID-19 pandemic. This program stands out from other wellbeing initiatives due to its comprehensive focus on mental health, particularly its proactive approach to emotional wellbeing. It encouraged open conversations around mental health, reducing stigma in the workplace.

4.6 Mahindra Group of companies has been proactive in creating a workplace that prioritizes wellbeing and inclusivity. One initiative taken by the organisation is the appointment of the 'Wellness Officer' (HR World, 2021, May 15) from 2021 onwards, whose role is to oversee the comprehensive wellness of all associates, ensuring access to medical care, hospitals, and essential supplies while also prioritizing the mental health of the Tech Mahindra family. The company extends their support to their partners and vendors also through this effort (Tech Mahindra, 2021, May 15). Tech Mahindra employs a comprehensive 360-degree approach to employee wellbeing, with a strong focus on mental health and wellness support to assist associates during challenging times like COVID pandemic. Their programs include regular outreach covering various wellness areas namely emotional, physical, spiritual, environmental, intellectual, social etc. which can be called as comprehensive "Wellness Framework". Another initiative that the group offered is their Mhealthy initiative, (Verma, 2020, August 03), a thorough COVID-19 risk screening tool which tests for antibodies and assesses vital health statistics related to COVID-19 comorbidities which is the presence of one or more additional conditions or diseases that occur alongside a primary condition. By providing real-time reports, this solution ensures that everyone entering Tech Mahindra's premises is in good health, contributing to a safe and secure work environment (Verma, 2020, August 03). Another notable initiative is the tie-up with Practo, an integrated healthcare company to provide health care support in the form of corporate wellness plans for all their employers, inclusive of their family members (Mahindraadmin, 2021, November 22). Overall, their wellness programs include activities such as health screenings, fitness challenges, wellness workshops, and sessions on stress management. Additionally, the company offers Mind@Ease, through their Tech Mahindra Foundation which is a CSR wing of Tech Mahindra. Mind@Ease provides aggregrated solutions across the country for all mental health and wellbeing initiatives. Mind@Ease aims to unite counseling service providers on a single platform, making their services easily accessible to users and raising awareness about the importance of mental health. This is an initiative by the group to extend wellness to the community itself, including their employees (Tech Mahindra Foundation, n.d.). Another initiative is their "Diversity and Inclusion" programs that focus on creating an inclusive environment where all employees feel valued and respected. Ultimately, the D&I program contributes to a positive and supportive work environment, driving both individual wellbeing and organisational success.

4.7 Patanjali Ayurved, a leading player in the natural and ayurvedic products industry, has taken a unique approach to employee wellbeing by integrating traditional wellness practices into their work environment with their, "Patanjali Corporate Wellness Program" (Jain, n.d.). They offer it to various corporates, targeting the employees of various corporate houses, about their wellness. It was launched in the early 2010s, integrating Ayurvedic principles, yoga, and dietary guidance tailored for corporate settings also part of Patanjali's broader initiative to enhance workplace wellness (Jain, n.d.). The organization integrates Ayurvedic principles into its health initiatives (Patanjali Wellness, n.d.), providing employees with access to Ayurvedic consultations, yoga classes, and herbal therapies. Furthermore, Patanjali advocates for a comprehensive approach to wellness by promoting a balanced lifestyle that encompasses nutritious eating and regular physical activity. This incorporation of traditional wellness practices not only enhances employee health but also resonates with the company's core values. The organization develops personalized wellness plans that cater to individual health requirements, utilizing Ayurvedic evaluations to formulate tailored programs. Additionally, they implement targeted stress management strategies, including mindfulness practices and relaxation techniques, to assist employees in effectively managing workplace stress.

Regular health screenings and assessments are conducted to monitor employees' health, enabling early detection and intervention of potential issues. Patanjali emphasizes holistic lifestyle programs that address not only physical health but also mental and emotional wellbeing, promoting a balanced approach to overall health (Jain, n.d.). Additionally, the company organizes wellness challenges and activities that encourage employees to adopt healthy habits, fostering a supportive community. Patanjali launched its "Patanjali Health Camps" initiative in the mid-2010s, offering free Ayurvedic consultations and treatments to both employees and the broader community. Recently, in March 2024, they organized free health camp in a remote village in Uttarakhand, providing villagers with health benefits and distributing Ayurvedic medicines. This initiative has been a part of their broader efforts to promote holistic health and wellness (The Statesman, 2024, March 23). Overall, these programs reflect Patanjali's commitment to integrating traditional wellness practices into modern work environments.

So, to summarize, around seven success stories are covered extensively in this section emphasizing the uniqueness of each of these success stories and the similarities in the wellbeing framework. But these cases are from private sector organisations. In India, several unique employee wellbeing programs have been introduced specifically for government employees, aimed at enhancing their overall health and wellbeing. In 1954, the central government established the Central Government Health Scheme (CGHS), providing comprehensive healthcare services to central government employees, pensioners, and their families. Under this scheme, outpatient and inpatient care, diagnostics, and drugs are included. CGHS has a well-integrated network of wellness centers and empanelled hospitals that provide a multi-faceted approach to health care. India's National Pension System (NPS) which is primarily a pension scheme, introduced in 2004, includes provisions for the wellbeing of government employees by ensuring financial security post-retirement. It provides a dedicated saving scheme for government employees, the benefits of which ranges from tax deduction to systematic pension payout benefits helping contribute to overall financial health in the long run. Through schemes to cover medical expenses, goods of education and assistance in emergency conditions, Employee Welfare Fund (EWF) in India provide support for the welfare. The benefits of these funds differ with each state, but these funds are generally aimed at improving the standard of living of the government staffs and their families. The specifics of these funds and their benefits vary by state, but they generally aim to improve the quality of life for government employees and their families.

5. DEVELOPING AND PROPOSING A "HAPPINESS WISDOM FRAMEWORK" FOR ORGANISATIONS

A framework is a structured approach of organizing ideas in a systematic and meaningful way. Along with ideas, it can be concepts, theories or steps and the objective is to break down the complexity of the content to more meaningful, systematic and structured way. This is also done to ensure all the points are covered giving a comprehensive way of presenting complex ideas, concepts and theories.

5.1 Introduction to the Proposed "Happiness Wisdom Framework"

Figure 1 presents a systematic and sequential approach to the Happiness Wisdom Framework, that is proposed for organisations. The happiness wisdom framework for organisations is a structure designed to help employees understand and achieve happiness by integrating various aspects of wellbeing. Though there are no universally defined framework with this exact name, the term generally refers to a holistic approach. Creating a Happiness Wisdom Framework in organisations is a must to improve not just organisational performance but also employee welfare. Satisfied employees are usually more charged up and more motivated, which results in more productivity and better quality of work. Such a positive environment that is created, not only attracts the best talent; but also ensures that your valuable employees do not leave, thus saving you on the high turnover and other associated costs. In addition to that, satisfied employees present novel ideas more often, and their stress and exhaustion will fall back, which will definitely lead to a greater culture and work environment. A wellbeing-oriented approach enhances a positive organisational culture, leading to improved collaboration and communication. Furthermore, happy employees deliver great customer support, which leads to customer satisfaction and loyalty. Ultimately, an organisation that ensures the wellbeing of its employees will pave the way for sustainable business growth, as it nourishes a workforce that is both resilient and adaptable.

For developing the proposed Happiness Wisdom Framework, two methods were employed. One, the best practices and strategies connected to employee happiness and wellbeing were identified in successful organisations renowned for fostering employee wellbeing and the key components adopted in each of the success stories were explored. Two, the ideas proposed by the Generation Z participants in each of the FGDs were captured and meaningful, feasible ideas are inducted in the framework. As of 2024, Generation Z makes up to approximately 20% of the current global workforce. This proportion is expected to grow significantly in the coming years, with estimates suggesting that Generation Z will constitute around

30-40% of the workforce by 2030. This increase will be driven by ongoing graduation rates and the gradual retirement of older generations, leading to a shift in workplace demographics and expectations. Hence listening to what they want in the happiness framework is quite significant for organisations to create and foster such a framework for their future employees and revisit their existing wellbeing practices. The proposed framework exclusively covers the preferences of Gen Z's though the inputs from the existing practices were taken for developing this model.

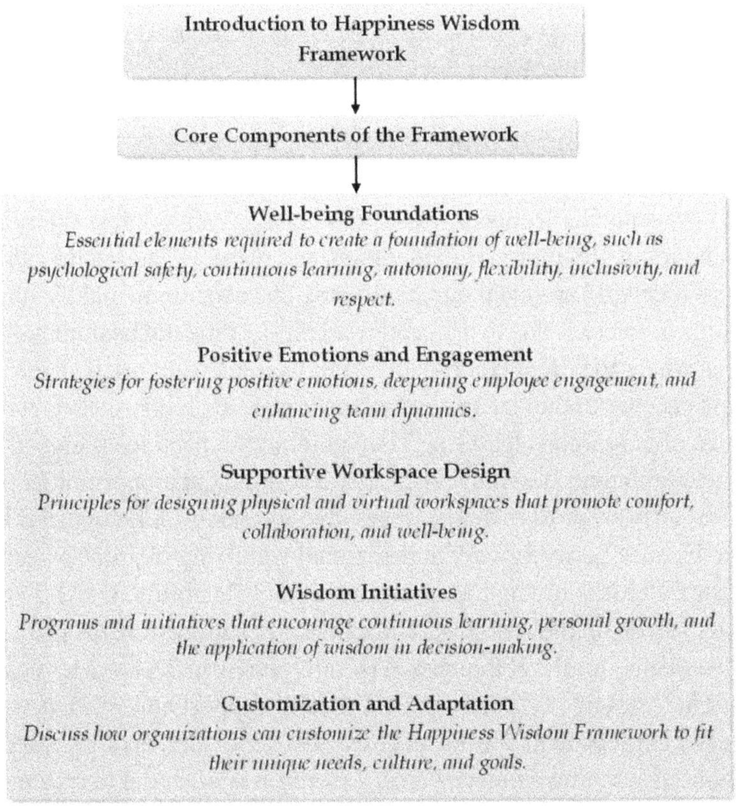

5.2 Core Components of the Framework

Figure 1 covers the core components of the framework namely the perceived foundations of wellbeing, strategies for fostering positive emotions, practices to be considered for designing supportive workspace, programs and initiatives that applies the gained wisdom in decision-making, and lastly how the organisations can customize and adapt the processes in the earlier steps to institutionalize the framework within their existing system. While developing a wellbeing framework, the first step is to understand the foundations upon which the wellbeing is built. So, what are the foundational principles Generation Z (Gen Z) would expect at their workplace is the question raised here. Understanding wellbeing foundations is crucial because they provide the core principles and factors that shape Gen Zs quality of life. By identifying these key elements, we can ensure that the framework addresses all essential areas of life that contribute to wellbeing. This understanding also helps in designing interventions and strategies that are holistic in nature. The Happiness Wisdom Framework for Generation Z (Gen Z) starts with integrating their unique values and needs they expect in the workplace which are the core elements that act as foundation for their wellbeing.

5.3 Wellbeing Foundations

Figure 1 presents the wellbeing bases of Gen Z, psychological safety, ongoing learning, autonomy, flexibility, consideration, and respect. Their values and what is happening in the world around them are shaping this generation and the importance of psychological safety is due to a greater awareness of mental health, making them crave places where they feel emotionally safe, well and supported. Their growing need for fast-paced adaptability and growth in an ever-evolving world that resonates with the idea of continuous learning. They point to the need for things like digital fluency and continuous learning and skill development opportunities that this generation of answering to computers and able to code as a recognized language values. The balance between work and personal wellbeing required to get through whatever comes next is crucial, as is autonomy and flexibility, which is why they are no longer staying in their old lives and careers. In summation, the primary foundations of wellbeing for the Happiness Wisdom framework as it relates specifically to Generation Z will need focus on mental health support and resilience-building to alleviate the unprecedented levels of stress this generation endures. Since Gen Z crave continuous learning and true career growth, it is essential to create opportunities for development. Moreover, creating a sense of purpose and alignment with organisational values helps Gen Z employees to stay engaged and motivated with their work, thereby improving job satisfaction and productivity.

The foundational wellbeing elements of Gen Z differ significantly from other generations due to their unique experiences and the world they have grown up in. Unlike older generations, especially Baby Boomers and Gen X, who valued stability, long-term career growth, and adherence to a traditional corporate structure, Gen Z is more interested in autonomy and flexibility and seeks a more fluid work environment with increased control over their time. But while Millennials prioritized work-life balance and group effort, Gen Z cuts straight to the chase with a focus on psychological safety and mental health, likely due to their increased exposure to mental health issues and social media's impact on self-image. Because Gen Z has to shovel new technology more constantly than previous generations, they also put a greater focus on continuous learning versus on more traditional career advancement. What truly distinguishes them is their deep commitment to inclusivity and social justice over self-reliance, overcoming the traditional focus of the generation on getting ahead, above and apart from the rest. Organisations that have implemented wellbeing practices over the years to fit the needs of earlier generations need to understand that these practices may not translate directly to Generation Z. Gen Z have a unique set of priorities around autonomy, psychological safety, inclusivity, and continuous learning, that need different wellbeing practices than those of other generations. To this end, the Happiness Wisdom Framework for Gen Z will have to embrace the changes that prioritizes mental health, flexible working conditions, and an inclusive, diverse culture. To realise their expectations, the framework must be recreated keeping emphasis on personal empowerment, social justice and growth opportunities, ensuring that wellbeing initiatives are aligned to the changing needs of, along with the values embraced by Gen Z.

5.4 Positive Emotions and Engagement

The second step in the framework involves setting up right approach and creating distinctive practices around the key elements identified as building blocks in the first step, for happiness and wellbeing of Gen Zs. Gen Z are guided by the values of psychological safety, autonomy, inclusivity, continuous learning, flexibility, and respect; hence the initiatives has to be matched to these values. Stress and negativity can be drained out of Generation Z by creating an ambience where mental health is given priority. This will lead to improved emotional security amongst them. Gen Z needs to feel stable, so clearly access to mental health resources with regular in-office outings and mental health days can set the bar straight. Providing flexibility, such as virtual therapy sessions to employees and implementing designated mental health days within their work week enables employees to focus on their wellness needs without experiencing additional barriers.

Work arrangements such as remote work or hybrid work arrangements cater to Gen Z's need for freedom and balance. For example, working from home three days a week and then coming to the office for meetings avoids burnout and allows the employee to steer through daily life, while still being productive. Eventually, organisations may be able to take hybrid work even further with the use of more advanced technology such as AI-driven workspace personalization, and VR (virtual reality) collaboration tools. Imagine, for example, that AI could customize remote work support systems to neutralize any potential distractors by, say, adjusting lighting, temperature, and ergonomic settings to individual preferences in real time. On the other hand, VR can reinvent the office experience by facilitating virtual office spaces that allow for more alive team meetings and collaboration sessions that authentically mimic in-person collaboration, making remote work more engaging and feeling less disconnected.

Teams will feel more engaged and included when we create diverse and respectful breeds and ensure all voices are expressed within those teams. One such concrete way to encourage inclusivity is to create feedback loops where every team member is actively given time to share their thoughts, opinions, and ideas, creating a well-rounded decision-making process that incorporates multiple perspectives. As a forward-thinking and more revolutionary future step, organisations could deploy AI-enabled sentiment analysis tools to gain insights into how teams interact and individuals engage, and instantaneously identify, and resolve inclusivity concerns and disparate impact in real time to help ensure that all voices within the organisation regularly get to be heard and appreciated.

Continuous learning and personal growth are essential, as well, so providing resources and opportunities to grow via mentorship, workshops, and development initiatives will keep them intellectually stimulated and emotionally engaged. As one particular example of how to encourage continuous learning, we can offer personalized learning paths that allow employees to select from a diverse range of courses and development programs according to their interests and career aspirations, thus strengthening positive emotions, engagement and satisfaction. One possible future innovation is AI powered learning platforms that would react to the developing skills of an employee and tailor their learning journey accordingly providing personalized learning experiences, virtual simulations tailored to their personal and professional ambitions. Also, acknowledgement of and respect for the contribution of others not only breeds respect and validation but also incites positive emotions that cause workers to engage better in the workplace.

In the end strategies and practices that targets in amplifying positive emotions echoes one specific kind of organisational culture. Therefore, the framework developed and adopted by organisations will have to focus on building such a culture in the workplace and the framework should not be merely a set of policies and practices adopted in the organisations. This has to be deeply ingrained to an organisation culture. When organisations promote positivity, they are creating a culture where the wellbeing of the worker community, along with the benefit of the entire team, is the focus. Some of these practices that are well ingrained may be celebrating success, providing constant feedback, giving employees a platform to express gratitude and appreciation.

Additionally, just to put another point across positive emotions will only elevate the morale which will ultimately result in creativity, increased productivity, and an overall sense of belonging. When people develop emotional attachment to their work and teams, employee engagement will accelerate, and it always leads to more collaboration and trust. Team-building activities, social events, and wellbeing programs can foster closer interpersonal connections. When employees interact more, they tend not to exit the job and these results in improved retention rate. Furthermore, employees that are engaged tend to work harder, which ultimately leads to a greater success of the organisation. When companies weave positivity and productive participation into the fabric of their culture and work environment, the result is the creation of a workforce that is persistent, evolving, inspired, and energized. Combining these will result in an organisation that aligns with the values and expectations of Gen Z and creates a suitable culture.

In the happiness wisdom framework for Gen Zs, supportive workspace design is proposed as the third step. Supportive workspace design is essential because it affects employee comfort, productivity levels, and overall wellbeing. Physical or virtual when designed well, it creates a good environment for work, a place where focus, creativity, and collaboration are part of the culture. Ergonomic furniture, natural lighting, and intuitive digital tools help reduce stress and increase job satisfaction. Meeting the need and preference of the employee in workspace design creates an environment that is more engaging and supportive, resulting in good emotions, positive engagement, more retention and performance. Designing a supporting workspace is extremely important for Gen Z because they thrive with flexibility and comfort and will feel more productive and positive in the work environment. When we meet their expectations quietly with ergonomic setups and digital tools, we improve their engagement and wellbeing by giving them what they need to cater to efficient, adaptable work environments. Providing such an office is great because it fosters a comfort zone making work easier irrespective of generation. It offers ergonomic design features that reduce physical stress and enhance work productivity, along with flexible digital tools that adapt to the changing tech gears of older populations. By designing workplaces that enable cross-team and cross-age collaboration, communication can further be fostered. Future workspaces may include smart adaptive workstations with smart desks and chairs that automatically adjust to accommodate an individual's ergonomic preference and health needs, sensors and AI will be used to adaptively optimize comfort levels and posture during the work day. Second, with virtual reality collaborations, organisations can have lifelike meeting rooms and create a shared space where remote and in-office employees interact as 3-D holographic co-workers and work materials, making collaboration and engagement easier. Third, organisations can create biofeedback-integrated environments, which means an organisation can use biofeedback technology to monitor an employee's stress levels and during stressful periods it can change environmental factors like light, temperature and sound to eliminate stress in real time and provide a calm and productive atmosphere. Fourth, organisations can create modular and dynamic spaces in their future offices, using modular furniture and movable partitions with customizable layouts, allowing teams to easily reconfigure their workspaces based on function, from team collaborations to quiet, focused work.

Overall if we add these new supportive workspace designs it will increasingly foster contentedness and spark positive emotions among all generations. Smart adaptive workstations and VR collaboration features, for instance, address the need for hybrid flexibility and advanced technology-driven comfort through an engaging work environment for Gen Z. The need for mental wellbeing is addressed in the form of biofeedback integrated environments with a responsive and stress-reducing environment. For example, modular spaces allow for the flexibility and customization they seek. These innovations also offer ergonomic designs that alleviate discomfort and strain for other generations with more flexibility and the collaborative aspect enabling communication and group work, resulting in employees feeling more satisfied with their job and, in turn, feeling more positive emotions.

5.5 Wisdom Initiatives

In this step, organisations should develop and implement structured programs like mentorship, specialized training, and leadership development, to support employees in their career advancement. Unlike the second step, wisdom initiatives will focus on equipping employees with the tools and experiences needed to make informed decisions. This involves creating a culture where knowledge sharing and personal development are prioritized, encouraging employees to seek out new challenges and apply their wisdom in their roles. Wisdom initiatives are deeply connected to the foundational elements of the proposed Happiness Wisdom Framework, as they build on and enhance those core aspects. One, in case of psychological safety, wisdom initiatives thrive in an environment where psychological safety is prioritized when employees feel safe to take risks and make mistakes, they are more likely to engage in continuous learning and apply their wisdom without fear of judgment. Two, organisations align wisdom initiatives with the foundational elements like continuous learning. This will encourage the employees to expand their skills and knowledge. Three, organisations should provide opportunities that will allow employees to take charge of their own career paths. Four, wisdom initiatives often involve flexible learning options, such as online courses or modular training programs. This will accommodate different learning styles and schedules, thus supporting the need for flexibility. Five, effective wisdom initiatives will have to be inclusive, ensuring that all employees have access to development opportunities and that diverse perspectives are considered. Six, wisdom initiatives also should reinforce respect by recognizing and valuing employees' efforts to grow and apply their wisdom. Overall, wisdom initiatives need to be built on the foundational elements by creating a supportive environment that nurtures ongoing learning, personal growth, and its application.

5.6 Customization and Adaptation

The framework concludes with adaptation and customization, the final part of proposed wellbeing. It covers on how one must fine-tune their wellbeing strategies in order to best satisfy unique groups within workforce. It is very important that wellness related steps are appropriate, useful beneficial for all. All these activities should be considered with a personalized learning and development path aligned to the career aspirations and interest area of Gen Zs.

The framework directly brings together different components into a seamless manner for establishing a healthy workplace. Fundamentally, the framework is centred around wellbeing fundamentals such as psychological safety and inclusivity & respect. One, these are basic building blocks that make sure the employees feel respected and a part of the crew. Building on this base the framework adds general strategies for increasing positive emotions and engagement like affirmations, meaningful work or empowerment. Employers enable deeper employee engagement and foster rapport at work. Further, the framework incorporates meaningful practices that encourage employees to continuously learn from their experiences and insights as well as reflect on them so they may apply these very same insights in decision making. Customization and adaptation are heavily stressed because the framework needs to be implemented in a way that can suit each organization's individual requirements, culture, goals etc. With ongoing evaluation and optimization of the framework, companies should be able to fulfil their changing needs over time leading them towards a team culture that involves employees who are well-engaged, supported by management systems & capable. An overview of the proposed happiness wisdom framework is presented in Figure 1.

Step 1: Understanding the Framework

Before implementation begins, leaders and key stakeholders need to thoroughly understand the proposed Happiness Wisdom Framework. As a first step, they have to familiarize themselves with the core principles and components of the framework, such as the focus on emotional wellbeing, resilience, and positive organisational culture. Organisations can consider conducting workshops and training sessions with key veterans in the organisation, internal and external experts recognized to pioneer the transformation and as an overall team must delve into the framework's philosophy and practical applications.

Step 2: Assess Current Organisational Climate

The team form in step 1 need to perform a thorough assessment of the existing organisational culture by conducting surveys, focus groups and one-on-one interviews to measure employee satisfaction, stress levels, and overall wellbeing. By assessing the current culture and where it requires development, existing metrics will serve as benchmarks for how effective proposed solutions of the Happiness Wisdom Framework are. Even greater, it can then be aligned to the climate and culture currently existing within the organisation.

Step 3: Develop a Customized Implementation Plan

The next step will be for the team to draft a detailed implementation plan customized to the organisation. That plan outlines what they would like to achieve, when and what resources are necessary. There are certain elements that need to be part of it, such as commitment from leadership and the support they have to provide; employee engagement strategies; a communication plan etc. At this juncture, the core team must determine and appoint a project team responsible for monitoring the implementation of this process to meet organisational objectives.

Step 4: Engage Leadership and Build Support

For the framework to be successful, as mentioned earlier, securing commitment from top leadership is essential. Leaders should publicly endorse the initiative and model the behaviors and attitudes promoted by the framework. They should be acting as role models for other employees to get inspired and replicate by imbibing the behaviours. The core team should be encouraging the leaders to participate in training sessions and actively engaging with employees to demonstrate their support and commitment.

Step 5: Launch Training and Development Programs

In this step, the core team will be focussing on implementing training programs that educate employees about the principles of the Happiness Wisdom Framework. These programs should cover topics such as emotional intelligence, stress management, and positive communication. Along with that, offering workshops, seminars, and online resources to ensure that all employees have access to the necessary tools and knowledge, whenever they require for upskilling. In total, this step will focus on building the required competencies needed for all the stakeholders in making this transformation.

Step 6: Integrate the Framework into Daily Practices

Now that all the organisational members are geared up with the required competencies to embrace the framework that is proposed, the core team should focus on embedding the principles of the framework into everyday organisational practices. This is to ensure that whatever got communicated in the training programs and workshops are practised so that the transformation is wholesome and here to stay. Also, this should be combined with revising policies to promote work-life balance, introducing flexible working arrangements, and fostering a supportive work environment. Lastly, though the core team and the project implementation team invest their efforts in this transformation process, they need to encourage managers to incorporate the framework's principles into their leadership styles and interactions with team members since they are the people who take such kind of initiatives and reach it to all the levels in the hierarchy.

Step 7: Foster a Positive Culture

To retain the attitude and behaviours that got promoted in the previous steps, the core team must develop and promote a culture of appreciation and recognition within the organisation for retaining it. The core team will need to implement programs that celebrate achievements, provide constructive feedback, and encourage collaboration. They will also be creating opportunities for employees to share their experiences and insights related to the framework, fostering a sense of community and shared purpose. This is a phase where the proposed framework gets cemented and becomes a system to be practised in a recurring manner.

Step 8: Monitor Progress and Gather Feedback

Once converted into a system, the core team must regularly evaluate the impact of the Happiness Wisdom Framework through surveys, feedback sessions, and performance metrics. Such an audit system can be evolved and at regular intervals, they can audit the system and the progress it has made along with the impact on the stakeholders. They can track key indicators like employee engagement, productivity, and wellbeing regularly to find out whether it is yielding them the results. Along with this the core team can also use data to make informed adjustments to the implementation strategy and address any emerging challenges.

Step 9: Sustain and Evolve the Framework

It is the core team's responsibility to ensure the framework's principles are integrated into the organisation's long-term strategy. They must continuously review and refine the approach based on feedback and changing organisational needs. At periodic intervals, when they are auditing to check the implementation process at various levels, they also must encourage ongoing learning and development to keep the framework relevant and effective.

Step 10: Celebrate Successes and Share Best Practices

Finally, assuming that the organisation has reached to the transformed stage, embracing all the previous steps, finally the core team needs to acknowledge and celebrate milestones and successes achieved through the implementation of the Happiness Wisdom Framework. They can share the best practices and success stories to the outside world. By sharing with other organisations in the industry they can demonstrate the framework's strength and feasibility of implementing it in practice. This approach would result in wider acceptance thereby encouraging wider adoption in other organisations. By following these steps, organisations can effectively implement the Happiness Wisdom Framework, leading to improved employee happiness, wellbeing and enhanced organisational culture.

6. CONCLUSION

The goal of this chapter has been to highlight possible ways towards a more flourishing and healthier work life by highlighting good practices from different organisations that can broaden the employees´ sphere of functioning, create positive emotions and facilitate engagement. Illustrating both proven case studies, as well as the methods to accomplish this goal the author has made it apparent that investing in these areas is beneficial not only for personal fulfillment but also contributes to performance. Developing the "Happiness Wisdom Framework" is a significant part in actually leveraging this insight into concrete, actionable guidelines. The framework provides organisations with an integrated tool for building a culture of wellbeing, happiness and positive culture. The framework provides a structured approach to embed happiness wisdom into the organisational ecosystem and build a brighter workplace with positive energy and engagement. Moving forward with these strategies, organisations will realize that investing in employee wellbeing is not just a moral responsibility but also a strategic benefit. All organisations that wish to develop a flourishing and resilient workforce would benefit from the practical insights presented in this chapter. Implementing these strategies and utilizing the Happiness Wisdom Framework enables organisations to create a more balanced work environment that promotes development, supports its individuals, and in turn fosters growth.

REFERENCES

Bhattacharyya, R. (2024, August 8). *Godrej Industries ramps up hiring at group companies to push growth.* ET Bureau. The Economic Times. Retrieved September 18, 2024 from https://economictimes.indiatimes.com/jobs/hr-policies-trends/godrej-industries-ramps-up-hiring-at-group-companies-to-push-growth/articleshow/112355460.cms

Castelino, L. M., & Shinde, R. (2022). Employee Engagement: A Key to Improve Performance–A Case Study on HCL. *International Journal of Case Studies in BusinessIT and Education*, 6(1), 566–577.

Chaudhury, N., & Modi, S. (2016). Employee Wellness Programs in the Context of an Emerging Epidemic of Lifestyle Diseases: What Works and What Doesn&t? *NHRD Network Journal*, 9(4), 33–38. DOI: 10.1177/0974173920160407

Ganesh, N. K. (2022). Avoiding stress, improving productivity: a study on stress management policies.

Godrej. (n.d.). *Our Goals*. Godrej. Retrieved September 18, 2024 from https://www.godrejenterprises.com/good-and-green

Infosys Employee Wellness. (n.d.). *Driving the Culture of Wellness.* Infosys Limited. Retrieved September 18, 2024, from https://www.infosys.com/about/esg/social/employee-wellbeing/driving-culture-wellness.html

Jain, H. (n.d.). *A complete guide on Corporate Yoga Programs in India.* MantraCare. Retrieved September 19, 2024, from https://mantracare.org/employee-wellness/corporate-yoga/corporate-yoga-india/

KV, L., & Misra, S. R. (2015). Social Career Navigation-HCL Experience. *NHRD Network Journal, 8*(1), 71-77.

Mahindraadmin. (2021, November 22). *Mahindra empowers its employees with Practo's Corporate Health Plans*. Mahindra & Mahindra Ltd. Retrieved September 19, 2024, from https://www.mahindra.com/news-room/press-release/en/mahindra-empowers-its-employees-with-practos-corporate-health-plans

Majumdar, A., & Kumar, S. (2022). Organisational justice and employee wellbeing in India: Through a psychological lens. *Business Perspectives and Research.*

Monteiro, E., & Joseph, J. (2022). Preventing Stress, Improving Productivity: A Case Study on Stress Management Policies of TCS and Infosys. *International Journal of Case Studies in BusinessIT and Education*, 6(1), 401–413.

Patanjali Wellness. (n.d.). Retrieved September 19, 2024, from https://patanjaliwellness.com/

Paul, B. (2023, April 30). *Infosys: Behind the iconic tech giant's drive to retain talent and push for growth.* Retrieved September 18, 2024, from https://www.businesstoday.in/magazine/deep-dive/story/infosys-behind-the-iconic-tech-giants-drive-to-retain-talent-and-push-for-growth-377639-2023-04-17

Perwez, S. K., & Ramasehan, H. (2016). Employee Counselling: Need and importance in the 21st century workplace. *International Journal of Physical and Social Sciences*, 6(10), 1–19.

Seetharaman, G. (2012, March 4). *TCS tops best companies to work for list.* Retrieved September 18, 2024, from https://www.businesstoday.in/magazine/cover-story/story/tata-consultancy-services-tcs-best-companies-to-work-india-28301-2012-02-16

Shergill, P., & Notra, K. (2015). The world's largest 'ideapreneurship™': Putting employees first so the customer never feels second! In *Business Models and People Management in the Indian IT Industry* (pp. 204–218). Routledge.

Tech Mahindra. (2021, May 15). *Tech Mahindra Announces Appointment of 'Wellness Officer'.* Tech Mahindra. Retrieved September 12, 2024, from https://www.techmahindra.com/insights/news/tech-mahindra-announces-appointment-wellness-officer/

Tech Mahindra Foundation. (n.d.). *Mind@Ease.* Tech Mahindra Foundation. Retrieved September 19, 2024, from https://mindatease.techmahindrafoundation.org/

The Economic Times. (2008, May 30). *Wipro launches Fit for Life for its employees.* The Economic Times. Retrieved September 18, 2024 from https://economictimes.indiatimes.com/tech/software/wipro-launches-fit-for-life-for-its-employees/articleshow/3086633.cms

The Statesman. (2024, March 23). *Patanjali Ayurved Hospital organises free health camp in Majri Imlikhera.* The Statemans News Service. Retrieved September 19, 2024 from https://www.thestatesman.com/india/patanjali-ayurved-hospital-organises-free-health-camp-in-majri-imlikhera-1503282980.html#google_vignette

The TCS Way. (n.d.). *Promoting good health and wellbeing at the workplace.* TATA Consultancy Services. Retrieved September 18, 2024, from https://www.tcs.com/who-we-are/tcs-way/case-study/employee-health-wellness-tcs-wellbeing

Verma, P. (2020, August 3). *Tech Mahindra launches Mhealthy to enable workforce and community safety against COVID-19.* The Economic Times. Retrieved September 19, 2024 from https://economictimes.indiatimes.com/tech/ites/tech-mahindra-launches-mhealthy-to-enable-workforce-and-community-safety-against-covid-19/articleshow/77330380.cms

World, H. R. (2021, May 15). *Tech Mahindra appoints Meghna Hareendran as Wellness Officer.* The Economic Times. Retrieved September 19, 2024, from https://hr.economictimes.indiatimes.com/news/industry/tech-mahindra-announces-appointment-of-wellness-officer/82655433

Yadav, S. K. S. (2016). Corporate social responsibility: how TCS is performing it well? *International Multidisciplinary Journal, 5*(5).

Chapter 19
What Makes a Wise Organization?
Characteristics and Benefits

Yassine Hassani Abou Mehdi
Sidi Mohamed Ben Abdellah University, Morocco

Allouani Saif Allah
https://orcid.org/0000-0002-2848-169X
Sidi Mohamed Ben Abdellah University, Morocco

Roqai Chaoui Mehdi
https://orcid.org/0009-0004-0034-4038
Sidi Mohamed Ben Abdellah University, Morocco

ABSTRACT

This chapter explores the concept of organizational wisdom, focusing on identifying core characteristics that define wise organizations in the face of global challenges and technological advancements. Drawing from frameworks such as collective phronesis, the three-dimensional wisdom model, and self-determination theory, it examines how wisdom emerges within organizations through both individual and collective dynamics. Key benefits, including enhanced well-being, improved decision-making, adaptability, and long-term sustainability, are discussed. The chapter also presents practical strategies for implementing wisdom-driven practices and addresses barriers to their adoption. Finally, it highlights emerging trends in organizational wisdom research, offering both theoretical insights and practical guidance to foster ethical, resilient, and impactful organizations.

DOI: 10.4018/979-8-3693-8457-2.ch019

INTRODUCTION

In an era of unprecedented global challenges and rapid technological change, the concept of organizational wisdom has gained increasing relevance and urgency. As businesses, institutions, and societies grapple with complex issues ranging from climate change to ethical dilemmas posed by artificial intelligence, there is a growing recognition that traditional models of organizational management and decision-making may be insufficient. This chapter explores the emerging field of organizational wisdom, with a central focus on addressing the key problematique: What are the main features that characterize wise organizations?

This question is crucial in today's interconnected and volatile world, as it seeks to identify the fundamental attributes that enable organizations to navigate complexity while maintaining ethical integrity and long-term sustainability. Organizational wisdom goes beyond mere knowledge management or collective intelligence. It encompasses a holistic approach to decision-making, problem-solving, and organizational culture that integrates cognitive understanding, ethical considerations, and a deep sense of responsibility towards all stakeholders.

By examining the main features of wise organizations, we aim to provide a framework for understanding how wisdom manifests in organizational settings. This exploration will consider various dimensions, including:

- Ethical decision-making processes
- Systems thinking and long-term perspective
- Adaptive learning and knowledge integration
- Stakeholder engagement and social responsibility
- Leadership practices that foster wisdom
- Organizational culture that supports wise behavior

This chapter aims to provide a comprehensive exploration of these features, their theoretical underpinnings, and their practical implications. We will begin by examining the theoretical foundations of organizational wisdom, drawing upon concepts such as collective phronesis, the Three-Dimensional Wisdom Model, and Self-Determination Theory. We will then analyze how these theories inform the key attributes that distinguish wise organizations.

Throughout the chapter, we will explore the dynamics of how wisdom manifests and develops within organizational settings, considering the interplay between individual and collective wisdom, as well as the role of organizational structures and processes in fostering wisdom. We will examine case studies of organizations that have successfully implemented wise practices, drawing lessons and best practices from their experiences.

Finally, we will evaluate the tangible benefits of cultivating these features of organizational wisdom, from improved employee well-being and decision-making capabilities to enhanced adaptability and long-term sustainability. The chapter will conclude with a discussion of future directions in the study and application of organizational wisdom, emphasizing its critical role in addressing the challenges of our time and fostering more ethical, resilient, and impactful institutions.

By addressing the central problematique of identifying the main features of wise organizations, this chapter aims to provide both theoretical insights and practical guidance for leaders, managers, and scholars seeking to foster wisdom in their own organizational settings and contribute to the development of more adaptive, ethical, and successful institutions in our rapidly changing world.

THE NEED FOR WISE ORGANIZATIONS IN THE MODERN CONTEXT

In an era characterized by unprecedented complexity, rapid technological advancement, and global interconnectedness, organizations face challenges that demand more than efficiency and profitability. The modern context requires a new paradigm of organizational thinking and behavior embodying wisdom (Nonaka & Takeuchi, 2011).

The need for wise organizations has never been more pressing. Organizations play a crucial role in shaping our collective future as we grapple with climate change, social inequalities, ethical dilemmas posed by emerging technologies, and the repercussions of global pandemics. Traditional management and decision-making models often fall short in addressing these multifaceted issues, highlighting the necessity for a more holistic, long-term, and ethically grounded approach (Rowley & Gibbs, 2008).

Wise organizations are better equipped to navigate uncertainty, balance competing stakeholder interests, and contribute positively to society while maintaining economic viability (Rooney et al., 2010). They can make decisions that consider immediate outcomes, long-term consequences, ethical implications, and the greater good.

Definition and Scope of Organizational Wisdom

Organizational wisdom extends beyond an institution's collective intelligence or knowledge management capabilities. It encompasses a dynamic interplay of cognitive, reflective, and compassionate dimensions that permeate all levels of organizational functioning (Ardelt, 2003).

What you should do is a quite exahaustive recession of organizational wisdom as it has been stated within the literature.

For the purposes of this chapter, we define organizational wisdom as:

"The collective capacity of an organization to leverage knowledge, experience, and ethical judgment to make decisions and take actions that balance short-term needs with long-term sustainability, consider diverse perspectives, and contribute positively to the well-being of its members, stakeholders, and the broader society."

This definition draws upon several theoretical frameworks, including collective phronesis (Nonaka & Takeuchi, 2011), the Three-Dimensional Wisdom Model (Ardelt, 2003), and Self-Determination Theory (Ryan & Deci, 2000). It emphasizes that organizational wisdom is not merely the sum of individual wisdom within an organization but rather an emergent property arising from the interactions, structures, and cultures that characterize the organization as a whole (Bierly et al., 2000).

The scope of organizational wisdom encompasses various aspects of organizational life, including:

- Decision-making processes
- Leadership practices
- Organizational culture and values
- Learning and adaptation mechanisms
- Stakeholder relationships
- Ethical considerations and social responsibility

Chapter Objectives and Roadmap

This chapter aims to provide a comprehensive exploration of wise organizations, their characteristics, and the benefits they offer to their members and society. Our objectives are to:

1. Elucidate the concept of organizational wisdom and its relevance in the modern context.
2. Identify and analyze the key characteristics that distinguish wise organizations.
3. Examine the role of leadership in fostering organizational wisdom (McKenna et al., 2009).

4. Explore the dynamics and systemic nature of wisdom within organizational settings.
5. Evaluate the tangible benefits of wise organizations for employees, stakeholders, and overall organizational performance.
6. Provide practical insights and strategies for cultivating wisdom in organizational contexts.
7. Explore the potential of "wise interventions" in organizational settings, drawing on recent research in psychological interventions that alter individuals' perceptions and behaviors in adaptive ways.
8. Examine the role of boundaries, phenomenal contracts, and shadow elements in developing and applying organizational wisdom.

To achieve these objectives, the chapter will proceed as follows:

First, we will delve into the theoretical foundations of organizational wisdom, drawing upon established models and concepts. Next, we will examine the defining characteristics of wise organizations, illustrating how they manifest in practice. We will then explore the complex dynamics that underpin organizational wisdom, including the interplay between individual and collective wisdom (Hays, 2007).

The chapter will subsequently analyze the multifaceted benefits of wise organizations, supported by empirical evidence and case studies. We will then offer practical guidance for implementing wisdom-oriented practices in organizations, addressing potential barriers and proposing strategies for overcoming them.

Finally, we will conclude by discussing future directions in the study and application of organizational wisdom, emphasizing its critical role in addressing the challenges of our time and fostering sustainable, ethical, and successful organizations.

THEORETICAL FOUNDATIONS OF ORGANIZATIONAL WISDOM

Collective Phronesis and the Three-Dimensional Wisdom Model

The concept of organizational wisdom is rooted in the ancient Greek notion of *phronesis*, or practical wisdom. Nonaka and Takeuchi (2011) expanded this idea to the organizational level, introducing the concept of collective *phronesis*. This collective form of practical wisdom is essential for organizations to make ethically sound decisions that contribute to the common good.

Building on this foundation, Monika Ardelt's Three-Dimensional Wisdom Model (3D-WM) provides a comprehensive framework for understanding wisdom at both the individual and organizational scales (Ardelt, 2003). The 3D-WM posits that wisdom comprises three interconnected dimensions:

- **Cognitive:** This dimension involves a deep understanding of life, including the ability to grasp the complexity of human nature and the limits of knowledge.
- **Reflective:** The reflective component emphasizes the importance of self-examination, self-awareness, and the ability to see phenomena from multiple perspectives.
- **Compassionate:** This dimension encompasses positive emotions and behaviors towards others, including empathy, compassion, and a genuine concern for well-being.

Figure 1. The three-dimensional wisdom model

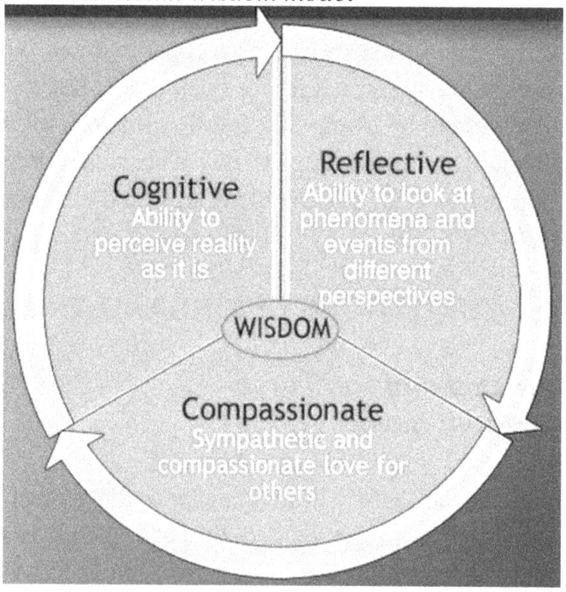

In the context of organizations, the 3D-WM suggests that wise organizations should cultivate these three dimensions collectively. They should foster a culture that values deep understanding, encourages reflective practices, and promotes compassionate action towards all stakeholders.

Self-Determination Theory and Its Relevance to Wise Organizations

Self-Determination Theory (SDT), developed by Ryan and Deci (2000), provides another crucial theoretical pillar for understanding wise organizations. SDT posits that individuals have three basic psychological needs:

- **Autonomy:** The need to feel in control of one's actions and decisions.
- **Competence:** The need to feel capable and effective in one's activities.
- **Relatedness:** The need to feel connected to others and part of a community.

Figure 2. Components of Self-Determination Theory (SDT)

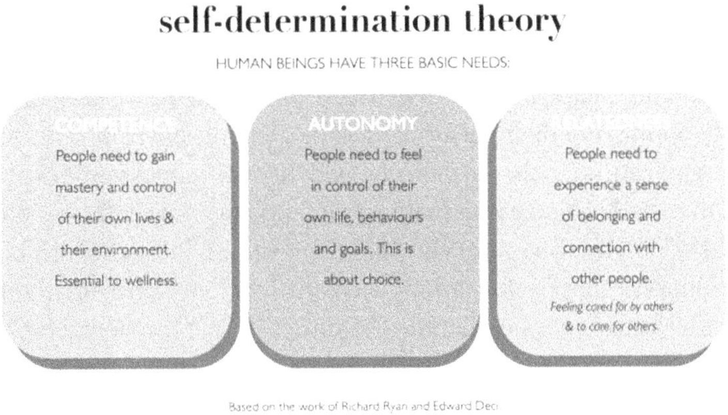

Wise organizations, as proposed by Ardelt and others, recognize the importance of fulfilling these basic needs. They create environments that support employee autonomy, foster competence through continuous learning and development, and promote a sense of community and belonging (Ardelt & all 2023)

The integration of SDT with organizational wisdom suggests that wise organizations not only make ethically sound decisions but also create conditions that allow their members to thrive. This approach aligns with the compassionate dimension of the 3D-WM, emphasizing the importance of considering the well-being of all organizational members.

Open Systems and Experiential Learning in Organizational Contexts

The concept of organizations as open systems, coupled with the importance of experiential learning, provides the third major theoretical foundation for understanding organizational wisdom. Open Systems Theory, as applied to organizations, posits that organizations are in constant interaction with their environment, exchanging resources, information, and energy (Scott, 1992). This perspective is crucial for understanding how organizations can develop and maintain wisdom in dynamic contexts.

Wise organizations, viewed through this lens, are those that can effectively sense and interpret changes in their environment. They possess a heightened awareness of external and internal shifts, enabling them to identify emerging trends, challenges, and opportunities. This ability to sense change is crucial for staying relevant and competitive in a rapidly evolving landscape. In addition to their perceptive capabilities, wise organizations are adept at adapting their structures and processes in response to these changes. They embrace flexibility and agility, making necessary adjustments to their operations, strategies, and organizational design to align with new realities. This adaptability allows them to remain resilient and responsive, continuously optimizing their performance in a dynamic environment. At the same time, wise organizations maintain their core identity and values while evolving. They understand that while change is essential, it should not come at the expense of their foundational principles. By preserving their core values, these organizations ensure that their evolution is purposeful and aligned with their long-term mission and vision.

Experiential learning, as explored by Kolb (1984) and others, emphasizes the importance of learning through reflection on concrete experiences. In the context of organizational wisdom, this theory suggests that organizations become wise not just through accumulating knowledge, but through actively reflecting on and learning from their experiences. Hays integrates these concepts in his dynamic model of organizational wisdom, emphasizing the role of reflection as a driver of continuous learning and improvement. This model suggests that wise organizations create spaces and processes for collective reflection, allowing them to derive meaningful insights from their experiences and translate these insights into effective actions. Furthermore, the notion of "wise interventions" is compatible with the principles of experiential learning. These interventions are intended to modify individuals' perceptions and behaviors in constructive ways and can be interpreted as systematically organized experiences aimed at cultivating personal and collective wisdom.

In conclusion, the theoretical foundations of organizational wisdom are informed by a range of disciplines, including philosophy, psychology, and organizational studies. By synthesizing concepts such as collective phronesis, the Three-Dimensional Wisdom Model, Self-Determination Theory, open systems thinking, and experiential learning, we can develop a comprehensive understanding of what characterizes a wise organization and the methods through which such wisdom can be fostered and preserved within dynamic organizational settings.

CHARACTERISTICS OF WISE ORGANIZATIONS

Balancing Cognitive, Reflective, and Compassionate Dimensions

Wise organizations integrate the cognitive, reflective, and compassionate dimensions of wisdom to create a balanced approach to decision-making and leadership (Ardelt, 2003). In the cognitive dimension, these organizations emphasize deep understanding, critical thinking, and intellectual humility. They encourage employees to explore complex issues, question assumptions, and accept uncertainty as part of the decision-making process. This dimension supports wise organizations in navigating challenges with informed judgment and foresight.

In the reflective dimension, wise organizations promote self-awareness and continuous learning. They foster environments where employees are encouraged to reflect on their experiences, successes, and failures, contributing to individual and organizational growth. Practices such as "lessons learned" sessions allow teams to critically assess past projects and refine their approaches for future endeavors. This reflective wisdom ensures that organizations adapt and improve continuously.

In the compassionate dimension, wise organizations prioritize empathy, care, and concern for all stakeholders, including employees, customers, and the broader community. Compassionate wisdom is evident in the focus on building positive social relationships, fostering mutual respect, and creating opportunities for collaboration and support. These organizations often implement policies that support work-life balance and social well-being, ensuring a holistic approach to employee satisfaction and organizational success.

Cultivating a Culture of Ethical Decision-Making and the Common Good

Wise organizations embed ethical values and considerations into all aspects of their decision-making processes. They cultivate a strong culture of collective phronesis—practical wisdom rooted in ethical and moral values shared by employees at all levels of the organizational hierarchy (Nonaka & Takeuchi, 2011). This commitment to shared values creates a sense of purpose and unity, aligning employees with the organization's mission to contribute to the common good.

Organizations that prioritize the common good make deliberate efforts to contribute to societal well-being through their products and services. They are driven by an intention to make the world a better place, not only through their external outputs but also by providing meaningful livelihoods to their employees (Bierly et al., 2000). Such organizations balance profit-making with a genuine commitment to positive societal impact, ensuring that their actions benefit both their internal and external communities.

Ethical decision-making in wise organizations goes beyond short-term gains. It involves a forward-thinking approach that considers the long-term implications of decisions on society, the environment, and future generations. This approach aligns with the organization's vision for sustainable and ethical growth, reinforcing its dedication to doing the right thing through reflection, learning, and synthesis of knowledge for the greater good (Nonaka & Toyama, 2007).

Fostering Supportive Leadership and Employee Autonomy

Wise organizations place a strong emphasis on supportive leadership, where leaders act as mentors and facilitators rather than authoritarian figures. These leaders exemplify ethical behavior and demonstrate genuine concern for the well-being of their employees (Bennis, 1997; Sternberg, 2018). By creating a nurturing and empowering work environment, leaders foster a culture of trust and collaboration.

Informed by insights from Self-Determination Theory (Ryan & Deci, 2000), some organizations strive to create environments that support employee autonomy, competence, and relatedness. These organizations may implement practices where leaders act as mentors and facilitators, providing guidance while encouraging independent thinking and decision-making.

In addition to autonomy, wise organizations provide opportunities for employees to grow both professionally and personally. Mentoring programs, apprenticeships, and continuous learning initiatives are implemented to encourage development, ensuring that employees remain engaged and motivated to contribute to the organization's success (Nonaka & Takeuchi, 2011).

Moreover, wise organizations prioritize trust and psychological safety, cultivating an environment where employees feel secure in expressing ideas, taking calculated risks, and learning from failures. This atmosphere of trust is crucial for innovation and continuous improvement, as it encourages open communication and collaborative problem-solving. A notable example of this approach is Google's "20% time" policy, which allowed employees to dedicate a portion of their work time to personal projects. This policy exemplifies how fostering autonomy and innovation can lead to breakthrough ideas and sustained organizational growth. By supporting employee autonomy, competence, and relatedness, wise organizations create a thriving workplace that benefits both individuals and the organization.

Embracing Complexity and Systems Thinking

Wise organizations understand the interconnectedness of modern challenges and adopt a systems thinking approach to navigate complexity. They cultivate a holistic perspective, considering the broader context and potential ripple effects of their actions on the external environment (Bertalanffy, 1968). This approach ensures that organizational strategies are aligned with both internal goals and the larger societal and environmental landscape.

By employing adaptive strategies, these organizations remain resilient in the face of uncertainty. They develop flexible approaches that allow them to respond to changing circumstances, emerging challenges, and new opportunities. Wise organizations also prioritize interdisciplinary collaboration, encouraging teams from different departments and expertise areas to work together to address complex problems (Lewin, 1947).

Furthermore, wise organizations emphasize the efficient application of knowledge to achieve desired goals. They integrate emotional intelligence into their actions, ensuring that decision-making processes take into account both rational analysis and human emotions (Nonaka et al., 2014). This synthesis of knowledge, judgment, and emotional intelligence helps organizations navigate complex business environments with agility and foresight.

Promoting Reflection and Continuous Learning

Wise organizations create a culture of continuous learning and improvement by embracing reflection and experiential learning as core components of their operations. They cultivate a learning culture where curiosity is encouraged, and learning is viewed as an ongoing process for all members of the organization. This commitment to learning ensures that individuals and teams remain engaged, adaptive, and innovative in the face of new challenges.

Reflective practices are deeply embedded in wise organizations, with regular reflection incorporated into their processes. This intentional focus on reflection allows for deep learning from experiences, helping the organization to identify patterns, uncover root causes, and make informed decisions that enhance future performance. These reflective practices contribute to a cycle of continuous improvement, where past experiences inform future actions.

In addition to fostering reflection, wise organizations prioritize knowledge sharing, ensuring that insights and learnings are disseminated across the organization rather than being confined to specific teams or individuals. By facilitating open communication and collaboration, they break down silos and create a more cohesive and informed workforce.

Furthermore, wise organizations emphasize experiential learning, creating opportunities for employees to learn through hands-on experiences and experimentation. This approach not only reinforces theoretical knowledge but also encourages innovation and creative problem-solving.

In summary, wise organizations support the flourishing of their employees across three key dimensions of wisdom. In the cognitive dimension, they enhance employees' competence and sense of accomplishment by offering meaningful work, role modeling, mentoring, and education and training programs. In the reflective dimension, they promote autonomy and flexibility, while fostering a community centered on mutual learning and reflection. Lastly, in the compassionate dimension, they create opportunities and environments that nurture positive social relationships, encouraging empathy, compassion, appreciation, respect, and support.

Table 1. Characteristics of Wise Organizations

Characteristics of Wise Organizations	Description
Ethical Foundation and Leadership	
Strong Culture of Collective Wisdom	Fostering shared ethical and moral values throughout the organization.
Ethical Leadership	Leaders exemplify honesty, fairness, compassion, and genuine concern for employee welfare.
Focus on Common Good and Stakeholder Well-being	
Prioritizing Societal Contribution	Organizational purpose centered on benefiting all stakeholders, including employees, customers, and the community.
Meaningful Work Environment	Fostering a sense of accomplishment and purpose among employees.
Employee Development and Empowerment	

continued on following page

Table 1. Continued

Characteristics of Wise Organizations	Description
Continuous Learning and Growth	Implementing mentoring programs, apprenticeships, and training initiatives.
Autonomy and Flexibility	Providing employees with self-directed task management opportunities and supporting work-life balance.
Inclusive and Supportive Organizational Culture	
Caring Work Environment	Cultivating mutual support, inclusivity, and participation.
Psychological Need Fulfillment	Addressing fundamental employee needs like understanding, self-integrity, and belonging.
Adaptive and Reflective Practices	
Open Systems Approach	Continuous interaction with and adaptation to the external environment.
Experiential Learning	Encouraging learning from real-life experiences and challenges.
Reflective Decision-Making	Engaging in interpretative processes to align organizational actions with broader ethical goals.
Innovative Intervention Strategies	
Tailored Wise Interventions	Implementing context-specific interventions sensitive to employee diversity.
Strategic Timing and Situational Awareness	Carefully considering when and how to implement interventions.
Practical Wisdom in Action	
Applied Phronesis	Integrating cognitive and relational qualities to navigate complex situations.
Ethical Decision-Making	Prioritizing moral considerations in organizational choices and character development.

THE DYNAMICS OF ORGANIZATIONAL WISDOM

Interplay Between Individual and Collective Wisdom

Organizational wisdom emerges from the complex interplay between individual wisdom and collective processes. Understanding this dynamic relationship is crucial for comprehending how wisdom operates within organizational contexts. Wise individuals bring personal experiences, insights, and ethical judgments to the organization, enriching the collective wisdom pool through diverse perspectives

(Ardelt, 2003). These individuals contribute unique viewpoints and problem-solving approaches that enhance the organization's ability to navigate complex challenges.

Organizational structures and processes can amplify individual wisdom, creating a collective intelligence greater than the sum of its parts. This amplification occurs through mechanisms such as knowledge sharing platforms, which facilitate the exchange of information and best practices across the organization (Nonaka & Takeuchi, 1995). These platforms enable individuals to share insights and learn from one another, leading to a more informed and capable organization. Additionally, cross-functional teams bring together diverse skill sets and viewpoints to tackle complex problems collaboratively (Edmondson & Harvey, 2018). By leveraging the strengths of various disciplines, these teams enhance the organization's ability to address multifaceted issues.

A continuous feedback loop exists between individual and collective wisdom. As individuals contribute to organizational wisdom, they are simultaneously influenced and shaped by the collective wisdom of the organization (Weick & Roberts, 1993). This reciprocal relationship ensures that both individual and collective wisdom evolve over time, reinforcing one another. For example, in a healthcare setting, a nurse's individual wisdom about patient care can inform hospital-wide protocols. These enhanced protocols then improve the practices and knowledge of all staff members, demonstrating the reciprocal relationship between individual and collective wisdom (Merriam & Bierema, 2013). This example illustrates how individual insights can lead to organizational improvements, which in turn enhance the wisdom and effectiveness of all members within the organization.

Navigating Organizational Boundaries and Social Contracts

Wise organizations effectively navigate various boundaries and social contracts that influence how wisdom is developed, shared, and applied. Task boundaries, which define the scope of work and responsibilities, are a critical aspect of this process. Wise organizations create permeable task boundaries that allow for the cross-pollination of ideas and collaborative problem-solving (Ashkenas et al., 2002). By facilitating collaboration across different roles and functions, these organizations foster innovative solutions and a more dynamic approach to addressing challenges.

Space boundaries, both physical and virtual, can significantly impact the flow of wisdom within an organization. Wise organizations design environments that encourage interaction, reflection, and knowledge sharing (Duffy, 1997). For example, open-plan offices and well-designed virtual collaboration tools can facilitate communication and the free exchange of ideas, contributing to a more connected and informed workforce.

Understanding boundaries relate to shared mental models and language within the organization. Wise organizations strive to create a common understanding while valuing diverse perspectives (Bolman & Deal, 2017). They work to ensure that all members have a shared vision and terminology, which enhances collaboration and reduces misunderstandings. At the same time, these organizations embrace different viewpoints to enrich organizational wisdom.

Phenomenal contracts, as discussed by Shotter and Tsoukas (2014), are the unwritten agreements and expectations that govern behavior within the organization. Wise organizations are adept at recognizing and managing these implicit contracts to foster trust and cooperation. They understand the importance of these unspoken rules in shaping organizational culture and ensuring that interactions are based on mutual respect and shared values.

For example, a tech company might implement open-plan offices and virtual collaboration tools to address space boundaries, while fostering a culture of open communication and shared goals to address understanding boundaries and phenomenal contracts. This approach enhances the flow of wisdom across the organization, demonstrating how thoughtful management of boundaries and social contracts can support organizational effectiveness (Olson & Olson, 2000).

Challenging assumptions is a practice that wise organizations regularly engage in to foster a culture of critical thinking and open-mindedness (Senge, 1990). By continuously examining and questioning underlying assumptions, these organizations avoid complacency and encourage innovative thinking. This approach helps in adapting to new information and perspectives, leading to more informed and effective decision-making.

Ethical frameworks play a pivotal role in guiding behavior and choices across the organization. Developing and consistently applying robust ethical frameworks ensures that decisions and actions are aligned with the organization's values and ethical standards (Trevino & Nelson, 2016). These frameworks provide a structured approach to evaluating situations and making decisions, reinforcing a commitment to ethical conduct.

For example, a financial institution might implement regular ethics training and establish an ethics committee to review complex decisions. This helps to align values and challenge biases throughout the organization, demonstrating how structured approaches to ethics and bias management can support organizational wisdom (Schwartz, 2013). This practice ensures that the organization maintains a high standard of ethical behavior and continuously improves its decision-making processes.

Addressing Shadow Elements and Unrecognized Influences

Wise organizations recognize that unacknowledged or "shadow" elements can significantly impact behavior and decision-making. One key aspect of this recognition is shadow identification. Wise organizations actively work to identify shadow elements—the unspoken, often unconscious aspects of organizational culture that influence behavior (Gabriel, 1999). By bringing these hidden elements into the open, they can address underlying issues that might otherwise distort decision-making and behavior.

Another crucial element is understanding power dynamics. Wise organizations are attuned to how formal and informal power structures affect the development and application of wisdom, striving for equitable and transparent power distribution (Pfeffer, 1992). By ensuring that power is distributed fairly and transparently, these organizations help prevent the concentration of influence that can lead to biased or unwise decisions.

Emotional undercurrents are also a significant consideration. Wise organizations acknowledge and address the role of emotions in organizational life, understanding how emotions can both enhance and hinder wise decision-making (Fineman, 2003). Recognizing the impact of emotions on decision-making processes allows organizations to create environments where emotional intelligence is leveraged to support better outcomes.

Attention to cultural artifacts is another important factor. Wise organizations pay close attention to symbols, rituals, and stories that convey implicit messages about organizational values and norms (Schein, 2010). These artifacts can reveal the underlying values and assumptions that guide behavior within the organization, helping leaders understand and shape the organizational culture more effectively.

Wise interventions are employed to address shadow elements and alter perceptions and behaviors in adaptive ways (Walton, 2014). For example, a corporation might use organizational network analysis to uncover informal influence networks. By designing targeted interventions, the corporation can ensure these networks are leveraged positively rather than becoming sources of dysfunction (Cross & Parker, 2004). This approach demonstrates how understanding and managing shadow elements can enhance organizational wisdom and effectiveness.

BENEFITS OF WISE ORGANIZATIONS

Enhanced Employee Well-Being and Job Fulfillment

Wise organizations prioritize the well-being and fulfillment of their employees, recognizing that a satisfied workforce is crucial for long-term success. By supporting psychological needs, such as autonomy, competence, and relatedness, organizations foster intrinsic motivation and well-being (Ryan & Deci, 2000). This approach creates an environment where employees feel empowered and engaged.

Promoting meaningful work is another essential factor. Encouraging work that aligns with personal values and contributes to a greater purpose enhances eudaimonic well-being, which encompasses personal growth and self-realization (Huta & Waterman, 2014). When employees find their work meaningful, it leads to greater satisfaction and a deeper sense of fulfillment.

Encouraging employee voice is also vital. Facilitating participation in decision-making processes leads to higher job satisfaction and lower turnover intentions (Gonzalez-Mulé & Cockburn, 2017). This inclusion ensures that employees feel valued and heard, which can significantly impact their engagement and loyalty to the organization.

For instance, companies that implement flexible work arrangements and opportunities for professional development demonstrate a commitment to employee well-being and fulfillment (Grant & Parker, 2009). Such practices show that organizations value their employees' growth and work-life balance, ultimately contributing to a more motivated and dedicated workforce.

Improved Decision-Making and Problem-Solving Capabilities

Wise organizations excel in decision-making and problem-solving by integrating multiple perspectives and considering long-term consequences. Practicing ethical decision-making through collective phronesis enables organizations to make ethically sound choices that serve the common good (Nonaka & Takeuchi, 2011). This ensures that decisions are aligned with moral values and societal benefits.

Balanced approaches are crucial for addressing complex problems. By incorporating cognitive, reflective, and compassionate dimensions, organizations develop more nuanced and effective solutions (Ardelt, 2003). This balance allows for a deeper understanding of issues and more comprehensive responses.

Navigating uncertainty is another essential capability. Wisdom-based approaches enhance the ability to manage ambiguity, leading to robust and adaptive strategies (Intezari & Pauleen, 2014). This adaptability is vital in today's rapidly changing world, where unforeseen challenges frequently arise.

For instance, organizations that utilize diverse teams and inclusive deliberation processes are better equipped to address multifaceted challenges and innovate effectively (Page, 2007). By drawing on a wide range of experiences and insights, these organizations can develop creative solutions and maintain a competitive edge.

Increased Adaptability and Resilience in the Face of Change

Wise organizations demonstrate greater adaptability and resilience due to their systems thinking approach and openness to learning. A learning orientation emphasizes continuous learning and adaptation, enabling organizations to respond effectively to changing environments (Senge, 1990). This focus on growth ensures that they remain agile and responsive.

Collective mindfulness is another key factor. By cultivating mindfulness and reflexivity, organizations are better prepared to handle unexpected challenges and maintain performance under stress (Weick & Sutcliffe, 2015). This mindset allows them to stay focused and calm in the face of adversity.

Resilient practices further enhance adaptability. Organizations fostering collective mindfulness exhibit greater resilience during industry disruptions and environmental changes (Vogus & Sutcliffe, 2012). This resilience helps them navigate uncertainties and emerge stronger.

For example, companies that conduct regular scenario planning and stress testing can quickly adjust strategies in response to market shifts and crises (Schwartz, 1991). These proactive measures enable them to anticipate potential challenges and respond effectively, ensuring long-term success.

Positive Impacts on Organizational Performance and Sustainability

The cultivation of organizational wisdom positively influences overall performance and long-term sustainability. One of the primary benefits is superior financial performance. Implementing evidence-based and wisdom-oriented management practices can lead to enhanced financial and operational outcomes (Rousseau et al., 2008). By making informed, strategic decisions grounded in wisdom, organizations are better positioned to achieve strong financial results and operational efficiency.

Enhanced corporate social responsibility (CSR) is another significant benefit. Wise organizations that focus on ethical decision-making and stakeholder consideration improve their CSR performance and bolster public trust (Wang et al., 2016). By prioritizing ethical practices and addressing the needs of various stakeholders, these organizations strengthen their reputation and build stronger relationships with the community and customers.

Long-term competitiveness is also positively impacted by organizational wisdom. Prioritizing employee well-being and sustainable practices contributes to sustained competitive advantage and market leadership (Pfeffer, 2010). Organizations that invest in their employees and commit to sustainable practices are more likely to maintain a strong position in the market over time, as they are perceived as responsible and forward-thinking.

For example, organizations integrating sustainability into their core strategies often experience increased investor confidence and customer loyalty, driving long-term success (Eccles et al., 2014). This integration not only enhances the organization's reputation but also attracts stakeholders who value sustainability, contributing to ongoing success and market leadership.

IMPLEMENTING WISDOM IN ORGANIZATIONS

Strategies for Overcoming Barriers to Organizational Wisdom

Implementing organizational wisdom often encounters obstacles ranging from entrenched mindsets to structural impediments. Recognizing and addressing these barriers is essential for cultivating wisdom.

Table 2. Strategies for Cultivating Organizational Wisdom

Strategy	Description	Example
Cultivating a Learning Culture	Fostering environments that encourage continuous learning and development.	Implementing double-loop learning to question underlying assumptions and values.
Fostering Psychological Safety	Creating a workplace where employees feel safe to express ideas and admit mistakes.	Leaders modeling vulnerability and openness to encourage safe communication.
Embracing Diversity and Inclusion	Recognizing and valuing diverse perspectives to enhance problem-solving and decision-making.	Implementing inclusive practices to support diversity and foster a more adaptable culture.
Implementing Reflective Practices	Incorporating reflection and introspection into organizational processes.	Conducting regular after-action reviews to learn from experiences and improve performance.
Addressing Power Dynamics	Reducing hierarchical structures and promoting participatory decision-making.	Flattening hierarchies to enable more open communication and shared decision-making.

continued on following page

Table 2. Continued

Strategy	Description	Example
Developing Systems Thinking	Understanding and managing complex interdependencies within organizations.	Providing training programs on systems thinking to equip employees with the necessary skills.
Challenging Assumptions	Questioning existing beliefs and exploring alternative perspectives.	Conducting scenario planning to challenge assumptions and prepare for uncertainty.

For exemple An organization facing market disruption might conduct comprehensive scenario planning and involve diverse stakeholders in strategy development, enabling it to pivot effectively and maintain resilience (Wack, 1985).

Designing and Implementing Wise Interventions

Wise interventions are carefully designed strategies aimed at positively influencing individual behavior and organizational culture. These interventions are grounded in psychological and organizational theories, ensuring their effectiveness and relevance. By employing targeted, theory-based techniques, organizations can cultivate a more wise and productive work environment.

One effective approach is to implement brief, targeted exercises that address specific psychological processes. These concise activities can have a significant and lasting impact on individual behavior and organizational outcomes. For instance, mindfulness training programs can help employees improve their focus, reduce stress, and make more thoughtful decisions.

Another valuable strategy is job crafting interventions. By allowing employees to redesign aspects of their work to better align with their strengths and values, organizations can enhance employee engagement and foster a wiser organizational culture. This approach empowers individuals to take ownership of their work and contribute more meaningfully to the organization's goals.

Creating Spaces for Reflection and Dialogue

To foster organizational wisdom, it is crucial to establish dedicated spaces and times for reflection and dialogue. These practices encourage continuous learning, collective intelligence, and deeper understanding.

The reflective practitioner approach encourages individuals to reflect on their experiences, promoting ongoing skill development and personal growth. Dialogue practices, such as facilitated conversations, enhance collective intelligence by fostering open and authentic communication. Additionally, work-based learning methods, like action learning sets and peer coaching, support ongoing development and wisdom cultivation.

By incorporating these practices into organizational culture, companies can create a more thoughtful, reflective, and intelligent workplace. For example, regularly scheduled "learning lunches" can provide a platform for employees to discuss challenges, share insights, and promote a culture of reflection and continuous improvement.

CASE STUDIES AND PRACTICAL EXAMPLES

Analysis of Organizations Successfully Implementing Wise Practices

Patagonia: Environmental Stewardship and Ethical Business

Patagonia, an outdoor clothing company founded by Yvon Chouinard in 1973, exemplifies organizational wisdom through its unwavering commitment to environmental sustainability and ethical business practices. The company has become a model for how businesses can thrive financially while prioritizing environmental and social responsibility.

Table 3. Key Wise Practices at Patagonia

Key Wise Practice	Explanation	Example
Long-Term Perspective	Patagonia's mission statement—"Build the best product, cause no unnecessary harm, use business to inspire and implement solutions to the environmental crisis"—reflects a dedication to long-term sustainability over short-term profits (Chouinard & Stanley, 2012).	In 2011, Patagonia launched its "Don't Buy This Jacket" campaign, actively discouraging excessive consumption during Black Friday. This counterintuitive marketing strategy demonstrated the company's commitment to reducing environmental impact, even at the potential cost of short-term sales.
Ethical Decision-Making	The company's "1% for the Planet" initiative, donating 1% of sales to environmental causes, showcases its commitment to the common good and ethical responsibility (Chouinard & Stanley, 2012).	In 2018, Patagonia announced it would donate the $10 million it saved from federal tax cuts to environmental groups, stating that the tax cut was "irresponsible" and the planet needed the money more.
Transparency and Reflection	Patagonia's "Footprint Chronicles" provides detailed information about the environmental and social impact of its products, demonstrating accountability and reflective practices (O'Rourke & Strand, 2017).	The company regularly publishes detailed reports on its supply chain, including information about working conditions in factories and the environmental impact of its materials. In 2019, Patagonia openly acknowledged its contribution to microfiber pollution and committed to finding solutions.
Innovation for Sustainability	Patagonia consistently invests in innovative technologies and practices to reduce its environmental footprint.	The company developed and patented Yulex, a plant-based replacement for neoprene used in wetsuits, reducing CO2 emissions in the manufacturing process by up to 80%. Patagonia then shared this technology with competitors to maximize its positive environmental impact.
Employee Empowerment	Patagonia fosters a culture that empowers employees to live the company's values and contribute to its mission.	The company offers on-site childcare, flexible working hours, and paid time off for environmental activism. In 2016, Patagonia closed all its stores on Election Day to encourage employees and customers to vote.
Stakeholder Engagement	Patagonia actively engages with various stakeholders, including customers, environmental groups, and even competitors, to further its mission.	Through its "Worn Wear" program, Patagonia encourages customers to repair, reuse, and recycle their clothing. The company provides repair guides, hosts repair events, and resells used Patagonia gear.

Despite (or perhaps because of) its unconventional approach, Patagonia has seen significant business success. The company's revenue grew from $540 million in 2015 to over $1 billion in 2019. More importantly, Patagonia has become a leader in sustainable business practices, influencing other companies and consumers to prioritize environmental responsibility.

Patagonia's case demonstrates how organizational wisdom, manifested through long-term thinking, ethical decision-making, transparency, innovation, and stakeholder engagement, can lead to both business success and positive societal impact. The company's approach offers valuable lessons for other organizations seeking to integrate wisdom into their practices and contribute to addressing global environmental challenges.

Google: Fostering Innovation and Employee Autonomy

Google, founded in 1998 by Larry Page and Sergey Brin, has become renowned for its innovative culture and employee-centric practices. The company's approach aligns closely with principles of organizational wisdom, particularly in fostering creativity, continuous learning, and employee well-being.

Table 4. Key Wise Practices at Google

Key Wise Practice	Explanation	Example
Employee Autonomy	Google's famous "20% time" policy allows employees to dedicate a portion of their work time to personal projects, fostering autonomy and innovation (Bock, 2015).	Many of Google's popular products, including Gmail, Google News, and AdSense, originated from 20% time projects. This policy demonstrates trust in employees and recognition of the value of intrinsic motivation.
Continuous Learning	Google emphasizes data-driven decision-making and experimentation, cultivating a culture of learning and adaptability (Garvin, 2013).	Google's "Test and Learn" approach encourages employees to run thousands of experiments annually. The company also offers extensive learning opportunities through its "Googler-to-Googler" program, where employees teach classes to their peers
Supportive Leadership	Project Oxygen, launched in 2008, identified key behaviors of effective managers, underscoring the importance of supportive and empowering leadership (Garvin, 2013).	Based on Project Oxygen findings, Google implemented leadership development programs focusing on coaching skills, empowering teams, and creating inclusive environments.
Work Environment	Google designs its workspaces to promote collaboration, creativity, and well-being.	Google offices feature open layouts, informal meeting spaces, and amenities like free meals, fitness centers, and relaxation areas. These design choices reflect an understanding of the link between employee well-being and productivity.

continued on following page

Table 4. Continued

Key Wise Practice	Explanation	Example
Diversity and Inclusion	Google has made significant commitments to fostering diversity and inclusion in the tech industry.	The company publishes annual diversity reports and has invested in programs like Howard West, a partnership with Howard University to increase African American representation in tech.
Long-term Thinking	Google X (now X Development) was established to work on "moonshot" projects that address major global challenges.	Projects like self-driving cars and Project Loon (internet-beaming balloons) demonstrate Google's commitment to long-term, transformative innovations.

Google's approach has led to consistent innovation, strong financial performance, and high employee satisfaction. However, the company has also faced challenges, including concerns about data privacy and workplace culture issues, highlighting the ongoing need for ethical reflection and adaptation.

Unilever: Sustainable Living Plan

Unilever, a multinational consumer goods company, launched its Sustainable Living Plan in 2010. This comprehensive strategy demonstrates a wise approach by balancing profitability with social and environmental responsibility.

Table 5. Key Wise Practices at Unilever

Key Wise Practice	Explanation	Example
Systems Thinking	Unilever's plan addresses interconnected issues such as health, hygiene, environmental impact, and livelihoods, illustrating a holistic approach to sustainability (Unilever, 2010).	The company's efforts to improve smallholder farmer livelihoods while also securing sustainable agricultural supplies demonstrate an understanding of the interconnectedness of social, environmental, and business systems.
Stakeholder Consideration	Unilever committed to improving the health and well-being of over a billion people, showing deep consideration for diverse stakeholders (Polman & Bhattacharya, 2016).	The company's handwashing promotion programs in developing countries, which aim to reduce diseases while also growing the market for soap products, illustrate a win-win approach to stakeholder value creation.
Long-Term Perspective	Unilever aimed to halve its environmental footprint while doubling its business, reflecting balanced attention to growth and sustainability (Polman & Bhattacharya, 2016).	The company has invested in sustainable agriculture practices and committed to sourcing 100% of agricultural raw materials sustainably by 2020, demonstrating a long-term view of supply chain resilience.

continued on following page

Table 5. Continued

Key Wise Practice	Explanation	Example
Transparency and Accountability	Unilever regularly reports on its progress towards Sustainable Living Plan goals, promoting transparency and accountability.	The company publishes detailed annual reports on its sustainability performance, including both successes and areas for improvement.
Innovation for Sustainability	Unilever invests in product and packaging innovations that reduce environmental impact.	The company developed compressed deodorants that use less packaging and propellant gas, reducing carbon footprint while maintaining product performance.
Organizational Integration	Sustainability is integrated into core business strategy and operations, rather than being treated as a separate initiative.	Sustainability criteria are incorporated into innovation processes, brand development, and performance evaluations across the organization.

Unilever's Sustainable Living Plan has driven significant progress in areas such as sustainable sourcing, waste reduction, and social impact. The company has also seen strong financial performance, with its "Sustainable Living" brands growing faster than the rest of the business. However, challenges remain in areas like plastic packaging reduction and scope 3 emissions, illustrating the ongoing nature of the sustainability journey.

These case studies of Google and Unilever, along with the previously expanded Patagonia example, provide a more comprehensive look at how different organizations implement wise practices in their unique contexts. They demonstrate that while the specifics may vary, common themes of long-term thinking, stakeholder consideration, and integration of social and environmental concerns into core business practices are hallmarks of organizationally wise approaches.

Lessons Learned and Best Practices

Table 6. Lessons and Best Practices for Cultivating Organizational Wisdom

Lesson	Lesson Explanation	Best Practice
Cultivate Psychological Safety	Creating an environment where employees feel safe to take risks, voice opinions, and admit mistakes is crucial for developing organizational wisdom.	Implement regular feedback mechanisms, celebrate learning from failures, and train leaders to respond constructively to vulnerability (Edmondson, 1999).
Integrate Diverse Perspectives	Wisdom emerges from synthesizing diverse viewpoints and considering multiple stakeholders	Establish advisory boards and cross-functional teams, and provide training in perspective-taking techniques (Page, 2007).
Prioritize Reflection and Learning	Continuous reflection and learning are essential for cultivating and maintaining organizational wisdom.	Dedicate time for reflection sessions, implement after-action reviews, and develop systems for capturing and sharing lessons learned (Schön, 1983).
Align Incentives with Wisdom Principles	Traditional incentive structures may prioritize short-term gains over long-term wisdom.	Integrate wisdom-related metrics—such as stakeholder impact and sustainability—into performance evaluations and reward systems (Kerr, 1995).
Develop Systems Thinking Capabilities	Understanding complex interdependencies is vital for wise decision-making	Provide systems thinking training and utilize systems mapping tools in strategic planning (Meadows, 2008).
Foster a Culture of Compassion	Compassion enhances collective wisdom by promoting understanding and ethical consideration.	Implement compassion cultivation programs and recognize compassionate behaviors within the organization (Kanov et al., 2004).
Foster a Culture of Compassion	Compassion enhances collective wisdom by promoting understanding and ethical consideration.	Implement compassion cultivation programs and recognize compassionate behaviors within the organization (Kanov et al., 2004).
Lead by Example	Organizational wisdom must be embodied and championed by leadership to take root.	Develop wisdom mentoring programs for leaders and ensure top-level decisions consistently reflect wisdom principles (Gandz & Bird, 2010).
Create Structures for Ethical Consideration	Wise organizations have formal processes for addressing ethical dilemmas.	Establish ethics committees and develop clear frameworks for ethical decision-making accessible to all employees (Trevino & Nelson, 2016).

continued on following page

Table 6. Continued

Lesson	Lesson Explanation	Best Practice
Balance Tradition and Innovation	Organizational wisdom involves honoring valuable traditions while embracing change and innovation.	Maintain repositories of institutional knowledge alongside innovation labs or change management teams to balance continuity and adaptation (Tushman & O'Reilly, 1996).
Measure and Monitor Wisdom	Developing metrics for organizational wisdom is essential for its cultivation and maintenance	Create a balanced scorecard incorporating measures of employee well-being, ethical decision-making, long-term thinking, and stakeholder impact (Kaplan & Norton, 1996).

These case studies and lessons learned illustrate that implementing organizational wisdom is a multifaceted endeavor requiring sustained effort and commitment. However, the benefits – including enhanced employee well-being, improved decision-making, and long-term sustainability – demonstrate the value of pursuing organizational wisdom as a core strategic priority.

FUTURE DIRECTIONS

Challenges and Opportunities for Future Exploration

- **Measuring Organizational Wisdom:** One significant challenge is developing robust, validated measures of organizational wisdom. Future research could focus on creating and refining assessment tools that capture the multidimensional nature of wisdom in organizational contexts (Glück et al., 2013).
- **Longitudinal Studies on the Development of Organizational Wisdom:** There is a need for long-term studies that track how wisdom develops and evolves within organizations over time. Such research could provide valuable insights into the factors that foster or hinder the growth of organizational wisdom (Yang, 2011).
- **Integrating Wisdom into Organizational Systems and Processes:** A key opportunity lies in exploring how wisdom can be systematically integrated into various organizational functions, from strategic planning to human resource management. This could involve developing practical frameworks and tools for implementing wisdom-oriented practices across different organizational levels (Rooney et al., 2010).
- **Exploring the Dark Side of Wisdom:** Future research could delve into potential negative consequences or misapplications of wisdom in organizational settings. This might include examining how perceived wisdom could lead to

complacency or how wisdom principles might be manipulated for unethical purposes (Linley, 2003).

SUMMARY AND SIGNIFICANCE

Summary of Key Insights

- **Theoretical Foundations:** This chapter has explored the multifaceted nature of organizational wisdom, drawing upon diverse theoretical foundations including collective phronesis (Nonaka & Takeuchi, 2011), the Three-Dimensional Wisdom Model (Ardelt, 2003), and Self-Determination Theory (Ryan & Deci, 2000). These frameworks collectively highlight the cognitive, reflective, and compassionate dimensions of wisdom in organizational contexts.
- **Characteristics of Wise Organizations:** We have identified key characteristics that distinguish wise organizations, including their ability to balance short-term needs with long-term sustainability, foster ethical decision-making, and create environments that support employee well-being and growth (Rooney et al., 2010).
- **Implementation Strategies:** The chapter has provided practical insights into implementing wisdom-oriented practices, including strategies for overcoming barriers, designing wise interventions, and aligning organizational structures with wisdom principles (Kessler & Bailey, 2007).
- **Benefits and Outcomes:** We have examined the tangible benefits of organizational wisdom, including enhanced employee well-being, improved decision-making capabilities, increased adaptability, and positive impacts on organizational performance and sustainability (Intezari & Pauleen, 2014).

Significance of Organizational Wisdom

- **Addressing Complex Global Challenges:** In an era characterized by unprecedented complexity and interconnectedness, organizational wisdom offers a crucial framework for addressing multifaceted global challenges. Wise organizations are better equipped to navigate the ethical dilemmas, environmental concerns, and social issues that define our time (Senge et al., 2008).
- **Enhancing Organizational Resilience:** The cultivation of wisdom within organizations significantly contributes to their resilience and adaptability. In a rapidly changing business landscape, this capacity for wise adaptation is

increasingly becoming a key determinant of long-term success and survival (Weick & Sutcliffe, 2015).

- **Promoting Ethical Business Practices:** By emphasizing the ethical dimension of decision-making and fostering a culture of reflection and consideration for diverse stakeholders, organizational wisdom provides a robust framework for promoting responsible and sustainable business practices (Küpers & Pauleen, 2013).
- **Fostering Innovation and Creativity:** Wise organizations, with their emphasis on diverse perspectives, reflective practices, and supportive environments, are well-positioned to foster innovation and creativity. This capacity for wise innovation is crucial in addressing the complex challenges of the 21st century (Nonaka et al., 2014).
- **Contributing to Societal Well-Being:** Beyond their immediate organizational boundaries, wise organizations have the potential to contribute significantly to broader societal well-being. By making decisions that consider long-term consequences and the common good, these organizations can play a crucial role in addressing societal challenges and promoting sustainable development (Kessler & Bailey, 2007).

Final Thoughts

The pursuit of organizational wisdom represents a paradigm shift in how we conceptualize and practice management and leadership. It calls for a move beyond narrow definitions of success to embrace a more holistic, ethical, and sustainable approach to organizational life.

As we face increasingly complex global challenges, from climate change to social inequalities, the need for wise organizations has never been more urgent. By cultivating wisdom at the organizational level, we can create institutions that not only thrive in a complex world but also contribute positively to shaping a better future for all.

CONCLUSION

This chapter has explored the evolving concept of organizational wisdom, highlighting its theoretical underpinnings, practical applications, and significance in addressing the multifaceted challenges of our time. The integration of wisdom into organizational practices offers a pathway toward creating more resilient, ethical, and innovative organizations. As we continue to navigate an increasingly complex global landscape, the pursuit of organizational wisdom will not only enhance organizational performance but also contribute to a more sustainable and equitable future. The journey towards wise organizations is challenging but essential for achieving long-term success and societal well-being.

The journey towards organizational wisdom is ongoing and demanding, requiring continuous learning, reflection, and adaptation. However, the potential rewards – for organizations, their members, and society at large – are immense. As we conclude this chapter, we invite scholars, practitioners, and leaders to embrace the challenge of fostering wisdom in their organizations, recognizing it as both a strategic imperative and a moral obligation in our interconnected world.

REFERENCES

Ardelt, M. (2003). Empirical assessment of a three-dimensional wisdom scale. *Research on Aging*, 25(3), 275–324. DOI: 10.1177/0164027503025003004

Argyris, C., & Schön, D. A. (1996). *Organizational learning II: Theory, method, and practice*. Addison-Wesley.

Bangen, K. J., Meeks, T. W., & Jeste, D. V. (2013). Defining and assessing wisdom: A review of the literature. *The American Journal of Geriatric Psychiatry*, 21(12), 1254–1266. DOI: 10.1016/j.jagp.2012.11.020 PMID: 23597933

Bierly, P. E.III, Kessler, E. H., & Christensen, E. W. (2000). Organizational learning, knowledge and wisdom. *Journal of Organizational Change Management*, 13(6), 595–618. DOI: 10.1108/09534810010378605

Cameron, K. S., Dutton, J. E., & Quinn, R. E. (Eds.). (2003). *Positive organizational scholarship: Foundations of a new discipline*. Berrett-Koehler Publishers.

Cooperrider, D. L., & Whitney, D. (2005). *Appreciative inquiry: A positive revolution in change*. Berrett-Koehler Publishers.

Edmondson, A. C. (2018). *The fearless organization: Creating psychological safety in the workplace for learning, innovation, and growth*. John Wiley & Sons.

Glück, J., König, S., Naschenweng, K., Redzanowski, U., Dorner, L., Straßer, I., & Wiedermann, W. (2013). How to measure wisdom: Content, reliability, and validity of five measures. *Frontiers in Psychology*, 4, 405. DOI: 10.3389/fpsyg.2013.00405 PMID: 23874310

Gonzalez-Mulé, E., & Cockburn, B. S. (2017). Worked to death: The relationships of job demands and job control with mortality. *Personnel Psychology*, 70(1), 73–112. DOI: 10.1111/peps.12206

Grant, A. M., Christianson, M. K., & Price, R. H. (2007). Happiness, health, or relationships? Managerial practices and employee well-being tradeoffs. *The Academy of Management Perspectives*, 21(3), 51–63. DOI: 10.5465/amp.2007.26421238

Hays, J. M. (2007). Dynamics of organisational wisdom. *Business Renaissance Quarterly*, 2(4), 77–122.

Huta, V., & Waterman, A. S. (2014). Eudaimonia and its distinction from hedonia: Developing a classification and terminology for understanding conceptual and operational definitions. *Journal of Happiness Studies*, 15(6), 1425–1456. DOI: 10.1007/s10902-013-9485-0

Intezari, A., & Pauleen, D. J. (2014). Management wisdom in perspective: Are you virtuous enough to succeed in volatile times? *Journal of Business Ethics*, 120(3), 393–404. DOI: 10.1007/s10551-013-1666-6

Isaacs, W. (1999). *Dialogue and the art of thinking together: A pioneering approach to communicating in business and in life*. Currency.

Kaplan, A., & Haenlein, M. (2020). Rulers of the world, unite! The challenges and opportunities of artificial intelligence. *Business Horizons*, 63(1), 37–50. DOI: 10.1016/j.bushor.2019.09.003

Katz, D., & Kahn, R. L. (1978). *The social psychology of organizations* (Vol. 2). Wiley.

Kessler, E. H., & Bailey, J. R. (Eds.). (2007). *Handbook of organizational and managerial wisdom*. Sage Publications. DOI: 10.4135/9781412982726

Kolb, D. A. (1984). *Experiential learning: Experience as the source of learning and development*. Prentice-Hall.

Küpers, W., & Pauleen, D. J. (2013). *A handbook of practical wisdom: Leadership, organization and integral business practice*. Gower Publishing, Ltd.

Laloux, F. (2014). *Reinventing organizations: A guide to creating organizations inspired by the next stage in human consciousness*. Nelson Parker.

McKenna, B., Rooney, D., & Boal, K. B. (2009). Wisdom principles as a meta-theoretical basis for evaluating leadership. *The Leadership Quarterly*, 20(2), 177–190. DOI: 10.1016/j.leaqua.2009.01.013

Meadows, D. H. (2008). *Thinking in systems: A primer*. Chelsea Green Publishing.

Meeks, T. W., & Jeste, D. V. (2009). Neurobiology of wisdom: A literature overview. *Archives of General Psychiatry*, 66(4), 355–365. DOI: 10.1001/archgenpsychiatry.2009.8 PMID: 19349305

Nonaka, I., Chia, R., Holt, R., & Peltokorpi, V. (2014). Wisdom, management and organization. *Management Learning*, 45(4), 365–376. DOI: 10.1177/1350507614542901

Nonaka, I., & Takeuchi, H. (2011). The wise leader. *Harvard Business Review*, 89(5), 58–67. PMID: 21548419

Page, S. E. (2007). *The Difference: How the Power of Diversity Creates Better Groups, Firms, Schools, and Societies*. Princeton University Press.

Pfeffer, J. (1992). *Managing with power: Politics and influence in organizations*. Harvard Business Press.

Pfeffer, J. (2010). Building sustainable organizations: The human factor. *The Academy of Management Perspectives*, 24(1), 34–45.

Raelin, J. A. (2002). 'I don't have time to think!' versus the art of reflective practice. *Reflections: The SoL Journal*, 4(1), 66–79. DOI: 10.1162/152417302320467571

Rooney, D., McKenna, B., & Liesch, P. (2010). *Wisdom and management in the knowledge economy*. Routledge. DOI: 10.4324/9780203852798

Rousseau, D. M., Manning, J., & Denyer, D. (2013). Evidence in management and organizational science: Assembling the field's full weight of scientific knowledge through syntheses. *The Academy of Management Annals*, 7(1), 79–100.

Rowley, J., & Gibbs, P. (2008). From learning organization to practically wise organization. *The Learning Organization*, 15(5), 356–372. DOI: 10.1108/09696470810898357

Ryan, R. M., & Deci, E. L. (2000). Self-determination theory and the facilitation of intrinsic motivation, social development, and well-being. *The American Psychologist*, 55(1), 68–78. DOI: 10.1037/0003-066X.55.1.68 PMID: 11392867

Schön, D. A. (1983). *The reflective practitioner: How professionals think in action*. Basic Books.

Scott, W. R. (1992). *Organizations: Rational, natural, and open systems*. Prentice-Hall.

Senge, P., Smith, B., Kruschwitz, N., Laur, J., & Schley, S. (2008). *The necessary revolution: How individuals and organizations are working together to create a sustainable world*. Doubleday.

Senge, P. M. (1990). *The fifth discipline: The art and practice of the learning organization*. Doubleday/Currency.

Vogus, T. J., & Sutcliffe, K. M. (2012). Organizational mindfulness and mindful organizing: A reconciliation and path forward. *Academy of Management Learning & Education*, 11(4), 722–735. DOI: 10.5465/amle.2011.0002c

Walton, G. M. (2014). The new science of wise psychological interventions. *Current Directions in Psychological Science*, 23(1), 73–82. DOI: 10.1177/0963721413512856

Walumbwa, F. O., Christensen, A. L., & Hailey, F. (2011). Authentic leadership and the knowledge economy: Sustaining motivation and trust among knowledge workers. *Organizational Dynamics*, 40(2), 110–118. DOI: 10.1016/j.orgdyn.2011.01.005

Wang, Q., Dou, J., & Jia, S. (2016). A meta-analytic review of corporate social responsibility and corporate financial performance: The moderating effect of contextual factors. *Business & Society*, 55(8), 1083–1121. DOI: 10.1177/0007650315584317

Weick, K. E. (1995). *Sensemaking in organizations*. Sage Publications.

Weick, K. E., & Sutcliffe, K. M. (2015). *Managing the unexpected: Sustained performance in a complex world*. John Wiley & Sons. DOI: 10.1002/9781119175834

Williams, T. A., Gruber, D. A., Sutcliffe, K. M., Shepherd, D. A., & Zhao, E. Y. (2017). Organizational response to adversity: Fusing crisis management and resilience research streams. *The Academy of Management Annals*, 11(2), 733–769. DOI: 10.5465/annals.2015.0134

Yang, S. Y. (2011). Wisdom displayed through leadership: Exploring leadership-related wisdom. *The Leadership Quarterly*, 22(4), 616–632. DOI: 10.1016/j.leaqua.2011.05.004

ADDITIONAL READING

Ardelt, M., & Oh, H. (2016). Wisdom: Definition, Assessment, and Its Relation to Successful Cognitive and Emotional Aging. In Pachana, N. (Ed.), *Encyclopedia of Geropsychology*. Springer.

McKenna, B., Rooney, D., & Kenworthy, A. L. (2013). Wisdom and Management: A Guest-Edited Special Collection of Resource Reviews for Management Educators. Academy of Management Learning & Education, 12(2), 306-311. DOI: 10.5465/amle.2013.0112

Nonaka, I., & Takeuchi, H. (2019). The Wise Company: How Companies Create Continuous Innovation. Oxford University Press.

Rooney, D., McKenna, B., & Liesch, P. (2010). *Wisdom and Management in the Knowledge Economy*. Routledge. DOI: 10.4324/9780203852798

Statler, M., & Roos, J. (2006). Reframing Strategic Preparedness: An Essay on Practical Wisdom. *International Journal of Management Concepts and Philosophy*, 2(2), 99–117. DOI: 10.1504/IJMCP.2006.010263

Sternberg, R. J., & Jordan, J. (Eds.). (2005). A Handbook of Wisdom: Psychological Perspectives. Cambridge University Press.

Weick, K. E. (2009). *Making Sense of the Organization: The Impermanent Organization* (Vol. 2). John Wiley & Sons.

KEY TERMS AND DEFINITIONS

Artificial Intelligence (AI): The simulation of human intelligence in machines that are programmed to think and learn, with a growing focus on integrating ethical and wise decision-making processes.

Collective Phronesis: A concept derived from Aristotle's notion of practical wisdom, referring to the collective capacity of an organization to make wise and ethical decisions.

Crisis Management: The process by which an organization deals with unexpected and disruptive events, with a focus on how wise practices can enhance organizational resilience.

Cross-Cultural Perspectives: An approach that examines how cultural values, beliefs, and practices influence the development and application of wisdom in organizational settings.

Dark Side of Wisdom: Potential negative consequences or misapplications of wisdom, such as complacency or manipulation, that could arise in organizational contexts.

Ethical Decision-Making: The process of making decisions that are consistent with ethical principles, including fairness, integrity, and respect for all stakeholders.

Innovation: The process of creating new ideas, products, or processes that bring value, often enhanced by the wisdom-oriented practices within an organization.

Longitudinal Studies: Research studies that follow the same subjects over a period of time, allowing for the observation of long-term effects and trends, particularly in the development of organizational wisdom.

Neuroscience: A branch of science that deals with the structure and function of the nervous system and brain, particularly how these relate to behavior and cognitive functions, including wisdom.

Organizational Wisdom: The collective ability of an organization to make decisions and take actions that are ethical, long-term focused, and contextually aware, balancing short-term objectives with long-term sustainability.

Phronesis: A Greek term often translated as "practical wisdom," referring to the moral and ethical insight needed to make the right decisions in complex situations.

Resilience: The capacity of an organization to recover quickly from difficulties, adapt to change, and continue functioning effectively under challenging conditions.

Self-Determination Theory: A psychological theory by Ryan & Deci (2000) that emphasizes the role of intrinsic motivation and autonomy in fostering personal and organizational well-being.

Sustainable Development: Development that meets the needs of the present without compromising the ability of future generations to meet their own needs, often facilitated by wise organizational practices.

Three-Dimensional Wisdom Model: A framework proposed by Ardelt (2003) that defines wisdom as a combination of cognitive, reflective, and compassionate dimensions.

Compilation of References

Abbott, B., Underwood, K., Seybold, E., Kincaid, D., Hamshaw, S., Lee, R., Rizzo, D., Brown, B., Toolin, R., Chorover, J., Li, L., Lewis, G., Sayedi, S. S., St. Clair, S., Buck, R., Aanderud, Z., Brahney, J., Nixon, R., Wang, W., & Perdrial, J. (2023). *Resistance, recovery, and resilience: Rethinking the three Rs of survival in the Anthropocene*. https://doi.org/DOI: 10.22541/essoar.167390526.69780816/v1

Abramson, T., & Schmidt, B. (2024, April 24). *Cultivating Psychological Resilience/ Elders*. https://generations.asaging.org/cultivating-psychological-resilienceelders

Achor, S. (2010). *The happiness advantage: The seven principles of positive psychology that fuel success and performance at work*. Crown Business.

Adams, R., & Miller, L. (2020). Recognition and rewards: Enhancing employee happiness. *Employee Relations*, 42(3), 595–610. DOI: 10.1108/ER-05-2019-0248

Adula, M., Birbirsa, Z. A., & Kant, S. (2023). The effect of interpersonal, problem solving and technical training skills on performance of Ethiopia textile industry: Continuance, normative and affective commitment as mediators. *Cogent Business & Management*, 10(3), 2286672. Advance online publication. DOI: 10.1080/23311975.2023.2286672

Ahsan, M. (2023). The role of emotional intelligence in effective corporate social responsibility leadership. *International Journal of Organizational Analysis*, 31(8), 75.91. DOI: 10.1108/ijoa.02.2023.3615

Aikens, K. A., Astin, J., Pelletier, K. R., Levanovich, K., Baase, C. M., Park, Y. Y., & Bodnar, C. M. (2014). Mindfulness Goes to Work: Impact of an Online Workplace Intervention. *Journal of Occupational and Environmental Medicine*, 56(7), 721–731. DOI: 10.1097/JOM.0000000000000209 PMID: 24988100

Akbari, M., Hooshmand, M., & Aletaha, S. H. (2019). Internal Marketing and the Internal Customers' Citizenship Behavior in Higher Education. *International Journal of Schooling*, 1(3), 15–28.

Aldahadha, B. (2023). Self-disclosure, mindfulness, and their relationships with happiness and well-being. *Middle East Current Psychiatry, Ain Shams University*, 30(1), 7. DOI: 10.1186/s43045-023-00278-5

Alegre, J., & Pasamar, S. (2018). Firm innovativeness and work-life balance. *Technology Analysis and Strategic Management*, 30(4), 421–433. DOI: 10.1080/09537325.2017.1337091

Alemayehu, E. (2021). Practices, obstacles and benefits of instructional leadership at private schools of Addis Ababa, Ethiopia. *Academy of Educational Leadership Journal*, 25, 1–18.

Algarni, M., & Alemeri, M. (2023). The role of employee engagement, job satisfaction and organizational commitment on happiness at work at a Saudi organization. *International Journal of Business and Management*, 18(2), 27. DOI: 10.5539/ijbm.v18n2p27

Alicja, D. (2023). *1. How Does Inclusion Impact Employees in Organisations?* Literature Review. Acta Universitatis Lodziensis. DOI: 10.18778/0208-6018.364.02

Ali, F., Rasoolimanesh, S. M., Sarstedt, M., Ringle, C. M., & Ryu, K. (2018). An assessment of the use of partial least squares structural equation modeling (PLS-SEM) in hospitality research. *International Journal of Contemporary Hospitality Management*, 30(1), 514–538. DOI: 10.1108/IJCHM-10-2016-0568

Ali, R., Ateeq, A., Ani, Z. A., & Ali, S. A. (2023). A Critical Review of Contemporary Trends and Challenges in Human Resource Management Article Information. *ResearchGate*, 4(2), 22–27. DOI: 10.11648/ IJIHRM.04.02.2023.003

Allan, B. A., Douglass, R. P., Duffy, R. D., & McCarty, R. J. (2016). Meaningful work as a moderator of the relation between work stress and meaning in life. *Journal of Career Assessment*, 24(3), 429–440. DOI: 10.1177/1069072715599357

Allen, T. D., Johnson, R. C., Saboe, K. N., & Cho, E. (2013). Work-family conflict and flexible work arrangements: A meta-analysis of the literature. *The Journal of Applied Psychology*, 98(6), 1011–1026.

Allman, P., McLaren, P., & Rikowski, G. (2018). *Critical education against global capitalism: Karl Marx and revolutionary critical education*. Sense Publishers.

AllVoices. (2023). What is continuous feedback and how can it transform your team? Retrieved from https://www.allvoices.co/blog/what-is-continuous-feedback

Alshammari, A. S., Piko, B. F., & Fitzpatrick, K. M. (2021). Social support and adolescent mental health and well-being among Jordanian students. *International Journal of Adolescence and Youth*, 26(1), 211–223. DOI: 10.1080/02673843.2021.1908375

Amabile, T. M., & Kramer, S. J. (2010). *The progress principle: Using small wins to ignite joy, engagement, and creativity at work*. Harvard Business Review Press.

Amabile, T. M., & Pratt, M. G. (2016). The dynamic componential model of creativity and innovation in organizations: Making progress, making meaning. *Research in Organizational Behavior*, 36, 157–183. DOI: 10.1016/j.riob.2016.10.001

Amdemaryam, Z. (2020). *The Effect of Organizational Justice on Organizational Performance. Employees Trust toward Their Leader as a Mediator.(Ethiopian Airline Group: Case of Bahirdar and Lalibela Branches)* (Doctoral dissertation).

American Institute of Stress. (n.d.). The benefits of stress management. Retrieved from https://www.stress.org/

American Psychological Association (APA). (2024). How these organizations are leading in making employee mental health a priority. Retrieved from https://www.apa.org/topics/healthy-workplaces/organizations-improving-employee-mental-health

American Psychological Association. (2024). *Resilience*. https://www.apa.org/topics/resilience

Andenæs, R., Jackowska, M., Steptoe, A., & Jackowska, M. (2016). Positive affect, psychological well-being, and good sleep. *Journal of Psychosomatic Research*, 84(9).

Andersen, E. (2016). Learning to learn. *Harvard Business Review*, 94, 19.

Anderson, N., & De Dreu, C. K. W. (2022). Innovation and creativity in organizations: The role of individual and group dynamics. *Journal of Organizational Behavior*, 43(2), 123–139.

Anderson, N., Potočnik, K., & Zhou, J. (2014). Innovation and creativity in organizations: A state-of-the-science review, prospective commentary, and guiding framework. *Journal of Management*, 40(5), 1297–1333. DOI: 10.1177/0149206314527128

Anseel, F., Lievens, F., Schollaert, E., & Choragwicka, B. (2015). Feedback-seeking behavior as a response to negative feedback: The role of feedback environment and personal attributes. *The Journal of Applied Psychology*, 100(1), 266–283. DOI: 10.1037/a0036832

Arakkathara, J. G., & Bance, L. (2019). Promotion of Well-Being, Resilience and Stress Management (POWER): An Intervention Program for Mothers of Children with Intellectual Disability: A Pilot Study. *Indian Journal of Positive Psychology*, 10(4).

Ardelt, M. (1997). Wisdom and life satisfaction in old age. *The Journals of Gerontology. Series B, Psychological Sciences and Social Sciences*, 52(1), 15–P27. DOI: 10.1093/geronb/52B.1.P15 PMID: 9008672

Ardelt, M. (2003). Empirical assessment of a three-dimensional wisdom scale. *Personality and Individual Differences*, 34(7), 1279–1293. DOI: 10.1016/S0191-8869(02)00158-6

Ardelt, M. (2003). Empirical assessment of a three-dimensional wisdom scale. *Research on Aging*, 25(3), 275–324. DOI: 10.1177/0164027503025003004

Ardelt, M. (2004). Wisdom as expert knowledge system: A critical review of a contemporary operationalization of an ancient concept. *Human Development*, 47(5), 257–285. DOI: 10.1159/000079154

Ardelt, M., & Bergsma, A. (2012). Self-Reported Wisdom and Happiness: An Empirical Investigation. *Journal of Happiness Studies*, 13(3), 481–499. DOI: 10.1007/s10902-011-9275-5

Argyle, M., Martin, M., & Crossland, J. (1989). Happiness as a function of personality and social encounters. *Recent Advances in Social Psychology: An International Perspective*, 189-203.

Argyle, M. (1989). *The Psychology of Happiness*. Routledge.

Argyle, M., & Crossland, J. (1987). The dimensions of positive emotions. *British Journal of Social Psychology*, 26(2), 127–137. DOI: 10.1111/j.2044-8309.1987.tb00773.x PMID: 3607389

Argyris, C., & Schön, D. A. (1996). *Organizational learning II: Theory, method, and practice*. Addison-Wesley.

Aristotle, . (1999). *Nicomachean ethics* (Irwin, T., Trans.). Hackett.

Arnetz, B. B. (1996). Techno-stress: A prospective psychophysiological study of the impact of a controlled stress-reduction program in advanced telecommunication systems design work. *Journal of Occupational and Environmental Medicine*, 38(1), 53–65. DOI: 10.1097/00043764-199601000-00017 PMID: 8871332

Aronsson, J., Clarke, D., Grose, J., & Richardson, J. (2020). Student nurses exposed to sustainability education can challenge practice: a cohort study. *Nursing and Health Sciences*, 22(3), 803.811. DOI: 10.1111/nhs.12734

Arthur, J., Kristjánsson, K., Walker, D., Sanderse, W., & Jones, C. (2015). Character education in UK schools.

Arthur, J., Kristjánsson, K., Harrison, T., Sanderse, W., & Wright, D. (2016). *Teaching character and virtue in schools*. Routledge. DOI: 10.4324/9781315695013

Arthur, M. M. (2003). Share price reactions to work-family initiatives. *Academy of Management Journal*, 46(4), 497–505. DOI: 10.2307/30040641

Asefa, A. (2023). Effect of Transformational Leadership on Organizational Performance: The Mediating Role of Employee Commitment and Expert Systems (AI) Inclusion in Ethiopia. *2023 International Conference on Communication, Security and Artificial Intelligence (ICCSAI)*, 305-310. DOI: 10.1109/ICCSAI59793.2023.10421269

Asefa, K., Debela, K. L., & Kant, S. (2023). Transformational Leadership effect on Organizational Performance with Mediation role of Employee Commitment in case of Public Sector in Oromia, Ethiopia. *Horn of African Journal of Business and Economics*, 6(2), 192–211.

Ashford, S. J., & DeRue, D. S. (2012). Developing as a leader: The power of mindful engagement. *Organizational Dynamics*, 41(2), 146–154. DOI: 10.1016/j.orgdyn.2012.01.008

Ashforth, B. E., & Mael, F. (1989). Social identity theory and the organization. *Academy of Management Review*, 14(1), 20–39. DOI: 10.2307/258189

Ashraf, M. (2019). The mediating role of work atmosphere in the relationship between supervisor cooperation, career growth and job satisfaction. *Journal of Workplace Learning*, 31(2), 78–94. Advance online publication. DOI: 10.1108/JWL-12-2017-0113

Asrini, M. (2024). *1. The Role of Human Resource Management in Employee Well-Being and Mental Health: A Systematic Literature Review*. Productivity. DOI: 10.62207/phea4z38

Atthayasai, J. (2023). Surgical nurses' perceptions of strategies to enhance pain management proficiency: a qualitative study. *Nursing Reports*, 13(2), 923.933. DOI: 10.3390/nursrep13020081

Aurelius, M. (2002). *Meditations* (Hays, G., Trans.). The Modern Library.

Avey, J. B., Luthans, F., Hannah, S. T., Sweetman, D., & Peterson, C. (2011). Impact of employees' character strengths of wisdom on stress and creative performance. *Human Resource Management Journal*, 22(2), 165–181. DOI: 10.1111/j.1748-8583.2010.00157.x

Avolio, B. J., & Gardner, W. L. (2005). Authentic leadership development: Getting to the root of positive forms of leadership. *The Leadership Quarterly*, 16(3), 315–338. DOI: 10.1016/j.leaqua.2005.03.001

Aznan, E., Kassim, A., Othman, N., Yusof, M., & Amir, N. (2019). The relationship between job satisfaction and social skill. *Jurnal Intelek*, 14(2), 251.256. DOI: 10.24191/ji.v14i2.258

Baehr, J. (2016). *Intellectual virtues and education*. Taylor & Francis.

Baer, M., & Oldham, G. R. (2006). The impact of negative workplace gossip on employee creativity. *The Journal of Applied Psychology*, 91(1), 109–118. DOI: 10.1037/0021-9010.91.1.109 PMID: 16435942

Baghdadi, N., Sankarapandian, C., Arulappan, J., Taani, M. H., Snethen, J., & Andargeery, S. Y. (2023). The association between nursing students' happiness, emotional intelligence, and perceived caring behavior in Riyadh city, Saudi Arabia. *Health Care*, 12(1), 67. DOI: 10.3390/healthcare12010067 PMID: 38200973

Bailey, C., Madden, A., Alfes, K., & Fletcher, L. (2017). The meaning, antecedents and outcomes of employee engagement: A narrative synthesis. *International Journal of Management Reviews*, 19(1), 31–53. DOI: 10.1111/ijmr.12077

Bai, Y., Wang, Z., Alam, M., Gul, F., & Wang, Y. (2022). The Impact of Authentic Leadership on Innovative Work Behavior: Mediating Roles of Proactive Personality and Employee Engagement. *Frontiers in Psychology*, 13, 879176. DOI: 10.3389/fpsyg.2022.879176 PMID: 35756212

Bajaj, B., Khoury, B., & Sengupta, S. (2022). Resilience and Stress as Mediators in the Relationship of Mindfulness and Happiness. *Frontiers in Psychology*, 13, 771263. DOI: 10.3389/fpsyg.2022.771263 PMID: 35185720

Bajaj, B., & Pande, N. (2016). Mediating role of resilience in the impact of mindfulness on life satisfaction and affect as indices of subjective well-being. *Personality and Individual Differences*, 93, 63–67. DOI: 10.1016/j.paid.2015.09.005

Bakker, A. B., & Demerouti, E. (2008). Towards a model of work engagement. *Career Development International*, 13(3), 209–223. DOI: 10.1108/13620430810870476

Baltes, P. B., & Staudinger, U. M. (2000). Wisdom: A metaheuristic (pragmatic) to orchestrate mind and virtue toward excellence. *The American Psychologist*, 55(1), 122–136. DOI: 10.1037/0003-066X.55.1.122 PMID: 11392856

Bangen, K. J., Meeks, T. W., & Jeste, D. V. (2013). Defining and assessing wisdom: A review of the literature. *The American Journal of Geriatric Psychiatry*, 21(12), 1254–1266. DOI: 10.1016/j.jagp.2012.11.020 PMID: 23597933

Bansal, G., & Punia, B. K. (2023). Precursors of workplace mindfulness: An exploration and conceptual modelling. In Narwal, K., Bhisnoi, V. K., Bhaker, S. K., & Saini, V. P. (Eds.), *Florilegium: Management theory, research and practices* (pp. 174–184). Arihant Books.

Barasa, E., Mbau, R., & Gilson, L. (2018). What Is Resilience and How Can It Be Nurtured? A Systematic Review of Empirical Literature on Organizational Resilience. *International Journal of Health Policy and Management*, 7(6), 491–503. DOI: 10.15171/ijhpm.2018.06 PMID: 29935126

Baregheh, A., Rowley, J., & Sambrook, S. (2009). Towards a multidisciplinary definition of innovation. *Management Decision*, 47(8), 1323–1339. DOI: 10.1108/00251740910984578

Bareket-Bojmel, L., Chernyak-Hai, L., & Margalit, M. (2023). Out of sight but not out of mind: The role of loneliness and hope in remote work and in job engagement. *Personality and Individual Differences*, 202, 111955. Advance online publication. DOI: 10.1016/j.paid.2022.111955

Bartels, M. (2015). Genetics of well-being and its components satisfaction with life, happiness, and quality of life: A review and meta-analysis of heritability studies. *Behavior Genetics*, 45(2), 137–156. DOI: 10.1007/s10519-015-9713-y PMID: 25715755

Basu, S., Thomas, S., & Khan, T. (2022). Impact of Digital Education on Learning Behavior of Undergraduates. *Journal of Higher Education Theory and Practice*, 22(11). Advance online publication. DOI: 10.33423/jhetp.v22i11.5421

Baumeister, R. F., & Leary, M. R. (2017). The need to belong: Desire for interpersonal attachments as a fundamental human motivation. Interpersonal development, 57-89.

Bazerman, M. H., & Tenbrunsel, A. E. (2011). *Blind spots: Why we fail to do what's right and what to do about it*. Princeton University Press. DOI: 10.1515/9781400837991

Bebeau, M. J. (2002). The role of ethics in clinical practice: Lessons from a case study. *Journal of Dental Education*, 66(12), 1297–1306.

Becker, J. M., Klein, K., & Wetzels, M. (2012). Hierarchical latent variable models in PLS-SEM: Guidelines for using reflective-formative type models. *Long Range Planning*, 45(5-6), 359–394. DOI: 10.1016/j.lrp.2012.10.001

Becker, J. M., Ringle, C. M., Sarstedt, M., & Völckner, F. (2015). How collinearity affects mixture regression results. *Marketing Letters*, 26(4), 643–659. DOI: 10.1007/s11002-014-9299-9

Beham, B., Prag, P., & Drobnič, S. (2012). Who's got the balance? A study of satisfaction with the work-family balance among part-time service sector employees in five western European countries. *International Journal of Human Resource Management*, 23(18), 3725–3741. DOI: 10.1080/09585192.2012.654808

Beine, M., de Groot, H. L., & van der Klauw, M. (2009). Determinants of study success in higher education. *Economics of Education Review*, 28(2), 123–134.

Bek Yağmur, Ö., & Aydıntuğ Myrvang, N. (2023). The effect of organizational agility on crisis management process and organizational resilience: Health sector example. *International Journal of Disaster Risk Reduction*, 96, 103955. DOI: 10.1016/j.ijdrr.2023.103955

Bellmann, L., & Hübler, O. (2021). Working from home, job satisfaction and work–life balance–robust or heterogeneous links? *International Journal of Manpower*, 42(3), 424–441. DOI: 10.1108/IJM-10-2019-0458

Beninger, S., & Francis, J. N. P. (2018). On being fair: Cultural self-construals and public engagement. *Journal of Business Research*, 82, 197–206. DOI: 10.1016/j.jbusres.2017.09.043

Benioff, M., & Adler, C. (2019). *Trailblazer: The power of business as the greatest platform for change*. Currency.

Bennis, W. (2009). *On becoming a leader* (4th ed.). Basic Books.

Berg, J. M., Dutton, J. E., & Wrzesniewski, A. (2013). Job crafting and meaningful work.

Berkowitz, M. W., & Bier, M. C. (2004). Based character education. *The Annals of the American Academy of Political and Social Science*, 591(1), 72–85. DOI: 10.1177/0002716203260082

Berku, D. W. (2024). Instructional Leadership Practice of Secondary School Principals to Deliver Quality Education in North Shewa Zone in Ethiopia. *Leadership and Policy in Schools*, 1–19. DOI: 10.1080/15700763.2024.2347912

Bersin, J. (2012). *The state of employee recognition in 2012*. Bersin & Associates.

BetterUp. (2021). Guide to conflict resolution skills — plus real world examples. Retrieved from https://www.betterup.com/blog/conflict-resolution-skills

BetterUp. (2022). 8 team bonding activities to increase engagement and belonging. Retrieved from https://www.betterup.com/blog/team-bonding

Betterworks. (2023). How to achieve transparency in the workplace. Retrieved from https://www.betterworks.com/magazine/workplace-transparency-alignment-trust/

Beyer, B. K. (1995). *Critical Thinking*. Phi Delta Kappa Educational Foundation.

Bhattacharyya, R. (2024, August 8). *Godrej Industries ramps up hiring at group companies to push growth.* ET Bureau. The Economic Times. Retrieved September 18, 2024 from https://economictimes.indiatimes.com/jobs/hr-policies-trends/godrej-industries-ramps-up-hiring-at-group-companies-to-push-growth/articleshow/112355460.cms

Bierly, P. E.III, Kessler, E. H., & Christensen, E. W. (2000). Organizational learning, knowledge and wisdom. *Journal of Organizational Change Management*, 13(6), 595–618. DOI: 10.1108/09534810010378605

Bishop, S. R., Lau, M., Shapiro, S., Carlson, L., Anderson, N. D., Carmody, J., Segal, Z. V., Abbey, S., Speca, M., Velting, D., & Devins, G. (2004). Mindfulness: A proposed operational definition. *Clinical Psychology : a Publication of the Division of Clinical Psychology of the American Psychological Association*, 11(3), 230–241. DOI: 10.1093/clipsy.bph077

Blaauw, D., Ditlopo, P., & Rispel, L. (2014). Nursing education reform in South Africa – lessons from a policy analysis study. *Global Health Action*, 7(1), 26401. Advance online publication. DOI: 10.3402/gha.v7.26401 PMID: 25537941

Blau, P. M. (1964). *Exchange and Power in Social Life*. John Wiley and Sons.

Bock, L. (2015). *Work rules! Insights from inside Google that will transform how you live and lead.* Twelve.

Bock, L. (2015). *Work rules!: Insights from inside Google that will transform how you live and lead.* Twelve.

Boku, G. G., Abeya, S. G., Ayers, N., & Abera, M. (2024). Leadership Commitment and the Quality of Adolescent-Friendly Sexual Reproductive Health Services in Public Health Facilities Among Pastoral Districts of Guji Zone, Ethiopia. *Journal of Healthcare Leadership*, 16, 53–66. DOI: 10.2147/JHL.S441951 PMID: 38370150

Bonde, E. H., Mikkelsen, E. G., Fjorback, L. O., & Juul, L. (2023). The impact of an organizational-level mindfulness-based intervention on workplace social capital and psychological safety: A qualitative content analysis. *Frontiers in Psychology*, 14(March), 1–13. DOI: 10.3389/fpsyg.2023.1112907 PMID: 36959993

Bonde, E. H., Mikkelsen, E. G., Fjorback, L. O., & Juul, L. (2024). Exploring an Organizational-Level Mindfulness-Based Intervention in Private Workplace Settings. *Mindfulness*, 15(6), 1453–1471. DOI: 10.1007/s12671-024-02375-w

Botha, F., & Booysen, F. (2014). Family functioning and life satisfaction and happiness in South African households. *Social Indicators Research*, 119(1), 163–182. DOI: 10.1007/s11205-013-0485-6

Boyle-Baise, M., & Langford, J. (2004). There are children here: Service learning for social justice. *Equity & Excellence in Education*, 37(1), 55–66. DOI: 10.1080/10665680490422115

Braskamp, L. A., Trautvetter, L. C., & Ward, K. (2006). *Putting students first: How colleges develop students purposefully*. Anker Publishing Company.

Brees, J. R., & Brees, D. S. (2014). *Managing employee performance: A practical approach*. Routledge.

Breevaart, K., Bakker, A. B., Demerouti, E., & Derks, D. (2014). Daily feedback and employee engagement: The role of work-related flow. *Journal of Occupational Health Psychology*, 19(4), 428–438. DOI: 10.1037/a0037196

Brief, A. P., & Weiss, H. M. (2002). Organizational Behavior: Affect in the Workplace. *Annual Review of Psychology*, 53(1), 279–307. DOI: 10.1146/annurev.psych.53.100901.135156 PMID: 11752487

Brodsky, A. E., & Cattaneo, L. B. (2013). A transconceptual model of empowerment and resilience: Divergence, convergence and interactions in kindred community concepts. *American Journal of Community Psychology*, 52(3–4), 333–346. DOI: 10.1007/s10464-013-9599-x PMID: 24057948

Brookey & Company. (2024). The benefits of an organizational assessment. Retrieved from https://www.brookeyco.com/blog/the-benefits-of-an-organizational-assessment

Brookfield, S. D. (2017). *Becoming a Critically Reflective Teacher*. Jossey-Bass.

Brown, A., & Lee, C. (2022). Positive psychology in the workplace: Applications and outcomes. *Journal of Organizational Behavior*, 43(2), 123–145.

Brown, A., & Wilson, T. (2023). The role of social well-being in employee engagement and performance. *Human Resource Management Review*, 33(1), 45–60.

Brown, B. (2018). *Dare to lead: Brave work. Tough conversations. Whole hearts*. Random House.

Brown, K. W., & Ryan, R. M. (2003). The benefits of being present: Mindfulness and its role in psychological well-being. *Journal of Personality and Social Psychology*, 84(4), 822–848. DOI: 10.1037/0022-3514.84.4.822 PMID: 12703651

Brown, K. W., Ryan, R. M., & Creswell, J. D. (2007). Mindfulness: Theoretical Foundations and Evidence for its Salutary Effects. *Psychological Inquiry*, 18(4), 211–237. DOI: 10.1080/10478400701598298

Brown, M. E., & Treviño, L. K. (2006). Ethical leadership: A review and future directions. *The Leadership Quarterly*, 17(6), 595–616. DOI: 10.1016/j.leaqua.2006.10.004

Brudney, J. L. (2005). The impact of organizational involvement in community service on the development of employee skills and relationships. *Public Administration Review*, 65(5), 545–556.

Brunelle, E., & Fortin, J. A. (2021). Distance Makes the Heart Grow Fonder: An Examination of Teleworkers' and Office Workers' Job Satisfaction Through the Lens of Self-Determination Theory. *SAGE Open*, 11(1). Advance online publication. DOI: 10.1177/2158244020985516

Brynjolfsson, E. (2014). The second machine age: Work, progress, and prosperity in a time of brilliant technologies.

Bukhari, S. R., & Afzal, F. (2017). Perceived social support predicts psychological problems among university students. *International Journal of Indian Psychology*, 4(2), 18–27.

Bunderson, J. S., & Thompson, J. A. (2009). The role of organizational membership in the relationship between personal and organizational values. *The Journal of Applied Psychology*, 94(4), 1014–1025.

Burch, T. (2018). Faculty workload: An analysis of perceived workload and its impact on job satisfaction. *International Journal of Educational Management*, 32(1), 145–158. DOI: 10.1108/IJEM-07-2017-0200

Burmann, C., & Zeplin, S. (2005). Building brand commitment: A behavioural approach to internal brand management. *Journal of Brand Management*, 12(4), 279–300. DOI: 10.1057/palgrave.bm.2540223

Burnard, K. J., & Bhamra, R. (2019). Challenges for organisational resilience. *Continuity & Resilience Review*, 1(1), 17–25. DOI: 10.1108/CRR-01-2019-0008

Burton, J. (2010). *WHO healthy workplace framework and model: background and supporting literature and practices*. World Health Organization. https://iris.who.int/handle/10665/113144

Butler, C., O'Shea, D., & Truxillo, D. (2021). *Adaptive and Proactive Coping in the Process of Developing Resilience* (Vol. 19). Research in Occupational Stress and Well Being. DOI: 10.1108/S1479-355520210000019002

Butt, A., Imran, F., Helo, P., & Kantola, J. (2024). Strategic design of culture for digital transformation. *Long Range Planning*, 57(2), 102415. DOI: 10.1016/j.lrp.2024.102415

Buzzanell, P. M., & Turner, L. H. (2003). Emotion work revealed by job loss discourse: Backgrounding-foregrounding of feelings, construction of normalcy, and (re) instituting of traditional masculinities. *Journal of Applied Communication Research*, 31(1), 27–57. DOI: 10.1080/00909880305375

Byrne, U. (2005). Work-life balance. *Business Information Review*, 22(1), 53–59. DOI: 10.1177/0266382105052268

Cable, D. M., & DeRue, D. S. (2002). The role of fit in organizational selection and work outcomes. *Organizational Behavior and Human Decision Processes*, 88(1), 294–311.

Cabrera.Aguilar, E., Zevallos-Francia, M., Morales-García, M., Ramírez-Coronel, A. A., Morales-García, S. B., Sairitupa-Sanchez, L. Z., & Morales-García, W. C. (2023). Resilience and stress as predictors of work engagement: The mediating role of self.efficacy in nurses. *Frontiers in Psychiatry*, 14, 1202048. Advance online publication. DOI: 10.3389/fpsyt.2023.1202048 PMID: 37649562

Cameron, K. S., Dutton, J. E., & Quinn, R. E. (2012). *Positive Organizational Scholarship: Foundations of a New Discipline*. Berrett-Koehler Publishers.

Cameron, K. S., Dutton, J. E., & Quinn, R. E. (Eds.). (2003). *Positive organizational scholarship: Foundations of a new discipline*. Berrett-Koehler Publishers.

Cameron, K., Mora, C., Leutscher, T., & Calarco, M. (2011). Effects of positive practices on organizational effectiveness. *The Journal of Applied Behavioral Science*, 47(3), 266–308. DOI: 10.1177/0021886310395514

Caprara, G. V., & Steca, P. (2006). The contribution of self–regulatory efficacy beliefs in managing affect and family relationships to positive thinking and hedonic balance. *Journal of Social and Clinical Psychology*, 25(6), 603–627. DOI: 10.1521/jscp.2006.25.6.603

Carlson, D. S., Grzywacz, J. G., & Kacmar, K. M. (2010). The relationship of schedule flexibility and outcomes via the work family interface. *Journal of Managerial Psychology*, 25(4), 330–355. DOI: 10.1108/02683941011035278

Carlson, D. S., & Kacmar, K. M. (2000). Work--family conflict in the organization: Do life role values make a difference? *Journal of Management*, 26(5), 1031–1054. DOI: 10.1177/014920630002600502

Carmeli, A., Brueller, D., & Dutton, J. E. (2009). Learning behaviours in the workplace: The role of high-quality interpersonal relationships and psychological safety. *Systems Research and Behavioral Science*, 26(1), 81–98. DOI: 10.1002/sres.932

Carmeli, A., Gilat, G., & Waldman, D. A. (2007). The role of perceived organizational performance in organizational identification, adjustment and job performance. *Journal of Management Studies*, 44(6), 972–992. DOI: 10.1111/j.1467-6486.2007.00691.x

Carmeli, A., & Spreitzer, G. M. (2009). Trust, connectivity, and creativity: The role of affective and cognitive trust in the workplace. *Journal of Organizational Behavior*, 30(6), 941–962. DOI: 10.1002/job.586

Carragher, J. & Gormley, K. (2016). Leadership and emotional intelligence in nursing and midwifery education and practice: a discussion paper. *Journal of Advanced Nursing*, 73(1), 85.96. DOI: 10.1111/jan.13141

Cartwright, S., & Holmes, N. (2006). The meaning of work: The challenge of regaining employee engagement and reducing cynicism. *Human Resource Management Review*, 16(2), 199–208. DOI: 10.1016/j.hrmr.2006.03.012

Caspi, A., Sugden, K., Moffitt, T. E., Taylor, A., Craig, I. W., Harrington, H., McClay, J., Mill, J., Martin, J., Braithwaite, A., & Poulton, R. (2003). Influence of life stress on depression: Moderation by a polymorphism in the 5-HTT gene. *Science*, 301(5631), 386–389. DOI: 10.1126/science.1083968 PMID: 12869766

Castelino, L. M., & Shinde, R. (2022). Employee Engagement: A Key to Improve Performance–A Case Study on HCL. *International Journal of Case Studies in BusinessIT and Education*, 6(1), 566–577.

Caulfield, A. (2015). *The contribution of the practice of mindfulness to stress reduction among school teachers: a qualitative study of Irish primary teachers* (Doctoral dissertation, University of Lincoln).

Centre for Research and Evidence on Security Threats. (2023). *A Communication Perspective on Resilience*. https://crestresearch.ac.uk/comment/a-communication-perspective-on-resilience/

Chakraborty, T., & Ganguly, M. (2019). Crafting Engaged Employees Through Positive Work Environment. *Advances in Human Resources Management and Organizational Development*, 180–198. Advance online publication. DOI: 10.4018/978-1-5225-7799-7.ch011

Chang, M. L. (2009). An appraisal perspective of teacher burnout: Examining the emotional work of teachers. *Educational Psychology Review*, 21(3), 193–218. DOI: 10.1007/s10648-009-9106-y

Chang, Y. Y., & Shih, H. Y. (2019). Work curiosity: A new lens for understanding employee creativity. *Human Resource Management Review*, 29(4), 100672. DOI: 10.1016/j.hrmr.2018.10.005

Chan, H. C., & Chu, K. M. (2024). A Multilevel Perspective on High-Performance Work System, Mindfulness, Employee Work Well-Being, and Employee Creative Engagement. *SAGE Open*, 14(2), 21582440241242206. DOI: 10.1177/21582440241242206

Charles, S. T., Reynolds, C. A., & Gatz, M. (2001). Age-related differences and change in positive and negative affect over 23 years. *Journal of Personality and Social Psychology*, 80(1), 136–151. DOI: 10.1037/0022-3514.80.1.136 PMID: 11195886

Charoensukmongkol, P., & Puyod, J. V. (2022). Mindfulness and emotional exhaustion in call center agents in the Philippines: Moderating roles of work and personal characteristics. *The Journal of General Psychology*, 149(1), 72–96. DOI: 10.1080/00221309.2020.1800582 PMID: 32748707

Chaudhry, S., Tandon, A., Shinde, S., & Bhattacharya, A. (2024). Student psychological well-being in higher education: The role of internal team environment, institutional, friends and family support and academic engagement. *PLoS One*, 19(1), e0297508. DOI: 10.1371/journal.pone.0297508 PMID: 38271390

Chaudhury, N., & Modi, S. (2016). Employee Wellness Programs in the Context of an Emerging Epidemic of Lifestyle Diseases: What Works and What Doesn&t? *NHRD Network Journal*, 9(4), 33–38. DOI: 10.1177/0974173920160407

Cheng, L., Yang, J., Li, M., & Wang, W. (2020). Mediating effect of coping style between empathy and burnout among Chinese nurses working in medical and surgical wards. *Nursing Open*, 7(6), 1936.1944. DOI: 10.1002/nop2.584

Cheng, H., Li, Z., Zhao, J., Wang, W., & Zou, R. (2022). The role of cognition, affect, and resources in the influence of unreasonable tasks on work engagement: A moderated chain mediation model. *Frontiers in Psychology*, 13, 1013773. Advance online publication. DOI: 10.3389/fpsyg.2022.1013773 PMID: 36275277

Cheng, J. C., & Chen, C. Y. (2017). Job resourcefulness, work engagement and prosocial service behaviors in the hospitality industry. *International Journal of Contemporary Hospitality Management*, 29(10), 2668–2687. DOI: 10.1108/IJCHM-01-2016-0025

Cheng, L., Huang, C.-C., & Sitar, S. (2023). Mindfulness and job performance in Chinese nonprofit workers: Mediation effects of PANA and work engagement. *Humanities & Social Sciences Communications*, 10(1), 871. DOI: 10.1057/s41599-023-02402-6

Chen, L., & Zhang, Y. (2017). Flexible work arrangements and their impact on employee happiness. *The Journal of Applied Psychology*, 102(5), 697–706. DOI: 10.1037/apl0000223

Cherniss, C. (2001). Emotional intelligence and organizational effectiveness. In Cherniss, C., & Goleman, D. (Eds.), *The emotionally intelligent workplace*. Jossey-Bass.

Chin, B., Slutsky, J., Raye, J., & Creswell, J. D. (2019). Mindfulness Training Reduces Stress At Work: A Randomized Controlled Trial. *Mindfulness*, 10(4), 627–638. DOI: 10.1007/s12671-018-1022-0 PMID: 30923585

Chin, W. W. (1998). The partial least squares approach to structural equation modeling. In Marcoulides, G. A. (Ed.), *Modern Methods for Business Research* (pp. 295–358). Erlbaum.

Chin, W. W., Gopal, A., & Salisbury, W. D. (1997). Advancing the theory of adaptive structuration: The development of a scale to measure faithfulness of appropriation. *Information Systems Research*, 8(4), 342–367. DOI: 10.1287/isre.8.4.342

Choi, E., Gruman, J. A., & Leonard, C. M. (2021). A balanced view of mindfulness at work. *Organizational Psychology Review*, 12(1), 35–72. DOI: 10.1177/20413866211036930

Choi, E., Leroy, H., Johnson, A., & Nguyen, H. (2022). Flaws and All: How Mindfulness Reduces Error Hiding by Enhancing Authentic Functioning. *Journal of Occupational Health Psychology*, 27(5), 451–469. DOI: 10.1037/ocp0000327 PMID: 35549505

Christensen, K. E., & Staines, G. (1990). Flextime: A viable solution to work/family conflict? *Journal of Family Issues*, 11(4), 455–477. DOI: 10.1177/019251390011004007

Chughtai, M. S., Syed, F., Naseer, S., & Chinchilla, N. (2023). Role of adaptive leadership in learning organizations to boost organizational innovations with change self-efficacy. *Current Psychology (New Brunswick, N.J.)*. Advance online publication. DOI: 10.1007/s12144-023-04669-z PMID: 37359696

Clampitt, P. G. (2016). *Communicating for managerial effectiveness*. SAGE Publications.

Clary, E. G., & Snyder, M. (1999). The Motivations to Volunteer: Theoretical and Practical Considerations. *Current Directions in Psychological Science*, 8(5), 156–159. DOI: 10.1111/1467-8721.00037

Clifton, T. J., & Shepard, E. (2004). Work and family programs and productivity: Estimates applying a production function model. *International Journal of Manpower*, 25(8), 714–728. DOI: 10.1108/01437720410570036

Cochis, C., Mattarelli, E., Bertolotti, F., Scapolan, A. C., Montanari, F., & Ungureanu, P. (2021). How perceptions of work-life balance and technology use impact upon creativity in collaborative spaces. In *Digital Transformation and Human Behavior: Innovation for People and Organisations* (pp. 217-234). Springer International Publishing. DOI: 10.1007/978-3-030-47539-0_16

Cohen, S., & McKay, G. (2022). Resources and support: Key factors in workplace well-being. *The Journal of Applied Psychology*, 107(5), 777–790.

Colby, A., & Sullivan, W. M. (2009). Strengthening the Foundations of Students' Excellence, Integrity, and Social Contribution. *Liberal Education*, 95(1), 22–29.

Compton, W. C. (2005). Love and well-being. In Compton, W. C. (Ed.), *An Introduction to Positive Psychology* (pp. 86–107). Wadsworth.

Condon, P. (2017). *Mindfulness-Compassion-and-Prosocial-Behavior*. Mindfulness in Social Psychology.

Confucius, . (1979). *The Analects* (Lau, D. C., Trans.). Penguin Classics.

Conroy, S., Henle, C. A., Shore, L., & Stelman, S. (2017). Where there is light, there is dark: A review of the detrimental outcomes of high organizational identification. *Journal of Organizational Behavior*, 38(2), 184–203. DOI: 10.1002/job.2164

Cooper, C. L., & Cartwright, S. (1994). Healthy mind; healthy organization: A proactive approach to occupational stress. In *Human Relations* (Vol. 47, Issue 4, pp. 455–471). Sage Publications. DOI: 10.1177/001872679404700405

Cooperrider, D. L., & Whitney, D. (2005). *Appreciative inquiry: A positive revolution in change*. Berrett-Koehler Publishers.

Costa, P. J., & McCrae, R. R. (1988). From catalog to classification: Murray's needs and the five-factor model. *Journal of Personality and Social Psychology*, 55(2), 258–265. DOI: 10.1037/0022-3514.55.2.258

Costa, T., Suardi, A. C., Diano, M., Cauda, F., Duca, S., Rusconi, M. L., & Sotgiu, I. (2019). The neural correlates of hedonic and eudaimonic happiness: An fMRI study. *Neuroscience Letters*, 712, 134491. Advance online publication. DOI: 10.1016/j.neulet.2019.134491 PMID: 31518675

Cowley, S. A., Tzouvara, V., & Horta Reis da Silva, T. (2023). Public Health: healthy ageing and well-being. In *Redfern's Nursing Older People*. Fifth edition. Elsevier.

Crego, A., Yela, J. R., Gómez-Martínez, M. Á., Riesco-Matías, P., & Petisco-Rodríguez, C. (2021). Relationships between mindfulness, purpose in life, happiness, anxiety, and depression: Testing a mediation model in a sample of women. *International Journal of Environmental Research and Public Health*, 18(3), 925. DOI: 10.3390/ijerph18030925 PMID: 33494471

Crompton, R., Lewis, S., & Lyonette, C. (Eds.). (2007). *Women, men, work and family in Europe* (pp. 159–182). Palgrave Macmillan. DOI: 10.1057/9780230800830

Cropanzano, R., & Wright, T. A. (2001). When a "happy" worker is really a productive worker: A review and further refinement of the happy-productive worker thesis. *Consulting Psychology Journal: Practice and Research, 53*(3), 182-199. DOI: 10.1037/1061-4087.53.3.182

Cropanzano, R., & Mitchell, M. S. (2005). Social exchange theory: An interdisciplinary review. *Journal of Management*, 31(6), 874–900. DOI: 10.1177/0149206305279602

Cropanzano, R., & Wright, T. A. (2001). When a "happy" worker is really a productive worker: A review of the literature and a theoretical framework. In Giacalone, R. A., & Jurkiewicz, C. L. (Eds.), *Handbook of workplace spirituality and organizational performance* (pp. 60–78). M.E. Sharpe.

Crowley, C., Kapitula, L. R., & Munk, D. (2022). Mindfulness, happiness, and anxiety in a sample of college students before and after taking a meditation course. *Journal of American College Health*, 70(2), 493–500. DOI: 10.1080/07448481.2020.1754839 PMID: 32369422

Csikszentmihalyi, M. (1990). *Flow: The psychology of optimal experience*. Harper & Row.

Csikszentmihalyi, M. (1996). *Creativity: Flow and the psychology of discovery and invention*. HarperCollins.

Çulha, Y., Turan, N., & Kaya, H. (2017). Entrepreneurship in nursing education. *Pressacademia*, 4(1), 50.53. DOI: 10.17261/Pressacademia.2017.516

CultureMonkey. (2024). The importance of feedback in the workplace. Retrieved from https://www.culturemonkey.io/employee-engagement/the-importance-of-feedback-in-the-workplace/

CultureMonkey. (2024). What is transparency at work: Benefits and top tips to practice. Retrieved from https://www.culturemonkey.io/employee-engagement/transparency-at-work/

da Silva, T. H. R. (2022). Emotional awareness and emotional intelligence. *British Journal of Community Nursing*, 27(12), 573–574. DOI: 10.12968/bjcn.2022.27.12.573 PMID: 36519463

Dagger, R. (1997). *Civic Virtues: Rights, Citizenship, and Republican Liberalism*. Oxford University Press. DOI: 10.1093/oso/9780195106336.001.0001

Dalton, D. R., & Mesch, D. J. (1991). On the extent and reduction of avoidable absenteeism: An assessment of absence policy provisions. *The Journal of Applied Psychology*, 76(6), 810–817. DOI: 10.1037/0021-9010.76.6.810

Dâmbean, C. & Gabor, M. (2021). Implications of emotional intelligence in human resource management. *Economics*, 9(2), 73.90. DOI: 10.2478/eoik.2021.0016

Dane, E. (2010). Paying Attention to Mindfulness and Its Effects on Task Performance in the Workplace. *Journal of Management*, 37(4), 997–1018. DOI: 10.1177/0149206310367948

Dane, E., & Brummel, B. J. (2014). Examining workplace mindfulness and its relations to job performance and turnover intention. *Human Relations*, 67(1), 105–128. DOI: 10.1177/0018726713487753

Daniel, C., Daniel, P. A., & Smyth, H. (2022). The role of mindfulness in the management of projects: Potential opportunities in research and practice. *International Journal of Project Management*, 40(7), 849–864. DOI: 10.1016/j.ijproman.2022.07.003

Danna, K., & Griffin, R. W. (1999). Health and well-being in the workplace: A review and synthesis of the literature. *Journal of Management*, 25(3), 357–384. DOI: 10.1177/014920639902500305

Danner, D. D., Snowdon, D. A., & Friesen, W. V. (2001). Positive emotions in early life and longevity: Findings from the Nun Study. *Journal of Personality and Social Psychology*, 80(5), 804–813. DOI: 10.1037/0022-3514.80.5.804 PMID: 11374751

Davaei, M. & Gunkel, M. (2023). The role of intelligences in teams: a systematic literature review. *Review of Managerial Science*, 18(1), 259.297. DOI: 10.1007/s11846.023.00672.7

Davenport, L., Allisey, A., Page, K., Lamontagne, A., & Reavley, N. (2016). How can organisations help employees thrive? The development of guidelines for promoting positive mental health at work. *International Journal of Workplace Health Management*, 9(4), 411–427. DOI: 10.1108/IJWHM-01-2016-0001

Davis, M., Jenkins, J., & Liu, Y. (2021). Psychological well-being and academic success: The role of self-efficacy and resilience. *Educational Psychology Review*, 33(4), 567–586.

Davis, R., & Kim, S. (2024). The future of work: Remote and hybrid models. *Workplace Research Journal*, 12(1), 45–67.

Day, D., Gronn, P., & Salas, E. (2004). Leadership capacity in teams. *The Leadership Quarterly*, 15(6), 857–880. DOI: 10.1016/j.leaqua.2004.09.001

De Giorgio, A., Barattucci, M., Teresi, M., Raulli, G., Ballone, C., Ramaci, T., & Pagliaro, S. (2023). Organizational identification as a trigger for personal well-being: Associations with happiness and stress through job outcomes. *Journal of Community & Applied Social Psychology*, 33(1), 138–151. DOI: 10.1002/casp.2648

De Simone, S. (2014). Conceptualizing well-being in the workplace. *International Journal of Business and Social Science*, 5(12), 118–122.

Deborah, B. (2022, July 03). Fiona, Buick., Michael, O'Donnell., Nabil, Adnan, Ilahee. (2022). 1. Changing the Conversation to Create Organizational Change. *Journal of Change Management*, 22(3), 252–272. Advance online publication. DOI: 10.1080/14697017.2022.2040570

Deci, E. L., Connell, J. P., & Ryan, R. M. (1989). Self-determination in a work organization. *The Journal of Applied Psychology*, 74(4), 580–590. DOI: 10.1037/0021-9010.74.4.580

Deci, E. L., & Ryan, R. M. (2000). The" what" and" why" of goal pursuits: Human needs and the self-determination of behavior. *Psychological Inquiry*, 11(4), 227–268. DOI: 10.1207/S15327965PLI1104_01

Delle Fave, A., Brdar, I., Freire, T., Vella-Brodrick, D., & Wissing, M. P. (2011). The Eudaimonic and Hedonic Components of Happiness: Qualitative and Quantitative Findings. *Social Indicators Research*, 100(2), 185–207. Advance online publication. DOI: 10.1007/s11205-010-9632-5

Demaray, M. K., Malecki, C. K., Davidson, L. M., Hodgson, K. K., & Rebus, P. J. (2005). The relationship between social support and student adjustment: A longitudinal analysis. *Psychology in the Schools*, 42(7), 691–706. DOI: 10.1002/pits.20120

Demerouti, E., Bakker, A. B., Nachreiner, F., & Schaufeli, W. B. (2001). The job demands-resources model of burnout. *The Journal of Applied Psychology*, 86(3), 499–512. DOI: 10.1037/0021-9010.86.3.499 PMID: 11419809

Demissie, A. D., Alemu, A. E., & Tensay, A. T. (2024). Servant Leadership and Organizational Citizenship Behavior: The Mediating Role of Perceived Organizational Politics and the Moderating Role of Political Skill in Public Service Organizations. *Employee Responsibilities and Rights Journal*, 1–39. DOI: 10.1007/s10672-023-09486-x

Denning, S. (2011). *The secret language of leadership: How leaders inspire action through narrative*. Jossey-Bass.

Dereso, C. W., Kant, S., Muthuraman, M., & Tufa, G. (2023). Effect of Point of Service on Health Department Student's Creativity in Comprehensive Universities of Ethiopia: Moderating Role of Public-Private Partnership and Mediating Role of Work Place Learning. In Proceedings of the International Health Informatics Conference. Lecture Notes in Electrical Engineering, vol 990. Springer, Singapore. DOI: 10.1007/978-981-19-9090-8_13

DeskAlerts. (2024). Best employee feedback tools to use in 2024. Retrieved from https://www.alert-software.com/blog/employee-feedback-tools

Dewan, N., Hossain, M. B., Kim, G. G., Dunay, A., & Illés, C. B. (2022). Transportation Mobile Applications Adoption Behavior Does Affect Overseas Residents' Life Satisfaction: Involvement as A Moderator. *Cogent Business & Management*, 9(1), 2096998. DOI: 10.1080/23311975.2022.2096998

Dewey, J. (1933). *How We Think*. D.C. Heath and Company.

Dharani, B. (2020). At the intersection of happiness and contentment at work. In *The Routledge companion to happiness at work* (pp. 61–75). Routledge. DOI: 10.4324/9780429294426-7

Diener, E. (1984). Subjective well-being. *Psychological Bulletin*, 95(3), 542–575. DOI: 10.1037/0033-2909.95.3.542 PMID: 6399758

Diener, E. (2006). Guidelines for national indicators of subjective well-being and ill-being. *Applied Research in Quality of Life*, 1(2), 151–157. DOI: 10.1007/s11482-006-9007-x

Diener, E., & Chan, M. Y. (2011). Happy people live longer: Subjective well-being contributes to health and longevity. *Applied Psychology. Health and Well-Being*, 3(1), 1–43. DOI: 10.1111/j.1758-0854.2010.01045.x PMID: 26286968

Diener, E., & Lucas, R. E. (2009). *Personality and subjective well-being. The science of wellbeing*. Springer.

Diener, E., & Oishi, S. (2018). Lessons learned from national subjective well-being studies. *Journal of Happiness Studies*, 19(3), 775–787. DOI: 10.1007/s10902-017-9862-3

Diener, E., Oishi, S., & Tay, L. (2018). Advances in subjective well-being research. *Nature Human Behaviour*, 2(4), 253–260. DOI: 10.1038/s41562-018-0307-6 PMID: 30936533

Diener, E., & Seligman, M. E. P. (2002). Very happy people. *Psychological Science*, 13(1), 81–84. DOI: 10.1111/1467-9280.00415 PMID: 11894851

Diener, E., & Seligman, M. E. P. (2004). Beyond money: Toward an economy of well-being. *Psychological Science in the Public Interest*, 5(1), 1–31. DOI: 10.1111/j.0963-7214.2004.00501001.x PMID: 26158992

Diener, E., Thapa, S., & Tay, L. (2020). Positive Emotions at Work. *Annual Review of Organizational Psychology and Organizational Behavior*, 7(1), 451–477. Advance online publication. DOI: 10.1146/annurev-orgpsych-012119-044908

Dirks, K. T., & Ferrin, D. L. (2002). Trust in leadership: Meta-analytic findings and implications for research and practice. *The Journal of Applied Psychology*, 87(4), 611–628. DOI: 10.1037/0021-9010.87.4.611 PMID: 12184567

Doerfel, M. L., Kim, M., Kwestel, M., Yoon, H., & Quow, J. (2022). Resilience organizing: A multilevel communication framework. *Journal of Communication*, 72(6), 605–618. DOI: 10.1093/joc/jqac027

Doğru, Ç. (2022). A meta.analysis of the relationships between emotional intelligence and employee outcomes. *Frontiers in Psychology*, 13, 611348. Advance online publication. DOI: 10.3389/fpsyg.2022.611348 PMID: 35548499

Drisko, J. W., & Maschi, T. (2016). *Content analysis*. Pocket Guide to Social Work Re.

Drummond, S., O'Driscoll, M. P., Brough, P., Kalliath, T., Siu, O. L., Timms, C., Riley, D., Sit, C., & Lo, D. (2017). The relationship of social support with well-being outcomes via work–family conflict: Moderating effects of gender, dependants and nationality. *Human Relations*, 70(5), 544–565. DOI: 10.1177/0018726716662696

Duchek, S. (2020a). Organizational resilience: A capability-based conceptualization. *Business Research*, 13(1), 215–246. DOI: 10.1007/s40685-019-0085-7

Duchek, S., Raetze, S., & Scheuch, I. (2020b). The role of diversity in organizational resilience: A theoretical framework. *Business Research*, 13(2), 387–423. DOI: 10.1007/s40685-019-0084-8

Duckworth, A. (2016). *Grit: The power of passion and perseverance* (Vol. 234). Scribner.

Dunn, E. W., Aknin, L. B., & Norton, M. I. (2008). Spending Money on Others Promotes Happiness. *Science*, 319(5870), 1687–1688. DOI: 10.1126/science.1150952 PMID: 18356530

Durga, P., Godavarthi, D., Kant, S., & Basa, S. S. (2024). Aspect-based drug review classification through a hybrid model with ant colony optimization using deep learning. *Discov Computing*, 27(1), 19. DOI: 10.1007/s10791-024-09441-w

Dvir, T., Eden, D., Avolio, B. J., & Shamir, B. (2002). Impact of transformational leadership on follower development and performance: A field experiment. *Academy of Management Journal*, 45(4), 735–744. DOI: 10.2307/3069307

Dweck, C. S. (2006). *Mindset: The new psychology of success.* Random house.

Dwivedi, D. (2011). Stress Management: How to Reduce and Manage Workplace Stress. Juris Ray. 5.

Dwivedi, D. (2014). New Dimensions of HRM: Performance Management.

Dwivedi, D. (2018). Stress Management in Software Industry.

Dwivedi, D. (2015). Impact of Information Technology on the Productivity of the Organization. *HR Journal of Management.*, 7, 77.

Dwivedi, D., & Agarwal, S. (2024). Green Technology and Its Effect on the Modern World. In *Green Innovations for Industrial Development and Business Sustainability* (pp. 120–126). CRC Press. DOI: 10.1201/9781003458944-8

Dziuba, S. T., Ingaldi, M., & Zhuravskaya, M. (2020). Employees' Job Satisfaction and their Work Performance as Elements Influencing Work Safety. System Safety Human - Technical Facility - Environment, 2(1), 18–25. DOI: 10.2478/czoto-2020-0003

Ebstein, R. P., Novick, O., Umansky, R., Priel, B., Osher, Y., Blaine, D., Bennett, E. R., Nemanov, L., Katz, M., & Belmaker, R. H. (1996). Dopamine D4 receptor (D4DR) exon III polymorphism associated with the human personality trait of novelty seeking. *Nature Genetics*, 12(1), 78–80. DOI: 10.1038/ng0196-78 PMID: 8528256

Edmondson, A. (1999). Psychological safety and learning behavior in work teams. *Administrative Science Quarterly*, 44(2), 350–383. DOI: 10.2307/2666999

Edmondson, A. (2019). *The fearless organization: Creating psychological safety in the workplace for learning, innovation, and growth*. Wiley.

Edmondson, A. C., & Harvey, J. F. (2017). *Extreme teaming: Lessons in complex, cross-sector leadership*. Emerald Publishing Limited. DOI: 10.1108/9781786354495

Edmondson, A., & Mogelof, J. P. (2006). Explaining psychological safety in the workplace: A conceptual model. *Journal of Organizational Behavior*, 27(3), 367–391. DOI: 10.1002/job.383

Eid, R., Al Zaabi, A., Alzahmi, R., & Elsantil, Y. (2019). Integrating internal branding antecedents, customer and job satisfaction in the public sector. *The International Journal of Organizational Analysis*, 27(5), 1480–1503. DOI: 10.1108/IJOA-09-2018-1548

Eisenberger, R., Huntington, R., Hutchison, S., & Sowa, D. (2001). Perceived organizational support. *The Journal of Applied Psychology*, 71(3), 500–507. DOI: 10.1037/0021-9010.71.3.500 PMID: 11302232

Elam, T., & Taku, K. (2022). Differences between posttraumatic growth and resiliency: Their distinctive relationships with empathy and emotion recognition ability. *Frontiers in Psychology*, 13, 825161. Advance online publication. DOI: 10.3389/fpsyg.2022.825161 PMID: 35418895

Epstein, R. M., & Street, R. L. (2011). Patient-centered communication in cancer care: Promoting healing and reducing suffering. National Cancer Institute. https://www.cancer.gov/about-cancer/coping/feelings/patient-centered-care

Erika & Jonathan. (2023). Conversation Analysis, Enacting Teams, and Displaying Team Spirit in a Decision-Making Episode of Talk. New perspectives in organizational communication, .DOI: 10.1007/978-3-031-30199-5_7

Espasandín-Bustelo, F., Ganaza-Vargas, J., & Diaz-Carrion, R. (2021). Employee happiness and corporate social responsibility: The role of organizational culture. *Employee Relations*, 43(3), 609–629. DOI: 10.1108/ER-07-2020-0343

Etezadi, S., & Pushkar, D. (2013). Why are wise people happier? An explanatory model of wisdom and emotional well-being in older adults. *Journal of Happiness Studies*, 14(3), 929–950. DOI: 10.1007/s10902-012-9362-2

Evenseth, L., Sydnes, M., & Gausdal, A. (2022). Building Organizational Resilience Through Organizational Learning: A Systematic Review. *Frontiers in Communication*, 7, 837386. Advance online publication. DOI: 10.3389/fcomm.2022.837386

Eysenck, M. W. (1995). *Personality and Individual Differences: Current Issues*. Wiley.

Facione, P. A. (2015). *Critical Thinking: What It Is and Why It Counts*. Measured Reasons.

Fallowfield, L., Jenkins, V., & Farewell, V. (2006). Eliciting patients' preferences for treatment: A review of the evidence for best practice. *Journal of Clinical Oncology*, 24(15), 2420–2426.

Fang, Y., Mirza, F., Chaudhary, N., Arshad, R., & Wu, Y. (2022). Impact of perceived skillset and organizational traits on digital wellbeing of teachers: Mediating role of resilience. *Frontiers in Psychology*, 13, 923386. Advance online publication. DOI: 10.3389/fpsyg.2022.923386 PMID: 35719496

Farhana, A. (2023). Effect of emotional intelligence on job satisfaction among nurses: descriptive study. *PJMHS*, 17(6), 127.129. DOI: 10.53350/pjmhs2023176127

Farmer, J., Mistry, M., & Jainer, A. (2020). Emotional intelligence for healthcare. *Sushruta Journal of Health Policy & Opinions,* 13(1), 26.27. DOI: 10.38192/13.1.8

Fathy El Dessouky, N., & Al-Ghareeb, A. (2020). Human Resource Management and Organizational Resilience in The Era of COVID-19: Theoretical Insights, Challenges and Implications. *2020 Second International Sustainability and Resilience Conference: Technology and Innovation in Building Designs(51154),* 1–6. DOI: 10.1109/IEEECONF51154.2020.9319967

Ferede, W. L., Endawoke, Y., & Tessema, G. (2024). Change management through strategic leadership: The mediating effect of knowledge management in public organizations, Ethiopia. *Future Business Journal*, 10(1), 93. DOI: 10.1186/s43093-024-00363-z

Fernando & Romana. (2023). Human Resources as a Factor of Influence and Inclusion in Companies: The Case of El Corte Ingles. European modern studies journal, DOI: 10.59573/emsj.7(4).2023.25

Field, L. K., & Buitendach, J. H. (2011). Happiness, work engagement and organisational commitment of support staff at a tertiary education institution in South Africa. *SA Journal of Industrial Psychology*, 37(1), 1–10. DOI: 10.4102/sajip.v37i1.946

Fisher, C. D. (2010). Happiness at Work. *International Journal of Management Reviews*, 12(4), 384–412. DOI: 10.1111/j.1468-2370.2009.00270.x

FitzGerald, S. (2012). *Using mindfulness to build a transformative school culture: A phenomenological study of elementary school principals who create an atmosphere of academic rigor and teacher effectiveness* (Doctoral dissertation, Argosy University/Seattle).

Fitzpatrick, J. M., Bianchi, L. A., Hayes, N., Da Silva, T., & Harris, R. (2023). Professional development and career planning for nurses working in care homes for older people: A scoping review. *International Journal of Older People Nursing*, 18(1), e12519. DOI: 10.1111/opn.12519 PMID: 36441621

Forbes. (2021). The costs and benefits of addressing mental health in the workplace. Retrieved from https://www.forbes.com/councils/forbesbusinesscouncil/2021/12/06/the-costs-and-benefits-of-addressing-mental-health-in-the-workplace/

Forbes. (2023). 19 effective strategies for building a culture of adaptability. Retrieved from https://www.forbes.com/councils/forbesbusinesscouncil/2023/06/12/19-effective-strategies-for-building-a-culture-of-adaptability/

Ford, M. T., Cerasoli, C. P., Higgins, J. A., & Decesare, A. L. (2011). Relationships between psychological, physical, and behavioural health and work performance: A review and meta-analysis. *Work and Stress*, 25(3), 185–204. DOI: 10.1080/02678373.2011.609035

Fornell, C. G., & Larcker, D. F. (1981). Evaluating structural equation models with unobservable variables and measurement error. *JMR, Journal of Marketing Research*, 18(1), 39–50. DOI: 10.1177/002224378101800104

Foster, K., Cuzzillo, C., & Furness, T. (2018). Strengthening mental health nurses' resilience through a workplace resilience programme: a qualitative inquiry. *Journal of Psychiatric and Mental Health Nursing*, 25(5.6), 338.348. DOI: 10.1111/jpm.12467

Fowers, B. J. (2008). From continence to virtue: Recovering goodness, character unity, and character types for positive psychology. *Theory & Psychology*, 18(5), 629–653. DOI: 10.1177/0959354308093399

Fowler, J. H., & Christakis, N. A. (2008). Dynamic spread of happiness in a large social network: Longitudinal analysis over 20 years in the Framingham Heart Study. *British Medical Journal*, 337(dec04 2), a2338. DOI: 10.1136/bmj.a2338 PMID: 19056788

Franken, E., Plimmer, G., Malinen, S., & Bryson, J. (2022). Growing and Adapting During Continuous Change: Building Employee Resilience in the Public Sector. In Pinheiro, R., Frigotto, M. L., & Young, M. (Eds.), *Towards Resilient Organizations and Societies: A Cross-Sectoral and Multi-Disciplinary Perspective* (pp. 143–170). Springer International Publishing. DOI: 10.1007/978-3-030-82072-5_6

Frantically Speaking. (2024). 11 effective communication strategies to resolve conflict. Retrieved from https://franticallyspeaking.com/11-effective-communication-strategies-to-resolve-conflict/

Fredrickson, B. L. (2001). The role of positive emotions in positive psychology: The broaden-and-build theory of positive emotions. *The American Psychologist*, 56(3), 218–226. DOI: 10.1037/0003-066X.56.3.218 PMID: 11315248

Freiberg, K., & Freiberg, J. (1998). *Nuts!: Southwest Airlines' crazy recipe for business and personal success*. Crown Currency.

Frey, B. S., Gallus, J., & Steiner, L. (2014). Open issues in happiness research. *International Review of Economics*, 61(2), 115–125. DOI: 10.1007/s12232-014-0203-y

Friedman, R. A., & Holtom, B. C. (2002). The effects of network groups on minority employee turnover intentions. *Human Resource Management*, 41(4), 405–421. DOI: 10.1002/hrm.10051

Frone, M. R. (2003). Work-family balance. In Quick, J. C., & Tetrick, L. E. (Eds.), *Handbook of Occupational Health Psychology*. American Psychological Association. DOI: 10.1037/10474-007

Frone, M. R., Russell, M., & Cooper, M. L. (1995). health : A test of identity theory. *Journal of Occupational and Organizational Psychology*, 68(1), 1–11. DOI: 10.1111/j.2044-8325.1995.tb00684.x

Frontiers. (2023). Changing the landscape of mental health among college students. Retrieved from https://www.frontiersin.org/journals/public-health/articles/10.3389/fpubh.2023.1175594/full

Gable, S. L., & Haidt, J. (2011). What (and Why) Is Positive Psychology? *Review of General Psychology*, 15(2), 103–111. DOI: 10.1037/1089-2680.9.2.103

Gabriel, Y. (2000). *Storytelling in organizations: Facts, fictions, and fantasies*. Oxford University Press. DOI: 10.1093/acprof:oso/9780198290957.001.0001

Gale, C. R., Booth, T., Mõttus, R., Kuh, D., & Deary, I. J. (2013). Neuroticism and extraversion in youth predict mental wellbeing life satisfaction 40 years later. *Journal of Research in Personality*, 47(6), 687–697. DOI: 10.1016/j.jrp.2013.06.005 PMID: 24563560

Galperin, B. L., Michaud, J., Punnett, B. J., Melyoki, L. L., Metwally, E., Mukanzi, C., Senaji, T. A., & Taleb, A. (2024). Towards Increased Understanding of Leadership in the African Context: Data From Seven Countries. *Journal of International Management*, 30(5), 101170. DOI: 10.1016/j.intman.2024.101170

Ganesh, N. K. (2022). Avoiding stress, improving productivity: a study on stress management policies.

Gao, C., Khalid, S., Lianyu, C., & Tadesse, E. (2024). Integrated leadership for coherent school improvement in Ethiopia: The moderating role of transformational leadership on the relationship between instructional leadership and student academic achievement mediated by school improvement process. *Psychology in the Schools*, 61(2), 455–474. DOI: 10.1002/pits.23065

Garas, S. R. R., Mahran, A. F. A., & Mohamed, H. M. H. (2018). Internal corporate branding impact on employees' brand supporting behaviour. *Journal of Product and Brand Management*, 27(1), 79–95. DOI: 10.1108/JPBM-03-2016-1112

Garcia, A. C. M., Ferreira, A. C. G., Silva, L. S. R., da Conceição, V. M., Nogueira, D. A., & Mills, J. (2022). Mindful Self-Care, Self-Compassion, and Resilience Among Palliative Care Providers During the COVID-19 Pandemic. *Journal of Pain and Symptom Management*, 64(1), 49–57. DOI: 10.1016/j.jpainsymman.2022.03.003 PMID: 35292366

Garcia, M., Patel, R., & Singh, A. (2021). Diversity and inclusion in workplace happiness research: A review. *International Journal of Human Resource Management*, 32(5), 789–812.

Garg & Punia, B.K. (2016). Exploring Social Exchange Theory in Indian Context, *XIBA. Business Review*, 2(2), 12–21.

Garg, N. (2022). Gratitude and work-family enrichment among Indian female workforce: Exploring the mediating role of psychological capital. *International Journal of Work Organisation and Emotion*, 13(1), 1–17. DOI: 10.1504/IJWOE.2022.121971

Garland, E. L., Geschwind, N., Peeters, F., & Wichers, M. (2015). Mindfulness training promotes upward spirals of positive affect and cognition: Multilevel and autoregressive latent trajectory modeling analyses. *Frontiers in Psychology*, 6, 15. DOI: 10.3389/fpsyg.2015.00015 PMID: 25698988

Garvin, D. A. (1993). Building a learning organization. *Harvard Business Review*, 71(4), 78–91. PMID: 10127041

Gase, L. N., Gomez, L. M., Kuo, T., Glenn, B. A., Inkelas, M., & Ponce, N. A. (2017). Relationships among student, staff, and administrative measures of school climate and student health and academic outcomes. *The Journal of School Health*, 87(5), 319–328. DOI: 10.1111/josh.12501 PMID: 28382671

Gergen, K. J., McNamee, S., & Barrett, F. J. (2001). Toward transformative dialogue. *International Journal of Public Administration*, 24(7-8), 679–707. DOI: 10.1081/PAD-100104770

Ghenaatgar, A., & Jalali, S. M. (2016). Study of the Effect of Internal Brand Management on Brand Citizenship Behavior in Presence of Brand Commitment and Job Satisfaction of Employees in Banking Industry. *International Business Management*, 10(18), 4200–4208.

Gibson, D. E., Berry, A. B., & Lewis, K. R. (2000). Wisdom in Action: The Role of Wisdom in Workplace Performance. *The Journal of Applied Psychology*, 85(2), 275–284.

Gilley, J. W., Gilley, A., & McMillan, H. S. (2010). Organizational Learning, Performance, and Change: How Managers Use Learning to Improve Performance. *International Journal of Business and Management*, 5(1), 63–70.

Gip, H., The Khoa, D., Guchait, P., Fernando Garcia, R. L., & Pasamehmetoglu, A. (2022). Employee mindfulness and creativity: When emotions and national culture matter. *Service Industries Journal*, 42(5-6), 383–411. DOI: 10.1080/02642069.2022.2037570

Girdhar, R., & Punia, B. K. (2023). Inclusion, Organisational identification, job satisfaction and task performance: Exploration and Outcome, *Empirical. Economics Letters*, 22(1), 1–18.

Giuseppe & Pirchio. (2019), Positive environments for children and adults. .DOI: 10.1007/978-3-662-58409-5_11

Glomb, T. M., Duffy, M. K., Bono, J. E., & Yang, T. (2011). Mindfulness at Work. In Joshi, A., Liao, H., & Martocchio, J. J. (Eds.), *Research in Personnel and Human Resources Management* (Vol. 30, pp. 115–157). Emerald Group Publishing Limited. DOI: 10.1108/S0742-7301(2011)0000030005

Glomb, T. M., & Liao, H. (2003). Interpersonal aggression in the workplace: A review and proposed framework. *The Academy of Management Annals*, 2(1), 225–266. DOI: 10.5465/19416520328158712

Glück, J., & Baltes, P. B. (2006). The two faces of wisdom: A framework for understanding the nature and development of wisdom. In Sternberg, R. J. (Ed.), *Handbook of wisdom: Theory, research, and applications* (pp. 215–236). Cambridge University Press.

Glück, J., & Bluck, S. (2011). Laypeople's conceptions of wisdom and its development: Cognitive and integrative views. *The Journals of Gerontology. Series B, Psychological Sciences and Social Sciences*, 66(3), 321–324. DOI: 10.1093/geronb/gbr011 PMID: 21398417

Glück, J., & Bluck, S. (2013). The MORE life experience model: A theory of the development of personal wisdom. In Ferrari, M., & Weststrate, N. M. (Eds.), *The scientific study of personal wisdom* (pp. 75–97). Springer.

Glück, J., König, S., Naschenweng, K., Redzanowski, U., Dorner, L., Straßer, I., & Wiedermann, W. (2013). How to measure wisdom: Content, reliability, and validity of five measures. *Frontiers in Psychology*, 4, 405. DOI: 10.3389/fpsyg.2013.00405 PMID: 23874310

Glück, J., & Weststrate, N. M. (2022). The Wisdom Researchers and The Elephant: An Integrative Model of wise Behavior. *Personality and Social Psychology Review*, 26(4), 342–374. DOI: 10.1177/10888683221094650 PMID: 35652684

Godrej. (n.d.). *Our Goals*. Godrej. Retrieved September 18, 2024 from https://www.godrejenterprises.com/good-and-green

Goleman, D. (2006). *Emotional Intelligence: Why It Can Matter More Than IQ*. Bantam Books.

Goleman, D. (2020). *Emotional intelligence: Why it can matter more than IQ*. Bloomsbury Publishing.

Gonzalez-Mulé, E., & Cockburn, B. S. (2017). Worked to death: The relationships of job demands and job control with mortality. *Personnel Psychology*, 70(1), 73–112. DOI: 10.1111/peps.12206

Good, D. J., Lyddy, C. J., Glomb, T. M., Bono, J. E., Brown, K. W., Duffy, M. K., Baer, R. A., Brewer, J. A., & Lazar, S. W. (2016). Contemplating mindfulness at work: An integrative review. In *Journal of Management* (Vol. 42, Issue 1, pp. 114–142). Sage Publications. DOI: 10.1177/0149206315617003

Google. (n.d.). Our mission. Retrieved from https://about.google/our-story/

Gottlieb, L. N., Gottlieb, B., & Bitzas, V. (2021). Creating Empowering Conditions for Nurses with Workplace Autonomy and Agency: How Healthcare Leaders Could Be Guided by Strengths-Based Nursing and Healthcare Leadership (SBNH-L). *Journal of Healthcare Leadership*, 13, 169–181. DOI: 10.2147/JHL.S221141 PMID: 34349581

Gouda, S., Luong, M. T., Schmidt, S., & Bauer, J. (2016). Students and teachers benefit from mindfulness-based stress reduction in a school-embedded pilot study. *Frontiers in Psychology*, 7, 590. DOI: 10.3389/fpsyg.2016.00590 PMID: 27199825

Grant, A. M. (2012). *Give and take: A revolutionary approach to success*. Viking.

Grant, A. M. (2012). Leading with meaning: Beneficiary contact, prosocial impact, and the performance effects of transformational leadership. *Academy of Management Journal*, 55(2), 458–476. DOI: 10.5465/amj.2010.0588

Grant, A. M., Christianson, M. K., & Price, R. H. (2007). Happiness, health, or relationships? Managerial practices and employee well-being tradeoffs. *The Academy of Management Perspectives*, 21(3), 51–63. DOI: 10.5465/amp.2007.26421238

Grant, A., O'Connor, S., & Studholme, I. (2019). Towards a Positive Psychology of Buildings and Workplace Community:the Positive Built Workplace Environment. *International Journal of Applied Positive Psychology*, 4(1-2), 67–89. DOI: 10.1007/s41042-019-00019-2

Grant, P., & McGhee, P. (2021). Hedonic versus (true) eudaimonic well-being in organizations. In Dhiman, S. (Ed.), *The Palgrave handbook of workplace well-being* (pp. 925–943). Palgrave Macmillan/Springer Nature., DOI: 10.1007/978-3-030-30025-8_37

Greco, L. M., Porck, J. P., Walter, S. L., Scrimpshire, A. J., & Zabinski, A. M. (2022). A meta-analytic review of identification at work: Relative contribution of team, organizational, and professional identification. *The Journal of Applied Psychology*, 107(5), 795–830. DOI: 10.1037/apl0000941 PMID: 34591563

Green, C., & Carter, J. (2015). Professional development opportunities and employee happiness. *The Career Development Quarterly*, 63(4), 340–354. DOI: 10.1002/cdq.12067

Greenhaus, J. H., & Allen, T. D. (2011). Work–family balance: A review and extension of the literature.

Grossmann, I., Na, J., Varnum, M. E., Park, D. C., Kitayama, S., & Nisbett, R. E. (2010). Reasoning about social conflicts improves into old age. *Proceedings of the National Academy of Sciences of the United States of America*, 107(16), 7246–7250. DOI: 10.1073/pnas.1001715107 PMID: 20368436

Growth Tactics. (2023). Benefits of transparent communication. Retrieved from https://www.growthtactics.net/benefits-of-transparent-communication/

Growth Tactics. (2024). 50 transformative team building games for students. Retrieved from https://www.growthtactics.net/team-building-games-for-students/

Grygorenko, Z., & Naydonova, G. (2023). The Concept Of "Resilience": History Of Formation And Approaches To Definition. *Public Administration And Law Review*, 76–88. DOI: 10.36690/2674-5216-2023-2-76-88

Grzywacz, J. G., & Marks, N. F. (2000). Reconceptualizing the work–family interface: An ecological perspective on the correlates of positive and negative spillover between work and family. *Journal of Occupational Health Psychology*, 5(1), 111–126. DOI: 10.1037/1076-8998.5.1.111 PMID: 10658890

Gu, M., Tan, C. M., Ho, Y. S., & Liu, L. (2022, August). Work–family conflict and happiness: the moderating role of national culture. In *Evidence-based HRM: a Global Forum for Empirical Scholarship*. Emerald Publishing Limited. DOI: 10.1108/EBHRM-01-2021-0001

Gupta, A., & Jain, R. (2019). Work-life balance and job stress among faculty members in higher education institutions. *Journal of Management Development*, 38(1), 70–80. DOI: 10.1108/JMD-05-2018-0184

Gupta, M., Shaheen, M., & Reddy, P. K. (2017). Impact of psychological capital on organizational citizenship behavior: Mediation by work engagement. *Journal of Management Development*, 36(7), 973–983. DOI: 10.1108/JMD-06-2016-0084

Gupta, N., & Sharma, V. (2018). The comparative analysis of employee engagement measures: A theoretical perspective. *International Journal of Management Practice*, 11(1), 42–68. DOI: 10.1504/IJMP.2018.088382

Gupta, R. (2023). Emotional intelligence for health professionals. *Journal of Internal Medicine and Health Affairs*, 2(3). Advance online publication. DOI: 10.58489/2836-2411/024

Gupta, S., Bhasin, J., & Mushtaq, S. (2021). Employer brand experience and organizational citizenship behavior: Mediating role of employee engagement. *Asia-Pacific Journal of Business Administration*, 13(3), 357–382. DOI: 10.1108/APJBA-08-2020-0287

Guyo, S. K., & Kero, C. A. (2023). Mediation of Marketing Intermediaries and AI Adoption Between Livestock Products Marketing and Economic Status of Pastoralist in Ethiopia. *2023 International Conference on Communication, Security and Artificial Intelligence (ICCSAI)*, 311-316. DOI: 10.1109/ICCSAI59793.2023.10421261

Gu, Z., Chupradit, S., Ku, K., Nassani, A., & Haffar, M. (2022). Impact of Employees' Workplace Environment on Employees' Performance: A Multi-Mediation Model. *Frontiers in Public Health*, 10, 890400. Advance online publication. DOI: 10.3389/fpubh.2022.890400 PMID: 35646787

Hackman, J. R., & Oldham, G. R. (1976). Motivation through the design of work: Test of a theory. *Organizational Behavior and Human Performance*, 16(2), 250–279. DOI: 10.1016/0030-5073(76)90016-7

Haddon, J. (2013). The Secret to Life Balance and Happiness. *Management Services*, 57(1), 30.

Haidt, J. (2006). *The happiness hypothesis: Finding modern truth in ancient wisdom*. Basic Books.

Hair, J. F. M., H. G. T., Ringle, C. M., & Sarstedt, M. (2017). A primer on partial least squares structural equation modeling (PLS-SEM) (2nd ed.). Sage Publications.

Hair, J. F.Jr, Howard, M. C., & Nitzl, C. (2020). Assessing measurement model quality in PLS-SEM using confirmatory composite analysis. *Journal of Business Research*, 109, 101–110. DOI: 10.1016/j.jbusres.2019.11.069

Hair, J. F., Risher, J. J., Sarstedt, M., & Ringle, C. M. (2019). When to use and how to report the results of PLS-SEM. *European Business Review*, 31(1), 2–24. DOI: 10.1108/EBR-11-2018-0203

Hair, J., Hult, G., Ringle, C., & Sarstedt, M. (2017). *A Primer on Partial Least Squares Structural Equations Modeling (PLS-SEM)* (2nd ed.). SAGE.

Hajibabaee, F., Farahani, M., Ameri, Z., Salehi, T., & Hosseini, F. (2018). The relationship between empathy and emotional intelligence among Iranian nursing students. *International Journal of Medical Education*, 9, 239.243. DOI: 10.5116/ijme.5b83.e2a5

Halpern, D. F. (2014). *Thought and Knowledge: An Introduction to Critical Thinking*. Psychology Press.

Hameed, I., Ijaz, M. U., & Sabharwal, M. (2022). The impact of human resources environment and organizational identification on employees' psychological well-being. *Public Personnel Management*, 51(1), 71–96. DOI: 10.1177/00910260211001397

Hammett, R. D., Arenas, F., & Scherer, J. (2018). Facilitating full.range leadership with emotional intelligence in the USAF Squadron Officer College. *The International Journal of Transformative Emotional Intelligence*, 5.

Hargadon, A., & Sutton, R. I. (2000). Building an innovation factory. *Harvard Business Review*, 78(3), 157–166. PMID: 11183977

Hargreaves, A., & Fullan, M. (2012). *Professional capital: Transforming teaching in every school. Teachers College Press.*

Harris, G. E., & Cameron, J. E. (2005). Multiple Dimensions of Organizational Identification and Commitment as Predictors of Turnover Intentions and Psychological Well-Being. *Canadian Journal of Behavioural Science/Revue canadienne des sciences du comportement, 37*(3), 159-169.

Harris, B., & Davis, E. (2014). Effectiveness of employee feedback systems on workplace happiness. *International Journal of Human Resource Management*, 25(12), 1746–1764. DOI: 10.1080/09585192.2013.866859

Harris, J., & Clark, D. (2023). Organizational transparency and its impact on employee happiness. *Journal of Business Ethics*, 183(2), 301–318. DOI: 10.1007/s10551-022-05223-7

Harrison, S. H., & Dossinger, K. (2017). Curiosity in the workplace: A model of curiosity and its role in work outcomes. *Journal of Organizational Behavior*, 38(1), 100–118.

Harter, J. K., Schmidt, F. L., & Hayes, T. L. (2002). Business-unit-level relationship between employee satisfaction, employee engagement, and business outcomes: A meta-analysis. *The Journal of Applied Psychology*, 87(2), 268–279. DOI: 10.1037/0021-9010.87.2.268 PMID: 12002955

Hartmann, S., Backmann, J., Newman, A., Brykman, K. M., & Pidduck, R. J. (2022). Psychological resilience of entrepreneurs: A review and agenda for future research. *Journal of Small Business Management*, 60(5), 1041–1079. DOI: 10.1080/00472778.2021.2024216

Harvard Business Review. (2021). The secret of adaptable organizations is trust. Retrieved from https://hbr.org/2021/03/the-secret-of-adaptable-organizations-is-trust

Harvard Business School. (2023). 5 strategies for conflict resolution in the workplace. Retrieved from https://online.hbs.edu/blog/post/strategies-for-conflict-resolution-in-the-workplace

Hasan, R. (2023). Work environment and job satisfaction among nurses in Jordan: A systematic literature review. *British Journal of Health Care Management*, 29(4), 1–7. Advance online publication. DOI: 10.12968/bjhc.2021.0128

Hasni, M. J. S., Salo, J., Naeem, H., & Abbasi, K. S. (2018). Impact of internal branding on customer-based brand equity with mediating effect of organizational loyalty: An empirical evidence from retail sector. *International Journal of Retail & Distribution Management*, 46(11/12), 1056–1076. DOI: 10.1108/IJRDM-07-2017-0148

Hattie, J., & Timperley, H. (2007). The power of feedback. *Review of Educational Research*, 77(1), 81–112. DOI: 10.3102/003465430298487

Hawkins, K. (2017). Mindful teacher, mindful school: Improving wellbeing in teaching and learning.

Hays, J. M. (2007). Dynamics of organisational wisdom. *Business Renaissance Quarterly*, 2(4), 77–122.

Heart It Out. (n.d.). Online counselling. Retrieved from https://heartitout.in/

Heckman, J. J., & Kautz, T. (2012). Hard evidence on soft skills. *Labour Economics*, 19(4), 451–464. DOI: 10.1016/j.labeco.2012.05.014 PMID: 23559694

Hegazy, A., Ibrahim, M., Shokry, W., & Shrief, H. (2021). *Work Environment Factors in Nursing Practice*. Menoufia Nursing Journal. DOI: 10.21608/menj.2021.206247

Helliwell, J. F., & Wang, S. (2017). Happiness and life satisfaction in the United States: The role of social capital. World Happiness Report, 2017, 36-49. https://worldhappiness.report

Helmi. (2023). Work Environment, Work Conflict, and Employee Performance: A Literature Review. International Journal of Advanced Multidisciplinary, DOI: 10.38035/ijam.v1i4.146

Henderson, R., & Steen, E. V. D. (2015). Why do firms have "purpose"? The firm's role as a carrier of identity and reputation. *The American Economic Review*, 105(5), 326–330. DOI: 10.1257/aer.p20151072

Hennink, M. M. (2013). *Focus group discussions*. Oxford University Press.

Henseler, J., Ringle, C. M., & Sarstedt, M. (2015). A new criterion for assessing discriminant validity in variance-based structural equation modeling. *Journal of the Academy of Marketing Science*, 43(1), 115–135. DOI: 10.1007/s11747-014-0403-8

Henseler, J., & Sarstedt, M. (2013). Goodness-of-fit indices for partial least squares path modeling. *Computational Statistics*, 28(2), 565–580. DOI: 10.1007/s00180-012-0317-1

Hermes, M., Hagemann, D., Naumann, E., & Walter, C. (2011). Extraversion and its positive emotional core—Further evidence from neuroscience. *Emotion (Washington, D.C.)*, 11(2), 367–378. DOI: 10.1037/a0021550 PMID: 21500905

Herodotou, C., Sharples, M., Gaved, M., Kukulska-Hulme, A., Rienties, B., Scanlon, E., & Whitelock, D. (2019, October). Innovative pedagogies of the future: An evidence-based selection. [). Frontiers Media SA.]. *Frontiers in Education*, 4, 113. DOI: 10.3389/feduc.2019.00113

He, Z., Huang, H., Choi, H., & Bilgihan, A. (2022). Building organizational resilience with digital transformation. *Journal of Service Management*, 34(1), 147–171. DOI: 10.1108/JOSM-06-2021-0216

Hill, E. J., Hawkins, A. J., Ferris, M., & Weitzman, M. (2001). Finding an extra day a week: The positive influence of perceived job flexibility on work and family life balance. *Family Relations*, 50(1), 49–58. DOI: 10.1111/j.1741-3729.2001.00049.x

Hofstede, G. (1984). The cultural relativity of the quality-of-life concept. *Academy of Management Review*, 9(3), 389–398. DOI: 10.2307/258280

Howitt, D. (2019). *Introduction to qualitative research methods in psychology*. pearson UK.

Hsieh, T. (2010). *Delivering happiness: A path to profits, passion, and purpose*.

Hsu, T., Rojas, C., & Luthra, M. (2018). The social media influence on happiness: A study on the effect of online social interactions. *Computers in Human Behavior*, 85, 163–171. DOI: 10.1016/j.chb.2018.03.024

Huang, H., Liu, L., Yang, S., Cui, X., Zhang, J., & Wu, H. (2019). Effects of job conditions, occupational stress, and emotional intelligence on chronic fatigue among Chinese nurses: a cross.sectional study;. *Psychology Research and Behavior Management*, 12, 351.360. DOI: 10.2147/PRBM.S207283

Huang, C. C., Chen, Y., Cheung, S., Hu, H., & Wang, E. (2021). Adverse childhood experiences, mindfulness and happiness in Chinese college students during the COVID-19 pandemic. *Child & Family Social Work*, 26(4), 677–686. DOI: 10.1111/cfs.12848 PMID: 34220280

Huang, Q. (2021). Can Curious Employees be More Innovative? Exploring the Mechanism of Intrinsic Motivation and Job Autonomy. *Psychology (Irvine, Calif.)*, 12(03), 425–440. DOI: 10.4236/psych.2021.123027

HubSpot. (2022). 16 employee feedback tools to track your team's engagement. Retrieved from https://blog.hubspot.com/agency/employee-feedback-engagement-tools

HubSpot. (2023). Open communication: Tips and examples for the workplace. Retrieved from https://blog.hubspot.com/sales/open-communication

Hu, L. T., & Bentler, P. M. (1998). Fit indices in covariance structure modeling: Sensitivity to underparameterized model misspecification. *Psychological Methods*, 3(4), 424–453. DOI: 10.1037/1082-989X.3.4.424

Hundie, Z. A., & Habtewold, E. M. (2024). The Effect of Transformational, Transactional, and Laissez-Faire Leadership Styles on Employees' Level of Performance: The Case of Hospital in Oromia Region, Ethiopia. *Journal of Healthcare Leadership*, 16, 67–82. DOI: 10.2147/JHL.S450077 PMID: 38380132

Huta, V., & Waterman, A. S. (2014). Eudaimonia and its distinction from hedonia: Developing a classification and terminology for understanding conceptual and operational definitions. *Journal of Happiness Studies*, 15(6), 1425–1456. DOI: 10.1007/s10902-013-9485-0

Hutchison, J. (2020). Transparent communication: Toward a respectful workplace. Retrieved from https://workplace.msu.edu/transparent-communication/

IBM. (n.d.). Diversity and inclusion. Retrieved from https://www.ibm.com/employment/inclusion/

Iheduru.Anderson, K., & Waite, R. (2022). Illuminating antiracist pedagogy in nursing education. *Nursing Inquiry*, 29(4), e12494. Advance online publication. DOI: 10.1111/nin.12494 PMID: 35543498

Indeed. (2024). 17 benefits of team building for your organization. Retrieved from https://www.indeed.com/career-advice/career-development/benefits-of-team-building

Indeed. (2024). Adaptability in the workplace: Benefits and importance. Retrieved from https://www.indeed.com/career-advice/career-development/adaptability-in-the-workplace

Indeed. (2024). Types of assessments for employees (with steps and tips). Retrieved from https://www.indeed.com/career-advice/career-development/assessment-for-employees

Indeed. (2024). What is open communication? (With benefits and importance). Retrieved from https://www.indeed.com/career-advice/career-development/what-is-open-communication

Infosys Employee Wellness. (n.d.). *Driving the Culture of Wellness.* Infosys Limited. Retrieved September 18, 2024, from https://www.infosys.com/about/esg/social/employee-wellbeing/driving-culture-wellness.html

Insight Global. (2024). Transparency in the workplace: Everything you need to know. Retrieved from https://insightglobal.com/blog/transparency-in-the-workplace/

Intezari, A., & Pauleen, D. J. (2014). Management wisdom in perspective: Are you virtuous enough to succeed in volatile times? *Journal of Business Ethics*, 120(3), 393–404. DOI: 10.1007/s10551-013-1666-6

Ipseeta. (2014). Work-Life Balance @ Working Couples - A Review of Literature. Asian Journal of Research in Social Sciences and Humanities,

Isaacowitz, D. M., Vaillant, G. E., & Seligman, M. E. (2003). Strengths and satisfaction across the adult lifespan. *International Journal of Aging & Human Development*, 57(2), 181–201. DOI: 10.2190/61EJ-LDYR-Q55N-UT6E PMID: 15151189

Isaacs, W. (1999). *Dialogue and the art of thinking together: A pioneering approach to communicating in business and in life*. Currency.

Jabo, B. B., & Kant, S. (2024). Impact of Technical CRM on Ethiopia Bank Human-Computer Interface and Competitive Advantage as Mediators of Performance. *2024 IEEE International Conference on Computing, Power and Communication Technologies (IC2PCT)*, 679-682. DOI: 10.1109/IC2PCT60090.2024.10486237

Jain, H. (n.d.). *A complete guide on Corporate Yoga Programs in India*. MantraCare. Retrieved September 19, 2024, from https://mantracare.org/employee-wellness/corporate-yoga/corporate-yoga-india/

Jain, S., & Nair, S. K. (2017). Work support and family support as predictors of work-to-family enrichment and family-to-work enrichment. *Global Business Review*, 18(5), 1307–1324. DOI: 10.1177/0972150917710332

James, G., Witten, D., Hastie, T., & Tibshirani, R. (2013). *An introduction to statistical learning: With applications in R*. Springer. DOI: 10.1007/978-1-4614-7138-7

Jawabri, A., Alarmoti, A., & Rehman, W. (2022). Impact of Remote Working Environment on Employee Motivation, Engagement, and Job Satisfaction: A Study of Service Sector from UAE. *Business and Economic Review*, 12(1), 82. Advance online publication. DOI: 10.5296/ber.v12i1.19679

Jennings, P., Lantieri, L., & Roeser, R. W. (2012). Supporting educational goals through cultivating mindfulness. *Handbook of prosocial education, 1*, 371.

Jeong, J. G., Kang, S. W., & Choi, S. B. (2020). Employees' weekend activities and psychological well-being via job stress: A moderated mediation role of recovery experience. *International Journal of Environmental Research and Public Health*, 17(5), 1642. DOI: 10.3390/ijerph17051642 PMID: 32138361

Jeong, J., Kang, S., & Choi, S. (2022). A multilevel study of the relationship between csr promotion climate and happiness at work via organizational identification: Moderation effect of leader–followers value congruence. *International Journal of Environmental Research and Public Health*, 19(11), 6637. DOI: 10.3390/ijerph19116637 PMID: 35682221

Jeste, D. V., & Vahia, I. V. (2008). Comparison of the conceptualization of wisdom in ancient Indian literature with modern views: Focus on the Bhagavad Gita. *Psychiatry*, 71(3), 197–209. DOI: 10.1521/psyc.2008.71.3.197 PMID: 18834271

Jobin, A., Ienca, M., & Vayena, E. (2019). The global landscape of AI ethics guidelines. *Nature Machine Intelligence*, 1(9), 389–399. DOI: 10.1038/s42256-019-0088-2

Johnson, P., & White, T. (2018). Workplace wellness programs and employee well-being. *Journal of Workplace Behavioral Health*, 33(1), 20–36. DOI: 10.1080/15555240.2018.1426701

Jonathan, D., & Dewi, Y. (2022). *Work From Home: The Influence of Work Motivation and Work Environment on Employee Work Spirit.* International Journal of Social Science and Business. DOI: 10.23887/ijssb.v7i1.52517

Joshi, R., & Kumar, V. (2020). Evaluating faculty performance in higher education: A study of stressors and their implications. *International Journal of Educational Management*, 34(5), 1237–1249. DOI: 10.1108/IJEM-10-2019-0378

Jubilee Centre for Character and Virtues. (2017). *A framework for character education in schools.* University of Birmingham.

Jubilee Centre for Character and Virtues. (2022). *A framework for character education in universities.* University of Birmingham.

Judge, T. A., & Bono, J. E. (2001). Relationship of core self-evaluations traits—self-esteem, generalised self-efficacy, locus of control, and emotional stability—with job satisfaction and job performance: A meta-analysis. *The Journal of Applied Psychology*, 86(1), 80–92. DOI: 10.1037/0021-9010.86.1.80 PMID: 11302235

Jufrizen, J., Khair, H., & Loviky, F. B. (2023). Work Engagement and Emotional Intelligence on Personnel Performance: The Mediating Role of Job Satisfaction. *International Journal of Business Economics (IJBE), 5*(1), 77.91. DOI: 10.30596/ijbe.v5i1.16499

Jung, H., & Kang, S. (2020). Collective efficacy and communication ability according to emotional intelligence in nursing students. *Indian Journal of Public Health Research & Development*. Advance online publication. DOI: 10.37506/ijphrd.v11i12.13232

Kabat-Zinn, J. (1990). *Full Catastrophe Living: Using the Wisdom of Your Body and Mind to Face Stress, Pain, and Illness*. Dell Publishing.

Kabat-Zinn, J. (2003). Mindfulness-based interventions in context: Past, present, and future. *Clinical Psychology : a Publication of the Division of Clinical Psychology of the American Psychological Association*, 10(2), 144–156. DOI: 10.1093/clipsy.bpg016

Kabat-Zinn, J. (2003). Mindfulness-based stress reduction (MBSR). *Constructivism in the Human Sciences*, 8(2), 73.

Kahneman, D., & Deaton, A. (2015). High income improves evaluation of life but not emotional well-being. *Proceedings of the National Academy of Sciences of the United States of America*, 107(38), 16489–16493. DOI: 10.1073/pnas.1011492107 PMID: 20823223

Kahn, W. A. (1990). Psychological conditions of personal engagement and disengagement at work. *Academy of Management Journal*, 33(4), 692–724. DOI: 10.2307/256287

Kahn, W. A. (2010). The Human Side of Enterprise Revisited: A 40-Year Journey. *Journal of Management*, 36(5), 1405–1431.

Kalev, A., Dobbin, F., & Kelly, E. (2006). Best practices or best guesses? Assessing the efficacy of corporate affirmative action and diversity policies. *American Sociological Review*, 71(4), 589–617. DOI: 10.1177/000312240607100404

Kalliath, T., & Brough, P. (2008). Work–life balance: A review of the meaning of the balance construct. *Journal of Management & Organization*, 14(3), 323–327. DOI: 10.5172/jmo.837.14.3.323

Kang, H. J. A., Kim, W. G., Choi, H. M., & Li, Y. (2020). How to fuel employees' prosocial behavior in the hotel service encounter. *International Journal of Hospitality Management*, 84, 102333. DOI: 10.1016/j.ijhm.2019.102333

Kant, S., & Adula, M. (2024). Human-Machine Interaction in the Metaverse in the Context of Ethiopia. In *Impact and Potential of Machine Learning in the Metaverse* (pp. 196–212). IGI Global. DOI: 10.4018/979-8-3693-5762-0.ch008

Kaplan, A., & Haenlein, M. (2020). Rulers of the world, unite! The challenges and opportunities of artificial intelligence. *Business Horizons*, 63(1), 37–50. DOI: 10.1016/j.bushor.2019.09.003

Kar, S., Kar, A., & Gupta, M. (2021). Industrial Internet of Things and Emerging Digital Technologies–Modeling Professionals' Learning Behavior. *IEEE Access : Practical Innovations, Open Solutions*, 9, 30017–30034. DOI: 10.1109/ACCESS.2021.3059407

Kashdan, T. B., & Fincham, F. D. (2004). Facilitating curiosity: A social and self-regulatory perspective for scientifically based interventions. Positive Psychology in Practice, 482-503.

Kashdan, T. B., Biswas-Diener, R., & King, L. A. (2008). Reconsidering happiness: The costs of distinguishing between hedonics and eudaimonia. *The Journal of Positive Psychology*, 3(4), 219–233. DOI: 10.1080/17439760802303044

Kashdan, T. B., Rose, P., & Fincham, F. D. (2004). Curiosity and exploration: Facilitating positive subjective experiences and personal growth opportunities. *Journal of Personality Assessment*, 82(3), 291–305. DOI: 10.1207/s15327752jpa8203_05 PMID: 15151805

Kashdan, T. B., Sherman, R. A., Yarbro, J., & Funder, D. C. (2013). On the uniqueness of joy: Examining the importance of distinguishing between joy and happiness. *The Journal of Positive Psychology*, 8(3), 221–232.

Kashdan, T. B., & Steger, M. F. (2007). Curiosity and pathways to well-being and meaning in life: Traits, states, and everyday behaviors. *Motivation and Emotion*, 31(3), 159–173. DOI: 10.1007/s11031-007-9068-7

Katz, D., & Kahn, R. L. (1978). *The social psychology of organizations* (Vol. 2). Wiley.

Katz, J. S., & Martin, B. R. (1997). What is research collaboration? *Research Policy*, 26(1), 1–18. DOI: 10.1016/S0048-7333(96)00917-1

Kaur, P., Malhotra, K., & Sharma, S. K. (2020). Moderation-mediation framework connecting internal branding, affective commitment, employee engagement and job satisfaction: An empirical study of BPO employees in Indian context. *Asia-Pacific Journal of Business Administration*, 12(3/4), 327–348. DOI: 10.1108/APJBA-10-2019-0217

Kebede, A. G., Terefe, S. D., & Ijigu, A. W. (2024). Ambidextrous leadership and academic staff innovative behavior at Debre Berhan University, Ethiopia: The mediating role of workplace happiness. *Cogent Business & Management*, 11(1), 2307564. DOI: 10.1080/23311975.2024.2307564

Kelloway, E. K., & Barling, J. (2010). Leadership Development as an Intervention in Occupational Health Psychology. *Work and Stress*, 24(3), 232–244. DOI: 10.1080/02678373.2010.518441

Keng, S.-L., Smoski, M. J., & Robins, C. J. (2011). Effects of mindfulness on psychological health: A review of empirical studies. *Clinical Psychology Review*, 31(6), 1041–1056. DOI: 10.1016/j.cpr.2011.04.006 PMID: 21802619

Kenrick, D. T., Griskevicius, V., Neuberg, S. L., & Schaller, M. (2010). Renovating the pyramid of needs: Contemporary extensions built upon ancient foundations. *Perspectives on Psychological Science*, 5(3), 292–314. DOI: 10.1177/1745691610369469 PMID: 21874133

Kere, Z. A. (2024). The Influence of Age on Emotional Intelligence Among NGO Leaders in Addis Ababa, Ethiopia. *JIM: Jurnal Ilmiah Mahasiswa Pendidikan Sejarah*, 9(1), 336–343.

Kernaghan, K. (2003). Integrating values into public service: The role of leadership. *Canadian Public Administration*, 46(4), 517–533. DOI: 10.1111/j.1754-7121.2003.tb01020.x

Kessler, E. H., & Bailey, J. R. (Eds.). (2007). *Handbook of organizational and managerial wisdom*. Sage Publications. DOI: 10.4135/9781412982726

Kets de Vries, M. F. R. (2006). The leadership mystique: Leading behavior in the human enterprise. Financial Times Prentice Hall.

Keye, M. D., & Pidgeon, A. M. (2013). Investigation of the relationship between resilience, mindfulness, and academic self-efficacy. *Open Journal of Social Sciences*, 1(6), 1–4. DOI: 10.4236/jss.2013.16001

Keyes, C. L., & Haidt, J. (2003). *Flourishing: Positive psychology and the life well-lived*. American Psychological Association. DOI: 10.1037/10594-000

Keyes, C. M., Kendler, K. S., Myers, J. M., & Martin, C. C. (2015). The genetic overlap and distinctiveness of flourishing and the big five personality traits. *Journal of Happiness Studies*, 16(3), 655–668. DOI: 10.1007/s10902-014-9527-2

Khan, A., Masrek, M. N., & Nadzar, F. M. (2017). Emotional intelligence and job satisfaction of academic librarians: An assessment of the relationship. *Journal of Librarianship and Information Science*, 49(2), 199–210. Advance online publication. DOI: 10.1177/0961000616650733

Khan, H., Ozkan, K. S. L., Deligonul, S., & Cavusgil, E. (2024). Redefining the organizational resilience construct using a frame based methodology: A new perspective from the ecology based approach. *Journal of Business Research*, 172, 114397. DOI: 10.1016/j.jbusres.2023.114397

Khan, T., & Thomas, S. (2022). Promoting Positive Education through Constructivist Digital Learning Heutagogy: An Intervention Outcome. *Journal of Learning for Development*, 9(2), 305–316. Advance online publication. DOI: 10.56059/jl4d.v9i2.646

Khoury, B., Lecomte, T., Fortin, G., Masse, M., Therien, P., Bouchard, V., Chapleau, M.-A., Paquin, K., & Hofmann, S. G. (2013). Mindfulness-based therapy: A comprehensive meta-analysis. *Clinical Psychology Review*, 33(6), 763–771. DOI: 10.1016/j.cpr.2013.05.005 PMID: 23796855

Kiishi, V. (2024). The role of emotional intelligence in effective leadership and its impact on team performance: a study of the university of Ibadan, Nigeria. *International Journal of Business and Management Review*, 12(2), 75.138. DOI: 10.37745/ijbmr.2013/vol12n275138

Kim, W. S. (2021). The Effect of Positive Psychological Art Program on Self-Efficiency and Job Satisfaction of Workers with Developmental Disabilities : Based on PERMA Model. *Culture and Convergence*, 43(1), 957–978. Advance online publication. DOI: 10.33645/cnc.2021.01.43.1.957

Kim, Y. (2021). Building organizational resilience through strategic internal communication and organization-employee relationships. *Journal of Applied Communication Research*, 49(5), 589–608. Advance online publication. DOI: 10.1080/00909882.2021.1910856

Kim, Y., & Anderson, M. (2017). The role of emotional intelligence in workplace happiness. *Journal of Organizational Behavior*, 38(4), 560–578. DOI: 10.1002/job.2144

King, L. A. (2001). The health benefits of writing about life goals.

Kiziloğlu, E., & Şahin, M. (2022). *The mediating role of burnout in the effect of emotional intelligence on job satisfaction: an application on coachs*. Equinox Journal of Economics Business and Political Studies. DOI: 10.48064/equinox.1060496

Kjell, O. N. E., Ali, A. N., Sverker, S., Trevor, A., & Danilo, G. (2013). Iranian and Swedish adolescents: Differences in personality traits and well-being. *PeerJ*, 1(1), 197. DOI: 10.7717/peerj.197 PMID: 24255812

Klajkó, D., Restás, P., Szabó, Z. P., & Czibor, A. (2019). The Effect of Organizational Culture on Employee Well-Being: Work- Related Stress, Employee. . . ResearchGate. https://www.researchgate.net/publication/339103130_The_Effect_of_Organizational_Culture_on_Employee_Well-Being_Work-_Related_Stress_Employee_Identification_Turnover_Intention

Kluger, A. N., & DeNisi, A. (1996). The effects of feedback interventions on performance: A historical review, a meta-analysis, and a preliminary feedback intervention theory. *Psychological Bulletin*, 119(2), 254–284. DOI: 10.1037/0033-2909.119.2.254

Kock, N. (2015). Common method bias in PLS-SEM. *International Journal of e-Collaboration*, 11(4), 1–10. DOI: 10.4018/ijec.2015100101

Kock, N., & Lynn, G. (2012). Lateral collinearity and misleading results in variance-based SEM: An illustration and recommendations. *Journal of the Association for Information Systems*, 13(7), 546–580. DOI: 10.17705/1jais.00302

Kolb, D. A. (1984). *Experiential learning: Experience as the source of learning and development*. Prentice-Hall.

Kolla, N., Prasad, R. V., & Geetha, K. V. (2019). Impact of Internal Branding on Employees' Job Satisfaction, Brand Commitment and Brand Citizenship Behaviour. *International Journal on Emerging Technologies*, 10(2), 435–439.

Kopelman, R., Protter, D. J., Thompson, C. A., & Jahn, E. W. (2006). A multilevel examination of work-Life practices: Is more always better? *Journal of Managerial Issues*, 18(2), 232–225.

Kossek, E. E., & Ozeki, C. (1998). Work-family conflict, policies, and the job-life satisfaction relationship: A review and directions for organizational behavior-human resources research. *The Journal of Applied Psychology*, 83(2), 139–149. DOI: 10.1037/0021-9010.83.2.139

Koutsioumpa, E. (2023). Development of emotional intelligence and leadership aspects applied in health professionals. a scoping review. *Technium Biochemmed*, 6, 22.36. DOI: 10.47577/biochemmed.v6i.9533

Kouzes, J. M., & Posner, B. Z. (2023). *The leadership challenge: How to make extraordinary things happen in organizations*. John Wiley & Sons.

KPMG. (2023, June 7). *KPMG Powered Enterprise Resilience—KPMG Global*. KPMG. https://kpmg.com/xx/en/home/insights/2021/02/powered-enterprise-resilience.html

Kristjánsson, K. (2020). Aristotelian character friendship as a 'method'of moral education. *Studies in Philosophy and Education*, 39(4), 349–364. DOI: 10.1007/s11217-020-09717-w

Kross, E., & Grossmann, I. (2012). Boosting wisdom: Distance from the self-enhances wise reasoning, attitudes, and behavior.

Kumari, A., & Singh, R. (2021). Research productivity and academic stress: A study of Indian higher education institutions. *Journal of Educational Planning and Administration*, 35(1), 67–80. DOI: 10.1177/0971685821996104

Kumar, V., & Pansari, A. (2016). Competitive advantage through engagement. *JMR, Journal of Marketing Research*, 53(4), 497–514. DOI: 10.1509/jmr.15.0044

Kumprang, K., & Suriyankietkaew, S. (2024). Mechanisms of Organizational Mindfulness on Employee Well-Being and Engagement: A Multi-Level Analysis. *Administrative Sciences*, 14(6), 121. Advance online publication. DOI: 10.3390/admsci14060121

Kun, A., & Gadanecz, P. (2019). Workplace happiness, well-being and their relationship with psychological capital: A study of Hungarian Teachers. *Current Psychology (New Brunswick, N.J.)*, 41(1), 185–199. DOI: 10.1007/s12144-019-00550-0

Kunzmann, U., & Baltes, P. B. (2003). Wisdom-related knowledge: Affective, motivational, and interpersonal correlates. *Personality and Social Psychology Bulletin*, 29(9), 1104–1119. DOI: 10.1177/0146167203254506 PMID: 15189607

Kuo, H. T., & Chang, H. H. (2015). How workplace aggression affects employee creativity: The moderating role of psychological safety. *International Journal of Conflict Management*, 26(3), 296–314. DOI: 10.1108/IJCMA-12-2014-0111

Küpers, W., & Pauleen, D. J. (2013). *A handbook of practical wisdom: Leadership, organization and integral business practice*. Gower Publishing, Ltd.

Kushlev, K., & Dunn, E. W. (2015). The benefits of taking breaks: Mindfulness and well-being. *Journal of Happiness Studies*, 16(3), 579–593. DOI: 10.1007/s10902-014-9524-

Kusuma, A. (2021). *Literature Study: The Effect of the Working Environment on Employee Performance*. Business and Entrepreneurial Review. DOI: 10.25105/ber.v21i1.8239

Kütük, H., Hatun, O., Ekşi, H., & Ekşi, F. (2023). Investigation of the relationships between mindfulness, wisdom, resilience and life satisfaction in Turkish adult population. *Journal of Rational-Emotive & Cognitive-Behavior Therapy*, 41(3), 536–551. DOI: 10.1007/s10942-022-00468-w PMID: 35909985

KV, L., & Misra, S. R. (2015). Social Career Navigation-HCL Experience. *NHRD Network Journal, 8*(1), 71-77.

Kwabena, F., Asare, K., & Ackah, R. (2022). Does emotional intelligence influence an employee's job satisfaction? an empirical assessment. *Asian Journal of Social Sciences and Management Studies,* 9(4), 75.84. DOI: 10.20448/ajssms.v9i4.4349

Lakhiara, M. (2021). *A Analysis of the relationship between the working environment and employee performance in selected construction firms in Karachi city*. Neutron. DOI: 10.29138/neutron.v21i1.86

Laloux, F. (2014). *Reinventing organizations: A guide to creating organizations inspired by the next stage in human consciousness*. Nelson Parker.

Lamb, S., Wocial, L., & McCormick, J. (2017). *Ethics Rounds: A Model for Teaching and Evaluating Ethics in Healthcare*. Springer.

Lapiso, T. L. (2023). The Effect Of Servant Leadership Style On Bank Performance: Evidences From Berhan Bank Of Ethiopia. *International Journal of Research Science and Management*, 10(11), 9–18.

Lateef, A., & Mhlongo, E. (2019). Factors influencing nursing education and teaching methods in nursing institutions: A case study of southwest Nigeria. *Global Journal of Health Science*, 11(13), 13. DOI: 10.5539/gjhs.v11n13p13

Latifah, Y., &Muafi, M. (2021). Examining the effect of internal branding on employee performance: Job satisfaction and employee engagement as mediation variables. *International Journal of Business Ecosystem & Strategy, 3*(4), 1-12.

Layous, K. (2019). Promoting happiness in the workplace. *Creating Psychologically Healthy Workplaces*, 171-195.

Leaders.com. (2022). The value of open communication in the workplace. Retrieved from https://leaders.com/articles/company-culture/open-communication/

Lecina-Diaz, J., Martínez-Vilalta, J., Lloret, F., & Seidl, R. (2024). Resilience and vulnerability: Distinct concepts to address global change in forests. *Trends in Ecology & Evolution*, 39(8), 706–715. DOI: 10.1016/j.tree.2024.03.003 PMID: 38531712

Lee, C. & Wong, C. (2017). The effect of team emotional intelligence on team process and effectiveness. *Journal of Management & Organization*, 25(6), 844.859. DOI: 10.1017/jmo.2017.43

Lee, E. S., Park, T. Y., & Koo, B. (2015). Identifying organizational identification as a basis for attitudes and behaviors: A meta-analytic review. *Psychological Bulletin*, 141(5), 1049–1080. DOI: 10.1037/bul0000012 PMID: 25984729

Lee, J. S., Back, K. J., & Chan, E. S. (2015). Quality of work life and job satisfaction among frontline hotel employees: A self-determination and need satisfaction theory approach. *International Journal of Contemporary Hospitality Management*, 27(5), 768–789. DOI: 10.1108/IJCHM-11-2013-0530

Lee, K. (2008). Opportunities for green marketing: Young consumers. *Marketing Intelligence & Planning*, 26(6), 573–586. DOI: 10.1108/02634500810902839

Lee, M. D., MacDermid, S., Williams, M., Buck, M., & Leiba-O'Sullivan, S. (2002). Contextual factors in the success of reduced-load work arrangements among managers and professionals. *Human Resource Management*, 41(2), 209–223. DOI: 10.1002/hrm.10032

Lee, S., & Kim, H. (2022). Workplace design and its effects on employee well-being. *Journal of Environmental Psychology*, 80, 101722. DOI: 10.1016/j.jenvp.2022.101722

Lee, Y. K., Kim, S., & Kim, S. Y. (2014). The impact of internal branding on employee engagement and outcome variables in the hotel industry. *Asia Pacific Journal of Tourism Research*, 19(12), 1359–1380. DOI: 10.1080/10941665.2013.863790

Leggett, W. (2022). Can mindfulness really change the world? The political character of meditative practices. *Critical Policy Studies*, 16(3), 261–278. DOI: 10.1080/19460171.2021.1932541

Le, N. H., Mai, M. Q. T., & Le, K. G. (2024). Mindfulness, resilience and the happiness of service employees working from home. *Journal of Services Marketing*, 38(4), 460–473. DOI: 10.1108/JSM-03-2023-0109

Leuhery, F., Hasan, S. Z., Mustari, V. H., Widaningsih, R. R. A., & Lubis, F. M. (2024). The Evolution of Work-Life Balance: Redefining Priorities in Human Resource Management. *Dinasti International Journal of Economics. Finance and Accounting*, 5(1), 23–34.

Lewis, M., & Thompson, H. (2020). Social connections at work and employee happiness. *Journal of Social and Personal Relationships*, 37(4), 1252–1270. DOI: 10.1177/0265407520928946

Li, X., Fang, X., Wang, L., Geng, X., & Chang, H. (2021). Relationship between emotional intelligence and job well-being in Chinese registered nurses: mediating effect of communication satisfaction. *Nursing Open*, 8(4), 1778.1787. DOI: 10.1002/nop2.820

Liang, S., Dong, M., Zhao, H., Song, Y., & Yang, A. (2022). Mindfulness and life satisfaction: The moderating effect of self-control and the moderated moderating effect of resilience. *Personality and Individual Differences*, 185, 111241. DOI: 10.1016/j.paid.2021.111241

Lickona, T. (1992). *Educating for character: How our schools can teach respect and responsibility*. Bantam.

Liesa-Orús, M., Latorre-Cosculluela, C., Vázquez-Toledo, S., & Sierra-Sánchez, V. (2020). The technological challenge facing higher education professors: Perceptions of ICT tools for developing 21st century skills. *Sustainability (Basel)*, 12(13), 5339. DOI: 10.3390/su12135339

Likierman, A. (2020, November 24). The elements of good judgment. Harvard Business Review. https://hbr.org/2020/01/the-elements-of-good-judgment

Lilgendahl, J., & McAdams, D. P. (2011). Constructing stories of self-growth: How individual differences in patterns of autobiographical reasoning relate to well-being in midlife.

Li, M., Qin, G., & Li, Y. (2022). Mediating effects of emotional intelligence on the relationship between empathy and humanistic care ability in nursing students: A cross.sectional descriptive study. *Medicine*, 101(46), e31673. DOI: 10.1097/MD.0000000000031673 PMID: 36401377

Lindsay, E. K., Chin, B., Greco, C., Young, S., Brown, K., Wright, A. G. C., Smyth, J. S., Burkett, D., & Creswell, D. (2018). How mindfulness training promotes positive emotions: Dismantling monitor and acceptance in two randomized controlled trials. *Journal of Personality and Social Psychology*, 115(6), 944–973. DOI: 10.1037/pspa0000134 PMID: 30550321

Lisa, F. (2024). Loving One Another in Healthcare: Power of the Positive Work Environment. DOI: 10.1007/978-3-031-52276-5_9

Lister, J., & Houghton, R. (2014). The impact of workplace happiness on employee performance and organizational outcomes. *Journal of Organizational Behavior*, 35(3), 423–439. DOI: 10.1002/job.1881

Litman, J. A. (2008). Interest and deprivation factors of epistemic curiosity. *Personality and Individual Differences*, 44(7), 1585–1595. DOI: 10.1016/j.paid.2008.01.014

Liu, H., Zhang, L., Yan, J., Huang, H., Yi, Q., & Peng, L. (2023). The relationship between social support, empathy, self.efficacy, and humanistic practice ability among clinical nurses in China: A structural equation model. *Journal of Nursing Management*, 2023(1), 9. DOI: 10.1155/2023/1378278

Liu, S., Liu, S., Liu, Z., Peng, X., & Yang, Z. (2022). Automated detection of emotional and cognitive engagement in MOOC discussions to predict learning achievement. *Computers & Education*, 181, 104461. DOI: 10.1016/j.compedu.2022.104461

Locke, E. A., & Latham, G. P. (2002). Building a practically useful theory of goal setting and task motivation: A 35-year odyssey. *The American Psychologist*, 57(9), 705–717. DOI: 10.1037/0003-066X.57.9.705 PMID: 12237980

Lodi-Smith, J., Geise, A. C., Roberts, B. W., & Robins, R. W. (2009). Narrating personality change.

Lomas, T., Medina, J. C., Ivtzan, I., Rupprecht, S., & Eiroa-Orosa, F. J. (2017). The impact of mindfulness on the wellbeing and performance of educators: A systematic review of the empirical literature. *Teaching and Teacher Education*, 61, 132–141. DOI: 10.1016/j.tate.2016.10.008

London, M. (2003). *Job feedback: Giving, seeking, and using feedback for performance improvement.* Lawrence Erlbaum Associates. DOI: 10.4324/9781410608871

London, M., & Smither, J. W. (1999). The role of performance feedback in developing employees' performance. *The Journal of Applied Psychology*, 84(3), 546–553. DOI: 10.1037/0021-9010.84.3.546

London, M., & Smither, J. W. (2002). Feedback orientation, feedback culture, and the longitudinal performance management process. *Human Resource Management Review*, 12(1), 81–100. DOI: 10.1016/S1053-4822(01)00043-2

Lowe, G., Schellenberg, G., & Shannon, H. (2003). Correlates of Employees' Perceptions of a Healthy Work Environment. *American Journal of Health Promotion*, 17(6), 390–399. DOI: 10.4278/0890-1171-17.6.390 PMID: 12858619

Lown, B. A., Rosen, J., & Marttila, J. (2011). The critical role of communication in patient-centered care. *Health Affairs*, 30(4), 628–633. DOI: 10.1377/hlthaff.2011.0019 PMID: 21471482

Lucas, R. E., & Baird, B. (2004). Extraversion and emotional reactivity. *Journal of Personality and Social Psychology*, 86(3), 473–485. DOI: 10.1037/0022-3514.86.3.473 PMID: 15008650

Luhmann, M., Hofmann, W., Eid, M., & Lucas, R. E. (2012). Subjective well-being and

Luhmann, M., Hofmann, W., Eid, M., & Lucas, R. E. (2012, March). adaptation to life events: A meta-analysis. *Journal of Personality and Social Psychology*, 102(3), 592–615. DOI: 10.1037/a0025948 PMID: 22059843

Lundqvist, D., & Wallo, A. (2023). Leadership and Employee Well-Being and Work Performance when Working from Home: A Systematic Literature Review. *Scandinavian Journal of Work and Organizational Psychology*, 8(1), 1–19. DOI: 10.16993/sjwop.199

Luthans, F., & Youssef, C. M. (2007). Emerging Positive Organizational Behavior. *Journal of Management*, 33(3), 321–349. DOI: 10.1177/0149206307300814

Luthans, F., Youssef, C. M., & Avolio, B. J. (2006). *Psychological capital: Developing the human competitive edge*. Oxford University Press. DOI: 10.1093/acprof:oso/9780195187526.001.0001

Lyddy, C., Good, D., Bolino, M., Thompson, P., & Stephens, J. (2021). The Costs of Mindfulness at Work: The Moderating Role of Mindfulness in Surface Acting, Self-Control Depletion, and Performance Outcomes. *The Journal of Applied Psychology*, 106(12), 1921–1938. Advance online publication. DOI: 10.1037/apl0000863 PMID: 33570968

Lynda, H. (2019). Does A Positive Age Environment Successfully Influence Negative Age Stereotypes from an Employee Perspective.

Lynn, T., Rosati, P., Conway, E., & Van Der Werff, L. (2023). The future of work. In Palgrave studies in digital business & enabling technologies. DOI: 10.1007/978-3-031-31494-0

Lyubomirsky, S., & Lepper, H. S. (1999). A measure of subjective happiness: Preliminary reliability and construct validation.

Lyubomirsky, S., King, L., & Diener, E. (2005). The benefits of frequent positive affect: Does happiness lead to success? *Psychological Bulletin*, 131(6), 803–855. DOI: 10.1037/0033-2909.131.6.803 PMID: 16351326

Lyu, Y., Zhu, H., Zhong, H. J., & Hu, L. (2016). Abusive supervision and customer-oriented organizational citizenship behavior: The roles of hostile attribution bias and work engagement. *International Journal of Hospitality Management*, 53, 69–80. DOI: 10.1016/j.ijhm.2015.12.001

Maassen, S., Oostveen, C., Vermeulen, H., & Weggelaar, A. (2021). Defining a positive work environment for hospital healthcare professionals: A Delphi study. *PLoS One*, 16(2), e0247530. Advance online publication. DOI: 10.1371/journal.pone.0247530 PMID: 33630923

Macey, W. H., & Schneider, B. (2008). Engaged in engagement: We are delighted we did it. *Industrial and Organizational Psychology: Perspectives on Science and Practice*, 1(1), 76–83. DOI: 10.1111/j.1754-9434.2007.00016.x

Machado, L., Reis de Oliveira, I., Peregrino, A., & Cantilino, A. (2019). Common mental disorders and subjective well-being: Emotional training among medical students based on positive psychology. *PLoS One*, 14(2), e0211926. Advance online publication. DOI: 10.1371/journal.pone.0211926 PMID: 30731006

MacIntyre, A. (2007). *After virtue: A study in moral theory*. University of Notre Dame Press.

Mael, F. A., & Tetrick, L. E. (1992). Identifying Organizational Identification. *Educational and Psychological Measurement*, 52(4), 813–824. DOI: 10.1177/0013164492052004002

Mael, F., & Ashforth, B. E. (1992). Alumni and their alma mater: A partial test of the reformulated model of organizational identification. *Journal of Organizational Behavior*, 13(2), 103–123. DOI: 10.1002/job.4030130202

Mahindraadmin. (2021, November 22). *Mahindra empowers its employees with Practo's Corporate Health Plans*. Mahindra & Mahindra Ltd. Retrieved September 19, 2024, from https://www.mahindra.com/news-room/press-release/en/mahindra-empowers-its-employees-with-practos-corporate-health-plans

Maira. (2022). Well-being at work: a literature review on the complex framework. DOI: 10.3846/bm.2022.843

Majumdar, A., & Kumar, S. (2022). Organisational justice and employee wellbeing in India: Through a psychological lens. *Business Perspectives and Research.*

Maltby, J., Day, L., & Barber, L. (2005). Forgiveness and happiness. The differing contexts of forgiveness using the distinction between hedonic and eudaimonic happiness. *Journal of Happiness Studies*, 6(1), 1–13. Advance online publication. DOI: 10.1007/s10902-004-0924-9

Maor, D., Park, M., & Weddle, B. (2022). *Building organizational resilience*. McKinsey. https://www.mckinsey.com/capabilities/people-and-organizational-performance/our-insights/raising-the-resilience-of-your-organization

Mariati, L., Jakri, Y., & Djerubu, D. (2022). The effect of emotional intelligence on nurse's communication skill. *Jurnal Ners Dan Kebidanan (Journal of Ners and Midwifery),* 9(2), 218.226. DOI: 10.26699/jnk.v9i2.art.p218.226

Martela, F., & Ryan, R. M. (2021). In selecting measures for a comprehensive assessment of well-being, it is essential to include indicators of psychological need satisfaction. In *Preventive Medicine Reports* (Vol. 23). DOI: 10.1016/j.pmedr.2021.101474

Martinez, A., & Robinson, J. (2023). Organizational culture and its impact on employee happiness. Journal of Organizational Culture. *Communications and Conflict*, 27(2), 185–199. DOI: 10.1108/JOCC-07-2022-0128

Martin, J. R. (1997). Mindfulness: A proposed common factor. *Journal of Psychotherapy Integration*, 7(4), 291–312. DOI: 10.1023/B:JOPI.0000010885.18025.bc

Marzuki, N. A. (2013). The impact of personality on employee well-being. *European Scientific Journal*, 9(20), 43–52.

Matanda, M. J., & Ndubisi, N. O. (2013). Internal marketing, internal branding, and organisational outcomes: The moderating role of perceived goal congruence. *Journal of Marketing Management*, 29(9-10), 1030–1055. DOI: 10.1080/0267257X.2013.800902

Mattarelli, E., Cochis, C., Bertolotti, F., & Ungureanu, P. (2024). How designed work environment and enacted work interactions impact creativity and work–life balance. *European Journal of Innovation Management*, 27(2), 648–672. DOI: 10.1108/EJIM-01-2022-0028

Maurer, T. J. (2001). Career-relevant learning and development, worker age, and beliefs about self-efficacy for development. *Journal of Management*, 27(2), 123–140. DOI: 10.1177/014920630102700201

Ma, Y., Zhang, H., & Dai, Y. (2021). How job creativity requirements Affects employee creativity: Evidence from a Across-Level analysis. *Frontiers in Psychology*, 12, 714886. Advance online publication. DOI: 10.3389/fpsyg.2021.714886 PMID: 35027897

Mayer, D. M., & Salvador, R. (2014). The role of workplace incivility in creativity: A longitudinal examination. *Journal of Management*, 40(1), 92–112. DOI: 10.1177/0149206312441022

Mayer, R. C., Davis, J. H., & Schoorman, F. D. (1995). An integrative model of organizational trust. *Academy of Management Review*, 20(3), 709–734. DOI: 10.2307/258792

Mayo Clinic. (n.d.). Stress management: Stress relief. Retrieved from https://www.mayoclinic.org/healthy-lifestyle/stress-management/basics/stress-relief/hlv-20049495

Mayo, A. R. P., Velaz, E. B., Nieto, N. R., & Sánchez, P. G. (2019). Working Happiness in the Human Resource of a University Organization Based on Seligman's PERMA Model. *International Journal of Human Resource Studies*, 9(4), 101. Advance online publication. DOI: 10.5296/ijhrs.v9i4.15718

Mazmanian, M., Orlikowski, W. J., & Yates, J. (2013). The autonomy paradox: The implications of mobile email devices for knowledge professionals. *Organization Science*, 24(5), 1337–1357. DOI: 10.1287/orsc.1120.0806

McCormack, B., & McCance, T. V. (2017). *Person-Centred Practice in Nursing and Health Care: Theory and Practice*. Wiley-Blackwell. DOI: 10.1002/9781119099635

McCormick, J., & Wocial, L. (2012). Ethics rounds: A model for interdisciplinary ethics education in health care. *The Hastings Center Report*, 42(5), 15–18.

McCrae, R. R., & Costa, P. T. (1989). The structure of interpersonal traits: Wiggins's circumplex and the five-factor model. *Journal of Personality and Social Psychology*, 56(4), 586–595. DOI: 10.1037/0022-3514.56.4.586 PMID: 2709308

McDarby, G., Seifeldin, R., Zhang, Y., Mustafa, S., Petrova, M., Schmets, G., Porignon, D., Dalil, S., & Saikat, S. (2023). A synthesis of concepts of resilience to inform operationalization of health systems resilience in recovery from disruptive public health events including COVID-19. *Frontiers in Public Health*, 11, 1105537. DOI: 10.3389/fpubh.2023.1105537 PMID: 37250074

McKenna, B., Rooney, D., & Boal, K. B. (2009). Wisdom principles as a meta-theoretical basis for evaluating leadership. *The Leadership Quarterly*, 20(2), 177–190. DOI: 10.1016/j.leaqua.2009.01.013

McLellan, J. (2004). Volunteering and community engagement: The role of the nonprofit sector in employee development. *Nonprofit and Voluntary Sector Quarterly*, 33(4), 573–594.

McNall, L. A., Masuda, A. D., & Nicklin, J. M. (2011). A meta-analysis of the relationship between work-to-family conflict and job performance. *The Journal of Applied Psychology*, 96(1), 193–207. DOI: 10.1037/a0020927

McWilliams, S. A. (2014). Foundations of mindfulness and contemplation: Traditional and contemporary perspectives. *International Journal of Mental Health and Addiction*, 12(2), 116–128. DOI: 10.1007/s11469-014-9486-1

Meadows, D. H. (2008). *Thinking in systems: A primer*. Chelsea Green Publishing.

Mebratie, E., & Shanbel, B. (2024). Identifying the prevalence of destructive leadership behavior and its determinants in northwest Ethiopia. *Cogent Business & Management*, 11(1), 2315696. DOI: 10.1080/23311975.2024.2315696

Medhn Desta, A. G., & Mulie, H. (2024). The effect of empowering leadership practices on employees performance with the mediating role of work engagement: The case of ethio-telecom. *Cogent Business & Management*, 11(1), 2307066. DOI: 10.1080/23311975.2024.2307066

Mediarti, D., Rehana, R., & Abunyamin, A. (2018). Nurses education and motivation towards nursing documentation. *Jurnal Ners*, 13(1), 31.35. DOI: 10.20473/jn.v13i1.3478

Medved, C. E. (2016). Stay-at-home fathering as a feminist opportunity: Perpetuating, resisting, and transforming gender relations of caring and earning. *Journal of Family Communication*, 16(1), 16–31. DOI: 10.1080/15267431.2015.1112800

Medvedev, O. N., & Landhuis, C. E. (2018). Exploring constructs of well-being, happiness and quality of life. *PeerJ*, 6, e4903. DOI: 10.7717/peerj.4903 PMID: 29876148

Meeks, T. W., & Jeste, D. V. (2009). Neurobiology of wisdom: A literature overview. *Archives of General Psychiatry*, 66(4), 355–365. DOI: 10.1001/archgenpsychiatry.2009.8 PMID: 19349305

Meghna. (2020), Exploring the relationship between Work Environment and Job Satisfaction.

Mehta, A., & Bhatia, S. (2020). Cultural expectations and academic stress among faculty in higher education. *International Journal of Educational Research*, 102, 101577. DOI: 10.1016/j.ijer.2020.101577

Meliana. (2018). A Literature Review of Quality of Work Life. .DOI: 10.33846/HN.V2I6.222

Men, L. R. (2014). Strategic internal communication: Transformational leadership, communication channels, and employee satisfaction. *Management Communication Quarterly*, 28(2), 264–284. DOI: 10.1177/0893318914524536

Men, L. R. (2014). The effects of organizational transparency on employees' trust and commitment. *Journal of Public Relations Research*, 26(2), 174–193. DOI: 10.1080/1062726X.2014.882571

Mercader.Rubio, I., Ángel, N. G., Teixeira, A., & Brito-Costa, S. (2023). Relationships between informal sports leadership and emotional intelligence: A cross. sectional study. *Sustainability (Basel)*, 15(19), 14571. DOI: 10.3390/su151914571

Mertler, C. A. (2009). *Action research: Teachers as researchers in the classroom.* Sage Publications.

Mewafarosh, R., Agarwal, S., & Dwivedi, D. (2024). Balancing FOMO and Digital Detoxification. In *Business Drivers in Promoting Digital Detoxification* (pp. 1–15). IGI Global. DOI: 10.4018/979-8-3693-1107-3.ch001

Michael, G. (2022, September 20). Positive psychology in the working environment. Job demands-resources theory, work engagement and burnout: A systematic literature review. *Frontiers in Psychology*, 13, 1022102. Advance online publication. DOI: 10.3389/fpsyg.2022.1022102

Michalak, J., Steinhaus, K., & Heidenreich, T. (2020). (How) do therapists use mindfulness in their clinical work? A study on the implementation of mindfulness interventions. *Mindfulness*, 11(2), 401–410. DOI: 10.1007/s12671-018-0929-9

Mickler, C., & Staudinger, U. M. (2008). Personal wisdom: Validation and age-related differences of a performance measure. *Psychology and Aging*, 23(4), 787–799. DOI: 10.1037/a0013928 PMID: 19140650

Microsoft. (n.d.). Flexible work. Retrieved from https://www.microsoft.com/en-us/flexible-work/

Miller, C. R., & Williams, J. D. (2015). Faculty stress and wellness: An exploration of faculty workload and wellness strategies. *Journal of Higher Education Policy and Management*, 37(2), 139–152. DOI: 10.1080/1360080X.2015.1011508

Min, H., Park, S.-H., Lee, S.-H., Lee, B.-H., Kang, M., Kwon, M. J., Chang, M. J., Negi, L. T., Samphel, T., & Won, S. (2024). Building resilience and social–emotional competencies in elementary school students through a short.term intervention program based on the see learning curriculum. *Behavioral Sciences (Basel, Switzerland)*, 14(6), 458. DOI: 10.3390/bs14060458 PMID: 38920790

Mischel, W. (2004). Toward an integrative model for CBT: Encompassing behavior, cognition, affect, and process. *Behavior Therapy*, 35(1), 185–203. DOI: 10.1016/S0005-7894(04)80011-X

Mittelstadt, B. D., Allo, P., Taddeo, M., Wachter, S., & Floridi, L. (2016). The ethics of algorithms: Mapping the debate. *Big Data & Society*, 3(2), 1–21. DOI: 10.1177/2053951716679679

Mizrak, K. (2024). *Crisis Management and Risk Mitigation: Strategies for Effective Response and Resilience* (pp. 254–278). DOI: 10.4018/979-8-3693-1155-4.ch013

Mobarakeh, M., Juhari, R., Yaacob, S., Redzuan, M., & Mobarakeh, S.(2015). The effects of personality traits and psychological well-being among Iranian adolescent migrants in Kuala-Lumpur, Malaysia. IOSR Journal of Humanities and Social Science, 20(7),25-28.

Mobarakeh, M., Juhari, R., Yaacob, S., Redzuan, M., & Mobarakeh, S. (2015). The effects of personality traits and psychological well-being among Iranian adolescent migrants in Kuala-Lumpur, Malaysia. *IOSR Journal of Humanities and Social Science*, 20(7), 25–28.

Moloney, W., Fieldes, J., & Jacobs, S. (2020). An integrative review of how health-care organizations can support hospital nurses to thrive at work. *International Journal of Environmental Research and Public Health*, 17(23), 8757. DOI: 10.3390/ijerph17238757 PMID: 33255725

Momodou. (2023). Examining the Impact of Team Dynamics in Agile Project Management Success in Software Development: A Systematic Literature Review. .DOI: 10.1109/IDAACS58523.2023.10348796

Monteiro, E., & Joseph, J. (2023). A Review on the Impact of Workplace Culture on Employee Mental Health and Well-Being. International Journal of Case Studies in Business, IT, and Education, 291–317. DOI: 10.47992/IJCSBE.2581.6942.0274

Monteiro, E., & Joseph, J. (2022). Preventing Stress, Improving Productivity: A Case Study on Stress Management Policies of TCS and Infosys. *International Journal of Case Studies in BusinessIT and Education*, 6(1), 401–413.

Mosteanu, N. R. (2024). Adapting to the Unpredictable: Building Resilience for Business Continuity in an Ever-Changing Landscape. *European Journal of Theoretical and Applied Sciences*, 2(1), 444–457. DOI: 10.59324/ejtas.2024.2(1).37

Moudatsou, M., Stavropoulou, A., Philalithis, A., & Koukouli, S. (2020). The Role of Empathy in Health and Social Care Professionals. *Health Care*, 8(1), 26. DOI: 10.3390/healthcare8010026 PMID: 32019104

Mudzi, P., & Bruce, J. (2023). How ready are nursing colleges to be integrated into higher education? a scoping review of influential factors. *Journal of Nursing Education and Practice*, 13(11), 1. DOI: 10.5430/jnep.v13n11p1

Mulyatsih, M., Nursalam, , Sriyono, , Duwiyani, N. N., & Siregar, S. (2023). Nurses' perception of caring.based nursing care for stroke patients with thrombolysis and influencing factors. *Journal of Law and Sustainable Development*, 11(11), e1268. DOI: 10.55908/sdgs.v11i11.1268

Mumford, M. D. (2011). *Handbook of organizational creativity*. Academic Press.

Munira, K., Rahman, D., & Akhter, S. (2022). Impact of emotional intelligence on sustainable leadership. *Business Perspective Review*, 4(2), 1.15. DOI: 10.38157/bpr.v4i2.446

Munoz, A., Billsberry, J., & Ambrosini, V. (2022). Resilience, robustness, and antifragility: Towards an appreciation of distinct organizational responses to adversity. *International Journal of Management Reviews*, 24(2), 181–187. DOI: 10.1111/ijmr.12289

Mussel, P. (2010). Epistemic curiosity and related constructs: Lacking evidence of discriminant validity. *Personality and Individual Differences*, 49(5), 506–510. DOI: 10.1016/j.paid.2010.05.014

Mussel, P. (2013). Introducing the construct curiosity for predicting job performance. *Journal of Organizational Behavior*, 34(4), 453–472. DOI: 10.1002/job.1809

Naimisha, M. (2023, October 1). Scoping Review of Employer-Led Research Using Employee Health Claims Data. *Population Health Management*, 26(5), 341–352. Advance online publication. DOI: 10.1089/pop.2023.0140

Nelson, B. B. (2012). 1501 ways to reward employees. Hachette UK.

Ngo, L. V., Nguyen, N. P., Huynh, K. T., Gregory, G., & Cuong, P. H. (2020). Converting internal brand knowledge into employee performance. *Journal of Product and Brand Management*, 29(3), 273–287. DOI: 10.1108/JPBM-10-2018-2068

Nguyen, L., & Patel, V. (2021). Workplace diversity and employee happiness. *Diversity and Inclusion*, 15(2), 89–102. DOI: 10.1108/DI-01-2021-0011

Nguyen, T., & Brown, J. (2021). The impact of team dynamics on workplace happiness. *Team Performance Management*, 27(1), 31–45. DOI: 10.1108/TPM-09-2020-0095

Nicholas, K. (2023, November). Being Thankful for What You Have: A Systematic Review of Evidence for the Effect of Gratitude on Life Satisfaction. *Psychology Research and Behavior Management*, 16, 4799–4816. Advance online publication. DOI: 10.2147/PRBM.S372432

Nikolaev, B. (2018). Does Higher Education Increase Hedonic and Eudaimonic Happiness? *Journal of Happiness Studies*, 19(2). Advance online publication. DOI: 10.1007/s10902-016-9833-y

Noe, R. A. (2020). *Employee training and development*. McGraw-Hill.

Nonaka, I., Chia, R., Holt, R., & Peltokorpi, V. (2014). Wisdom, management and organization. *Management Learning*, 45(4), 365–376. DOI: 10.1177/1350507614542901

Nonaka, I., & Takeuchi, H. (2011). The wise leader. *Harvard Business Review*, 89(5), 58–67. PMID: 21548419

Norris, G. (2019). *Adaptability and mindfulness of Chinese knowledge workers in multinational companies* (Doctoral dissertation, Edinburgh Business School).

Nouri, B. A., Abbasgholizadeh, N., Oleykie, F., & Nemati, V. (2021). The effect of transformational leadership style on organizational happiness and the mediating role of job passion in hospitals of Ardabil. *Journal of Health*, 12(3), 368–384. DOI: 10.52547/j.health.12.3.368

Nye, C., Tengelin, E., & Somayaji, D. (2022). Developing a theory of norm.criticism in nursing education. *Advances in Nursing Science*, 46(2), E66.E79. DOI: 10.1097/ANS.0000000000000440

Nyoach, T. D., Lemi, K., Debela, T., & Kant, S. (2024). Does Organizational Commitment Mediate the Relationship between Employee Relationship Management and Bank Performance? The Case of Banks in Ethiopia. *International Journal of Organizational Leadership*, 13(2), 355–376. DOI: 10.33844/ijol.2024.60419

Occupational Safety and Health Administration (OSHA). (n.d.). A safe workplace is sound business. Retrieved from https://www.osha.gov/safety-management

Occupational Safety and Health Administration (OSHA). (n.d.). Safety and health programs step-by-step guide. Retrieved from https://www.osha.gov/safety-management/step-by-step-guide

Ogawa, R., & Bossert, S. (1995). Leadership as an Organizational Quality. *Educational Administration Quarterly*, 31(2), 224–243. DOI: 10.1177/0013161X95031002004

Onesti, G. (2023). Exploring the impact of leadership styles, ethical behavior, and organizational identification on workers' well-being. *Administrative Sciences*, 13(6), 149. DOI: 10.3390/admsci13060149

Onesti, G., & Palumbo, R. (2023). Tone at the Top for Sustainable Corporate Governance to Prevent Fraud. *Sustainability (Basel)*, 15(3), 2198. DOI: 10.3390/su15032198

Onyebuchi. (2023). Team Building in Organizations: Benefit and Challenge - A Review. International Journal Of Social Sciences And Management Research. DOI: 10.56201/ijssmr.v9.no3.2023.pg42.52

Onyema, E. M. (2020). Integration of emerging technologies in teaching and learning process in Nigeria: The challenges. *Central Asian Journal of Mathematical Theory and Computer Sciences*, 1(1), 35–39.

Opalo, K. O., & Smith, L. (2021). Ideology and succession politics in Ethiopia: Autocratic leadership turnover and political instability. *Democratization*, 28(8), 1463–1482. DOI: 10.1080/13510347.2021.1929178

Organ, D. W., Podsakoff, P. M., & MacKenzie, S. B. (2005). *Organizational citizenship behavior: Its nature, antecedents, and consequences*. Sage Publications.

Osei-Owusu, B. (2022). Impact of Professional Development Programmes on Teachers' Knowledge and Academic Performance of Senior High School Students in Ghana. *European Journal of Education and Pedagogy*, 3(2), 60–69. Advance online publication. DOI: 10.24018/ejedu.2022.3.2.276

Özçelik, G., & Fındıklı, M. A. (2014). The relationship between internal branding and organizational citizenship behaviour: The mediating role of person-organization fit. *Procedia: Social and Behavioral Sciences*, 150, 1120–1128. DOI: 10.1016/j.sbspro.2014.09.127

Page, S. E. (2007). *The Difference: How the Power of Diversity Creates Better Groups, Firms, Schools, and Societies*. Princeton University Press.

Palumbo, R. (2020). Let me go to the office! An investigation into the side effects of working from home on work-life balance. *International Journal of Public Sector Management*, 33(6–7), 771–790. Advance online publication. DOI: 10.1108/IJPSM-06-2020-0150

Palumbo, R. (2024). Making sense of the relationship between involvement and work–life balance: Empirical insights from the public sector. *International Journal of Public Administration*, 47(10), 663–679. DOI: 10.1080/01900692.2023.2166065

Pan, T., Trakulmututa, J., & Youravong, N. (2020). Self.perception of leadership style of dentists: heads of dental departments in community hospitals, southern Thailand. *International Dental Journal*, 70(3), 193.200. DOI: 10.1111/idj.12544

Panda, G., Dash, M. K., Samadhiya, A., Kumar, A., & Mulat-weldemeskel, E. (2024). Artificial intelligence as an enabler for achieving human resource resiliency: Past literature, present debate and future research directions. *International Journal of Industrial Engineering and Operations Management*, 6(4), 326–347. DOI: 10.1108/IJIEOM-05-2023-0047

Pandya, M., & Korat, N. (2015). Personality traits and psychological wellbeing among youths of Rajkot district. *International Journal of Indian Psychology*, 2(2), 19–23.

Panigrahi, A., Pati, A., Sahu, B., Das, M. N., Nayak, D. S. K., Sahoo, G., & Kant, S. (2023). En-MinWhale: An ensemble approach based on MRMR and Whale optimization for Cancer diagnosis. *IEEE Access : Practical Innovations, Open Solutions*, 11, 113526–113542. DOI: 10.1109/ACCESS.2023.3318261

Papla, R., Yeltayeva, D., & Pak, D. (2022). Strategic Agility Or Resilience: What Should Smes Focus On During The Crisis? *InterConf*, 18(95), 82–91. DOI: 10.51582/interconf.19-20.01.2022.007

Park, J. & Park, J. (2022). Identifying the knowledge structure and trends of nursing informatics. *Cin Computers Informatics Nursing*, 41(1), 8.17. DOI: 10.1097/CIN.0000000000000919

Parke, M. R., Tangirala, S., & Hussain, I. (2021). Creating organizational citizens: How and when supervisor-versus peer-led role interventions change organizational citizenship behavior. *The Journal of Applied Psychology*, 106(11), 1714–1733. DOI: 10.1037/apl0000848 PMID: 33090860

Parnham, N. (2023). *Resilience—Self-awareness and self-connection*. https://ninaparnham.com/resilience-self-awareness-and-self-connection

Patanjali Wellness. (n.d.). Retrieved September 19, 2024, from https://patanjaliwellness.com/

Patel, S., & Gupta, R. (2016). Job satisfaction and its correlation with workplace happiness. *Human Resource Management Review*, 26(2), 275–286. DOI: 10.1016/j.hrmr.2015.08.002

Patel, S., & Verma, K. (2018). Interpersonal relationships and faculty stress: A study of Indian higher education institutions. *Asian Journal of Education and Training*, 4(3), 273–280. DOI: 10.20448/journal.522.2018.43.273.280

Paul, B. (2023, April 30). *Infosys: Behind the iconic tech giant's drive to retain talent and push for growth.* Retrieved September 18, 2024, from https://www.businesstoday.in/magazine/deep-dive/story/infosys-behind-the-iconic-tech-giants-drive-to-retain-talent-and-push-for-growth-377639-2023-04-17

Paul, R., & Elder, L. (2006). *Critical Thinking: Tools for Taking Charge of Your Professional and Personal Life*. Pearson.

Pečiuliauskienė, P. (2021). Emotional intelligence and transformational leadership of gymnasium teachers'. *Society Integration Education Proceedings of the International Scientific Conference*, 2, 457.467. DOI: 10.17770/sie2021vol2.6194

Pedroso, T., Pedrão, L., & Perroca, M. (2020). Approaches to workload in psychiatric and mental health nursing. *Revista Brasileira De Enfermagem*, 73(suppl 1). DOI: 10.1590/0034.7167.2019.0620

Peláez.Fernández, M., Mérida.López, S., Sánchez-Álvarez, N., & Extremera, N. (2021). Managing teachers' job attitudes: The potential benefits of being a happy and emotional intelligent teacher. *Frontiers in Psychology*, 12, 661151. Advance online publication. DOI: 10.3389/fpsyg.2021.661151 PMID: 34017291

People Managing People. (2024). 10 best employee feedback software of 2024. Retrieved from https://peoplemanagingpeople.com/tools/best-employee-feedback-software/

Perry-Smith, J., & Blum, T. (2000). Work-family human resource bundles and perceived organizational performance. *Academy of Management Journal*, 43(6), 1107–1117. DOI: 10.2307/1556339

Perry, W. G. (1970). *Forms of Intellectual and Ethical Development in the College Years: A Scheme*. Holt, Rinehart and Winston.

Pertheban, T. R., Thurasamy, R., Marimuthu, A., Venkatachalam, K. R., Annamalah, S., Paraman, P., & Hoo, W. C. (2023). The Impact of Proactive Resilience Strategies on Organizational Performance: Role of Ambidextrous and Dynamic Capabilities of SMEs in Manufacturing Sector. *Sustainability (Basel)*, 15(16), 16. Advance online publication. DOI: 10.3390/su151612665

Perwez, S. K., & Ramasehan, H. (2016). Employee Counselling: Need and importance in the 21st century workplace. *International Journal of Physical and Social Sciences*, 6(10), 1–19.

Peterson, C., & Seligman, M. E. P. (2004). *Character strengths and virtues: A handbook and classification*. Oxford University Press.

Peterson, C., & Seligman, M. E. P. (2004). *Character strengths and virtues: A Handbook and Classification*. Oxford University Press.

Peterson, C., & Seligman, M. E. P. (2004). *Character Strengths and Virtues: A Handbook and Classification*. Oxford University Press.

Pettersen Gould, K. (2019). Precursor Resilience in Practice – An Organizational Response to Weak Signals. In *Exploring Resilience* (pp. 51–58). Springer. DOI: 10.1007/978-3-030-03189-3_7

Pfeffer, J. (1992). *Managing with power: Politics and influence in organizations*. Harvard Business Press.

Pfeffer, J. (2010). Building sustainable organizations: The human factor. *The Academy of Management Perspectives*, 24(1), 34–45.

Pless, N., & Maak, T. (2004). Building an inclusive diversity culture: Principles, processes and practice. *Journal of Business Ethics*, 54(2), 129–147. DOI: 10.1007/s10551-004-9465-8

Podsakoff, P. M., MacKenzie, S. B., Moorman, R. H., & Fetter, R. (1990). Transformational leader behaviors and their effects on followers' trust in leader, satisfaction, and organizational citizenship behaviors. *The Leadership Quarterly*, 1(2), 107–142. DOI: 10.1016/1048-9843(90)90009-7

Podsakoff, P. M., MacKenzie, S. B., & Podsakoff, N. P. (2016). Recommendations for creating better concept definitions in the organizational, behavioral, and social sciences. *Organizational Research Methods*, 19(2), 159–203. DOI: 10.1177/1094428115624965

Pollock, N. C., Noser, A. E., Holden, C. J., & Zeigler-Hill, V. (2016). Do orientations to happiness mediate the associations between personality traits and subjective well-being? *Journal of Happiness Studies*, 17(2), 713–729. DOI: 10.1007/s10902-015-9617-9

Positive Psychology. (2024). 14 conflict resolution strategies for the workplace. Retrieved from https://positivepsychology.com/conflict-resolution-in-the-workplace/

Positive Psychology. (n.d.). How to plan a mindfulness workshop: Best ideas for success. Retrieved from https://positivepsychology.com/mindfulness-workshop/

Pradhan, R. K., Panda, P., & Jena, L. K. (2017). Purpose, passion, and performance at the workplace: Exploring the nature, structure, and relationship. *The Psychologist Manager Journal*, 20(4), 222–245. DOI: 10.1037/mgr0000059

Prado, J., Zárate-Torres, R., Tafur-Mendoza, A., Prada-Ospina, R., & Sarmiento, C. (2022). Impact of leadership practices on manager's pathways to goal attainment: the mediating effect of emotional intelligence. *International Journal of Organizational Analysis*, 31(7), 2889.2902. DOI: 10.1108/ijoa.01.2022.3110

Prado.Gascó, V., Giménez.Espert, M., & Valero-Moreno, S. (2019). The influence of nurse education and training on communication, emotional intelligence, and empathy. *Revista Da Escola De Enfermagem Da USP*, 53. DOI: 10.1590/s1980.220x2018015903465

Pratibha. (2017). Review of Literature on Work Life Balance Policies and Practices. Asian Journal of Research in Business Economics and Management, DOI: 10.5958/2249-7307.2017.00067.6

Pratt, M. G. (1998). To be or not to be: Central questions in organizational identification. Identity in organizations: Developing theory through conversations, 171-207.

Pratt, M. G., & Ashforth, B. E. (2003). Fostering meaningfulness in working and at work. Positive organizational scholarship: Foundations of a new discipline, 309, 327.

Pressman, S. D., & Cohen, S. (2005). Does positive affect influence health? *Psychological Bulletin*, 131(6), 925–971. DOI: 10.1037/0033-2909.131.6.925 PMID: 16351329

Prihandhani, I., & Hakim, N. (2022). Training course on emotional intelligence effect of nurses' interpersonal relationship style on Tabanan general hospital. *International Journal of Research in Medical Sciences*, 10(9), 1878. DOI: 10.18203/2320-6012.ijrms20222262

Proactive, M. D. (n.d.). How to perform an ergonomic assessment in the workplace. Retrieved from https://proactive-md.com/how-to-perform-an-ergonomic-assessment-in-the-workplace/

Psychologist, R. T. (2024, June 26). The Classification of Character Strengths and Virtues. PositivePsychology.com. https://positivepsychology.com/classification-character-strengths-virtues/

Psychology Today. (2024). Managing conflict resolution effectively. Retrieved from https://www.psychologytoday.com/us/blog/the-wisdom-of-anger/202401/managing-conflict-resolution-effectively

Pulakos, E. D., Mueller-Hanson, R., & O'Leary, R. (2015). *Performance management: A roadmap for developing, implementing and evaluating performance management systems*. SHRM Foundation.

Punjaisri, K., & Wilson, A. (2017). The role of internal branding in the delivery of employee brand promise. *Advances in corporate branding*, 91-108.

Punjaisri, K., Evanschitzky, H., & Wilson, A. (2009). Internal branding: An enabler of employees' brand-supporting behaviours. *Journal of Service Management*, 20(2), 209–226. DOI: 10.1108/09564230910952780

Putnam, R. D. (2000). *Bowling alone: The collapse and revival of American community*. Simon and Schuster.

QuestionPro. (2023). Continuous feedback: Definition, management, and benefits. Retrieved from https://www.questionpro.com/blog/continuous-feedback/

Raelin, J. A. (2001). Public reflection as the basis for learning. *Management Learning*, 32(1), 11–32. DOI: 10.1177/1350507601321002

Raelin, J. A. (2002). 'I don't have time to think!' versus the art of reflective practice. *Reflections: The SoL Journal*, 4(1), 66–79. DOI: 10.1162/152417302320467571

Rafferty, A., Maben, J., & West, E. (2005). What makes a good employer? Academic Press.

Rafiq, M., & Ahmed, P. K. (1993). The scope of internal marketing: Defining the boundary between marketing and human resource management. *Journal of Marketing Management*, 9(3), 219–232. DOI: 10.1080/0267257X.1993.9964234

Ragins, B. R., & Dutton, J. E. (2017). Positive relationships at work: An introduction and invitation. In *Exploring positive relationships at work* (pp. 2–24). Psychology Press. DOI: 10.4324/9781315094199-2

Raj, A. B. (2020). Employee well-being through internal branding: An integrated approach for achieving employee-based brand outcomes. *Global Business Review*, 21(4), 1065–1086. DOI: 10.1177/0972150918779161

Randall, P. W. (2019). *Teacher stress in rural schools: A phenomenological study on stress and its effect on teacher-perceived physical and mental well-being* (Doctoral dissertation, Northwest Nazarene University).

Ranjan, S., & Mukherjee, A. (2018). Understanding faculty stress: Insights from Indian higher education. *Educational Studies*, 44(2), 144–160. DOI: 10.1080/03055698.2017.1394086

Raquel, R.-C., Bernardo, M.-J., Sara, R.-H., Abraham, Á.-B., & Ana Isabel, S.-V. (2010). Positive Psychology at Work: Mutual Gains for Individuals and Organizations. *Journal of Work and Organizational Psychology*, 26(3), 235–253. Advance online publication. DOI: 10.5093/tr2010v26n3a7

Rashmi, K., & Kataria, A. (2022). Work–life balance: A systematic literature review and bibliometric analysis. *The International Journal of Sociology and Social Policy*, 42(11/12), 1028–1065. DOI: 10.1108/IJSSP-06-2021-0145

Rasoolimanesh, S. M., Taheri, B., Gannon, M., Vafaei-Zadeh, A., & Hanifah, H. (2019). Does living in the vicinity of heritage tourism sites influence residents' perceptions and attitudes? *Journal of Sustainable Tourism*, 27(9), 1295–1317. DOI: 10.1080/09669582.2019.1618863

Rasool, S. F., Wang, M., Tang, M., Saeed, A., & Iqbal, J. (2021). How toxic workplace environment effects the employee engagement: The mediating role of organizational support and employee wellbeing. *International Journal of Environmental Research and Public Health*, 18(5), 2294. DOI: 10.3390/ijerph18052294 PMID: 33652564

Rastogi, M. (2020). A psychometric validation of the happiness at workplace scale. *Industrial and Commercial Training*, 52(1), 15–34. DOI: 10.1108/ICT-04-2019-0034

Raziq, A., & Maula-Bakhsh, R. (2015). Impact of Working Environment on Job Satisfaction. *Procedia Economics and Finance*, 23, 717–725. DOI: 10.1016/S2212-5671(15)00524-9

Reb, J., Allen, T., & Vogus, T. J. (2020). Mindfulness arrives at work: Deepening our understanding of mindfulness in organizations. *Organizational Behavior and Human Decision Processes*, 159, 1–7. DOI: 10.1016/j.obhdp.2020.04.001

Rechtschaffen, D. (2014). *The way of mindful education: Cultivating well-being in teachers and students*. WW Norton & Company.

Reese, E., Myftari, E., McAnally, H. M., Chen, Y., Neha, T., Wang, Q., Jack, F., & Robertson, S.-J. (2017). Telling the tale and living well:Adolescent narrative identity, personality traits, and well-being across cultures. *Child Development*, 88(2), 612–628. DOI: 10.1111/cdev.12618 PMID: 27637177

Reichheld, F. F. (2004). The one number you need to grow. *Harvard Business Review*, 82(6), 133–133. PMID: 14712543

Reio, T. G.Jr, & Callahan, J. L. (2004). Affect, curiosity, and socialization-related learning: A path analysis of antecedents to job performance. *Journal of Business and Psychology*, 19(1), 3–22. DOI: 10.1023/B:JOBU.0000040269.72795.ce

Reio, T. G.Jr, Petrosko, J. M., Wiswell, A. K., & Thongsukmag, J. (2006). The measurement and conceptualization of curiosity. *The Journal of Genetic Psychology*, 167(2), 117–135. DOI: 10.3200/GNTP.167.2.117-135 PMID: 16910206

Reis da Silva Tiago. (2024d) The Value of Emotional Intelligence in Midwifery: Enhancing Care and Outcomes for Mothers and Infants through Sustainable Development Goals and Leadership. *Journal of Womens Healthcare & Midwifery Research*. https://www.onlinescientificresearch.com/articles/the.value.of.emotional.intelligence.in.midwifery.enhancing.care.and.outcomes.for.mothers.and.infants.through.sustainable.developme.pdf

Reis da Silva, T. (2024a). The Evolution of Nursing for Older Adult: A Historical Perspective. *Associative J Health Sci*. 3(3). AJHS. 000561. 2024. https://crimsonpublishers.com/ajhs/pdf/AJHS.000561.pdf

Reis da Silva, T.H. (2024k) Pharmacokinetics in older people: an overview of prescribing practice. *Journal of Prescribing Practice*. 6(9). 374.381. DOI: 10.12968/jprp.2024.6.9.374

Reis da Silva, T. (2024j). Can supplementing vitamin B12 improve mental health outcomes?: A literature review. *British Journal of Community Nursing*, 29(3), 137–146. DOI: 10.12968/bjcn.2024.29.3.137 PMID: 38421889

Reis da Silva, T. H. (2024c). Oncology and Cancer Medicine: Understanding the complexities in Older Patients. *Biomedical Journal of Scientific & Technical Research*, 55(3), 2024. DOI: 10.26717/BJSTR.2024.55.008720

Reis da Silva, T. H. (2024e). Navigating Healthcare Complexity: Integrating Business Fundamentals into Nursing Leadership. In Sedky, A. (Ed.), *Resiliency Strategies for Long.Term Business Success. Pp. 145.168.* IGI Global. DOI: 10.4018/979-8-3693-9168-6.ch006

Reis da Silva, T. H. (2024f). Integrating business essentials into Gerontological Nursing: Enhancing Care for Older Adults in Diverse Settings. In Sedky, A. (Ed.), *Resiliency Strategies for Long.Term Business Success. Pp. 283.316.* IGI Global. DOI: 10.4018/979-8-3693-9168-6.ch011

Reis da Silva, T. H. (2024i). Loneliness in older adults. *British Journal of Community Nursing*, 29(2), 60–66. DOI: 10.12968/bjcn.2024.29.2.60 PMID: 38300245

Reis da Silva, T. H., & Mitchell, A. (2024a). Integrating Digital Transformation in Nursing Education: Best Practices and Challenges in Curriculum Development. In Lytras, M., Serban, A. C., Alkhaldi, A., Malik, S., & Aldosemani, T. (Eds.), *Digital Transformation in Higher Education, Part B Cases, Examples and Good Practices.* Emerald Publishing Limited.

Reis Da Silva, T. H., & Mitchell, A. (2024b). Simulation in nursing: The importance of involving service users. *British Journal of Nursing (Mark Allen Publishing)*, 33(5), 262–265. DOI: 10.12968/bjon.2024.33.5.262 PMID: 38446515

Reis, , & da Silva, T. H. (2024a). Gender Equity In Healthcare: Integrating Emotional Intelligence To Achieve The United Nations Sustainable Development Goals. *J Comm Med and Pub Health Rep*, 5(12). Advance online publication. DOI: 10.38207/JCMPHR/2024/JUL051202106

Rhoades, L., & Eisenberger, R. (2002). Perceived organizational support: A review of the literature. *The Journal of Applied Psychology*, 87(4), 698–714. DOI: 10.1037/0021-9010.87.4.698 PMID: 12184574

Richardson, K. M., & Rothstein, H. R. (2008). Effects of occupational stress management intervention programs: A meta-analysis. *Journal of Occupational Health Psychology*, 13(1), 69–93. DOI: 10.1037/1076-8998.13.1.69 PMID: 18211170

Riivari, E., & Lämsä, A. M. (2017). Organizational Ethical Virtues of Innovativeness. *Journal of Business Ethics*, 155(1), 223–240. DOI: 10.1007/s10551-017-3486-6

Risely. (2024). 6 benefits of conflict resolution for effective managers. Retrieved from https://www.risely.me/6-benefits-of-conflict-resolution-in-the-workplace/

Robbins, S. P., & Judge, T. A. (2012). *PerilakuOrganisasi, OrganizationalBeahavior, Buku 1, Edisi 12.* SalembaEmpat.

Roberts, B. W., Walton, K. E., & Viechtbauer, W. (2006). Patterns of mean-level change in personality traits across the life course: A meta-analysis of longitudinal studies.

Roberts, B. W., Walton, K. E., & Viechtbauer, W. (2006, January). Patterns of mean-level change in personality traits across the life course: A meta-analysis of longitudinal studies. *Psychological Bulletin*, 132(1), 1–25. DOI: 10.1037/0033-2909.132.1.1

Robertson, I. T., & Cooper, C. L. (2010). Full engagement: The integration of employee engagement and psychological well-being. *Leadership and Organization Development Journal*, 31(4), 324–336. DOI: 10.1108/01437731011043348

Robinson, A., & Walker, T. (2019). Managerial support and its influence on employee happiness. *Management Decision*, 57(6), 1495–1508. DOI: 10.1108/MD-07-2018-0843

Robinson, D., Perryman, S., & Hayday, S. (2004). *The drivers of employee engagement*. No Title.

Román, S., Cuestas, P. J., & Fenollar, P. (2008). An examination of the interrelationships between self-esteem, others' expectations, family support, learning approaches and academic achievement. *Studies in Higher Education*, 33(2), 127–138. DOI: 10.1080/03075070801915882

Romme, G., van den Berg, J., Blanc, P. M., & Alblas, A. (2019). Do Empowered Employees Boost Organizational Resilience? A Case Study in the Dutch Home Care Industry. *Academy of Management Annual Meeting Proceedings, 2019*, 19138. DOI: 10.5465/AMBPP.2019.19138abstract

Rooney, D., McKenna, B., & Liesch, P. (2010). *Wisdom and management in the knowledge economy*. Routledge. DOI: 10.4324/9780203852798

Roqai, M. C., Ennida, K., & Allouani, S. A. (2024). Promoting Character Education in Business Schools from an Integral Perspective: A Conceptual Paper. *Open Journal of Social Sciences*, 12(7), 534–549. DOI: 10.4236/jss.2024.127038

Rosenberg, M. J., & Heimler, R. (2016). *E-learning: Strategies for delivering knowledge in the digital age*. Palgrave Macmillan.

Rosso, B. D., Dekas, K. H., & Wrzesniewski, A. (2010). On the meaning of work: A theoretical integration and review. *Research in Organizational Behavior*, 30, 91–127. DOI: 10.1016/j.riob.2010.09.001

Rothbard, N. P. (2001). Enriching or depleting? The dynamics of engagement in work and family roles. *Administrative Science Quarterly*, 46(4), 655–684. DOI: 10.2307/3094827

Rousseau, D. M., Manning, J., & Denyer, D. (2013). Evidence in management and organizational science: Assembling the field's full weight of scientific knowledge through syntheses. *The Academy of Management Annals*, 7(1), 79–100.

Rowland, S. (2010). The importance of recognition in faculty satisfaction. *Higher Education Research & Development*, 29(5), 509–520. DOI: 10.1080/07294360.2010.501246

Rowley, J., & Gibbs, P. (2008). From learning organization to practically wise organization. *The Learning Organization*, 15(5), 356–372. DOI: 10.1108/09696470810898357

Rožman, M., Oreški, D., & Tominc, P. (2022). Integrating artificial intelligence into a talent management model to increase the work engagement and performance of enterprises. *Frontiers in Psychology*, 13, 1014434. Advance online publication. DOI: 10.3389/fpsyg.2022.1014434 PMID: 36506984

Rumanti, A. A., Rizana, A. F., & Achmad, F. (2023). Exploring the role of organizational creativity and open innovation in enhancing SMEs performance. *Journal of Open Innovation*, 9(2), 100045. DOI: 10.1016/j.joitmc.2023.100045

Ryan, F. (2024, August 15). They do not deserve your thanks! Witness reactions to leader-directed expressions of gratitude. *The Journal of Applied Psychology*. Advance online publication. DOI: 10.1037/apl0001228

Ryan, R. M., & Deci, E. L. (2000). Self-determination theory and the facilitation of intrinsic motivation, social development, and well-being. *The American Psychologist*, 55(1), 68–78. DOI: 10.1037/0003-066X.55.1.68 PMID: 11392867

Ryan, R. M., & Deci, E. L. (2001). On happiness and human potentials: A review of research on hedonic and eudaimonic well-being. *Annual Review of Psychology*, 52(1), 141–166. DOI: 10.1146/annurev.psych.52.1.141 PMID: 11148302

Ryff, C. D. (1989). Happiness is everything, or is it? Explorations on the meaning of psychological well-being. *Journal of Personality and Social Psychology*, 57(6), 1069–1081. DOI: 10.1037/0022-3514.57.6.1069

Ryff, C. D., & Keyes, C. L. M. (1995). The structure of psychological well-being revisited. *Journal of Personality and Social Psychology*, 69(4), 719–727. DOI: 10.1037/0022-3514.69.4.719 PMID: 7473027

Ryff, C. D., & Singer, B. (2000). The role of purpose in life in psychological well-being. *Psychology and Aging*, 15(2), 206–220. DOI: 10.1037/0882-7974.15.2.206

Sadeghi, T., Kiani, M., Saeidi, M., Moghaddam, H., Ghodsi, M., & Hoseini, R. (2018). The relationship between emotional intelligence with administrators' performance at Mashhad university of medical sciences. *Electronic Physician*, 10(3), 6487.6493. DOI: 10.19082/6487

Sadore, A. A., Kebede, Y., & Birhanu, Z. (2024). Effectiveness of engaging religious leaders in maternal health education for improving maternal health service utilization in Ethiopia: Cluster randomized controlled trial. *Frontiers in Public Health*, 12, 1399472. DOI: 10.3389/fpubh.2024.1399472 PMID: 39135926

Safaria, T. (2014). Forgiveness, Gratitude, and Happiness among College Students. *International Journal of Public Health Science*, 3(4), 241. Advance online publication. DOI: 10.11591/.v3i4.4698

SafetyCulture. (n.d.). Health and safety program: A brief guide. Retrieved from https://safetyculture.com/topics/occupational-health-and-safety/health-and-safety-program/

Sahoo, S. R., & Mohanty, S. (2019). Antecedents and Dimensions of Internal Branding. An Overview. *RevistaEspacios, 40*(37).

Saidi, N., Michael, F., Sumilan, H., Lim, S., Jonathan, V., Hamidi, H., & Ahmad, A. (2019). The Relationship Between Working Environment and Employee Performance. Journal of Cognitive Sciences and Human Development. .DOI: 10.33736/jcshd.1916.2019

Salajeghe, S., Farahbakhsh, A., &Sohi, Z. (2014). Explaining the relationship between internal marketing activities with organizational citizenship behavior among employees of tejarat bank.

Salas-Vallina, A., & Fernandez, R. (2017). The HRM-performance relationship revisited: Inspirational motivation, participative decision making and happiness at work (HAW). *Employee Relations*, 39(5), 626–642. DOI: 10.1108/ER-12-2016-0245

Salavera, C., Usán, P., & Teruel, P. (2020). The mediating role of positive and negative affects in the relationship between self-esteem and happiness. *Psychology Research and Behavior Management*, 13, 355–361. Advance online publication. DOI: 10.2147/PRBM.S240917 PMID: 32425623

Saleem, F. Z., & Iglesias, O. (2016). Mapping the domain of the fragmented field of internal branding. *Journal of Product and Brand Management*, 25(1), 43–57. DOI: 10.1108/JPBM-11-2014-0751

Salesforce. (n.d.). Equality at Salesforce. Retrieved from https://www.salesforce.com/company/equality/

Salovey, P., Mayer, J., Caruso, D., & Yoo, S. (2009). The positive psychology of emotional intelligence., 236.248. DOI: 10.1093/oxfordhb/9780195187243.013.0022

Sapp, A. L., Kawachi, I., Sorensen, G., LaMontagne, A. D., & Subramanian, S. (2010). Does workplace social capital buffer the effects of job stress? A Cross-Sectional, multilevel analysis of cigarette smoking among U.S. manufacturing workers. *Journal of Occupational and Environmental Medicine*, 52(7), 740–750. DOI: 10.1097/JOM.0b013e3181e80842 PMID: 20595910

Sarstedt, M., Ringle, C. M., & Hair, J. F. (2021). Partial least squares structural equation modeling. In *Handbook of market research* (pp. 587–632). Springer International Publishing. DOI: 10.1007/978-3-319-05542-8_15-2

Satena, A. A., Damessa, D. D., Dadiye, T. A., & Kant, S. (2024). Effect of Servant Leadership Style on Organizational Performance Among University Employees In Ethiopia. *International Journal of Social Science. Management and Economics Research*, 2(2), 42–63.

Saunders, J., Sridaromont, K., & Gallegos, B. (2020). Steps to Establish a Healthy Work Environment in an Academic Nursing Setting. *Nurse Educator*, 46(1), 2–4. DOI: 10.1097/NNE.0000000000000829 PMID: 33283997

Scandura, T., & Lankau, M. J. (1997). Relationships of gender, family responsibility and flexible work hours to organizational commitment and job satisfaction. *Journal of Organizational Behavior*, 18(4), 377–391. DOI: 10.1002/(SICI)1099-1379(199707)18:4<377::AID-JOB807>3.0.CO;2-1

Schaufeli, W. B., Leiter, M. P., & Maslach, C. (2009). Burnout: 35 years of research and practice. *Career Development International*, 14(3), 204–220. DOI: 10.1108/13620430910966406

Schaufeli, W. B., Salanova, M., Gonzalez-Roma, V., & Bakker, A. B. (2002). The measurement of engagement and burnout: A confirmative analytic approach. *Journal of Happiness Studies*, 3(1), 71–92. DOI: 10.1023/A:1015630930326

Schaufeli, W. B., & Taris, T. W. (2014). A critical review of the Job Demands-Resources Model: Implications for improving work and health. In *G. Bauer, & O.Bridging occupational, organizational and public health* (pp. 43–68). Springer. DOI: 10.1007/978-94-007-5640-3_4

Schein, E. H. (2010). *Organizational culture and leadership*. Jossey-Bass.

Schmutte, P. S., & Ryff, C. D. (1997). Personality and well-being: Reexamining methods and meanings. *Journal of Personality and Social Psychology*, 73(3), 549–559. DOI: 10.1037/0022-3514.73.3.549 PMID: 9294901

Schnettler, B., Denegri, M., Miranda, H., Sepúlveda, J., Orellana, L., Paiva, G., & Grunert, K. G. (2015). Family support and subjective well-being: An exploratory study of university students in southern Chile. *Social Indicators Research*, 122(3), 833–864. DOI: 10.1007/s11205-014-0718-3

Schön, D. A. (1983). *The reflective practitioner: How professionals think in action*. Basic Books.

Schön, D. A. (1983). *The Reflective Practitioner: How Professionals Think in Action*. Basic Books.

Schwartz, B., & Sharpe, K. (2011). *Practical wisdom: The right way to do the right thing*. Penguin.

Scott, B. B., & Manning, M. R. (2022). Designing the Collaborative Organization: A Framework for how Collaborative Work, Relationships, and Behaviors Generate Collaborative Capacity. *The Journal of Applied Behavioral Science*, 60(1), 149–193. DOI: 10.1177/00218863221106245

Scott, J., & Miller, P. (2018). Job design and its effects on employee happiness. *Journal of Vocational Behavior*, 104, 1–10. DOI: 10.1016/j.jvb.2017.10.001

Scott, S. G., & Bruce, R. A. (1994). Determinants of innovative behavior: A path model of individual innovation in the workplace. *Academy of Management Journal*, 37(3), 580–607. DOI: 10.2307/256701

Scott, W. R. (1992). *Organizations: Rational, natural, and open systems*. Prentice-Hall.

Seetharaman, G. (2012, March 4). *TCS tops best companies to work for list.* Retrieved September 18, 2024, from https://www.businesstoday.in/magazine/cover-story/story/tata-consultancy-services-tcs-best-companies-to-work-india-28301-2012-02-16

Sekerka, L. E., & Bagozzi, R. P. (2007). Moral courage in the workplace: Moving to and from the desire and decision to act. *Business Ethics (Oxford, England)*, 16(2), 132–149. DOI: 10.1111/j.1467-8608.2007.00484.x

Seligman, M. (2018). PERMA and the building blocks of well-being. *The Journal of Positive Psychology*, 13(4), 333–335. Advance online publication. DOI: 10.1080/17439760.2018.1437466

Seligman, M. E. (2002). Positive psychology, positive prevention, and positive therapy. In Snyder, C. R., & López, S. J. (Eds.), *Handbook of positive psychology* (pp. 3–9). Oxford University Press.

Seligman, M. E. P. (2002). *Authentic Happiness: Using the New Positive Psychology to Realize Your Potential for Lasting Fulfillment*. Free Press.

Seligman, M. E. P. (2011). *Flourish: A Visionary New Understanding of Happiness and Well-being*. Free Press.

Seligman, M. E. P. (2012). *Flourish: A visionary new understanding of happiness and well-being*. Free Press.

Seligman, M. E. P., & Csikszentmihalyi, M. (2000). Positive psychology: An introduction. *The American Psychologist*, 55(1), 5–14. DOI: 10.1037/0003-066X.55.1.5 PMID: 11392865

Senge, P. M. (1990). *The fifth discipline: The art and practice of the learning organization*. Doubleday/Currency.

Senge, P., Smith, B., Kruschwitz, N., Laur, J., & Schley, S. (2008). *The necessary revolution: How individuals and organizations are working together to create a sustainable world*. Doubleday.

SessionLab. (2024). 66 team building activities to bring your team together. Retrieved from https://www.sessionlab.com/blog/team-building-activities/

Setyorini, D. M., Shodiqoh, A. I., Naufalani, N. A., Saputra, D., Pribadi, H. C., & Qomariah, N. (2023). Relationship Between Family Support and Work Family Balance in Career Women. *Journal of Economics. Finance and Management Studies*, 6(2), 978–981.

Seyal, A. H., & Afzaal, T. (2013). An Investigation of Relationship among Emotional Intelligence, Organizational Commitment and Job Satisfaction: Evidence from Academics in Brunei Darussalam. *International Business Research*, 6(3). Advance online publication. DOI: 10.5539/ibr.v6n3p217

Shankland, R., Tessier, D., Strub, L., Gauchet, A., & Baeyens, C. (2021). Improving Mental Health and Well-Being through Informal Mindfulness Practices: An Intervention Study. *Applied Psychology. Health and Well-Being*, 13(1), 63–83. DOI: 10.1111/aphw.12216 PMID: 32851775

Shapiro, S. L., Astin, J. A., Bishop, S. R., & Cordova, M. (2005). Mindfulness-based stress reduction for health care professionals: Results from a randomized trial. *International Journal of Stress Management*, 12(2), 164–176. DOI: 10.1037/1072-5245.12.2.164

Sharma, N., & Nayak, P. (2016). Study on Work Life Balance and Organisation Policy in IT Sector in NCR. *Amity Global Business Review, 11.*

Sharma, S., & Singh, N. (2017). Resource constraints and faculty stress in Indian universities: An empirical study. Higher Education, 74(3), 481-497. DOI: 10.1007/s10734-016-0016-4

Sharma, J., & Dhar, R. L. (2016). Factors influencing job performance of nursing staff: Mediating role of affective commitment. *Personnel Review*, 45(1), 161–182. DOI: 10.1108/PR-01-2014-0007

Sharma, V., & Handa, A. (2019). Job insecurity and its impact on academic staff in higher education institutions. *Indian Journal of Higher Education*, 11(1), 47–56. DOI: 10.1177/23476311211012345

Sheldon, K. M., & Krieger, L. S. (2014). Walking the talk: Value importance, value enactment,and well-being. *Motivation and Emotion*, 38(5), 609–619. DOI: 10.1007/s11031-014-9424-3

Sheldon, K. M., Ryan, R., & Reis, H. T. (1996). What makes for a good day? Competence and autonomy in the day and in the person. *Personality and Social Psychology Bulletin*, 22(12), 1270–1279. DOI: 10.1177/01461672962212007

Shepherd, T. (2021). The influence and interplay of emotional intelligence and leadership type on early childhood educators' organizational commitment. *International Journal of Business and Management Research,* 9(2), 168.177. DOI: 10.37391/IJBMR.090207

Shergill, P., & Notra, K. (2015). The world's largest 'ideapreneurship™': Putting employees first so the customer never feels second! In *Business Models and People Management in the Indian IT Industry* (pp. 204–218). Routledge.

Shibata, K., Naruse, K., & Boonyanurak, P. (2020). Does the mutual recognition agreement on nursing services accelerate nurse migration in member countries of the association of southeast Asian nations?. *Nursing Open*, 7(4), 1187.1196. DOI: 10.1002/nop2.504

Shirley, D., & MacDonald, E. A. (2016). *The mindful teacher*. Teachers College Press.

Shmueli, G., & Koppius, O. R. (2011). Predictive analytics in information systems research. *Management Information Systems Quarterly*, 35(3), 553–572. DOI: 10.2307/23042796

Shore, L. M., Randel, A. E., Chung, B. G., Dean, M. A., Ehrhart, K. H., & Singh, G. (2011). Inclusion and diversity in work groups: A review and model for future research. *Journal of Management*, 37(4), 1262–1289. DOI: 10.1177/0149206310385943

Shrestha, M. and Mandal, P. (2021). Emotional intelligence among nursing students of a government campus in eastern Nepal. *Journal of Kathmandu Medical College*, 10(1), 39.42. DOI: 10.3126/jkmc.v10i1.38970

Shukla, A., & Gupta, A. (2018). Factors influencing job stress among faculty members in higher education institutions: A study of Indian universities. *Journal of Higher Education Policy and Management*, 40(4), 392–404. DOI: 10.1080/1360080X.2018.1510172

Simons, P., Linden, J., & Duffy, T. (1999). New Learning: Three Ways to Learn in a New Balance. .DOI: 10.1007/0-306-47614-2_1

Singh, R., & Gupta, P. (2020). Administrative pressures and their impact on academic stress among university teachers in India. *International Journal of Educational Management*, 34(1), 12–23. DOI: 10.1108/IJEM-07-2019-0260

Singh, S., & Ryhal, P. C. (2021). The Influence of Teachers' Emotional Intelligence on Academic Performance With Mediating Effect of Job Satisfaction. *Journal of Education*. Advance online publication. DOI: 10.1177/00220574211032314

Sipe, W. E., & Eisendrath, S. J. (2012). Mindfulness-based cognitive therapy: Theory and practice. *Canadian Journal of Psychiatry*, 57(2), 63–69. DOI: 10.1177/070674371205700202 PMID: 22340145

Sirgy, M. J. (2012). *The psychology of quality of life: Hedonic well-being, life satisfaction, and eudaimonia* (Vol. 50). Springer science and business media. DOI: 10.1007/978-94-007-4405-9

Sirota, D., Mischkind, L. A., & Meltzer, M. I. (2005). *The enthusiastic employee*. Wharton School Publishing.

Sisto, A., Vicinanza, F., Campanozzi, L. L., Ricci, G., Tartaglini, D., & Tambone, V. (2019). Towards a Transversal Definition of Psychological Resilience: A Literature Review. *Medicina*, 55(11), 745. DOI: 10.3390/medicina55110745 PMID: 31744109

SiteDocs. (n.d.). How to create a safe work environment: Best practices. Retrieved from https://www.sitedocs.com/blog/safe-work-practices/

Slutsky, J., Chin, B., Raye, J., & Creswell, J. D. (2019). Mindfulness training improves employee well-being: A randomized controlled trial. *Journal of Occupational Health Psychology*, 24(1), 139–149. DOI: 10.1037/ocp0000132 PMID: 30335419

Smith, B. W., Ford, C. G., Erickson, K., & Guzman, A. (2021). The Effects of a Character Strength Focused Positive Psychology Course on Undergraduate Happiness and Well-Being. *Journal of Happiness Studies*, 22(1), 343–362. Advance online publication. DOI: 10.1007/s10902-020-00233-9

Smither, J. W., London, M., & Reilly, R. R. (2005). *Performance appraisal: State of the art in practice*. Jossey-Bass.

Smith, J., & Jones, L. (2023). Predictive analytics in employee engagement: Innovations and challenges. *Human Resource Management Review*, 33(3), 456–478.

Soelton, M. (2023). How Did It Happen: Organizational Commitment and Work-Life Balance Affect Organizational Citizenship Behavior. *Journal of Database Management*, 14(1), 149–164.

Soner. (2024). A Systematic Literature Review of Machine Learning Applications for Team Formation Problems. International Journal Of Informatics Technologies, DOI: 10.17671/gazibtd.1414527

Soto, C. J. (2015). Is happiness good for your personality? Concurrent and prospective relations of the big five with subjective well-being. *Journal of Personality*, 83(1), 45–55. DOI: 10.1111/jopy.12081 PMID: 24299053

Southwick, F., Martini, B., Charney, D., & Southwick, S. (2017). *Leadership and Resilience*. DOI: 10.1007/978-3-319-31036-7_18

Southwick, S. M., Bonanno, G. A., Masten, A. S., Panter-Brick, C., & Yehuda, R. (2014). Resilience definitions, theory, and challenges: Interdisciplinary perspectives. *European Journal of Psychotraumatology*, 5. DOI: 10.3402/ejpt.v5.25338

Srivastava, S. (2007). Women in workforce: Work and family conflict. *Management and labour studies, 32*(4), 411-421.

Srivastava, A. P., Mani, V., & Yadav, M. (2019). Evaluating the implications of stakeholder's role towards sustainability of higher education. *Journal of Cleaner Production*, 240, 118270. DOI: 10.1016/j.jclepro.2019.118270

Srivastava, A., & Dey, D. K., & MS, B. (2020). Drivers of brand credibility in consumer evaluation of global brands and domestic brands in an emerging market context. *Journal of Product and Brand Management*, 29(7), 849–861. DOI: 10.1108/JPBM-03-2018-1782

Stacey. (2016). Positive employment relations: An exploratory study.

Starbucks. (n.d.). Diversity and inclusion. Retrieved from https://www.starbucks.com/responsibility/diversity-and-inclusion/

Staudinger, U. M., & Glück, J. (2011). Psychological wisdom research: Commonalities and differences in a growing field. *Annual Review of Psychology*, 62(1), 215–241. DOI: 10.1146/annurev.psych.121208.131659 PMID: 20822439

Steelman, L. A., Levy, P. E., & Snell, A. F. (2004). The feedback environment scale: Construct definition, measurement, and validation. *Educational and Psychological Measurement*, 64(1), 165–184. DOI: 10.1177/0013164403258440

Steffens, N. K., Haslam, S. A., Schuh, S. C., Jetten, J., & van Dick, R. (2017). A meta-analytic review of social identification and health in organizational contexts. *Personality and Social Psychology Review*, 21(4), 303–335. DOI: 10.1177/1088868316656701 PMID: 27388779

Steger, M. F. (2016). Creating meaning and purpose at work. The Wiley Blackwell handbook of the psychology of positivity and strengths-based approaches at work, 60-81 DOI: 10.1002/9781118977620.ch5

Steger, M. F., Dik, B. J., & Duffy, R. D. (2012). Measuring meaningful work: The work and meaning inventory (WAMI). *Journal of Career Assessment*, 20(3), 322–337. DOI: 10.1177/1069072711436160

Stepanikova, I., & Karriker-Jaffe, K. J. (2020). Social networks and health: A longitudinal study of emotional well-being in social contexts. *Health & Place*, 61, 102265. DOI: 10.1016/j.healthplace.2019.102265

Sternberg, R. J., Jarvin, L., & Reznitskaya, A. (2008). Teaching for wisdom through history: Infusing wise thinking skills in the school curriculum. *Teaching for wisdom: Cross-cultural perspectives on fostering wisdom*, 37-57.

Sternberg, R. J. (1998). A balance theory of wisdom. *Review of General Psychology*, 2(4), 347–365. DOI: 10.1037/1089-2680.2.4.347

Sternberg, R. J. (2003). *Wisdom, intelligence, and creativity synthesized*. Cambridge University Press. DOI: 10.1017/CBO9780511509612

Sternberg, R. J. (2012). The assessment of creativity: An investment-based approach. *Creativity Research Journal*, 24(1), 3–12. DOI: 10.1080/10400419.2012.652925

Sternberg, R. J. (2017). ACCEL: A new model for identifying the gifted. *Roeper Review*, 39(3), 152–169. DOI: 10.1080/02783193.2017.1318658

Stone, D., & Heen, S. (2014). *Thanks for the feedback: The science and art of receiving feedback well.* Penguin Books.

Stoner, A. M., & Cennamo, K. S. (2018). *Enhancing reflection within situated learning: Incorporating mindfulness as an instructional strategy.* Springer. DOI: 10.1007/978-3-319-70326-8

Submitter, G. A. T. R., Bello, Z., & Tanko, G. I. (2020). Review of work-life balance theories. *Journals and Bello, Zainab and Tanko, Garba Ibrahim, Review of Work-Life Balance Theories.*

Suhail, K., & Chaudhry, H. R. (2004). Predictors of subjective well-being in an Eastern Muslim culture. *Journal of Social and Clinical Psychology*, 23(3), 359–376. DOI: 10.1521/jscp.23.3.359.35451

Sullivan, O., & Coltrane, S. (2008, April). Men's changing contribution to housework and childcare. *Prepared for the11th Annual Conference of the Council on Contemporary Families.*

Surf Office. (2024). 18 benefits of team building in any working environment. Retrieved from https://www.surfoffice.com/blog/team-building-benefits

Surjit, S. (2024), Nurturing Positive Organizational Climates to Enhance Work Success. Advances in human resources management and organizational development book series, DOI: 10.4018/979-8-3693-1524-8.ch004

T. (2016). Quality of Work Life Components: A Literature Review. DOI: 10.25215/0401.042

Tang, Y., Huang, X., & Wang, Y. (2017). Good marriage at home, creativity at work: Family–work enrichment effect on workplace creativity. *Journal of Organizational Behavior*, 38(5), 749–766. DOI: 10.1002/job.2175

Tara, . (2018). Using a positive practice environment framework to support recruitment. *Nursing Times.*

Taşdelen-Karçkay, A., & Bakalım, O. (2017). The mediating effect of work–life balance on the relationship between work–family conflict and life satisfaction. *Australian Journal of Career Development*, 26(1), 3–13. DOI: 10.1177/1038416216682954

Taufik, T., Dumpratiwi, A. N., Prihartanti, N., & Daliman, D. (2021). Elderly muslim wellbeing: Family support, participation in religious activities, and happiness. *The Open Psychology Journal*, 14(1), 76–82. DOI: 10.2174/1874350102114010076

Tay, L., & Diener, E. (2011). Needs and subjective well-being around the world. *Journal of Personality and Social Psychology*, 101(2), 354–365. DOI: 10.1037/a0023779 PMID: 21688922

Taylor, C., Harrison, J., Haimovitz, K., Oberle, E., Thomson, K., Schonert-Reichl, K., & Roeser, R. W. (2016). Examining ways that a mindfulness-based intervention reduces stress in public school teachers: A mixed-methods study. *Mindfulness*, 7(1), 115–129. DOI: 10.1007/s12671-015-0425-4

teambuilding.com. (2024). 24 team bonding activities, games & ideas for work. Retrieved from https://teambuilding.com/blog/team-bonding-ideas

Teame, K., Debie, A., & Tullu, M. (2022). Healthcare leadership effectiveness among managers in Public Health institutions of Addis Ababa, Central Ethiopia: A mixed methods study. *BMC Health Services Research*, 22(1), 540. DOI: 10.1186/s12913-022-07879-6 PMID: 35459173

Tech Mahindra Foundation. (n.d.). *Mind@Ease*. Tech Mahindra Foundation. Retrieved September 19, 2024, from https://mindatease.techmahindrafoundation.org/

Tech Mahindra. (2021, May 15). *Tech Mahindra Announces Appointment of 'Wellness Officer'*. Tech Mahindra. Retrieved September 12, 2024, from https://www.techmahindra.com/insights/news/tech-mahindra-announces-appointment-wellness-officer/

Tellegen, A., Lykken, D. T., Bouchard, T. J., Wilcox, K. J., Segal, N. L., & Rich, S. (1988). Personality similarity in twins reared apart and together. *Journal of Personality and Social Psychology*, 54(6), 1031–1039. DOI: 10.1037/0022-3514.54.6.1031 PMID: 3397862

Ten Brummelhuis, L. L., & Bakker, A. B. (2012). A resource perspective on the work–home interface: The work–home resources model. *The American Psychologist*, 67(7), 545–556. DOI: 10.1037/a0027974 PMID: 22506688

The Economic Times. (2008, May 30). *Wipro launches Fit for Life for its employees.* The Economic Times. Retrieved September 18, 2024 from https://economictimes.indiatimes.com/tech/software/wipro-launches-fit-for-life-for-its-employees/articleshow/3086633.cms

The Statesman. (2024, March 23). *Patanjali Ayurved Hospital organises free health camp in Majri Imlikhera.* The Statemans News Service. Retrieved September 19, 2024 from https://www.thestatesman.com/india/patanjali-ayurved-hospital-organises-free-health-camp-in-majri-imlikhera-1503282980.html#google_vignette

The TCS Way. (n.d.). *Promoting good health and wellbeing at the workplace.* TATA Consultancy Services. Retrieved September 18, 2024, from https://www.tcs.com/who-we-are/tcs-way/case-study/employee-health-wellness-tcs-wellbeing

TherapyRoute. (n.d.). Therapists in Bangalore, India. Retrieved from https://www.therapyroute.com/therapists/india/bangalore/1

Thomas, D. A. (1990). The impact of diversity on organizational behavior. *Harvard Business Review*, 68(5), 107–119. PMID: 10106515

Thomas, M. L., Bangen, K. J., Ardelt, M., & Jeste, D. V. (2017). Development of a 12-item abbreviated Three-Dimensional Wisdom Scale (3D-WS-12): Item selection and psychometric properties. *Assessment*, 24(1), 71–82. DOI: 10.1177/1073191115595714 PMID: 26209513

Tichy, N. M., & Bennis, W. (2007). *Judgment: How winning leaders make great calls*. Portfolio.

Tidwell, M. V. (2005). A social identity model of prosocial behaviors within non-profit organizations. *Nonprofit Management & Leadership*, 15(4), 449–467. DOI: 10.1002/nml.82

Tinto, V. (2003). Learning better together: The impact of learning communities on student success. Higher Education Monograph Series, 3, 1-12. Retrieved from https://eric.ed.gov/?id=ED476810

Toscano, F., & Zappalà, S. (2021). Overall Job Performance, Remote Work Engagement, Living with Children, and Remote Work Productivity during the COVID-19 Pandemic: A Mediated Moderation Model. *European Journal of Psychology Open*, 80(3), 133–142. Advance online publication. DOI: 10.1024/2673-8627/a000015

Trumpold, K., Kern, M., & Zapf, D. (2021). Emotion regulation and service-related attitudes: Connecting customer orientation and service organization identification with customer interactions. *SMR-Journal of Service Management Research*, 5(4), 270–286. DOI: 10.15358/2511-8676-2021-4-270

Tuckey, M., Sonnentag, S., & Bryan, J. (2018). Are state mindfulness and state work engagement related during the workday? *Work and Stress*, 32(1), 1–16. DOI: 10.1080/02678373.2017.1420707

Tushman, M. L., & O'Reilly, C. A. (1996). Ambidextrous organizations: Managing evolutionary and revolutionary change. *Organization Science*, 7(6), 665–684.

Tushman, M. L., Smith, W. K., Wood, R. C., Westerman, G., & O'Reilly, C. A. (2010). Organizational designs and innovation streams. *Industrial and Corporate Change*, 19(5), 1331–1366. DOI: 10.1093/icc/dtq040

U.S. Department of Labor. (n.d.). Flexible schedules. Retrieved from https://www.dol.gov/general/topic/workhours/flexibleschedules

Ullah, P. S., Jamal, W., & Naeem, M. (2018). The Relationship of Employee Engagement, Organizational Commitment, and Organizational Citizenship Behavior. *Jinnah Business Review*, 6(1), 35–41. DOI: 10.53369/ZHCF6210

Vakilzadeh, K., & Haase, A. (2021). The building blocks of organizational resilience: A review of the empirical literature. *Continuity & Resilience Review*, 3(1), 1–21. DOI: 10.1108/CRR-04-2020-0002

Valerie, J. (2014, November). Promoting Work-Family Balance Through Positive Psychology: A Practical Review of the Literature. *The Psychologist Manager Journal*, 17(4), 221–244. Advance online publication. DOI: 10.1037/mgr0000023

Varughese, J. and Rema, M. (2021). Perceived stress, emotional intelligence and self.efficacy among nursing students during the covid.19 pandemic. *International Journal of Research and Studies Publishing*, 11(4), 201.207. DOI: 10.29322/IJSRP.11.04.2021.p11225

Vazquez, A. C. S., Ferreira, M. C., & Mendonça, H. (2020). Advances in positive psychology: Well-being, engagement and job crafting. *Avaliação Psicológica*, 18(4). Advance online publication. DOI: 10.15689/ap.2019.1804.18859.02

Veenhoven, R. (2008). Happiness in nations. In *Happiness studies: A second generation of research* (pp. 1-24). https://www.eur.nl/en/research/happiness-research

Verma, P. (2020, August 3). *Tech Mahindra launches Mhealthy to enable workforce and community safety against COVID-19.* The Economic Times. Retrieved September 19, 2024 from https://economictimes.indiatimes.com/tech/ites/tech-mahindra-launches-mhealthy-to-enable-workforce-and-community-safety-against-covid-19/articleshow/77330380.cms

Viac, C., & Fraser, P. (2020). Teachers' well-being: A framework for data collection and analysis.

Villagran, M. A. L., & Martin, L. (2022). Academic librarians: Their understanding and use of emotional intelligence and happiness. *Journal of Academic Librarianship*, 48(1), 102466. Advance online publication. DOI: 10.1016/j.acalib.2021.102466

Villar, A., Paladini, S., & Buckley, O. (2023). Towards Supply Chain 5.0: Redesigning Supply Chains as Resilient, Sustainable, and Human-Centric Systems in a Post-pandemic World. *Operations Research Forum*, 4(3), 60. DOI: 10.1007/s43069-023-00234-3

Visser, W., & Jacobs, S. (2019). *Multi-level Resilience: A Human Capital Perspective*. University of Antwerp.

Vogus, T. J., & Sutcliffe, K. M. (2012). Organizational mindfulness and mindful organizing: A reconciliation and path forward. *Academy of Management Learning & Education*, 11(4), 722–735. DOI: 10.5465/amle.2011.0002c

Vries, M. (1994). The leadership mystique. *The Academy of Management Perspectives*, 8(3), 73–89. DOI: 10.5465/ame.1994.9503101181

Vroom, V. H., & Jago, A. G. (1988). *The new leadership: Managing participation in organizations*. Prentice-Hall.

Wahba, M. A., & Bridwell, L. G. (1976). Maslow reconsidered: A review of research on the need hierarchy theory. *Organizational Behavior and Human Performance*, 15(2), 212–240. DOI: 10.1016/0030-5073(76)90038-6

Wałaszek, M., Jaślan, D., Kołpa, M., Wójowska.Mach, J., Gniadek, A., & Różańska, A. (2021). Nurses' views on and compliance with the guidelines of hand hygiene, including nail hygiene in a multi.profile hospital in lesser Poland province – the evidence for need of continuous education and training. *Pielegniarstwo Xxi Wieku / Nursing in the 21st Century*, 20(3), 180.189. DOI: 10.2478/pielxxiw.2021.0029

Waldemar, J. O. C., Rigatti, R., Menezes, C. B., Guimarães, G., Falceto, O., & Heldt, E. (2016). Impact of a combined mindfulness and social–emotional learning program on fifth graders in a Brazilian public school setting. *Psychology & Neuroscience*, 9(1), 79–90. DOI: 10.1037/pne0000044

Walton, G. M. (2014). The new science of wise psychological interventions. *Current Directions in Psychological Science*, 23(1), 73–82. DOI: 10.1177/0963721413512856

Walumbwa, F. O., Avolio, B. J., Gardner, W. L., Wernsing, T. S., & Peterson, S. J. (2008). Authentic leadership: Development and validation of a theory-based measure. *Journal of Management*, 34(1), 89–126. DOI: 10.1177/0149206307308913

Walumbwa, F. O., Christensen, A. L., & Hailey, F. (2011). Authentic leadership and the knowledge economy: Sustaining motivation and trust among knowledge workers. *Organizational Dynamics*, 40(2), 110–118. DOI: 10.1016/j.orgdyn.2011.01.005

Walumbwa, F. O., Mayer, D. M., Wang, P., Wang, H., Workman, K., & Christensen, A. L. (2011). Linking ethical leadership to employee performance: The roles of leader–member exchange, self-efficacy, and organizational identification. *Organizational Behavior and Human Decision Processes*, 115(2), 204–213. DOI: 10.1016/j.obhdp.2010.11.002

Wang, X. (2024). Nurses' personality traits and perceived work environments during public health emergencies: implications for nursing workforce planning. *Risk Management and Healthcare Policy*, 17, 1199.1209. DOI: 10.2147/RMHP.S458235

Wang, H., Wang, L., & Liu, C. (2018). Employee competitive attitude and competitive behavior promote Job-Crafting and performance: A Two-Component dynamic model. *Frontiers in Psychology*, 9, 2223. Advance online publication. DOI: 10.3389/fpsyg.2018.02223 PMID: 30524335

Wang, L. (2023). The beneficial effect of empathy on work related quality of life among oncology nurse: mediating role of resilience. DOI: 10.21203/rs.3.rs.3327160/v1

Wang, Q., Dou, J., & Jia, S. (2016). A meta-analytic review of corporate social responsibility and corporate financial performance: The moderating effect of contextual factors. *Business & Society*, 55(8), 1083–1121. DOI: 10.1177/0007650315584317

Wang, W., Kang, S. W., & Choi, S. B. (2021). Effects of employee well-being and self-efficacy on the relationship between coaching leadership and knowledge sharing intention: A study of UK and US employees. *International Journal of Environmental Research and Public Health*, 18(20), 10638. DOI: 10.3390/ijerph182010638 PMID: 34682385

Webster, J. D. (2003). An exploratory analysis of a self-assessed wisdom scale. *Journal of Adult Development*, 10(1), 13–22. DOI: 10.1023/A:1020782619051

Weeden, K. A. (2005). Is there a flexiglass ceiling? Flexible work arrangements and wages in the United States. *Social Science Research*, 34(2), 454–482. DOI: 10.1016/j.ssresearch.2004.04.006

Wegge, J., Van Dick, R., Fisher, G. K., Wecking, C., & Moltzen, K. (2006). Work motivation, organisational identification, and well-being in call centre work. *Work and Stress*, 20(1), 60–83. DOI: 10.1080/02678370600655553

Weick, K. E. (1995). *Sensemaking in organizations*. Sage Publications.

Weick, K. E., & Sutcliffe, K. M. (2015). *Managing the unexpected: Sustained performance in a complex world*. John Wiley & Sons. DOI: 10.1002/9781119175834

Weisbrod, A. V., Bohman, L. C., & Ramdial, K. J. (2024). From theory to practice: A novel meditation program at a global corporation. *Current Psychology (New Brunswick, N.J.)*, 43(5), 4266–4283. DOI: 10.1007/s12144-023-04516-1 PMID: 37359588

Wellable. (n.d.). 30 holistic wellness activities for the workplace. Retrieved from https://www.wellable.co/blog/30-holistic-wellness-activities-for-the-workplace/

Wilber, K. (2001). *A theory of everything: An integral vision for business, politics, science, and spirituality*. Shambhala Publications.

William, A. (2013). Career Conversations in Small- to Medium-Sized Businesses: A Competitive Advantage. Canadian Journal of Counselling and Psychotherapy.

Williams, T. A., Gruber, D. A., Sutcliffe, K. M., Shepherd, D. A., & Zhao, E. Y. (2017). Organizational response to adversity: Fusing crisis management and resilience research streams. *The Academy of Management Annals*, 11(2), 733–769. DOI: 10.5465/annals.2015.0134

Wolle, G. (2024). Gender stereotypes and contributing factors for the gender gap in the school leadership position in North Wello Zone: Ethiopia. *Cogent Education*, 11(1), 2375482. DOI: 10.1080/2331186X.2024.2375482

Wong, K. P., Lee, F. C. H., Teh, P. L., & Chan, A. H. S. (2021). The interplay of socioecological determinants of work–life balance, subjective wellbeing and employee wellbeing. *International Journal of Environmental Research and Public Health*, 18(9), 4525. DOI: 10.3390/ijerph18094525 PMID: 33923234

Woolley, A. W., Chabris, C. F., Pentland, A., Hashmi, N., & Malone, T. W. (2010). Evidence for a collective intelligence factor in the performance of human groups. *Science*, 330(6004), 686–688. DOI: 10.1126/science.1193147 PMID: 20929725

WorkHound. (2023). How an employee feedback platform boosts employee engagement. Retrieved from https://workhound.com/blog/how-an-employee-feedback-platform-boosts-employee-engagement/

World Economic Forum. (2022). *Risk Proof: A Framework for Building Organizational Resilience in an Uncertain Future*. https://www.weforum.org/publications/risk-proof-a-framework-for-building-organizational-resilience-in-an-uncertain-future/

World, H. R. (2021, May 15). *Tech Mahindra appoints Meghna Hareendran as Wellness Officer.* The Economic Times. Retrieved September 19, 2024, from https://hr.economictimes.indiatimes.com/news/industry/tech-mahindra-announces-appointment-of-wellness-officer/82655433

Wright, T. A., & Cropanzano, R. (2007). Psychological well-being and job satisfaction as predictors of job performance. *Journal of Occupational Health Psychology*, 12(2), 112–123. DOI: 10.1037/1076-8998.12.2.93 PMID: 17469992

Wright, T. A., & Huang, C. (2012). The many benefits of employee well-being in organizational research. *Journal of Organizational Behavior*, 33(8), 1188–1192. DOI: 10.1002/job.1828

Wrzesniewski, A., & Dutton, J. E. (2001). Crafting a job: Revisioning employees as active crafters of their work. *Academy of Management Review*, 26(2), 179–201. DOI: 10.2307/259118

Wrzesniewski, A., Dutton, J. E., & Debebe, G. (2003). Interpersonal sensemaking and the meaning of work. *Research in Organizational Behavior*, 25, 93–135. DOI: 10.1016/S0191-3085(03)25003-6

Xiao, L., & Cao, H. (2017). Organizational Resilience: The Theoretical Model and Research Implication. *ITM Web of Conferences, 12*, 04021. DOI: 10.1051/itmconf/20171204021

Xu, J., Zhang, L., Ji, Q., Ji, P., Chen, Y., Song, M., & Guo, L. (2023). Nursing students' emotional empathy, emotional intelligence and higher education.related stress: A cross.sectional study. *BMC Nursing*, 22(1), 437. Advance online publication. DOI: 10.1186/s12912-023-01607-z PMID: 37981672

Yadav, S. K. S. (2016). Corporate social responsibility: how TCS is performing it well? *International Multidisciplinary Journal, 5*(5).

Yalew, M. T. (2024). Development of relations between Ethiopia and China during Emperor Haile Selassie: A product of timing or the leadership? *Cogent Social Sciences*, 10(1), 2333082. DOI: 10.1080/23311886.2024.2333082

Yang, R., Gao, Y., & Ji, Z. (2023). The relationship between self.regulated learning, mindful agency, and psychological resilience in Chinese master of nursing specialists: A cross.sectional study. *Frontiers in Psychology*, 14, 1066806. Advance online publication. DOI: 10.3389/fpsyg.2023.1066806 PMID: 37008842

Yang, S. Y. (2011). Wisdom displayed through leadership: Exploring leadership-related wisdom. *The Leadership Quarterly*, 22(4), 616–632. DOI: 10.1016/j.leaqua.2011.05.004

Young, T., Macinnes, S., Jarden, A., & Colla, R. (2020). The impact of a wellbeing program imbedded in university classes: The importance of valuing happiness, baseline wellbeing and practice frequency. *Studies in Higher Education*. Advance online publication. DOI: 10.1080/03075079.2020.1793932

Zarate, K., Maggin, D. M., & Passmore, A. (2019). Meta-analysis of mindfulness training on teacher well-being. *Psychology in the Schools*, 56(10), 1700–1715. DOI: 10.1002/pits.22308

Zavvy. (2024). How to build robust employee feedback systems in your company. Retrieved from https://www.deel.com/blog/employee-feedback-system/

Zellars, K. L., Perrewé, P. L., & Rossi, A. M. (2005). Stressors, leadership, and wellness: A longitudinal assessment of stress, leadership style, and emotional response in a health care environment.

Zhang, D., Lee, E. K. P., Mak, E. C. W., Ho, C. Y., & Wong, S. Y. S. (2021). Mindfulness-based interventions: An overall review. *British Medical Bulletin*, 138(1), 41–57. DOI: 10.1093/bmb/ldab005 PMID: 33884400

Zhou, J., & George, J. M. (2001). When job dissatisfaction leads to creativity: Encouraging the expression of voice. *Academy of Management Journal*, 44(4), 682–696. DOI: 10.2307/3069410

Zoogah, B. D. (2020). Companionate leadership: A shemswian perspective. *Africa Journal of Management*, 6(3), 214–247. DOI: 10.1080/23322373.2020.1779944

Zubair, A., Kamal, A., & Artemeva, V. (2018). Mindfulness and resilience as predictors of subjective well-being among university students: A cross cultural perspective. *Journal of Behavioural Sciences*, 28(2), 1.

Zutshi, A., Mendy, J., Sharma, G. D., Thomas, A., & Sarker, T. (2021). From Challenges to Creativity: Enhancing SMEs' Resilience in the Context of COVID-19. *Sustainability (Basel)*, 13(12), 6542. Advance online publication. DOI: 10.3390/su13126542

About the Contributors

Minh Tung Tran gains (his 1st Doctoral Degree) a Doctor of Business Administration (DBA Degree) in Marketing Management from University of Technology and Management (UITM), Poland and a Master of Science in Business Information Systems from Heilbronn University, German. He is currently Acting Director of Swinburne Vietnam – Danang Location cum Media and Business Lecturer. He has over 18 years of work experience and over 12 years in teaching and sharing at both over 40 Enterprises and over 22 Higher Educational Institutions in Vietnam. His research interests are in Social Media, PR, Marketing, Marketing in Higher Education, Innovation Teaching Methodology, Data Driven Marketing, Information Systems, Standards Based Curriculum, Experience Learning and Gamification in Education. Recently, he has completed and obtained (his 2nd and 3rd Doctoral Degree) EdD - Professional Doctorate in Educational Administration & Leadership and Doctor of Philosophy (Ph.D.) in Media and Communication from European International University, EIU-Paris, France, in 2023 which can assist him in his personal development plan (PDP) and professional career in current role in leading and administrating international higher education as well as teaching Media and Business.

* * *

Yassine Hassani Aboumehdi is a Ph.D. student specializing in the study of wisdom across cultures at Sidi Mohamed Ben Abdellah University. He also serves as a Professor Assistant at the National School of Commerce and Management. His research delves into the comparative analysis of wisdom traditions across different cultures, exploring how these insights can inform contemporary practices and understanding. In his academic journey, Yassine Hassani Aboumehdi has developed a keen interest in how cultural contexts shape philosophical and practical notions of wisdom. His work aims to bridge cultural perspectives and contribute to a more nuanced understanding of wisdom in a globalized world.

Shivani Agarwal is an Associate Professor, Galgotias University, Greater Noida, India. She has earned her PhD from Indian Institute of Technology (IIT, Roorkee) in Management. She has completed the executive programme in HR Analytics from IIM Ahmedabad. She has more than 13 years of experience in teaching and in handling various administrative positions. She also presented several research papers at national and international conferences. Dr. Agarwal has contributed chapters to different books published by Taylor and Francis, Springer and IGI Global. She has conducted and attended various workshops, FDPs and MDPs. She is the Book Series Editor of Information Technology, Management & Operations Research Practices, CRC Press, Taylor & Francis Group, USA. She is a guest editor with IGI-Global, USA. She can be contacted at jindal.shivani24@gmail.com.

Saif Allah Allouani is an Associate Professor of Intercultural Management and Organizational Behavior at the Business School- ENCG- Sidi Mohammed Ben Abdellah University- FES, Morocco. His teaching and research focus on Human flourishing, particularly emphasizing Well-being, Practical Wisdom, and Character Education. A seasoned counselor and trainer, he leverages his experience to craft specific coaching and training programs with a broad societal outreach. His latest book, "You Shall not Languish, an anti-guide for Wisdom and Well-being," features some of his key ideas about the ailment of our educational system and some directions for corrective actions. He works with the Wisdom and Culture Lab of the University of Waterloo to develop a culturally grounded understanding and measurement of constructs related to wisdom, character, and culture.

K. Balaji is an Assistant Professor in Business and Management, Christ University, Bangalore. He did Ph.D. from KLU Business School, KL University, Vijayawada. He is having 12 years of teaching experience. He has to his credit 23 Research Articles published in reputed National and International Journals. He has participated and presented more than 12 papers in both National and International Seminars/Conferences and also attended more than 50 workshops/FDPS organized by various reputed organizations. He has also participated in more than 50 seminars / webinars organized by various reputed organizations. He has also attended in 6 Short Term Training programs. He has successfully conducted 3 webinars, one 5 day FDP and one International Conference on Reimaging marketing in New Normal. He is a ratified as Assistant Professor by both JNTUH, JNTU Anantapur and Sri Venkateswara University, Tirupati. His specialized areas include, Accounting and

Financial management, Marketing Management, Retailing Management, Consumer Behavior studies, Entrepreneurship and Business Laws.

Garima Bansal is a research scholar in Guru Jambheshwar University of Science & Technology, Hisar and pursuing PhD under the supervision of Prof. B.K. Punia. Her research domain focuses on leadership, prosocial service behavior, and mindfulness. She has presented research papers in national and international conferences. She has also bestowed with "Naari Shakti Samaan" Award from "Sadhbhawana Welfare Society", Hisar because of her remarkable contribution in the upliftment of underprivileged children in Hisar district. Her research journey has been centered around the exploration of mindfulness and life awakening experiences. She has also attended various mindfulness workshops and meditation sessions. She is an active volunteer in an NGO Foundation– "Bhikh Nahi Kitaab Do" from last 4 years.

Phuong Cao is currently a PhD Candidates of Development Economics Department, International Institute of Social Studies, part of Erasmus University Rotterdam, the Netherlands. She earned her Master's degree in Public Health at the KIT Institute, Amsterdam, the Netherlands in 2018. Her research interests are in Public Health, Health Development, Health Economics, Mental Health, Health Policy and Management.

Mehdi Chaoui Roqai is a PhD student in management sciences at Sidi Mohammed Ben Abdellah University. He holds a Master's degree in Organization Management and Audit. His research focuses on character education in universities. He is a member of the Moroccan Inter-University Research Initiative for Character Education (MIRICE) and is certified as a coach by the Human Flourishing Engineering Institute (HFEI) and the Asian Regional Training and Development Organization (ARTDO).

Lan Dang is currently the Head of the Language Center and Foundation Year of the Vietnamese-German University (VGU) in Vietnam. . She earned her Master's degree in Educational Management and Human Resource Development at the University of Sydney in Australia in 2002, and her doctoral degree in Higher, Adult, and Lifelong Education at Michigan State University (MSU) in 2012. Her research interests are in gender issues, academic women and leadership, administration, governance, and quality assurance and accreditation in higher education.

Saumendra Das is presently working as an Associate Professor at the School of Management Studies, GIET University, Gunupur, Odisha. He has more than 21 years of teaching, research, and industry experience. He has published more than

105 articles in national and international journals, conference proceedings, and book chapters. He also authored and edited sixteen books. Dr Das has participated and presented many papers in seminars, conferences, and workshops in India and abroad. He has organized many FDPs and workshops in his career. He is an academician, author, and editor. He has also published two patents. He is an active member of various professional bodies such as ICA, ISTE and RFI. In the year 2023, he was awarded as the best teacher by Research Foundation India.

Deeksha Dwivedi is a Software Engineer at Leslie's, USA. She is a former Asst. Professor in the Department of Management, HRIT, Ghaziabad. She holds PhD in management. Her research focuses primarily on stress management, talent management, knowledge management and artificial Intelligence. Dr. Deeksha is author of more than 12+ research papers published in national and international journals. Her book "Stress Management in Software Industry: Indian context" is published in multiple languages. Her hobbies include hiking, gardening, traveling, and cooking.

Kenza Ennida is a PhD student at the Sidi Mohamed Ben Abdellah University (National School of Business and Management of Fez, Morocco) and human resources professional in the public sector. Member of the Moroccan Interuniversity Research Initiative for Character Education (MIRICE) and the American Psychological Association. Passionate about and certified in the fields of work psychology and organizational behavior.

Radhika Girdhar is a research scholar in Guru Jambheshwar University of Science & Technology, Hisar and pursuing PhD under the supervision of Prof. B.K. Punia in the field of Human Resource Management. She served as an Assistant Professor in management college for more than 1 year. She has also received "Best Paper Presentation Award" in the International Conference on "Building A Resilient Economy: Policies And Strategies For Sustainable Growth" organized by Jaipuria Institute of Management, Indirapuram, Ghaziabad on 6th July, 2024

Madhu Giri is a licensed Clinical Psychologist, and she earned her M.phi lin Clinical Psychology from Gautam Buddha University. Driven by an unwavering commitment to make a lasting impact, Madhu Giri embarked on her doctoral journey at the Department of Psychology, Christ University, India. Under the guidance of esteemed mentors, she delved into the uncharted territories of positive psychology, exploring the profound effects of gratitude and mindfulness on mental well-being. As a JRF at the Department of Psychology, Christ University, Madhu plays a pivotal role in fostering a culture of academic excellence. Her multifaceted responsibilities include conducting independent research, assisting in teaching undergraduate and postgraduate courses, and providing counseling to help students to strive through their academic journey. She is widely regarded as a compassionate mentor, offering guidance and support to students eager to embark on their own journeys of discovery.

Tiago Horta Reis da Silva is a Lecturer in Nursing Education (AEP) at King's College London, with a range of qualifications including BSc in Nursing, BSc in Traditional Chinese Medicine, MSc in Emotional Intelligence, Counselling and NLP, a Master of Business Administration, and MSc in Traditional Chinese Medicine. He has experience in other Higher Education Institutions and NHS and is a member of the Adult Nursing department, assisting with the running, development, and administration of BSc and MSc programmes. He also assists with teaching other modules' content and assists with interviews and assessment matters for other courses. Tiago is a Senior Fellow in Higher Education, a Fellow of the Royal Society of Medicine, and a Fellow for Faculty Nursing and Midwifery at the Royal College of Southern Ireland. https://www.kcl.ac.uk/people/tiago-horta-reis-da-silva. https://orcid.org/my-orcid?orcid=0000-0001-5220-1718. https://www.researchgate.net/profile/Tiago-Horta-Reis-Da-Silva.

Hieu Huynh is currently an anesthesiologist, lecturer and researcher at University Medical Center, a part of Medicine and Pharmacy University, Ho Chi Minh City, Vietnam. He is teaching and coaching medical students in anesthesiology at graduate and post-graduate levels. His research interests are related to health sciences, anesthesiology, health management and leadership in Vietnam.

Parveen Singh Kalsi holds a PhD from IKG Punjab Technical University, Jalandhar, and has accumulated 19 years of experience in the education sector. He is presently working as an Associate Professor at GNA University, Phagwara. He has made significant contributions to his field with various research publications. In addition to his academic achievements, Dr. Kalsi has actively participated in various faculty development programs to enhance his professional growth. He has also completed the prestigious Professional Certificate Program (eMDP) in Business Analytics from the Indian Institute of Management, Kozhikode, further expanding his expertise in data-driven decision-making.

James Kanda is an Assistant Professor at GNA University, Phagwara, known for his expertise and contributions to the field of management education. He completed his MBA in Marketing from Punjab Technical University, Jalandhar, which laid the foundation for his career in academia. In 2012, Mr. Kanda further distinguished himself by clearing the prestigious UGC NET in Management, a national-level qualification that showcases his strong command over his subject. With over 11 years of teaching experience, Mr. Kanda has honed his skills in imparting knowledge and mentoring students in various management disciplines. He has also published 5 research papers in reputed international and UGC-recognized journals, contributing valuable insights to the academic community.

Tam Nguyen is currently the Head of Business Department, Swinburne Vietnam Alliance Program, FPT University. She is teaching management, leadership, and entrepreneurship, as well as training soft skills for students in Global Citizen Education Programs at university level. Her research interests are related to education, organizational culture, motivation, and leadership in Asia and Australia.

Swati Pathak has experience in de-addiction counselling, family therapy, adolescent counselling, research and training. Have published various research articles in reputed scopus indexed journals. Area of research interest lies in gender and sexuality, counselling psychology, male mental health, women reproductive issues. Member of various national psychological associations and have been contributing to varied course developments.

B. K. Punia is well renowned in the field of human resource management and organizational behavior. He has numerous research papers to his credit in diverse areas and has been chairing expert sessions in various national and international conferences. Apart from being a respectable researcher, he is a great administrator too. He held the prestigious post of Vice chancellorship of famous Maharshi Dayanand University, Rohtak, Haryana. Prior to MDU, he also worked as Dean, Haryana School of Business and also as founding director, Academic Staff College, Guru Jambheshwar University of Science and Technology.

Vandana Punia, Co-director of ICSSR Research project, is the Dean & Head Faculty of Education, Guru Jambheshwar University of Science &Technology, Hisar, Haryana. She is having 20 yrs of experience in teaching & research. She worked as a Content writer, Content presenter and Content reviewer in ARPIT 2018, ARPIT 2019. She has also developed an OER and MOOC course on " Happiness: Education of 21st Century from lenses of Happiness" under the aegis of OE4BW, an UNESCO initiative. She has completed two UGC sponsored Major Research Projects and two MHRD Digital Initiatives SWAYAM ARPIT 2018 & 2019. She has authored two books published by reputed National Publisher. Edited two books published by reputed National Publishers. Published more than eighty research papers in various National and International Journals, Developed and published Five Research Tools and one Training Module. She had been awarded Bharat Shiksha Ratan Award (2012), University Gold Medal in M.A. Journalism and Mass Communication, CDLU, Sirsa (2012), Innovative Res. Developers & Publishers–Teaching and Research Excellence Award (2017) & Dr. Radhakrishnan Award for

Teaching, Learning and Innovation. Her interests are in Faculty Development and Empowerment Psychology of Teaching and Learning, Technology Integration & Educational Technology. Devoted to upholding professional standards of conduct and ethical conduct. Proficient in accommodating the varied learning methods of students. Constantly on the lookout for the most recent advancements in the field of education.

Sethumadhavan R. is a seasoned academician and management expert with 23 years of experience in the field. He currently serves as a faculty member at the School of Management, Presidency University in Bangalore, Karnataka. Holding a PhD in Management, Dr. R. Sethumadhavan brings a wealth of knowledge and expertise to his teaching and research endeavors. His extensive experience spans various aspects of management, making him a valuable resource for students and professionals alike. orcid. ID 0000-0002-0508-2143.

Reena Rani, Ph.D., is working as an Assistant Professor at Mittal School of Business, Lovely Professional University, India. She has worked as Vice Principal at CT Group of Engineering, Management and Technology. She completed her Doctorate in Management from Punjab Technical University, Jalandhar. She has completed her MBA in Finance/HRM from Punjab Technical University, Jalandhar. She also did M. Com from Guru Nanak Dev University. She also cleared 2 National Level tests –UGC NET in Commerce and UGC NET with JRF in Management. She has more than 8 years of teaching experience, attended more than 13 conferences and summits, and has 18 publications (In Scopus (Emerald, IGI Global), International, and UGC journals. She has attended 8 FDPs and various workshops. Her interest areas for research are finance, banking, and the stock market. She has given guest lectures and organized events.

S. Sahoo, Associate Professor and Head of Economics, School of Management Studies at GIET University, Gunupur, has 24 years of academic experience and holds a Design Patent for a “Teaching Device for Students.” He earned the first Ph.D. in Economics from North Orissa University in 2011, focusing on “Micro Credit and Rural Development: Role of Voluntary Organizations in Rayagada District of Orissa.” He also holds a Master’s in Economics from Utkal University and an MBA in HR from IGNOU. Dr. Sahoo's expertise includes Econometrics, Statistics, Research Methodology, Micro Economics, and Managerial Economics. He has published over 25 research papers and guides six Ph.D. scholars. His research interests are in Entrepreneurship, Microfinance, Developmental Economics, Rural and Tribal Development, and Green Economics. He has designed curricula for MBA, BBA, and B.Tech courses and manages NBA accreditation and NIRF ranking at GIET University. A life member of ISTE, OEA, CSI, and SOEA, he actively participates in several national and international FDPs, conferences, and seminars.

Smruti Rekha Sahoo is currently serving as an Assistant Professor at the School of Management Studies, GIET University, Gunupur. She has a 9 years of rich experience in academics and research. Dr.Smruti Rekha Sahoo has published quality articles in journals and recognized conferences. She has also published 6 patents. She has also presented articles in seminars, conferences in India.

Neyyila Saibabu is an Assistant Professor at Aditya Institute of Technology and Management, Tekkali, Andhra Pradesh. He holds a post-graduate degree in M. Com, MBA, PGDIM and PhD from Acharya Nagarjuna University, Andhra Pradesh. He has published more than 12 articles in reputed national and international journals. He has participated in and presented many papers at national and international conferences. He has taught post-graduate and undergraduate subjects such as Accounting, Finance, Economics and Marketing. Additionally, he passed the Andhra Pradesh State Eligibility Test (APSET) in the management and commerce disciplines. He had authored 7 books in his career enhancement process.

Heni Dwi Windarwati is an esteemed nursing lecturer at the Faculty of Health Sciences of Universitas Brawijaya. She has an impressive educational background, having completed her undergraduate nursing program, nursing program, master's program specializing in psychiatric nursing, psychiatric nursing specialist program, and doctoral nursing program at the prestigious University of Indonesia.

Index

H

I

J

K

L

M

N

O

P

S

T

W

www.ingramcontent.com/pod-product-compliance
Lightning Source LLC
LaVergne TN
LVHW080615300926
849162LV00005B/1174
* 9 7 9 8 3 6 9 3 8 4 5 7 2 *